Political Business Cycles

Political Business Cycles

The Political Economy of Money, Inflation, and Unemployment

Edited by Thomas D. Willett

A Pacific Research Institute for Public Policy Book

Published by Duke University Press

Durham and London 1988

Acknowledgements

I have accumulated many debts in the preparation of this volume. I should like to particularly acknowledge the patience and cooperativeness of the contributors to the volume, the financial assistance from the Pacific Research Institute and Claremont Center for Economic Policy Studies which made the preparation of the volume possible, the able research assistance from a number of Claremont graduate students, especially Massoud Darbandi and Pamela Martin, and the helpful comments on individual papers from colleagues and students too numerous to name, including many of the contributors to this volume. I should like to especially thank Greg Christainsen, Charles Wainhouse, Eugenia Toma, and Edward Tower who read and made valuable suggestions on the entire manuscript and Keith Acheson, King Banaian, and Thomas Borcherding for many discussions which have substantially helped clarify (I hope) my thinking on the interrelationships among public choice analysis, information and rational expectations, and political competition and policy outcomes. Once again Lori Harnack proved invaluable with her prompt and efficient typing and editorial assistance in preparing the manuscript.

Thomas D. Willett

Contents

Part Four Proposals for Reform

Tables and Figures

Tables

Figures

Foreword

Axel Leijonhufvud

The performance of the American economy during most of the past twenty years has been disappointing. A slowdown in real growth has gone hand in hand with high and variable inflation rates and growing signs of financial instability in the United States and many other countries. On the world markets these problems have been accompanied by wide swings in exchange rates.

At home, the Reagan administration has succeeded in reducing the inflation rate from double digits to what now seems a more tolerable level. But nothing at all has been done in the way of reforming our monetary system so as to ensure for ourselves a future of continuing monetary stability. Federal budget deficits have been so huge that many observers fear they will be financed at least in part by creating new money. It remains to be seen whether the Gramm-Rudman deficit reduction bill, passed in 1985, will provide a way out of the budgetary impasse that has so far defied resolution.

Why has the record, national and international, been on the whole so dismal since the late 1960s? (Why not before?) The failures are very largely failures of policy—they are man-made. How did we slip into this stagflation syndrome of slow growth coupled with financial instability? Why are we so helpless to improve performance? Any number of reform proposals have been put forward, many of which would clearly improve on our recent record. Yet we are not making much headway with any of them.

Questions such as these have become steadily more pressing as the sorry record of stagflation has lengthened. The economics profession is thus forced to pay increasing attention to the social and political dimensions of the theory of macroeconomic policy. This collective venture by macroeconomists into political economy has been slow in coming, but the caliber of the contributors to the present volume as well as the range of their contributions prove that it is now gathering momentum.

The traditional breakdown of the social sciences into separate disciplines now works to our disadvantage. Out of the totality of interactions among individuals in society, we abstract (by none-too-clearly articulated rules) the "economic," the "political," and the "social." The workings of the "economy" are then analyzed as if interactions with the "polity" and "society" can be ignored. The political and social settings of economic problems are among the ceteris paribus assumptions.

Now it is fortunately true that many useful things can be said about asset prices, for instance, while abstracting from the mating rituals of yuppie stockbrokers. Financial theory is no doubt further advanced today for having made that abstraction. The same conclusion applies to economic theory in general—it has progressed as far as it has in large measure by ignoring complications that could not have been rigorously handled in any case. Like physics in the natural sciences, economics made the most rapid progress in the social sciences by being first to pick the easy problems (and especially the easily quantifiable problems) and leaving the intractable ones to others.

The price for these advantages of disciplinary specialization, however, turns out to be a certain trained incapacity on the part of most economists to think straight about problems that involve interactions between the economic and the political or social spheres. In the areas of public choice and of law and economics, it is true, economists have achieved a good deal toward remedying the situation. But these developments have only very recently begun to touch macroeconomics.

The interactions go both ways, of course. Economic policies have social and political consequences; social and political conditions constrain or impel economic policy. The policies of five, ten, and twenty years ago are a very large part of today's economic policy problems. And if these past policies have left us a troublesome legacy, economists must share the blame. The economics profession at large certainly did not oppose with convincing argument the policies whose longer-term consequences we now lament.

The generalities made above will be illustrated below with regard to the problem of monetary instability. The political economy of stagflation is not altogether a matter of monetary mismanagement and how to end it. The oil shocks of the 1970s, for instance, also played a role—when society turns its attention from labor-saving to energy-saving innovation, it is not surprising to find that the growth of productivity per man-hour slows down. But even here, it is mainly the financial aspects of the oil shocks that have left us with lasting problems of major consequences. Another important element in the present picture is the failure of many countries in Europe and elsewhere to adapt in the face of the extraordinary export performance of Japan and other East Asian economies. There are basically only two ways to adapt: either you meet the competition by lowering your own costs or else you reallocate resources from industries recently rendered uncompetitive into new areas of comparative advantage. The refusal to do either one can only result in unemployment and stagnation. Such a refusal to face unpalatable realities is not at bottom a monetary or financial problem, of course. But efficient adaptation to the changing structure of international trade is made far more difficult by wide and largely unpredictable swings in exchange rates. So, while monetary instability is not our only problem, we run across its ramifications in connection with virtually all our macroeconomic problems.

The American economics profession, in my opinion, bears a heavy responsibility for the great inflation that we have been through. Yet this responsibility is not direct or focused upon particular individuals. President Johnson's economic advisers in the late sixties, for instance, counseled against the guns-*and*-butter policies which shoved us into serious inflation. Rather, the responsibility is indirect and widely shared. Economists in general held and taught a most inadequate inflation theory which, in particular, was totally misleading with regard to the economic costs and social consequences of inflation. On the basis of then-accepted theory, there were, on the whole, no strong reasons not to inflate. So, naturally, policy analysts and decision makers were ready to risk inflation if, for example, some temporary employment gain could be hoped for.

This inflation theory focused on the question of the social costs of some given (not too high), foreseen, constant inflation rate. The answer, not surprisingly, is that the economic costs are trivial and the social consequences nil; and it is, indeed, the correct answer—albeit to the wrong question. The question presumes that the "typical" inflation (if there is such a thing!) takes place under conditions that are, in all essentials, those of a regime of perfect monetary stability—except for the peculiar happenstance that it is the rate of depreciation of the purchasing power of money, rather than that purchasing power itself, that is being managed so as to stay constant and foreseeable.

Actual inflationary regimes are not like that. Not one bit. We get a bit closer to real-world inflation if we assume that the inflation rate evolves as a random walk and that this is foreseen by the public. This captures the fact that monetary policy in inflationary regimes tends to be a sequence of shortsighted measures, each one a compromise formed by the economic exigencies and political pressures of the moment. The determinants of this random walk process, moreover, are themselves subject to change in ways that cannot be entirely foreseen and may be difficult to detect at an early stage. The exchange rate between two currencies each one of which is on its own "random walk monetary standard" may, therefore, be subject to large and sudden swings as the market registers perceived changes in the random walk process governing one or the other currency. This is the reason why flexible exchange rates have not been the unmixed blessing preadvertised, in particular, by monetarist economists.

The uncertainty over the future purchasing power of money under random walk monetary standards is not necessarily greater over the near term than in other practicable monetary regimes, but it is much larger over the longer term. This forces private sector agents into shorter-term planning and shorter-term contracting. Moreover, different agents will allocate resources intertemporally on the basis of divergent "best guesses" about the evolution of the price level. Hence, random walk regimes tend to reduce capital accumulation and to allocate capital inefficiently. For these reasons, and others, they tend to be stagflationary.

The efficiency losses imposed by inflation are not without social and political consequences but are less important in this regard than its distributive implications. These distributive implications make monetary stabilization politically more difficult to achieve when the economy has been in random walk inflation for a prolonged period. They help explain, therefore, why a country may blunder on with random walk monetary mismanagement for a prolonged period even when it has become apparent that an inflationary regime of this variety has significant costs in terms of economic efficiency.

Consider an economy where the inflation rate has been wandering around, say, 15 percent for a while and where modal market opinion expects this rate to continue over the short term. If, then, the government decided to stabilize at a 15 percent inflation rate "forever," this would legitimate currently held expectations (and should avoid, therefore, any adverse unemployment effects). But there may still be a large volume of mortgages, life insurance policies, bonds, and other claims outstanding in the economy carrying nominal interest rates embodying past states of inflation expectations of 0 percent, of 10 percent, of 20 percent, etc. A decision to stabilize at 15 percent is a boon to creditors holding the contracts concluded on the basis of a 20 percent expected inflation rate; it is a disaster for those still holding claims contracted on the presumption of price stability. A decision to go for stability at a 0 percent rate, on the other hand, redistributes wealth from debtors to creditors on all contracts embodying expectations of a positive inflation rate. Given these past states of expectations still embedded in "live" contracts, *any* decision to follow a particular price level path from now on entails an infinitely complex pattern of wealth redistributions. If such a decision were announced today, and were credible, it would be known what these redistributions were to be—and the decision would unavoidably become the focus of swirling political controversy. As long as you simply blunder on one period at a time, the redistributions are revealed piecemeal and today's losers can still hope for "better" government policy in coming periods. Once in a random walk inflation, therefore, it is politically easier to continue your rake's progress than to reform.

The redistributive consequences of monetary policy—of *any* monetary policy—in the random walk setting entail also the politicization of the central bank. It may indeed suit the administration and Congress to stress the "independence" of the Federal Reserve, but this is done in large part so that the Fed can serve as scapegoat to dilute the responsibility that elected officials would otherwise have to bear. The central bank obviously cannot be "independent" in the sense of being left alone to make decisions that have large and complex redistributive consequences. It must instead make monetary policy "a little bit at a time," watch for the resulting shifts in political pressures upon itself, and bend with them. Since no one group controls it, it may be surrounded by politicians (and economic experts) decrying its "independence" out of genuine frustration, but the status of this intensely politicized institution bears really no resemblance to the traditional concept of an independent central bank, staffed by professional experts and standing apart from politics.

It is also most unlikely that stricter subordination of the central bank to political authority would produce an improvement in monetary stability. To depoliticize money, on the other hand, means either to find a safe way to privatize the money supply or else to choose an objective rule, a monetary constitution, such as could be administered by an independent body of accountable professional experts.

Dissatisfaction and exasperation with the monetary instability of the last twenty years has stimulated numerous proposals for monetary policy reform. Constant monetary growth rules, price level targeting, a return to the gold standard, and the denationalization of money are among the most familiar, but there are also a great many less sweeping reform proposals having to do with the particulars of Federal Reserve governance or operating procedures. The number of proposals that have been advanced has long since reached the point where everybody's striving for the best has become the enemy of the merely good. Would-be reformers probably outnumber defenders of the status quo (if any!) by a considerable margin. But we are getting precisely nowhere.

Is it possible to find some feasible "good" reform that is not the enemy of anyone's "best"? I have one candidate. This proposal does not require us to choose sides, all at once, on all the issues that divide Keynesians, monetarists, Austrians, new classicists, and supply-siders. Nor does it commit us to a radical restructuring of present institutions or policy procedures. It lacks the appeal, perhaps, of those radical reforms that promise "optimal" results. But it is definitely a step in the right direction—and it will permit the continuation of the debate over whose optimum to go for.

The proposal is that Congress should legislate a *maximum* for the monetary base that the Federal Reserve could have in existence at any given time. On the date that the legislation takes effect, the legal maximum base should be set at some value a few percentage points (10–15 percent?) above the actual base. From then on, the *base ceiling* should be computed using a growth rate rule from the initial date.

The base ceiling idea does not come down on either side of the age-old "rules versus discretion" debate. It sets a *limit* to the discretion allowed. But this limit could initially be set so as to leave considerable scope for discretion. At the same time, implementation of the base ceiling would not preclude other measures to limit discretion or to improve accountability. The proposal, therefore, could be supported, at least on an interim basis, by most people on both sides of the rules versus discretion issue.

Similarly, a legislated base ceiling leaves open the choice both of short-term policies and of operating procedures. As long as the Federal Reserve finds itself well below the ceiling, it can expand or contract, and it can execute either policy by using either quantity targets or interest rate targets. It could be supported, therefore, by people with quite divergent ideas about what the best central bank operating procedures would be.

If, then, the base ceiling proposal leaves undecided all the more important monetary policy issues debated in recent years, what earthly good could it possibly be? The main purpose is to reduce the prevailing uncertainty about the dollar price level over the medium and longer term. A credible commitment to a base ceiling by the U.S. authorities would accomplish this. Admittedly, the Fed would retain short-term discretion as long as it is below the ceiling. But the ceiling precludes the possibility that U.S. monetary policy will come to follow a long sequence of predominantly inflationary moves.

Reducing the uncertainty about the value of the dollar over the long term will increase the volume of long-term bond financing and, at the same time, help bring down nominal interest rates by reducing or, in the best case, even eliminating the inflation premium. More predictable future dollar prices will improve the allocation of real investment resources in the country. It is perhaps not too much to hope that, over the somewhat longer run, personal saving which has declined so much in our monetary mismanagement period will also revive, as the American public relearns that we cannot all get rich from real estate speculation or being smart at inflationary finance. In these ways U.S. capital accumulation would be put on a sounder footing than past policies of steep tax incentives for investment combined with high real rates of interest to attract the requisite financing through foreign capital inflows.

Although reducing long-term nominal uncertainty is the main purpose of the base ceiling proposal, it is plausible that it will also reduce the amount of short-term speculation on the course of monetary policy. The market's intense fascination with month-by-month (or even week-by-week) variations in the growth rate of the money supply is a fairly recent phenomenon which is itself an adaptation to the random walk monetary environment. Once it becomes clear that the Thursday money supply announcements do not signal changes in the stance of the monetary authorities over the longer term, inflation expectations will become less volatile. This would carry with it two benefits.

First, the less volatile and more coherent the inflation expectations of the public are, the better we will be able to predict the consequences of macroeconomic policy measures. This, therefore, will make possible more rational stabilization policy—which, being more nearly foreseeable, will stabilize expectations further. When the interaction between the policy authorities and the private sector becomes more reliable in this way, both sides find themselves better able to anticipate the actual outcome of their actions. Second, increased stability of inflation expectations should also reduce the volatility of exchange rates and, thereby, help create a less uncertain environment for the sectors of the economy most exposed to foreign competition here or abroad.

Monetary policy can probably never be completely removed from politics. But the month-to-month conduct of it can be more or less insulated from immediate political pressures. A monetary constitution which makes the price level fairly predictable and keeps interest rate movements within reasonably narrow bounds would shackle the redistributive powers of the central bank. That, of course, is the main prerequisite for depoliticizing central banking.

My base ceiling idea is not the only proposal that could produce these effects, and it may not be the best of those that would. It is, however, in this direction that we should move. That is the main thing. The United States has disinflated during the 1980s, successfully if not painlessly. But this has been seen around the world as being due primarily to the individuals serving as president (Ronald Reagan) and chairman of the Federal Reserve Board (Paul Volcker). Monetary stability should rest on institutional arrangements, not be left contingent on personalities. The inflation rate may be lower now, but monetary reform is still needed.

Introduction and Summary

Patricia Dillon and Thomas D. Willett

While the strong U.S. anti-inflationary measures of the early 1980s succeeded in halting the continual escalation of international inflation of the preceeding two decades, the costs of this inflationary binge, including those of stopping it, have been enormous. The contributors to this volume seek to diagnose the causes of this dark episode in economic history and consider ways in which we can reduce the probabilities of a repeat in the future. Their contributions are grouped into four categories, starting with reasons for the great stagflation and ending with proposals for monetary reform.

The first set of papers compares and assesses theories on the causes of inflation, and emphasizes that both economics and politics are important in explaining inflation and in developing policy prescriptions. The second section of the volume examines a particular source of inflationary bias, the political business cycle: how it is modeled and how significant it has been in modern American economic history. The political economy of monetary policy-making is the subject of the third section. Finally, the last section of the book is devoted to a critical look at proposals for reform.

The first section of this introduction offers a brief background perspective on the political economy of the emergence of macroeconomic instability. The following section presents summaries of the individual papers. The introduction concludes with a summary of key points suggested by the analysis presented in the volume.

A Perspective on the Political Economy
of Macroeconomic Instability

Almost all economists, Keynesian as well as monetarist, agree that in the longer run inflation is essentially a monetary phenomenon, hence the heavy emphasis on monetary issues in this volume. But recognition of this crucial linkage is just the beginning, not the end, of the explanation for why inflation escalated. One also needs to explain the factors which influenced monetary policy and hence induced or at least allowed inflation to escalate.

It should not be surprising from the title of this volume that its contributors see the determinants of inflation as going beyond pure economics. It can certainly be argued that a nontrivial part of the increasing macroeconomic miseries of this period were due to adverse economic shocks such as the OPEC price hikes and to mistakes in economic analysis such as a tendency toward overly optimistic forecasts. However, much more important underlying factors were at work, which created in the United States and other major industrial countries politicized elements in those systems that perpetuated and magnified inflationary pressures.

While the worldwide character of this inflationary binge quite reasonably led many writers to seek its major source in the operation of the international monetary system, more detailed research suggests that for most countries this has not been the major cause. International economic interdependence has become important for issues of short-run macroeconomic management even for large countries like the United States. It has been argued that the international liquidity explosion accompanying the breakdown of the Bretton Woods international monetary system in the early 1970s resulted in vicious circles of inflation and depreciation under the new system of flexible exchange rates. The further claim that these factors caused the worldwide escalation of inflation during the 1970s is based on oversimplified analysis which does not stand up to careful inspection.

The similarity in inflationary experiences across countries was due for the most part to similar national developments in domestic political and economic pressures and attitudes. In this regard the international transmission of ideas probably made a much greater contribution to continuing inflation than the direct international transmission of economic disturbances emphasized in most of the economics literature.

The spread of the Keynesian notions that governments could and should use macroeconomic policy to offset short-run increases in unemployment, combined with a range of institutional developments that reduced the downward flexibility of wages and prices, generated a dynamic which we can see in hindsight was bound to create the gradual emergence of a strong inflationary bias. This was complemented by decreasing concerns among economists and the general public about the effects of government budget deficits, which contributed to the escalation of these deficits over time. Although it can be argued that Keynesian analysis itself contains an inflationary bias, this was not the major culprit. It was the interaction of Keynesian economics with democratic politics which was the real problem. Had the policy advice of Keynesian economists been followed consistently when they called for restrictive rather than expansionary policy, the inflation and unemployment suffered over the last two decades undoubtedly would have been far lower.

As the contributors to this volume show, a powerful inflationary bias was created when the politicization of macroeconomic policy combined with the short time horizon typically displayed in the political process. There is growing recognition that over the long run higher inflation cannot buy lower unemployment. Indeed, typically the reverse holds: higher inflation will contribute to keeping unemployment high. However, in the short run, a trade-off still does exist. The benefits (expanding employment and rising wages and profits) tend to come first under expansionary economic policies; most of the costs (in terms of rising inflation) come later. With contractionary policies the slump in the economy comes first and the reductions in inflation come later. The effects of monetary policy on interest rates work in the same way. Monetary expansion can hold down interest rates in the short run, but in the longer run they rise with escalating inflationary expectations. With restrictive monetary policies interest rates rise before they begin to fall. Thus focusing on short-term effects generates a substantial inflationary bias.

The creation of an independent Federal Reserve to make monetary policy in the United States was designed to overcome these political difficulties. As a number of contributors point out, however, in practice the independence of the Federal Reserve from political pressures has been more of a myth than a reality. Political considerations can initiate as well as perpetuate inflationary pressures. The technical literature on the political business cycle has shown that there can be strong incentives for governments to destabilize the economy for political gain rather than to stabilize the economy by offsetting instability in the private sector as envisioned in Keynesian theory. By overexpanding the economy just before an election, incumbent politicians can take advantage of favorable short-run effects, relying on the adverse inflationary side effects to be delayed until safely after the election.

The topic of political business cycles has generated considerable academic controversy among economists and political scientists. Much of this controversy has centered around two issues: how consistently the political business cycle game has been played and how successfully the public's process of rational learning will limit the political gain derived from playing the game. Much of this debate has focused on issues of minor relevance. It does not require the sophisticated statistical techniques often utilized to recognize that such behavior occurs sometimes but not always. In this volume we interpret political business cycles in a broader sense, to refer to the range of political considerations which influence macroeconomic policy-making. From this perspective we view the political business cycle as only one of a number of relevant pressures. Furthermore, much sophisticated analysis which has appeared in the recent literature predicts that we should not expect to see this particular type of political business cycle at every election. Still, even in this narrow sense, the empirical work presented and surveyed in this volume shows it to have been an important influence on the escalation of inflation in the United States, at least as significant as the supply shocks emphasized by many Keynesian economists.

While critical of much traditional Keynesian analysis, a number of contributors also criticize the strong forms of the monetarist rational expectations models which have become so popular in recent years. Drawing upon public choice analysis to consider the incentives for individual behavior in decentralized situations, we see that a rational basis can often be ascribed to behavior which appears to be irrational at the aggregate level, and indeed would be if the public comprised a single organized entity. From this perspective both cost-push activities by individual unions and considerable voter ignorance can be quite rational. It does not require assumptions of irrational nonmaximizing behavior to believe that the economy behaves in a Keynesian manner in the short run and that the incentives for political manipulation of the economy in harmful ways can continue for quite a while.

Where these contributors differ most strongly with traditional Keynesian analysis is in emphasizing that the problems of coordination which give Keynesian policies the potential for enhancing economic stability create political incentives to adopt quite different types of policies. For example, the substantial inflationary pressures kindled by the financing of the Vietnam War resulted primarily not from the influence of Keynesian economics but rather from the failure, for "good" political reasons, of President Johnson to follow the recommendations of his Keynesian advisers.

The analysis presented here suggests that it is dangerous to conclude that the recent success of our anti-inflationary policies implies that we need not worry about a serious resurgence of inflation. We do not doubt that learning from past mistakes contributes to improvements in policy-making; but the frequency with which elected and appointed officials in the past have ignored the recommendations of their economic advisers for "good" short-term political reasons suggests that we cannot safely rely on such learning to prevent the reemergence of inflationary problems. Given the complexity of the short-run behavior of the economy, it is unlikely that politically induced tendencies to err on the inflationary side are quickly detected by the general public. While recent experience has shown that democratic politics does not imply ever-increasing inflation, there is good reason to believe that an inflationary bias will continue to operate over the long run, resulting in both higher inflation and higher (not lower) unemployment.

Thus it is important to consider possible institutional reforms to constrain and/or tilt the balance of policy-making incentives against this bias. The attention span in Washington and other capitals is often rather short. It may prove a hopeless task to attempt to focus sufficient attention on avoiding future macroeconomic instability when the current inflation rate is low. We still believe the effort should be made.

Current concerns about limiting budget deficits are a hopeful sign, both in terms of political attention to long-run issues and because reduced deficits would in themselves reduce inflationary pressures. The analysis in this book shows that these pressures come from a wide variety of sources, however, so that bringing budget deficits under control would be far from sufficient to eliminate serious inflationary biases.

Ideally, the way to correct biases is to remove their sources. For example, efforts to increase public understanding of the longer-run consequences of playing the political business cycle game would be all to the good; so would attempts to improve policies which influence the micro-economic operation of our economy to increase productivity growth and reduce cost-push pressures. Most of the contributors to this volume are doubtful that such efforts would be sufficient, however. Perhaps most essential is the need to consider fundamental reform of our monetary institutions in order to constrain the ability of the monetary authorities to stimulate or accommodate escalating inflation. An effective system of constraints offers the prospect of ultimately limiting the accommodation of inflation and at the same time of creating a better set of incentives for the operation of the political process and the private economy.

The nature of such a constraint system is not a minor technical detail, and monetary reform is not a step to be taken lightly or revised frequently. One of the reasons that monetary reform has not received more active attention is that the two most widely known proposals, a return to a gold standard and the adoption of a simple monetary rule, have been subjected to considerable criticism by economists. Many economists believe that variability in the velocity of money and/or the demand and supply of gold would cause such systems to generate instability. Others, while concerned about the problem of long-run inflationary bias, would not like to see all scope for discretionary monetary policy eliminated. Thus there has been considerable disagreement even among those who agree on a serious need for major reform.

Fortunately, economists in recent years have developed a wider menu of proposals for fundamental reform, many of which are immune to the criticisms of the earlier gold standard and monetary rule proposals and offer greater scope to accommodate compromises between contending points of view. Such issues are considered in the papers in the concluding section of this volume. Our contributors are far from being of a single mind as to desirable reform, but they are all agreed that this is an issue which should receive serious attention. They agree also that the adoption of a political economy perspective, rather than a narrower economic prospective, is essential if reform is going to be acceptable as well as effective.

Summaries of Contributions

The Political and Economic Causes of the Great Stagflation

Willett and Banaian argue in "Explaining the Great Stagflation: Toward a Political Economy Framework" that economic analysis is an essential but incomplete guide to understanding the causes and the progress of inflation, and that any discussion of inflation must be couched in terms of factors that stimulate it in the first place and factors that sustain it afterwards. The paper reviews standard economic treatments of inflation (e.g., the Phillips curve—which it is argued is still useful if carefully interpreted—and the quantity theory) and the anti-inflationary macropolicy measures usually exercised.

In contrasting Keynesian and monetarist approaches, the authors point out that Keynesian explanations tend to emphasize elements that stimulate inflation, and monetarist explanations tend to emphasize elements that sustain it. Their political economy synthesis also includes the role of political and social factors, arguing that their interaction with economic elements is necessary for an adequate understanding of the onset of inflation and its continuance, and arguing that sociological, political, and economic considerations, if properly framed, can be seen as complementary rather than competitive explanations of the inflationary process. They include in their explanation of recent American inflation a careful look at the political process itself, as well as its outcome.

Their discussion of international inflation also relies on the integration of various sorts of pressures beyond economic ones, emphasizing throughout initiating versus sustaining elements. There is a strong element of the public choice approach in the paper; the authors encourage the reader to focus on the analysis of individual agents' or groups' actions and on the role of institutions. They conclude that despite the success of recent anti-inflation efforts, the current institutional environment likely contains a serious inflationary bias over the long run.

In "Inflation and Politics: Six Theories in Search of Reality," political scientist William Mitchell concentrates on the political content of the major macroeconomic theories of stagflation. He recognizes that economists' notions of the political business cycle and public choice analysis both take explicit account of political elements, but that most other economic theories do not deal with them systematically. His paper is a survey of six sets of ideas about how the economy works.

Keynesian theories of inflation argue for economic causes but imply political solutions; they express a faith in and reliance upon the wisdom and competence of democratic government. Rigidities in the system are seen to be on the side of the private sector (e.g., in wage levels). Keynesians believe in the efficiency of political processes but expect that markets may fail to be efficient and may need to be controlled by government. Both demand-pull and cost-push theories of inflation involve pressures generated by markets. Keynes's anti-inflation policies, both macro and micro, are described by Mitchell as neglecting the possibility of a political interest in preserving inflation.

Monetarists include political theory in their explanation of inflation, blaming government for both inflation and unemployment. Mitchell notes their belief in the existence of a political bias toward loose money and rising prices. Money is in fact the source of inflation pressure, and monetarists distrust monetary authorities. They see the government's job as the facilitation of free exchange in free markets and thus typically advocate fundamental reforms of various political institutions. Such reform is usually designed to get rid of discretionary policy in favor of a predetermined rule. For monetarists, the causes of and the cures for inflation are both political and economic.

In contrast, believers in the school of rational expectations have no political theory of inflation. Whether individuals are involved in economic or political activities, they rely heavily on information, the best they can get, and they learn. In fact, they learn to counteract government policy changes. Government therefore cannot eliminate inflation (or unemployment), but it can make things worse. Its best choice, then, is to behave predictably, according to predetermined rules. Mitchell argues that rational expectationists have a primitive conception of politics.

The public choice approach systematically includes political theory; its primary emphasis is on rational, self-interested actors within government. It has no specific theory of inflation. Some public choice models are voter-driven (the "median voter"), and some are supplier-driven (where the government is the influential determinant of policy). Mitchell suggests that before an election the former might be more appropriate to characterize political behavior, and after an election the latter better characterizes the government's behavior. Virtually all advocates of the public choice approach would agree that political actors find it easier to spend than to tax and may have vested interests in inflation, at least in the short run.

The notion of the politically manipulated business cycle is currently very fashionable. Inflation is explained as dependent upon whether voters are oriented to short-run issues or are strategically minded. The myopic voter will not recognize the connection between voter welfare and government policies. The theory is not clear about policy motives or implications; it argues that incentives exist to stimulate inflation before an election and to contract the economy after the election.

Insofar as there is a sociological analysis of inflation, it is based on the study of the structure of society in terms of power. The upper classes are assumed to dominate social and economic institutions, and the state serves the ruling class. Society is in perpetual conflict over the distribution of power, wealth, and income, and this is a primary source of inflation pressure. This analysis is often (but not exclusively) a Marxist one.

Mitchell concludes by noting that theorists in sympathy with the less well-off (e.g., Keynesians and Marxists) tend to find the causes of inflation within an unstable private economy. Others find fault with the political system instead, preferring a more powerful and independent market system and a reduced role for government.

The third paper (another by Willett and Banaian) is called "Models of the Political Process and Their Implications for Stagflation: A Public Choice Perspective." It offers, as its title suggests, a taxonomy of the major types of models of the political process, including their implications for the analysis of stagflation and for macroeconomic policy. The authors emphasize the distinction between normative economic analysis (which refers to arguments about the desirability of particular policy strategies) and normative public choice analysis (involving arguments about the desirability of the operation of the policy process).

The first of the classifications includes models that argue for efficient outcomes from political processes. Keynes believed in the efficient operation of the democratic process and in enlightened political action. The new Chicago school sees political markets functioning efficiently, just as do economic markets; if inflation persists for a very long time, it is a result of unsystematic errors or of efficient financing of a growing government sector. In contrast, the old Chicago school believes that self-interested behavior by political officials can lead to "political failure," analogous to market failure.

The second type of model is labeled leviathan and refers to the characterization of government as self-interested (versus being public-interested). The electoral check does not exist. Interest group models are currently popular, applied by economists in public choice analysis. These models are used to explain deviations from the wishes of the median voter and are characterized by rent seeking on the parts of individuals and of groups. Inflation, in fact, is explained as a result of the process of redistributional rent seeking. The last type of model is built around bureaucratic and independent regulatory behavior and typically is used to argue for structural reform to modify a perceived inflationary bias.

Willett and Banaian structure their paper around the median voter criterion for efficiency in decision making—i.e., whether voters are evenly balanced on either side of the "average" voter. They note that outcomes may persistently differ from this efficient one based on the distribution of political power, which may give rise to a systematic bias, and based on the poor information and short time horizon that are typical of voters. The reasons for such deviations are examined (why isn't the will of the people carried out?) in terms of costliness of monitoring officials, the decision process itself, and the usual formation of distributional coalitions.

Furthermore, there are few powerful incentives for the voter to become well-informed—votes of informed voters count for no more than any others—and the voting process itself generates a classic free rider problem. Willett and Banaian agree with the rational expectations school that the more systematically the government indulges in highly visible self-interested policies (such as the political business cycle), the more likely voters are to become sensitized to the issue, but they stress that many other inflationary biases in the discretionary stabilization policy process will persist.

An appendix to the paper ("An Overview of Political Business Cycles" by King Banaian) presents a more detailed review of political business cycle theory and includes a critical discussion of some of the recent controversies surrounding this theory. The role of government myopia and/or voter myopia in generating the political business cycle is given particular attention, along with strategies of voting and the formation of voter expectations.

In "The Keynesian Legacy: Does Countercyclical Policy Pay Its Way?" Thomas Mayer assesses the Keynesian legacy, that is, discretionary demand management, and finds it lacking. He argues that government efforts may be ineffective just because of lack of knowledge of *how* to stabilize the economy. Other contributing factors are covered: various lags, the existence of vested interests, forecasting errors, errors about magnitudes of change, and government irrationality (as opposed to individual rationality). Fiscal policy fails to stabilize the economy largely because both conservatives and liberals prefer (for different reasons) large deficits over the alternatives.

Monetary policy fails, and may even be destabilizing, because of difficulties in timing policy actions correctly and because of social and political incentives to rely on expansionary policy. Mayer also emphasizes the historical tendency to underestimate the costs of inflation, and the recent and growing acceptability of large deficits.

Gottfried Haberler's paper, "Wage and Price Rigidities, Supply Restrictions, and the Problem of Stagflation," revisits the question of the failure of the economy's self-corrective mechanisms. In other words, why stagflation? He reviews explanations of inflexibility in wages and prices, from those of extreme Keynesian to extreme monetarist-rational expectations. The many microeconomic barriers to flexibility fall into two categories: instances of market interference (e.g., price supports, regulation) and instances of monopoly power in both product and factor markets. The author provides thorough reviews of the various positions—monetarist, rational expectations, and Keynesian—on reasons for sluggishness of market adjustments; and he decides that although the world is neither completely classical nor completely Keynesian, classical policy prescriptions lead to fewer problems.

In addressing the issue of increasingly rigid wages and prices and inflationary pressures, Haberler provides international comparisons (especially between Europe and the United States) of the role of unions, minimum wages, and unemployment benefits. Supply shocks are analyzed as another element, especially important in recent years.

The author supports anti-inflationary monetary policy, backed by appropriate fiscal policy *and* microeconomic measures, including deregulation and free trade. Government is, after all, "the worst offender in distorting product and labor markets."

In "The Inflation Tax" McClure and Willett provide a review of the literature on that subject. Following this, they emphasize the distinction between the rate of inflation which maximizes government revenues and the (lower) so-called optimal rate of inflation which equalizes the marginal deadweight costs of inflation with those of other forms of taxation. Despite the popularity of discussions of this source of inflationary pressures, the authors argue that the inflation tax is not a terribly important consideration for the United States. It can be very important for many other countries, however, especially less-developed ones. The major criticism levied against the inflation tax literature is that it typically assumes perfect anticipation of inflation, and so the uncertainty costs of inflation are ignored and efficient levels of inflation are substantially overestimated. McClure and Willett look at two additional sources of greater revenues, namely bracket creep and unanticipated inflation. They conclude that short time horizons on the part of government policymakers and slow adjustments by the public to changing rates of inflation both contribute to perpetuation of inflationary pressures. Inflation generates more inflation.

In their review of the debate on the role of gold ("The Decline of Gold as a Source of Monetary Discipline"), Briggs et al. argue that the portrayal of relatively good macroeconomic performance under the Bretton Woods international monetary system is inappropriate as an example of the benefits of gold. The authors provide a brief history of gold in American and monetary history and a statistical analysis of the relationships between gold and the behavior of the U.S. money supply. Although it is true that the last vestiges of gold were not purged from the system until after the gold window was shut for official international transactions in 1971, the U.S. gold stock had little (if any) effective influence on the behavior of the money supply after World War II.

Nor can fixed exchange rates be credited as the primary explanation for different average levels of macroeconomic performance before and after the Bretton Woods exchange rate system. The escalation of stagflation had begun well before the switch from pegged to flexible rates and in fact contributed to the breakdown of the pegged rate system. The authors conclude that neither pegged rates nor flexible gold arrangements will effectively restrain inflation, without direct mechanisms to control the growth of the money supply.

In "Inflation Hypotheses and Monetary Accommodation: Postwar Evidence from the Industrial Countries," Willett et al. survey four popular single-factor explanations for the behavior of monetary authorities, reflected in changes in monetary aggregates, and test the explanatory power of those four factors: international liquidity increases, import price shocks, wage-push pressures, and budget deficits.

The authors find no factor dominant across countries or time periods, but emphasize that almost all factors have some explanatory power for particular times and places. They observe that a wider set of variables would produce stronger results; monetary authorities do not always respond to a particular sort of change in the same way, monetary officials themselves change and learning goes on for every newcomer and group, and decision procedures also change from time to time. Monetary reaction functions do not tend to be of the stable, easily discoverable variety often assumed in rational expectations models.

Willett et al. find considerable evidence of monetary accommodation of wage increases and budget deficits but conclude that it is dangerous to focus on any single factor as the predominant cause of inflation or to base analysis on the assumption that wage and price shocks will always be validated with monetary accommodation. They also find evidence that although international reserve increases have often been a significant determinant of monetary expansion in other industrial countries, monetary authorities still have a good deal of scope for independent national actions if they so choose. They are not subject to domination by international economic developments to the degree suggested by global monetarist and vicious circle views of world inflation. International developments can be important even for as large an economy as the United States. Witness, for example, the substantial impact which the appreciation of the dollar under President Reagan has had in slowing the rate of inflation much more rapidly than is suggested by most domestic macroeconomic models. But sustained inflation is still primarily a national responsibility except in the smallest, most open economies, since they typically find it too costly to adopt flexible exchange rates.

The Political Business Cycle

The basic idea of the political business cycle literature is that because the typical lags in adjustment of inflation to changes in macroeconomic policy are longer than for unemployment, a carefully engineered economic expansion can give incumbent politicians the advantage of a booming economy just before an election, while most of the associated inflationary costs do not follow until the election is safely over. With less than full information and a short horizon on the part of the public, political incentives exist to destabilize the economy and in the process generate an inflationary bias.

Many models of the relationship between business fluctuations and elections have been constructed and tested. Schneider and Frey, in "Politico-Economic Models of Macroeconomic Policy: A Review of the Empirical Evidence," suggest that most of these have been too simple; they ignore, for example, the possibility that political business cycle behavior may be more pronounced in an election that is close, as opposed to a safe one where ideological objectives may guide the government. The authors provide an extensive survey of voter behavior models wherein voters are influenced by the state of the economy; voters influence the government, which in turn influences the economy. The usual variables representing the state of the economy are inflation, unemployment, and the growth of real income. Although the importance of these variables differs between countries and at different times, most of the studies find a statistically significant and persistent relationship between the economic situation and voters' evaluations of government.

Despite the overwhelming evidence that macroeconomic conditions do play an important role in public opinion polls and presidential voting, the studies which have investigated the prevalence of political business cycles have often found negative results. An explanation offered by Schneider and Frey is complemented by another in the next paper, "Does the Political Business Cycle Dominate U.S. Unemployment and Inflation? Some New Evidence" by Stephen Haynes and Joe Stone, having to do with important neglected variables. Casual observation strongly suggests that governments in the United States and abroad have not attempted to generate political business cycles on every possible occasion. As Schneider and Frey stress, there is another strand of literature on the political economy of macroeconomic policy which stresses ideological or class-based macroeconomic policy. Conservative parties are more concerned with inflation, while liberal and labor parties are more concerned with unemployment. Drawing on their earlier work on this subject, the authors show how these two approaches can be integrated in a political-economic model which predicts ideological behavior by an incumbent party when an election looks like it will be safe and political business cycle behavior when it is expected to be close. They show that there is considerable empirical support for this more sophisticated synthesis.

Several disaggregated studies are reviewed and yield interesting but not surprising results: low-income voters are more concerned about unemployment, and high-income voters are more concerned about inflation.

Econometric studies of governments' utility maximizing behaviors are also surveyed. One clear result emerges from them: If the government in a representative democracy is in fear of losing its position, it will tend to switch to fiscal policy preferred by most voters. After the election, the government is likely to move back to more ideologically motivated objectives. An equivalent politico-economic cycle has been found in various eastern European authoritarian regimes, even in the absence of elections. Apparently no government is altogether independent of the support of the populace. The dictatorial regime balances the costs of suppressing discontent (in order to avoid being overthrown) against what is involved in improving economic and political conditions.

Schneider and Frey lastly survey recent related research which brings in other actors, such as the central bank, or various political interest groups (e.g., trade unions, protectionists). They conclude with a suggested agenda for further research.

Modeling of political business cycles can be grouped into studies of the demand for electoral cycles (by voters) and studies of the supply of such cycles (by governments). Haynes and Stone argue that most tests of responses of voting behavior to economic conditions are supportive of the demand-side hypothesis, challenged only by the rational expectations school and some political scientists. Similarly, most recent research on the supply side of electoral cycles shows that electoral variables significantly affect policy reaction functions.

But evidence that economic outcomes—inflation and unemployment rates—follow an electoral cycle is weak. Most recent studies have failed to find a simple recurring electoral cycle. Haynes and Stone argue that this is the result of using inappropriate statistical methods and that tests of electoral influence on inflation and on unemployment have so far been misspecified. They typically ignore two important factors: first, there are *many* sources of variation in inflation and unemployment; second, these outcomes are sluggish and must be studied over a whole presidential term (not just around elections). The authors undertake to correct this, and in the process of explaining their model provide detailed criticism of econometric procedures employed in other studies.

The results of their tests show strong four-year cycles for unemployment and inflation, and patterns in the timing of maximum and minimum values of both that are aligned with presidential elections. They conclude that cyclical variation in unemployment and inflation in America between 1951 and 1980 was due more to politically induced macropolicy than to often-discussed supply shocks (like OPEC). They also find evidence for a short-run Phillips curve; the short-term inflation-unemployment trade-offs which create the incentives for political business cycles and biases toward accommodative rather than restrictive policies are still alive and well, despite the blows they have received from rational expectations economists in recent years.

In "Political Business Cycles and the Capital Stock: Variations on an Austrian Theme," Peter Lewin attempts to integrate Austrian theory with public choice theory to describe how political decisions can distort the capital structure and thereby exaggerate (if not cause) economic cycles. That distortion is a result of government-financing activities, according to Austrian theory, and one result of political decisions and processes, according to public choice theory.

Although Lewin sees cycles as inevitable in market economies, his argument is that economic policy exacerbates, or even generates, those cycles. In a majoritarian democracy, votes are bought with subsidies that create government debt and therefore inflation. But the real value of subsidies (to their recipients) declines over time, partly because subsidized projects tend to be losers in the first place. This leads to increased pressures for higher nominal subsidies, so government debt grows, taxation increases, and inflation escalates. These can bring on a political crisis or a stock market panic. Hence the pressures for and creation of subsidies sow the seeds of recession as well. Lewin's analysis supports the existence of the political business cycle.

The Political Economy of Monetary Policy

In "Problems Inherent in Political Money Supply Regimes: Some Historical and Theoretical Lessons," Lawrence White argues that "political money supply regimes are radically flawed," and goes on to explore a number of theories explaining why undesirable political influence may be inherent in the government supply of money. He first traces the history of central banks, noting that they are political in origin, created typically to meet the fiscal needs of government. Further, they may respond to various political incentives, for example, in transferring wealth from the private to the public sector by inflating the money supply via monetization of government debt, or by increasing the money supply in order to influence macroeconomic conditions before an election, to benefit either Congress or the president.

The persistence of inflation and an increasing monetary base through time can partly be explained in terms of government incentives to raise revenues by means of seigniorage; but since a reputation for being moderate is important for future success, the government will not typically expand the money base at a short-run seigniorage-maximizing rate. The roles of central bank interest in its own profits and of government incentives for generating election cycles in money growth are also considered.

The popular myths to which Thomas Havrilesky's paper "Two Monetary and Fiscal Policy Myths" refers are that the Fed is an independent and politically neutral agency and that the objective of monetary and fiscal policies is the maximization of social welfare. In doing away with the first myth, the author argues convincingly for greatest influence on monetary policy coming from the administration; in fact, he tests this hypothesis empirically and finds statistically significant effects on monetary policy by the administration (but not by Congress).

The political business cycle literature emphasizes the payoffs to an administration from control over monetary variables. On the other hand, costs of resisting the administration are extremely high for the Fed. The Fed performs a valuable service to the administration by issuing ceremonial warnings against easy money and low interest rates, which gives the administration an excuse not to ease the money supply and sets the stage for successful monetary surprises when they are needed. Moreover, all this enhances the Fed's nonpartisan image. Congress is much less likely to exercise much direct influence on the Fed since encounters are costly:

issues are complex and usually technical, and direct contact is usually limited to hearings and the like.

A major implication of Havrilesky's paper is that the political business cycle is an incidental effect of the Fed's pursuit of other objectives. Fiscal redistributive policies put parties in power in the first place, and the role of monetary policy is to compensate for expected vote losses as a result of those redistributive policies. That is, monetary supply explosions are attempts to generate periods of apparent prosperity in order to alleviate the electoral consequences of voters' alienation resulting from redistribution; the explosions of this century did not develop out of monetary authorities' desire to counter recession. Switches between efforts to counteract government redistributive policies on the one hand and to build credibility on the other would generate monetary policy behavior consistent with a political business cycle.

In spite of a great body of research it remains unclear whether monetary policy has in recent decades moderated or aggravated instability. Many critics argue that monetary policy has been procyclical in the short run and inflationary in the long run. Raymond Lombra, in "Monetary Policy: The Rhetoric versus the Record," takes us on a tour through the world of policy-making to help us understand why policy outcomes have frequently differed so much from stated intentions. Throughout his discussion of monetarist and nonmonetarist explanations for inflation he emphasizes that the economic *and* political environments faced by policymakers are inadequately accounted for, and that understanding policy problems requires a combination of political and economic analysis.

The political aspects of monetary policy-making influence the selection of policy actions. This bears little resemblance to the scientific approach typically envisioned by economists. Problems are complex, individuals' priorities differ, goals are typically not explicit, and muddling through is about the best that can be hoped for. This being the case, the selection of intermediate targets is no better; but Lombra argues that this is deliberate. Monetary authorities prefer to shift attention to technical issues (about means) and away from sensitive political issues (about ends). Political incumbents prefer the vagueness, too. They can claim some credit if policy succeeds or claim the Fed ignored their urgings after policies fail. Edward Kane makes the same point in a later paper.

In executing policies the Fed reacts primarily to short-run domestic pressures (both political and economic), but not according to any simple rules. There is a tendency to try to stabilize the short-run environment, thereby risking long-run destabilization.

The economic factors that condition monetary policy are numerous and account for much divergence between rhetoric and results. Lombra discusses four: lags exist in the process, short-run effects of a policy are not the same as long-run, uncertainty about effects—or even about key structural relationships—is pervasive, and the open economy is a source of many complicating factors.

The author analyzes the 1970s and concludes that both economic and political factors persistently resulted in shortsightedness on the part of the Fed. That period is in part responsible for current efforts to reform the Fed toward more policy coordination and/or improved accountability. Lombra much prefers the latter.

The factors that in the past contributed to a short time horizon and erratic policies from within the Fed still persist. Forecasts are often poor; policymakers ignore the role of expectations of the public and vacillate about the significance of influential variables. They operate in an atmosphere of great uncertainty with respect to important structural relationships and the path of a dynamic economy. They usually (and understandably) confine their efforts to stabilizing short-run nominal interest rates. Both political and economic factors—institutional structure and incentives—are essential elements in the explanation of the Fed's short time horizon and lack of concern with the longer term.

Economics explains the effects of policies, but we must look to politics to explain why policy is chosen. In "Politics and Monetary Policy," Nathaniel Beck provides a wide-ranging survey of political theories of central bank behavior, none of which relies upon the traditional public interest theory of political behavior. The Fed is seen as nonpartisan but not apolitical.

One set of explanations involves the relationship between the bank and the executive, with the bank seen as the agent of the executive. The authority of the Fed versus that of the president is at issue when the two disagree; when the Fed and the executive cooperate, the issue becomes the creation of political business cycles. The general conclusion is that the Fed is not completely dominated by the president, but its powers vis-à-vis the executive are limited.

Another set of models, either leader- or voter-driven, addresses the question of the use of monetary policy to maximize the probability of reelection. Beck surveys the political business cycle literature and concludes that no unequivocal evidence for the cycle exists.

A third political approach to monetary policy is the party control model. Political parties are characterized as stable coalitions with clear policy preferences. This approach, like the earlier ones, offers additional insights but takes inadequate account of too many important factors—for example, the complexities of political entrepreneurship. A president may be pushed by domestic or international forces into actions that go against the interests of his coalition.

Another rich set of explanations is built around the organizational and bureaucratic aspects of the central bank. Organizational theories emphasize internal politics and incentives that lead to "disjointed incrementalism": the bank continues doing whatever it was doing last month, making small changes to head off perceived problems, checking the effects, then going back to the initial iterative sequence of trial-and-error behavior. Procyclical effects of policy changes can be explained simply by adding the existence of lags. Bureaucratic theories are related, but they see central bankers as rational individuals intent on minimizing costs of policy changes and on maximizing personal interests—perhaps budget size, flexibility, or future job opportunities. Beck urges cautious use of this personal interest model, suggesting that it may be less powerful a predictor than a political interest approach, described next.

The last group of models considers the formation of monetary policy in the context of various interest groups and Congress. The Fed is often characterized as the agent of congressional committees, especially the Senate Banking Committee. Beck argues that the Fed has fought to maintain its independence from Congress (but may have an increasingly difficult time as its political visibility increases) and that Congress has apparently preferred to stay out of monetary policy-making. The Fed should not be characterized as just another federal agency. There is widespread agreement on the importance of a sound currency and agreement that monetary policy should not be made via normal political processes. There are current pressures, however, to give political authorities more control over the Fed. These should be viewed cautiously, according to Beck; although central banks must in the long run obey the dictates of the political system, in the short to medium run they do have some flexibility.

Proposals for Reform

In "Evaluating Proposals for Fundamental Monetary Reform," Mayer and Willett begin the section with an overview and critical analysis of the most popular proposals for fundamental monetary reform and find difficulties with them all, but they acknowledge the instability and inflationary tendencies inherent in the present system and argue that reform is needed. Arguments *against* reform typically point up the usefulness of the flexibility in a discretionary system, and Mayer and Willett agree. Flexibility, however, also has costs—for example, the uncertainty that it generates.

The most popular approaches to monetary reform all make specific assumptions about the stability of some parameters or functions and instability of others. For example, a simple monetary rule combined with flexible exchange rates assumes that the demand for money is relatively stable while equilibrium real exchange rates fluctuate. Arguments for fixed exchange rate systems, on the other hand, tend to assume instability in national demand for money functions and relative constancy of equilibrium real exchange rates.

Perhaps the most popular plan for reorganizing the monetary system, and certainly the longest-lived, is for the establishment of a monetary growth rate rule. This alternative would impose definite restraints upon the scope of monetary authorities' discretion but carries with it the potential danger of generating recession or inflation if velocity is in fact seriously unstable. Growth rate rules are meant to help control inflation, but they make no provision for discretionary action when it is needed—for example, in response to supply shocks. The various proposals for narrow constitutional constraints are subject also to the criticism of lack of flexibility in the face of unusual situations. The uncertainty about how any of the strictly defined rules would work is very great.

What is left? Mayer and Willett favor reform and suggest that some rule setting is in order. But they advocate a constraint rather than an optimal policy rule approach. The constraint approach would certainly be both more complex and more workable—for example, a target range for the average rate of growth of nominal income, with constraints on the rate of monetary growth implemented when the target range is violated. Any new system should enjoy widespread support, and that will require a spirit of compromise by all parties involved. But the system would be no one's ideal, because it would provide more discretion than monetarists would like and more restraints on discretion than Keynesians would like. Nevertheless, the possibility exists for structuring a system that would avoid a repeat of the escalating inflation while still being able to deal with shocks.

Greg Christainsen's paper, "Fiat Money and the Constitution: A Historical Review," argues that the founding fathers did not intend the federal government to have the power to issue fiat money. For many years it has been the government's interpretation that the Constitution explicitly forbids states to issue fiat money but does not prohibit Congress from doing so; but the granting of legal tender status to paper money was not a power enumerated to Congress in the Constitution, and the founding fathers intended to limit government to clearly enumerated powers.

The issue reached the Supreme Court when Civil War greenbacks were challenged as legal tender. The issue of fiat money was debated in several subsequent cases, until the granting of legal tender status to the greenback was decided to be an inherent power of the government. Not until 1968 did Congress complete the transition to fiat money by declaring that silver certificates would no longer be redeemed by the government in silver.

Why not privately produced money instead of the usual government monopoly? Michael Melvin's analysis ("Monetary Confidence, Privately Produced Monies, and Domestic and International Monetary Reform") raises questions about the desirability of the private provision of money. The reasons for a government monopoly are political as well as economic, and the single most important element of those reasons is public confidence. Melvin first analyzes a group of proposals for alternative monetary systems and then analyzes various empirical studies of demand for competing currencies as a function of inflation differentials. There is some support for the fact that currencies compete on the basis of variability of inflation. Many currency competition advocates, however, have tended to overestimate the degree of competition. Consumer confidence is crucial and costly to develop; there is considerable historical evidence that switching to a new medium of exchange is highly inelastic with respect to a currency's inflation rate (between the currencies of different countries). This is not the case, however, for money as a store of value.

Among the arguments for and explanations of government monopoly which Melvin surveys, one of the strongest (but nevertheless still controversial) is that money production is a natural monopoly. Confidence-creating selling costs mean that fixed costs are large, while the marginal costs of increasing output are small; a single currency in a trade area is efficient. The long history of government monopoly is not the result of societal ignorance (as has been argued). Private solution to money production is possible, but private issuers would have to receive a premium sufficient to exceed the gain from deceptive overissue or contract defaults would be highly likely. Melvin argues that government money should be able to survive competition because it is more socially efficient. This does not mean, however, that unconstrained discretionary money creation is the optimal form of government production.

Lawrence White supports privately produced money in "Depoliticizing the Supply of Money," and undertakes to build a case for it by analyzing the potential failure of current suggestions for reforming the Federal Reserve system. Proposals to make the Fed more independent presume that having the Fed beholden to commercial banks is somehow preferable to having the Fed beholden to Congress. Legislatively created central banks have weak incentives to resist political pressure.

On the other hand, proposals for fixed rules to restrain the Fed are unlikely to be any more successful; White doubts the possibility of an apolitical agency that controls the money supply. There are no historical precedents. Furthermore, two conditions would have to hold. First, effective monitoring of the agency (and enforcement) would have to be carried out. The free rider problem makes this unlikely. Second, the public would have to perceive this rule to be politically stable in the long run, also unlikely.

Given the widely recognized drawbacks of our current political monetary regime, White argues for free market provision of money, specifically attacking the two primary elements of the theoretical case for government control, public good/externality arguments and the natural monopoly argument presented in the preceding paper by Melvin. With respect to the latter, White sees Melvin's "confidence-creating" costs as proportional to the real money balances the issuer has in circulation, and therefore not fixed. The premium that Melvin says must be paid to issuers (to make one-shot money supply increases unprofitable) are no greater than those necessary for the government money producer if the government has uncertain tenure and therefore a short time horizon. The "protection" premiums to issuers are no longer necessary if private money is redeemable into specie. Contract costs are much lower. And the opportunity costs of holding currency would be lower under a gold-standard free-banking system than is now the case, since lower inflation implies a lower nominal rate of interest on alternative assets. Convertibility makes desirable money behavior credible for competitive private issuers of money. White is skeptical about the possibility of depoliticizing the banking functions of government and thinks it too difficult to believe that government can be more easily held to its promises than can private firms in a competitive environment.

In "Fedbashing and the Role of Monetary Arrangements in Managing Political Stress," Ed Kane analyzes criticisms of Federal Reserve behavior and emphasizes that the tendency of critics to adopt particular narrow economic perspectives has generated the appearance of a wide range of technical disagreement and contradictory proposals. This has contributed to the Federal Reserve's ability to deflect criticisms and justify its traditional defenses of its discretionary policies as necessary to deal with the complexities of monetary issues.

The political relationships between Congress, the executive, and the Fed are not clearly defined, and for good reason. Washington is full of Fedbashers, and the Fed seems to be willing to absorb critical blows, again for good reason. Kane presents arguments that the looseness of the aforementioned relationships serves several real purposes. It leaves room for politicians to blame the Fed for unpopular policies or outcomes and allows the Fed to preserve its privileges—of budgetary autonomy, public recognition, broad policy capabilities, and so on. Although many preferable systems could be devised whereby the Fed was more accountable to Congress, none of the three groups is interested in changing the system. The Fed's wide range of policy discretion and the lack of clear accountability procedures allows Congress and the president to Fedbash when politically expedient. Successful monetary reform would have to undo a number of incentives that make present arrangements convenient for all three groups.

The executive and Congress try to influence the Fed's policy goals, but they want to be able to avoid blame for unpopular policies. The existence and the status of the Fed depend on rules set by Congress. That fact and a whole set of other sticks and carrots keep the Fed in line to a great extent. The Fed faces conflicts in having commitments to fight inflation and to keep financial institutions liquid. No one—not even Congress—

can examine the Fed's policy priorities, since board and Open Market Committee policy debates are secret.

Monetary reformers interested in establishing nondiscretionary monetary rules favor "naive, brute-force" ways to reduce the short-run bias that political pressures and lags give monetary policy. Such a rule would ensure consistent decisions across business and electoral cycles but would require Congress constantly to review the appropriateness of the rule, the levels for policy triggers, and compliance of the Fed with the rule. It would be harder for Congress to avoid blame for unpopular political outcomes, a cost that elected officials are unwilling to bear.

Kane explores a number of other methods of putting more explicit short-run political pressures on the Fed which would make politicians less able to disclaim responsibility for policies—in other words, which would introduce incentives to look past the current stage of the business cycle. Unfortunately, reformers have not managed to present a unified front or speak in a single voice, and their many suggestions tend not only to cancel each other out but also to bury real concerns about the absence of political accountability for actions by the Fed.

With the increasing recognition that the Federal Reserve is not really independent of political pressures (emphasized also in the papers by Beck and Lombra), critics from both the right (such as Milton Friedman) and from the left (such as Lester Thurow) have suggested that the Fed be made more directly accountable to elected officials. These officials could then be held directly responsible for their monetary performance by the public at the ballot box. Such proposals have considerable appeal, but the weight of the analysis presented earlier on political business cycles suggests the likelihood of substantial inflationary biases in the operation of the democratic political process which would limit the effectiveness of the electoral check against inflationary performances by monetary authorities.

This presumption is reinforced by the analysis presented in "Subordinating the Fed to Political Authorities Won't Control Inflationary Tendencies" by Banaian, Laney, McArthur, and Willett. They argue that the primary issue with respect to the need for monetary reform is *not* the independence of the Federal Reserve system as a reasonable structure; indeed, it may be desirable to insulate monetary decision making from the political process. They briefly review the historical debate over the desirability of the independence of the Fed and critically analyze recent arguments that bureaucratic incentives to maximize budgets have been an important explanation for inflation in the U.S. They note that while greater political control over the Fed would reduce the scope for bureaucratic expansion, it would at the same time increase political pressure for inflationary policies. They point out that in fact the majority of the central banks in the industrial countries have relatively little independence and that these countries have tended to have higher rates of money growth and inflation than those whose central banks have greater independence. They present a statistical analysis which incorporates other influences on the rate of inflation and find that independence still has large negative effects on inflation rates.

They conclude that the performance of the Federal Reserve comes closer to those of the most independent central banks, in Germany and Switzerland, than to the more politically accountable central banks in the other industrial countries. Thus while the current degree of political independence of the Federal Reserve has not been an effective check against inflationary pressures, attempts to make the Federal Reserve more directly politically accountable would appear to be a move in the wrong direction.

As a reading of the papers in this section makes clear, there is no simple institutional solution to the problem of monetary instability. All of the contributors to this volume share the view, however, that the success of anti-inflationary policies in the first half of the 1980s should not lull us into a false sense of security that the great stagflation of the 1970s was merely a historical accident, or that our current institutional structure for macroeconomic policy-making is fundamentally sound.

A Summary of Key Points

The contributions summarized above are wide-ranging, diverse, sometimes even in disagreement with each other. Nevertheless, certain fundamental ideas emerge. The following fifteen points present what we see as some of the most important conclusions to be drawn from the analysis presented in this volume.

1. Despite the frequency of criticisms and controversies, *mainstream economic analysis provides a useful and indeed essential framework for understanding the development of stagflation.*

Inflation is essentially a monetary phenomenon in the sense that expansionary monetary and/or fiscal policy are both necessary and sufficient conditions for inflation. Increasing inflationary expectations help explain why we developed simultaneous high rates of inflation and unemployment. However, to explain inflation economic analysis must be complemented with social and political analysis in order to understand why the expansionary macroeconomic policies necessary to sustain inflation are adopted. While adverse economic shocks and policy mistakes due to faulty economic analysis and/or forecasting errors explain a nontrivial portion of the acceleration of inflation, political incentives to inflate and to avoid disinflation have been even more important.

2. *Control of inflation is largely a national responsibility.*

While the growth of international economic interdependence has increased the influence of international developments on national macroeconomic conditions, for most countries these effects are not so strong that they dominate the domestic economy. While changes in the international monetary system have affected stagflation and macroeconomic policies, they have not been the dominant explanation of the acceleration of world inflation as has been suggested by global monetarists and by vicious-circle arguments. International developments may have stabilizing as well as destabilizing effects, and flexible exchange rates may help disinflation rather than just being an engine of inflation as has been frequently alleged.

3. *The trend of recent economic research suggests that the costs of inflation are greater and the benefits are less than has commonly been thought by economists during most of the postwar period.*

While there is still scope for governments to raise revenue through the inflation tax, recent research suggests that the use of inflationary finance is much more costly than has been suggested by conventional analysis. Both theoretical research and empirical research have undercut the view that inflation can facilitate permanent increases in employment. Furthermore, because high rates of inflation are difficult to forecast accurately, they impose uncertainty and instability costs on the economy and are much more important than the allocative inefficiency costs of perfectly anticipated inflation which were stressed in much of the earlier postwar economic literature. There is now evidence that over the longer term higher rates of inflation may lead to lower rather than higher levels of output and employment; for example, inflation can interact with the tax system to create perverse incentive effects that can distort the output mix so as to reduce employment.

4. *Many of the disagreements in economists' analyses of inflation concern differences (often implicit) in the time period being considered.*

For example, in the very short run a considerable portion of price-level changes may not be closely related to changes in aggregate demand, and considerable unpredictable variability in velocity and the monetary aggregates make precise government control of the economy impossible. Over longer periods these difficulties decline tremendously in importance. Likewise, in many dimensions the economy behaves in a much more Keynesian manner the shorter the period being considered, and it behaves in a more monetarist manner the longer the period in question.

5. *In general, it is not useful to try to find a single dominant cause of inflation; rather, we need to focus on the combinations of elements which result in inflation.*

For example, high wage settlements cannot by themselves be a cause of sustained inflation, but they can give rise to pressures for monetary accommodation which do stimulate an ongoing inflation. In such a case there is no logical basis for singling out either the initial cost push or the monetary accommodation as being the *real* cause of inflation. Both aspects are important.

6. *In explaining inflation it is useful to distinguish between **initiating** and **sustaining** factors.*

Initiating factors which stimulate monetary accommodation may include such factors as wage and commodity price pushes, increased government spending and budget deficits, political business cycles, and devaluations and international liquidity increases.

Sustaining factors which tend to perpetuate inflation include the adjustment of inflationary expectations and desires to avoid the temporary (but nontrivial) increases in interest rates and unemployment which generally accompany slowdowns in the rate of monetary expansion. In ongoing inflation these interactions make it difficult or impossible to make a clear distinction between demand-pull and cost-push inflation.

7. *The integration of economic and political analysis is necessary for the understanding of both initiating and sustaining factors, and these can be studied productively at many different levels of analysis.*

Thus, for example, at one level we can investigate how budget deficits and wage increases influence monetary expansion, while at another we can seek to explain how the wage increases and budget deficits came about. These in turn can be explained in a number of different ways. Within an appropriate political economy framework, economic, political, and sociological analysis can be viewed as complementary rather than necessarily conflicting approaches to the study of inflation.

Disputes should focus primarily on the quality of particular analysis rather than the general superiority or inferiority of different disciplinary approaches. Marxist analysis correctly points to the role that distribution conflicts can play in the generation of stagflation, but it is seriously deficient in analyzing the full nature of these conflicts and the ways in which they operate through the political process.

8. *Due to problems of information costs, coordination, and collective decision making, the pursuit of rational self-interest by individuals and groups may lead to outcomes which are irrational or inefficient from an aggregate perspective.*

These insights from public choice analysis imply that such factors as wage push, differences between short-term and long-term inflation-unemployment trade-offs, and political business cycles which would not persist in simple rational expectations models may be consistent with rational behavior in more complex views of the political economy. Further research on the political economy of the inflationary process needs to focus on how various important individuals and groups perceive their interests, the factors which offset the comparative effective political influence of these groups, and the interactions which may exist among the major actors.

9. *The demand for inflation is largely a derived demand.*

While there are distribution gains to some from inflation, adjustments in inflationary expectations and other factors have generally kept inflation from having strong predictable income redistribution effects among income or functional groups in the economy. (The main exception is the generation of government revenue.) While propensities to inflation may be heavily influenced by distributional battles, these are generally not direct demands for more inflation, but are instead demands for greater government spending, lower taxes, lower interest rates, higher wages, and lower unemployment which create more inflation as a by-product. This helps explain why inflation often continues, even though it is viewed as undesirable by a vast majority of the public.

10. *The democratic process is likely to contain serious inflationary biases in the absence of a well-informed public.*

The sources of such inflationary biases include the disportionate influence which government officials and organized interests may have in the political process, and the ballot box rewards which rationally ignorant members of the public give incumbent politicians when the economy is booming at election time as well as (and perhaps more importantly) the costs they levy when the economy is in recession. Combined with a short time horizon on the part of a significant number of voters, differences between short-term and longer-term inflation-unemployment relationships give political incentives for governments to expand the economy before elections, as depicted in models of the political business cycle, and impose strong political constraints on the pursuit of disinflationary policies. Both aspects have had important real world effects, although the limitations to the pursuit of disinflation appear to have been a more persistent consideration.

11. *Incentives to stimulate a political business cycle still exist.*

Political business cycles have not occurred regularly at every election. In fact, as rational expectations theorists emphasize, if such cycles did occur each time, learning by the public over time could be expected to eliminate any possible political gains from such a strategy. Ironically, because the political business cycle game has been played only sometimes but not always, the scope for political gain from such behavior still exists. The political business cycle is but one example of the more general problem of the inflationary bias which exists in modern politicized economies.

12. *Institutional arrangements can have important influences on the operation of the inflationary process.*

This can clearly be seen in cross-country comparisons. Differences in collective bargaining arrangements, the degree of political independence of central banks, and the effective distribution of political power among different groups can all have important influences.

13. *The independence of the Federal Reserve is a partial myth.*

Central banks need to be considered as an important element in the inflationary process whose behavior may differ at times from that desired either by government officials or important private interests. The view that Federal Reserve decision making is dominated by technical expertise operating independently of political pressures is a myth. The Federal Reserve is often heavily influenced by pressures from Congress, the executive branch, and private interests, but it is not a simple captive of any of these groups; nor are all political pressures partisan ones. Direct study of the behavior of monetary authorities is a crucial aspect of the political economy of inflation.

14. *As a result of the above considerations, a strong case can be made that we need major institutional reforms to reduce current inflationary propensities. Unfortunately, all of the simplest types of proposals which have become popular suffer from serious deficiencies which would make them very risky strategies to pursue.*

This applies to the major proposals for a return to gold, the substitution of private for government money, making the Federal Reserve more directly responsible to the voters, and simple monetary growth rules.

15. *As a consequence, it is important to consider more complicated compromise proposals.*

While a strong case exists against the degree of discretionary macroeconomic policy-making which we have had in the past, there are plausible scenarios under which any of the various proposals which completely eliminate discretion would not work well. What is needed is agreement on the development of automatic limits on the range of permissible discretion. For such an approach to be feasible, it will be necessary for the proponents of the different main schools of economic thought to adopt a constitutional approach toward considering acceptable "second best" safeguards, rather than continuing to be concerned primarily only with their own conflicting minority views of first-best reforms.

Part One

The Political and Economic Causes of

the Great Stagflation

1 Explaining the Great Stagflation: Toward a Political Economy Framework

Thomas D. Willett and King Banaian

The difficulty facing the typical citizen in understanding the causes of inflation can be substantial. Popular treatments indicate a vast number of different possible causes—budget deficits, monetary expansion, OPEC, commodity shortages, consumerism, big business monopoly, decline of the work ethic, irresponsible labor unions, capital shortage and productivity growth slowdown, social tensions (perhaps inherent in capitalism), growth of the welfare state, defense spending, lack of political discipline, the adoption of Keynesian economics, loss of a gold anchor, the breakdown of the international monetary system—to name a few. The confusion which can be generated by such a broad list of factors frequently held responsible for inflation is compounded by the frequent absence of accompanying discussion of how the different explanations interrelate and by the tendency of many commentators to focus on some one particular factor as the "real" cause or major explanation of inflation.

In this paper we present a relatively simple framework which helps us see how the different major explanations of inflation relate to one another. One of the virtues of adopting such an approach is that it clearly shows the difficulties of attempting to meaningfully discuss any one single factor as the real cause of inflation. In general, we will see that where ongoing inflation is at issue there need to be at least two types of factors at work: those which initiate inflationary pressures and those which lead to the accommodation of these pressures and create sustained inflation.

This simple distinction between initiating and sustaining factors helps to explain a good deal of the difference in emphasis between monetarists and Keynesians in their analysis of cost-push inflation. In textbook treatments of inflation, we often refer to inflation as being either cost-push or demand-pull. Pure cost-push inflation occurs when the prices of factors of production rise independently of developments in the macroeconomy, as in the case of a supply shortage. On the other hand, increases in prices due to increased spending, that is, a demand increase along a given supply schedule, is labeled demand-pull inflation. Both schools agree that cost-push pressures cannot create a sustained inflation by themselves without monetary accommodation, but many Keynesians place their emphasis on the initial behavior of wages or commodity prices as the key causal link—assuming that accommodative monetary policy will naturally follow—while monetarists tend to place their emphasis on the monetary accommodation as the key factor without which sustained inflation would not occur.[1]

As this example illustrates, the debate over the real causes of inflation is to some extent just a semantic one. But it is much more. It also concerns important issues of empirical fact, conceptual analysis, and normative judgments about the behavior of the economy, the polity, and government.[2] Thus, for example, economists who focus on high wage demands as the real cause of inflation tend to recommend direct actions on wages and prices through such measures as incomes policies, while economists who emphasize the necessity of monetary accommodation for ongoing inflation tend to emphasize monetary control as the appropriate policy remedy.

It is important to stress, however, that while an understanding of the nature of the causes of inflation is usually quite important for the discussion of policy cures, it is not always true that the best cure should be designed to operate directly on the cause. For example, the basis for the common Keynesian policy prescription that macroeconomic policies should be used to fight demand inflation and that incomes policies should be used to fight cost inflation breaks down during a sustained inflation in which inflationary expectations play an important role in nominal wage demands.[3] In such a situation high wage increases may be a purely passive response to past and expected future macroeconomic developments. Still, if these wage increases are not validated by monetary expansion, unemployment will initially rise just as in the autonomous cost-push scenario. Thus governments committed to the goal of continuous full employment in the short run would be induced to fuel ongoing inflation. In such a world, incomes policy would be unlikely to be very effective, and the costly traditional medicine of tight macroeconomic policies would be the only effective cure.

There is an interesting pattern of selectivity in the ways in which traditional monetarists and Keynesians have approached macroeconomic issues. Keynesians have tended to focus on the decentralized decision-making problems of private sector adjustments to macroeconomic shocks and the roles which labor unions, industrial market power, and other institutional factors can play in generating short-run wage-price rigidities and cost-push pressures, while giving relatively little attention to analytically similar problems operating in the government process. With monetarists just the opposite has been emphasized. Labor unions and other sociological and institutional factors which can generate cost-push pressures have been ascribed relatively little importance in monetarists' thinking, while the role of perceived inflationary biases in the operation of the political process which determine macroeconomic policies has been highlighted.[4] Thus while Keynesians have tended to think primarily in terms of private market failures and benign and enlightened government policies, monetarists have tended to focus on perceived government instability and private sector stability. The new rational expectations models have tended to focus on efficiency in both private and public sector behavior.[5] From a public choice perspective, however, we see important problems operating in both public and private sector behavior. The failures may be pervasive.

Thus while we share the view that sustained inflation is ultimately the government's responsibility in the sense that it cannot be maintained for long without accommodative macroeconomic policies, we see a wide range of factors which can contribute to the development of prolonged inflation. The development of effective strategies to control inflation on a sustained basis requires a broad understanding of the major political and economic factors which have contributed to the generation of inflationary pressures. Even though inflation is essentially a monetary phenomenon, we must also understand what factors have influenced the course of monetary policy. This requires a blending of political and economic analysis.

A Public Choice Approach to the Political
Economy of Inflation

It is possible to develop a synthesis of important aspects of mainstream monetarist and Keynesian thinking as well as some of the underlying social and political considerations emphasized by many political scientists and sociologists (as well as some economists).[6] One crucial aspect of the development of such a political economy synthesis is recognition of the limitations of the single, well-informed rational actor model which underlies much of the monetarist and rational expectations analysis. The mechanism of collective decision making, especially democratic vote aggregation, can lead rational individuals in a collective setting to generate outcomes that would be deemed irrational behavior of a single rational actor. This problem can be complicated by relatively weak incentives for the individuals in the collective to acquire and assimilate information about the issues confronting them, as each individual's influence over the outcome is relatively small. Both of these difficulties have been stressed in the public choice literature.[7] From this standpoint, a rational basis can be ascribed to much of the analysis of union wage-push behavior and downward inflexibilities of wages and prices which would be incompatible with the behavior of a single rational actor. Likewise, this perspective helps explain why many voters may be relatively uninformed and may not provide an effective check on inflationary tendencies. These possibilities have been overlooked by many monetarist and rational expectations writers who frequently describe such behavior as implying irrationality and hence being incompatible with the economic approach.[8]

The public choice perspective also provides useful criticisms on much of the class-based analysis in Marxist and sociological writings which fail to see the conflicts as well as the commonalities of interests within broad-based social groups.[9] Likewise, mainstream economics provides a useful reminder that the operation of the economic system can be a positive-sum game generating net productivity, so that relations between social classes can have important cooperative elements—not just the conflicts emphasized in Marxist and some of the sociological writings. Thus we believe that much of both the monetarist and rational expectations literature on the one hand and the Marxist and sociological treatments on the other have suffered from focusing on overly aggregate levels of analysis. The incentives for cooperation and conflict are more complex and are more dependent on the nature of the institutional environment than is recognized in the "hard-line" versions of these approaches. The basis for synthesis rests largely in the study of rational behavior at more disaggregate levels of analysis and recognition of the need to link analysis of distributional conflicts to the behavior of macroeconomic policy.

In undertaking such a synthesis it is important to maintain a middle position between the extreme propositions that wage behavior is completely independent of macroeconomic policy and that wage behavior is completely determined by macroeconomic conditions.[10] For example, while monetarists have correctly attacked the former view, they have at times tended to jump from their demolitions of the first view to implicit acceptance of the second view. The empirical evidence, however, supports neither extreme view.[11] While monetary developments are crucial for explaining long-run behavior, their short-term linkage to wage behavior is somewhat loose. There is scope for at least semiautonomous wage developments to place short-run pressures on monetary authorities which may in turn induce monetary expansion.

To answer both the positive questions of the causes of our inflationary experiences and the normative questions of whether the current institutional framework of our political economy contains a serious inflationary bias and if so how we might best go about trying to correct this, we need to understand the major political and economic factors which have influenced the formulation of macroeconomic policies. This in turn requires knowledge about such factors as the patterns of shocks or disturbances and the structure of the economy, the beliefs of various actors about values and economic and political analysis, and the way in which the institutional structure of the political economy aggregates these individually perceived interests to determine patterns of effective influence.

The Role of Economic Analysis
of Money and Inflation

In taking such a broad political economy approach, traditional economic analysis remains an essential but incomplete guide. With respect to the economic part of the analysis it is useful to distinguish between those factors which influence the total level of spending in the economy (aggregate demand) and how changes in spending are divided between changes in prices and output—the short-run inflation-unemployment trade-off, or Phillips curve.[12] Changes in spending move us along the short-term inflation-unemployment trade-off[13] which itself then may shift up and down over time in response to shocks, institutional changes, and increases or decreases in inflationary expectations.

While it has become fashionable in some quarters to criticize Phillips curve analysis, we believe that properly used it is a valuable tool for analysis. Criticisms of the early formulations which assumed an unchanging permanent trade-off between inflation and unemployment are quite valid, but modern versions discuss how the relationships change over time in response to shocks and shifts in inflationary expectations. Today most (but not all) Keynesians as well as monetarists agree that there is no long-run trade-off which allows higher rates of inflation to buy permanently lower unemployment. Many rational expectations theorists have argued that there is, likewise, no policy-exploitable trade-off even in the short run. This conclusion, however, does not hold even with rational expectations if there are short-term wage and price rigidities, and the weight of recent empirical research suggests that changes in government macroeconomic policies do still have real effects in the short run such as are depicted by movements along a short-run Phillips curve.[14] There is still considerable uncertainty about the exact shapes of these trade-offs and the speed with which they shift over time so that short-term forecasts of inflation and unemployment are subject to considerable error, but such forecasting difficulties should not be confused with the usefulness of the Phillips curve concept as a framework for helping to analyze macroeconomic developments. A macroeconomic expansion, for example, would initially move the economy up a given short-run curve, as illustrated in figure I by the movement from a to b on SR^1. As inflation increased so would inflationary expectations, shifting up the curve to SR^2. Conversely, deflationary policies would move the economy along the new, higher short-run Phillips curve causing unemployment, point d, while inflation was still high, that is, what has been inelegantly termed stagflation. Over time the curve will begin to shift down as inflationary expectations are lowered, ultimately allowing full employment to be restored at a lower rate of inflation, point a again, on the long-run (approximately vertical) Phillips curve (LR).

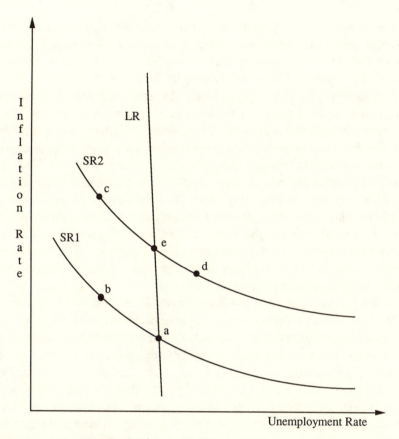

Figure 1.1   The Phillips Curve

The speed of this process and the magnitude of transitional unemployment generated is a source of considerable dispute among economists, but the nature of the general process is not. The way in which expectations are formed and institutional factors such as the degree of indexing and length of labor union contracts will influence the steepness of the short-run curve and the speed with which it adjusts. For such reasons, short-run Phillips curves appear to differ considerably from one country to another. In the United States both the changing composition of the labor force and government policies such as minimum wage rates and unemployment insurance have caused the long-run Phillips curve to shift to the right substantially over time, further contributing to the worsening of stagflation, while particular estimates of the level of unemployment at which inflation would remain steady have risen from 4 percent or below in the early 1960s to 6 percent or above by the 1980s.[15]

Stagflation may also be generated by economic shocks which directly shift the short-run curve up. For example, a major oil price increase or unusually high real wage settlements would shift the curve up directly, yielding both higher unemployment and prices for a given level of aggregate demand shifting the economy from, say, point a to point d. Thus, as was discussed in the introduction, cost-push and sustained demand-pull inflation may both generate stagflation. To keep unemployment from rising in the short run, expansionary monetary and/or fiscal policies would not be adopted, moving the economy out along the worsened Phillips curve SR^2 to point e, and further increasing inflation. Thus, microeconomic shocks may set off a longer-run inflationary dynamic if accommodative macroeconomic policies are followed.

While some incentives for macroeconomic expansion may be direct, such as the use of inflation as a tax to finance government spending and the adoption of expansionary macroeconomic policies before elections to woo voters, many are the result of *indirect* pressures to avoid other developments, particularly increases in interest rates and unemployment. For example, cost-push pressures emanating from domestic labor unions or international commodity prices cannot by themselves cause sustained inflation, but by worsening short-run inflation-unemployment tradeoffs they can induce monetary and fiscal authorities to adopt more expansionary policies to hold down unemployment and thus convert short-term to longer-term inflationary pressures. Likewise, concern with the costs which higher interest rates would impose on the housing sector may be an important reason why monetary authorities often finance government budget deficits with monetary expansion.

While inflation can of course have important distributional effects, these are often difficult to trace by researchers, much less by the general public, and do not appear usually to be heavily concentrated on particular interest groups or social and economic classes. Even the traditionally stressed distributional conflict between debtors and creditors applies primarily only to unanticipated changes in the rate of inflation. Thus the pressures for expansionary policies come largely as the by-product of the pursuit of other objectives such as avoiding unemployment and holding down interest rates.[16]

Economists normally define inflation as continuing increases in the aggregate level of prices. While it is common to speak of any major price increase as being inflationary, it is important to distinguish between changes in relative prices and changes in the general price level. Inflation refers to the rate of change in that general price level. With aggregate demand and supply held constant and flexible wages and prices, increases in the prices of some particular goods and services would be offset by a fall in the price of others. Relative prices would change while keeping the aggregate price level approximately constant.

Where there is a lack of downward flexibility in wages and prices, the increases in the prices of particular goods might cause the whole price level to rise. While the process might take place over a period of time, this would still be essentially a one-shot increase in the price level. Only if this leads to a continued increase in prices over time would most economists speak of a "problem of inflation." It is such sustained increases in the price level with which this volume is primarily concerned and which form the basis of the economists' contention that in an important sense inflation is essentially a monetary phenomenon.[17]

In the very short run the linkage between monetary conditions and inflation may be quite low. For example, we are used to the newspaper reports of the monthly price index reports discussing inflation in terms of increases in housing costs, farm prices, public transit price hikes, etc. Often these changes will have little relation to the overall state of the economy. But as the relevant time period lengthens, we find a tendency for these specific or microeconomic causes of price changes to tend to cancel out, leaving more persistent patterns generated primarily by macroeconomic conditions. In some cases, a relative price change initiated by microeconomic phenomena will lead to macroeconomic policy decisions. The decision of whether or not to accommodate the rapid increase in the price of oil in 1973–74 by expanding demand in order to avoid or reduce induced increases in unemployment is a case in point.[18] Relative price changes alone cannot be sustaining factors of inflation, but by themselves they may be initiating factors.

Both monetary and fiscal policy can influence aggregate demand, although the relative strength of their effects has been a major issue of dispute between monetarists and Keynesians. We can look at these issues from the standpoint of the quantity theory of money.

It is true by definition that

$$MV = PY$$

i.e., that the money supply (M) times its velocity (V), which is one way of looking at nominal income or aggregate demand, is equal to the price level (P) times the level of real income (Y), which is another way of looking at nominal income.[19] This is a tautology but a very useful one, even if one does not accept the monetarists' empirical assumptions.

If we have a constant level of output and of velocity, then there will be a one-to-one relationship between changes in the rate of growth of the money supply and the rate of inflation, which leads to the popular definition of inflation as "too much money chasing too few goods." Notice, however, that it is the rate of monetary expansion relative to the other variables in the equation which determines inflation. Thus for a given rate of monetary expansion, more rapid real income growth will "cause" less inflation. Thus we can see the argument that a slowing of the rate of productivity growth, with its corresponding reduction in the rate of growth of real output, is a "cause" of inflation. This conclusion depends on the assumption that the rate of growth of MV is held constant. If we want to keep the rate of inflation from increasing when productivity growth slows we can do so by lowering the rate of monetary expansion. This may be politically difficult to do, but from a logical standpoint the cause of inflation would be the failure of the variables to adjust to each other in a noninflationary manner.

In this framework fiscal expansion would cause an increase in V and/ or M. Pure fiscal policy would cause an increase in V (small and temporary according to many monetarists and large and continuing according to many Keynesians). Unless there is considerable slack in the economy this fiscal expansion would put upward pressure on interest rates. If the monetary authorities follow a policy of attempting to limit short-term interest rate variability this would in turn induce monetary expansion. Thus even from a monetarist perspective budget deficits could play an important initiating role in the inflationary process, while even from a Keynesian perspective without monetary accommodation it would require ever-growing fiscal deficits to cause continuing inflation. Thus we may view the role of fiscal policy as being primarily an initiating rather than a sustaining cause of inflation, although of course continued large deficits will continue the pressure for accommodation. This explains why, when considering problems of secular inflation, Keynesians as well as monetarists tend to adopt a monetary approach.

Much of the criticism of taking a monetary approach to inflation rests on beliefs that velocity is highly unstable and/or that the monetary authorities cannot effectively control the money supply.[20] Such concerns point to very legitimate limitations on the ability of monetary authorities to fine-tune the economy in the short run. They are very misleading, however, as critiques of the types of longer-run monetary analysis undertaken in this volume.

From a medium- and long-run perspective, changes in the behavior of velocity can be offset by changes in the rate of monetary expansion. Should we consider the development of the Eurocurrency market and other financial innovations which increase velocity as being inflationary? Not necessarily. If such developments are recognized by the monetary authorities, as over the longer term they should be, then ceteris paribus the monetary authorities should reduce the rate of monetary expansion that would have otherwise achieved a given rate of growth of aggregate nominal income. As long as the monetary authorities do not lose their ability to control the monetary aggregates, such financial innovations need not be a cause of sustained inflation. Indeed, in the short term (as measured by a few weeks or months), monetary authorities do not have the technical capability of controlling monetary aggregates within a very narrow margin of error. In this sense, the critics who argue that central banks cannot control the money supply are quite correct, just as are those who see scope for price changes unconnected to overall monetary conditions. But this is not of major importance to the study of inflationary trends. Generally on a two-quarter basis (and certainly on an annual basis) major central banks have the technical capability of hitting fairly narrow targets for average rates of monetary expansion with a high degree of accuracy.[21] The major reason that central banks have so often failed to meet announced target rates of monetary growth has been the switching of objectives, not lack of technical capabilities.

From the standpoint of medium-term and longer-term inflation analysis, international considerations generate the major circumstances under which reasonable control of monetary aggregates may be lost. With very high international capital mobility, attempts to change the domestic money supply under fixed exchange rates could be almost entirely offset by international capital flows, destroying the central banks' ability to control national monetary conditions.

Such a view of the world has underlain a good deal of international monetarist analysis of the development of worldwide inflation.[22] In this view, pegged exchange rates and high international capital mobility caused inflationary pressures in the United States to be transmitted to the rest of the world in the early 1970s via huge U.S. balance of payments deficits and the consequent international liquidity explosion. This in turn led to rapid monetary expansion and inflation abroad and the breakdown of the Bretton Woods international monetary system. There is certainly some explanatory power in this hypothesis about the escalation of worldwide inflation, but a good deal of careful empirical research suggests that the quantitative importance of this causal chain has frequently been greatly exaggerated.[23]

Most of the industrial countries have shown their considerable ability and willingness to neutralize (the technical term is "sterilize") most of the effects of international capital flows on domestic monetary aggregates. Only in very small open economies are international economic developments so dominant that there is little scope for independent national monetary policy actions.

The other circumstances in which countries will not have effective control over their national money supplies is when they are on a system of genuinely fixed exchange rates. Under such a fixed rate system, of which the gold standard is a popular prototype, maintenance of long-run balance of payments equilibrium (gold convertibility) is a binding constraint over the behavior of the national money supply, and the domestic economy must adjust to the world rate of inflation. Thus under fixed rates inflation is primarily a global phenomenon, while under flexible exchange rates inflation is primarily a national issue.[24]

The abandonment of the Bretton Woods system has frequently been charged with contributing substantially to the subsequent escalation of worldwide inflation. Such analysis is misleading, however, because Bretton Woods was not a system of genuinely fixed rates and, as is discussed in chapter 7 of this volume, the discipline that gold exerted on U.S. domestic monetary policy during the postwar period was minimal. The major forces generating the escalation of inflation in the industrial countries had been set in motion while the Bretton Woods system was in place, not after it broke down, and reflected domestic political and economic forces.[25]

The similarity of the patterns of accelerating inflation among industrial countries was much higher than would be expected by chance. Thus, the search for an international explanation is quite understandable. We believe, however, that much more important than the direct international transmission of economic and financial disturbances stressed in most of the economic literature was the international transmission of ideas and social concerns which led to similar types of political economy pressures across a number of countries.[26] The form of the particular initiating developments which played a major role in starting disturbances varied across countries; for example, wage-push pressures appear to have been important initiating factors in several European countries but not in the United States. The forces which kept inflation going were similar.

The Political Economy Approach Applied:
Explaining the U.S. Inflation

From this approach we see that there are many different levels at which the "causes" of inflation can be discussed.[27] For example, besides looking at how different developments such as budget deficits or high wage settlements induced monetary expansion, we may also be interested in what caused the budget deficits and high wage settlements. The causes of these developments can in turn be studied at different levels and from different approaches involving economic, political, and social analysis. For example, at one level, economic analysis and quantitative methods can be used to try to explain wage behavior in terms of economic variables, indices of the extent of unionization and union militancy, and the structure of collective bargaining arrangements.[28] At a "deeper" level, there may be emphasis on the nature of class attitudes, social tensions, and aspirations gaps,[29] and then in turn on the factors on which these depend.

Viewed from this perspective there is no necessary conflict between those taking a technical economic approach and those taking a broader social and political approach.[30] What is important is that analysis clearly indicate how the different types of analysis relate to one another within a broad political economy framework. There typically will not be any one single factor which can meaningfully be called "the cause" of inflation. In general, there will be two or more factors which, when brought together, cause sustained inflation. An explosion may be caused by the combination of the gas leak and the lighted match; in the absence of the other, neither would have provoked the explosion. We can discuss events such as an autonomous wage push or a politically motivated fiscal deficit as being an initiating factor, but where monetary accommodation is required for substantial inflation to result there are only emotional, not logical, reasons for singling out one of these developments as being the "real" cause of the subsequent inflation as has so often been done.[31] It is the combination which is jointly responsible. Thus we believe that in general it is most useful to think of the causes of inflation in terms of a chain rather than a single link.

Consider for example concerns with promoting short-term interest rate stability. Monetary authorities have frequently had such concerns not only because of the Keynesian orientation of many central bank officials but also because of the "political" pressures against such fluctuations generated by the financial community and other interest groups. Further, these concerns with promoting interest rate stability have been somewhat asymmetrical, with groups (such as the various components of the housing industry) more concerned with interest rate increases than declines.

The rationale of the traditional greater emphasis by Keynesians on interest rate than money supply stability depends crucially on the pattern of disturbances to which the economy is subjected. For example, if shifts in the demand for money are the dominant type of disturbance, a constant interest rate strategy with a variable money supply will help promote economic stability, while if shifts in private saving and investment or overly expansionary fiscal policy were the dominant disturbance, a greater emphasis on monetary aggregates would be called for.[32]

Note that because of the effects of an excess supply of money on aggregate demand and inflationary expectations a one-time monetary mistake could become self-perpetuating as long as a policy of holding down interest rates is followed. The initial expansion would, with a lag (which may be very short according to some monetarist analysis), generate an increase in the demand for money and hence generate either an interest rate increase or further monetary expansion which of course continues the process. As inflationary expectations mount, even with rising interest rate targets, this process can continue as long as the targets are not raised sufficiently rapidly. There can be little question that this process played a nontrivial role in the escalation of U.S. inflation.

Ceteris paribus, the greater the concern of the monetary authorities with stabilizing interest rates in the short term, the greater the chances of a cumulative monetary explosion being generated. However, in the heyday of official U.S. concerns with maintaining constant low interest during the 1950s such cumulative expansion did not turn out to be a major problem. Even in the early 1960s, with the economy well below full employment the accompaniment of the Kennedy tax cut with accommodative monetary policy seemed quite appropriate. However, the concerns with interest rate stability, even though they had slightly weakened, became very costly in the face of the rapid expansion of government spending in 1965 associated with Vietnam which occurred after the economy had returned to close to full employment. With an increase in taxes or cut in other government expenditures ruled out on political grounds, the resulting large budget deficits placed substantial upward pressure on interest rates and induced considerable monetary accomodation. Note that this monetary accommodation could be induced by concerns with limiting interest rate increases without the need for the "independent" Federal Reserve to have any partisan concerns with the president's political objectives. In a similar manner, politically motivated fiscal deficits in election years can produce an accommodative political business cycle in monetary policy even if the Federal Reserve were entirely free of partisan political concerns.[33]

In turn, a lessening of concerns with short-run interest rate stability by the monetary authorities because of the adoption of a longer-run perspective and more monetarist-oriented technical views, and/or adoption of a tougher attitude toward external pressures, would reduce the linkage between fiscal pressures and monetary accommodation. Thus we can see that there can be important interactions between exogenous developments, deep-level factors such as foreign policy attitudes and the psychology of the president, short-term political considerations which kept the president from asking Congress for a tax increase and sparking a debate over the war, and the influence of economic doctrines and external pressures on the monetary authorities. Each of these made an important contribution to the development of escalating inflationary pressures in the United States.

It should be noted here that the development of the large budget deficits associated with Vietnam went directly against the advice of President Johnson's Keynesian-oriented Council of Economic Advisors.[34]

While it has become common to criticize Keynesians' overoptimism about their ability to fine-tune the economy, had monetary and fiscal policy during the Vietnam period been made by a set of truly independent Keynesian experts, not only would the tax increase have come much sooner but the proportion of any remaining budget deficit financed by monetary accommodation would likely have been much smaller. To the extent that the Keynesian revolutionaries were guilty of hubris, the (implicit) belief that economic experts would dominate the policy process was perhaps a more serious shortcoming than overoptimism about the technical ability of economic policies to be fine-tuned to promote macroeconomic stability.[35]

The weakening of public concern about budget deficits per se (brought about in large part by the functional finance ideas of the Keynesian revolution) unleashed political propensities for deficit finance whose negative effects on macroeconomic stability may have more than outweighed the positive contributions to our economic understanding. A similar argument can be made about the decline in the mystique of gold and the abandonment of gold as a constraint on monetary policy.[36] Our point is not that the net effects are conclusive one way or the other but that the effects of advances (or changes) in economic analysis may depend importantly on the uses made of them by the participants in the political process.

Unfortunately, the more government has evidenced a concern about unemployment, the less credible will be its announcements that antiinflationary policies will be sustained and the greater will be the transitional unemployment costs generated in the disinflationary process.[37] This cruel fact is a large part of the basis for views that the generation of widely held expectations that governments are responsible for assuring full employment is a sustaining and perhaps the major "cause" for the acceleration of inflation in most industrial countries over the last several decades.

One of the keys to this process is the interaction of the behavior of short-term inflation-unemployment trade-offs with the very short time horizon which characterizes the operation of a substantial portion of the political process.[38] The shorter the effective time horizon adopted, the more attractive appear the benefits of accommodation relative to its costs; likewise the greater seem the costs of disinflation relative to the benefits. Keynesians tend frequently to adopt a shorter time horizon for analysis than do monetarists. Often, political officials may have incentives to adopt even shorter time horizons than most Keynesian economists, not extending much beyond the next election or crucial congressional vote. Since we find that employment and output typically tend to respond more rapidly to changes in macro policy than does inflation (reflected in the relatively flat slope of the short-run inflation-unemployment trade-off), a short time horizon can impart a substantial expansionary bias to macro-economic policy-making.

Several of the papers in this volume discuss in some detail how this can create vote-seeking incentives to generate political business cycles by timing expansions to bring most of the favorable employment effects prior to the election while most of the unfavorable effects of inflation would come after the election.[39] Here we wish to emphasize the complementary and perhaps more empirically important role which this asymmetry can play in sustaining an inflationary process. Whatever the initial cause of inflation, as it continues workers will demand higher nominal wages and firms will expect to be able to pass through these higher costs in higher prices without hurting sales, so the inflation-unemployment trade-off will shift upward. If disinflationary policies are then applied, there will be lags due to contracts and sluggish adjustment of expectations so that the initial effects of more restrictive macroeconomic policies fall heavily on unemployment.[40]

It seems likely that it is through their contribution to slowing the adjustment process and flattening the short-term inflation-unemployment trade-off and consequently strengthening the forces which sustain ongoing inflation that unions have contributed most to inflation in the United States, rather than in the more frequently discussed role of initiators of cost-push pressures.[41] The same holds, with respect to the role of "administered" business prices, in the more oligopolistic segments of the economy.[42] On the other hand, floating exchange rates, while often maligned as a cause of inflation, may actually instead make some contribution to reducing inflation by speeding up price responses and steepening short-run inflation-unemployment trade-offs.[43]

President Nixon, impatient with his anti-inflationary policies under pegged exchange rates and concerned that high unemployment would substantially harm his chances for reelection, dramatically adopted wage and price controls in 1971. Behind this smoke screen, restrictive macroeconomic policies were abandoned and economic stimulus applied.[44] This gave a pattern of policy behavior consistent with the theory of political business cycles discussed above. Nixon's motivation may have been more to avoid the political costs of continued disinflation than to overtly engage in direct political manipulation for vote gains. In either case, however, the result was the same: a further escalation of inflation in response to perceived political pressures. On the other hand, under flexible exchange rates President Reagan's anti-inflation policies began to reduce inflation much more quickly and thus contributed to his ability to carry them through rather than giving up in midstream as President Nixon did.

Concluding Remarks

In this chapter we have presented a sketch of a political economy framework and illustrated how it can be used to consider the key interrelationships among many of the major factors mentioned as causes of inflation. Inflation may be initiated either by demand-pull factors (such as the Vietnam expenditure increase and President Nixon's initiation of a political business cycle) or by cost-push factors such as increases in administered prices or commodity price shocks, or increased union militancy. Whatever the initial source, ongoing inflation requires continued expansionary macroeconomic policy. This process causes supply curves to shift upward over time so that the process has the traditional symptoms of a cost-push inflation whether demand or supply factors were the initiating factors. While inflation has often been a desirable short-run mechanism for relieving social tensions and avoiding making explicit distributional considerations, this shock-absorber effect does not work over the longer run. Indeed, continued inflation tends to contribute to rather than relieve social and political tensions.

Concerns with increases in interest rates and unemployment provide powerful short-run incentives to continue accommodative policies. It may be plausibly argued that this response mechanism, which to varying degrees has operated in all of the industrial countries, has been as much or more responsible for the escalation of inflationary problems than the particular incidents which initiated the process.

The types of underlying factors stressed by the sociological approach can be important and complementary to standard economic analysis. These can have a number of economic manifestations, ranging from pressures to increase various types of government social welfare expenditures and the stimulation of greater worker militancy and higher wage demands as initiating factors to the increased social and political intolerance of unemployment which increased the pressures for the adoption of accommodative macroeconomic policies.

While the United States has certainly not been entirely free from the strong social tensions emphasized in some of the sociological literature, our overview of the process of escalating stagflation in the United States suggests that such considerations, as evidenced for example by autonomous wage-push pressures, have probably been a good deal less important for the United States than for some European countries.[45] There can be little question, however, that in the last several decades there was a substantial shift in most Western countries in the attitude of society toward government as a focus for resolving distributional concerns. The resulting combination of pressures for increased government spending, low taxes and interest rates, and the maintenance of full employment have produced political economies which are highly prone to sustain inflation once it is initiated (although not to the extent of the earlier European hyperinflations and the triple-digit rates reached in some Latin American countries). While many have seen inflation as a type of safety valve which can help to resolve distributional conflicts, we have seen that just as with the static Phillips curve, these potentially desirable effects accompanying inflation do not tend to last long.[46] Over time, continuing inflation loses its effectiveness as a safety valve and, indeed, appears to contribute further to social current and distributional conflict.

While most of the policy analysis in this volume deals with proposals for monetary reforms to reduce the tendencies for money supply increases to initiate and/or accommodate inflation, we should stress that microeconomic proposals to increase productivity and wage and price flexibility can be important complements to monetary reform. Even if one accepts our conclusion that wage push has not played a major role in initiating inflationary pressures in the United States, it has played a major sustaining role and numerous government policies have contributed to a worsening of short-run inflation-unemployment trade-offs. In chapter 5 of this volume Gottfried Haberler discusses a number of proposals for increasing the efficiency and flexibility of the economy and in turn making inflation-unemployment trade-offs more favorable.

While anti-inflationary reforms are difficult to achieve at both the micro- and macroeconomic levels, there are signs that the costs of these cumulative stagflationary processes of the 1960s and 1970s have generated a substantial revision in attitudes by government officials, economists, and the general public alike. This has reflected not only the increasing concerns with inflation as its rate rose but also greater recognition of the full range of costs of inflation, especially its uncertainty costs.[47] In the 1960s many economists viewed these costs as slight and believed that higher rates of inflation could be permanently traded off to obtain lower unemployment. Today there is much wider recognition that higher inflation will not buy lower unemployment over the long run and that indeed because of uncertainty effects higher inflation is likely to depress employment.[48]

Such perceptions of the high cost of inflation have spread beyond academia. Social analysts in the 1960s and 1970s would have been shocked by the failure of the voters to throw Mr. Reagan and Mrs. Thatcher out of office following their prolonged anti-inflation policies. We cannot be confident, however, that this political check will be more than temporary. While probably somewhat dampened, most of the mechanisms which contributed to the escalation of inflation in the 1960s and 1970s still remain in place. Thus we believe that it would be most unfortunate if the current lull in inflation should deflect attention from the types of fundamental reforms in the macroeconomic policy-making process addressed by the papers in part 4 of this volume.

Notes

1   For example, contrast the rebuttals by monetarist Harry G. Johnson, "What Is Right with Monetarism," *Lloyds Bank Review,* April 1976, and J. Michael Parkin, "Where Is Britain's Inflation Going?" *Lloyds Bank Review,* July 1975, to the analysis of Keynesian Sir John R. Hicks, "Mr. Keynes and the Classics: A Suggested Interpretation," *Econometrica* 5 (April 1937): 147–59, and Lord R. A. Kahn, "Thoughts on the Behavior of Wages and Monetarism," *Lloyds Bank Review,* January 1976.

2   The terms of the debate on this issue have often been quite sharp. There have been strong allegations of ideological biases and lack of scientific content among some of the key disputants. The fervor and hostility with which such charges are exchanged clearly shows that there are some strong emotional and ideological elements to much of the debate. For examples, see Karl Brunner, "Comment: The Demand and Supply of Inflation," *Journal of Law and Economics* 18 (December 1975): 837–49; David P. Calleo, *The Imperious Economy* (Cambridge: Harvard University Press, 1983); Nicholas Kaldor, *The Scourge of Monetarism* (Oxford: Oxford University Press,

1982); and Sidney Weintraub, "Monetarism's Muddles," *Kredit und Kapital* 14, no. 1 (1982): 463–95.

3   For further recent discussion and references on the cost-push debate, see Frederic Mishkin, "The Causes of Inflation," in *Price Stability and Public Policy* (Symposium sponsored by the Federal Reserve Bank of Kansas City, Jackson Hole, Wyo., August 2–3, 1984), pp. 1–24; and Thomas D. Willett and Leroy O. Laney, "Monetarism, Budget Deficits, and Wage Push Inflation: The Cases of Italy and the U.K.," *Banca Nazionale del Lavoro Quarterly Review*, no. 127 (December 1978): 315–31.

4   Often monetarists charge that such analysis is based on highly fallacious reasoning. See, for example, Brunner, "Comment"; Robert J. Gordon, "The Demand and Supply of Inflation," *Journal of Law and Economics* 18 (December 1975): 807–36; and the discussion of monetarist views on this issue by Gottfried Haberler, "Some Currently Suggested Explanations and Cures for Inflation," in *Institutional Arrangements and the Inflation Problem*, ed. Karl Brunner and Allan H. Meltzer, Carnegie-Rochester Conference Series on Public Policy, vol. 3 (New York: North-Holland, 1976), pp. 143–77. For examples of sociological analysis, see Colin Crouch, "Inflation and the Political Organization of Economic Interests," in *The Political Economy of Inflation*, ed. Fred Hirsch and John Goldthorpe (Cambridge: Harvard University Press, 1978), pp. 217–39; idem, "The Conditions for Trade-Union Restraint," in *The Politics of Inflation and Economic Stagnation*, ed. Leon N. Lindberg and Charles S. Maier (Washington, D.C.: Brookings Institution, 1985), pp. 105–39; and John H. Goldthorpe, "The Current Inflation: Towards a Sociological Account," in *Political Economy of Inflation*, ed. Hirsch and Goldthorpe, pp. 186–213. For examples of sociological type analysis by economists, see John T. Addison and John Burton, "The Sociopolitical Analysis of Global Inflation: A Theoretical and Empirical Examination of an Influential Basic Explanation," *American Journal of Economics and Sociology* 42 (January 1983): 13–28; John T. Addison and John Burton, "The Sociopolitical Analysis of Inflation," *Weltwirtschaftliches Archiv* 120, no. 1 (1984): 90–119; Robert Heilbroner, "Inflationary Capitalism," *New Yorker*, December 1979; and Peter Wiles, "Cost Inflation and the Theory of the State," *Economic Journal* 83 (1973): 377–98.

5   For discussion and references to the rational expectations approach, see Steven M. Sheffrin, *Rational Expectations* (Cambridge: Cambridge University Press, 1983).

6   An important early effort toward developing elements of such a synthesis is made in the contributions in Hirsch and Goldthorpe, *Political Economy of Inflation*. For a political-institutional approach which has many similarities with the approach taken in this volume, see the contributions in Lindberg and Maier, *Politics of Inflation and Economic Stagnation*. While in agreement with criticisms of the excessive narrowness of many standard economic analyses of inflation, we do not agree with many of the criticisms of public choice analysis offered there. We likewise disagree with the conclusion that economic models do not explain well the recent experiences of inflation and unemployment. We believe that such criticism often comes from a failure to distinguish between failures of short-term forecasting accuracy, which are considerable, and the ability to explain the general course of economic developments; as we hope this paper illustrates, we believe that our recent stagflation (the combination

of high inflation and high unemployment) illustrates the usefulness of economic analyses.

For these and other reasons we do not share the Brookings volume's disagreement with "the received wisdom that attributes the blame for inflation to government" (p. 573). If the conclusion read "all of the blame," the analysis presented here would be in agreement. Other factors have clearly been important, but our analysis suggests that these have not been sufficient to absolve governments of a major share of the responsibility. For further critical analysis of parts of *The Politics of Inflation and Economic Stagnation,* see Thomas D. Willett, "National Macroeconomic Policy Preferences and International Coordination Issues," (Paper presented at the National Bureau of Economic Research Interdisciplinary Conference on the Political Economy of International Macroeconomic Policy Coordination, Andover, Mass., November 1987, available as a Claremont Working Paper).

7   See, for example, Mancur Olson, *The Logic of Collective Action* (Cambridge: Harvard University Press, 1965); idem, *The Rise and Decline of Nations* (New Haven: Yale University Press, 1983); and chapter 3 of this volume. We should note that while many sociological analyses of inflation strongly eschew rational maximizing explanations, not all sociologists adopt such an approach. See, for example, Mark Granovetter, "Toward a Sociological Theory of Income Differences," in *Sociological Perspectives on Labor Markets,* ed. Ivan Berg (New York: Academic Press, 1981), pp. 11–47.

8   See particularly the contrasting comments by Brunner, "Comment," and Mancur Olson, "The Demand and Supply of Inflation: Comment," *Journal of Law and Economics* 18 (December 1975): 850–56. While these points are particularly easy to see by those coming from a public choice perspective, they are appreciated by economists from a wide range of orientations. For example, see Axel Leijonhufvud, *Information and Coordination: Essays in Macroeconomic Theory* (New York: Oxford University Press, 1981); Arthur M. Okun, *Prices and Quantities* (Washington, D.C.: Brookings Institution, 1982); and chapter 5 of this volume. Note that such analysis implies that one need not rely on the assumption of money illusion to argue that the transitional unemployment associated with forcing down real wages is likely to be less if this comes about through price level increases rather than nominal wage decreases in a decentralized setting.

9   For examples of Marxist analysis of inflation, see Raford Boddy and James Crotty, "Class Conflict and Macro-Policy: The Political Business Cycle," *Review of Radical Political Economy* 7 (Spring 1975): 1–19; Pat Devine, "Inflation and Marxist Theory," *Marxism Today,* March 1974; James Harvey, "Theories of Inflation," *Marxism Today,* January 1977, 24–29; and James R. O'Connor, *The Fiscal Crisis of the State* (New York: St. Martin's Press, 1973). Much of the Marxist analysis argues that capital is inherently more powerful than labor because of the importance of investment in stimulating economic growth and high employment. This follows, however, only if business can operate as an effective unified force. Such views overlook the conflicting interests of capitalists on many issues as well as the incentives particular subsets of labor and capital have to cooperate on particular political economy issues. For further references and critiques of the Marxist theory of the state as

applied to economic policy issues, see Olson, *Logic of Collective Action;* Kerry Schott, *Policy, Power, and Order: The Persistence of Economic Problems in Capitalist States* (New Haven: Yale University Press, 1984); Martin Staniland, *What Is Political Economy?* (New Haven: Yale University Press, 1985); and Thomas D. Willett, "The Public Choice Approach to International Economic Relations," Claremont Center for Economic Policy Studies Working Paper (Claremont, Calif.: Claremont Graduate School, 1981).

10 For examples of the almost complete independence view, see Peter Wiles, "Cost Inflation," and Sir John R. Hicks, "What Is Wrong with Monetarism?" *Lloyds Bank Review,* October 1975.

11 See, for example, the analysis and references in Arthur J. Brown, *World Inflation since 1950: An International Comparative Study* (Cambridge: Cambridge University Press, 1985); and Michael Bruno and Jeffrey D. Sachs, *Economics of Worldwide Inflation* (Cambridge: Harvard University Press, 1985). We should also note that a belief that wage-push is sometimes important need not logically imply that wage and price controls or incomes policies are desirable or effective. Evidence presented by monetarists against these latter propositions, while an appropriate point of debate against the positions of a number of post-Keynesian economists, is not evidence against all aspects of cost-push analysis. For discussions of and references to the literature on the effectiveness (and lack thereof) of incomes policies and their relation to macroeconomic policy, see Martin Neil Baily, *Workers, Jobs, and Inflation* (Washington, D.C.: Brookings Institution, 1982); and Shlomo Maital and Irwin Lipnowski, eds., *Macroeconomic Conflict and Social Institutions* (Cambridge, Mass.: Ballinger, 1985). Almost all economists agree that to have any chance of working, incomes policies need to be used as a complement to, not a substitute for, anti-inflationary macroeconomic policies.

12 Strictly speaking, the Phillips curve refers to the relationship of unemployment to wage rather than price inflation. For recent surveys of the vast technical literature on the economics of inflation, unemployment, and inflation-unemployment relationships, see Brown, *World Inflation;* Helmut Frische, *Theories of Inflation* (Cambridge: Cambridge University Press, 1983); John Hudson, *Inflation: A Theoretical Survey and Synthesis* (London: George Allen and Unwin, 1982); James J. Hughes and Richard Perlman, *The Economics of Unemployment: A Comparative Analysis of Britain and the United States* (New York: Cambridge University Press, 1984); David E. W. Laidler and Michael Parkin, "Inflation—A Survey," *Economic Journal* 85 (December 1975): 741–809; and Andrew J. Pierre, ed., *Unemployment and Growth in the Western Economies* (New York: Council on Foreign Relations, 1984). For discussion of the distinctive Austrian approach to inflation analysis, see Llewellyn H. Rockwell, Jr., ed., *The Gold Standard: An Austrian Perspective* (Lexington, Mass.: Lexington Books, 1985), and chapter 11 of this volume.

13 While for simplicity we shall refer to inflation-unemployment relationships through this paper, unemployment should be understood as referring to the broad array of aspects of fluctuations in economic activity. Recent studies suggest that published unemployment rates often are not the best measure to use in wage and price equations (see, for example, Baily, *Workers, Jobs, and Inflation*) and that the political

effects of macroeconomic fluctuations are influenced as much or more by the corresponding fluctuations in real incomes and growth as by actual and expected unemployment. On these latter issues, see chapter 9 of this volume and the references cited there.

14 See, for example, the analysis and references in Frederic S. Mishkin, *A Rational Expectations Approach to Macroeconometrics* (Chicago: University of Chicago Press, 1983).

15 See, for example, Pierre, *Unemployment and Growth.*

16 See, for example, Gordon, "Demand and Supply of Inflation"; Robert J. Gordon, "Alternative Responses to Policy and Supply Shocks," *Brookings Papers on Economic Activity* 1 (1975): 183–204; and Charles S. Maier, "The Politics of Inflation in the Twentieth Century," in *Political Economy of Inflation,* ed. Hirsch and Goldthorpe, pp. 37–72. One can find differing results on the effects of inflation on the income distribution by changing the income concept. On a purely cash income basis, popular analyses which conclude that inflation has helped the rich at the expense of the poor are quite correct. Lester C. Thurow, *The Zero-Sum Society* (New York: Basic Books, 1980), and idem, "Stagflation and the Distribution of Real Economic Resources," in *DRI Readings in Macroeconomics,* ed. A. Sanderson (New York: McGraw-Hill, 1981) provide a quite careful treatment of this case. However, when one also looks at assets that do not provide cash income until their sale, a markedly different pattern emerges. Joseph J. Minarik, "The Size Distribution of Income during Inflation," *Review of Income and Wealth* 25 (December 1979): 377–92, and Edward N. Wolff, "The Distributional Effects of the 1969–75 Inflation on Holdings of Household Wealth in the United States," *Review of Income and Wealth* 25 (June 1979): 195–208 show that the marked increase in value of housing—which constitutes an enormous portion of the working poor's portfolio—leads to the conclusion that recent inflationary redistribution in the United States has been toward the center of the income distribution.

17 This view is held by most Keynesians as well as monetarists. See, for example, Alan Blinder, *Economic Policy and the Great Stagflation* (New York: Academic Press, 1979), and Gordon, "Demand and Supply of Inflation."

18 For discussion of the factors influencing the costs and benefits of accommodating commodity shocks, see Bruno and Sachs, *Economics of Worldwide Inflation;* Brunner, "Comment"; Gordon, "Demand and Supply of Inflation"; idem, "Alternative Responses"; and John B. Taylor, "The Role of Expectations in the Choice of Monetary Policy," in *Monetary Policy Issues in the 1980s* (Symposium sponsored by the Federal Reserve Bank of Kansas City, Jackson Hole, Wyo., August 9–10, 1982), pp. 47–76.

19 Expressed in terms of rates of change (denoted by $\cdot$), the equation becomes $\dot{M} + \dot{V} = \dot{P} + \dot{Y}$.

20 See, for example, Kaldor, *Scourge of Monetarism.*

21 For recent discussions and references to the literature on the limits of monetary control and evaluations of alternative control techniques, see Ralph C. Byrant, *Money and Monetary Policy in Interdependent Nations* (Washington, D.C.: Brookings Institution, 1980); idem, *Controlling Money: The Federal Reserve and Its Crit-*

ics (Washington, D.C.: Brookings Institution, 1983); and William G. Dewald, *Making Monetary Policy in the United States,* supplement to the *Journal of Money, Credit, and Banking* 14, pt. 2 (November 1982).

22 See, for example, David I. Meiselman and Arthur B. Laffer, eds., *The Phenomenon of World Wide Inflation* (Washington, D.C.: American Enterprise Institute, 1975). For critical discussion and further references, see Thomas D. Willett, *International Liquidity Issues and the Evolution of the International Monetary System* (Washington, D.C.: American Enterprise Institute, 1980), and idem, "U.S. Monetary Policy and World Liquidity," *American Economic Review* 73 (May 1983): 43–47.

23 See the analysis and references in chapter 8 of this volume.

24 This does not mean, however, that international developments may not have significant short-run influences on national economies even under flexible rates. See, for example, Sven Arndt, Richard J. Sweeney, and Thomas D. Willett, *Exchange Rates, Trade, and the U.S. Economy* (Boston: Ballinger [for the American Enterprise Institute], 1985) for further discussion, evidence, and references.

25 For evidence on this, again see chapter 8 of this volume.

26 This argument is made in Richard J. Sweeney and Thomas D. Willett, "The International Transmission of Inflation: Mechanisms, Evidence, and Issues," Special Supplement to *Kredit und Kapital* (1977): 441–517.

27 Debate on a causal framework for inflation analysis has been carried forward by D. Rhys and D. Berry, "The Current Inflation: Causation and Mechanics," *International Journal of Social Economics* 3, no. 1 (1976): 45–62; John T. Addison, John Burton, and Thomas S. Torrance, "On the Causation of Inflation," *Manchester School of Economics and Social Studies* 48 (June 1980); idem, "On the Causation of Inflation: Some Further Clarification," *Manchester School of Economics and Social Studies* 49 (December 1981): 355–56; and David Cobhan, "On the Causation of Inflation: Some Comments," *Manchester School of Economics and Social Studies* 49 (December 1981): 348–54.

28 For examples and references to the literature on such issues by economists and sociologists, see Bruno and Sachs, *Economics of Worldwide Inflation;* Crouch, "Inflation and Political Organization"; idem, "Conditions for Trade Union Wage Restraint"; George Perry, "Determinants of Wage Inflation around the World," *Brookings Papers on Economic Activity* 2 (1975): 403–47; and Andrew Tylecote, *The Causes of the Present Inflation* (New York: Academic Press, 1981). There is considerable evidence, for example, that differences in collective bargaining arrangements across countries contribute significantly to differences in the inflation-unemployment tradeoffs.

29 For examples of sociological and aspirations gap analysis, see Milivoje Panic, "The Origin of Increasing Inflationary Tendencies in Contemporary Society," in Hirsch and Goldthorpe, *Political Economy of Inflation;* Goldthorpe, "The Current Inflation"; Thomas Havrilesky, "The Discordance-Inequality Tradeoff," *Public Choice* 35 (1980): 371–77; and Addison and Burton, "Sociopolitical Analysis of Global Inflation."

30 On this issue, see the exchange between Ira Kaminow, "Politics, Economics, and Procedures of U.S. Money Growth Dynamics," in *The Political Economy of Inter-*

national and Domestic Monetary Relations, ed. Raymond Lombra and Willard Witte (Ames: Iowa State University Press, 1982), pp. 181–96; and Thomas D. Willett and Leroy O. Laney, "Technical versus Political Causes of Monetary Expansion," in *Political Economy of Monetary Relations,* ed. Lombra and Witte, pp. 203–7.

31 For examples of such real cause analysis, see Hicks, "What Is Wrong with Monetarism?" and Kaldor, *Scourge of Monetarism.*

32 See, for example, Bryant, *Money and Monetary Policy.*

33 See Leroy O. Laney and Thomas D. Willett, "Presidential Politics, Budget Deficits, and Monetary Policy in the United States: 1960–1976," *Public Choice* 40 (1983): 53–69; and John T. Woolley, *Monetary Politics: The Federal Reserve and the Politics of Monetary Policy* (New York: Cambridge University Press, 1984).

34 One can sense the frustrations of advisors Walter W. Heller, *New Dimensions in Political Economy* (New York: Cambridge University Press, 1966) and Arthur M. Okun, *The Political Economy of Prosperity* (New York: W. W. Norton, 1970) with the recalcitrance of Congress to impose the tax surcharge when it was proposed in late 1965. A longer historical perspective is offered by advisor Herbert Stein, *Presidential Economics* (New York: Simon and Schuster, 1984).

35 On the hubris of Keynesian economics and its relation to politics, see chapters 2 and 4 of this volume.

36 On both of these causes, see James M. Buchanan and Richard E. Wagner, *Democracy in Deficit: The Political Legacy of Lord Keynes* (New York: Academic Press, 1977) and Sam Brittain, "Inflation and Democracy," and Fred Hirsch, "The Ideological Underlay of Inflation," both in *Political Economy of Inflation,* ed. Hirsch and Goldthorpe, pp. 161–85 and 263–84, respectively.

37 For discussions of credibility effects and their relation to the adaptive and rational expectations views, see William Fellner, *Towards a Reconstruction of Macroeconomics* (Washington, D.C.: American Enterprise Institute, 1976); Bennett T. McCallum, "Credibility and Monetary Policy," in *Price Stability and Public Policy,* pp. 105–128; and (in the same volume) Mishkin, "Causes of Inflation."

38 Phillip Cagan makes a similar argument in his contribution, "The Conflict between Short-Run and Long-Run Objectives," in *Alternative Monetary Regimes,* ed. Colin D. Campbell and William R. Dugan (Baltimore: Johns Hopkins University Press, 1986), pp. 31–37. On the short time horizon of the political process, see, for example, Michael J. Mumper and Eric M. Uslaner, "The Bucks Stop Here: The Politics of Inflation in the United States," in *The Politics of Inflation: A Comparative Analysis,* ed. Richard Medley (New York: Pergamon Press, 1982), pp. 104–26.

39 See chapter 3 and part 2 (chaps. 9–11) of this volume.

40 In organized segments of the economy, employment relationships are often based on custom or contracts shaped around longer-run expectational developments. Such sluggishness of response to disinflationary policies is likely even if rational expectations are held by most economic agents. See, for example, Okun, *Prices and Quantities.*

41 For a similar view see Brittain, "Inflation and Democracy." This is consistent with our empirical findings in chapter 8 of this volume. For evidence of slower adjustment

in the unionized than in the ununionized sectors of the U.S. economy, see Daniel J. B. Mitchell, *Unions, Wages, and Inflation* (Washington, D.C.: Brookings Institution, 1980). We should note that in economies where bargaining is more centralized and the typical contract period is shorter, short-run inflation-unemployment trade-offs tend to be considerably steeper. See, for example, Bruno and Sachs, *Economics of Worldwide Inflation;* Jeffrey Sachs, "Wages, Profits and Macroeconomic Adjustment," *Brookings Papers on Economic Activity* 2 (1979): 269–319; Tylecote, *Causes of the Present Inflation;* and Lars Calmfors, "The Roles of Stabilization Policy and Wage Setting for Macroeconomic Stability—The Experiences of Economies with Centralized Bargaining," *Kyklos* 38 (1985): 329–47.

42   For the classic statement of the administered prices inflationary thesis, see Gardiner C. Means, *Industrial Prices and Their Relative Inflexibility,* 74th Cong., 1st sess., 1935, U.S. Senate Document 13; for a more recent treatment in this vein see W. David Slawson, *The New Inflation: The Collapse of Free Markets* (Princeton: Princeton University Press, 1981). For critical empirical analysis on the thesis that American business has been a major initiating force in U.S. inflation, and evidence that more heavily concentrated industries do tend to show less rapid adjustment, see Philip Cagan, *Persistent Inflation* (New York: Columbia University Press, 1982).

43   See Thomas D. Willett and John Mullen, "The Effects of Alternative International Monetary Systems on Macroeconomic Discipline and the Political Business Cycle," in *Political Economy of International and Domestic Monetary Relations,* ed. Lombra and Witte, pp. 143–55. For further discussion of the effects of flexible exchange rates on world inflation, see Andrew Crockett and Morris Goldstein, "Inflation under Fixed and Flexible Exchange Rates," *International Monetary Fund Staff Papers* 23 (November 1976): 509–45; Thomas D. Willett and Matthias Wolf, "The Vicious Circle Debate: Some Conceptual Distinctions," *Kyklos* 36 (1983); and the vast literature referenced in these papers.

44   For discussions of this episode, see Blinder, *Economic Policy;* Robert R. Keller and Ann Mari May, "The Presidential Political Business Cycle for 1972," *Journal of Economic History* 44 (June 1984): 265–76; Stein, *Presidential Economics;* and Edward R. Tufte, *Political Control of the Economy* (Princeton: Princeton University Press, 1978).

45   On the costs of inflation, see the discussion and references in Axel Leijonhufvud, "Inflation and Economic Performance," in *Money in Crisis,* ed. B. Siegel (Cambridge, Mass.: Ballinger, 1984), pp. 19–36; Stanley Fischer, "The Benefits of Price Stability," in *Price Stability and Public Policy,* pp. 33–50; and chapter 6 of this volume.

46   On the relationships between inflation and distributional conflict, see, for example, Albert Hirschman, "Reflections on the Latin American Experience," in *Politics of Inflation,* ed. Lindberg and Maier, pp. 53–77; Brittain, "Inflation and Democracy"; and Hirsch, "Ideological Underlay of Inflation."

47   This conclusion is consistent with the recent study by Arthur J. Brown, *World Inflation since 1950.* For case studies of inflation in a number of European countries, see Lawrence B. Krause and Walter S. Salant, eds., *Worldwide Inflation* (Washington,

2 Inflation and Politics: Six Theories in Search of Reality

William C. Mitchell

The persistence of substantial unemployment and inflation in western nations has created not only an enormous literature on stagflation but altered some long-held beliefs on the part of both economists and political scientists. The latter no longer ignore economic matters, public finance, and economic reasoning about nonmarket phenomena. Economists, on the other hand, no longer regard politicians, bureaucrats, voters, and governments as exogenous variables and, therefore, immune to economic analysis. This shift of intellectual and professional gears in the social sciences is of momentous importance because such a shift offers hope for a genuine integration of political economy. Viewing politics as a rational endeavor is nothing less than a "sea change" in economics because voters were often thought to leave their good sense at home when voting while politicians were considered to be so idiosyncratic that rational explanations became impossible. The advent of public choice has altered all this and made economists acutely self-conscious about political life and its role in economic matters.

In this chapter I explore the political content of the dominant economic theories of stagflation. Political causes of stagflation include constraints and choices originating in the political system as contrasted with causes endogenous to the economy. These political elements may be treated quite explicitly and even formally as is the case with theories of the "political business cycle" and public choice. With other theories and theorists, the political element is left in a somewhat inchoate state and must be ferreted out by way of inference.

As the chapter title suggests, I will consider six theories pertaining to macroperformance and stagflation in particular. All but one are well known among economists: Keynesian approaches to output fluctuations and price determination; monetarist views of the supply and demand for money; rational expectations and policy impotence; public choice and the fiscal and monetary behavior of governments; the political business cycle and myopic electoral influences on macropolicies; and, finally, the least well-known approach—the Marxist-influenced "sociology" of inflation.

Each of these theories casts a powerful light on some aspect of the political setting of macropolicies and the functioning of our economy, but that powerful light has its limitations both for our understanding of inflation and for making appropriate policy advice. Because reality is so complex it is entirely possible to construct explanations that are at once mutually contradictory and yet persuasive. No theory, it seems, can be totally dismissed by some crucial experiment or other empirical test. On the other hand, a vacuous acceptance of all approaches is unsatisfactory and is not found in these pages.

The models and images considered are not without normative or policy significance; indeed, one might well contend that what many theorists wish to be the case dictates how they see politics. An examination of constitutional, institutional, and policy reforms pertaining to inflation can be a fruitful source of views about how the economy and polity function. Accordingly, I consider typical fiscal reforms advanced as solutions to our problems. Indeed, it may be claimed that like macroeconomics, generally, most inflation theories are essentially normative in purpose and structure. In any event, I consider both positive and normative matters.

Some caveats: I am a political scientist. I am a sojourner in economics and especially in the area of macroeconomics. As such I cannot claim detailed technical knowledge of the theories I consider, but that very innocence may save me from mistaking the trees for the forest. While not an economist I do have a fine appreciation for economics if not for all economists. In writing this chapter I have had occasion to selectively review far more macroeconomics than I had wished; nevertheless, that review has reinforced a belief that very little of macroeconomic theory is positive and that far too much of it proceeds in ignorance of well-established microassumptions, theorems, and empirical knowledge. Still, the theories of economics, whether micro or macro, have a logical structure unapproached in political science. The very best of political theory is still no match for the rigor found in an elementary economics text. Accordingly, economists are able to specify their differences and agreements to a degree unattained in the other social sciences. Finally, I should note that I do not emphasize intraschool differences nor consider the evolution of opinion, methods, proofs, techniques of analysis, etc., in my account. It is challenge enough to just discover the political elements.

From Keynes to Zero-Sum Games

Virtually all contemporary discussions of inflation begin with Keynes for the simple and good reason that we have lived with and under Keynesian doctrines for over forty years. And, while Keynes's classic did not address itself to inflation, it does have an implicit but obvious policy message re inflation and the role of government. His successors have developed policy strategies for dealing with underemployment and inflation to such a level that even the ordinary freshman in a principles class now "knows" about IS/LM analysis and what government should do to "manage" demand.

The Keynesian apparatus used to explain inflation is advanced in either of two forms: "demand-pull" or "cost-push" explanations. Each attempts to get at a causal explanation that may be better recognized as examples of the well-known prisoners' dilemma.[1] While there are crucial differences in both causes and effects, both explanations are basically applications of game theory. It should be noted that while the two theories stress economic causes both offer political solutions.

Demand-pull theorists claim that changes in the price level are caused by increases in aggregate demand that exceed supply gains during periods of full employment—thus, "excess demand." Accordingly, prices for limited goods and services are bid upward which, in turn, cause suppliers to offer higher bids to holders of resources and their prices are, in turn, increased. Of course, this says nothing about the causes of the excess demand, whether found in individual markets or aggregate demand. Some analysts argue that the causes are found in autonomous expenditures, others in an increase in the money supply. While the dispute over ultimate causes continues, the mechanism or process by which the increasing demands are felt and are converted into price increases is clear. Once prices begin their upward movement, the rational buyer expects that the price rise will continue and, that being the case, the intelligent thing to do is buy now. But when everyone entertains the same expectations and acts accordingly, expectations are reinforced and become reality; everyone is made worse-off.

Of course, Keynes himself is famous for his depiction of the opposite situation, i.e., the demand-pull deflationary game in which consumers expecting price decreases await the new lower prices. Again, if every consumer or buyer acts accordingly, collective disaster results because no one buys and aggregate demand suffers. The only apparent solution for the sellers is to lower prices still more, but this reinforces the expectations that price reductions will continue. The phenomenon is better known as Keynes's savings paradox. It is a version of the more general prisoners' dilemma.

Even if the diagnoses and prescriptions of demand-pull theories are economically correct there is little incentive for the politicians, voters, and bureaucrats to pursue anti-inflation policies. A constituency for global efficiency exists, but it is rarely a very large one. Policies that reduce unemployment are understandably popular since they impose no immediate sacrifices; policies that discourage inflation are distinctly costly in the short run and promise but a generalized public good to be enjoyed only in the long run. Demand-pull theories have a good deal of intuitive appeal for the conservative citizen because they seem to focus responsibility for inflation on the consumer and government rather than on producers. Interestingly, Keynes spawned not only demand-pull theories and policies but cost-push analyses as well. His more conservative followers, it would seem, prefer the demand-pull versions, and are often downright hostile toward cost-push analysis, whereas the more radical post-Keynesians prefer cost-push approaches to inflation. Strong distributional preferences are characteristic of the latter school.

The spiral of self-defeating choices can occur on the supply side of the market as well; ironically, this particular game has been advanced mostly but not exclusively by more radical theorists. Cost-push theories also admit of a greater complexity in inflationary moves and mechanisms. Gylfason and Lindbeck, for example, depict three categories (causes) of cost-push inflation and depict no less than five distinct subtypes of inflation in their second and most important category, i.e., attempts of organized groups of income earners and profit seekers to advance their own relative positions.[2] And within this latter category the most significant are those involving the efforts of unions to keep up with one another's contract demands; in their terms it is a "wage-wage" game. The payoff matrix is identical to that of demand-pull games, except that the actors are powerful unions making competing demands for wage improvements. Other variations include firms and their associations bidding up the prices they charge. These same writers also note that governments can participate in these games because governments make their own demands for tax dollars and, thereby, influence private settlements. Cost-push tendencies, in any case, are said to be products of an oligopolistic, price-administered economy of huge firms and unions. This analysis, while characteristic of such stalwarts of the Left as Galbraith, Heilbroner, and Lekachman, is also suggestive of certain institutional economists of the Right. Cost-push analyses are normal components in Austrian explanations of inflation (such as those of Hayek) as well as those of Alchian, Phelps, and others usually considered contributors to a new microeconomic explanation of inflation based on recent Chicago theories of industrial organization.[3] Whereas Galbraithians emphasize the power of the business firm to manipulate output and prices independently of demand, Phelps et al. and some Keynesians, notably the late Arthur Okun, focus on the rigidities of labor contracts and markets, many of which are consequences of public policy. Closed shops, restrictive practices, strikes and slowdowns, etc., are all effective means of increasing union bargaining power. Additionally, government policies lower the costs of unemployment to the worker.

Cost-push theories have some merit for they consider some of the more apparent basic conditions of modern economies, and they do recognize that politics and policies have much to do with shaping the structure of and decisions in the economy. Unlike the demand-pull version, cost-push does note that prices can continue to rise even with lessening demand and growing unemployment. Cost-push writers of the Right also observe that in increasing areas of the economy and, especially in service industries and the public sector, the scope for increasing productivity is exceedingly low. As Baumol and others have shown, wages and salaries are the major costs in these labor-intensive industries. Wages are almost completely rigid downward, but highly flexible upward. This being the case, if unions demand higher wages, they get them, but at the cost of higher prices and profits to be paid for by innocent and powerless consumers and taxpayers. Both versions of inflation theory, but especially the cost-push, emphasize social conflicts over the distribution of income, wealth, and power.[4] In this struggle are the seeds of ideological commitment.

Some Keynesians believe that unless government regulates certain crucial prices the outcome of the distributional conflict will be decided by the distribution of political power, and they see the corporations as ultimate victors. Austrians and others of the Right see victories by coalitions of unions, lower-income citizens, liberal politicians, and bureaucrats. This latter coalition introduces serious perversities and distortions into markets, weakens them, and eventually enhances the power of governments. Prices, national income, the allocation of resources, and the distribution of income now become the prerogatives of the state. Inflationary finance soon follows.

While cost-push analyses have some well-known and profound shortcomings they are not without significant policy and strategic relevance. Cost-push theories have strategic attractiveness in the political arena because they are so intuitively appealing and simple to understand and propogate. Since cost-push analysis is based on the widespread belief that human action is motivated or purposive, politicians and ideologists can assign the role of devil to whomever will prove appealing on the electoral trail. If unions or business have the power to initiate price increases, they will use it and they will frequently succeed. Needless to say, advocacy of political controls over unethical monopolists has great appeal among voters. And this raises the questions of what should be done about such inflations.

Having been worked out for more than forty years, Keynesian policy proposals—macro and micro—are well known. Whether cast in terms of income policies, wage-price controls, jawboning, recontracting, TIP (Tax-based Income Policy), all micropolicies appear to entail significant participation by government. This reliance on government stems from a combination of factors, the most important of which include the definition of the problem as a prisoners' dilemma and a benign faith in the omniscience and omnicompetence of democratic governments. At another, more implicit level is a belief, especially among British Keynesians, in the global efficiency of political processes, more generally, and a powerful disinclination to view the market as an effective and fair institution for distribution. Finally, and ironically, Keynesian aggregate demand policies can only be successful if suppliers *fail* to correctly perceive the effects on the price level of policy changes. The New Classical economists as we shall see avoid this dilemma. We turn now to the political consequences of Mr. Keynes.

If inflation is viewed as a prisoners' dilemma or zero-sum game, it is clear to many, including such notable economists as Lester Thurow, that some sort of social contract and outside coercion is necessary to resolve attendant difficulties.[5] Hobbesian solutions are, indeed, highly popular among students of such games. The interesting thing about this approach is the convenient assumption that those involved in the presumed zero-sum market setting will be able to escape playing the same game in the political arena.

The idea of a "social contract" has enormous appeal based as it is on the simplistic notion that business, labor, and government can "sit down" and talk out a long-term agreement. Good will can overcome the inherent conflicts of interest that exist on the supply side of the market. And, in one sense they can, i.e., if the parties form a cartel that obtains its gains at the expense of consumers and taxpayers who, interestingly enough, are not formally represented at the bargaining table. Social contract discussions also tend to overlook the extraordinary power of government as well as its own discernible interests in maintaining power, increasing revenue, and spending more money. The government has at least as much incentive to break the contract as labor and management. In any case, if the government has the power to enforce its will why go through the motions of enacting a social contract?

Keynesians and game theorists alike seem fascinated with the puzzle of finding ways out of the prisoners' dilemma. Thus, they call for educational campaigns for enlarging the time frames of people, changing the payoffs, teaching reciprocity, and informing people of the bad consequences of failure to cooperate. Seldom does it occur that the best institution for furthering cooperation is that least known and appreciated institution—the market. Keynesians and Pigouvians may have their theoretical differences, but on one thing they seem united, the failures of the market to be efficient. Interestingly, markets are not thought to be corrigible; government on the other hand is so viewed and especially in overcoming the cyclical behavior of capitalism. Accordingly, markets cannot be improved; they can only be controlled, minimized, or supplanted.

Occasionally, resolution is thought possible by calling on the participants to see the folly of their ways: President Ford's WIN Campaign

(Whip Inflation Now) and the incessant jawboning of recent presidents are ready examples. In any event, Keynesian game players view inflation as more insidious and unfair than the loss of personal liberty stemming from increasing government controls. The allocative inefficiencies of anticipated inflation are quite properly considered insignificant. It should be noted that Keynesians do worry about inflation; indeed, the adverse effects on distributional patterns of unanticipated inflation has provided a clarion call for more government.

What few Keynesians seem to realize is that the political process itself will exacerbate the very game it is entrusted to control; at least that seems to be the case whenever liberal and socialist governments are in power. Even conservative governments—witness Thatcher!—have considerable difficulty in resisting the universal distributive impulse of powerful competing claims to greater shares of the national income. In fact, politicians and bureaucrats become spokesmen or representatives of the rent-seekers. And, were they not, they still act as though they—the governors—have a vested interest in preserving inflation as, indeed, in the short run, they do.

And that raises another problem—the proper strategy for a government favoring at least some disinflation. Basically, such a government can pursue either a policy of gradualism or administer some form of "shock treatment." With the conspicuous exception of Hayek, most economists, including both Keynesians and macroeconomists influenced by Keynes, have favored a policy of gradualism mostly because of the much higher costs associated with the "cold turkey" treatment. But such gradualism as has been pursued and the manner in which it has been done poses not only the normal expected unemployment costs but creates a credibility problem for citizen and government alike. Long, drawn-out efforts to combat inflation typically lead the citizenry to question the commitment of the government. Policymakers are seen as weak backsliders as they cope with the contradictory demands of unemployment and inflation. Consistent firmness and effectiveness in policy-making are difficult to achieve and easy to lose. Myopic politics and long-run economic losses are always with us. Regrettably, too, Keynesians of all persuasions have had enormous difficulty in accepting this obvious premise.

That Keynesians oppose constitutional amendments constraining the choices of governments should hardly occasion surprise.[6] Why limit redistribution opportunities and shackle political efficiency? What is surprising is the Keynesian argument that governments will find ways around any and all proposed constitutional fiscal constraints. One might expect more conservative and libertarian thinkers to be cynical on this matter, but not liberal economists. Liberal thinkers contend on the one hand that governments *should not* be constrained during rapidly changing circumstances while on the other hand they maintain that governments *cannot* be constrained. If the latter be the case, why worry? But, they do worry because they believe that such constraints are, in fact, apt to be ineffective and likely to lead to cynicism on the part of citizen and ruler alike. There is some merit to this argument; one should at least be suspect of any dramatic political change such as Prohibition which is likely to affect everyone in substantial ways. But Prohibition was a restriction on private citizens; contemporary constitutional reform of fiscal activity is control *over* government, not unlike the constraints already found in the Constitution, the Bill of Rights, and other amendments having to do with the powers of government. Then, too, it is always possible to craft constitutional changes more or less skillfully.

Finally, it should be noted that the game theories that have evolved from Keynes's analysis of less than full employment equilibrium also constitute efforts to explain inflation. Conservative analysts maintain that these game analyses do not explain how inflation and substantial unemployment can occur simultaneously, nor, as Hayek has long contended, given the political domination of our times appear inevitable. Others might argue that the shift up in the Phillips curve caused by cost-push may lead to partial rather than complete validation, resulting in increases in both inflation and unemployment. In any case the recognition of questionable compatibility has come slowly through the reluctant rejection of the Phillips curve. For nearly twenty years the Phillips dilemma, in which politicians face a Hobson's choice, constituted fashionable policy wisdom. Which bad is deemed worse depends on the constituency one represents, but in any case, sophisticated policies are called for which elicit an optimal combination of the bads. Phillips and his Keynesian followers did not fully understand either the economic or political relationships between unemployment and inflation; it was only later, with the advent of revised theories of unemployment referred to above, that public choice and the revived Austrian approach enabled some fresh assaults on the political economy of stagflation. I should also emphasize the crucial role played by monetarists in undermining previous misunderstandings. And it is to the monetarists that we now turn to discover some new and even paradoxical understandings of our fiscal plight.

The Monetarists' Polity

Unlike their chief antagonists, the Keynesians, monetarists have actually developed something in the nature of a political theory of inflation. While these political elements have not been formalized they are set forth with considerable clarity and some rigor by such well-known monetarists as Friedman, Brunner, Meltzer, and Parkin. These analysts not only lay the blame for inflation and unemployment on governmental policy but, unlike Keynesians, explain why governments adopt the wrong monetary and fiscal policies or having chosen the right policies do so at the wrong times. Their explanations are complementary to and, indeed, have much in common with those of public choice. Having read little public choice, some monetarists appear to have reinvented the wheel even after the car has been popularized.[7] In any event, some place little reliance on the existing literature of public choice and concentrate, instead, on the erratic record of monetary authorities and the technical difficulties of data gathering, interpretation, and implementation of monetary policy.

Monetarists maintain that inflation is a monetary phenomenon to be discussed in the context of the well-known Fisher equation ($MV = PT = Y$). What distinguishes modernized versions of the equation is a concern over difficult questions having to do with the changing quantities of money and the output of goods and services. Since the quantity of money is largely a political responsibility and output of goods a private one the analyst must account for both political and private decisions. Indeed, even the latter decisions are profoundly affected by both macro- and micropolicies. Modern monetary theorists, therefore, examine why governments are led inexorably to expand the supply of money while adopting micropolicies that discourage production. Both strategies are rooted in electoral necessities.

Inflation is seen as the major product of government efforts to cope with electoral imperatives and their own incentives to be reelected. According to this analysis, politicians learn that they are entrepreneuers competing in a volatile market for votes and influence. As such, they offer policy proposals that range from explicit redistributions to vague and vacuous patriotism. They soon learn that redistributive policies are apt to garner more support than providing public goods and that among these policies are proposals to expand the benefits of increasing numbers of beneficiaries who, typically, are better organized, better informed, and more influential than the anonymous taxpayers who provide the resources. Policy costs and benefits are asymmetrically distributed as are the costs of information about those costs and benefits. Politicians quickly adapt themselves to these constraints and, thereby, lend their own support to those demands which, on average, expand benefits of the most visible kind. These same politicians also learn that as the expenditures of government rapidly exceed revenues, inflationary possibilities are enhanced. And while inflation is often regarded as a public bad, it is a private good for some citizens and most politicians for it can be readily and easily employed to finance the inevitable deficits resulting from so-called functional finance. The monetizing of the debt is an ingenious political solution to outstanding problems of providing both guns and butter. Monetizing the debt does not, however, solve the resource allocation problem nor the Phillips dilemma.

Although the Federal Reserve Board can technically control the supply of money to a reasonable approximation over the medium term, this is no simple matter to be resolved by fiat. The incentives of most public officials and many important citizens are such that policies appealing to them are also policies that tend to increase the supply of money while decreasing the incentives and means for controlling that supply. Accordingly governments, once they are entrapped by the Phillips dilemma of increasing inflationary expectations, find it virtually impossible to resist pressures to engage in a stop-go set of actions that lead to increasing both the money supply and public expenditures while attempting to reduce the costs of unemployment. Having increased the potential for inflation they tend to overreact, at least, at higher levels of inflation and install politically popular but ineffectual policies designed to reduce inflationary pressures but which seldom reduce the long-run level of either unemployment or inflation. So the political bias is for still more money and inflation. Complicating this perverse process is a perceptual problem induced by the realization that the benefits of diminished inflation are a public good to be realized by the many in the long run while the costs are immediate and dramatic, as in the case of increased unemployment, among the few.

Then, too, the effects of a business downturn are broader than just the unemployed involved. Profits, inventories, and overtime work fall, only to create greater apprehension.

As noted above, many modern monetarists spend almost as much time explaining the political sources of inefficient micropolicies as on the inefficient macropolicies explaining the overall supply of money. Monetarists complain about the new protectionism designed to shelter virtually every powerful interest. Such measures restrict the flow of free trade, reduce the mobility of resources and competition, raise prices, reduce consumption, and ultimately reduce the incentives to be productive, i.e., the right-hand side of Fisher's identity equation (PT). These negative-sum games in which politicians enact measures that take from some citizens in order to give to others lead to a smaller GNP than would otherwise be achieved.

In this general analysis of inflation we detect the roots of public choice. But, unlike many public choice analysts, monetarists are not at all reluctant to prescribe alternative policies nor to advocate fundamental reform of political institutions.

Although many monetarists despair of the possibilities of reversing inflationary tendencies, some, including Friedman, will not admit of defeat. How else can we account for his prolific and essentially optimistic effort to educate the citizenry and officialdom on changing our emphasis from fiscal to monetary policy and from one kind of the latter to another? Friedman, in particular, never tires of pointing out the follies of expanding the role of government, the logrolling tendencies of legislatures that increase expenditures, the perverse results of public regulations, etc. In all this, Friedman is profoundly aware not only of the importance of discouraging but the necessity of restraining governments from greater spending and taxing; in this critique he accepts Hayek's belief that it is the *size* of government and not the deficit that is critical in the long run.[8] Government is inherently inefficient, yet powerful enough to endanger the liberties of citizens for whom it presumably exists to serve. Thus, Friedman and other monetarists wish to see the growth of government reduced, the use and value of money stabilized, the free market revitalized. Government's major responsibility is not to ensure full employment but to facilitate free exchange.

For monetarists the best way to accomplish their monetary ends is to end the shortsighted, discretionary, and destabilizing powers of the monetary authorities by the adoption of some rule enabling control of the money supply. This approach gets at the most immediate and visible of money problems. A return to a gold standard, privatizing the money supply, and enacting a fixed rule for monetary growth are among the best known major proposals. It will also be useful to give the president an item veto and index taxation and incomes for the protection of all adversely affected by inflation. But most important of all feasible reforms is the addition of a constitutional amendment that would get at the problem pointed to above, namely, the expanding state.

Friedman would like to see an amendment that would limit federal government spending as a fraction of the national income and require balanced budgets. The pursuit of balanced budgets to the exclusion of the size of those budgets is, in Friedman's view, rather shortsighted.[9] Such a requirement does not prevent government from growing, though it may induce some greater attention to efficiency. In 1978 Friedman stated, "I would far rather have total federal spending at $200 billion with a deficit of $100 billion than a balanced budget at $500 billion."[10] Still, Friedman regards tax limitation laws not as cure-alls but as stopgaps until public opinion changes. As to be expected, he has been guardedly optimistic about that possibility.

Now, however, we read that budget reforms are "losing steam" as the campaign for a constitutional convention to write a balanced budget amendment is falling short of the necessary state endorsements. Only two more states are required, but they are apt to be difficult ones and still other states may withdraw previous support. Ironically, Reagan's considerable success in reducing inflation also reduces the demand for a budgetary amendment to the constitution. If inflationary tendencies of governments can be harnessed by ordinary policies, why enact rigid constitutional reforms not all of whose consequences may be known?

While the more purely monetary reforms offered by monetarists are their most obvious and compelling reforms, they are not the only ones. Most monetarists are firm believers in the efficiency of free exchange and free markets. They believe that inflation would not be so serious a problem if such exchange were permitted to once more prevail and flower. It follows that Friedman and his colleagues are strong advocates of any market reforms that will strengthen competition and facilitate resource mobility. Labor markets are considered especially obnoxious in this regard. Curtailing the power of unions in both the market and the polity is high on the agenda of reforms. Unions bear a special responsibility for the enactment of full employment policies and the perversities that goal has introduced into our political and economic lives. The political-business cycle—to be considered below—may well be an inadvertent intellectual product of a powerful labor movement.

Monetarists believe, correctly, that the enactment of the necessary anti-inflation policies and constitutional reforms is a demanding and time-consuming task. Few such reforms are apt to prove popular among voters, politicians, and bureaucrats. Acceptance of temporary but higher unemployment, reduced government expenditures, reduction of credit, and controls over the discretion of officials cannot have much appeal. And this is the source of the monetarist dilemma; they advocate that which few want. In a democracy that may be fatal.

Rational Expectations: Policy Impotence?

Because of its totally unexpected yet rigorous course of argument, the rational expectations school or New Classical Economics is in some ways the most fascinating theory.[11] Simple-minded theorists can easily generate simple-minded policy and develop logical constitutional implications from their premises. Since rational expectations is a highly sophisticated, and to some degree counterintuitive, theory, any layman who thinks he understands or is able to predict the next stage of the argument is usually wrong. And that perplexity makes our task somewhat more difficult and ultimately disappointing because the New Classical Economics is precisely that; it is without a political theory of inflation.

According to rational expectations theory, all "macroproblems" such as inflation and large-scale, persistent unemployment are in need of drastic redefinition, and what may then remain is subject to an entirely different sort of analysis. In the new classical analysis, information is assumed to be the linchpin of everything. Economic agents in both their market and political activities act on the basis of the very best information (past and forecasts) available, but what is available is rarely ever complete or costless. So we have the partially blind leading the blind in both the economy and polity! In spite of this ubiquitous blindness, economic agents do act rationally and rapidly; they may learn in discontinuous rather than adaptive ways, but they learn well. No matter what occurs they are assumed to respond appropriately given the circumstances. The capacity of

Keynesian agents to learn and forecast is distinctly limited; that is why they are viewed as "adaptive" rather than "rational." If exogenous events occur that are relevant, the agent amends his behavior in the proper ways. One such exogenous shock is a change in government policy. Investors, consumers, labor, etc., all learn how to *counter* whatever governments intend to do. The countercyclical policies of Keynesians are, therefore, doomed to failure. Since everyone internalizes the changing expected values in their decisions, whatever government attempts is effectively countered and little is gained; indeed, something is lost because of wasted efforts on the part of the government.

But now the unexpected! If the government were to alter course in some dramatic way, that would be the equivalent of a random shock and such a shock could make things worse if the government were to follow the dramatic policy. So, pessimism to end all pessimism, the rational expectations analysts inform us that government should continue its previous policies, unless they were random, so that its actions will be predictable. A government cannot reduce unemployment or inflation by changes in policy to offset shocks but it *can make things worse* by adding instability from government policies to whatever instabilities arise from the private sector.

What is of greatest concern to us is not the intricate general equilibrium theory of rational expectations and its employment in macroeconomics, but the views of government and politics held by that school. No member of the school excepting, perhaps, Robert Barro has made any systematic contribution to the study of public choice.[12] Although I find many of the views of the New Classicists reasonable, their conception of politics is as primitive as that of many Keynesians. Indeed, the basic ideas of equilibrium, expectations, learning, risk, and uncertainty seem to have been applied almost exclusively to the market and not extended to the choices and strategies of voters and the government. We never learn why governments tax and spend as they do. But what would such an extension entail?

Insofar as political science has a theory of politicians it might best be summarized as one of adaptive expectations or, in the language of the political scientist, as an "incremental" theory.[13] Voters and politicians learn and act as though the immediate past is likely to continue without major alteration. In budgetary studies, where this theory is most often applied, it is concluded that most changes are highly predictable. Although incrementalism has held sway for quite some time, it has been modified on theoretical and challenged on empirical grounds as inapplicable to new allocations.[14] And "exogenous shocks," a term rarely if ever used in political science, suggests another phenomenon that incrementalism ignores. In any case, in democracies stability of policy and budgetary expectations is usually assumed by political scientists. This is also said to be true of changes in administrations or democratic governments more generally. Things do not change very often or by very much.

Standard public choice and many electoral studies in political science display a distinct tendency to model voters, especially, as uninformed, past- rather than future-oriented, and subject to all sorts of fiscal and other illusions. The reduction of these costs is considered too high. Politicians, bureaucrats, and interest groups, on the other hand, having more direct interests in being more substantially informed, may also be less than perfectly informed, but they do have distinct advantages over the voters. Originally formulated by Downs, "rational ignorance" is now an unquestioned theorem of public choice and even some American Government textbooks.

Obviously, if the rational expectationists extend their logic to that of the public sector then it also follows that the voters, politicians, interest groups, and bureaucrats are themselves rational in their political expectations. They will all make the best of whatever they confront. They will, like their market counterparts, make errors but not systematic, persistent errors. Still, the rational expectationist might well contend that there is more risk or less certainty in the polity and that would account for a greater incidence of inefficient policy choices and organizational behavior in the public sector. Faced with many more random shocks, correct anticipations and learning become less certain and ever more costly.

Incrementalism, public choice, and the adaptive expectations school would all seem to view the relationships between government and citizen as one of imbalance, inequality, and admitting of manipulation. The citizen is at a distinct disadvantage in confrontations with the government. Most rational expectations analysis, however, assumes otherwise. (For recent exceptions to this generalization, see the discussion and references in chapter 3 of this volume.)

Although the New Classicists have advice for governments, they do not have a realistic model of actual government choice and behavior. They tend to view government as independent of the electorate. Oddly, then, in one important sense they are very Keynesian! More important, and unlike Keynesians, they arrive at the paradoxical conclusion that government is impotent! The reason is obvious: whereas Keynesians assume an omnicompetent government that can "manipulate" the electorate and economy, the new classicists match an omniscient government against omniscient citizens and economic agents, with the latter able to both anticipate and correct for any policy change. If this state of affairs were indeed true the principle would surely be one of the most important and devasting of all "impossibility" theorems. Among other things, in most of its versions it would do away with the political business cycle! Informed rational individuals and organizations are simply unable to control their collective destinies. This fascinating and disturbing problem will be considered further when we examine public choice and the theory of the political business cycle.

The more supply-oriented analysts of public choice and even some Marxist revisionists question all this.[15] They maintain that the government not only has an effect but powerful effects on the market and society and that due to the workings of the political process these effects are usually inefficient and/or inequitable. And worse, monopolistic government has powerful incentives and the resources to successfully manipulate the citizenry. Both bureaucrat and politician have superior informational resources as well as the ultimate power of state authority and coercion. But to say more is to anticipate our discussion of public choice.

With the possible exception of Robert E. Hall, the academic New Classicists have not been in the forefront of popular policy debate nor appeared as energetic sponsors of constitutional amendments; they have opted instead to pursue their mathematical truths.[16] Of course, normative and strategic implications do emerge, sometimes directly from the pens of these theorists. Rational expectations as well as supply-side arguments lay behind the preparation of the Reagan administration's so called Rosy Scenario in which, counter to the conventional economic wisdom of monetarists and Keynesians alike, inflation and unemployment were forecast to fall simultaneously.

At this stage it seems that the best we can elicit from the approach are certain precautions re policy-making, cautions that sound conservative even when they are not derived from explicit conservative premises. In any event, these theorists appear to favor policies that are less activist, less discretionary, more stable, and based on a respect for consumer rather than governmental sovereignty and omnicompetence. Because we know so little about the so-called macroevents we should be extremely cautious about efforts to control them. Ironically, much of the rationalist attack on Keynes is based on the assumption that even mathematical economists know little about how individuals respond to activist policy changes. When one knows so little, being less ambitious and less confident seems in order. Like many Austrians and public choice theorists, rational expectations analysts envisage pervasive perversity or at least the high probability of unintended consequences.

Recent Reagan administration policy changes may be good cases in point since many administration forecasts have not worked out as planned and hoped. Admittedly, economists are not always in a good position to predict the income and substitution effects of new policies. While Keynesians may chide Reagan forecasters, few economists seem to accept these criticisms of their profession.

Since we know so little about aggregate policies and their micro-effects, the rationalists advocate greater stability in whatever policies are adopted. Frequent changes with the hope of finding dramatic solutions will not do. While this may sound like a policy of despair, it really isn't. Rational citizens may not make systematic errors, but why confront them with the opportunities to tax their already burdened cognitions? Frequent policy changes will do that and will have certain known but undesirable consequences. Some citizens will profit more than others, and they may be selected on random grounds. If policies are altered frequently, citizens will spend more time anticipating policy changes than in productive effort. And perhaps they will also attempt to gain important information earlier and by illegal means. In any event, when policy-making changes create so much uncertainty and conflict, distrust between citizens and governments is apt to increase. One has the feeling if not evidence that stability is so critical that any rule, so long as it is stable, is preferable to changing rules and policies, even if some are more efficient than existing practices. Is this "Second Best" doctrine?

Much of this overall line of reasoning is based on the fundamental assumption or belief that the private market economy is a stable and marvelously efficient institution. The market clears, and when and where it does not is a normal result of government interference. Unlike Keynesians, rationalists have a certain nonrational faith in both the allocative and distributive workings of general equilibrium. Just why the political system has become so pervasive becomes a bit of a problem; if the private economy has worked so well, how can we explain the greater use and substitution of the political process? Perhaps it is due to the informational disparities and inequities that some economic agents feel should and can be rectified by government. After all, the rationalists do not claim that all involuntary unemployment and persistent general rises in price levels are simply definitional and statistical quirks.[17] Or do they? No, they don't. We are told that sticky labor contracts are problematic, as are the errors of some people mistaking movements in money prices for relative price changes.

Public Choice: The Political Institutions of Inflation

The theories of inflation thus far considered accord a kind of begrudging recognition to the pervasive role of politics in inflation and an analytical indifference to the role of specific political institutions in generating and maintaining an inflationary regime. The indifference is particularly marked in the case of the Keynesians, post and classical. After two decades of public choice, their continued faith in the efficacy of government to pursue correct countercyclical policies would be comical were it not so tragic. Perhaps this political faith yet curious indifference to policy failure stems from the origins of the theory in a depression when increasing faith in government was so politically sensible or expedient. Fighting inflation, however, usually requires political suicide or at least a severe case of electoral illness. In any event, Keynesians, the New Classicists, monetarists, and Austrians alike have yet to produce a full-blown positive theory of politics and inflation. At best, certain monetarists including Brunner, Meltzner, Parkin, and Friedman have made spasmodic positive efforts to account for the powerful role and operations of the political process.[18] And Austrian polemics about bureaucratic politics and planning have proven to be remarkably good positive theory. While all are highly critical of politics as the major culprit in the business cycle, it has remained for another group of economists—the public choice theorists—to fully elaborate an agenda of research and provide systematic political theory. Among the thousand or more members of the Public Choice Society, but a handful, largely from or stimulated by those who founded the Society at Virginia Polytechnic Institute in Blacksburg, Virginia, dominate. The leading figures have been and remain James M. Buchanan and Gordon Tullock.

The positive theory of public choice is still very much in its infancy, but the major outlines are quite clear and have pronounced implications for the analysis of inflation. While the public choice paradigm was not devised to account for inflation and other macroeconomic phenomena, its application to the former as well as to many micromarket regulations was not long in developing; in fact, little more than a decade elapsed between the publication of *The Calculus of Consent* (1962) and the publication of *Democracy in Deficit* (1977). Needless to say, many fiscal research endeavors form the link between the two books. Buchanan in particular had long been concerned with the fiscal and monetary problems of democracy and has consistently identified himself as outside the Keynesian circle. We should not underestimate the impetus inflation has provided for at least some public choice analysts.

Our discussion of the public choice explanation of inflation is based mostly on two books: *Democracy in Deficit: The Political Legacy of Lord Keynes,* coauthored by James M. Buchanan and Richard E. Wagner (New York: Academic Press, 1977), and *The Power to Tax: Analytical Foundations of a Fiscal Constitution,* written by Geoffrey Brennan and James Buchanan (New York: Cambridge University Press, 1980). Three themes are advanced in the former volume: (1) a story and an explanation of why Keynesian ideas came to prevail and supplant the neoclassical analyses and public policies, (2) a public choice theory of the inflationary tendencies of democratic governments, and (3) a program of constitutional reforms for guiding governmental policies. One is tempted to revise the phrase they borrowed from Roy Harrod to describe Keynes's commitments and say "the presuppositions of Blacksburg" in setting forth their three theses. Of the three inquiries we are chiefly concerned with the second and third. *The Power to Tax* is considered below.

Keynesian ideas came into popularity during and after the worst depression the world has known. That Keynes should have elicited so much favorable attention is perfectly understandable since he offered a sensible, understandable means of rapidly overcoming an agreed-upon bad. That Keynes offered economists a theory worthy of their skills is obvious; he also provided them a new political importance. Perhaps more importantly, policies entailed by Keynesian analysis provide the perfect electoral strategies. With so many things going for it one cannot be amazed at its all-encompassing victories in the halls of government as well as the groves of academe. Those suspicious of the market and capitalism likewise found refuge in a highly persuasive and supportive ideology. The recurring crises of capitalism need not be explained in alien Marxist terms. And best of all, crises need not be inevitable.

The chief presuppositions of Keynes were the inherent instability of capitalism, the possibility of technical knowledge regarding the economy, and the omniscience of government in enacting policies that are based on that technical knowledge. Public choice theorists reject the first and third and some are ambivalent about the second premise. Of the three questioned premises the one indigenous to public choice is the last one. Politicians, bureaucrats, and voters are said to follow a different set of decision rules from those honored whenever they act in market roles. While buyers and sellers are no different in terms of their motivations than are their political equivalents, all are constrained utility maximizers who prefer more to less, now rather than later, etc. But, unlike the heavily disciplined market choices, the political are made without certain fundamental constraints such as price tags, limited income, competition, property rights, and contracts operating within continuous markets. Accordingly, the utility-maximizing efforts of political man are less constrained and, therefore, conducive of less economically efficient and responsible choices. The unseen hand in the market is not only a powerful integrator of diverse performances but unsurpassed in its ability to convert individual selfishness into social good.

Paul Samuelson and other authors of texts on macroeconomics have perpetuated (inadvertently, one hopes) the notion that governments convene to enact macropolicies advocated by disinterested Keynesian policy advisers. In this rarified setting policies are designed to affect the great aggregates of consumption, investment, savings, etc. as though these aggregates were real and unrelated to the particular interests of consumers, producers, savers, and investors who face daily the uncertainties of particular markets. The fact is, neither policymakers nor citizens live in this contrived universe of abstract aggregate economic functions; instead, they deal with their own wages, salaries, prices, etc., and attempt to advance their interests in both the market and polity. Politicians have a superb feeling for these concerns and their vote implications. Accordingly, politicians enact not grandiose laws affecting the macroaggregates but mundane legislation that will grant advantages to particular groups in their own constituencies and impose disadvantages elsewhere. It is the sum total of the contradictory redistributive micropolicies that inform and constitute our macroresponses to political and economic life. And these policies are chosen not for their macroresults but their microredistributive market and political benefits. How then, asks the public choice theorist, can we expect Keynesian doctrines to provide a meaningful operational guide to policymakers?

In terms of the inflation problem we can readily observe that virtually all political actors have short-run vested interests in promoting fiscal and monetary policies that worsen rather than improve matters. Governments would much rather spend money than tax and so are easily if not inevitably led to promote "easy" money, fiscal illusions, increases in and monetization of the debt, and, generally, adoption of policies that fail to enhance productivity. Instead of pursuing policies that promote efficiency in resource allocation, governments are trapped in a redistributionist, prisoners' dilemma. Each of these political responses adds to whatever inflationary potential may already be inherent in the economy.

While the incentive structures of politics are now well known, less known are the mechanisms through which these incentives are worked out within the institutional arrangements. Here, Buchanan and Wagner and many others have performed a distinct service, for they have shown how majority rule, logrolling practices, budgetary processes, single-representative constituencies, and "winner take all" promote inflationary policies. Like the Keynesians, Buchanan and others of the Virginian School of public choice have demystified an entire set of social institutions, in this case the political. Whereas Keynes made a stable monetary constitution, once a noble responsibility of government, into an ordinary policy choice that officials could rationally manipulate,[19] the Virginians have dethroned the notion of high-minded officials pursuing the public interest by showing how and why they act as mere vote-maximizing politicians. Ironically, the effect of this dethronement has provided a new but more sophisticated rationale for the old-fashioned, resident myth that Keynes demystified, namely, the almost religious compulsion to balance the budget, restrict the size of government and otherwise enact prudent policies.

Ever larger governments deciding policy meant that all political institutions could now aid and abet the causes of inflation. When Congress spent but a few million each year, the need for logrolling could not have been great; but when governments consist of hundreds of thousands of elective officials and millions of bureaucrats and all must somehow curry the favor of their constituents, one can see how logrolling becomes institutionalized and undisciplined spending arises. And when a government begins to tax significant portions of personal income it is easy to grasp why the shaping of taxes becomes a most difficult political process and dilemma. In short, once a government begins to grow, something akin to a prisoners' dilemma sets in to reinforce and speed the process of growth and rent-seeking. Everyone must become politicized or lose out in the political competition. Pursuit of advantages and the avoidance of disadvantage soon become the political preoccupation. Ironically, the traditional tasks of the government including the provision of such basic public goods as a stable monetary system and economic rules of the games (property rights and contracts) are themselves swallowed up in citizen rent-seeking and the political aspirations of politicians. The result: still greater instability.[20] One further consequence of note, observed mostly by Austrians, is the highly differential and arbitrary effect of inflation on the allocation of resources and the distribution of wealth and income. Scarce resources no longer gravitate toward their most valued productive uses as they would in free markets; instead they end up in hedges, speculation, and a vast underground economy not subject to the regular laws. Some thinkers, including Gunnar Myrdal, also contend that such activity seriously weakens the moral foundations of society, capitalism, and democracy itself.

If one regards inflation and/or other macrophenomena as products of unstable markets, changes in governmental control and policy will usually be thought sufficient to ameliorate the situation. If instability of markets is so great that Keynesian ministrations are considered trivial, one must consider revolution and some new social system. But if one considers the source of the problems as inherent in an otherwise worthy polity as do many public choice theorists, solutions are sought not so much in changes of policy and certainly not in revolution but in constitutional provisions that proscribe and prescribe governmental responsibilities and limitations on fiscal authority and discretion. Buchanan in particular has been most insistent in his advocacy of additional and novel constitutional constraints on the fiscal powers of the government. He views himself as simply advocating what our Founding Fathers did when they defended the new Constitution as a set of rules which specifies both how the political process is to operate and how basic rights of citizens are protected. Accordingly, the powers of government must be clearly defined.

Buchanan worries about the power of government and rights of citizens.[21] Due process is an important protection for citizens. Unfortunately, the power to tax which is so closely related to the due process clause is not so similarly restrained by constitutional dictate. There is no constitutional limit on the power of government to tax; the only constraint is that taxes be uniform. Buchanan's apprehensions about this unconstrained power are not ill-founded; the proportion of income being taxed has increased notably during the past twenty-five years. To tax someone is not only to deprive them of income but to prevent them from directly controlling the use or disposition of those tax revenues. Of course, governments do not tax away all of their subjects' income; that they do not has something to do with their own self-interests and the interests of the taxpayers. Even highly inefficient political processes protect taxpayers in general if not in particular. While public choice analysts do not know the optimal tax burden, they surely know that it is not confiscation of all wealth. Our governors do have an interest in a productive economy, for it is the golden goose.

So what is to be done? Constitutionally oriented public choice theorists rely on constitutional revisions and amendments.[22] They believe that governments can be more effectively controlled, especially in their fiscal activities. That we control government through constitutional means hardly requires examples; that we control governmental fiscal operations is clearly shown at the state and local levels, where balanced budgets are the norm. Constitutional limitations on tax increases, budget increases, and bonding requirements are all widely accepted basic constraints. And a few states even tie increases in their budgets to some growth index of the economy.

While hardly in agreement, many public choice theorists (some are totally indifferent to such matters) support a balanced budget rule, a limitation on the growth rate of government expenditures and the money supply, and a more demanding majority rule, usually two-thirds, on fiscal issues in Congress. In *The Power to Tax,* Brennan and Buchanan go still further, perhaps, because they choose to adopt a "deliberately cynical model of government," i.e., a "revenue-maximizing Leviathan." Adopting the Rawlsian strategy they ask what rational citizens might adopt in the way of a fiscal constitution if choosing behind a veil of ignorance.

Since the government is assumed to be revenue rather than welfare maximizing, little imagination is required to envisage all sorts of government stratagems designed to obtain the revenue. Like Downs, Brennan and Buchanan predict that under majority rule electoral strategies enabling the last party to announce its platform will redistribute benefits in such a way that minimal winning coalitions are formed and elections won. What Brennan and Buchanan add to the Downsian analysis is the further and crucial implication that once in office the government will continue to pursue such policies and, indeed, to so redistribute benefits that it maximizes its *own* share.[23]

Monopoly government emerges, then, even out of simple majority rule. Policies are patently non-Paretian. But things are still more dire; politicians can create and manipulate fiscal illusions, and bureaucrats uncontrolled by elections can pursue policies at still greater variance from those desired by majorities. Thus, it is within this unhappy setting that the model of "natural government" or Leviathan is erected and against which rational citizens contend. No benign politics here! Fundamental constitutional reform is required. Choosing behind the veil of ignorance, voters would reject most standard liberal fiscal proposals and adopt a minimax strategy. Eschewing a policy but not an analytical concern for particular tax proposals, especially of the postconstitutional variety, Brennan and Buchanan claim to have provided a sound basis for adoption of rigorous fiscal constraints in general, and especially those affecting the tax base, protection afforded by "loopholes," rate restrictions, and procedural limits such as qualified majorities and budget balancing. Their analysis, rooted as it is in public choice, is probably the most significant analytical and normative theorizing in public finance since Keynes. It simply cannot be ignored. And, like Keynes of the *General Theory*, it ain't easy reading!

A final note on public choice: Although I have treated public choice as a more or less homogeneous body of thought, it is clear that serious analytical fissures exist and that they may have consequences for our understanding of inflation as well as other policies of government. I like to contrast models that are voter-driven, as best exemplified by the "median voter" theorem, with models that are basically supplier-driven. Whereas governments are conditioned if not controlled in demand models, the government itself is the controller or most influential policymaker in supply-side models. Theories of politically based inflation ought to recognize these different sources of inflationary policies. Inflation's causes, paths, and the reforms vital to its control are apt to differ somewhat in each model. Just how these models of inflation work out and whether they can even be reconciled has yet to be achieved. On a purely impressionistic basis I am inclined to believe that demand models are most relevant during election periods, while supply models best portray the periods after or between elections. Politicians are apt to be most sensitive to voter concerns when they are pleading for their votes and least sensitive after elections. It is not that median voters are powerless during the longer interelection periods but rather that voter demands find more efficient expression through the activities of specialized interest groups. The electorate and the organized interest sector are not, however, composed of the same citizens. Accordingly, governments hear different voices over the electoral cycle. Whereas the median voter counts for more during elections, it is the more intensely committed whose voices otherwise prevail. These voters are found at the tail ends of the familiar median voter curves. It would be strange indeed if the politicians in office did not promise one thing during campaigns and enact different policies once in authority. This strong possibility suggests something in the nature of a political business cycle.

Politically Manipulated Business Cycles

One of the more fashionable developments in recent public choice has been the elaboration and testing of models designed to account for plausible relationships between the electoral cycle of national governments and the fiscal and monetary policies pursued by those governments. While the basic idea that governments can directly affect economic conditions has been around since at least the time of Keynes and Kalecki, the actual formulation of the precise relationship and its rigorous testing is a product of the past decade. In short, a political business cycle is said to exist—one whose basic parameter is the length of the electoral term of office. Preelection policy stimuli and postelection contraction producing greater inflation in the first instance and greater unemployment in the second are said to be not only the motivations of the ruling party but within their power.

Students of macroeconomics will quickly recognize that the political business cycle is based on the famous Phillips curve, which postulates a short-run trade-off between the rates of unemployment and inflation and a long-run curve of steeper slope. The trade-off presents the authorities with an unfortunate choice—a Hobson's choice of two bads with the actual choice being some hopefully optimal combination of the two evils. Political business cycle theorists claim that the lesser of the evils before an election is an increase in the inflation rate while the lesser evil after an election is greater unemployment. The political business cycle produces a sequence of contradictory policies.

Increasing unemployment and inflation are the results. How the spiral of Hobsonian choices is explained depends on how the investigator(s) treat the voters, i.e., as basically short-run oriented (Nordhaus)[24] or strategically minded (MacRae).[25] This latter point is of importance not only in the context of interpreting the political business cycle literature but also, as we have seen, in rational expectations analysis. Oddly, MacRae maintains that voters are myopic during some periods and strategic during still others. This seems strange, but then the data are aggregate and the voting population constantly changes in composition so that a constant rate of learning becomes impossible. Other students of voting would complicate matters by stipulating a past- or future-oriented voter.[26]

The intuitive appeal of the political business cycle model and partial confirmation of it by various statistical tests is not something to be ignored. The basic logic of the model(s) is in accord with what ordinary insight might suggest about the behavior of politicians and what public choice theory clearly indicates to be the case. Still, these studies abstract a great deal from the richness of actual polities, in particular the capacities of governments to know how to deal with both inflation and unemployment as well as their authority and power to enact appropriate measures. Governments may be powerful in even the least stable democracies, but they are constrained by information limitations, theoretical inadequacies, and, of course, all sorts of institutional limitations on their discretionary choices. This latter constraint is particularly crucial in the United States with its separation of powers, federalism, divided party control, and constitutionally defined fiscal powers. In addition to these limitations one must also not overlook the perversity of some politicians and the stupidity of still others. And as governments cannot fine-tune Keynesian instruments of policy, so too they cannot fine-tune the responses of voters as they reward or punish governments for past actions, express current preferences, and make demands for future policies.

The studies of Nordhaus and Tufte tend to view voters as truly myopic, an assumption that seems in accord with much of the public choice tradition but one which seems to be going against a distinctly different thrust in the theory of rational expectations and recent political science.[27] Several political scientists including Fiorina and Kiewiet, previously cited, are now concluding that voters are economically "sophisticated" and understand the connection between their own welfare and the policies of government. They may not grasp the theoretical subtleties but they are not stupid. And they most certainly are not naive about the objectives of politicians interested in retaining office.

We need not exaggerate the intelligence and information of voters to make the point. Unless convulsed by ideology, individual voters are more attuned to particular policies than to general fiscal policies, and they are probably more sensitive to recent than long-run changes in their situation, but catastrophic changes such as the Great Depression have their lasting impact. The general price level is likely to be of less concern than are prices of goods and services purchased, while one's own income is unquestionably of greater importance than a government's overall incomes policy. However the theorist may feel about these matters, politicians seem to assume such priorities to be true for most voters.[28] And they act accordingly.

There is a bit of paradox here. Governments, especially of the civics book and Keynesian kind, are considered to be desirous and capable of overcoming the business cycle by countercyclical policies. A generation or more of voters have been so taught. Yet voters learn from reality that governments consist of partially and ill-formed electoral maximizers whose own interests may run counter to their own. These interests may dictate not stabilizing but destabilizing the economy. Creating a crisis in international politics is a well-known instrument of politicians for domestic survival. Politicians have long known of the electoral power of not only taking advantage of crises but of creating them. So we should not be surprised to find this insight applied to fiscal operations. And it does seem to explain some policy shifts.

We cannot ignore the empirical tests since as is often the case in social sciences the tests may not be entirely valid, i.e., do not test what the theorists argue should be tested. And analysts employ different tests. In the immediate instance it is clear that the political business cycle people are mostly testing actual changes in the economy and not the intentions of politicians and/or what politicians have in fact done by way of macropolicy manipulation. In other words, unemployment and inflation figures may be the product more of autonomous economic changes than of deliberate policy alterations. If the tests do not contain these two elements then the tests are not entirely valid. The use of data pertaining to actual economic changes is, of course, shaped by the availability of such data. Since economists prefer to assume political objectives, investigating motives is ruled out, while identifying policy actions presents almost insuperable obstacles for controlling the variables in the tests.

Students of the political business cycle have not been particularly concerned with the policy or constitutional implications of their models. Normative concern seems to be a separate matter, one that cannot be logically derived from empirical tests and positive theory, or so the econometrician would contend. On the other hand, normative students might well attempt to draw various implications from empirical work or at least attempt to document their own concerns with "evidence" and logic from the political business cycle literature. And that is what I shall do.

If it is true that voters are myopic and that governments base policies on this fact, then in the context of the electoral cycle it would seem to follow that relatively little can be done to alter the shortsightedness of voters but that something could be done to change the strategic choices of the politicians, if one finds the cycle to be disturbing. Policy choices could conceivably be somewhat more stabilized if the electoral periods were lengthened. Antiunemployment and anti-inflation policies could be permitted to work out their effects over a longer phase and might therefore have a better chance at becoming effective.[29] Of course, the cycle would not be eliminated (at least in democracies), but the sudden vacillations would be dampened. Likewise, one might conclude that removing some policy choices from the purview of the elected officials would serve to mitigate policy oscillations. If this be the case, then it might be argued that certain constitutional changes are in order. Limitations on spending and/or taxation would seriously reduce the capacity of politicians to affect the political business cycle. And placing basic monetary choices in the hands of truly independent agents or constraining monetary growth by constitutional means would seem consistent applications of lessons learned from political business cycle theorists. Of course, if the claims of these theorists are somewhat less impressive than has been thought to be the case, then reform may have to be sought elsewhere.

Some theorists, including the influential Bruno Frey, have seriously qualified their own work by stressing the importance of ideologies in a government's policy selection.[30] Similarly, it has been observed that exogenous forces of international trade and politics place severe limitations on the ability of governments to manipulate the economy and therefore the cycle. If the sources of fiscal instability are found outside a nation, reform of the fiscal and monetary processes is somewhat irrelevant. For the moment we cannot ascribe policy motives to cycle theorists nor can we confidently deduce policy implications and reforms.

The Sociology of Inflation

Although most social scientists share the economists' belief that the study of inflation is a property right of economists, there has emerged a challenge to those rights, a challenge that has come, interestingly, not so much from political scientists as from sociologists. And sociologists with a particular perspective—that of Marxism. To complicate things still further, one should note that many of those who stress "sociological" factors in their economic analyses are actually economists and not card-carrying sociologists.[31] Sociology, as such, does not have a theory of inflation nor indeed does it have much professional interest in the phenomenon. The same can be said about political science, psychology, and anthropology. Nevertheless, something akin to a sociological analysis of inflation has emerged during the past decade or so. It deserves some attention.

The economic analysis of anything differs greatly and markedly from that of sociology. This is no more apparent than in the writings of Gary Becker, who has seen fit to confront the very core of sociological explanations of social status, social structure, family, crime, etc.[32] What distinguishes the sociological approach is its substitution of groups, organizations, norms, status, and, above all, power for the categories of methodological individualism one finds in conventional economics. Becker, of course, maintains that the basic units of sociology can themselves be renamed and specified in economic terms and explanations. And that he does, much to the consternation of sociologists.

The sociologists of inflation begin their analyses not by a rigorous treatment of the marketplace but through a power approach to the structure of society. Interestingly and paradoxically, sociologists share the economists' assumption that people are interested in their material welfare and that they pursue that interest in a rational manner. But these assumptions are rarely stated in any explicit way; rather they appear to be implicit, otherwise the actions of the various status groups and economic organizations make little sense. Society is characterized by having different social classes whose income, wealth, status, and power vary greatly. The basic condition is one of inequality in a largely zero-sum contest. Thus far, the upper classes have predominated and, thereby, ensured that they not only monopolize social and economic institutions but have managed to control the political as well. Life, then, is a vast organizational and class struggle over the distribution of limited property rights and actual income and wealth. But like the Marxists, the modern sociologist of inflation abhors this historical evolution and usually assumes or predicts that it will end. Most of the pathologies of society, including inflation, are blamed on the workings of capitalism.

While the actual processes of inflation typically are not specified by sociologists as they are by economists, it is clear that inflation is set off and maintained by an intense distributional conflict that is not unlike the one portrayed in cost-push theories. However, the latter lack the biting edge of the sociological version. Galbraith does not much write of "the class struggle." And the cost-push versions also seem less deterministic, less the product of historical forces; accordingly, such theorists advocate changes in governmental policies, not in the basic structure of society. No cost-push theorist believes in revolution and the dictatorship of the proletariat.

A skeptical student might well ask why capitalism or the capitalists should permit inflation, particularly when inflation has devastating consequences for at least some capitalists and capitalist institutions. The answer was provided by a Marxist economist over forty years ago, one not much cited by the modern sociologists: Michal Kalecki. According to Kalecki, inflation and unemployment are not simply manifestations of capitalism but tools of control for the exploitation of workers.[33] But Kalecki went far beyond traditional Marxism; Kalecki was, in fact, the originator of the political business cycle analysis. In his theory, however, business interests prevail over the political institutions; it is not so much the politicians who initiate and manipulate the electoral cycle as it is the capitalist class which manipulates the economy and politicians. Unemployment is the major means of disciplining the workers. Kalecki was not entirely wrong; unemployment does place a powerful constraint on union demands. Unfortunately, Kalecki like most Marxists never spelled out the political mechanism by which the capitalists are able to implement their economic policies. But they didn't need to in a society with a small political sector; they could act directly over the economy by their own investment decisions.

Modern sociologists have a finer appreciation of political institutions if not a very good understanding of the economic. In any event, the sociologists see inflation as the product of distributional concerns, and the responses of social groups and individuals to inflation as fairly rational. In these respects, one might say that such analysts share some of the perspectives of the monetarists, cost-push theorists, public choice, and even the New Classical approach. While the differences, however, are far more pronounced, the Marxist approach is not without a theory of inflationary finance in which the state plays a major role.

James O'Connor, for example, maintains that the state engages in inflationary activities because a "structural gap" has developed between the rising expenditures demanded by capitalists and the limited capacity of the state to raise revenues.[34] Marxists term these various expenditures as "social investment" (public goods?) and "social consumption" (welfare). The productivity of the private sector rises at a lower rate than the expenditures, leading to the occurrence of fiscal crises and the resort to inflationary finance. While this analysis is superficially similar to others we have examined, it must be noted that the Marxists see the economy as monopoly based; the capitalists are in a position to exploit and counter unfavorable state policies and, of course, dominate ineffectual political institutions. Marxists do not examine the workings and consequences of majority rules, agenda setting, the divorce of costs and benefits, etc.— the core of public choice. It is the class struggle that looms ever present. The vast variety of competing interest groups most observers of democracy see are not present in the Marxist vision. The modern state may be bureaucratic, but it too is inconsequential or, more accurately, serves the interests of the ruling class. Since bureaucracy does not have interests of its own it cannot be a cause of inflationary finance. Little in the monetarist or public choice analyses of politics is to be found in the Marxist approach. That modern democracy carries the seeds of its own fiscal destruction does not suggest any tendencies toward analytical convergence between Marxism and public choice.

Conclusions

The several theories of inflation addressed in this chapter all testify to the importance of inflation among economists and citizens alike. While we concentrated on the role of political forces in both the causes and cures for inflation, we did not make an effort to discuss the popularity of each theory among different segments of society. Such considerations cannot be ignored, for no matter how technical the exposition of theories there is always the haunting question of who gains and loses from pursuing different policies under different rules of the game.

Most analysts tend to believe that inflation, at least the unanticipated kind, benefits debtors and penalizes creditors. Most analysts believe that holding certain assets, especially real estate, gold, and other precious commodities is encouraged under inflation. Most believe that fixed income recipients will suffer. Some believe that holding money makes little or no sense. Not all or even many believe that wages lag behind prices. Few believe that savings are automatically eroded. Yet most citizens probably believe the exact opposite and therefore demand many of the policies that post-Keynesians advocate.

And again, as in solving the tragedy of the commons, many people argue that what is needed to reduce the inflation tax is for the government to make still more money available. While inflation is viewed as a major problem of our time, some analysts and citizens contend that it is better than unemployment and that it can continue indefinitely. Whether the latter is true or not, the cost of reducing inflation significantly is thought by radicals and many liberals to be too high and far too concentrated on the less well-off. For the sociological theorists, the elimination of inflation attacks the symptoms, not the cause. Closing off the pressure valve of inflation may have dire consequences. Conservatives, on the other hand, tend to view inflation as tragic not only because of its economic consequences but because of the erosion of moral and ethical standards. And most conservatives believe that inflation benefits the government at the cost of misallocated or wasted resources, enhanced government power, and reduced individual liberties. Some, particularly Friedman and Hayek, contend that not only does inflation produce unemployment but that the latter may be expected to occur simultaneously with inflation. The malcoordination of productive processes and the distortions introduced into the pricing mechanism ensure such eventualities. Wage-price controls would only exacerbate these misallocations.

While theorists debate over the causes and cures for inflation, they do so because of the alleged consequences, some of which have been depicted above. It seems clear in such debates that the distributional effects are of primary importance. Those analysts who, like the Keynesians and Marxists, sympathize most with the less well-off tend to develop theories that find final causes in the unstable private economy, while those who voice less concern over the poor produce theories that find fault with the nature of the political system. These latter analysts include the monetarists, rational expectations theorists, Austrians, and public choice analysts. All would prefer to have a more independent and powerful market system, a reduced political system, and quite different fiscal and monetary policies than have been pursued since World War II. It is not that these antigovernmental theorists object to improving the welfare of some. Rather, they feel that most policies are actually perverse and do not, in fact and in the long run, benefit the intended poor. The battle over inflation policy like all other policies has its distributional objectives and consequences. They cannot be ignored in either the evaluation of competing theories or public policy. This writer sides with those analysts who treat inflation as the paramount *political* problem of our time.

Notes

1 Shlomo Maital and Yael Benjamin, "Inflation as Prisoner's Dilemma," *Journal of Post Keynesian Economics* 2 (1981–82): 459–81.

2 Thorvaldur Gylfason and Assar Lindbeck, "The Political Economy of Cost Inflation," *Kyklos* 35 (1982): 430–55. The three basic types include (a) exogenous cost increases; (b) attempts by interest groups to maintain or enhance their relative positions; and (c) attempts, whether organized or not, to maintain or enhance their positions in *real* terms.

3 See Edmund S. Phelps, ed., *Microeconomic Foundations of Employment and Inflation Theory* (New York: W. W. Norton, 1970).

4 An especially good exposition of this point may be found in James J. Rakowski, "Income Conflicts, Inflation, and Controls," *Journal of Post Keynesian Economics* 4 (1983): 590–602.

5 Cf. Lester Thurow, *The Zero-Sum Society* (New York: Basic Books, 1980), especially chapter 3, and his *Dangerous Currents* (New York: Random House, 1983), also chapter 3, on inflation.

6 A sampling of views on constitutional limits may be found in W. S. Moore and

Rudolph G. Penner, eds., *The Constitution and the Budget* (Washington, D.C.: American Enterprise Institute, 1980). Another, more technical set of papers, mostly anti-Keynesian, is offered by Helen F. Ladd and T. Nicolaus Tideman, eds., *Tax and Expenditure Limitations* (Washington, D.C.: Urban Institute Press, 1981).

7　A good sample is found in Karl Brunner's "Comment" on the well-known paper by Robert J. Gordon, "The Demand for and Supply of Inflation," *Journal of Law and Economics* 18 (1975): 807–37; the "Comment" follows on pp. 837–57.

8　Milton Friedman, "The Limitations of Tax Limitations," *Policy Review* 5 (1978): 7–14.

9　On balanced budgets, see especially Richard Wagner, "The Balanced Budget Amendment," *Policy Report* 1 (June 1979): 1–5; idem, "Limiting Government Budgets: The Misplaced Emphasis," *Policy Report* 1 (October 1979): 1–7; and idem, "Spending Limitation, the Constitution, and Productivity: A Response to James Tobin," *Taxing and Spending* 3 (1980): 59–71. In addition to Friedman's reservations about balanced budgets, consider William A. Niskanen, "A Friendly Case against the Balanced Budget," *Taxing and Spending* 3 (1980): 41–48.

10　Friedman, "Limitations," p. 12.

11　Fortunately, the nonprofessional reader of economics can now gain a decent understanding of rational expectations from a number of primers, including David K. H. Begg, *The Rational Expectations Revolution in Macroeconomics* (Baltimore: Johns Hopkins University Press, 1982); Stanley Fischer, ed., *Rational Expectations and Economic Policy* (Chicago: University of Chicago Press, 1980); and, most accessible of all, Steven M. Sheffrin, *Rational Expectations* (Cambridge: Cambridge University Press, 1983). A brief but lucid account is set forth by Mark H. Willes, "Rational Expectations as a Counterrevolution," *The Public Interest,* special edition, 1980, pp. 81–96.

12　Robert Barro, "The Control of Politicians: An Economic Model," *Public Choice* 14 (1973): 19–42.

13　While the literature in political science dealing with incrementalism is enormous, still the best treatments are to be found in two articles by the economist turned political scientist, Charles E. Lindblom: "Policy Analysis," *American Economic Review* 48 (1958): 298–312; and "The Science of Muddling Through," *Public Administration Review* 19 (1959): 79–88.

14　Oliver E. Williamson, "A Rational Theory of the Federal Budgetary Process," *Public Choice* 2 (1977): 71–89; and John E. Jackson, "Politics and the Budgetary Process," *Social Science Research* 1 (1972): 35–60. Both show how the incremental view can be reconciled with rational models.

15　In addition to much of the work by Buchanan and Tullock, attention is here called to an early but unappreciated classic of "supply-side" public choice—Randall Bartlett's *Economic Foundations of Political Power* (New York: Free Press, 1973). The book did not go far enough and is somewhat marred by a slight Marxist "bias." Another lesser-known "supply-sider" is Albert Breton, *The Economic Theory of Representative Government* (Chicago: Aldine, 1974).

16　Robert E. Hall and Alvin Rabushka, *Low Tax, Simple Tax, Flat Tax* (New York: McGraw-Hill, 1983), make a superb polemical statement for tax reform. For useful insights into the primacy of theoretical interests for most of the academic members of the rational expectations school, see Arjo Klamer, ed., *Conversations with Economists* (Totowa, N.J.: Rowman and Allanheld, 1984).

17 Political scientists do not take kindly to Robert E. Hall's notion that unemployment may be a form of "idleness," nor to Robert Lucas's contention that cyclical unemployment is a form of "leisure."

18 Karl Brunner's most extensive contribution to public choice is noted above, in note 7. While Friedman has written often about politics, he has not set forth a systematic statement except, perhaps, in his recent volume with Rose Friedman, *Tyranny of the Status Quo* (New York: Harcourt Brace Jovanovich, 1984). More rigorous attempts at exploring certain aspects of public choice have been advanced by Allan H. Meltzer and Scott F. Richard, "Why Government Grows (and Grows) in a Democracy," *The Public Interest* (1978): 109–18.

19 I cannot think of a more profound analysis on this demystification of money and its consequences than the slender volume by S. Herbert Frankel, *Two Philosophies of Money: The Conflict of Trust and Authority* (New York: St. Martin's Press, 1977).

20 One of the very best analyses on the destabilizing effects of politics is that of Richard E. Wagner, "Economic Manipulation for Political Profit: Macroeconomic Consequences and Constitutional Implications," *Kyklos* 30 (1977): 394–410.

21 A good introduction to Buchanan's constitutional views is contained in his Frank M. Engle Lecture presented on January 21, 1981, in Tulsa, Oklahoma. The lecture has been printed under the title "Constitutional Restrictions on the Power of Government" (Bryn Mawr, Pa.: The American College, 1981).

22 A representative sample of views on constitutional issues should include these three volumes: James M. Buchanan and Richard E. Wagner, eds., *Fiscal Responsibility in Constitutional Democracy* (Boston: Martinus Nijhoff Social Science Division, 1978); Richard E. Wagner, Robert D. Tollison, Alvin Rabushka, and John T. Noonan, Jr., *Balanced Budgets, Fiscal Responsibility, and the Constitution* (Washington, D.C.: CATO Institute, 1982); and a book by the well-known political scientist Aaron Wildavsky, *How to Limit Government Spending* (Berkeley: University of California Press, 1980). Rumor has it that Wildavsky has been persuaded by William A. Niskanen that deficits are not quite as important as he had formerly believed to be the case.

23 Brennan and Buchanan, *Power to Tax*, p. 21.

24 William Nordhaus, "The Political Business Cycle," *Review of Economic Studies* 42 (1975): 169–90.

25 C. Duncan MacRae, "A Political Model of the Business Cycle," *Journal of Political Economy* 85 (1977): 293–363.

26 See especially Morris P. Fiorina, *Retrospective Voting in American National Elections* (New Haven: Yale University Press, 1981), and D. Roderick Kiewiet, *Micro-Economics and Micro-Politics* (Chicago: University of Chicago Press, 1983).

27 Edward R. Tufte, *Political Control of the Economy* (Princeton: Princeton University Press, 1978).

28 Comparative public opinion data for a number of Western democracies are presented and interpreted by Robert D. Putnam in *The Beliefs of Politicians* (New Haven: Yale

University Press, 1973) and by Joel D. Alberbach, Robert D. Putnam, and Bert A. Rockman, *Bureaucrats and Politicians in Western Democracies* (Cambridge: Harvard University Press, 1981).

29 William R. Keech and Carl P. Simon conclude that there is no single best-term length of office for all conditions. See "Inflation, Unemployment, and Electoral Terms: When Can Reform of Political Institutions Improve Macroeconomic Policy?" in *The Political Process and Economic Change,* ed. Kristen R. Monroe (New York: Agathon Press, 1983), pp. 77–107.

30 Much of Bruno Frey's work is conveniently summarized in two of his recent books: *Modern Political Economy* (New York: John Wiley & Sons, 1978) and *Democratic Economic Policy* (New York: St. Martin's Press, 1983). A critique of Frey's work is set forth by James E. Alt and K. Alec Chrystal, *Political Economics* (Berkeley: University of California Press, 1983). This same volume may be usefully consulted on many other macroeconomic issues.

31 The classic presentation is a collection of papers edited by Fred Hirsch and John H. Goldthorpe, *The Political Economy of Inflation* (Cambridge: Harvard University Press, 1978). Another important work is that of Paul Peretz, *The Political Economy of Inflation in the United States* (Chicago: University of Chicago Press, 1983).

32 Much of Gary S. Becker's challenging work is contained in *The Economic Approach to Human Behavior* (Chicago: University of Chicago Press, 1976). Various other sociological concerns are addressed from the same economic approach by Reuven Brenner, *History—The Human Gamble* (Chicago: University of Chicago Press, 1983).

33 "Political Aspects of Full Employment," *Political Quarterly* 4 (1983): 322–31. A first-rate intellectual biography of Kalecki has been written by George R. Feiwel, *The Intellectual Capital of Michal Kalecki* (Knoxville: University of Tennessee Press, 1975); chapter 9 deals with Kalecki's theory of the political business cycle.

34 James O'Connor, *The Fiscal Crisis of the State* (New York: St. Martin's Press, 1973).

3 Models of the Political Process and Their Implications for Stagflation: A Public Choice Perspective

Thomas D. Willett and King Banaian

Introduction

Analysis of the causes of stagflation and issues of monetary reform are often based on widely differing views of the operation of the political process. Frequently these differences in assumptions about political constraints are implicit rather than explicit. Even when political assumptions are spelled out clearly, much less attention is given to the importance of these assumptions than to debate about differences in market analysis. Yet the range of assumptions commonly made about the operation of the political process is at least as wide as those about market behavior. This implies differences in both positive and normative analyses of economic policy-making that may easily be as great as those between monetarist and Keynesian analysis of the behavior of the macroeconomy.

One of the major reasons for the paucity of careful analysis of the political assumptions underlying economists' analysis of inflation issues is the relative newness of the field of public choice analysis. The number of economists interested in monetary and macroeconomic issues who also have a background in public choice analysis is quite limited. In hopes of stimulating increased attention to such issues we present in this paper an overview of the major types of public choice models of the operation of the political process.[1] We combine this with discussion of some of the major implications of these different models for the analysis of macroeconomic policy and the political economy of inflation and unemployment. We make no attempt here to convince the reader that one particular model of the political process is the best for dealing with macroeconomic issues. We are still far from having conclusive empirical evidence on this issue.[2] Our analysis suggests, however, that the empirical support for models which do not produce some type of inflationary bias is particularly weak. Thus, while further research is certainly needed, based on our current knowledge, we find little basis for optimism that our present institutional structure provides sufficient safeguards against political incentives to create and/or to accommodate excessive rates of inflation on average.

We often find that economists fail to recognize the difficulties of aggregating individual rational choices to yield results that can be considered efficient. In the last section we discuss a number of reasons why models which conclude that the political process can generate persistent inefficiencies over time may be plausible and need not be inconsistent with the assumption of rational individual behavior. This is one of the most important insights of public choice theory. We cannot be confident that under our current institutional arrangements the invisible hand operates fully in the political market to assure that individual rational behavior will lead to efficient aggregate outcomes.

Types of Possible Biases in the Political Process

Models of the political process can be used both for positive analysis to explain and predict patterns of policy outcomes and for normative analysis concerning the desirability of the existing decision-making structure and possible alternatives.[3] While traditional normative economic analysis is based on arguments about the desirability of particular policy strategies, normative public choice analysis is based on arguments about the desirability of the operation of the decision-making process which leads to policy outcomes.

Thus at the level of normative economic analysis one might argue that there has been too much inflation because the inflation rate has been higher than what one personally judges to have been optimal based on positive economic analysis of the effects of inflation and normative evaluations of these effects. Normative public choice analysis would tend to focus rather on the question of whether the political decision-making process under a particular set of institutions is likely to aggregate perferences efficiently or instead generate systematically biased outcomes.

Of course, we must ask what is our benchmark for judging bias. The choice of a benchmark is clearly in itself a normative decision and one on which we could not expect to secure complete agreement. Differences in views about how the powers of decision making should be distributed is one of the most persistent reasons for political disagreements. For example, who should be enfranchised and to what extent should elected officials lead or follow the wishes of the public? At one extreme, we may have the advocacy of a benevolent dictatorship, perhaps in the form of government by experts.[4] At the other, we have democratic control by the voter. Not all voters are likely to agree. Thus from this perspective, we should not judge the efficiency of the decision-making process in terms of the number of unhappy voters. Rather we should see whether those who disagree are relatively evenly balanced on each side of the outcome, i.e., does the outcome conform to the wishes of the average (median) voter. A good deal of public choice analysis, both positive and normative, focuses on such median voter outcomes. Thus one sense in which we may speak of biases in the operation of the political process refers to outcomes which tend to systematically differ from those desired by the median potential or actual voter.[5]

Even if the median voter does tend to dominate political outcomes, the possibility of a second type of bias persists. The voter may not be well informed about the full range of the costs and benefits of particular policy actions. As will be discussed in some detail in the next section, the typical voter may have little direct incentive to become well informed about most policy issues. Rational perceptions may be based on relatively poor information. Thus, as Anthony Downs pointed out in one of the important early contributions to the development of public choice analysis, where the average voter is more aware of the costs of his or her taxes than the benefits of public spending, the size of the public sector would be biased downwards.[6] Likewise, an overallocation would be expected where the perceived benefits of public spending were exaggerated and/or the costs not fully perceived.

It is this type of model of the political process on which the initial formal models of the political business cycle were based.[7] As is discussed in more detail in the Appendix, with voters having short time horizons and relatively little knowledge of macroeconomic analysis, there would be incentives for vote-seeking incumbent politicians to generate macroeconomic cycles. This would also cause an inflationary bias as compared with the benchmark inflation rate "demanded" by well-informed voters.

In the short run, unanticipated changes in macroeconomic policies tend to influence employment and output more quickly than prices. Thus, unless fully anticipated by the public, an economic expansion shortly before an election would yield a high portion of its political benefits (employment expansion) before the election while most of the costs (inflation) would come after. If a substantial proportion of voters react primarily to the current state of the economy, then this would be a vote-gaining strategy. On the other hand, with the types of well-informed, forward-looking individuals typically assumed in recent rational expectations models of the macroeconomy, such destabilizing actions would be punished rather than rewarded at the ballot box. However, the public good nature of electoral decisions leaves one sanguine of the likelihood that those voters at the margin will be well informed. Since the probability of one's vote being decisive is minimal, direct incentives to acquire information for political purposes will likewise approach zero. Voters who are well informed for other reasons, for example, as a result of their economic activities, seem as likely to be on the edges of the political spectrum as at the middle, and the strong mechanisms for good information to drive out bad which exist in private markets are not present.

Thus we may think of two major types of potential biases, one involving the distribution of effective political power and the other caused by lack of good information and/or shortsightedness. As we shall discuss below, recognition of these two types of problems goes a long way toward explaining the differences in view of those who see the major cause of inflation as "too much democracy" and those who see it as the lack of a sufficient democratic check.

Major Types of Models of the Political Process

With this background, we turn to a more systematic review of major types of models of the political process. We begin with those which assume or predict a tendency for efficient outcomes.

Efficiency Models

There has been an interesting evolution in the views of Keynesian and Chicago economists on the operation of the political process generating economic policy outcomes. Lord Keynes's recommendations of policy activism were based not only on his views of instabilities in the operation of the private sector but also on his assumption, implicitly or explicitly shared by most of the technical writings on the theory of economic policy, that the policy process would tend to generate the adoption of policies that promoted aggregate efficiency. Keynes's faith in the enlightened operation of the policy process was based on a benign technocratic view. Given his famous comment that not one man in a million is able to diagnose the inflationary process, he could not have had much confidence in the role of the public as a check on inflation.[8] His elite ruling-class background likewise supports the view that he thought in terms of government by experts at both the positive and normative levels. American Keynesians have tended to share Keynes's view that the government will tend to follow economically desirable policies, but often this was based on faith in the relatively efficient operation of the democratic process in following the wishes of the public (i.e., a median voter model).[9]

Such assumptions that the macroeconomic policy process would tend to be dominated by public interest considerations (either because of benign experts or efficient political checks) has been challenged both by monetarists and by many public choice theorists. In light of this, it is somewhat ironic that what has been called the new Chicago school sharply disagrees with the older Chicago-type monetarist and public choice views. An older generation of Chicago-oriented economists such as James Buchanan, Ronald Coase, Milton Friedman, and Gordon Tullock argued that the pursuit of self-interest by government officials generated policy outcomes that often resulted in "political failure."[10] This deviated substantially from the implications of the public interest assumptions underlying Keynesian thinking as well as much of the traditional political science and public administration literature.

In contrast, the new Chicago school has applied the traditional Chicago skepticism toward allegations of private market failure to the operation of the political market as well.[11] This gives rise to the skepticism of the rational expectations school that vote-gaining incentives for political business cycles could long endure.[12] This split in "conservative" Chicago views and the prominence of a political liberal such as Mancur Olson[13] in contributing to analysis consistent with the old Chicago views should give some pause to those who have suggested that public choice analysis is just a facade for conservative ideology.

Where the new Chicago school does differ from the traditional benign public interest views of government is that its adherents do see the political process as being dominated by distributional conflict. Thus they are more inclined to see the income redistribution generated by government as resulting more from the actions of self-interested pressure groups than from public-interest motivated views of equity. For example, while the new Chicago perspective suggests that the operation of pressure groups in the democratic process can lead to an overexpansion of government as compared with some normative public interest benchmark, competition among pressure groups would create a tendency for redistribution to take place in relatively efficient ways.[14]

This new Chicago view suggests that without an alteration of the distribution of effective political power, reformist policy proposals will not be productive. In terms of macroeconomic issues, the new Chicago view would seem to imply explanations of the inflation of the past two decades primarily in terms of unsystematic mistakes and efficient financing of the growth of government. Some of these economists have argued recently, however, that in the absence of governments being bound by enforceable contracts (a kind of market failure?), credibility and reputation problems will create an inflationary bias which presents a case for a monetary rule.[15]

There is certainly an important truth in the argument that ceteris paribus we should expect to see such transfers have a tendency to take more efficient forms, as this would allow gains to be shared between the payers and receivers. Traditional public choice analysis, however, has frequently focused on the difficulties of designing efficient compensation mechanisms for transfers to take place in ways which minimize deadweight efficiency costs. Frequently, the success of special interests in securing transfers relies in part on the effects not being clearly seen by the general public or the typical member of Congress. While economic analysis typically suggests that lump sum transfers are the most efficient form of redistribution,[16] these appear to be more the exception than the rule in actual governmental distributive politics.

We believe that a major explanation for this is that the visibility of such economically efficient transfers would make them much more difficult for interest groups to secure. Most interest groups try to cloak their lobbying efforts in public interest rhetoric, and we suspect that the ability to do so often carries considerable weight in securing their passage. For example, while there is a presumption that the replacement of import quotas with a direct subsidy could frequently make both producers and consumers better-off, there is little evidence of producers trying to receive their political rents in this form. They may be concerned both that the costs of their subsidy would be more apparent to those who might oppose such transfers and that efforts to cloak their lobby in public interest rhetoric would lose considerable credibility.

It is important to remember that in the political process successful coalition formation in large groups often requires a substantial number of relatively passive participants who help ratify the proposals emanating from the intense bargaining of subgroups. While the operation of "informational fog factors" is usually pierced by those intensely interested in an issue, such considerations may be important in securing support or lack of opposition from those less intensely interested. If such relatively passive support is important and the most efficient forms of transfers have greater visibility and less ease of cloaking in public interest appeals, then the tendency toward the adoption of efficient forms of transfers and regulation as posited by the new Chicago school will be muted.[17]

Leviathan

At the other extreme of political models are those based on the self-interest of governments combined with little or no effective check from the voting public. Such views frequently underlie the arguments of gold standard advocates that governments have inherently inflationary tendencies. Thus while the public interest and new Chicago views tend to predict optimum rates of inflation, i.e., efficient inflation taxes, the autonomous, self-interested government view predicts the much higher revenue-maximizing rates of inflation since the government cares about costs imposed on the economy only as they lead to lower government revenues.[18] While such analysis is most applicable to monarchies and dictatorships, some public choice theorists such as Brennan and Buchanan have argued that this view of a lack of any effective electoral check, while of course overstated, still has considerable explanatory power in today's democracy.[19] It would be consistent with Keynes's own views of the political process that if self-interested politicians did gain control of the government there would be little effective public check on their inflationary proclivities.

*Interest Groups and Deviations from
the Median Voter Model*

The traditional public choice literature emphasizes two types of models. One is the median voter model discussed above. The second, in the tradition of Buchanan and Tullock and Mancur Olson, highlights ways in which the distribution of effective political power may deviate substantially from the one person–one vote democratic norm. This type of public choice analysis emphasizes the free rider problem, which creates a divergence between individual and group interests and often results in small, well-organized pressure groups winning out in the political process against the interests of large but unorganized groups.[20] Thus while a simple median voter model would predict that government policies with wide benefits and concentrated costs would be likely to achieve a majority vote, Mancur Olson's analysis predicts that policies which have concentrated benefits (to organized pressure groups) and widely dispersed costs (to a rationally apathetic public) would be more successful.

Such analysis also suggests that the simple Marxist class conflict models of political economy are seriously deficient in that they overlook the conflicts of interest which exist within the capital and the labor classes.[21] Public choice analysis helps explain, for example, why we often see both labor and management in a particular interest lobbying for and sometimes securing trade restrictions to reduce import competition at the expense of workers, capitalists, and consumers in the rest of the economy.[22]

While occasionally groups have sought inflation as a source of income redistribution from creditors to debtors, this seems unlikely to have been a major source of direct inflationary pressure in the postwar United States. In general, in comparison with unemployment the distributional consequences of inflation are difficult to determine.[23] They will vary depending on the particular causes of the inflation and the degree to which inflation is anticipated or not. Thus it is not surprising that we find much less difference across income groups in attitudes toward inflation than toward unemployment.[24] Redistributional rent-seeking activities are primarily indirect sources of inflation.[25] They operate to increase government spending and budget deficits and to pressure the monetary authorities to hold down interest rates. In the private sector they can be sources of wage-push which raise nominal wages above equilibrium levels and force a short-run dilemma on monetary authorities of having to choose between higher inflation and higher unemployment. As is discussed in chapter 1 of this volume, these combinations would tend to generate monetary expansion and inflation.

The Marxist rationale for political business cycles is that in order to keep workers docile and ever mindful of the reserve army of the unemployed, the government as the agent of the capitalist class will periodically and deliberately generate a recession.[26] Thus while in the orthodox political business cycle models it is the expansionary phase which is the motivating factor, in the Marxist analysis it is the downswing which is the prime incentive for the political cycle. While there is survey evidence of class-related differences in attitudes toward unemployment with higher-income individuals showing somewhat less concern, we find little evidence of the business support for recession implied by the Marxist analysis.

Bureaucratic and Independent Regulatory Behavior

The Keynesian and traditional political science–public administration assumptions that government consists primarily of public-interest motivated experts have been commonly applied to the operation of the government bureaucracy and independent regulatory commissions. Indeed, the versions of this approach which are skeptical of the operation of direct democratic politics lead naturally to the idea of independent regulatory commissions in which experts can pursue the public interest freed of the pressures of political considerations. Such thinking has been reflected in the establishment of a number of "independent" regulatory agencies in the United States and in the structure of the Federal Reserve system.

Public choice–type analysis has again challenged these public interest views. While granting that public-spirited motivations may not be entirely absent, these approaches emphasize the pursuit of personal interests and the capacity of individuals to convince themselves that their private interests coincide closely with the public interest.[27]

Much of the early literature in this tradition by both economists and political scientists treated government bureaus and regulatory agencies as being relatively autonomous from the formal political process.[28] These were seen as being motivated primarily by their own bureaucratic interests and the interests of client groups in the private sector, with relatively few checks from the president and Congress. The independent regulatory agencies were seen as being "captured" by the industries they were set up to regulate. Revisionist analysis was even able to argue that industries themselves sometimes had a hand in setting up their regulation in order to limit private sector competition.[29] While some of the bureaucratic literature emphasized budget enhancement in order to increase power and perks as the major objective of bureaucratic behavior, and this assumption has been applied to the behavior of the Federal Reserve by some writers,[30] other writers have stressed that bureaus and regulatory agencies may have a wide range of goals which do not always correlate with expenditure increases. These objectives can include gaining and maintaining prestige and standing among groups outside of the bureaucracy, the enjoyment of a wide range of discretionary authority, and the avoidance of having to say no too often to powerful lobbying groups.[31]

The recent trend in bureaucratic and regulatory analysis has been to see a greater role for elected government officials. As is reflected in the discussion and references in chapters 14, 15, and 20 of this volume, the analysis of the politics of the Fed has become a substantive growth industry. The emphasis on the role of formal politics on the behavior of both government bureaucrats and "independent" regulatory agencies has not led to a reemergence of belief in public interest outcomes. Rather these have tended to emphasize the importance of pressure groups acting both on the bureaus and regulatory agencies and on elected officials. In such analysis the role of oversight committees in Congress often receives considerable attention. It generally is argued that such committees have considerable power and that membership is heavily self-selected from those with particular political interests who serve as supporters rather than watchdogs over spending and interest groups in the areas of their committee jurisdiction.[32]

This perspective suggests skepticism that technical changes in operating procedures would make major differences in the general course of monetary policy. Thus the logic of these views is that much of the technical economic debate over monetary policy is largely irrelevant and that more fundamental reforms in institutional structure and the distribution of effective power would be required to substantially change the inflationary propensities of monetary policy-making.

Arguments for Deviations from
Informed Median Voter Outcomes

As was discussed in the first section, beliefs that political outcomes in a democracy may systematically differ from the interests of the average voter require arguments that the average voter is not well informed or does not act in his or her interest and/or that the median voter is frequently not decisive in determining the trend of policy outcomes. In this section, we consider some of the reasons why these may be plausible assumptions in many instances.

Causes of Deviations from Median Voter Outcomes

We shall discuss below why voters may be rationally poorly informed about the costs and benefits of alternative government actions. We begin here by considering reasons why political outcomes can deviate from median voter interests with a well-informed electorate.[33]

One major reason is that most political decisions are based on decisions by elected or appointed officials rather than direct referenda by the public. The direct voting check is generally exercised only periodically and only in the form of the choice between a limited number of candidates. Even if the voters have good knowledge of how candidates would vote on all future policy issues, they are left with the problem that there will be many different issues and no candidate is likely to fully reflect their own preferences. Thus they can only choose from a set of alternative policy preferences the one that comes the closest to their own preferences. This can easily leave scope for all candidates to deviate substantially from median voter interests on many issues. While the ballot box might be a relatively strong influence on a limited number of big issues, it would still leave considerable scope for slippage on an array of smaller issues.

This suggests considerable scope for effective interest groups lobbying for pork barrel redistributive measures, whose individual effects do not influence many votes adversely. Thus even apart from the effects of campaign contributions in influencing votes, we can see how minority interest groups could have a substantial impact on a president's, and even more on a farm district legislator's, chance of reelection. Suppose that farmers constitute only 5 percent of voters, but that for them the farm bill is an extremely important determinant of their vote. Thus voting against a general farm bill would substantially affect the vote calculus of farmers. The other 95 percent of the voters may have gained, so that in a narrow, self-interest-based referendum vote the cut in spending would pass overwhelmingly. But in a presidential vote, for how many voters would opposition to the farm bill be decisive in influencing their vote? Probably only a handful. Thus even in a strict one person–one vote model we can see how such special interest bills can be politically attractive. The addition of lobbying and campaign contribution considerations of course only serves to reinforce this conclusion.

So does our form of geographic representation. Particular political districts often have only a few major economic interests. Congress has developed the tradition of giving committees substantial power in spending decisions. The memberships of these committees are largely self-selected on the basis of the "interests" of the members of Congress. Risk aversion contributes to an attitude that "I'll go along with your district's particular interest if you go along with mine." Thus each member can run on his or her record of securing local benefits. It is true, of course, that the local benefits ceded to all the other districts may impose aggregate costs to the home district greater than these localized benefits (pork barrel is usually a negative-sum game). But even if this is recognized by the voters, it may not be a vote-losing strategy. The gains for the particular winners will be greater than their share of the costs in the vote decision, while concerns about the excessive costs of government may be less decisive in the calculus of other voters.

Furthermore, even if the cost cutters do succeed in electing their own candidate, unless a substantial proportion of other districts do likewise, the likely outcome is the reduction in home district pork barrel programs with little overall reduction in the costs from benefits to other districts. The costs of monitoring and exposing such pork barrel activities increases this problem. Of course if things get too out of hand, cost-cutting moves may become politically popular at times. This has been part and parcel of President Reagan's agenda. Even with considerable voter attention focused on this issue, Reagan's failure to halt the rise in government spending indicates just how difficult it can be to undo the distributional coalitions which have formed around government benefit programs.

The difficulties of holding public attention on such issues help explain why efforts at fundamental institutional reforms such as balanced budget amendments and monetary rules could be both feasible and desirable. Some have argued that the recent taxpayer revolts and support for anti-inflation policies show that the electoral check does punish major economic abuses, albeit with some lag. History suggests, however, that it is often difficult to maintain the type of widespread active attention which would prevent the original tendencies from reemerging. Idealized views of public monitoring would suggest that the imposition of institutional constraints would be unnecessary and undesirable. Views that there is virtually no electoral check would imply that there is no chance the imposition of such reforms would ever be politically feasible. However, an intermediate view of the operation of the electoral check which suggests that it works for a limited number of "hot" or big issues at any particular time implies that efforts to design and implement institutional checks may at times be feasible.

From the standpoint of a simple median voter model it can be argued that the political democratic process will have an anti-inflation, prounemployment bias. After all, everyone is hit directly by inflation, while even with very high unemployment less than 10 percent of the public would be directly affected. Even after allowing for those who expect distributional gains from inflation, those directly hurt by inflation would typically exceed those directly hurt by unemployment by a factor of five times or more. By the same logic we would almost never have trade barriers erected because the gainers from maintaining free trade would greatly exceed the losers. This illustrates the importance of the intensity of effects in influencing voting and lobbying behavior discussed above. Most of the public does oppose inflation. This comes through clearly in public opinion polls. But the decisiveness of this in influencing voting and lobbying behavior may be a good deal less than for those hard hit by recessions, just as consumers of farm products frequently have less influence than producers, even though consumers are many times more numerous.

Furthermore, it is important to remember that unemployment is typically not generated in a vacuum. The short-run trade-off is not just inflation versus unemployment but inflation versus tight macroeconomic policies which will generate a recession, the costs of which go far beyond those directly unemployed. Profits and real wage increases for employed workers will also decline. Furthermore, the numbers of workers and managers who will fear being unemployed in a downswing will typically be considerably greater than the number who actively become unemployed.

While typical rational expectations formulations may be too strong, many voters clearly look forward as well as backward. This is one of the major reasons that vote and popularity studies find the rates of change as well as the levels of economic variables such as economic growth and unemployment to be important. Considering the much quicker effects of changes in macroeconomic policy on output and employment than on inflation and the relatively short time horizon which tends to operate in the political process, we see little basis for concluding that on balance the concentrated effects of unemployment are sufficient to create a deflationary bias in macroeconomic policy-making under democratic institutions.

Incentives for Being Well Informed

Generally, in microeconomic models economists assume that consumers and producers tend to be well informed, relying upon our standard self-interest assumption that buyers and sellers have incentives to be well informed. While many more detailed analyses do focus on information costs and how they influence microeconomic allocation,[34] most orthodox economists appear to believe that it is reasonable to assume that the economic actors are reasonably well informed for a wide range of microeconomic activities. Such a view is reflected as well in the common assumptions that financial markets behave with a high degree of informational or speculative efficiency. The supporting empirical evidence which has been generated is not surprising.

Many economists have assumed or argued, however, that many product and labor markets behave with considerably less informational efficiency than do financial markets. More analysis is needed on the incentives for and costs or difficulties of information processing in different types of markets. Economic rationality does not preclude markets with different structures from behaving differently, and one must be wary of unwarranted extrapolation of results from one market to another.

This is particularly true when moving from economic to political markets, for here in addition to all of the difficulties of acquiring good information, there is the added problem that there is little direct incentive either to acquire or act on this information. There is a classic free-rider, public-goods problem in operation. While there would be widespread agreement that well-informed voting would be in "the public interest," the likelihood that any one individual's actions would influence political outcomes is so low that there is little direct incentive to be informed or for that matter even to vote. Indeed, on the basis of narrow self-interest reasoning the surprising question is not why election turnouts are so small but rather why they are as large as they are.[35] In reality, the electorate is better informed and more politically active than a narrow economic model of individual self-interest maximization would imply because many individuals will engage in the relatively low-cost activity of voting for reasons other than the differential benefits of electing one's preferred candidate. Such voting is likely to incorporate a good deal of information which was a free or low-cost by-product of other activities.[36]

Likewise, the existence of organized interest groups presents additional low-cost information and increased incentives to vote, although at the likely cost of moving one away from median potential voter outcomes. Still, when one reads public opinion polls which report on the low levels of economic literacy of the general public, one may question the efficiency of the electoral check on government macroeconomic policies.[37] Likewise, it should not be surprising to find that adaptive expectations play a more prominent role in political markets than in many economic markets.

Of course, if all economic markets displayed the characteristics assumed in the strong form rational expectations approach, this would probably be sufficient to remove most incentives for socially costly political manipulation of the economy. In other words, while the data might give the appearance of a short-run inflation-unemployment trade-off because of unanticipated developments, the government could not systematically exploit this observed statistical relationship in order to play the political business cycle game. Strong form rational expectations theorists have offered empirical evidence in support of this view, and there is a general consensus that there is less scope for policy exploitation of short-run trade-offs than was commonly thought a decade ago. However, the recent trend in econometric research is to find short-term real effects from anticipated as well as unanticipated monetary changes. There is some evidence that this is due primarily to short-term wage and price stickiness in many markets rather than substantial biases in expectations formation in economic markets, but this question needs a good deal more research.[38] We believe that most economists still hold the view that there is scope for government macropolicies to influence the real side of the economy in a politically profitable manner because such policy is unlikely to be predictable and/or anticipated policy changes can still have significant short-run effects on output and employment (albeit less strong than for unanticipated policy changes).

The analytic point to be made here, however, is that the best defense of the public against these manipulations rests on the direct reactions of the economy. If, in fact, the behavior of the economy does offer exploitable short-run inflation-unemployment trade-offs, we could not reasonably expect a majority of the voting public to look beyond this and punish rather than reward governments at the ballot box for such activity. Of course this could be likely to occur for some voters who are well informed because of their economic activities or general interest in such issues. Voters of this nature would then engage in "strategic voting," casting ballots to induce incumbents toward long-run equilibria. This can be done if voters are aware of the long-run trade-off between inflation and unemployment, or more generally, if voters exhibit preferences for contractionary policies during periods of high inflation (i.e., they do not punish incumbents for increases in unemployment during these times.)[39]

Public choice analysis of voter incentives makes one doubtful that individuals as voters would show better foresight than individuals as economic actors, since the benefits of additional information seeking would generally be quite small relative to the costs. Furthermore, while there is a strong tendency for those who are best informed to dominate price setting in competitive economic markets, the same mechanism does not hold in competitive political markets. While there may be some tendency for those who typically vote to be somewhat better informed about national issues than those who don't, the actions of an informed voter count for no more or less than those of an ignorant or misinformed voter. For the democratic check to be assured of working well, a much broader diffusion of general information is necessary than is required for most economic markets.

Recent developments certainly suggest that democratic politics does not inevitably force ever-increasing rates of inflation over time. The rational expectations approach is undoubtedly correct in emphasizing learning behavior on the part of the public.[40] In recent years there have been discussions of political business cycle tendencies in the popular press. The more predictably the political business cycle game is played, the greater awareness of this there will be in both economic decision making and voting. The short-run trade-offs in response to such policy behavior would be less favorable, and voters would be less likely to reward governments for exploiting short-run trade-offs which did remain. But there is quite a difference between showing that you cannot fool all of the people all of the time with the same trick, and showing that you cannot fool enough of the people enough of the time so that a bias toward excessive inflation will continue on average over time. This will be particularly true if, as the empirical evidence suggests and the more sophisticated later generations of political business cycle models predict, such behavior does not accompany every election.[41] We cannot safely predict that the anti-inflationary developments of the first half of the 1980s will endure. Unfortunately the permanent removal of substantial incentives to engage in political business cycle behavior requires not only considerable learning but also long memories on the part of the public. The disastrous hyper-inflation in Germany after World War I does appear to have generated such memories for the German public to a substantial degree. We may hope, but cannot be confident, that the American public will display a similar memory from the much milder but still highly costly inflationary excesses of the 1960s and 1970s.

Appendix: An Overview of Political Business Cycle Models
King Banaian

As was discussed in the text, with expansionary macroeconomic policies a disproportionate amount of the desirable effects of expanded output and employment tends to show up first, while the costs of higher inflation are more heavily concentrated in later periods. With contractionary policies, just the reverse is the case. If the political process does indeed operate with a short time horizon the result is a bias toward expansionary over contractionary policies. There is scope for political advantage from exploiting the difference between short-run and long-run inflation-unemployment trade-offs, a policy strategy which results in both excessive volatility and higher rates of inflation than would occur with an informed median voter benchmark. This bias will be greater, the flatter is the policy exploitable short-run Phillips curve and the more myopic is the voting public.

The Mechanics of the Basic Argument

This point is demonstrated formally in the literature on political business cycles (PBCS) and is illustrated in figures 3.1 and 3.2.[42] Consider the situation where the political party in power maximizes a quadratic vote function whose arguments are the rates of unemployment and of inflation.[43] Each of the set of indifference or iso-vote curves labeled V_1 shows the different combinations of inflation, p, and unemployment, u, which will yield some particular percentage of the votes cast for the incumbent at the next election. The lower are p and u, the larger is the vote share of the party in power in the coming election. Thus points on indifference curves (iso-vote lines) closer to the origin are preferred to ones further away. The party in power is assumed able to set unemployment at any desired rate, but it is constrained by a short-run Phillips curve which shifts over time. Thus it may lower the unemployment rate in the short run but it pays a double price in terms of higher inflation now and a worse short-run inflation-unemployment trade-off in the next period. In the figures, LR repre-

Figure 3.1 Inflation-Unemployment Trade-Offs and Short-Run Political Equilibrium

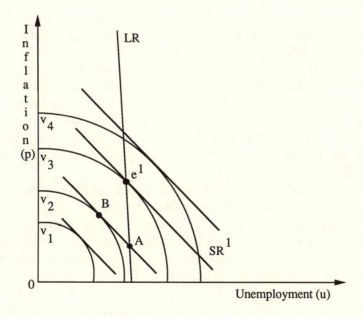

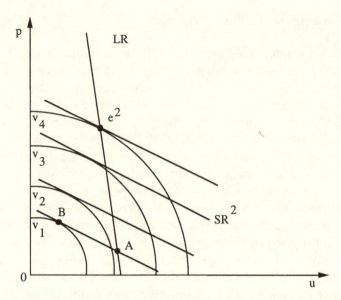

Figure 3.2   Inflation-Unemployment Trade-Offs and Long-Run Political Equilibrium

sents the long-run Phillips curve (drawn with a slight negative slope to illustrate that the analysis does not require a vertical long-run curve). The SR^1 and SR^2 curves represent two different families of short-run inflation-unemployment trade-offs, with the SR^1 curves having a steeper slope than the SR^2 curves. Attempts to exploit short-run points to the left of the long-run curve will shift out the short-run curve over time, while the adoption of points to the right of the long-run curve would shift the short-run curve in. Long-term equilibrium occurs where the long-run and short-run curves intersect on an indifference curve, at points e^1 and e^2 respectively in the figures.

Let the initial inflation-unemployment values be those given by point A in each figure. In both of these cases the party in power is able to increase its vote share in the next election by moving along the relevant short-run trade-off to point B, which is tangent to a more southwesterly dashed indifference or iso-vote curve. In each case there are incentives to inflate prior to the election. Note, however, that the flatter the short-run trade-off curves, the greater the long-run inflation rate (e^2 is higher than e^1). The effects of the slopes of the short-run curves on the political equilibrium rate of inflation have not been emphasized in the early treatments of the political business cycle.

The greater the short-run flexibility of wages and prices and the less sluggish the adjustment of expectations, the steeper will be SR and hence, the less will be the incentives for overexpansion. This implies that rather than being the engine of inflation that many have charged, flexible exchange rates may help reduce inflationary tendencies. This is because the rapid adjustment of exchange rates tends to speed up the price effects of changes in macroeconomic policy and, hence, steepen SR.[44]

Given the diversity of preferences of the public, we would say public choice analysis finds that the Nordhaus model contains a perfect competitive check on independent political behavior which forces government behavior to conform to median voter preferences, thus avoiding an inflationary bias according to one standard norm (i.e., a non–median voter outcome). But this is not the median voter outcome that would occur if all voters were fully informed of the long-run effects of expansionary policies. This outcome would occur at the point of tangency of the long-run Phillips curve to the lowest iso-vote contour possible. The inflationary bias away from this point is greater, the less informed and the more myopic the general public.

The Different Roles of Myopia and Issues of Expectations Formation

The term myopia has been defined differently by many economists in discussing PBCs, and these differences have created confusion in critiquing the literature. Both the government and voter may suffer from myopia. Governmental myopia implies that incumbents attach zero value to macroeconomic outcomes past the election date. Thus Nordhaus describes a "purely myopic policy" where "planners apply infinite discount rates in evaluating policy."[45] This would not preclude perfect foresight of incumbents: models of incumbent myopia are consistent with the recent work of Barro and Gordon and of Backus and Driffill, which emphasizes a democratic government's inability to be bound by contract to socially optimal policies even when it desires to do so.[46] The PBC literature of this variety presumes that incumbents instead are vote maximizers.

Government myopia is common to most but not all PBC models. The most notable exception is the work by Frey in which ideological goals (whose benefits for the incumbent fall partly in future periods) are pursued given reasonable assurance of reelection.[47] The adherence to ideological positions at the expense of capturing votes near the median can be seen as an investment in political capital. Its return would be greater electoral prospects in future elections. Minford and Peel also use ideology to differentiate parties, so that some measure of benefits in future periods is considered by voters in evaluating the incumbent.[48]

Voter myopia may arise in two distinct ways: retrospectively and prospectively. In what can be called "retrospective voter myopia," voters base their political decision about incumbent reelection upon an assessment of past macroeconomic performance.[49] The voter offers a "report card" on the incumbents' ability to manage the economy. In prospective voter myopia, voters employ data of past macroeconomic performance to construct an expectation of likely future macroeconomic performance under the current policy regime with current policymakers. Obtaining and assimilating information to form alternative estimates for different regimes and policymakers may be exceedingly difficult. Hence both types of voter myopia suggest the same information set for the electorate, but with two distinct uses.

The difference is not trivial: the data appropriate for grading past performance may be unrelated to the data needed to form expectations. Changes in inflation rates may provide good guides to future rates but not much information about the performance by the incumbent. One may also ask questions about the effect of supply shocks on the popularity of incumbents. If a negative shock raises the inflation rate, retrospective voter myopia may predict punishment of the incumbent (voters may or may not be forgiving), while prospective voter myopia implies that voters will screen out the effects of past shocks and not defect from incumbent support.

The bifurcation of voter myopia presents interesting insights. Chappell, for example, while granting voters sophistication in understanding macroeconomics, uses a policy feedback rule as the mechanism by which a retrospective judgment is made.[50] Likewise, in chapter 9 of this volume, Schneider and Frey assume "voters . . . evaluate the government in terms of its past performance over the last legislative period, or even longer." Kiewiet also may be categorized as retrospective.[51] Into the prospective camp we can place authors who draw on the seminal works of Gerald

Kramer and Anthony Downs, who insisted that voters employ past actual performance as a proxy for future performances.[52] Kirchgässner uses this definition in developing alternative models of PBCs.[53]

The confusion between these items becomes apparent in discussions of strategic voting. Strategic voting implies that voters are fully aware of the long-run Phillips trade-off, and thus vote so as to lead incumbents to a point on the long-run curve that yields the minimum vote loss to the incumbent.[54] But government myopia may still exist.

Henry Chappell provides an interesting analysis of strategic voting.[55] He compares the model of voters who are naive with respect to the Phillips curve with one in which voters reward incumbents for following a feedback rule which calls for contractionary policies when inflation is high. Thus Chappell eliminates one type of myopia, insofar as voters understand long-run trade-offs. But they continue to discount past outcomes and continue to make retrospective judgments of incumbent performance. The election remains a "yes-no" referendum on the president. The models are roughly comparable in explaining presidential popularity (with adjusted r-squares of .63 for the naive model versus .65 for the sophisticated model). He finds that the amount of memory decay, or past performance discounting, is 3 percent per quarter. This does imply, however, that the events of the first quarter are weighed as 62 percent of the weight given to events in the last quarter of a presidential term. This result could be consistent with MacRae's myopic model if one attaches a step slope to the Phillips curve. MacRae also finds that strategic voting explains certain administrations but not others.[56] All told, the aggregate evidence for more sophisticated voting is ambiguous: while its predictions are consistent with American voting data at some times, the naive model predicts roughly as well. Incentives for cycle creation could come from memory decay or myopia. And the lack of incentives for informed voting on such issues may make one skeptical that strategic voting is of importance where the number of voters is large.

The confusion over different concepts of myopia is compounded by some misinterpretations. Noteworthy is the recent work of Brian Barry, who argues that the Nordhaus model contains an internal inconsistency.[57] Barry asserts that political business cycle models are constructed under the assumption that the incumbent cannot move the short-run curve substantially during its tenure. Nothing could be further from the truth. Were it true, there would be no cycle; government would move to a position

like point *A* in figure 3.1 and stay there. This would imply that government suffers from a myopia of the nature of the short- versus long-run
trade-off. Nordhaus does not assume this, but uses a fixed short-run curve
as pedagogy to illustrate the incentives government has for exploitation.[58]

Others have persisted in assuming away voter memory decay. This
is not necessary for the cycle, though it does add incentives. Stigler even
takes this step so far as to deny that voting can be influenced by short-run
economic conditions.[59] Yet his empirical results actually find statistically
significant relationships between votes received by incumbents and annual changes in real income and inflation. He then moves to two-year
changes, along with a respecification of the dependent variable. While
inflation is no longer a significant explanation of the revised vote share
for the incumbent, two-year changes in real income continue to be
strongly correlated to incumbent votes.

The majority of studies since Stigler's have found significant effects
of macroeconomic conditions on voting and public opinion polls at the
presidential level.[60] But we still are uncertain about the relative importance of different types of macroeconomic variables and the ways in
which voters form their expectations and make judgments about past and
expected future performance. These are important issues for continued
research.

Notes

1 For alternative characterizations of the main types of public choice models and more
   detailed references to this literature, see Ryan Amacher, Robert Tollison, and
   Thomas D. Willett, "Budget Size in a Democracy: A Review of the Arguments,"
   Public Finance Quarterly (April 1975): 99–122, reprinted in *The Economic Approach to Public Policy,* ed. Ryan Amacher, Robert Tollison, and Thomas D. Willett
   (Ithaca, N.Y.: Cornell University Press, 1976); William C. Mitchell, "Fiscal Behavior of the Modern Democratic State: Public Choice Contributions and Perspectives,"
   in *Political Economy,* ed. Larry L. Wade (Boston: Kluwer-Nihoff, 1983), pp. 69–
   114; and Dennis Mueller, *Public Choice* (Cambridge: Cambridge University Press,
   1979).

2 Indeed, in contrast to general discussion of the politics of macropolicy and inflation
   there have been very few efforts so far to analyze macroeconomic policy-making or
   outcomes in terms of the comparative explanatory power of alternative theories of
   political behavior. There are notable exceptions: Paul Peretz, *The Political Economy
   of Inflation in the United States* (Chicago: University of Chicago Press, 1983), presents a judgmental case study assessment of pluralist, elitist, and Marxist class mod-

els (he concludes that all have some explanatory power but none do very well). Henry W. Chappell, Jr., "Presidential Popularity and Macroeconomic Performance: Are Voters Really So Naive?" *Review of Economics and Statistics* 65 (August 1983): 385–92, and C. Duncan MacRae, "A Political Model of the Business Cycle," *Journal of Political Economy* 85 (November 1977): 506–22, compare political business cycle and strategic voting models, again not finding a clear dominance of one over the other. This paucity of research in the domestic macro area contrasts sharply with the substantial number of such studies on international economy policies. See, for example, the analysis and references in John Odell, *U.S. International Monetary Policy* (Princeton: Princeton University Press, 1982).

3 Contrast the following three examples, all of which deal with the behavior of central banks: Keith Acheson and John F. Chant, "Bureaucratic Theory and the Choice of Central Bank Goals," *Journal of Money, Credit, and Banking* 5 (May 1973): 637–55; Ira Kaminow, "Politics, Economics, and Procedure of U.S. Money Growth Dynamics," in *The Political Economy of International and Domestic Monetary Relations,* ed. Raymond E. Lombra and Willard E. Witte (Ames: Iowa State University Press, 1982), pp. 181–96; and Thomas D. Willett and John Mullen, "The Effects of Alternative International Monetary Systems on Macroeconomic Discipline and the Political Business Cycle," in Lombra and Witte, *Political Economy,* pp. 143–55.

4 Lord Keynes is a leading example of this view. Sir Roy Harrod, *The Life of John Maynard Keynes* (London: Macmillan, 1951), pp. 192–93, gives a clear statement of these presuppositions of the policy process. See also James M. Buchanan and Richard E. Wagner, *Democracy in Deficit: The Political Legacy of Lord Keynes* (New York: Academic Press, 1977), especially chaps. 3 and 4.

5 Contrast the views offered on this issue by Arthur Burns and Paul Samuelson, "Two Views of the Budget Balancing Debate," *AEI Economist,* April 1979, 1–6.

6 Anthony Downs, *An Economic Theory of Democracy* (New York: Harper and Row, 1957), pp. 69–71.

7 William Nordhaus, "The Political Business Cycle," *Review of Economic Studies* 42 (April 1985): 169–90; and C. Duncan MacRae, "A Political Model of the Business Cycle," *Journal of Political Economy* 85 (November 1977): 506–22.

8 *Collected Writings of John Maynard Keynes,* vol. 2, *The Economic Consequences of the Peace (1919)* (London: Macmillan–St. Martin's for the Royal Economic Society, 1971), p. 221.

9 See, for example, Samuelson, "Two Views," p. 5. See also Brian Barry, "Does Democracy Cause Inflation? Political Ideas of Some Economists," in *The Politics of Inflation and Economic Stagnation,* ed. Leon N. Lindberg and Charles S. Maier (Washington, D.C.: Brookings Institution, 1985), pp. 280–317, which argues against the view that the political process operates with an inflationary bias. Barry correctly argues that the existence of inflation per se cannot be taken as a political failure and that we do not have hard objective evidence that a bias exists, but parts of his arguments are technically flawed (see appendix), and we do not believe that he adequately addresses the arguments that we present in this volume for believing that there is a tendency toward inflationary bias. Barry does not give a balanced assessment of the arguments, treating inflation as if its costs were minor and charg-

ing those concerned with inflation and possible needs for institutional reform with "scaremongering" (p. 291) to advocate "reactionary twaddle" (p. 317).

10 Buchanan and Wagner, *Democracy in Deficit;* James M. Buchanan and Gordon Tullock, *The Calculus of Consent* (Ann Arbor: University of Michigan Press, 1962), chap. 3; and Milton Friedman, "Government Revenue from Inflation," *Journal of Political Economy* 79 (August 1971): 846–56, are but three examples.

11 See Melvin W. Reder, "Chicago Economics: Permanence and Change," *Journal of Economic Literature* 20 (March 1983): 25–28.

12 See, for example, George Stigler, "General Economic Conditions and National Economic Elections," *American Economic Review* 63 (May 1973): 160–67; and Bennett T. McCallum, "The Political Business Cycle: An Empirical Test," *Southern Economic Journal* 45 (October 1978): 504–15.

13 See his classic, Mancur Olson, *The Logic of Collective Action* (Cambridge: Harvard University Press, 1968).

14 See Gary S. Becker, "A Theory of Competition among Pressure Groups for Political Influence," *Quarterly Journal of Economics* 98 (August 1983): 371–400.

15 See, for example, Robert J. Barro and David B. Gordon, "Rules, Discretion, and Reputation in a Model of Monetary Policy," *Journal of Monetary Economics* 12 (July 1983): 101–22, and "A Positive Theory of Monetary Policy in a Natural Rate Model," *Journal of Political Economy* 91 (August 1983): 589–610; and Barro, "Rules versus Discretion," in *Alternative Monetary Regimes*, ed. Colin D. Campbell and William Dugan (Baltimore: Johns Hopkins University Press, 1986), pp. 1–15. For critical reviews of these papers see Alex Cukierman, "Central Bank Behavior and Credibility: Some Recent Theoretical Developments," Federal Reserve Bank of St. Louis *Review,* May 1986, pp. 5–17; Axel Leijonhufvud, "Rules with Some Discretion," in *Alternative Monetary Regimes,* pp. 38–43; and Kenneth Rogoff, "Reputational Constraints on Monetary Policy," *Carnegie-Rochester Conference Series on Public Policy* 26 (1987): 141–82.

16 But not always. See Becker, "Theory of Competition," pp. 388–91.

17 For a recent public choice analysis arguing that instead there will be a tendency toward increased inefficiency over time, see Mancur Olson, *The Rise and Fall of Nations* (New Haven: Yale University Press, 1982).

18 For discussion and empirical estimates of these concepts of optimal and revenue-maximizing rates of inflation, see chapter 6 of this volume.

19 Geoffrey Brennan and James M. Buchanan, *The Power to Tax: Analytical Foundations of a Fiscal Constitution* (New York: Cambridge University Press, 1980), chaps. 3, 8, and 10.

20 There has been considerable recent debate about the actual importance of free or cheap riding. See, for example, Oliver Kim and Mark Walker, "The Free Rider Problem: Experimental Evidence," *Public Choice* 43, no. 1 (1984): 3–24; and R. Mark Isaac, James M. Walker, and Susan H. Thomas, "Divergent Evidence on Free Riding: An Experimental Examination of Possible Explanations," *Public Choice* 43, no. 2 (1984): 113–49, and the references cited therein.

21 For examples of Marxist analysis of macroeconomic issues, see Raford Boddy and

James Crotty, "Class Conflict and Macro Policy: The Political Business Cycle," *Review of Radical Political Economy* 7 (Spring 1975): 1–19; and James Harvey, "Theories of Inflation," *Marxism Today* 21 (January 1977): 24–29.

22 See, for example, Ryan C. Amacher, Robert Tollison, and Thomas D. Willett, "The Divergence between Theory and Practice," in *Tariffs, Quotas, and Trade,* ed. Walter Adams et al. (San Francisco: Institute for Contemporary Studies, 1978), pp. 55–66.

23 For an excellent discussion of the difficulties in mobilizing distributional coalitions around inflation, see Charles Maier, "The Politics of Inflation in the Twentieth Century," in *The Political Economy of Inflation,* ed. Fred Hirsch and John H. Goldthorpe (Cambridge: Harvard University Press, 1978), pp. 37–72.

24 See Stanley Fischer and John Huizinga, "Inflation, Unemployment, and Public Opinion Polls," *Journal of Money, Credit, and Banking* 14 (February 1982): 1–19; Douglas A. Hibbs, Jr., "Inflation, Political Support, and Macroeconomic Policy," in *The Politics of Inflation and Economic Stagnation,* ed. Leon N. Lindberg and Charles S. Maier (Washington, D.C.: Brookings Institution, 1985), pp. 173–95, and "Public Concern about Inflation and Unemployment in the United States," in *Inflation,* ed. Robert E. Hall (Chicago: University of Chicago Press, 1982); and Peretz, *Political Economy of Inflation.* An examination of British class attitudes can be found in James E. Alt, *The Politics of Economic Decline* (Cambridge: Cambridge University Press, 1979).

25 See Robert Gordon, "The Demand for and Supply of Inflation," *Journal of Law and Economics* 18 (December 1975): 808–11. However, many sociological views cite this as a primary direct source of inflationary pressure. See John H. Goldthorpe, "The Current Inflation: Towards a Sociological Account," in *Political Economy of Inflation,* ed. Hirsch and Goldthorpe, pp. 186–213; and Colin Crouch, "Conditions for Trade Union Restraint," in *Politics of Inflation and Economic Stagnation,* ed. Lindberg and Maier, pp. 105–39.

26 Boddy and Crotty, "Class Conflict"; and Michael Kalekci, "Political Aspects of Full Employment," *Political Quarterly* 14 (October 1943): 322–31.

27 To wit, "Decisions as to which political party will do the most for the 'public good' are difficult to make. Both parties will be claiming that they will make more of a contribution than the opposition. The private benefits, on the other hand, are relatively easy to work out. The voter is likely to have figured out which side would have given him the most personally and then permitted himself to be convinced that this side was also the best for the country." Gordon Tullock, *Towards a Mathematics of Politics* (Ann Arbor: University of Michigan Press, 1977), p. 112.

28 See William A. Niskanen, Jr., *Bureaucracy and Representative Government* (Chicago: Aldine Atherton, 1971); and Thomas E. Borcherding, ed., *Budgets and Bureaucrats: The Sources of Government Growth* (Durham, N.C.: Duke University Press, 1977).

29 For a useful survey of the regulation literature, see Barry M. Mitnick, *The Political Economy of Regulation* (New York: Columbia University Press, 1980).

30 Marc Toma, "The Inflationary Bias of the Federal Reserve System: A Bureaucratic Approach," *Journal of Monetary Economics* 10 (September 1982): 163–90; and Wil-

liam F. Shughart and Robert D. Tollison, "Preliminary Evidence on the Use of Inputs by the Federal Reserve System," *American Economic Review* 73 (June 1983): 291–304. For critical analysis of these papers, see chapter 21 of this volume.

31   Important early contributions applying bureaucratic theory to the study of monetary policy-making are presented in the work by Acheson and Chant. See, for example, Keith Acheson and John F. Chant, "Bureaucratic Theory and the Choice of Central Bank Goals," *Journal of Money, Credit, and Banking* 5 (May 1973): 637–55. Recent examples include N. T. Skaggs, "A Theory of the Bureaucratic Value of Federal Reserve Operating Procedures," *Public Choice* 43 (1984): 65–76.

32   Tom Havrilesky reports findings of little effectiveness of congressional oversight in chapter 13 of this volume. Other writers have offered a mixed set of views, with most arguing that the influence of the executive branch is considerably greater than that of Congress. See Robert E. Weintraub, "Congressional Supervision of Monetary Policy," *Journal of Monetary Economics* 4 (April 1978): 341–62; James L. Pierce, "The Myth of Congressional Supervision of Monetary Policy," *Journal of Monetary Economics* 4 (April 1978): 363–70; Steven M. Roberts, "Congressional Oversight of Monetary Policy," *Journal of Monetary Economics* 4 (August 1978): 543–56; Kevin Grier, *Congressional Preference and Federal Reserve Policy*, Washington University, Center for the Study of American Business Working Paper no. 95 (St. Louis, 1985); and the discussions and additional references in chapters 14, 15, and 20 of this volume.

33   For further discussion of these issues, see Olson, *Rise and Fall of Nations;* and Dennis C. Muller, Robert D. Tollison, and Thomas D. Willett, "Solving the Intensity Problem in Representative Democracy," in *Economic Approach to Public Policy,* ed. Amacher, Tollison, and Willett, pp. 444–73.

34   George Akerloff, "The Market for Lemons: Qualitative Uncertainty and the Market Mechanism," *Quarterly Journal of Economics* 84 (August 1970): 488–500; and Armen A. Alchian, "Information Costs, Pricing, and Resource Unemployment," *Western Economic Journal* 7 (June 1969): 109–28, are two classics in this field.

35   See, for example, Robert Tollison and Thomas D. Willett, "Some Simple Economics of Voting and Not Voting," *Public Choice* 16 (Fall 1973): 58–71, reprinted in Amacher, Tollison, and Willett, *Economic Approach to Public Policy.*

36   See Tullock, *Mathematics of Politics,* pp. 82–114; and King Banaian, "First Differences versus Levels in the Political Economy of Inflation" (Ph.D. dissertation, Claremont Graduate School, 1986), chap. 3.

37   For discussion of the low levels of macroeconomic knowledge evidenced in most public opinion surveys, see Peretz, *Political Economy of Inflation.*

38   See Frederic S. Mishkin, *A Rational Expectations Approach to Macroeconometrics* (Chicago: University of Chicago Press, 1983); and Mohammad R. Safarzadeh and Thomas D. Willett, *Inter-Industry Differences in Responses to Anticipated and Unanticipated Money Supply Changes in the United States,* Claremont Center for Economic Policy Studies Working Paper (Claremont Graduate School, 1984), and the references cited therein.

39   MacRae, "Political Model," pp. 251–54, is an example of the former, and Chappell, "Presidential Popularity," of the latter.

40 A good deal of political science literature also suggests a more sophisticated and forward-looking process of expectations formation by voters than was assumed in the initial political business cycle models. For discussion and references, see Michael M. Gant and Dwight Davis, "Mental Economy and Voter Rationality: The Informed Citizen Problem in Voting Research," *Journal of Politics* 46 (1984): 132–53; and Norman J. Vig, "Post-Keynesian Economics and Politics," *World Politics*, 1981: 62–89. Note that the method of learning by the public may be as crucial as the content of the information. See Lawrence H. Meyer and Charles Webster, Jr., "Monetary Policy and Rational Expectations: A Comparison of Least Squares and Bayesian Learning," *Carnegie-Rochester Conference Series on Public Policy* 17 (Autumn 1982): 67–97, and the accompanying comments by Marc Rush and Peter Howitt. It is argued therein that least-squares learning implies adjustments to policy by the public that are so slow as to leave policy effective over many years. Bayesian learning dictates much quicker adjustments and far less scope for governmental manipulation. For an interesting recent theoretical treatment of uncertainty and learning behavior in this context, see Alex Cukierman and Allan H. Meltzer, "A Positive Theory of Discretionary Policy, the Cost of Democratic Government and the Benefits of a Constitution," *Economic Inquiry* 24 (July 1986): 367–88.

41 One such variant of the model assumes incumbents have ideological concerns but face the constraint of periodic reelection. When reelection is assured, incumbents cease to be concerned with macroeconomic conditions and return to pursuit of ideological goals. See Bruno S. Frey and Hans-Jürgen Ramser, "The Political Business Cycle: A Comment," *Review of Economic Studies* 43 (October 1943): 554–55; and Bruno Frey and Friederich Schneider, "An Empirical Study of Politico-Economic Interaction in the United States," *Review of Economics and Statistics* 60 (May 1978): 174–83.

42 See Nordhaus, "Political Business Cycle," and MacRae, "Political Model."

43 This model is employed by MacRae, "Political Model," p. 241.

44 See Willett and Mullen, "Alternative Monetary Systems."

45 Nordhaus, "Political Business Cycle," pp. 176–77.

46 See Barro and Gordon, "Rules, Discretion, and Reputation"; and David Backus and John Driffill, "Inflation and Reputation," *American Economic Review* 75 (June 1985): 530–38. Backus and Driffill, for example, contend that the reason for the run-up of inflation at the end of the term is that government is concerned with employment and finds no need for assumptions of voter myopia. Such manipulation is possible simply because voter/agents do not have the information about government's intentions or preferences. They acquire this information by observation of policy behavior; the longer government adheres to a noninflationary policy, the more credible the policy is, and inflationary expectations are dampened. The longer the noninflationary policy is kept intact, then, the greater is the payoff to governments concerned about employment to inflate the economy. Thus a government desirous of creating PBCs will adopt a noninflationary stance to create a reputation of not being concerned with employment. Should they persevere through an entire electoral cycle, the payoffs may be even greater at the next reelectoral juncture.

47 Frey and Ramser, "Political Business Cycle"; Frey and Schneider, "Politico-Economic Interaction."

48 Patrick L. A. Minford and David A. Peel, "The Political Theory of the Business Cycle," *European Economic Review* 17 (1982): 253–70.

49 While the best-known work in the genre is likely Gerald H. Kramer, "Short Run Fluctuations in U.S. Voting Behavior, 1896–1964," *American Political Science Review* 65 (March 1971): 131–43, one should also see Morris P. Fionina, *Retrospective Voting in American National Elections* (New Haven: Yale University Press, 1981).

50 Chappell, "Presidential Popularity."

51 D. Roderick Kiewiet, *Macroeconomics and Micropolitics: The Electoral Effects of Economic Issues* (Chicago: University of Chicago Press, 1983).

52 Kramer, "U.S. Voting Behavior"; Downs, *Economic Theory of Democracy.*

53 See Gebhard Kirchgässner, "On the Theory of Optimal Government Behaviour" (Swiss Federal Institute of Technology, Zurich, 1981, mimeographed), and "The Political Business Cycle If the Government Is Not Myopic," *Mathematical Social Sciences* 4 (July 1983): 243–60. For another alternative formation of a political business cycle model which sees unsophisticated governments being pressured into expansion shortly after being elected rather than waiting until the next election approaches as predicted in the original models, see Martin Paldam, "An Essay on the Rationality of Economic Policy: The Test Case of the Election Cycle," *Public Choice* 36 (1981): 43–60, and "The Political Dimensions of Wage Dynamics," in *The Political Process and Economic Change,* ed. Kristen R. Monroe (New York: Agathon Press, 1983), pp. 43–76.

54 If there is no trade-off, that point would be the natural rate of unemployment and zero inflation. With some long-run trade-off remaining, a positive inflation rate is optimal.

55 Chappell, "Presidential Popularity."

56 MacRae, "Political Model," p. 261.

57 Barry, "Does Democracy Cause Inflation?" pp. 280–317, esp. p. 314.

58 He dispenses of this tool thus: "We have assumed up to now that within an electoral period there is a fixed economic trade-off and *therefore a fixed policy.* We now employ the more realistic continuous model," which is a Phillips curve with adaptive expectations (Nordhaus, "Political Business Cycle," p. 182 [emphasis added]). The reader should compare this to Barry, "Does Democracy Cause Inflation?" p. 314, n. 61.

59 Stigler, "General Economic Conditions," pp. 163–68.

60 See the survey by Schneider and Frey in chapter 9 of this volume. For a recent critique of Stigler's paper, see Richard C. K. Burdekin, *Fluctuations in U.S. Voting Behavior: Evidence from Presidential Elections,* Federal Reserve Bank of Dallas Research Paper (Dallas, 1985).

4 The Keynesian Legacy: Does Countercyclical Policy Pay Its Way?

Thomas Mayer

Two generations ago, in 1923, Keynes first advocated what was to become the basis of contemporary macroeconomic policy: that the government should offset fluctuations in aggregate demand.[1] A few years afterward the Great Depression made this idea acceptable both to economists and the general public. The previous belief in the need to give primacy to balance of payments considerations disappeared as various nations left the gold standard. In addition, belief in the need to balance the budget faded away as the undesirability of raising taxes or cutting government expenditures in the midst of the Great Depression became more and more evident. In the United States the Employment Act of 1946 enshrined the notion that macroeconomic policy was one of the government's prime duties.

Apart from the harrowing experience of the Great Depression, the growth of the Keynesian consensus had several other causes. On a moral level there was a shift in emphasis from rectitude to compassion (Yes, Virginia, major changes in economic policies are grounded just as much, if not more, in a changing moral outlook as in new systems of differential equations). Within the confines of economics the new consensus was based on Keynes's magnificent *General Theory of Employment, Interest and Money* (1936), which taught that the capitalist system is not just subject to occasional recessions but is inherently unstable—that the invisible hand does not ensure that the economy is operating at an acceptable level of unemployment. Although the evidence presented for this view hardly suffers from excessive rigor, the experience of the Great Depression was dramatic enough to ensure that it would be widely accepted.

With the invisible hand unable to provide the right level of employment, this task was assigned to the visible hand of government. Monetary and fiscal policies were to even out business cycles. Moreover, since aggregate demand is likely to be too weak secularly, these policies were—on the average and over the long run—to keep interest rates low and the deficit high. Since it subsequently turned out that aggregate demand was *not* insufficient in the long run, the emphasis shifted almost entirely to short-run stabilization. With long-run aggregate demand not a serious problem, little attention was paid to the long run. The long run, being nothing but a combination of short runs, would take care of itself if the government did the right thing in the short run. At a time when "the end of ideology" was widely proclaimed, it is hardly surprising that such myopic pragmatism dominated.

This emphasis on the short run, and on dealing today with today's problems rather than with the problems of the next decade, might nowadays seem natural. But it is in sharp contrast to the previous attitude, when the need to adhere to principles that were painful in the short run but necessary for the long run set sharp limits on what short-run policy was allowed to do. Then, it was believed that it is the short run that would take care of itself if the government would do what was right for the long run. Given a sound currency and a balanced budget, a revival of business confidence would soon end a recession. Hence macroeconomic policy debates dealt with issues such as bimetallism and banking reform rather than what to do about next quarter's shortfall in GNP.

In the summer of the Keynesian revolution the old benighted attitude of "stick with the principles, never mind the current facts" was fit only for ridicule. But it is not just nostalgia that now makes many people surmise that the old-fashioned approach was not so silly after all.

Whether or not macroeconomic policy in the United States did succeed in significantly reducing unemployment is an issue that economic historians could debate for a long time. But what is clear is that any progress on the unemployment front that did occur was bought at the cost of substantial secular inflation. Whether this was due to a fault in the underlying economic analysis or to the way in which the government misapplied the teachings of economists is an interesting question. But it should not be allowed to detract attention from the more practical question of whether the government should continue to adhere to the Keynesian notion of stabilization policy. Economic policy advice may be founded on correct theory and yet be worse than useless if it asks the recipient of the advice to do something that is beyond his capability. Those of limited competence—such as governments—may be better off with simple, even naive policies than with sophisticated ones. The time has come to reconsider the Keynesian policy consensus.

The Keynesian Consensus

A decision to abandon the Keynesian policy consensus should not be taken lightly since there is much to be said in its favor. One can hardly deny that the American economy has in the past suffered from substantial fluctuations in output and employment. Even monetarists like Milton Friedman, who attribute most of this to the government's failure to maintain a stable money growth rate, do not deny that with a stable money growth rate *some* fluctuations would occur. Many other economists believe that the interaction between the multiplier and the accelerator ensures that, in the absence of government stabilization policy, a capitalist economy would suffer substantial fluctuations. But while monetarists and Keynesians disagree about how great such fluctuations would be if the government kept the money growth rate stable and the budget balanced, even relatively small fluctuations cause much suffering. With a labor force of around 110 million, a rise in unemployment by only half a percent implies that over half a million workers lose their jobs and, counting family members, that over a million people are made miserable.

It is therefore hardly surprising that most economists eagerly advocated countercyclical stabilization policy once Keynesian theory and the Great Depression freed them from the mental blinders of the gold standard and the balanced budget. It seems obviously better to use monetary policy to reduce unemployment than to have the money stock growing, regardless of the economy's need, either at a fixed rate or in accordance with gold flows. Similarly, instead of balancing the budget each year, why not have the government increase aggregate demand in periods of high unemployment by raising expenditures or cutting taxes? If there is no invisible hand that maintains full employment, it seems inhuman not to use the readily available visible hand of government. To argue against countercyclical policies therefore seems to imply either lack of ordinary decency or blind dogmatism.

This approach to policy deserves an A for effort but an F for hubris. It dismisses as unworthy of consideration the possibility that there is a large gap between the knowledge required to stabilize the economy and what we actually do know. If one's ignorance is great it is often better to do nothing; a person who knows little about first aid is not heartless if he refrains from moving an injured person whose back might be broken.

The danger that monetary and fiscal stabilization policies will actually be destabilizing can hardly be dismissed as implausible. Both monetary and fiscal policies take a long time to have their main impact on the economy. Suppose the administration decides that the economy is in a recession, or will shortly be in one, and hence asks Congress to cut taxes. It will take some time for Congress to comply, particularly if the tax cut is proposed before or in early stages of a recession. Congress responds more to actual problems than to hypothetical ones. Once taxes are cut it may, or may not, take some time for taxpayers to respond to lower taxes by raising their expenditures—we don't really know. By the time they do, the economy could well have recovered, and the tax cut, coming at a time when demand is already excessive, could worsen the inflation that accompanied the expansion. The same problem arises if instead of cutting taxes government expenditures are raised. Once an expenditure program is approved it usually takes a long time to get started and actually generate expenditures. It may seem that there is an obvious solution to the latter problem: prepare plans, etc., so that in the next recession there is a shelf of public works ready to go. But this does not work; not only do plans become obsolete, but once a project has been planned there may well be irresistible pressure to undertake it right away.

Moreover, fiscal policy faces a much more serious difficulty if its task is to curb, rather than to expand, aggregate demand. Obviously politicians are much more reluctant to raise taxes than to lower them. Similarly, it is difficult to cut off public works projects before they are completed. Social expenditure programs are also hard to terminate or reduce once they are underway and generate a constituency and a feeling that recipients have a right to them. Vested interests are not just the province of the rich. Hence, what is intended to be countercyclical fiscal policy is likely to be a one-way street.

Monetary policy too faces a severe problem of lags. To be sure, the

Fed can change monetary policy fairly quickly, but there is a substantial lag until changes in interest rates and in the money growth rate affect expenditures. Many economists have tried to estimate the length of this lag. Some believe that it is about half a year or less, but others, particularly those using large-scale econometric models, estimate that it takes more than a year before a change in monetary policy has its main impact on GNP. Not only is there much disagreement among these studies, but every one of them is subject to serious criticism.

Couldn't one avoid the difficulty that long lags create by changing fiscal and monetary policies well ahead of time? Unfortunately, there are some serious problems with this. First, it assumes that we can predict accurately enough what income will be at the time the policy becomes effective. Our ability to forecast GNP is rather limited, and with so much uncertainty about how long it takes monetary and fiscal policies to have their main effects on income we don't know very well for what date in the future we are supposed to forecast income. Moreover, there is the problem of selecting a policy of the right strength. When the Fed undertakes, say, a billion dollar open market operation, or when taxes are cut by a billion dollars, we know only approximately by how much this will change GNP. Hence, the policy may be too weak to do much good, or it may be too strong and thereby worsen fluctuations, for example, turning a mild recession into a much too great and inflationary expansion. It does not take much error in forecasting the strength of the policy, or the future course of income, for a strong stabilization policy actually to exacerbate income fluctuations. For a weak policy that tries to do little this danger is less, but then so is the potential payoff.[2]

Lags in the impact of policy and limited ability to forecast are only part of the problem. To predict what a countercyclical policy regime does to the economy one should not assume that such policy is made in an antiseptic environment in which policymakers formulate their goals; economists use sophisticated models to determine the best policy to attain these goals, and policymakers then adopt these policies. Economists have a strong bias towards this picture of policy-making. Not only does it emphasize the role of economists, but it greatly facilitates the analysis of policy-making. If one assumes that government agencies adopt the best policies, then by determining what the best policy is, one can predict what the agencies will do. By contrast, once one assumes that an agency behaves irrationally it becomes much more difficult to predict its actions.[3]

Moreover, the assumption of rational behavior has proven a powerful tool in analyzing the behavior of firms. But this does not mean that it is also a good tool for understanding the actions of government agencies. First, it is much easier for firms than for government agencies to be rational maximizers because they have only two goals, maximum profits and minimum risk; government agencies, on the other hand, have a multitude of goals. Second, for firms one can rely on a Darwinian argument; those firms that do not maximize profits efficiently are either driven out of business or taken over by others. But there is no rival central bank that can drive out the Federal Reserve. Hence, in analyzing stabilization policy one must step outside the economist's usual rationalistic framework.

This is something that Keynesian economists have generally been reluctant to do. Thus a leading Keynesian, Franco Modigliani, wrote, "I have personally no reason to believe that the United States government . . . is not able to attract able people who are interested in the common welfare and can do a good job."[4] That the government can attract able people is true, but it does not necessarily follow that they "can do a good job." For reasons that are not well understood the decisions that emerge from the deliberations of able people are frequently of a much lower caliber than one would expect given the quality of the people involved— as is well illustrated by most faculty meetings.

This problem is a familiar and much-discussed one with respect to elected officials. We are frequently told that they are unable to take an objective view because they have to worry about the next election. In addition, they are overly influenced by the narrow interests of pressure groups. In a more subtle view they have to act as brokers between various groups. Since the relative power of these groups often does not correspond to the worthiness of their causes, the public interest is sometimes (or often) only imperfectly represented in the compromises that shape policy. Moreover, given the difficulty of arranging side payments, compromises that would be in everyone's interest are sometimes not achievable. For example, a bill to cut taxes in a recession may fail because it cannot obtain the support of a particular constituency, a constituency that actually favors the tax cut but is holding out for a larger share than the other members of the coalition are willing to agree to. To blame politicians and their concern with reelection for such failures is simplistic. The wish to be reelected usually induces them to do what the public wants, something which good democrats can hardly condemn out of hand! But regardless of who should be blamed, when there are many contending groups with diverse interests, the optimal solution may simply be unattainable. Economic policies that will work only if the political process is a perfect conductor that provides no resistance to the public welfare may be worthwhile exercises in economic analysis, but they may make poor policy recommendations.

The standard answer to the inefficiency of the political process is to take decisions out of the political arena and have them made instead by expert civil servants. But as discussed below with respect to monetary policy, while the faults of the administration's experts are perhaps less dramatic and obvious than the faults of Congress, they are not necessarily less damaging.

Fiscal Policy

Turning to the specifics of fiscal policy, experience suggests, at least in the United States with its separation of legislative and executive powers, that fiscal policy cannot be used as an effective stabilization tool. Politics is concerned not just with economic stabilization but also with the redistribution of income—and the federal budget is a major tool for that. During a recession, discussions of whether taxes should be cut can easily get lost in the clamor about whose taxes should be cut. It is therefore not surprising that fiscal policy has generally not been used as a discretionary stabilization tool. Instead, changes in taxes and expenditures have at times been aimed toward balancing the budget and at other times have followed their own imperatives, with expenditures rising when there was a perceived need for more government services and taxes cut when the public complained about high taxes. Only the 1964 tax cut and the 1968 tax surcharge were primarily undertaken for the purpose of stabilization, and the latter took a year and a half to get through Congress.

The large deficits generated in the early 1980s by the Reagan tax cut and the recession were widely believed to be dangerous. But little was done until the Gramm-Rudman-Hollings Act at the close of 1985, and it is too early to tell if this act will be effective. If fiscal policy were oriented toward macroeconomic goals, these deficits would surely have been cut substantially in the early 1980s. But with conservatives preferring large deficits to tax increases, and with liberals preferring large deficits to reducing social expenditures, the macroeconomic effects of the deficits elicited much concern but little action. Moreover, if politicians were to pay more attention to the macroeconomic effects of fiscal policy, this attention *might* have an unwelcome consequence. It might lead to the political business cycle discussed in other essays in this volume.

Monetary Policy

How about monetary policy? Here the focus is obviously more on stabilization than it is in the case of fiscal policy, and the political pressures on the Fed are less, though on major issues the Fed does take its marching orders from the White House.[5] But the Fed's relative isolation from political pressures is not sufficient to validate the Keynesian picture of policymakers deciding upon goals, and then following the advice of their technical experts. The Fed simply does not work that way. Several studies that have looked at the minutes of the Federal Open Market Committee (FOMC) or the board of governors show the Fed making little use of the staff's highly capable economic analysis, but proceeding instead in a seat-of-the-pants fashion.[6]

Moreover, there are several reasons why the Fed is likely to be too slow in changing policy as economic conditions change. One factor is that, given the lag in the effect of monetary policy, a restrictive policy should probably be adopted at a time when unemployment is still high, and an expansionary policy while the inflation rate is accelerating. But it would take a great deal of courage and self-confidence for the Fed to adopt a restrictive policy despite high unemployment, or an expansionary policy at a time when the inflation rate is still accelerating. If the Fed had great trust in its forecasts it might perhaps find this courage, but given the precariousness of its forecasts such confidence may not be there.

A second reason why the Fed might be slow to change policy is that both the old policy and the new policy impose substantial costs; an expansionary policy hurts fixed income groups, and a restrictive policy hurts those whose jobs it will eliminate. To make a decision that imposes suffering is not easy and tends to be put off as long as possible. To be sure, if the old policy is not changed this imposes suffering too, but somehow one feels more responsibility for errors of commission than for errors of omission.

Third, there may be an institutional detail that inhibits prompt Fed action: the votes at FOMC meetings are published. Hence to obtain public credence the FOMC wants to make its decisions by unanimous or nearly unanimous votes. It may therefore be reluctant to change policy until the need for the new policy is clear enough to convince all, or most, of those who initially opposed the new policy.[7] This fact alone *might* delay policy changes sufficiently to make monetary policy procyclical. Whether this is actually so is hard to say. Perhaps the chairman's power and influence suffice to swing enough votes to the new policy right away. Perhaps the threat to break ranks and vote as a minority by those who advocate the new policy offsets the threat of others to vote against a new policy. We know much too little about FOMC interactions to be able to judge how great a problem the desire for near unanimity creates. But that is no reason to ignore this threat.

The factors that interfere with the correct timing of monetary policy are not the only ones that inhibit the effective application of policy. Another one is that once the Fed has made a wrong decision, for example, using an interest rate target instead of a money growth rate target, or a money growth rate target instead of a nominal GNP target, it will be reluctant to reverse this decision. For to do so would often require FOMC members to admit, at least to themselves, that they have made a mistake and caused damage, perhaps raising the inflation rate or throwing people out of work unnecessarily. Obviously, they are reluctant to do this.[8]

Another problem, quite apart from timing, is that it is only natural to pay more attention to those costs that are obvious and immediate rather than to those that are more remote, hidden, and hypothetical. This tempts the Fed to overemphasize the impact of its policies on the stability and efficiency of financial markets and to underplay the impact on aggregate demand. Moreover, there is always the temptation to focus on current problems at the expense of those that will arise only in the future. Beyond this—rightly or wrongly—a number of economists have argued that the Fed's actions reflect its self-interests.[9]

Optimists might respond that all of these problems are solvable—just appoint the right people to the board of governors. But this is a snake oil remedy. The intellectual caliber of the current governors is high. If they behave in certain ways that have undesirable consequences it is because the pressures under which they work induce such behavior. And the obvious way to remove these pressures is to eliminate countercyclical stabilization from their job descriptions.[10]

As long as the Fed pursues countercyclical policies, these pressures will inhibit the effectiveness of monetary policy. Hence it is unreasonable to expect monetary policy to reduce the fluctuations of nominal GNP to the extent that it could if forecasting errors were the only errors inhibiting monetary policy. Since the extent to which the just-discussed administrative problems inhibit monetary policy cannot be quantified, it is far from clear whether monetary policy actually stabilizes or destabilizes the economy.

One might therefore conclude that while no good case can be made in favor of countercyclical monetary policy, neither can a good case be made for eliminating it. But this is not so. With respect to short-run stability the match between the supporters and opponents of countercyclical policy has ended in a zero-zero draw. But long-run considerations argue strongly in favor of abandoning countercyclical policy. To be sure, it is hardly an example of exemplary rigor to argue that since we do not know which policy is better for the short run, we can simply ignore the short run and make the decision on the basis of long-run considerations. But rigorous or not, what else can one do?[11]

Secular Inflation

Turning therefore to the secular behavior of the postwar economy the salient factor is that inflation accelerated, with some interruptions, until the 1981–82 recession. To be sure, part of the secular inflation was due to supply shocks. But while supply shocks account for some of the spikes in the inflation rate, they do not account for its secular upward drift. This drift is explained much more by the secular acceleration in the money growth rate.

Such an acceleration of the money growth rate is hardly surprising; it follows naturally from the victory of the Keynesian consensus. First, the Keynesian consensus, or more generally the pragmatic ethos in which it is embedded, focuses attention on the short run. This makes it tempting to use a more expansionary monetary policy to trade off current unemployment against future inflation.

On a more technical level, at least until recently, Keynesians greatly underestimated the expansionary impact of a higher monetary growth rate, and hence called for too much monetary expansion. In addition, Keynesians overestimated the beneficial effects—and underestimated the deleterious effects—of a higher monetary growth rate because they misinterpreted the slope of the Phillips curve. They believed not only that you can buy a reduction in the unemployment rate by tolerating a little inflation, but they also believed that the terms of this trade-off are stable. They did not consider that a higher inflation rate would cause workers and employers to agree upon wage increases that took into account the likely rise in prices. How a profession that is so insistent on rational maximizing behavior could do this is hard to understand, but it did. As the subsequent behavior of the economy was to show, it was not the public but economists who suffered from a money illusion.

Furthermore, economists underestimated the cost of inflation. A major part—probably *the* main part—of this cost is the uncertainty that inflation creates. But this uncertainty cannot be expressed in dollar terms and hence is hard for economists to take into account. Thus, some Keynesians argued that inflation merely redistributes income, while unemployment reduces aggregate income. But to people whose real incomes are cut by inflation it does little good to be told: "Don't worry about the inflation cutting your real income; it is raising someone else's real income instead, so that total income is constant." Hence, they worry about inflation, and this worry and uncertainty is clearly a cost of inflation.

Beyond this, let us see how the choice between an expansionary and a more restrictive monetary policy looks to a policymaker imbued with the Keynesian consensus. As aggregate demand expands, policymakers have to decide at one point or other that demand now threatens to become excessive and that restrictive policies are called for. But they do not know where this point is; they are uncertain about how much income will expand on its own, and they do not know what the natural rate of unemployment is. But they do know that if they make a mistake and switch to restrictive policies too soon, they are responsible for many thousands of people being unnecessarily thrown out of work. This can never be made up. By contrast, if they continue their expansionary policy when it is inappropriate and allow the money supply to grow too fast, then they can hope to make up for this by lowering the money growth rate later on. As a description of economic reality this statement is probably wrong, since its validity depends on a peculiar assumption about the slope of the Phillips curve. But I am trying to describe not what actually happens but what seems to go on in the minds of policymakers. Moreover, the misery and waste created by unemployment are easier to visualize than are the more diffuse losses caused by inflation. In general, policies that err on the side of expansion and lower unemployment seem to appeal to our sense of decency more effectively than do policies that err on the side of caution and price stability. Add to this the political pressures for low interest rates, and it is hardly surprising that monetary policy has not been a two-way street, that it has imparted a secular upward drift to the inflation rate.

As a result the value of money lost its anchor, and with the inflation rate, and not just the price level, rising over the long run, there are legitimate fears about where it will all end. Will we return to double digit inflation a few years from now when the memory of the great postwar inflation has faded, and the current problem is a slow recovery that needs to be aided by a highly expansionary policy?

This is not the place to discourse on the evils of inflation. But they are large. When one considers these evils, plus the previously discussed fact that countercyclical monetary policy could easily be destabilizing rather than stabilizing, then the case for the Keynesian consensus on monetary policy looks weak; its benefits are uncertain, while its costs are substantial.

Deficits

How about fiscal policy? As already discussed, it has been used for stabilization purposes only infrequently. But by undermining the case for an annually balanced budget, the Keynesian consensus has done two things. First, it has allowed the budget to operate as an automatic stabilizer. This has been to the good. Few economists object to the deficits that occur automatically as a result of recessions. However, since the mid-1960s countercyclical fiscal policy has been a one-way street. Deficits have occurred not only in recessions, but have been the normal course of events.

These deficits have been damaging in several ways. First, they have raised interest rates, and since rising interest rates increase the velocity of money, they have played at least some direct role in inflation. If—and this is a debated issue—the Fed responds to deficits by raising the money growth rate, then here is a second way in which deficits are inflationary.

Beyond this, deficits have sapped fiscal discipline. Efficient resource allocation requires that (after adjustment for externalities) the output of each good and service is set at the level where its marginal utility is just equal to its marginal cost. In the private sector, this rule prevails only imperfectly, but the market mechanism ensures that it *does* prevail after a fashion. In the government sector there is only a much weaker mechanism at work since those who receive the benefit of government programs usually pay only a small part of the cost. This naturally sets up a clamor for additional government expenditures, and this clamor is stalemated at some level of government expenditures and taxes by the rival clamor of taxpayers. If the taxpayers do not assert themselves, then (taking the public's utility function as given) the level of government expenditures is too large. The traditional and seemingly naive fear of deficits, whatever else its faults, therefore did serve the useful function of invoking the power of the taxpayers against the power of the spenders. But this constraint has now given way. Instead of having to overcome taxpayer resistance, a new program can now be financed by raising the deficit. If deficits are neither illegal, immoral, or fattening, why not indulge in the moral impulse of telling the government to spend more to help the poor, as well as in the less moral but more profitable impulse of having the government help middle-class people like oneself?

To be sure, the legitimization of deficits since the 1960s should not be overstated; had it gone all the way, taxes would surely have been cut more substantially. There are obviously still serious limits to the size of the acceptable deficit, so that at the margin the spenders still had to fight the taxpayers. But all the same, the constraint has eroded. The greater and more frequent the deficits of previous years, the more acceptable become large deficits this year. If a conservative Republican like President Reagan can accept a $200 billion deficit, how big a deficit will it take to constrain the propensity to spend of the next liberal Democrat in the White House? One can imagine such a trend leading to an almost complete breakdown of fiscal discipline, with a great increase in government expenditures, in Federal Reserve monetization of government debt, and in greater inflation.

The lesson from this is once again that "a little learning is a dang'rous thing." Economists succeeded in teaching the public that the government is not like a family, that it cannot go bankrupt due to too large a (domestically held) debt, and that deficit spending does not impoverish future generations. But the lesson was not so easily absorbed that deficit spending should be limited because of the dangers of inflation and of crowding out too much private investment, as well as due to the need to limit government spending.

Currently, the wheel *may* be turning again. The public now believes that high interest rates are due in large part to the high projected deficits. But can one rely on this belief to restrain excessive government expenditures in the future? If real interest rates fall, opposition to large deficits may decline again. Besides, the deficits that are projected in the current budget are unusually large by historical standards—but once they actually occur, historical standards will have changed.

Thus, while having only arguable benefits in the short run, the Keynesian consensus has deplorable long-run effects. But if it is to be discarded, what should be put in its place? One possibility is to preach to politicians, government officials, and the public that countercyclical policy is not likely to work, and that we should adopt instead policies oriented toward the longer run that are likely to curb inflation and government deficits. Such an approach would try to change people's beliefs but would not require great changes in laws. Another approach is to change our laws and institutions so that the possibility of adopting too expansionary macropolicies simply does not arise. Such issues are considered in the chapters in part four.

Notes

1 John Maynard Keynes, *A Tract on Monetary Reform* (London: Macmillan, 1923). In this book Keynes advocated a countercyclical monetary policy; he developed a belief in countercyclical fiscal policy only in the 1930s.

2 This problem of whether a stabilization policy is stabilizing or is actually destabilizing has been elegantly formalized by Milton Friedman, *Essays in Positive Economics* (Chicago: University of Chicago Press, 1953), pp. 117–32. He shows that economic fluctuations can be thought of as resulting from two variances, the variance in income that would exist in the absence of policy (σ_x^2) and the variance of income introduced by stabilization policy to offset the existing variance of income (σ_y^2). If one adds these two variances to find the total variance in income when stabilization policy is used (σ_z^2), then one gets: $\sigma_z^2 = \sigma_z^2 + \sigma_x^2 + \sigma_y^2 + 2R\sigma_x\sigma_y$, where R is the coefficient of correlation between the two variances. Efficient policy makes R negative by adding to income when income would otherwise be low and subtracting from income when it would otherwise be high. For policy to do much good R must be strongly negative. For example, if $R = -0.7$, then a policy of the right size will cut the variance of income in half. But suppose that R is only -0.4 and that the government uses a policy that, if correctly timed (that is if R were -1) would offset all the fluctuation in income. Substitution in the above equation shows that a policy would actually destabilize income and thus be worse than no policy at all.

3 There is another feasible alternative. This is to assume that the agency tries to maxi-

mize its own budget. But this is not relevant to the Fed since it determines its own budget. Another possibility is to view a central bank as trying to maximize its power, prestige, etc. See, for instance, Keith Acheson and John Chant, "Bureaucratic Theory and the Choice of Central Bank Goals: The Case of the Bank of Canada," *Journal of Money, Credit, and Banking* 5 (May 1973): 637–56.

4　Franco Modigliani and Milton Friedman, "The Monetarist Controversy," Federal Reserve Bank of San Francisco *Economic Review,* Spring 1977, *Supplement,* p. 21.

5　See Robert Weintraub, "Congressional Supervision of Monetary Policy," *Journal of Monetary Economics* 4 (April 1978): 341–62; John Woolley, *Monetary Politics* (New York: Cambridge University Press, 1985).

6　See Karl Brunner and Allan Meltzer, *Some General Features of the Federal Reserve's Approach to Policy,* House Committee on Banking and Currency, 88th Cong. 2d sess., 1964; Raymond Lombra and Michael Moran, "Policy Advice and Policymaking at the Federal Reserve," in Karl Brunner and Allen Meltzer, *Carnegie-Rochester Conference Series on Public Policy* 13 (Autumn 1980): 9–68; Thomas Mayer, "Federal Reserve Policy in the 1973–75 Recession: A Case Study of Fed Behavior in a Quandary," in *Crises in the Economic and Financial Structure,* ed. Paul Wachtel (Lexington, Mass.: Lexington Books, 1982), and "A Case Study of Federal Reserve Policymaking: Regulation Q in 1966," *Journal of Monetary Economics* 10 (November 1982): 259–71.

7　See Robert Shapiro, "Politics and the Federal Reserve," *The Public Interest,* Winter 1982, 119–39.

8　I am indebted for this point to Richard Thaler.

9　See, for instance, Karl Brunner, "The Case against Monetary Activism," *Lloyds Bank Review* 139 (January 1981): 29–30; and Acheson and Chant, "Bureaucratic Theory."

10　One problem could, however, be ameliorated easily. The FOMC should not report by how many votes it adopts policies.

11　It may seem that one could answer the question of whether monetary and fiscal policies have been stabilizing by seeing whether the private sector is inherently stable. If the overall economy is more stable than the private sector would be on its own, then public sector policies must have been stabilizing. But unfortunately there is no convincing evidence on whether the private sector is stable. See Thomas Mayer, "Some Reflections on the Current State of the Monetarist Debate," *Zeitschrift für Nationalökonomie* 38, nos. 1–2 (1978): 72–75. Another approach, favored by many monetarists, is to argue that in the postwar period monetary policy has generally been procyclical since the money stock has risen at a faster rate in expansions than in recessions. But there are problems with this argument. First, the extent to which the monetary growth rate had behaved procyclically depends in part on how one measures cycles, whether from peak to peak or from trough to trough. Cf. Robert J. Gordon, "Lessons from Postwar Business Cycles for the Conduct of Monetary Policy" (1983, typescript, Northwestern University). Second, a procyclical monetary growth rate is not *necessarily* inconsistent with monetary policy being countercyclical. What matters is not when the money growth rate increases but when this increase had its main effect on income. However, to assume that the lags are just of the right length to transform a procyclical money growth rate into a countercyclical monetary policy is to make too much of a claim on nature's scarce stock of serendipity. Third, a well-timed stabilization policy does *not* lower income throughout the expansion and raise it throughout the recession. With a sinelike cycle, during half the expansion phase income is still below its mean, and during half the recession phase it is still above the mean. Hence, even if monetary policy raises income by more in the expansion phase than in the recession phase, so that it is procyclical in the usual sense of the term, this is not necessarily destabilizing.

5   Wage and Price Rigidities, Supply Restrictions, and the Problem of Stagflation

Gottfried Haberler

The Dilemma of Stagflation

The appearance for the first time on a large scale of stagflation, the co-existence of high inflation and high unemployment, posed serious new problems for economists and policymakers. The policymaker who had just mastered the principles of modern "Keynesian" macroeconomics was confronted with a nasty dilemma: if he applied expansionary measures to reduce unemployment he would accelerate inflation, and if he adopted restrictive measures to curb inflation he would exacerbate unemployment. This dilemma did not exist in such an acute form before World War II. In earlier business cycles prices and wages declined significantly during recessions. This flexibility in prices and wages helped to remove imbalances between supplies and demands in the various product and labor markets. To a large extent, a competitive market system could be viewed as a self-correcting mechanism.

The difficulties posed by stagflation for economic theory stem from the fact that traditionally, explicitly or implicitly, the microfoundation of macroeconomic theory has, in fact, been that of a competitive market system.[1] The assumption of perfect competition in the labor market is inconsistent with persistent unemployment and stagflation. In terms of general, abstract theory, unemployment can be defined as an excess of the supply of labor over demand. There are more job seekers than jobs. Elementary economic theory teaches that under competition excess supply will drive down the price until demand and supply come into equilibrium. Unemployed workers will compete for scarce jobs; the wage will decline relative to prices until full employment is restored.

That this is an inadequate picture of reality has been realized for a long time and was once more dramatically demonstrated by the long period of stagflation, which in recent years has given rise to a flood of more or less sophisticated attempts to account for an apparent *inflexibility* of wages and prices and to explain the stagflation riddle.

Some Proposed Solutions of the Dilemma

It will be useful to start by identifying two extreme attempts to solve the riddle. On the one hand some monetarists and some members of the rational expectations school have stuck to the assumption of perfect competition by demonstrating, to their own satisfaction, that even "massive" and "persistent" unemployment is after all quite compatible with perfect competition and "instantaneous clearing of all markets."

At the other extreme is a view deriving from Keynes that assumes with a minimum of theoretical underpinning that real wages are in fact rigid because, even if money wages are allowed to decline, prices will fall pari passu so that real wages would remain unchanged.[2]

Between these monetarist–rational expectations and Keynesian extremes lies a large literature that tries to identify and evaluate deviations from the competitive ideal that account for the persistence of unemployment and stagflation. Among the factors mentioned are monopolies and oligopolies in product and labor markets, union power, government regulation, minimum wages, price supports, and so on.[3]

The Monetarist Position

Let me make it quite clear near the outset that I fully agree with the monetarists that inflation, including stagflation, is basically a monetary phenomenon in the sense that there has never been a significant inflation or stagflation—prices rising by, say, 4 percent or more a year for several years—without a significant growth in the supply of money. The velocity of circulation of money is, of course, subject to change. But apart from extreme circumstances, such as hyperinflation or wartime price control and rationing, changes in velocity are not large enough to invalidate the basic proposition of the quantity theory of money as stated above.

Of course, a *reduction* in the money supply and, in turn, total spending will not immediately be fully reflected in a fall in prices. Measures such as those initiated during the New Deal reduced price and wage flexibility, at least in a downward direction. Thus, a decrease in aggregate spending now finds expression to a large extent in quantities—declining output and employment—rather than in declining prices.

It should be noted that Frank Knight, like Henry Simons, Jacob Viner, and other members of the older generation of the Chicago school, did not ignore or minimize the great importance of the growing rigidity of wages and prices for the smooth working of an economic system. Knight wrote, "In a free market these differential changes [between prices of 'consumption goods' and 'capital goods' on the one hand, and the prices of 'productive services, especially wages,' on the other hand] would be temporary, but even then might be serious, and with important markets [especially the labor market] as unfree as they actually are, the results take on the proportion of a disaster."[4] Knight wrote with the deflation of the 1930s in mind, but what he said about wage and price rigidity applies equally to the recessions of the 1970s and 1980s.

In this vein, Keynes unfairly criticized the "classical" economists for recognizing only "voluntary" unemployment, but he was prophetically right about some present-day monetarists.[5] Actually, classical economists had often made a distinction between "voluntary" and "involuntary," though they in many cases used other words in discussions of the unemployment problem. In fact, the archclassical A. C. Pigou, who was one of the main targets of Keynes's criticism, used the very words "involuntary idleness" in a popular book on unemployment in 1914[6] and had an excellent discussion of the distinction in his monograph *The Theory of Unemployment*.[7] D. H. Robertson, another classical economist, used the words "involuntary unemployment" in his *Study of Industrial Fluctuations*.[8] No wonder that Richard Kahn, Keynes's devoted disciple and assistant, "suffered a shock" when he discovered that what was regarded as one of the master's important discoveries was in many of the classical writings that he had criticized.[9]

Keynes's definition of involuntary unemployment is that "Men are involuntarily unemployed if, in the event of a small rise in the price of wage-goods relative to the money wage, both the aggregate supply of labor willing to work for the current money wage and the aggregate demand for it at that wage would be greater than the existing volume of employment."[10] Elsewhere I expressed the opinion that this definition is unnecessarily complicated; that the commonsense definition is quite satisfactory—to wit, that a man is involuntarily unemployed if he cannot find a job although he is willing and able to work at the ruling wage and work conditions for the type of work for which he is qualified.[11]

The Keynesian definition has been defended, however, by Alchian[12] and others on the ground that it makes the important distinction between a reduction of the real wage due to (a) a rise in prices and (b) a reduction in the money wage. Workers "as a rule" accept the former but resist the latter. The reason for this behavior is said to be that a rise in the price level affects all wage earners alike, while reductions in money wages are never across the board and, therefore, alter relative wages. The consequence is that workers resist a reduction of their wages because nobody likes to be singled out for a wage cut.

There may be some truth in this argument. But the other half of the old Keynesian theory is hard to accept. In our age of persistent inflation, widespread indexation, and sensitized inflationary expectations, it cannot be assumed that workers meekly and ignorantly accept a reduction in their real wage through inflation. Keynes himself was more cautious than Alchian. He speaks of a "small" rise in prices and says "as a rule" and "unless they [the reductions in real wages] proceeded to an extreme degree" (p. 14). If Keynes had lived longer, he surely would have amended his theory to take account of persistent inflation. As Axel Leijonhufvud has shown, we have to distinguish between Keynesian economics and the economics of Keynes.[13] The fact is that, excepting the period in the 1930s when he wrote *The General Theory,* Keynes was all his life concerned about inflation. In 1937, one year after the publication of *The General Theory,* he wrote three articles in the *Times* in which he urged a change in policy to fight inflation, although unemployment was still high and inflation comparatively low by post-World War II standards.[14]

Rational Expectations

Before discussing further the rigidity of wages, I will discuss the modern theory of rational expectations and contrast it with the Keynesian position. The theory of rational expectations is an offshoot of monetarism. The basic tenet of the school is that market participants, households, and firms must be assumed to act, by and large, rationally; they make use of all available information to form a judgment of future events, including the likely course of government macroeconomic policy and its impact on the economy. Specifically, market participants do not simply extrapolate the current price trend (inflation rate), but base their expectations of future inflation on an appraisal of a much broader kind.

Put in these terms, the theory is now widely accepted by many Keynesians as well as monetarists and may even be regarded as self-evident. But this was not the case a few years ago. Let us not forget that what Harry Johnson called "the monetarist counterrevolution" and, we may add, its offshoot, the rational expectations theory, were a reaction to the Keynesian downgrading of the importance of monetary policy and its lack of concern about inflation.

From what I call the "basic tenet," rational expectations theorists have drawn radical, even astonishing, conclusions that are quite controversial, to put it mildly. What has been called the "hard-line" (unqualified) version of the theory[15] asserts flatly that macroeconomic policies—more precisely, systematic, that is to say predictable, macropolicies—have no effect on the real economy (output and employment), but only on prices, money wages, and nominal interest rates. The argument is often described in the following way: Suppose the government embarks on an expansionary monetary-fiscal policy to stimulate production and employment. The market participants will figure out exactly what the effects on the price level will be. Financial markets will react almost instantaneously, pushing up interest rates. Commodity markets will follow suit, with wholesale prices in the vanguard. Workers and their unions will press for higher wages. Higher interest and labor costs will inhibit an expansion of output. The conclusion of the hard-line rational expectations theory is that this will happen so fast that it can be said that macropolicies are ineffective, even in the short run, as far as the real economy is concerned. This sounds rather implausible, to put it mildly.

However, the hard-line version of the theory has been softened considerably in later contributions. It is now often conceded that after a policy change there may be a transition period because it takes some time for market participants to figure out what the authorities are up to.

Furthermore, the ineffectiveness applies only to "systematic," "predictable" policies. The theory does not deny that unsystematic, unpredictable policy changes do have an effect on the real economy. The trouble with this argument, however, is that it is impossible to divide policies into two watertight compartments, wholly predictable and entirely unpredictable ones. It is a question of more or less predictable, not one of either-or. Suppose the general thrust of a policy change, whether it is expansionary or contractionary, is not in doubt. Still, the vigor and persistence with which the policy will be pursued is always uncertain and the assessments of different market participants will diverge. To assume, as some members of the school seem to, that the average or collective judgments will be exactly right because errors made by individuals will cancel out, is entirely unconvincing. The possibility of bandwagon effects and of cumulative and self-reversing errors of optimism and pessimism, which have played a great role in older business cycle theories,[16] cannot be excluded.

The most serious weakness of the hard-line version of the rational expectations theory and of the ineffectiveness hypothesis is that it pays no attention to wage and price rigidities. The theory is essentially one of perfect competition, of instantaneously clearing markets. This assumption, too, has been softened. It is now said that the theory can accommodate minor deviations from the competitive ideal.[17] Widespread rigidity of wages as we find it in the modern world is, however, an altogether different matter. Wage and price rigidity make it impossible for monetary-fiscal policy, even if entirely systematic and correctly perceived by the public, to be neutral (ineffective) with respect to the real economy as claimed by the rational expectations school.

Let me illustrate this by means of an extreme example: In the early 1930s during the period of mass unemployment in the Great Depression wages were rigid even in the upward direction. In other words, the supply of labor was highly, if not infinitely, elastic. Would anybody doubt that under such conditions a policy of boosting the aggregate demand for goods and services, as recommended by Keynes and many other economists at that time, would boost output and employment even if, or perhaps especially if, fully perceived by the public? The expansionary policies followed from 1933–37 were indeed very effective in reviving the real economy. True, they also boosted prices, as we have seen. But this was due in no small way to the cost-raising policies of the New Deal and had little or nothing to do with the reactions described by the rational expectations theory.

The present situation is, of course, entirely different from that of the 1930s. Unemployment in the postwar period has been much lower than in the 1930s, and inflationary expectations have been sensitized by years of intermittent inflation. Even so, one cannot say that expansionary policies have been entirely ineffective in the postwar period as far as the real economy is concerned. Cyclical recoveries after recessions have been initiated or speeded up temporarily by expansionary policies. To say, as rational expectations theorists are inclined to do, that these effects were due to the unsystematic parts of the expansionary policy does not help in view of the fact that systematic and unsystematic policy measures are in most cases not separable. At any rate, it takes time to figure out what the authorities are up to, and the learning process will not be the same for all market participants. Measures that appear systematic and predictable to some market participants may appear unsystematic and surprising to others.

The most startling conclusion of the rational expectations school is the so-called Ricardian equivalence theorem, which states that it makes no difference whether the government finances a deficit by taxes or by borrowing.[18] The theorem is based on the assumption that rational "agents," firms and households, realize that government debts have to be serviced; government borrowing will lead to higher taxes in the future. Increased future tax liabilities will induce rational people to save more so that they will be able to meet these liabilities. In this way, the increased supply of bonds resulting from government deficits and borrowing will be matched, dollar for dollar, by an increased demand for bonds on the part of the savers. Hence, deficits do not push up interest rates.

If the reader is surprised by how much knowledge people are supposed to have, he or she should know that this is not all. To counter the possible objection that the taxes to service the debt may fall on future generations of taxpayers, an "intergenerational" extension of the theory argues that the present taxpayers not only know how much their future tax will be, but also what the tax of their children and grandchildren will be, and will save enough to protect them from the extravagances of the present generation.

I can only repeat what I have said elsewhere: This is rational expectations gone wild. *Difficile est satiram non scribere!*[19]

*The Evolution of Keynesian Views on
Inflation and Unemployment*

Whereas some rational expectations theorists have simply denied the existence of sluggish price and wage adjustments, Keynesians for a long time downplayed dangers of an opposite sort: general, rapid upward movements in prices, i.e., inflation. The Keynesian unconcern about inflation and neglect of inflationary expectations is highlighted by the development of the theory of the Phillips curve, which postulated a more or less permanent trade-off between unemployment and inflation; lower levels of unemployment could be obtained by accepting higher levels of inflation. This theory for years dominated the Keynesian discussions of inflation. I cite two prominent examples. In 1960 Paul Samuelson and Robert Solow in a widely acclaimed article, "Analytical Aspects of Anti-Inflation Policy," presented a "Modified Phillips Curve for the United States" which they described as "the menu of choice[s] between different degrees of unemployment and price stability" (fig. 5.1).[20] The authors mentioned specifically two "obtainable" choices: (A) price stability with 5.5 percent unemployment and (B) 3 percent unemployment with 4.5 percent inflation per annum. They did not say whether they regarded other points on their curve, for example (C) 1.5 percent unemployment with 10 percent inflation, "obtainable" choices.

As we see it now, point (C) would not be "obtainable." With 10 percent inflation, the short-run Phillips curve would not stay put. Changes in inflationary expectations leading to anticipatory action by market participants would shift the curve up. But the authors, although they envisage shifts of the curve due to structural changes in the economy, do not point out that increases in inflationary expectations would shift the curve.[21] It is true that there is a brief reference to inflationary expectations, but it comes earlier in the paper and is not related to the Phillips curve. The authors say that inflationary expectations would be caused by "a period of high demand and rising prices." Inflationary expectations would "bias the future in favor of further inflation." But the importance of the matter is immediately played down by saying, "Unlike some other economists, we do not draw the firm conclusion that unless a firm stop is put, the rate of price increase must accelerate. We leave it as an open question: It may be that creeping inflation leads only to creeping inflation" (p. 185).

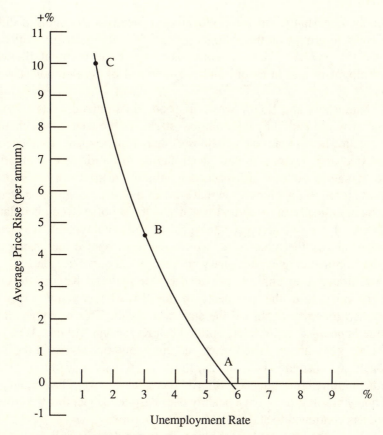

Figure 5.1 Modified Phillips Curve for the United States

It can be argued that Samuelson and Solow were right in the case of very low inflation rates, say, not more than 2 or 3 percent, or even a little higher provided they do not last too long. Maybe the authors meant that by "creeping."

I think enough has been said to justify the conclusion that the paper by Samuelson and Solow illustrates my point that Keynesian economics was characterized by unconcern about the dangers of inflation and neglect of inflationary expectations.

Now my second example. As late as 1972, shortly before inflation in the United States and other industrial countries soared into the two-digit range, James Tobin extolled the virtues of inflation in adjusting "blindly, impartially and non-politically the inconsistent claims of different pressure groups on the national product."[22] Tobin later gracefully admitted that he had "been overoptimistic about the trade-off [between unemployment and inflation] and too skeptical of accelerationist warnings."[23]

Samuelson and Solow wrote in 1960 when inflation was low. The surge of world and U.S. inflation that started in the later 1960s changed the picture. Inflationary expectations of market participants have become sensitized and economists have been alerted to the danger of inflation. The change in outlook has reached its climax in the theory of rational expectations. But we have seen that Keynes himself recognized a change in climate already in 1937 and urged a shift in policy to curb inflation without, of course, giving up the goal of full employment. Keynesian economists, on the other hand, were slow to recognize the change and were recommending expansionary policies in and out of season.

A dramatic example is provided by the fact that Keynesians completely misjudged the prospects of the British economy when the Thatcher government shifted the stance of policy. This was pointed out by the *Economist* in an article entitled "UnKeynesian Britain." When the Thatcher government raised taxes and cut public borrowing in the 1981 budget, 364 academic economists, most Keynesians, issued a manifesto predicting dire consequences. Shortly thereafter recovery began, and the economy is still growing at a healthy pace despite the fact that the government has continued to shrink public sector borrowing.

One of the 364 was Lord Kaldor. Two years later he still did not face the facts. In the introduction to his pamphlet *The Economic Consequences of Mrs. Thatcher* he quotes the following passage from a famous speech by Keynes in the House of Lords on May 25, 1944, in which he defended the Bretton Woods agreement on the International Monetary Fund against its critics.[24]

The experience of the years before the war has led most of us, though some of us late in the day, to certain firm conclusions. Three, in particular, are highly relevant to this discussion. We are determined that, in the future, the external value of sterling shall conform to its internal value, as set by our own domestic policies, and not the other way around. Secondly, we intend to retain control of our domestic rate of interest, so that we can keep it as low as suits our own purpose, without interference from the ebb and flow of international capital movements, or flights of hot money. Thirdly, whilst we intend to prevent inflation at home, we will not accept deflation at the dictate of influences from outside. In other words, we adjure the instruments of the Bank rate and credit contraction operating through the increase in unemployment as means of forcing our domestic economy into line with external factors.

Kaldor claims that this passage presents "the best account of the essential features underlying the consensus" that guided British economic policies of both labor and conservative governments in the postwar period. According to Kaldor, Keynesian policies that had served the country so well had been "completely repudiated" by the Thatcher government with disastrous consequences. This view calls for some critical comment.

To begin, it is true that Britain and all other industrial countries, as well as most less-developed countries, had experienced for about twenty years an almost unprecedented prosperity. Whether this was due to "enlightened Keynesian policies" is questionable. But the "enlightened Keynesian policies" had certainly led to high, unsustainable inflation before Mrs. Thatcher came to power.

Mrs. Thatcher's policy certainly was not flawless. For example, it was a great mistake to grant, that early in the game, an excessive wage increase of over 20 percent to public sector workers. But the overall performance of the economy has been by no means bad. Inflation has come down from 20 percent in mid-1979 to the 5 percent area. The economy has been expanding since the middle of 1981 and has continued to grow, albeit slowly, even during the 1982 recession in the United States, Japan, and Europe. In 1983 its growth rate was the highest among the countries in the European Community and was one of the highest in 1984. Productivity in manufacturing has increased briskly. Unemployment has remained high (about 12 percent) but employment has been increasing for some time now.

I now come to Keynes's statement. What he recommends is that Britain, while "preventing inflation at home," should under no circumstances allow deflation to be imported from abroad. The clear implication is that, if necessary, the exchange rate should be changed; in his words, "the external value of sterling should conform to the internal value."

Keynes's recommendation is the same as that of Thomas Willett and myself to the U.S. government when the dollar was weak in the 1970s: a policy of "benign neglect" of the balance of payments.[25] Contrary to what Kaldor said, there is no conflict between that recommendation and the policy of the Thatcher government. This is precisely what the Thatcher government has done; it has abolished exchange control and allowed sterling to float in the foreign exchange market with a minimum of official interventions.

Thus Kaldor's criticism completely falls to the ground.

After criticizing Keynesians for past sins and misconceptions, it is time to note that at long last they have become aware that the economic climate has changed.

It was mentioned earlier that James Tobin gracefully acknowledged that in earlier statements he had not given sufficient attention to the warnings of "accelerationists" such as William Fellner that inflation would accelerate because there is no permanent trade-off between unemployment and inflation.

My prime example, however, is the arch-Keynesian Paul Samuelson. In his sparkling contribution to the Keynes Centenary Conference in Cambridge in 1983 he found that in the present world neither the "depression Keynesian model" of the *General Theory* nor "the market clearing new classical theory model" work well any more. He concludes: "If I had to choose between these two extreme archetypes, a ridiculous Hobson's choice, I fear that the one to jettison would have to be the Ultra-Keynesian model" and "people learn faster these days and the easy Keynesian victories are long behind us."[26] I myself have expressed the same idea by saying that today the world is closer to the classical position than to the Keynesian one. As mentioned, Keynes himself had recognized already in 1937 that the economic climate had changed when he argued that it was time to switch policy from fighting unemployment to curbing inflation.

Thus it can be seen that the current group of Keynesian economists, exemplified by Samuelson, are at long last catching up with the views of the master.[27]

When Keynes became involved during the war in planning for postwar economic reconstruction, he at first strongly opposed the liberal trade policy proposed by the U.S. State Department. In a memo of October 1943 he wrote: "I am a hopeless skeptic about a return to 19th century laissez faire for which the State Department seems to have such nostalgia.

I believe the future lies with (I) state trading for commodities, (II) international cartels for necessary manufactures, and (III) quantitative import restrictions for non-essential manufacturers."[28] Harrod writes: "In the preceding ten years he [Keynes] had gone far in reconciling himself to a policy of planned trade: these ideas had sunk deeply in. Even for him with . . . his power of quick adaptation, it was difficult to unlearn so much."[29]

Another great admirer of Keynes, Lionel Robbins, wrote: "Even Keynes succumbed to the [then] current insanity. . . . A sad aberration of a noble mind."[30] Keynes later changed his mind, but many of his followers, notably Nicholas (Lord) Kaldor and the new Cambridge school, have consistently followed the protectionist line.

The Increase in Wage Rigidity

Wages have always been sticky, even before labor unions became as powerful as they are in many countries today. But there can be no doubt that in the post–World War II period they became much more sticky than they were earlier.

The growing rigidity of wages and the resulting decline in the responsiveness of wages and prices to the decline in economic activity during recessions were widely noted in the literature. I cite two papers that I found especially important, one by Phillip Cagan and the other by Jeffrey Sachs.[31]

Phillip Cagan concluded that "wholesale prices show a smaller decline in the recessions after 1948–49 than formerly," and that "there has clearly been a gradual decline in price response to recessions over the postwar period, except mainly for raw materials prices" (pp. 54–55).

Sachs used two methods to demonstrate the decreasing responsiveness of inflation to changes in aggregate demand with special emphasis on wage behavior. The first approach followed Cagan's method and led to the same conclusion for a longer period. A striking finding was that "for mild contractions, downward price flexibility seems to have ended with the pre–World War II period. For moderate and severe contractions, similarly, the response of wages and prices has fallen significantly since 1950" (p. 81).

The second approach can be described as an econometric Phillips curve estimation. The finding that the short-run Phillips curve had become flatter strongly supported the hypothesis of decreasing responsiveness of wages to declines in economic activity.

The causes of this development were fairly obvious. The increased strength of labor unions that goes back largely to the New Deal legislation of the 1930s is surely basic. That union wages are stickier than nonunion wages is notorious; that they seem to be stickier also on the up side of the cycle was more than amply compensated by the sharp increase in the lengths of union contracts providing hefty wages increases for each year. The overlapping and leapfrogging of union wage contracts was another factor that greatly exacerbated wage inflation.[32] In other industrial and industrializing countries, too, the power of labor unions increased sharply; so did wage-push and what J. R. Hicks has called "real wage resistance." Naturally, the pattern and force of this development varied from country to country, depending on the structure of the economy, the history of the labor movement, and its alliance in many countries with political, mainly socialist, parties.

Without going into too many details, it should be mentioned that in most European countries a much larger percentage of the labor force is unionized than in the United States and that in some countries, Austria and Sweden for example, there exist central organizations that represent labor as a whole and allow it to speak with almost one voice. Whether the existence of strong centralized organizations of labor increases or decreases the dangers of inflationary wage-push, compared with the U.S. decentralized system of essentially independent unions, is difficult to say. On the one hand it increases the power of unions and their political clout. But on the other hand it eliminates leapfrogging, and the leaders of an all-embracing organization of labor may perhaps be assumed to be more responsible and more aware of the general good of the population as a whole than the bosses of independent unions.

International comparisons could throw some light on these questions. But I must confine myself to two remarks. First, international comparisons are complicated by the fact that union power depends also on the structure of the economy. For example, it is well known that unions are more moderate in small countries where competition from world markets is strong because foreign trade plays a much greater role than in large countries. Second, Japan is a special case that merits close attention. Wages of Japanese workers are much more flexible than in Europe and the United States because Japanese workers receive a substantial part of their earnings in the form of a bonus whose size varies to some extent with the level of profits. Thus in recessions, when profits are low, wages and labor costs automatically decline. This is one of the reasons why unemployment is lower in Japan and why the economy rebounds more quickly from recessions than in most other industrial countries.

Another factor that derives its importance in part from the existence of powerful unions was the rise of Keynesianism and the resulting emphasis on antidepression and antirecession policy. This had a double inflationary effect: it reduced the price decline in the downswing of the business cycle and stiffened the resistance of workers and their unions to wage cuts, because they could assume that unemployment caused by large wage boosts would not last long—in other words, that government policy would bail them out if they caused unemployment by excessive wage demands.

Other policies that strengthened union power and produced unemployment were minimum wages, especially when indexed, and generous unemployment benefits and welfare payments. These measures reduced the responsiveness of wages and prices to recession by diminishing the incentive for individual workers to accept lower paid jobs and of unions to make wage concessions, especially if striking workers were eligible for unemployment benefits.

Geoffrey Moore has presented some very interesting figures that throw much light on the importance of large unemployment benefits for the rate of unemployment and the cyclical unresponsiveness of wages.[33] The author finds that both in 1929, a boom year, and 1982, a recession year, 58 percent of the population sixteen years old and over was employed. The 42 percent who were not working fall into two groups, the unemployeds (not working but seeking work) and those who neither work nor seek work. Now the interesting finding is that in 1929, 2 percent of the population was unemployed and 40 percent was not working nor seeking work, while in 1982 6 percent was unemployed and 36 percent was neither working nor seeking work.[34]

What explains the much higher unemployment percentage in 1982 than in 1929 despite the fact that the employment rate was the same in both years? Moore asks the question the other way round: "What explains the increase in the desire to work on the part of the non-working population?" There are several reasons, but a major reason is that "in 1982 unemployeds were much better supported than in 1929. Fifty years ago none of the unemployed received unemployment insurance benefits from the government, since there was no insurance program." Moore says that "the average weekly benefit paid to the insured unemployeds in 1982 was as high, in real terms, as the average weekly pay of all employed persons in 1929." Since "total compensation per worker employed in 1982 was roughly three times as high as in 1929, *after* allowing for inflation," in 1982 average weekly unemployment benefits amounted to roughly a third of the average compensation per worker.

This is a strong incentive to remain as long as possible in the ranks of the unemployed. If the unemployed in 1929 had had access to the benefits available to the insured unemployed today, unemployment would have been much higher and the percentage of nonworkers counted as not seeking work would have been lower.

Fortunately, wage rigidities seem to have been less pronounced in recent years. In the United States the unexpectedly vigorous cyclical expansion that began in November 1982 was accompanied by more moderate wage pressures than earlier recoveries in the post–World War II period. Wage costs per unit of output did not rise much and, as a consequence, inflation remained relatively low. There is strong evidence that the relatively consistent policy of disinflation that was pursued in the United States in the early part of the decade improved the trade-off between unemployment and inflation. In a study conducted by Phillip Cagan and William Fellner, the authors concluded, "In our appraisal, the data suggest an improved 'trade-off' for the past two years. By this we mean that during this period we obtained more disinflation per unit of economic slack (unemployment) than would be suggested by the same type of trade-off for the 1970s."[35]

But it is probably too optimistic to conclude that inflation has been definitely stopped; it may well accelerate again if the expansion continues, and the support the anti-inflation policy has enjoyed will not last forever. Moreover, the U.S. labor picture is not uniformly bright. For example, in two major industries, automobiles and steel, powerful unions have still managed to keep wages more than 70 percent higher than the average wage in U.S. manufacturing industries. This would not have been possible without strong support from the government through severe restrictions on imports of Japanese automobiles.

In its infinite wisdom the government chose the worst possible method of protection in the auto case, namely the so-called voluntary restrictions imposed on foreign exporters. Any import restriction, tariff or nontariff, drives a wedge between the price inside and outside the country. Under an import tariff the price difference goes to the U.S. Treasury as a duty and so ultimately to the U.S. taxpayer. But under the method of "voluntary" export restraints, the price difference goes to foreign exporters. This means that foreign exporters receive a large subsidy at the expense of the U.S. consumer. Robert Crandall has estimated that the Japanese automobile firms received an annual subsidy of at least $2 billion a year from the United States because of the increased price of Japanese cars. The total "cost to the [American] consumer in 1983 was $4.3 billion plus additional losses in consumer welfare due to the constraint on the choice of cars. The cost per job saved [in the U.S. automobile] industry therefore was at least $160,000 per year." Crandall adds, "Employment creation at this cost is surely not worth the candle."[36] A similar system has been used for steel imports.

The system has a serious, corrupting side effect. It is natural that foreign exporters quickly learn to like the system and no longer have any incentive to fight for free trade. They thus become accomplices of domestic protectionists, the U.S. automobile firms and the United Auto Workers (UAW).

Yet the fact remains that the performance of the U.S. economy has, on the whole, been much better than expected, and especially remarkable and instructive is the contrast between Europe and the United States. The European economic picture has been much less bright, the recovery from the recession started later and has been slower than in the United States, and unemployment is higher and there is more inflation in most European countries than in the United States.

What accounts for this contrast? There are basic structural differences which have been very well presented by Stephen Marris, the former chief economic advisor of the Organization of Economic Cooperation and Development (OECD).[37] I quote some salient facts described by Marris:

> European economies are in important respects less flexible than the American economy. . . . European workers are generally better protected against economic misfortune than their American counterparts. Collective agreements and government regulations give them more job security. But this makes it more difficult and expensive for European employers to lay off workers when demand weakens. And

they are more reluctant to take on new workers when demand picks up, preferring instead to work overtime. Provisions for unemployment are also more generous in Europe. Laid-off workers have more time to look around for a new job. But, by the same token, this slows down the movement of labor from declining to expanding industries.

Labor mobility is also inhibited in Europe by the greater rigidity of the *relative* wage structure between industries, occupations and regions. It is more difficult for employers in expanding industries to bid up wages to attract labor, or for laid-off workers in declining industries to bid down wages to get their jobs back.

. . . The main culprit is the downward rigidity of real wages, coupled with the high taxes. . . . Between 1960 and 1983 the ratio of general government expenditure to gross national product (GNP) in the European Community rose from 32 percent to 52 percent.

. . . In America the overall burden of taxation is lower, and real income seems to have adjusted more flexibly to the shocks of the 1970s. Twenty million new jobs have been created in America since 1972. . . . Against this, there was a net *loss* of around 2.5 million jobs in the European Community over the same period. Compared with Europeans, Americans coming into the labor force have been more willing to accept whatever level of real wages was necessary to induce employers to hire them; in other words, to 'price themselves' into jobs.

The European Common Market was supposed to institute freer and more vigorous trade among the members of the European Community (EC). But there still exist many impediments to the free movement of commodities. Some members, notably France, have had tight exchange control—a major obstacle to trade—although its purpose is ostensibly "merely" directed at capital transactions. Exchange control makes integration of financial markets impossible—a most serious handicap. Customs formalities and inspection at the border are still in place, and controllers and custom officials are very active to justify their existence.[38]

Equally important, European countries are burdened by the existence of national public monopolies in the areas of transportation, communications, and electric power (national airlines, railroads, etc.). These public monopolies suffer in various degrees from bureaucratic inefficiencies and are impervious to international competition. In addition, there are numerous nationalized industries that suffer from the same handicap.

Marris, however, is not satisfied with the structural explanation of the contrast between Europe and the United States. He insists that a basic difference between European and American macropolicies is equally if not more responsible. While the United States has run huge budget deficits, Europe's "recovery is being held back" by low structural deficits. In other words, European policies are not sufficiently expansionary ("Keynesian").

This I find unconvincing for two reasons. First, European macropolicies are by no means uniform. For example, there was, at least early in the decade, a sharp contrast between the two largest economies—France and West Germany. In France the Socialist government of François Mitterrand pursued a more "Keynesian" policy, running large budget deficits and, as a consequence, huge trade deficits, high inflation, and slow growth. Germany, on the other hand, pursued a much more cautious policy; inflation is much lower than in France, and the German economy staged a recovery, although unemployment is still high by German standards.[39] The second reason why Marris's theory is unconvincing is that, given the structural rigidities and immobility of labor as described by him, an expansionary ("Keynesian") macropolicy would quickly reignite inflation as exemplified by France, as pointed out by Helmut Schlesinger.[40] Schlesinger made clear that the Bundesbank would stick to its cautious policy, because accelerated inflation would soon be followed by a recession.

Supply Shocks and Wage Problems

After discussing the wage factor, let us consider how supply shocks fit into the picture.

The two oil shocks, the quadrupling of the price of crude oil in 1973 and the doubling of the price in 1979–80, were and still are widely regarded as by far the most important causes of two-digit inflation in 1974 and 1980–81 and the subsequent recessions. This surely is a great exaggeration. The first oil shock was preceded and accompanied by a highly inflationary commodity boom which, in turn, was superimposed on an inflationary groundswell that encompassed the whole postwar period and went into high gear in the 1960s.[41] In the United States inflation was fueled by huge public borrowing to finance the escalating cost of the war in Vietnam and the equally costly Great Society programs of the Johnson administration. There was also, of course, an accommodative monetary policy.

There is no doubt that the oil price rise had an inflationary impact, but the magnitude of the burden for the industrial countries has been greatly exaggerated. For the United States the additional oil import bill of the first oil shock was about $20 billion a year. This is a large sum but not more than about 1.22 percent of the GNP at that time, or less than half of the normal annual increase in GNP. It follows that a once-for-all decrease of about 1.22 percent in the wage level, or more generally money incomes, would have taken care of the problem, or assuming that money wages were rigid downward, a once-for-all increase in the price level of about 1.22 percent would have solved the problem.[42] An additional increase in inflation by 1.22 percentage points is a matter of minor importance in a period of two-digit inflation.

For other industrial countries the oil levy was a greater burden than for the United States, because they depend more heavily on imports. The jump in the oil import bill from 1973 to 1974 was 4.31 percent of GNP for Japan, 3.96 percent for Italy, 3.73 percent for the United Kingdom, and 2.17 percent for Germany.[43] This was not a negligible burden, but it was not an intolerable one; for all OECD countries as a group it was less than one year's normal growth. Hence a suspension of wage (income) growth for less than a year or a mild once-for-all rise in the price level would have taken care of the problem.

The conclusion I draw is that if one wants to assign to the oil price rise a major role in inflation and recession, it must be done by stressing *indirect* effects, for example, by assuming what Hicks has called "real wage resistance," workers resisting not only money but real wages, which would be brought about by widespread indexation of wages (and other incomes).

It is now widely recognized that wage rigidity, real as well as nominal, is the most serious impediment to a return to price stability at high rates of employment and growth. In recent years more and more economists have come to the conclusion that a decisive and *lasting* recovery from the world recession requires restructuring real wages to stimulate investment and growth; "wages," of course, include salaries.

What is said about the adverse effect of wage rigidity and real wage resistance applies also to other incomes or prices that have been made rigid by government action, especially by indexation, ranging from farm supports to social benefits of various kinds.

I cite a few examples of this trend in thinking about wages. A few years ago a group of prominent German economists, several of them of monetarist persuasion, issued a statement urging a temporary wage freeze to let inflation bring down real wages. The plea was not heeded; wages continued to rise and unemployment reached the two-digit level. Herbert Giersch, an author with monetarist leaning, argued in several important articles that most industrial countries, especially in western Europe, suffer from excessively high real wages and too low profits.[44]

The main argument against cutting money wages as a recovery measure is that it reduces total spending by reducing the money income of labor, and thus is a deflationary factor that intensifies a recession. This argument, however, is fallacious and rests on a misunderstanding of what a wage cut is supposed to achieve. The purpose would be not to reduce effective demand (nominal GNP); if such a reduction is necessary, it should be done by monetary-fiscal measures. The purpose of cutting money wages would be to boost profits and stimulate investment, employment, and growth by making labor more competitive with robots and other machines—in other words, with capital. Suppose hourly wage rates are cut by 10 percent—that does not necessarily mean that the wage bill and spending power of labor is reduced. If the elasticity of demand for labor is greater than unity, employment (in terms of hours) will rise by more than 10 percent and the wage bill and spending, too, will rise. True, if employment rises by less than 10 percent, labor incomes will decline, but that does not mean that total incomes and spending, too, will decline. A shift to profits will stimulate investment, employment, and growth. This tendency could be assisted by monetary expansion, for the reduction of unit labor costs would reduce the inflationary danger of easier money.

What these statements of the problem have in common is that they assume that market forces can, in due course, bring about the necessary restructuring of the economy to achieve essentially full employment, provided a moderate cut in some wages is achieved and macroeconomic levers are set right.

This optimistic conclusion will be challenged by the "structuralists." Thus, in the 1930s it was widely believed that part of the unemployment problem was that labor-saving inventions had reduced the demand for labor or that the "structure of production" had been distorted in some other way. In other words, it was argued that a large part of unemployment was "technological" and "structural," requiring large-scale reallocation of factors of production, a time-consuming, painful process. There can be no doubt that subsequent developments were entirely at variance with that structuralist theory. Experience has shown that as soon as deflation was stopped, the huge structural distortions that had been diagnosed by theorists during the depression had shriveled as quickly as they had surfaced earlier. What was called "secondary deflation" turned out to be a much more important cause of high unemployment than structural distortions.[45] In other words, there would have been some "structural" unemployment even if there had been no deflation (no contraction of the money stock), but the great bulk of unemployment was "Keynesian," or monetarist, if you like, not structural.

Extreme structuralist views can be heard again today. It is said that robots and other "smart" machines have put human labor in the same position as horses were when tractors came into wide use. This is, however, a very misleading analogy. Tractors replaced not only horsepower but also manpower. But unlike horses, human labor could be shifted to producing tractors.

This is not to deny that technological progress may require reallocations of factors of production that may cause some structural unemployment and at least a temporary decline of labor's share in GNP until the transfer and retraining of labor has been carried out. A modest decline of the share of labor in the national product may be required at the present time. But it is most unlikely that a large permanent reduction of the marginal productivity of labor, an intolerable drop in the real wage, and a massive decline of the share of labor (and salaries) would occur, as the analogy with the horses suggests. The share of labor in the national product has remained remarkably stable over the long pull—apart from cyclical fluctuations—despite the tremendous technological changes, including mechanization and automation, that have occurred since the industrial revolution in England.

I conclude that the present-day gloomy forecasts of disaster that will befall us unless radical reforms are undertaken involving massive redistribution of income to spread work—an argument often made in Europe—will turn out to be totally unfounded; these forecasts will share the fate of earlier, similarly gloomy prophecies which regularly made their appearance in periods of depression, beginning with those underlying the Luddite movement in the early nineteenth century to the most famous one, Karl Marx's theory of the immiseration of the working classes—prophecies that were completely disproved and discredited by subsequent developments.

Policy Implications

The policy implications of our analysis are straightforward. Before going into details, two general observations.

First, the emphasis must be on anti-inflation policy. This assertion should not be interpreted to deny that the *real* economy—output, employment, and growth—is intrinsically much more important than price stability. It rather reflects the conviction that we have learned from long, painful experience that chronic inflation is no cure for unemployment. There is no long-run trade-off between unemployment and inflation.

The second general observation is to repeat that inflation is in the long run a monetary phenomenon; monetary restraint and monetary stability are essential.

In a sense, monetary restraint is not only a necessary condition for holding down inflation but also a sufficient condition, namely, in the sense that sufficient monetary restraint can bring down inflation, irrespective of union strength, cost-raising policies of the government, and the size of the government budget deficit. However, the greater the resistance to wage and price reductions on the part of unions, other pressure groups, and the government, and the stronger the cost-raising measures of the government, the *stronger* must be monetary restraint to hold down inflation. And the greater the transitional unemployment and output loss of a strong anti-inflation policy, the harder it is politically to carry out such a policy to a successful conclusion.

Likewise, large budget deficits make it politically and economically more difficult to stop inflation. They drive up interest rates and crowd out productive private investment. The political pressure on the central bank to bring down interest rates by expansionary measures is bound to increase. Moreover, the rate of growth of real GNP will decline if and when productive private investment is reduced. As a consequence, a larger reduction in monetary growth will be required to promote price stability.

The policy conclusions are straightforward. For best results monetary policy should be supplemented and assisted by an appropriately tight fiscal policy and by *microeconomic* measures to make the economy more flexible in order to improve the trade-off between prices and quantities. Thus, in a period of expansion, the hope would be that any increase in nominal GNP would be reflected in rising quantities rather than in rising prices. In a period of disinflation, on the other hand, the necessary decline in nominal GNP growth should be reflected in prices rather than quantities (output and employment).

This general prescription has been discussed and spelled out, in roughly similar ways, under different headings. What gave rise to these discussions was the poor performance of most industrial economies in the late 1970s and early 1980s, stagnant output and high unemployment, even in nonrecession years. This experience has shaken confidence in exclusive reliance on government management of the aggregate demand for goods and services and has spurred the search for an explanation of the slowdown and a cure. One answer has been that what is required is the adoption of "adjustment policies" to speed up the economy's adaptability to changing conditions.[46] Advocates of incomes policy say that this is exactly what incomes policy is all about. The trouble is that incomes policy means different things to different people. It is often being interpreted as more or less comprehensive wage and price controls. In that form incomes policy must be rejected. Wage and price controls are too crude; they deal with symptoms only, distort the economy, and have never worked.[47]

I myself have distinguished between Incomes Policy I, and Incomes Policy II. The former is defined as more or less comprehensive wage and price control; the latter is a bundle of measures designed to move the economy closer to the competitive ideal. Such supply-oriented policies should not be regarded as alternatives or antitheses to "demand-side economics" (demand management). They are complements, not substitutes. It should be noted that a supply-oriented policy is a much broader concept than supply-side economics, which asserts that by reducing taxes it is possible to stimulate the economy to such an extent that tax revenues do not decline or may even rise.

Reducing high marginal tax rates to stimulate saving and investment is one measure among many others of a supply-oriented policy. This is a vast area; only a few basic facts and principles can be dealt with here. To bring the economy closer to the competitive ideal, all forms of monopolies and restrictions of trade should be attacked. It will be convenient to deal separately with business or industrial monopolies (including oligopolies and cartels), labor monopolies (labor unions), and the government.

The rules of conduct of business and labor monopolies are rather different. But they have this in common: they restrict supply, keep prices and wages higher than they would be under competition, and slow down productivity growth. In my opinion, in the present-day world, labor unions, at least in Europe, are much more powerful, present a greater danger for price stability and full employment, and are much more difficult to deal with than business monopolies.

Compared with labor unions, private business or industrial monopolies are really not much of a problem, except in the area of public utilities. The most effective antimonopoly policy, which is at the same time easy to carry out from the economic and administrative point of view (though not politically), is free trade. Given the enormous growth of world trade, especially of manufacturers in the last forty years, the great advances in the technology of transportation, communication, and information, and the emergence of new industries in scores of developed and developing countries, few if any monopolies would survive in a free trade world (outside the area of public utilities, where prices are under public control anyway).

Free trade policy must, of course, be interpreted broadly. It would include not only the phasing out of tariffs, import quotas, and exchange control but also elimination of administrative protectionism, the so-called voluntary restrictions imposed on foreign exporters (often called "orderly marketing agreements," OMAS), and the taking over of noncompetitive firms by government and operating them with great losses at the expense of the taxpayer. A policy along these lines would not require any new government bureaus or larger bureaucracies. On the contrary, it would reduce government activities, shrink the public sector, and lighten the tax burden.

I now come to the problems of the labor market. To begin with, liberalizing internal and international trade would go a long way to curb any monopoly power of labor unions. Unions know or quickly find out that striking against world markets is risky. This again is the reason why labor unions in small countries where the international sector is a large fraction of the economy are usually much more reasonable and moderate than in large countries where the international sector is small.

Union responsiveness is strikingly illustrated by a development of recent years, though not one from the international area: the deregulation in the United States of the trucking and airline industries. Until recently the two industries were tightly regulated by two huge federal bureaucracies. The dismantling of the controls is equivalent to the introduction of internal free trade. Deregulation—internal (domestic) free trade—changed the structure of the two industries dramatically. New, largely nonunionized firms—regional airlines—with lower cost and dynamic management sprang up, providing better and much cheaper service to the public. In both cases the power of the unions was sharply reduced. The wage rates and wage costs of the new airlines are much lower than those of the old ones. It is not surprising that the unions are strongly opposed to deregulation.

Finally, I mention specific measures that would reduce the monopoly power of labor, promote efficiency of the labor market, and increase overall labor productivity. Minimum wage laws, for one, should be repealed. Legal minimum wages do not, on the whole, benefit disadvantaged workers. On the contrary, it has been plausibly argued that in the United States the legal minimum wage is partly responsible for the shockingly high unemployment of teenagers. These young people are thus deprived of the on-the-job training that is so important to their future careers.[48]

There also exist laws, like the Davis-Bacon Act in the United States, that obligate the government to buy only from firms that pay union wages. Given the large size of the public sector and the huge volume of government purchases, ranging from paper and pencils to trucks and turbines, these laws add considerably to the monopoly power of unions—and to the size of the government budget. Such laws, too, should be abrogated.[49]

It should be clear from all this that government itself is the worst offender in distorting product and labor markets. The list of misdeeds is very long indeed. Public policy is largely responsible for the power of private monopolies and unions. We have seen that without protection from imports few if any private monopolies, oligopolies, or cartels would exist outside the public utility area, where prices are controlled anyway. In fact, in most countries public utilities, postal services, railroads, and telephone and telegraph services are government monopolies. Prices in this area are notoriously rigid and in many countries these public enterprises operate inefficiently and add substantially to the deficit of the government budget, crowding out productive private investment. Add to this the enormous burdens of the welfare state—overregulation of industry and a tax burden that blunts incentives to work, save, and invest.

When producers are too numerous to organize themselves to cut production and raise prices, the government steps in and does for them what unions do for their members. Farm price supports are perhaps the most notorious, though not the only, example.

There are thus virtually limitless opportunities for "adjustment policies" and "supply-oriented policies" to improve economic performance by making markets more competitive. The irony in all this is that most of these measures consist in *undoing* past policy interventions that had been rationalized as a way to cope with less than perfectly competitive markets. In the real world, free markets will never fully meet the standards of perfect competition, and difficult macroeconomic problems will arise, but we should have learned by now that the best thing government can do is simply to refrain from multiplying market imperfections.

Notes

1   This is true also of Keynes's *General Theory* (New York: Harcourt, Brace, 1935). James Tobin has said, "It is unfortunate that Keynes, in spite of the Chamberlin-Robinson revolution that was occurring in microeconomics at the same time he was making his macro revolution, chose to challenge orthodoxy on its own microeconomic ground of competitive markets." James Tobin, "Okun on Macroeconomic Policy: A Final Comment," in *Macroeconomics, Prices, and Quantities: Essays in Memory of Arthur M. Okun,* ed. James Tobin (Washington, D.C.: Brookings Institution, 1983), p. 299. Actually Keynes's position is ambivalent. He often simply assumed rigid *money* wages and prices, which is inconsistent with perfect competition. At the same time he accepted the classical position that real wages are determined by the marginal productivity of labor. That Keynes, as a rule, assumed rigid wages is the central theme of John R. Hicks's contribution to "The Keynes Centenary" in *The Economist,* June 18, 1983. The truth is that he simply was neither much interested nor well versed in microeconomics.

2   This does not do full justice to Keynes. The above is the theory he puts forward in the first part of his *General Theory,* which he restates again and again. But in chapter 19, "Changes in Money Wages," Keynes concludes that full employment may eventually be restored if and when money wages are driven down by competition, because the real value of the money stock would increase, which would push down interest rates and stimulate investment.

3   The literature has become very large. No attempt will be made to review it. A major contribution is the posthumously published book by Arthur M. Okun, *Prices and Quantities: A Macroeconomic Analysis* (Washington, D.C.: Brookings Institution, 1981).

4   Frank H. Knight, "The Business Cycle, Interest, and Money," *Review of Economics and Statistics* 23 (May 1941). Reprinted in Frank H. Knight's *On the History and Methods of Economics* (Chicago: University of Chicago Press, 1956), p. 224. See also p. 211: "Wages are notoriously sticky, especially with respect to any downward change of the hourly wage rates."

5   See, for example, Armen Alchian, "Information Costs, Pricing, and Resource Unemployment," *Western Economic Journal* 7 (June 1969).

6   Arthur C. Pigou, *Unemployment* (London: Howe University Library, 1914), p. 17

7   Arthur C. Pigou, *The Theory of Unemployment* (London: Howe University Library, 1933).

8   Dennis H. Robertson, *A Study of Industrial Fluctuations* (London: Aldwych, 1948).

9   See Richard Kahn, "Unemployment as Seen by the Keynesians," in *The Concept and Measurement of Involuntary Unemployment,* ed. G. D. N. Worswick (London: Allen and Unwin, 1975), p. 20. Kahn's paper presents an excellent analysis of the concept of involuntary unemployment in Keynes's *General Theory* and of subsequent developments of Keynes's thinking.

10 Keynes, *General Theory,* p. 15.

11 See my paper "The Economic Malaise of the 1980s: A Positive Program for a Benevolent and Enlightened Dictator," in *Essays in Contemporary Economic Problems, Demand, Productivity, and Population* (Washington, D.C.: American Enterprise Institute, 1981–82). For the empirical application of these concepts further specifications are required, and the borderline between voluntary and involuntary unemployment is not always clearly marked. On this point, see the careful analysis by Herbert Giersch, *Konjunktur- und Wachstumspolitik in der offenen Wirtschaft* (Wiesbaden: Dr. Th. Gabler, 1977), pp. 254–57. I was glad that Richard Kahn, too, reached the conclusion that Keynes's definition was "unnecessarily complicated." He points out that elsewhere in *The General Theory* a simpler definition is used.

12 Alchian, "Information Costs," p. 122.

13 See Axel Leijonhufvud, *On Keynesian Economics and the Economics of Keynes: A Study in Monetary Theory* (New York: Oxford University Press, 1968).

14 Keynes's three articles in the *Times* are reprinted in T. W. Hutchison, *Keynes versus the Keynesians? An Essay on the Thinking of J. M. Keynes and the Accuracy of Its Interpretation by His Followers* (London: Institute of Economic Affairs, 1977). For further details, see T. W. Hutchison, *On Revolution and Progress in Economic Knowledge* (Cambridge: Cambridge University Press, 1978), especially chap. 6, "Demythologizing the Keynesian Revolution," pp. 175–199. For Keynes's view on inflation, see Thomas M. Humphrey, "Keynes on Inflation," Federal Reserve Bank of Richmond *Economic Review* 67, no. 1 (January/February 1981): 3–13.

15 See especially William Fellner, "The Valid Core of Rationality Hypotheses in the Theory of Expectations," *Journal of Money, Credit, and Banking* 12, no. 4, pt. 2 (November 1980). That issue of the journal presents the proceedings of a full-dress

review of the rational expectations theory at a seminar sponsored by the American Enterprise Institute with contributions also by Bennet T. McCallum, Robert J. Barro, James Tobin, Edwin Burmeister, Arthur Okun, Phillip Cagan, and Gottfried Haberler. Another comprehensive review can be found in Stanley Fischer, ed., *Rational Expectations and Economics Policies,* National Bureau of Economic Research, Conference Report (Chicago: Chicago University Press, 1980).

16 See especially A. C. Pigou, *Industrial Fluctuations,* 2d ed. (London: Macmillan, 1929). Pigou's theory of the business cycle is often described as "psychological." This is, however, inappropriate. Errors of optimism and pessimism are only one factor among others in Pigou's theory. For example, he attributes equal weight to "monetary and banking policy."

17 See especially Bennet T. McCallum's contribution to the American Enterprise Institute seminar on rational expectations theory, "Rational Expectations and Macroeconomic Stabilization Policy: An Overview," *Journal of Money, Credit, and Banking* 12 (November 1980): 716–46, and his papers, "Price-Level Stickiness and the Feasibility of Monetary Stabilization Policy with Rational Expectations," *Journal of Political Economy* 85 (June 1977): 627–34, and "Monetarism, Rational Expectations, Oligopolistic Pricing, and the MPS Econometric Model," *Journal of Political Economy* 87 (February 1979): 57–73.

18 It is called Ricardian because it has been attributed to David Ricardo, but it should be noted that after Ricardo formulated the theorem, he rejected it as unrealistic.

19 The main references are Robert J. Barro, "Are Government Bonds Net Wealth?" *Journal of Political Economy* 82 (November/December 1974): 1095–1117, and *Macroeconomics* (New York: John Wiley & Sons, 1984), pp. 380–93. For further details see my "International Issues Raised by Criticisms of the U.S. Budget Deficits," in *Contemporary Economic Problems 1984–1985* (Washington, D.C.: American Enterprise Institute, 1985).

20 See the *American Economic Review* 50 (May 1960): p. 192, fig. 1.

21 There is reference to expectations in connection with the Phillips curve: "It might be that the low-pressure demand would so act upon wage and other expectations as to shift the curve downward in the longer run—so that over a decade, the economy might enjoy higher employment with price stability than our present-day estimate would indicate" (p. 193). But the reference is to *deflationary* expectations, and it is described as a long-run phenomenon. Inflationary expectations are not a truly *long*-run phenomenon. This makes the absence of any reference to inflationary expectations all the more conspicuous.

22 See Tobin's brilliant presidential address, "Inflation and Unemployment," *American Economic Review* 62 (March 1972): 13.

23 See Tobin's "Comment of an Academic Scribbler," *Journal of Monetary Economics* 4 (1978): 622.

24 Nick Butler, ed., *Speeches in the House of Lords 1979–1982,* pp. 1–2. Keynes's speech is reprinted in *Collected Writings of John M. Keynes,* vol. 26 (Cambridge: Cambridge University Press, 1980), p. 16.

25 See Gottfried Haberler and Thomas Willett, *A Strategy for U.S. Balance of Payments Policy: Special Analysis* (Washington, D.C.: American Enterprise Institute, 1971).

See also Gottfried Haberler, *U.S. Balance of Payments Policy and the International Monetary System*, Reprint no. 9 (Washington, D.C.: American Enterprise Institute, 1973).

26   See Paul Samuelson's "Comment," in *Keynes and the Modern World,* ed. David Worswick and James Trevithick (Cambridge: Cambridge University Press, 1983), p. 212.

27   I should note that it may be misleading to contrast Keynes's macroeconomics with Marshallian, Walrasian, and other neoclassical microeconomics as Samuelson and other Keynesians do. This ignores the fact that Marshall and Walras wrote extensively on money, banking, credit, and economic fluctuations. In other words, there exists a Marshallian and Walrasian macroeconomics. See Alfred Marshall, *Principles of Economics* (New York: Macmillan, 1890), on the one hand, and *Money, Credit, and Commerce* (London: Macmillan, 1923) and Marshall's *Official Papers* (London: Macmillan, 1926), on the other. See also Leon Walras's *Eléments d'économie politiques pure* (Lausanne, Rouge, 1896), on the one hand, and his *Etudes d'économie politique appliqués* (Lausanne, Rouge, 1898), on the other. It is worth noting that Marshall and Walras, along with acknowledged scholars like F. Y. Edgeworth, H. G. Pierson, and Irving Fisher, supported bimetallism (or symmetallism) in somewhat heretical opposition to the orthodoxy of the gold standard. This should help to dispel the myth propagated by the Keynesians, with their limited historical horizon, that Keynes was the only reputable economist (apart from Silvio Gesell, Major Douglas, and scores of others whose views could be dismissed as those of monetary cranks) who offered a responsible opposition to the prevailing orthodoxy.

28   Quoted in Roy F. Harrod, *The Life of John Maynard Keynes* (New York: Macmillan, 1951), pp. 567–68.

29   Ibid.

30   Lionel Robbins, *Autobiography of an Economist* (London–New York: Macmillan, 1971), p. 156.

31   See Phillip Cagan, "Changes in the Recession Behavior of Wholesale Prices in the 1920's and Post–World War II," in *Explorations in Economic Research,* National Bureau of Economic Research, Occasional Papers, vol. 2, no. 1 (Cambridge, Mass., 1975); and Jeffrey Sachs, "The Changing Cyclical Behavior of Wages and Prices: 1890–1976," *American Economic Review* 70 (March 1980): 78–90. Sachs's paper has extensive references to the literature. See also James E. Price, "The Changing Cyclical Behavior of Wages and Prices, 1890–1976: Comment," *American Economic Review* 72 (December 1982): 1188–90; and Jeffrey Sachs's reply, "The Changing Cyclical Behavior of Wages and Prices, 1890–1976: Reply," *American Economic Review* 72 (December 1982): 1191–93.

32   On this point, see John A. Taylor, *Union Wage Settlements during a Disinflation,* National Bureau of Economic Research, *Working Paper no. 985* (Cambridge, Mass., 1982), and the specialized literature quoted in the paper.

33   Geoffrey Moore, "Another 1929?" (Center for International Business Cycle Research, Graduate School of Business, Columbia University, New York, June 3, 1983, mimeographed).

34 The author explains that his figure for unemployment (6 percent in 1982) differs from the usually quoted official figure (almost 10 percent for 1982) because he prefers to express unemployment in percent of the *total* population of sixteen years or older, while the usually quoted figure is expressed in percent of the *labor force*, which is defined as the employeds plus the unemployeds. Those neither working nor seeking work (because of age, inability to work, etc.) are not considered part of the labor force. The difference in the definition does not affect the rest of the argument.

35 See Phillip Cagan and William Fellner, "The Cost of Disinflation, Credibility, and the Deceleration of Wages 1982–1983," in *Essays in Contemporary Economic Problems: Disinflation* (Washington, D.C.: American Enterprise Institute, 1984), p. 7.

36 Robert Crandall, "Import Quotas and American Industry: The Costs of Protectionism," *Brookings Review,* Summer 1984, 16. See also the excellent, comprehensive study by William Cline, *Exports of Manufactures from Developing Countries—Performance and Prospects for Market Access* (Washington, D.C.: Brookings Institution, 1984).

37 "Why Europe's Recovery Is Lagging Behind. With an Unconventional View of What Should Be Done about It," in *Europe: Magazine of the European Community,* March/April 1984. Since this paper was written, an important, wide-ranging paper by Ambassador Arthur F. Burns, "The Economic Sluggishness of Western Europe" (Dunlap Distinguished American Lecture, University of Dubuque, Iowa, September 5, 1984) has become available. Burns presents a thorough analysis of the structural handicaps of Europe as compared with the United States and vividly describes the excesses of the welfare state and the oppressive regulatory climate in many European countries.

38 True, tariffs and import quotas have largely been abolished between the members of the EC. But there has been a strong tendency to substitute more or less subtle administrative restrictions on intra-European trade (See *The Economist,* June 23, 1984, p. 29, for details).

39 On the scope, speed, and prospects of the German recovery see the statement by Helmut Schlesinger, vice president of the German central bank, "Bundesbankpolitik auch 1985 für Wachstum bei Stabilitat," *Deutsche Bundesbank Auszüge aus Presseartikeln,* no. 96 (December 12, 1984): 1–2.

40 Ibid.

41 See *International Financial Statistics, Supplement on Price Statistics,* no. 2 (Washington, D.C.: International Monetary Fund, 1981).

42 If one accepts what might be called "the rational expectations" interpretation of the Keynesian theory—that workers do not accept a reduction in their real wage if it comes in the form of a reduction of the money wage, because money wage reductions are never across the board—then the wage reduction imposed by the oil price increase would be an exception, for this reduction in wages clearly was across the board. An objection to this reasoning might be that there was a change in relative wages after all, because wages in the domestic oil and oil-related industries might not go down. But this, surely, would be spinning out things too finely.

43 Based on OECD data. See Organization for Economic Cooperation and Development, *Economic Outlook,* no. 17 (July 1973): 56, table 21.

44   See Herbert Giersch, "Arbeit, Lohn, und Productivität," *Weltwirtschaftliches Archiv* 119, (1983): 1–18, and the empirical literature quoted there, and "Prospects for the World Economy," *Skandinaviska Enskilda Banken Quarterly Review*, 1982, 104–10.

45   "Secondary" meant that the primary cause was some initial shock that was supposed to have triggered the deflationary spiral. This is certainly a possible explanation, keeping in mind what Milton Friedman and Anna Schwartz say in their classic *Monetary History of the United States 1867–1960* (Princeton: Princeton University Press for the National Bureau of Economic Research, 1963) that small events may have large consequences since there are such things as chain reactions and cumulative forces.

46   See *Adjustment, Trade, and Growth in Developed and Developing Countries*, General Agreement on Tariffs and Trade, Studies in International Trade, no. 6 (Geneva, 1978); and *Positive Adjustment Policies: Managing Structural Change* (Paris: Organization for Economic Cooperation and Development, 1983).

47   This negative judgment also applies to the so-called tax-oriented incomes policy (TIP), which substitutes tax incentives and deterrents for absolute controls. TIP would be an administrative nightmare; for that reason it has never been tried. Wage and price "freezes" have been tried, but never with success. For a more detailed criticism of these policies, see my *Economic Growth and Stability: An Analysis of Economic Change and Policies* (New York: Nash, 1974), and "Reflections on the U.S. Trade Deficit and the Floating Dollar," in *Contemporary Economic Problems 1978* (Washington, D.C.: American Enterprise Institute, 1978), pp. 233–38, "A Digression on Inflation."

48   For an exhaustive discussion of these problems, see Simon Rottenberg, ed., *The Economics of Legal Minimum Wages* (Washington, D.C.: American Enterprise Institute, 1981); and Masanori Hashimoto, *Minimum Wages and On-the-Job Training* (Washington, D.C.: American Enterprise Institute, 1981).

49   See John P. Gould and George Bittlingmayer, *The Economics of the Davis-Bacon Act: An Analysis of Prevailing Wage Laws* (Washington, D.C.: American Enterprise Institute, 1980).

6   The Inflation Tax

J. Harold McClure, Jr., and Thomas D. Willett

Economists have long been interested in the inflation tax as a source of government revenue, and a substantial literature has developed on the subject. While much of this literature is quite technical, the basic ideas involved are straightforward. One strand of the literature implicitly or explicitly assumes a government facing little or no democratic check on its inflationary propensities and investigates what rates of inflation would maximize a government's revenues.[1] Another strand assumes a benevolent dictatorship or an efficient democratic check and focuses on so-called optimal rates of inflation, where optimality is defined in terms of minimizing the efficiency costs of financing government expenditures.[2]

Insights from the Inflation Tax Literature

While we believe that the tax aspects of inflation have probably received disproportionate attention from economists and are typically only a minor part of the explanation of the inflationary propensities of the industrial countries during the postwar period, we argue in the following section that this body of literature does provide a number of useful insights into the inflationary process. We then go on to argue, however, that by focusing on perfectly anticipated inflation, this literature has contributed to a highly exaggerated view of the benefits of inflation relative to the costs. Taking into account that real-world inflation is not steady and that higher average rates of inflation have tended historically to generate more uncertainty, we find that calculations of efficient levels of inflation are drastically lowered, usually to zero. Thus we conclude that the conflict between economists' gut instincts that high inflation rates are quite costly and the estimates from the technical academic literature that "efficient" rates of inflation were often in the double-digit range was due to serious deficiencies in the models used to calculate such optimal inflation rates.

Difficulties in Traditional Calculations of Optimal Rates of Inflation

Most of this literature has focused on steady-state, fully anticipated rates of inflation. Where the payment of interest on money holdings is prohibited or regulated so that interest rates do not adjust to changes in inflation, then inflation acts as a tax on cash balances. Higher rates of inflation increase the cost of holding money and thus reduce the quantity demanded. This gives rise to the concept of the revenue-maximizing rate of inflation, that at which the additional gain in revenues from nominal money expansion is just offset by the reduction in the demand for real money holdings generated by the consequent inflation. Long before the Laffer curve depicting maximum revenue explicit tax rates was popularized, this concept had been standardly applied in the inflation tax literature. This literature has shown the commonsense propositions that the revenue-maximizing rate of inflation will be higher when the demand for money is steeper (i.e., less interest-elastic), the domestic growth rate less rapid, and the real rate of interest lower.

Writings from a public interest standpoint stress that revenue maximization is not an appropriate goal for a government interested in promoting economic efficiency. This literature argues that the inefficiency cost of reduced money holdings should be taken into account and shows that efficient government financing requires equalizing the marginal efficiency costs of all different forms of government financing.[3]

This literature points to a number of interesting conclusions. It shows that welfare maximizing or efficient levels of inflation will lie well below revenue-maximizing rates of inflation, but that they in general will not be zero. From this perspective optimal rates of inflation will be higher, the higher is the level of government expenditure and the higher are the marginal costs of other forms of taxation. These considerations may help explain why substantial increases in government expenditures during wartime are usually accompanied by increased inflation, even though increased government expenditures could be financed in a non-inflationary manner through higher taxes.[4] They may also help explain why many developing countries with relatively underdeveloped and inefficient tax systems tend to have higher rates of inflation than most industrial countries with well-developed tax systems. It may even help explain why Italy, with its citizens' notorious propensity for tax evasion, has tended to have one of the highest rates of inflation among the industrial countries.

In general, however, with the exception of helping to explain the inflation typically accompanying rapid increases in government expenditures, we do not believe that such revenue considerations have played a major part in explaining the inflationary experiences of the industrial countries. Table 6.1 shows that actual seigniorage gains average around only one percent of GNP for the industrial countries, although for some countries such as Italy the figure is a good bit higher.[5] Table 6.2 uses high and low estimates of the interest elasticity of money demand and the implied revenue-maximizing rate of inflation. In general we do not find a strong correlation across the industrial countries between actual inflation rates and traditional calculation of optimal inflation rates.

Indeed, in general we find that actual average rates of inflation in the industrial countries over the past several decades have fallen considerably below many of the calculations of optimal rates of inflation. At first

Table 6.1 Average Percentage of GNP Captured by Monetary Growth, 1961–85

	Monetary base	M1 concept of money
Canada	0.44%	1.34%
France	0.64	2.31
Germany	0.62	1.08
Italy	2.21	5.90
Japan	0.94	3.31
United Kingdom	0.47	1.31
United States	0.40	1.05

Source: International Financial Statistics tape.
Note: Figures are annual change in nominal monetary series divided by gross national product.

Table 6.2   Revenue-Maximizing Inflation Rates (π^*) under Low and High
Estimates of Money Demand Semielasticity (β)

	Low elasticity estimate			High elasticity estimate			Average inflation
	Elasticity	Implied $\hat{\beta}$	$\pi^* = 1/\hat{\beta}$	Elasticity	Implied $\hat{\beta}$	$\pi^* = 1/\hat{\beta}$	1961–85
Canada	0.06	0.81	123.5%	0.30	4.04	24.8%	5.81%
France	0.19	2.32	43.1	0.21	2.56	39.1	7.42
Germany	0.07	1.28	78.1	0.35	6.40	15.6	3.85
Italy	0.41	3.02	33.1	0.41	3.02	33.1	9.92
Japan	0.10	1.31	76.3	0.34	4.45	22.5	6.51
United Kingdom	0.27	3.22	31.1	0.66	7.88	12.7	8.60
United States	0.04	0.62	161.3	0.24	3.70	27.0	5.35

Notes: Source of elasticity estimates is James Boughton, "The Demand for Money in Major OECD Countries," *OECD Economic Outlook: Occasional Studies*, 1979, 35–57, who reports only one study for Italy. Implied β is calculated as elasticity divided by average short-term interest rate for 1961–85.

thought this would seem to present strong evidence against the arguments presented in several chapters of this volume that we have suffered from the operation of various inflationary biases. Instead, however, we believe that such calculations substantially overestimated desirable rates of inflation.

One consideration, which has been stressed only in recent literature, is that with fractional reserve banking systems such as exist in most countries, government revenues from money creation will be substantially lower than in calculations which ascribed government seigniorage to the full money stock.[6] Such fractional reserve banking need not affect the revenue-maximizing rate of inflation, but as is illustrated in table 6.3, it substantially reduces optimal rates of inflation.

A more fundamental qualification concerns the measure of the costs of inflation used. The optimal inflation tax literature has mirrored much of the technical economic literature of the last several decades which ascribed relatively low costs to inflation. By focusing on the efficiency costs of perfectly anticipated inflation, this literature assumes away the most important economic costs of inflation, the uncertainty and unpredictability which it generates, with the consequent increase in economic miscalculations and diminution in the effectiveness of the operation of the price

Table 6.3   Welfare-Maximizing Inflation Rates

	M1/ Monetary Base (Z)	Standard calculation of optimal inflation	Revised calculation with fractional reserve
Canada	2.52	13.7%	6.8%
France	2.92	13.6	6.0
Germany	1.54	8.7	6.4
Italy	2.56	11.0	5.4
Japan	3.59	11.6	4.2
United Kingdom	2.50	6.0	3.0
United States	2.73	15.4	7.2

Note: These optimal inflation rates are calculated as $(MC/\beta)/(Z+MC)$, where *MC* is the marginal cost of taxation taken to be 0.5 and β is the average of the high and low values in table 6.2.

system. There is a considerable body of evidence suggesting that, on average, higher rates of inflation tend to be more variable and less pre-dictable.[7] As Logue and Willett pointed out,[8] to the extent that such a relationship exists, taking the uncertainty and variability costs of inflation into account will substantially lower welfare-maximizing rates of infla-tion. Recently several estimates of these costs have been made for the United States.[9] Including these in optimal inflation rate calculations, we find that for countries like the United States the public interest efficiency case for a substantial positive rate of inflation disappears. For example, using conservative estimates of the output effects for the United States we find that this consideration lowers the optimal rate of inflation from the double-digit range to only 1 percent.[10]

Other Sources of Government Revenue Gains

Apart from direct seigniorage, two other forms of possible gains for gov-ernment revenue have been emphasized. One is the gains from bracket creep. With progressive taxation and no indexation, inflation will force individuals into ever-higher tax brackets even though their real income remains unchanged. This can provide a sizable source of government revenue and has caused some economists such as Milton Friedman to strongly urge indexation not only to promote economic efficiency but also to diminish the government's incentives for inflationary finance.[11] We doubt that this has been a major cause of the propensity to inflate in the United States. Typically legislators have responded to bracket creep by periodically cutting nominal tax lines in a loose form of longer-run index-ation. Thus it seems unlikely that there has not been at least some modest contribution to inflationary tendencies from this source.

Another potential source of government revenue comes from un-anticipated inflation.[12] This will increase seigniorage gains because the real quantity of money demanded does not fall as much. Furthermore, unanticipated inflation redistributes wealth from lenders to borrowers.[13] In this regard the U.S. government was a major gainer during the 1960s and 1970s. While inflation rose substantially over this period, most stud-ies find that on average actual inflation was higher than anticipated. Table 6.4 uses the difference between actual inflation and the Livingston series on expected inflation multiplied by the government debt as an estimate of this transfer of wealth. Note that this transfer exceeded $30 billion for 1978.

Table 6.4   U.S. Government Debt Transfers from Unexpected Inflation

	Actual inflation	Expected inflation	Unexpected inflation	Government debt in billions $	Implied transfer
1969	5.37	1.09	4.28	381.22	15.89
1970	4.86	1.18	3.67	400.82	14.00
1971	4.58	1.94	2.64	434.35	10.60
1972	4.17	2.35	1.82	460.24	7.92
1973	6.85	2.90	3.95	480.66	18.19
1974	9.68	3.38	6.30	503.99	30.29
1975	7.40	3.56	3.84	587.58	19.34
1976	4.55	3.51	1.04	664.79	6.10
1977	5.93	3.40	2.53	729.16	16.81
1978	8.14	4.59	3.55	797.69	25.86
1979	7.84	7.42	0.42	852.18	3.37
1980	9.68	5.74	3.94	936.69	33.58
1981	8.57	5.26	3.30	1,034.72	30.94
1982	4.17	5.96	− 1.79	1,201.90	− 18.55

Notes: Actual inflation is the percentage change in the GNP deflator. The government debt is the December value from the previous year. Both series are taken from the Citibase tape. Expected inflation is the average of the two semiannual data from the Livingston survey.

During disinflationary periods such as the early 1980s, just the reverse occurs. A sizable portion of the high real interest rates and increasing budget deficits of this period were the legacy of the unanticipated inflation and corresponding low and often negative ex post real interest rates of the previous decade. For 1982 table 4 shows an estimate of a negative $18 billion. Here we see another example of how inflation generates reactions which increase incentives for its continuation. In terms of political business cycle theory, even the inflation which occurs after the election from preelection expansion will have some favorable side effects for the government. The shorter the government's time horizon (i.e., the higher its discount rate) and the more slowly the public's expectations adjust to changing rates of inflation, the greater are the incentives to engage in such inflationary finance. Thus we see another channel through which a short time horizon in the political process can contribute to inflationary pressures.

Notes

1 Milton Friedman, "Government Revenue from Inflation," *Journal of Political Economy* 79 (July/August 1971): 846–56; and Geoffrey Brennan and James Buchanan, *The Power to Tax* (Cambridge: Cambridge University Press, 1980).

2 Martin J. Bailey, "The Welfare Cost of Inflationary Finance," *Journal of Political Economy* 64 (April 1956): 93–110, was the seminal paper, with the marginal conditions developed by Edward Tower, "More on the Welfare Cost of Inflationary Finance," *Journal of Money, Credit, and Banking* 4 (November 1971): 850–60, and Robert Gordon, "The Demand for and Supply of Inflation," *Journal of Law and Economics* 18 (December 1975): 807–36.

3 Efficiency also requires that the marginal benefit of government spending equals this marginal cost. Pushing any tax to its Laffer limit is therefore inefficient unless the marginal benefit of government spending is infinite. One rationale for the Reagan plan to cut taxes and monetary growth may be based upon a notion that these marginal benefits are below the marginal costs of taxation and inflationary finance. Of course, the only plan consistent with long-run equilibrium would be to cut government spending by more than the cut in tax revenues.

4 While seigniorage concerns may help explain the inflationary effects of the Vietnam War, we believe much more important was President Johnson's reluctance to raise taxes on political grounds combined with the concern by the Federal Reserve about high interest rates, which induced them to accommodate a considerable portion of the resulting budget deficits with monetary expansion.

5 For additional calculations including a number of developing countries, see Stanley

Fischer, "Seigniorage and the Case for a National Money," *Journal of Political Economy* 90 (April 1982): 295–313.

6 See, for example, J. Harold McClure, Jr., "Welfare Maximizing Inflation Rates under Fractional Reserve Banking with and without Deposit Rate Ceilings," *Journal of Money, Credit, and Banking* 18 (May 1986): 233–38; and Jeremy Siegel, "Inflation, Bank Profits, and Government Seigniorage," *American Economic Review* 71 (May 1981): 352–55.

7 A useful recent survey of this literature is given in Steven Holland, "Does Higher Inflation Lead to More Uncertain Inflation?" Federal Reserve Bank of St. Louis *Review*, February 1984, 15–26.

8 Dennis Logue and Thomas D. Willett, "A Note on the Relation between the Rate and Variability of Inflation," *Economica* 43 (May 1976): 151–58.

9 For discussion and references to this literature, see Deborah Frohman, Leroy O. Laney, and Thomas D. Willett, "Uncertainty Costs of High Inflation," *Voice* of the Federal Reserve Bank of Dallas, July 1981, 1–9. We should note that not all economists argue that the uncertainty costs of higher rates of inflation are substantial. For a dissenting view, see Stanley Fischer, "The Benefits of Price Stability," in *Price Stability and Public Policy* (Symposium sponsored by the Federal Reserve Bank of Kansas City, Jackson Hole, Wyo., August 2–3, 1984), pp. 33–50.

10 In our "Inflation Uncertainty and the Optimal and Revenue-maximizing Inflation Taxes" Claremont Center for Economic Policy Studies Working Paper (Claremont Graduate School, 1986), we derive the optimum inflation rate to be:

$$\frac{mc - f(1 + t \cdot mc)}{(1 + mc)(\beta + f)}$$

where β is the interest semielasticity of money demand (taken to be -2.5), f is the Friedman effect, t is the income tax rate (let $t = 0.2$), and MC is the marginal cost of explicit taxation (let $MC = 0.56$). If f is set at zero, then optimal inflation is 14 percent, while if $f = -0.1$, then optimal inflation is 1 percent.

11 He also discusses the transfers from unanticipated inflation when the nominal interest rate on government bonds does not rise with inflation. See Milton Friedman and Rose Friedman, *Free to Choose* (New York: Harcourt Brace Jovanovich, 1980), chap. 9.

12 For example, see Leonardo Auernheimer, "The Revenue-Maximizing Inflation Rate and the Treatment of the Transition to Equilibrium," *Journal of Money, Credit, and Banking* 15 (August 1983): 368–78; Harry Johnson, "A Note on the Dishonest Government and the Inflation Tax," *Journal of Political Economy* 3 (July 1977): 375–77; and Brennan and Buchanan, *Power to Tax*.

13 Franco Modigliani and Lucas Papademos, "Optimal Demand Policies against Inflation," *Weltwirtschaftliches Archiv*, 1978, 736–82, suggest that private financial wealth is about 1.5 times nominal GNP in the United States, so that each point of unexpected inflation represents transfers of 15 percent of GNP. In terms of a $4 trillion economy, this transfer would be almost $60 billion. It should be noted, however, that most households and firms are both creditors and debtors so that part of this transfer cancels out.

It also should be noted that the standard optimal inflation tax approach, including that presented here, must assume that monetary services enter directly into utility functions. As is stressed in the general theory of optimal taxation, taxes should not be levied on intermediate products. Thus in theories where money is treated only as a constraint or intermediate product, the optimal inflation tax is zero. On the general theory of optimal taxation, see Peter A. Diamond and James A. Mirrlees, "Optimal Taxation and Public Production, I: Production Efficiency, and II: Tax Rules," *American Economic Review* 61 (1971): 8–27, 261–78. For applications to optimal taxes on money balances, see Ira N. Gang and Edward Tower, "Differential Cash-in-Advance Constraints: A Good Reason for Protection in LDCs?" *Eastern Africa Economic Review* 2, no. 2 (1986): 193–95; and Kent P. Kimbrough, "The Optimum Quantity of Money Rule in the Theory of Public Finance," *Journal of Monetary Economics* 18 (1986): 277–84.

7 The Decline of Gold as a Source of U.S. Monetary Discipline

John Briggs, D. B. Christenson,
Pamela Martin, and Thomas D. Willett

The decline of the role of gold in our monetary system is often seen as a major cause of the secular rise in average rates of inflation over the past century. Some have gone even further and argued that the albeit limited role of gold in the postwar Bretton Woods international monetary system provided a major check against inflationary tendencies. A simple comparison of average rates of inflation for the decades before and after the breakdown of Bretton Woods supports this belief. We argue in this chapter, however, that such a conclusion is highly misleading. We present both institutional and statistical analysis to show that gold had no significant influence on U.S. monetary policy during the postwar period and did not constrain the buildup of inflationary pressures in the 1960s that contributed to the rapid rates of inflation of the 1970s.

This comparison of the pre– and post–Bretton Woods systems is only one of a number of episodes where judgments differ over whether particular monetary regimes should be considered as some form of gold standard. Such classifications are often made on the basis of a historical comparison of economic performance under gold and nongold monetary systems. Frequently it seems that advocates of gold classify ambiguous periods as being on gold if macroeconomic performance was good and off gold if it was poor. Critics of gold standards tend to do just the opposite. We suggest that a more appropriate method for classifying the "goldness" of monetary regimes is to consider the tightness of the linkage between gold reserves and the behavior of the domestic money supply.

Overview of the Nineteenth-Century Gold Standard

Looking at the heyday of the gold standard in the nineteenth century we do find a positive linkage between gold and the behavior of the U.S. money supply, but one which is much weaker than that implied by the classical rules of the game for the gold standard. Furthermore, prices did rise or fall for prolonged periods of time under the gold standard. Such developments were often the cause of a good deal more political controversy at the time than idealized accounts by advocates of gold typically acknowledge. Still, the Great Inflation and Great Deflation of the eighteen hundreds reflected average annual rates of price change which were quite low in comparison with the inflation of the last two decades.[1] Until the current century, gold standards, once adopted, displayed considerable durability and typically were abandoned only during wartime. Thus one can argue that gold-based monetary systems did succeed in that they were relatively successful in producing stable price expectations,[2] and that analyses which point to the decline in the discipline of gold as a major factor contributing to the inflation of the twentieth century have a sound basis.

Acceptance of this view does not, of course, logically imply that a return to gold would be desirable. Not only should one consider the costs as well as the benefits of a return to gold, but these should be weighed against the costs and benefits of alternative monetary systems. Furthermore, as the brief review in the Appendix suggests, there is good reason to believe that gold has in this century lost much of its magic as a disciplinary device. In the interwar period both the United States and the United Kingdom went off the gold standard without the presence of a wartime crisis, indicating that the strength of the political commitment to gold had waned substantially. The history of the U.S. commitment to gold during the postwar period was one of continual erosion in the strength of the formal linkages, terminating with President Nixon's breaking of the last ties to gold in his dramatic New Economic Policy of August 1971.

Pre- and Post-Bretton Woods Comparisons and the Classification of Monetary Regimes

Many of the proposals to return to gold envision linkages much less strong than those which obtained under the classical gold standard, but comparison of American postwar economic performance before and after 1971 suggests that even the weak ties to gold which the United States maintained under the Bretton Woods international monetary system had a desirable effect. The period after 1971 has recorded substantially higher rates of both inflation and unemployment than the earlier postwar period. Consequently, a number of economists have argued that cutting the last links to gold was a major contribution to the subsequent inflationary binge. For example, Robert Barro has argued that

> What is certainly clear is that before 1971 most economists under-estimated the extent to which the international system of fixed exchange rates with some role for gold served, although imperfectly, to restrain growth in the world money supply and thereby the world price level. Since the move in 1971 toward flexible exchange rates and the complete divorce of United States monetary management from the objective of a pegged gold price, it is clear that the nominal anchor for the monetary system—weak as it was earlier—is now entirely absent.[3]

While plausible on a priori grounds, such analysis is dead wrong. Where gold continues to play some statutory role in the monetary system, but the broad convertibility provisions of the classical gold standard are absent, it can be difficult to classify the degree of effective "goldness" from an analysis of the formal legal provisions alone, and there have been considerable differences in the way scholars have treated such intermediate gold systems.[4] In such circumstances, we suggest that the most effective way to classify periods is to study how closely gold holdings have influenced the behavior of the money supply, in other words, how closely the operation of the system has approximated that of the "rules of the game" of the classical gold standard under which the domestic money supply was supposed to rise or fall in line with changes in the gold holdings of the monetary authorities.

Nineteenth-Century U.S. Gold-Money Linkages

Earlier research focused quite heavily on the extent to which these rules were followed under the classical gold standard and found that the linkage between money supply behavior and gold was much weaker than had generally been supposed.[5] Interestingly, however, the strength of such linkages has received relatively little attention in much of the recent work on the gold standard, which has focused directly on the relationships between gold and prices.[6] The linkage for the United States was far from tight even during the 1879–1913 period of the gold standard.[7] As is shown in figures 7.1 and 7.2, there was considerable variability in both the ratio of high-powered money to gold and the ratio of the money supply to gold. Initially the money supply grew much less rapidly than gold stocks, leading to a fall in the money supply–gold multiplier from over 7 in 1879 to a little over 5 by 1888 (see figure 7.2). Then from the late 1880s to the mid-1890s the money supply grew much more rapidly than gold, with the multiplier rising to over 8 in 1895. For the rest of the century the multiplier fell to 7 in 1899, then rose in the early 1900s, peaking at 10.65 in 1906, then fell again to 7 in 1908. The money supply to gold ratio at the end of the gold standard period was at approximately the same level as its peak in the mid-1890s. This experience might be interpreted as a tendency for the money supply to be, on average, a multiple of seven to eight times the stock of gold with large fluctuations which tended to be reversed over a period of a decade or so. The number of cycles is too small, however, for us to be able to put great confidence in such a self-reversing property of large fluctuations in the money supply to gold ratio. Thus, the actual amount of monetary discipline exerted by gold over this period must remain an open question. Still, there was on average a positive relationship between changes in gold holdings and changes in the money stock.[8]

U.S. Gold-Money Linkages under Bretton Woods

For the postwar Bretton Woods period there is no such relationship, however. Nor did the balance of payments display any significant systematic influence on the behavior of the U.S. money supply. The international convertibility of the dollar into gold caused American officials considerable worry but had little influence on the actual course of monetary policy. This can be seen quite vividly in figure 7.3, which shows the ratio of the U.S. money supply (M2) to official gold holdings. What we see is a steady rise in the ratio with little tendency for changes to be reversed as would be necessary for the level of gold stocks to have a significant relation to the behavior of the money supply.[9] While this lack of relationship could have been due to the looseness in the relationship between U.S.

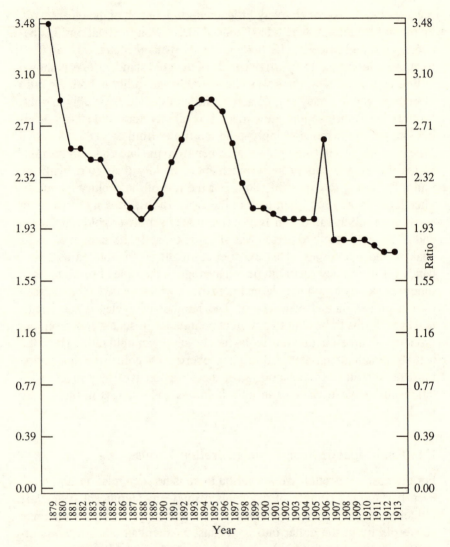

Figure 7.1   Ratio of U.S. High-Powered Money to Official Gold Stock, 1879–1913

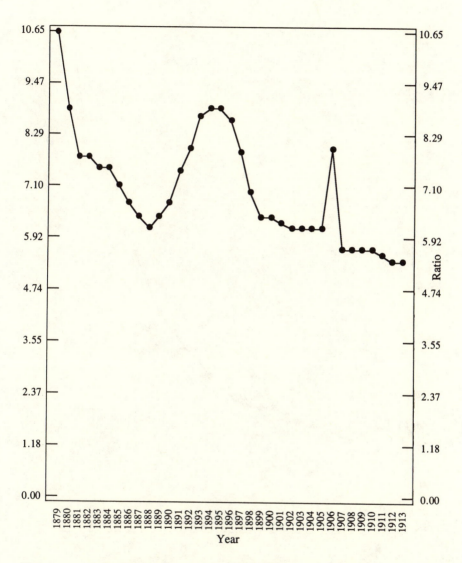

Figure 7.2   Ratio of U.S. Money to Official Gold Stock, 1879–1913

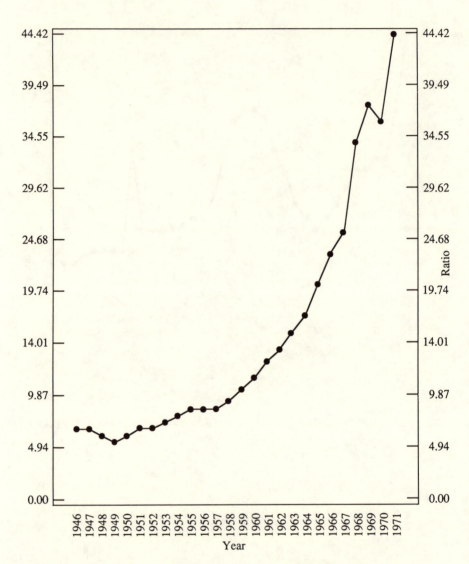

Figure 7.3   Ratio of U.S. Money Supply (M2) to Official Gold Stock, 1946–1971

balance of payments surpluses and deficits and gold flows, statistical analysis shows that the balance of payments did not have a systematic influence on the U.S. monetary supply either.[10] Worries about balance of payments deficits were reflected in a host of controls and other selective measures designed to reduce the deficit,[11] but the effects of payments imbalances on the domestic money supply were automatically sterilized, and only for short periods did international concerns contribute to tighter discretionary monetary policy. Indeed, international considerations appear to have played a stronger, although still typically weak, role in influencing American monetary policy since we moved to flexible exchange rates.[12]

Concluding Remarks

If anything, rather than providing discipline over American monetary policy, the Bretton Woods pegged exchange-rate system facilitated monetary accommodation by allowing the United States in the short run to export some of the inflationary consequences of its financing of the Vietnam War. The acceleration of inflation in the United States and in many European countries began while the Bretton Woods system was still in place.[13] This suggests that in the absence of direct mechanisms to control money growth, neither pegged exchange rates nor flexible gold trappings will by themselves provide an effective restraint on inflation.

Appendix: A Brief Review of the Role of Gold in U.S. Monetary Arrangements

An examination of the periods when the United States went off the gold standard shows that until the twentieth century the gold standard was suspended only in time of war. The adoption of a fiduciary standard in response to economic pressures or as a permanent standard was not seen until after World War I and perhaps reflects an increased concern with internal economic stability and a greater unwillingness to subordinate domestic goals to balance of payments considerations and international gold flows. In contrast, the major goal of economic policy before 1914 had been to maintain convertibility of the dollar at the legal parity.

The monetary history of the United States opened with the widespread issue of inconvertible paper currency to finance the Revolutionary

War and also the country's first and only hyperinflation. In 1792 a bimetallic standard fixing the value of the dollar in terms of silver and gold was adopted. The Mint Act fixed the price of gold at $19.39 an ounce; between 1834 and 1837 the price was gradually revised upward to $20.67. This price remained in effect until December 1861 when unbacked currency was issued to finance the Civil War and conversion of currency into specie was suspended. In 1873 the United States began implementing steps to restore convertibility. A de facto gold standard was instituted in January 1879, when gold convertibility for dollars was reestablished at the prewar price and the silver dollar was dropped from coinage. The Congress legislatively ratified this action with the Gold Standard Act of 1900. When the Federal Reserve system was established in 1914, its banks were required to back their notes and deposit liabilities with gold certificate reserves.[14]

The classical gold standard functioned until the outbreak of the First World War in 1914, when most of the major European countries went off the standard. The United States remained on a gold standard, but suspended foreign convertibility by forbidding the export of gold.

Successive decades saw gradual modifications of the gold standard in favor of greater flexibility and discretionary action. Even prior to 1914 many countries had held a mixed basket of the major gold-redeemable currencies as part of their reserve assets. The Gold Exchange Standard in 1925 substituted a similar gold standard in which the United States and Great Britain held gold reserves, but other countries were permitted to hold gold and dollars or pounds as reserves. The new standard differed from the old in that during the war most countries (except the United States) had withdrawn gold coins from circulation and gold holdings had been concentrated in the hands of the authorities. In Britain and other European nations the currency was now redeemable only in gold bullion of a minimum weight, in effect limiting the use of gold to official international settlements. In addition, nations frequently engaged in substantial sterilization to protect their domestic money supplies from the effects of gold flows. The Gold Exchange Standard lasted only until 1931, when chronic gold outflows forced Great Britain off the standard and the international economy entered a decade and a half of managed money.[15]

These years saw a retreat from the discipline of gold in the United States as well. The United States maintained full convertibility until March 1933, when the government suspended convertibility completely.

The use of gold in private domestic transactions was made illegal and gold coinage discontinued, but in February 1934 gold convertibility was restored for foreign monetary authorities following the devaluation of the dollar to $35 per ounce. Even this level of convertibility was not mandated by law, but was an administrative decision on the part of the Treasury. A more basic change was that after 1934 gold reserves were no longer allowed to influence the money supply.[16] Under the Banking Act of 1934, gold reserve requirements for the Federal Reserve banks were set at 35 percent against deposit liabilities and 40 percent against outstanding notes. In 1945 reserve requirements were reduced to 25 percent for both notes and deposits.

In 1944 President Truman restored gold-dollar convertibility, which had been suspended during the war. The Bretton Woods agreement taking effect in 1946 established an international payments system in which the dollar was held as the key reserve currency. Under the agreement only the United States accepted the obligation to hold gold reserves and convert foreign official dollar holdings at a fixed price for gold. Other currencies were pegged directly to the dollar and indirectly to gold through a system of fixed, but adjustable, exchange rates. These countries held convertible dollars as part of their monetary reserves and used dollars to settle transactions among themselves. Such a system required the United States to maintain sufficient gold reserves to ensure convertibility for the worldwide stock of dollars at the official price of $35. Equality of the official and private-market price in London was maintained by sales from or additions to the gold reserves as necessary. Maintenance of this price equality became increasingly difficult in the 1960s as the United States' balance of payments deficits mounted. Reduced American gold reserves and the rapid growth of dollar assets held abroad led foreign governments to convert increasing quantities of dollars into gold and to question the future ability or willingness of the United States to redeem dollars on demand. Indeed, the loss of confidence abroad and the need to slow the depletion of American gold reserves in the last years of the Bretton Woods era forced the U.S. government to press foreign monetary agencies not to convert their dollar holdings into gold.[17]

As economic pressures mounted through the 1960s, the tie to gold was further loosened. In March 1965 the gold reserve requirement against the Federal Reserve banks' deposit liabilities was eliminated, and gold backing for Federal Reserve notes was dropped in March 1968. In that year the United States and the other major industrial nations ceased selling in the London gold pool, thereby abandoning the effort to peg the private market price of gold at the official price. Thereafter, a two-tier system was adopted in which the official price was maintained for official transactions only and the private gold price was left to find its own level. By this time the low level of American gold reserves relative to official liabilities had rendered the dollar de facto inconvertible for large conversions by major countries. The worsening trade performance of the United States in the 1960s had by 1971 also resulted in congressional pressure for a devaluation of the dollar to improve the competitiveness of American exports. A report released on August 7, 1971, by the Joint Congressional Economic Subcommittee on Exchange and Payments recommended exchange rate adjustments and unilateral devaluation by the United States if necessary. This triggered massive speculative selling of the dollar in anticipation of devaluation.

On August 15 President Nixon announced the United States would no longer convert foreign-held dollars into gold, stating that "the time has come for exchange rates to be set straight" and citing the necessity to "take action . . . to defend the dollar against speculators."[18] As a consequence of the American renunciation of its convertibility obligation, foreign nations were no longer obligated to peg their currencies to the dollar. In December of the same year the official price of gold was raised to $38 as a part of the Smithsonian agreement to realign exchange rates. March 1973 saw the exchange rates of the major industrial countries set afloat and the final breakdown of the Bretton Woods system, signaling the end of a monetary role for gold.[19] There were efforts to produce a new, highly structured international monetary system based on convertibility into SDRs, the new international reserve instrument created in the late 1960s, but these proved to be in vain and the Jamaican Agreement of 1977 ratified the new system of flexible exchange rates.[20]

Notes

1 Michael Bordo has examined the stability of prices and real output in the United States and Great Britain for the period 1800–1979. He finds that the period before 1914 was characterized by long-run price stability, the period between the wars showed substantial deflation, and the post-World War II years persistent inflation. He concludes that long-run price stability was greater under the gold standard, but

at a cost to short-run real output, and short-run price stability was less. See Michael Bordo, "The Gold Standard: Myths and Realities," in *Money in Crisis,* ed. Barry Siegel (Cambridge, Mass.: Ballinger, 1984), pp. 197–237. Also see Alan Reynolds, "Why Gold?" *Cato Journal* 3 (Spring 1983): 211–32. For opposing viewpoints see Edward Bernstein, "Back to the Gold Standard?" *Brookings Bulletin* 17 (Fall 1980): 8–12; and Richard N. Cooper, "The Gold Standard: Historical Fact and Future Prospects," *Brookings Papers on Economic Activity* 1 (1982): 1–45.

2 There is some question whether market participants tended to expect price level changes to reverse themselves over time. See, for example, the contrasting analysis and conclusions drawn by Cooper, "Gold Standard," and Benjamin Klein, "Our New Monetary Standard: The Measurement and Effects of Price Uncertainty, 1800–1973," *Economic Inquiry* 13 (December 1975): 461–84. Clearly, however, rates of price change were not widely expected to continue for substantial periods as became the case with the escalating inflation of the 1960s and 1970s.

3 Robert Barro, "United States Inflation and the Choice of Monetary Standard," in *Inflation: Causes and Effects,* ed. Robert Hall (Chicago: University of Chicago Press, 1982), p. 105. For similar statements, see Samuel Brittain, "Inflation and Democracy," in *The Political Economy of Inflation,* ed. Fred Hirsch and John H. Goldthorpe (Cambridge: Harvard University Press, 1978), pp. 177–78; and James M. Buchanan and Richard E. Wagner, *Democracy in Deficit: The Political Legacy of Lord Keynes* (New York: Academic Press, 1977), pp. 71–72, 121–22.

4 While there is general agreement in classifying the period from 1879 to World War I as a gold standard, the following years saw a gradual removal of the constraints of the gold system and the wider adoption of discretionary monetary management. As a result, the end of the gold standard is pegged at different points. Richard Cooper uses World War II as his dividing point and Michael Bordo the termination of the Bretton Woods agreement. Benjamin Klein divides the years from 1880 to 1972 into three periods—a gold standard era from 1880 to 1915, a transitional period from 1916 to 1955, and a new standard since 1956. William Fellner defines a gold standard simply as the maintenance by monetary authorities of equality between a fixed official price and the private market price of gold. By this definition the United States was on a gold standard with the price of gold fixed at $20.67 from 1879 until March 1933, and again on one from February 1934, when the price of gold was fixed at $35 an ounce, until 1968. See Cooper, "Gold Standard"; Bordo, "Gold Standard"; Klein, "New Monetary Standard"; and William Fellner, "Gold and the Uneasy Case for Responsibly Managed Fiat Money," in *Essays in Contemporary Economic Problems: Demand, Productivity, and Population* (Washington, D.C.: American Enterprise Institute, 1981).

5 See, for example, Arthur I. Bloomfield, *Monetary Policy under the International Gold Standard* (New York: Federal Reserve Bank of New York, 1959); idem, *Short-Term Capital Movements under the Pre-1914 Gold Standard,* Princeton Studies in International Finance, no. 11 (Princeton: Princeton University Press, 1963); and Leland Yeager, *International Monetary Relations: Theory, History and Policy* (New York: Harper and Row, 1976), pp. 302, 306–7, 332–34.

6 See, for example, Bordo, "Gold Standard."

7 Despite the empirical evidence on the looseness of the relationship between the size of gold reserves and money supply behavior under the gold standard, most of the theoretical models of the gold standard have assumed a fixed relationship. For a recent exception which stresses the role of discretionary monetary policy, see Gertrud M. Fremling, "A Specie Flow Model of the Gold Standard," *Journal of International Money and Finance* 5 (March 1986): 37–55. For discussion of the looseness of the gold–money supply linkage under the pre–Civil War gold standard in the United States in the absence of a central bank, see Thomas D. Willett, "International Specie Flows and American Monetary Stability, 1834–1860," *Journal of Economic History,* March 1968, 28–50.

8 Regressions of high-powered money on gold and money on gold reveal that there was a positive relationship between gold and both high-powered money and money (money is M2, i.e., currency held by the public plus adjusted deposits at all commercial banks, less large negotiable CDs since 1961) during the gold standard era (1879–1913). However, the relationship weakens somewhat when we go from high-powered money to money. Because of the inherent problems with time series regressions done in levels (spurious correlations, growth over time, and possible third variable influences), the regressions were also run with changes and growth rates. This did not vitiate the results of a positive relationship between gold and the money supply for the gold standard era, but the strength of the relationship was much lower than we would expect from the discussion of figures 7.1 and 7.2 presented in the text. These regression results are available upon request from the Claremont Center for Economic Policy Studies, Claremont Graduate School, Claremont, Calif. 91711. Data sources for these regressions and the charts in the text are as follows: high-powered money and the money supply come from Milton Friedman and Anna J. Schwartz, *Monetary Trends in the United States and the United Kingdom* (Chicago: University of Chicago Press, 1982), pp. 122–29, table 4.8; and the monetary stock of gold comes from U.S. Bureau of the Census, *Historical Statistics of the United States, Colonial Times to 1970,* Bicentennial ed., pt. 2, ser. X417 (Washington, D.C.: U.S. Government Printing Office, 1976).

9 Regressions of high-powered money on gold and money on gold for the postwar era (1946–1971) actually indicate a slightly negative (though statistically insignificant) relationship between gold and both measures of money. What was happening during this period, especially during the latter part, was that the money supply was growing rapidly and there were slight drains on the gold stock from conversions. This led to the slightly negative relationship between gold and money during these years.

10 See the statistical results in chapter 8 of this volume. Similar results are found by Michael Darby, "The United States as an Exogenous Source of World Inflation under the Bretton Woods System," in *The International Transmission of Inflation,* ed. Michael Darby et al. (Chicago: University of Chicago Press, 1983), pp. 478–90.

11 For discussion of these measures, see Gottfried Haberler and Thomas D. Willett, *U.S. Balance of Payments Policies and International Monetary Reform: A Critical Analysis* (Washington, D.C.: American Enterprise Institute, 1968).

12 The tightening of U.S. monetary policy in response to the plunge of the dollar in the late 1970s is an example. See, for example, the discussion in Steven W. Kohlhagen,

"The Experience with Floating: The 1973–1979 Dollar," in *The International Monetary System: A Time of Turbulence,* ed. Jacob Dreyer, Gottfried Haberler, and Thomas D. Willett (Washington, D.C.: American Enterprise Institute, 1982), pp. 142–79. W. Douglas McMillin has found evidence of Granger-causality from the dollar devaluation on Federal Reserve behavior in the same period. See McMillin, "Federal Deficits, Macrostabilization Goals, and Federal Reserve Behavior," *Economic Inquiry,* April 1986, 257–69.

13 See the discussion in chapters 1, 3, and 8 of this volume.

14 For a history of the gold standard, see Leland Yeager, *International Monetary Relations: Theory, History, and Policy* (New York: Harper and Row, 1976), chaps. 15–17, and the references cited there.

15 Sweden, Norway, and Denmark left the gold standard within a week of Britain. Between 1929 and 1933 over thirty countries worldwide were driven off gold. The currencies of the major European nations still tied to gold maintained their existing parity until 1935. Between 1935 and 1939 France, Belgium, Switzerland, and the Netherlands devalued or went off the gold standard. See Yeager, *Monetary Relations,* pp. 341–76, and Arthur Bloomfield, "Gold Standard," in *Encyclopedia of Economics,* ed. Douglas Greenwald (New York: McGraw-Hill, 1981), p. 452.

16 For a description of U.S. monetary policy in the 1930s, see Cooper, "Gold Standard," pp. 9–10, and Yeager, *Monetary Relations,* pp. 346–56.

17 See Yeager, *Monetary Relations,* p. 575, for the details of this de facto end of convertibility. Also see Thomas D. Willett and Lawrence H. Officer, "Reserve Asset Preferences and the Confidence Problem in the Crisis Zone," *Quarterly Journal of Economics,* November 1969, 688–95; and idem, "The Interaction of Adjustment and Gold-Conversion Policies in a Reserve-Currency System," *Western Economic Journal,* March 1970, 47–60.

18 *New York Times,* August 15, 1971, 1, 14.

19 For a discussion of the events leading to the breakdown of the Bretton Woods system, see Yeager, *Monetary Relations,* chaps. 27–28; and Thomas D. Willett, *Floating Rates and International Monetary Reform* (Washington, D.C.: American Enterprise Institute, 1977), chap. 1.

20 For discussions of these reform negotiations see John Williamson, *The Failure of World Monetary Reform, 1971–1974* (New York: New York University Press, 1977); and Willett, *Floating Rates,* chap. 3.

8 Inflation Hypotheses and Monetary Accommodation: Postwar Evidence from the Industrial Countries

Thomas D. Willett, King Banaian,
Leroy O. Laney, Mohand Merzkani,
and Arthur D. Warga

One can find a number of explanations for the substantial worsening of inflation that occurred in the major industrial countries beginning in the late 1960s and early 1970s. It was commonplace during and following this period to encounter both formal and informal analyses attributing the surging inflation rate to some single cause. Wage-push explanations were prevalent in the late 1960s, especially in Europe, followed by interpretations relying on commodity price increases and international reserve explosions in the early 1970s.[1] Shortly thereafter the two oil price shocks led many writers to look toward supply shocks as explanations of inflation. The advent of flexible exchange rates in 1973 revived arguments that depreciating exchange rates put upward pressure on domestic prices. Finally, the development of large public sector fiscal deficits in most industrial countries in the 1970s widened internationally the concerns about the inflationary effects of budget deficits, which had already begun in the United States with the Vietnam deficits in the mid- and late 1960s.[2]

Various schools of economic thought have offered different analytical explanations of the inflationary process. Almost all economists, however, would agree that substantial inflation is a monetary phenomenon in the sense that inflationary pressures must be accommodated by monetary expansion. Private sector behavior can cause changes in velocity and money multipliers which make control of any particular measure of the money supply difficult in the very short run for monetary authorities, and the money stock might not precisely determine aggregate spending over longer periods. Still, the monetary authorities in most industrial countries are capable of controlling the average annual rate of monetary growth within fairly tight limits if they so choose, and monetary targets can in turn be adjusted to offset any sustained shifts in velocity.[3] Thus differences in average rates of monetary expansion are by far the single most important explanation of differences in average rates of inflation across countries and over time.[4] This view leaves open, however, the important question of what actually determines the behavior of the monetary authorities.[5] There is substantial disagreement among researchers over this point.

Traditionally, monetarists have tended to stress the role of government spending and budget deficits, while British Keynesians and American post-Keynesians have tended to focus on the role of cost-push factors, particularly wages and import prices.[6] The monetary accommodation of import price increases has also been emphasized in discussions of the inflationary impact of oil price hikes and in debates about the alleged vicious circle of inflation and currency depreciation under flexible exchange rates.[7] Writers known collectively as global or international monetarists, on the other hand, have stressed the role of international reserve increases in stimulating worldwide inflation.[8] There have been many adherents to Robert Triffin's conclusion that the international liquidity explosion in the early 1970s associated with the breakdown of the Bretton Woods international monetary system was "undoubtedly the biggest factor in triggering the worst global inflation in history."[9]

In this chapter we investigate the extent to which there is empirical support for these various single-factor explanations of inflation. We include measures for each of these four types of inflationary pressures in regression equations explaining annual rates of monetary growth for most major industrial countries over the past three decades. We place particular emphasis on the distinctions between initiating and sustaining aspects of wage-push pressures and between the actual and full employment budget deficits as sources of pressure for monetary accommodation.

There was considerable variability in the behavior of monetary authorities and their governments from country to country and over time. None of these popular single-factor explanations were dominant across countries and time periods, suggesting that one should regard with suspicion claims that the monetary authorities must systematically accommodate some particular type of inflationary shock. Considerable caution should be exercised in interpretation of the specific results, because they were often sensitive to the choice of time periods, proxy variables, and the particular specification used. However, there was sufficient evidence to suggest that monetary authorities often do succumb to the incentives to accommodate various pressures. We also found in general that despite the greatly increased focus in recent years on international causes of inflationary pressures, domestic pressures received greater amounts of monetary accommodation in the industrial countries.[10]

The Basic Equations

In this section the rationale underlying the four hypothesized causes of inflation under investigation are presented. Most recent analyses of the international transmission of inflationary pressures have focused on two major channels. One channel traces the effects of changes in international reserves on domestic money supplies. Keynesian analysis has traditionally assumed that monetary authorities typically sterilize (neutralize) the effects of reserve flows on domestic money supplies by taking offsetting actions. This view is supported by a number of empirical studies. Analysis based on the monetary approach to the balance of payments generally assumes that because of high international capital mobility, monetary authorities are typically unable to effectively sterilize reserve flows. Even if they can neutralize reserve flows, concern about avoiding prolonged payments disequilibrium will keep the authorities from following persistent sterilization. Thus in this view the modern international monetary system operates much like a gold standard, with balance of payments deficits (reserve declines) leading to domestic monetary contraction, and payments surpluses (reserve increases) stimulating monetary expansion. Consistent sterilization of reserve flows, on the other hand, would lead to little correlation between reserve flows and the monetary aggregates.

The second major channel of imported inflation concerns direct price effects. Under pegged exchange rates, foreign inflation will bid up the prices of a country's tradable goods, which in turn may stimulate higher domestic wage demands. Failure to validate such higher wage demands would in turn increase unemployment. If the monetary authority responds only to wage changes, this channel would manifest itself in a reaction function only as a domestic pressure, with wage changes correlating to increased money supply. Thus in our reaction function, this channel may

exist even if we do not find import price increases to be positively correlated with money supply growth. However, this type of shock could manifest itself in other ways. The adoption of flexible exchange rates could
insulate the domestic economy from the effects of general inflation
abroad, but flexible rates cannot insulate the economy completely from
the effects of price shocks in particular important commodities like oil.
This concern could cause monetary authorities to accommodate before
wages rise. Furthermore, it has been argued that flexible rates contribute
additional inflationary pressures of their own through a vicious circle of
depreciation and inflation.

If such pressures have a strong influence on policymakers, we would
expect increases in import prices to lead to higher monetary expansion.
On the other hand, a central bank concerned with inflation or the balance
of payments may respond to import price rises by decreasing money
growth, in an attempt to head off any upward movement in the general
price level. If the monetary authority responds only to wage changes, this
channel would manifest itself in a reaction function only as a domestic
pressure, with wage changes correlating to increased money supply. Thus
in our reaction function, this channel may exist even if we do not find
import price increases to be positively correlated with money supply
growth. However, this type of shock could manifest itself in other ways.

On the domestic side, one argument stressed especially by the post-
Keynesians is that monetary authorities will increase monetary expansion
as wage rates rise in order to avoid increases in unemployment. For example, Moore argues,

> [The monetary authorities] must accommodate to wage-push pres-
> sure if they are to fulfill their basic commitment to orderly financial
> markets, but the result will be persistence in the rate of inflation and
> a worsening of the position of fixed income groups. Moreover, they
> can fulfill their underlying obligation to resist the depreciation of the
> monetary unit, to the extent that this is consistent with the mainte-
> nance of financial stability, only by abandoning their full employ-
> ment commitment and permitting the unemployment rate to rise.[11]

This validation view contrasts with the more traditional normative view
that macroeconomic policy, if it is to be active at all, should follow the
countercyclical pattern. Under this view, cyclical upturns and accompanying wage and price increases would call for more restrictive monetary

policy. Thus the validation view suggests a positive coefficient on wage increases while the countercyclical view suggests a negative coefficient.

There has been a good deal of confusion generated in the discussions of wage-push validation by the failure to distinguish between initiating and sustaining aspects of the inflationary process. Most of the discussions of wage-push inflation have focused on the role of autonomous wage increases caused by such factors as increases in labor union militancy. However, as Willett and Banaian discuss in chapter 1 of this volume, wage increases can also play an important endogenous role in sustaining inflationary momentum. Even where labor has no increase in monopoly power, nominal wages will tend to increase over time in response to ongoing inflation. Failure to accommodate these induced wage increases will cause the same type of short-run increases in unemployment as would the failure to accommodate autonomous wage-push.

Thus, in ongoing inflations the distinction between demand-pull and cost-push inflation breaks down.[12] Concern about unemployment can cause wage behavior to stimulate monetary accommodation even where wages play little role in initiating inflationary pressures. In a crude attempt to distinguish between the possible initiating and sustaining roles of wage behavior in inducing monetary expansion, we include measures of the behavior of real wages as an indicator of the initiating role of wages in creating or increasing inflationary pressures and measures of nominal wage behavior as an indicator of the sustaining role of wage increases.

The last major hypothesis tested here is that of deficit financing. In this view, which has been particularly advocated by monetarists, it is the preference for orderly financial markets in terms of stable interest rates and asset prices and concerns about the distributional effects of high interest rates that lead to accommodation.[13] High interest rates tend to depress residential construction and other industries with sales that are sensitive to interest rates. High rates also could cause financial disintermediation (especially before the removal of regulation Q in the United States), and have been shown to be negatively related to profits for thrift institutions. Deficit financing through government bond sales will tend to drive up interest rates. In order to avoid such interest rate increases, the monetary authorities will purchase government bonds, reducing interest rates by expanding the money supply.

The effect of budget deficits on interest rates and monetary expansion has been the subject of considerable controversy in recent years. In response to concerns about the huge U.S. budget deficits, many supply-siders have argued that farsighted citizens will increase their savings to offset the effects of the expected increase in future taxes needed to re-pay the deficit. If this did occur, there would be no tendency for interest rates to rise and hence no pressures for monetary accommodation via this channel.[14]

We have included two different measures of the deficit in our esti-mates. One is the actual deficit, the balance of expenditures less receipts of all levels of government. This measure has been used in most popular discussions of the effects of government deficits on inflation. Economic analysis suggests, however, that the effects of budget deficits on interest rates and hence on monetary expansion will depend on the state of the economy. A budget deficit generated by the fall of tax receipts in a reces-sion typically will be associated with low rather than high interest rates. This relationship has led to analysis by supply-side economists that bud-get deficits do not cause high interest rates. A much better gauge of the interest rate pressures of budget deficits is the full employment or cycli-cally adjusted deficit. Such measures attempt to estimate what the budget position would be when the macroeconomy is operating at a high level of employment. Use of this concept removes a potential confounding factor in estimating whether budget deficits influence interest rates and mone-tary expansion.[15]

The empirical evidence presented here consists of regressions of an-nual data explaining rates of growth in narrow and broad monetary aggre-gates for twelve industrial countries.[16] For convenience these narrow and broader aggregates are labeled M1 and M2 respectively, but in several countries the broader measure bears another name.[17] Many preceding monetary reaction function studies specified some interest rate as the de-pendent variable and used monthly and quarterly data.[18] While this is an appropriate procedure for examining the immediate short-term influences on the behavior of the monetary authorities, our concern is with persistent accommodation of internal and external pressures over a longer time ho-rizon.[19] For this level of analysis, focusing on money supply behavior seems more appropriate.[20]

It is not necessary for the purposes of this investigation that the mon-etary authorities have any particular monetary target at all.[21] Indeed, in many instances this was not an important direct objective of the authorities. But because ex post it is behavior of the money supply that is the major determinant of inflationary trends, it is useful to investigate how various intermediate-level factors correlate with rates of monetary expansion.[22]

Our objective is to focus on the extent to which these frequently hypothesized causes of inflation are consistent with the actual behavior of monetary expansion. For this reason, the reported equations have not been manipulated to improve overall goodness of fit. While several equations may suffer from significant serial correlation in the residuals, ordinary least squares (OLS) estimates are reported without autocorrelation correction. The presence of any such serial correlation does not bias OLS coefficient estimates, and while correction procedures would be likely to increase the explanatory power of the overall equation, the result could give a misleading impression of the significance of the basic explanatory variables. Because of the limited number of explanatory variables available for each country, a better understanding of the underlying behavioral processes would be unlikely. Similarly, lagged values of the independent variables were not included because with annual data it was generally hypothesized that monetary policy would respond to the pressure variables primarily during the current year.

The estimated equations regress the rate of growth of the narrow and broad monetary aggregates as a function of the size of the budget deficit relative to a country's GNP, the change in the international reserve holdings of the central bank as a share of its money supply, and the rates of growth of wages and import prices.[23] We have included a variable that allows for a break in the trend of money growth after 1973 (a year which saw both a change in the international monetary system and a large increase in oil prices). As mentioned above, various measures of the independent variables have been employed. We report separate estimates for actual and cyclically adjusted budget deficits, and for real and nominal wage growth. Also, we have reported separate equations using two different measures of import price pressure: one which measures the rate of growth of import prices alone and a second which measures the change in import prices less the change in the overall price level. This latter measure represents a crude attempt to identify import price shocks coming from abroad, i.e., import price inflation different from that which would be generated by domestic inflationary pressures.

Empirical Results

In this section, we present and discuss the results for reaction function equations for twelve countries—Austria, Belgium, Canada, France, Germany, Italy, Japan, the Netherlands, Sweden, Switzerland, the United Kingdom, and the United States. The empirical results are presented in tables 8.1–8.8 (Appendix). Because our primary purpose is to investigate the consistency of various inflation hypotheses with the rates of monetary expansion rather than to present a detailed analysis of monetary policy, we analyze our results by variable[24] and place the emphasis in our discussion on the significance of the estimated coefficients as measured by the reported t-statistics. The latter need not give an accurate picture of the relative contributions of the various pressure variables to monetary growth. For example, a highly significant positive coefficient would not identify them as a major source of variations in money growth if the budget deficits themselves varied little. The commonly used measure for the contribution of the movement of an independent variable to the explanation of the behavior of a dependent variable is the beta coefficient, which adjusts for the variability in the independent variable. We thus report beta coefficients as well.[25] We also compare our results to other empirical studies for the industrial countries.[26]

The 1973 Shift

Because of the substantial acceleration in monetary expansion for most industrial countries over the past decade and the potentially important impact of the change in the international monetary system, we included a shift variable to test whether higher rates of monetary expansion could be explained by constant reaction to the pressure variables or whether basic rates of monetary expansion had shifted upward significantly. To coincide both with the change in the international monetary system and the OPEC oil shock, we took 1973 as the year for this shift.

There is admittedly some arbitrariness in choosing this date. The years 1970 or 1971 would also be plausible dates. The entire period 1970–73, when the Bretton Woods international monetary system showed increasing signs of collapse, might best be treated as a separate transitional period. We have undertaken some preliminary experimentation with this and plan to pursue it in future research. We are also investigating possible shifts in the coefficients of the international variables after the initiation of floating exchange rates. In general, we find little evidence of significant shifts in the coefficients of the import price variables, suggesting that our negative findings on the vicious circle hypotheses are not due to combining pegged and flexible rate periods in the equations reported here. There is more evidence of a shift on the reserve variable, with the coefficients tending to be higher under pegged rates than during the flexible rate period. This is consistent with the view that flexible rates have offered many countries greater short-run monetary independence than under pegged rates, but differences have not been as dramatic as others have suggested.[27]

The results show little significant shift in the trend of monetary growth rates after 1973, with the exception of the United Kingdom for M1, where growth increased. For the broader aggregate M2, increases in trend growth were found for Belgium, Canada, and Italy, and a decrease was found for Germany. The case of Italy may reflect also the move toward indexed wage contracts, *la scala mobile,* after 1973.

In earlier work using absolute rather than percentage changes in monetary aggregates, we found the trend shift coefficient to be often quite significant, and without the shift variable, problems of serial correlation of the residuals were quite severe. This may have occurred in part because a constant percentage rate of growth implies increasing absolute changes. Differencing the data in percentage terms yielded considerably less evidence of nonstationarity problems in the data than did absolute differencing.

International Reserves

Our results suggest that international reserve flows as a share of the relevant monetary aggregate have not had a large persistent impact on monetary expansion in most of the countries tested, with Austria and Switzerland being consistent exceptions. The M2 regressions show far less support for the global monetarist view than those for the narrower aggregate. The M1 regressions offer some confirmation for the results of Gordon, who found that Germany, Japan, and the United Kingdom did not sterilize international reserve flows.[28] We do not confirm his results for Germany, and our results for the United Kingdom suggest some, though not perfect, sterilization. We do, however, find some confirmation for Japan. Gordon's results for Germany are confirmed by Beck but not by Sheehey and Kreinin.[29] Black finds that increases in reserves led to declines in money growth in Germany, but his independent variable is presented as a share of imports.[30] Comparisons are therefore difficult. Darby et al. find virtually complete short-run sterilization for all of the industrial countries they studied, but also found evidence of lagged effects of the balance of payments on monetary expansion in most of the countries in their sample.[31] The latter finding suggests that concerns with promoting long-run balance of payments equilibrium may have had an influence on the course of monetary policy.

Import Prices

We do not find any case where the persistence of monetary accommodation in response to import price changes is supported by the evidence. This is consistent with the results of Gordon and of Sheehey and Kreinin.[32] In fact, we find four relatively open economies—Belgium, Germany, Italy, and Switzerland—in which import price hikes are more often associated with decreases in monetary growth rates. In most other cases the coefficients, while not statistically significant, show a negative sign.[33] This may be caused by monetary authorities not reacting to import price pressures until they are manifested in higher wages.

Wage-Push Arguments

The results show that positive relationships exist between money and nominal wages for six of the countries under study. In no case do we see negative relationships. These results are generally consistent with those of Moore for the United States and of Sheehey and Kreinin for all countries except Germany.[34] Black and Gordon, on the other hand, found much less accommodation.[35] This is not surprising since their methods of estimation required more stringent conditions for positive evidence of wage-push accommodation. The evidence for real wage accommodation is much weaker. Belgium and Italy show signs of real wage accommodation that are significant for M1, and results which are close to significant for Italy in the M2 regressions. For Belgium, the results show one significant positive estimate for M2, and one significantly negative.[36] Combining these results leads us to believe that persistent as opposed to occasional episodes of real wage-push has not been a major initiating factor in the inflationary process in the industrial countries, but that the dynamics of inflation as reflected in the tendency for nominal wages to adjust upward in response to past inflation did play an important role in sustaining inflation.

Careful examination of specific episodes reinforces the general picture of variability in the behavior of monetary policy presented by our regression results. For example, while the cost-push hypothesis would have predicted widespread accommodation of the oil price shocks of 1973–74 and the accompanying escalation of nominal wage increases, this was not in general the case. While some countries such as Sweden did clearly accommodate, others such as Germany, Japan, and the United States did not. Still others such as Italy, France, and the United Kingdom tended to vacillate in their responses, ultimately providing considerable accommodation but less than their highly accommodative policies of the late 1960s. In general the industrial countries were even less accommodative to the second oil price shock. Furthermore the partial nonaccommodation to the first shock contributed to much milder wage responses to the second shock. This is consistent with the learning behavior emphasized in the rational expectations literature, but not with the predictable policy regimes also stressed in many versions of rational expectations analysis.[37]

Budget Deficits

Our results, while not as strong as those found in our earlier work, still suggest that budget deficits are frequently accommodated by increased monetary expansion.[38] We again find very strong results for the United States. There is also considerable support for deficit accommodation views in the data for Canada, Italy, Sweden, and the United Kingdom. There is little evidence of persistent accommodation for the other countries in the sample, however. These results follow the same broad outline found by prior researchers, with Gordon and Sheehey and Kreinin generally finding the same mixed patterns.[39]

Concluding Remarks

As indicated in the introduction, the poor statistical fit of many of the equations and frequent lack of significance of the predicted coefficients should make one very skeptical of the commonly seen statements that such pressures as wage escalation and budget deficits must always be validated by monetary accommodation in all democratic countries. Nor can one conclude that in our increasingly integrated world economy international developments will dominate national ones.

However, there may be considerable merit to looser forms of some of these arguments. Our work in this area convinces us that almost all of these pressures have at least some explanatory power for particular episodes. There is considerable empirical evidence to contradict views of some extreme cost-push advocates that macroeconomic conditions have negligible influence on union wage rates, but there is also evidence to support more eclectic views that at particular times factors other than microeconomic conditions may have significant influences on wage behavior. The magnitude of the wage increases in the late 1960s in Europe is an important case in point.[40] However, even before the recent disinflationary episodes in the United States and the United Kingdom under Mr. Reagan and Mrs. Thatcher, respectively, there was little basis for the strong view that: "The wage level in the modern economy is indeterminant because in the final analysis the monetary authority must—for political reasons—provide a money supply adequate to ratify any given level of money wages, no matter how it is reached, in order to avoid excessive unemployment."[41]

An interpretation that high wage increases do place pressures on the monetary authority to adopt more expansionary policies to avoid the increase in unemployment which would otherwise be likely to result does seem valid. We do find that the European wage bursts in the late 1960s were generally accompanied by more rapid monetary expansion, and we are thus led to believe that this process may explain as much or more of the rapid European monetary expansion of the early 1970s as does the international liquidity explosion of that period, although the effects of the latter were certainly not trivial. However, due in part to increasing concerns with inflation on the part of national governments and monetary authorities, the huge oil price increases in 1973–74 were followed by monetary deceleration rather than acceleration in most countries—even though the oil shock was accompanied by substantial nominal wage increases.

The relatively poor performance of our estimated equations is related in part to the difficulties of constructing good quantitative indicators of monetary policy and pressure variables. A more important reason for the loose fit of our estimates is that discretion means case-by-case decision making. Monetary authorities and their governments do not have fixed feedback rules and do not always respond to the behavior of pressure variables in the same way. Not only are there frequent changes in the political officials who most heavily influence monetary policy-making, there is often considerable learning behavior and changes in view by officials over time. Changes in operating procedures may also have an influence.

Monetary behavior patterns are neither completely determinant and invariable nor infinitely malleable. We need to develop a better understanding of the factors which cause changes in such behavior over time. Progress in this direction will require a careful blending of the methods of the historian and the econometrician within a conceptual framework drawn from political economy.

Appendix: Some Methodological Issues— Causation and Simultaneity Bias

Bidirectional causation is a possibility in the specification used in this paper. While it is reasonable to hypothesize wage increases causing monetary validation, monetary expansion will also cause wage increases through effects on inflationary expectations and aggregate demand. Most available evidence suggests that monetary expansion in a particular year affects wage increases in subsequent years, however, so that this aspect may not constitute a serious problem. Still, because simultaneity bias is a possibility here, results should be viewed as a check on the consistency of the wage-push hypothesis rather than a verification of causal direction. While the econometric causality tests developed by Granger and Sims can be useful for some aspects of the question considered here, they can test only for the initiating and not the sustaining aspects of wage-push inflation. It should be noted that econometric causality does not always correspond to our normal concepts of behavioral causality in economic analysis. It is in essence a sophisticated statistical analysis of lead-lag relationships and hence is fully subject to the *post hoc, ergo propter hoc* fallacy (as its developers, but not all of its users, were fully aware).[42]

The international reserve coefficients are more subject to bias, although in this case two-way causation would likely result in downward rather than upward bias. While the global monetarist school emphasizes causation running from reserve increases to money supply increases, an exogenous increase in the rate of monetary expansion would—from the other direction—lead to balance of payments deficits and reserve losses.

The correlation between reserve and money supply changes depends in part on the pattern of disturbances, and a fully and properly specified reaction function should minimize this problem. But to the extent our reported equations may omit some domestic causes of monetary expansion, a downward bias in the reserve coefficients may result. While the rudimentary nature of this reaction function specification suggests a possibly serious problem here, the general consistency of our results with more detailed studies of sterilization coefficients reduces our concern.

There may also be some downward bias in coefficients on the budget deficit term. Like other cross-national studies, the method of cyclical adjustment used was relatively rudimentary; more extensive efforts at cyclical adjustment for each country may lead to a finding of stronger effects for the deficit term.

As with the wage variable, one might expect upward bias in the import price terms if monetary expansion generates import price increases in the concurrent period, especially with possible exchange rate depreciation under flexible rates. The general outcomes here find very few positive coefficients and many negative ones on the import price terms, however. Thus, this constitutes strong evidence that this is not an important channel of inflation causation, despite the popularity of allegations of imported inflation.[43]

These reaction function estimates, even if accurate, do not represent direct estimates of policymakers' preference functions. They reflect rather the combined influences of these preferences and the trade-offs imposed by the operation of the economy.[44] Thus, for example, central bankers in country A might weigh the costs of inflation relative to unemployment more heavily than those in country B but still follow more accommodative policies due to a worse short-run inflation-employment trade-off. Both public choice analysis of encompassing groups and the political science and sociological literature on corporatism suggest and the available empirical estimates confirm that short-run inflation-unemployment trade-offs can differ considerably across countries.[45] This helps explain some of our empirical findings. For example, most estimates suggest that the United States has a flatter short-run inflation-unemployment trade-off than Germany. This could help explain why we find significant nominal wage accommodation in the United States, without the Federal Reserve necessarily assigning different weights to the costs of inflation versus unemployment relative to the German central bank (although we cannot exclude this latter possibility).

Table 8.1 Correlates with Narrow Money Growth: Specification 1

Country	Const	C = DM Intercept Shift	RDM1 Foreign Assets	İI Import Prices	IC
		Foreign Variables			
Austria	.037	−.051	.37	−.38	
	(1.47)	(−1.48)	(3.08)	(−1.35)	
		[−.44]	[.51]	[−.36]	
Belgium	−.008	−.004	.18	−.29	
	(−.34)	(−.17)	(.96)	(−2.40)	
		[−.044]	[.16]	[−.53]	
Canada	.04	−.10	.10	.11	
	(.82)	(−1.17)	(.18)	(.30)	
		[−.44]	[.034]	[.072]	
France	.09	−.004	.02	.08	
	(2.07)	(−.12)	(.11)	(.63)	
		[−.045]	[.026]	[.20]	
Germany	.08	−.026	.031	−.074	
	(2.69)	(−1.06)	(.28)	(−.59)	
		[−0.28]	[.057]	[−.132]	
Italy	.09	−.034	.15	−.13	
	(3.02)	(−.46)	(.59)	(−1.41)	
		[−.30]	[.11]	[−.40]	
Japan	.11	−.02	.66	−.15	
	(4.90)	(−.52)	(2.37)	(−2.01)	
		[−.10]	[.25]	[−.15]	
Netherlands	.015	−.009	−.06	−.13	
	(.34)	(−.31)	(−.25)	(−.83)	
		[−.09]	[−.05]	[−.21]	
Sweden	.01	−.004	.27	.17	
	(.27)	(−.11)	(1.38)	(.84)	
		[−.055]	[.32]	[.27]	
Switzerland	.03	−.005	1.17	−.22	
	(3.30)	(−.32)	(6.49)	(−2.25)	
		[−.036]	[.72]	[−.24]	
United Kingdom	.03	.02	.18	.001	
	(1.44)	(.44)	(1.02)	(.009)	
		[.14]	[.20]	[.0015]	
United States	.0032	−.012	−.27	−.027	
	(.25)	(−.72)	(−.46)	(.027)	
		[−.21]	[−.077]	[−.11]	

Notes: The top number in each column for each country is the estimated coefficient, the second number (in parentheses) is the *t*-statistic, and the bottom number (in brackets) is the beta coefficient.

Transformed variables: RD = percentage change in foreign assets; $\dot{W}$ = percentage change in nominal wages; $\dot{WRP}$ = percentage change in real wages; $\dot{II}$ = percentage change in import prices; $C\dot{C}$ = percentage change

| | Domestic Variables | | | | | |
$\overset{\bullet}{W}$ Nominal Wages	$\overset{\bullet}{WRP}$ Real Wages	DG Actual Govt. Deficit	DDIG Adjusted Deficit	DW	R²	Interval
.0064		− .31		2.38	.33	1956–81
(2.41)		(− .32)				
[.35]		[− .074]				
.007		.31		2.53	.38	1957–82
(3.85)		(.94)				
[.74]		[.24]				
.32		2.11		2.2	− .049	1949–82
(.44)		(1.83)				
[11.14]		[.46]				
.0003		.96		1.56	− .19	1960–82
(.07)		(.98)				
[.031]		[.26]				
.001		.41		2.06	− .025	1951–82
(.48)		(.51)				
[.11]		[.146]				
.004		.24		1.29	.33	1956–82
(1.84)		(.44)				
[.62]		[.22]				
.0046		− .49		2.15	.51	1956–79
(2.66)		(− .72)				
[.26]		[− .11]				
.008		.4		2.4	.10	1961–82
(2.32)		(.59)				
[.60]		[.16]				
.003		.75		1.80	.33	1960–80
(1.10)		(1.52)				
[.18]		[.55]				
− .0005		− .03		1.65	.62	1950–82
(− .67)		(− .03)				
[− .051]		[− .0040]				
.0007		1.00		2.07	.23	1956–82
(.26)		(1.20)				
[.023]		[.42]				
.60		.65		1.59	.31	1949–83
(2.36)		(1.92)				
[.57]		[.43]				

in consumer price index; IC = defined as ($\overset{\bullet}{II}$-$\overset{\bullet}{CC}$(− 1)), the contribution of the import price change to the domestic inflation rate; DG = ratio of the actual deficit (or surplus) to national income; $DDIG$ = ratio of the cyclically adjusted deficit to national income in the equation in which a shift of the slope of real income was allowed; DW = Durbin-Watson statistic

Table 8.2 Correlates with Narrow Money Growth: Specification 2

| Country | Const | Foreign Variables | | | IC |
		C = DM Intercept Shift	RDM1 Foreign Assets	II Import Prices	
Austria	.038	−.06	.36	−.35	
	(1.86)	(−2.19)	(3.06)	(−1.43)	
		[−.51]	[.50]	[−.34]	
Belgium	.006	.01	.13	−.26	
	(.37)	(.57)	(.17)	(−2.07)	
		[.11]	[.11]	[−.42]	
Canada	.092	−.019	.064	−.009	
	(1.72)	(−.25)	(.10)	(−.047)	
		[−.08]	[.021]	[−.006]	
France	.07	−.005	.02	−.03	
	(1.56)	(−.14)	(.11)	(−.26)	
		[−.057]	[.026]	[−.07]	
Germany	.07	−.008	.012	−.11	
	(2.76)	(−.36)	(.10)	(−.91)	
		[−.09]	[.022]	[−.19]	
Italy	.11	−.014	.26	−.14	
	(4.6)	(−.32)	(1.12)	(−1.99)	
		[−.12]	[.20]	[−.42]	
Japan	.09	−.03	.67	−.14	
	(3.51)	(−1.33)	(2.38)	(−1.94)	
		[−.15]	[.25]	[−.27]	
Netherlands	.033	−.001	−.083	−.13	
	(.89)	(−.04)	(−.30)	(−.82)	
		[−.01]	[−.067]	[−.21]	
Sweden	.06	.02	.18	.20	
	(1.54)	(.63)	(.92)	(1.01)	
		[.28]	[.21]	[.32]	
Switzerland	.04	−.01	1.11	−.25	
	(3.41)	(−.83)	(5.96)	(−2.53)	
		[−.072]	[.10]	[−.27]	
United Kingdom	.04	.04	.17	−.02	
	(2.30)	(1.28)	(1.09)	(−.21)	
		[.28]	[.18]	[−.030]	
United States	.01	.002	−.33	−.017	
	(1.48)	(.20)	(−.60)	(−.43)	
		[.035]	[−.10]	[.067]	

Note: See notes to table 8.1.

$\overset{\bullet}{W}$ Nominal Wages	$\overset{\bullet}{WRP}$ Real Wages	DG Actual Govt. Deficit	DDIG Adjusted Deficit	DW	R^2	Interval
Domestic Variables						
.005			.26	2.3	.36	1956–81
(2.24)			(.74)			
[.27]			[.15]			
.006			− .03	2.45	.36	1957–82
(3.97)			(− .44)			
[.63]			[− .077]			
− .035			.188	2.3	− .14	1949–82
(− .047)			(.85)			
[− 1.22]			[.17]			
.002			− 1.02	1.44	− .21	1960–82
(.48)			(− .93)			
[.20]			[− .38]			
.001			− .31	2.08	.17	1951–82
(.52)			(− 1.10)			
[.11]			[− .20]			
.004			.84	1.58	.34	1956–82
(1.96)			(2.35)			
[.62]			[5.00]			
.0052			− .010	2.09	.50	1956–79
(2.90)			(− .57)			
[.30]			[− .07]			
.007			.05	2.5	.07	1961–82
(2.23)			(.28)			
[.52]			[.50]			
.001			.11	1.89	.19	1960–80
(.36)			(.51)			
[.061]			[.15]			
− .0004			.60	1.74	.63	1950–82
(− .54)			(1.00)			
[− .041]			[.10]			
.001			.40			
(.74)			(2.44)	2.03	.36	1956–82
[.008]			[.74]			
.52			.21	1.96	.36	1949–83
(2.09)			(2.54)			
[.44]			[.30]			

Table 8.3   Correlates with Narrow Money Growth: Specification 3

Country	Const	Foreign Variables			IC
		$C = \dot{D}M$ Intercept Shift	RDM1 Foreign Assets	$\dot{\Pi}$ Import Prices	
Austria	.048	−.018	.36		−.26
	(1.93)	(−.61)	(2.77)		(−1.06)
		[−.15]	[.50]		[−.22]
Belgium	.003	.02	.19		(−.23)
	(.11)	(1.11)	(.92)		(−2.12)
		[.22]	[.17]		[−.40]
Canada	.063	−.07	.12		.09
	(1.27)	(−1.18)	(.21)		(.24)
			[.041]		[.055]
France	.10	.001	.01		.08
	(2.98)	(.07)	(.07)		(.66)
		[.011]	[.013]		[.18]
Germany	.09	−.030	.05		−.017
	(3.55)	(−1.15)	(.46)		(−.17)
		[−.32]	[.09]		[−.027]
Italy	.076	−.03	.27		−.04
	(2.92)	(−.54)	(1.10)		(−.50)
		[−.26]	[.21]		[−.08]
Japan	.14	.003	.76		−.06
	(6.16)	(−.08)	(2.45)		(−.88)
		[−.014]	[.30]		[−.11]
Netherlands	.070	.005	−.046		−.13
	(1.65)	(.16)	(−.16)		(−.84)
		[.05]	[−.040]		[−.20]
Sweden	.03	.02	.27		.11
	(1.30)	(.59)	(1.26)		(.66)
		[.27]	[.32]		[.16]
Switzerland	.02	−.008	1.18		−.15
	(2.43)	(−.47)	(4.93)		(−1.41)
		[−.058]	[.73]		[−.17]
United Kingdom	.04	.01	.32		.01
	(2.74)	(.43)	(1.94)		(.12)
		[.070]	[.33]		[.013]
United States	.032	.0081	.23		.051
	(4.32)	(.49)	(.36)		(.94)
		[.14]	[.065]		[.20]

	Domestic Variables					
• W Nominal Wages	• WRP Real Wages	DG Actual Govt. Deficit	DDIG Adjusted Deficit	DW	R²	Interval
	.0061 (1.39) [.25]	−.19 (−.19) [−.045]		2.18	.24	1956–81
	.008 (2.79) [.48]	.24 (.65) [.20]		2.58	.27	1957–82
	.12 (.09) [2.24]	1.97 (1.54) [.43]		2.1	−.07	1949–82
	−.002 (−.17) [−.087]	1.05 (.96) [.28]		1.56	−.19	1960–82
	.0003 (.095) [.032]	.37 (.47) [.132]		2.03	−.040	1951–82
	.007 (2.97) [.45]	.65 (1.26) [.60]		1.63	.30	1956–82
	.0037 (1.18) [.11]	−.93 (−1.21) [−.22]		1.86	.37	1956–79
	.005 (.93) [.31]	−5.0 (−.09) [−2.00]		2.15	−.10	1961–82
	.003 (.70) [.20]	.81 (1.57) [.60]		1.86	.28	1960–80
	−.0005 (−.31) [−.042]	−.30 (−.34) [−.040]		1.58	.58	1950–82
	−.008 (−1.99) [−.27]	1.0 (1.70) [.42]		2.16	.37	1956–82
	.10 (.40) [.07]	.56 (1.38) [.37]		1.27	.31	1949–83

Table 8.4 Correlates with Narrow Money Growth: Specification 4

Country	Const	C = DM Intercept Shift	RDM1 Foreign Assets	II Import Prices	IC
			Foreign Variables		
Austria	.052	−.030	.35		−.24
	(2.67)	(−1.32)	(2.79)		(−1.14)
		[−.25]	[.48]		[−.21]
Belgium	.01	.03	.15		−.21
	(.81)	(1.66)	(.75)		(−1.92)
		[.33]	[.13]		[−.36]
Canada	.011	−.02	.076		−.14
	(2.30)	(−.51)	(.12)		(−.37)
		[−.09]	[.026]		[−.086]
France	.11	.008	−.03		−.05
	(3.38)	(.37)	(−.17)		(−.38)
		[.091]	[−.040]		[−.11]
Germany	.08	−.013	.029		−.053
	(3.22)	(−.49)	(.26)		(−.54)
		[−.14]	[.053]		[−.085]
Italy	.011	.023	.32		−.09
	(6.64)	(1.19)	(1.56)		(−1.56)
		[.20]	[.24]		[−.19]
Japan	.13	−.035	.77		−.021
	(4.53)	(−1.09)	(2.35)		(−.32)
		[−.17]	[.30]		[−.040]
Netherlands	.07	.001	−.07		−.13
	(2.13)	(.04)	(−.24)		(−.77)
		[.009]	[−.058]		[−.20]
Sweden	.08	.03	.15		.13
	(3.40)	(1.11)	(.77)		(.75)
		[.42]	[.17]		[.20]
Switzerland	.03	−.01	1.18		−.14
	(2.59)	(−1.06)	(5.07)		(−1.41)
			[.733]		[−.16]
United Kingdom	.06	.06	.27		−.04
	(4.05)	(3.05)	(1.83)		(−.38)
		[.072]	[.28]		[−.053]
United States	.043	.014	.021		.015
	(5.47)	(1.24)	(.036)		(.38)
		[.24]	[.060]		[.060]

	Domestic Variables					
• W Nominal Wages	• WRP Real Wages	DG Actual Govt. Deficit	DDIG Adjusted Deficit	DW	R^2	Interval
	.0055		−.33	2.15	.27	1956–81
	(1.26)		(.90)			
	[.23]		[.20]			
	.007		−.26	2.50	.26	1957–82
	(2.96)		(−.34)			
	[.42]		[−.67]			
	−.76		.16	2.3	.14	1949–82
	(−.61)		(.67)			
	[−14.23]		[.14]			
	−.004		−1.06	1.48	−.20	1960–82
	(−.54)		(−.97)			
	[−.17]		[−.40]			
	.001		−.30	2.05	−.008	1951–82
	(.25)		(−1.02)			
	[.106]		[−.20]			
	.007		.091	1.95	.45	1956–82
	(3.32)		(2.84)			
	[.44]		[.53]			
	.003		−.0046	1.78	.32	1956–79
	(1.15)		(−.022)			
	[.20]		[−.0031]			
	.005		.04	2.17	−.11	1961–82
	(1.14)		(.20)			
	[.31]		[.40]			
	−.0004		.13	2.07	.17	1960–80
	(−.10)		(.56)			
	[−.026]		[.17]			
	−.001		.60	1.61	.59	1950–82
	(−.63)		(.82)			
	[−.085]		[.10]			
	−.005		.41	1.92	.43	1956–82
	(−1.48)		(2.37)			
	[−.17]		[.74]			
	.48		.22	1.60	.18	1949–83
	(.19)		(1.97)			
	[.37]		[.32]			

Table 8.5 Correlates with Broad Money Growth: Specification 1

Country	Const	C = DM Intercept Shift	RDM1 Foreign Assets	İl Import Prices	IC
			Foreign Variables		
Austria	.090	− .014	.52	− .15	
	(7.00)	(− .81)	(2.74)	(− 1.08)	
		[− .25]	[.48]	[− .30]	
Belgium	.34	.003	.06	− .21	
	(2.07)	(.24)	(.34)	(− 2.70)	
		[.045]	[.049]	[− .51]	
Canada	.06	.06	.25	.01	
	(2.70)	(1.67)	(.46)	(.09)	
		[.46]	[.06]	[.012]	
France	.09	− .03	.19	.004	
	(2.79)	(− 1.16)	(.77)	(.04)	
		[− .43]	[.17]	[.012]	
Germany	.14	− .034	.25	− .28	
	(6.97)	(− 1.97)	(1.42)	(− 3.37)	
		[− .38]	[.20]	[− .52]	
Italy	.14	.09	− .21	− .14	
	(7.09)	(1.85)	(− .69)	(− 2.17)	
		[1.03]	[− .12]	[− .56]	
Japan	.15	− .01	− 1.61	− .16	
	(2.96)	(− .22)	(− 1.06)	(− .99)	
		[− .07]	[− .37]	[− .43]	
Netherlands	.11	.029	− .48	− .02	
	(4.74)	(1.78)	(− 1.41)	(− .34)	
		[.45]	[− .25]	[− .052]	
Sweden	.06	− .008	.45	− .13	
	(2.47)	(− .32)	(.85)	(− 1.01)	
		[− .07]	[.20]	[− .30]	
Switzerland	.07	− .004	.93	− .27	
	(6.03)	(− .22)	(1.82)	(− 2.47)	
		[− .037]	[3.05]	[− .38]	
United Kingdom	.05	.039	− .29	.087	
	(2.12)	(.63)	(− .72)	(.50)	
		[.27]	[− .13]	[.11]	
United States	.037	− .02	1.41	.059	
	(2.64)	(− 1.43)	(1.41)	(1.03)	
		[− .11]	[.07]	[.07]	

| | Domestic Variables | | | | | |
W Nominal Wages	WRP Real Wages	DG Actual Govt. Deficit	DDIG Adjusted Deficit	DW	R²	Interval
.002 (1.96) [.225]		.54 (1.15) [.268]		1.76	.31	1956–81
.005 (4.90) [.699]		.13 (.61) [.136]		2.3	.54	1957–82
.09 (.28) [5.48]		.34 (.65) [.13]		1.88	.32	1949–82
.004 (1.03) [.51]		.05 (.06) [.017]		1.32	− .16	1960–82
− .0031 (−1.41) [−.36]		.23 (.41) [.086]		1.56	.59	1951–82
.0004 (.24) [.008]		− .13 (−.35) [−.16]		.79	.33	1956–82
.003 (.90) [.24]		− .76 (−.49) [−.25]		2.91	− .060	1956–79
.002 (1.29) [.23]		− .40 (−2.33) [−.15]		1.27	.33	1961–82
.0001 (.04) [.009]		1.06 (3.13) [1.13]		1.36	.39	1960–80
− .0005 (−.62) [−.066]		.20 (.19) [.23]		1.30	.18	1950–82
.0024 (.72) [.18]		.19 (.18) [.07]		1.04	.17	1956–82
.12 (.43) [0.33]		1.85 (4.87) [0.40]		1.74	.54	1949–83

Table 8.6 Correlates with Broad Money Growth: Specification 2

Country	Const	C = DM Intercept Shift	RDM2 Foreign Assets	$\dot{\text{II}}$ Import Prices	IC
			Foreign Variables		
Austria	.10	−.002	.56	−.23	
	(9.40)	(−.19)	(2.82)	(−1.85)	
		[−.035]	[.52]	[−.46]	
Belgium	.04	.008	.04	−.22	
	(4.06)	(.65)	(.27)	(−2.79)	
		[.12]	[.032]	[−.53]	
Canada	.084	.06	.42	.03	
	(3.76)	(2.16)	(.81)	(.22)	
		[.46]	[.045]	[.034]	
France	.07	−.03	.19	−.08	
	(2.05)	(−1.38)	(.81)	(−.79)	
		[−.43]	[.17]	[−.24]	
Germany	.14	−.024	.21	−.31	
	(7.38)	(−1.50)	(1.12)	(−3.61)	
		[−.27]	[.16]	[−.58]	
Italy	.14	.07	−.15	−.13	
	(7.79)	(2.34)	(−.50)	(−2.30)	
		[.80]	[−.10]	[−.52]	
Japan	.15	−.05	−1.69	−.13	
	(2.39)	(−.99)	(−1.04)	(−.84)	
		[−.35]	[−.40]	[−.35]	
Netherlands	−.08	.004	−.58	−.0017	
	(−3.83)	(.23)	(−1.42)	(−.017)	
		[.062]	[−.31]	[−.0044]	
Sweden	.13	.02	−.07	−.09	
	(4.89)	(1.00)	(−.14)	(−.67)	
		[.20]	[−.23]	[−.21]	
Switzerland	.09	−.02	.57	−.34	
	(6.90)	(−1.28)	(1.16)	(−3.30)	
		[−.18]	[1.87]	[−.48]	
United Kingdom	.05	.038	−.25	.080	
	(2.43)	(.81)	(−.65)	(.48)	
		[.27]	[−.11]	[.11]	
United States	.074	.021	.81	−.07	
	(4.63)	(1.60)	(.79)	(−1.50)	
		[.12]	[.04]	[−.09]	

| Domestic Variables | | | | | | |
W $\overset{\bullet}{}$ Nominal Wages	WRP $\overset{\bullet}{}$ Real Wages	DG Actual Govt. Deficit	DDIG Adjusted Deficit	DW	R^2	Interval
.0028 (2.09) [.31]			.043 (.23) [.052]	1.64	.27	1956–81
.005 (5.30) [.70]			.040 (.86) [.041]	2.32	.55	1957–82
.011 (.03) [.67]			.17 (1.93) [.07]	2.28	.39	1949–82
.006 (1.55) [.77]			− 1.30 (1.62) [− .60]	1.48	− .22	1960–82
− .0031 (− 1.45) [− .36]			− .18 (− .89) [− .12]	1.63	.60	1951–82
.0001 (.08) [.002]			.01 (.39) [.077]	.78	.33	1956–82
.003 (.92) [.24]			.05 (.12) [.05]	2.92	− .073	1956–79
.004 (2.39) [.48]			.10 (.99) [.16]	1.42	.11	1961–82
− .003 (− 1.32) [− .26]			.23 (1.44) [.45]	1.68	.14	1960–80
− .0001 (− .21) [− .013]			− 1.0 (− 2.39) [− .23]	1.41	.32	1950–82
.002 (.85) [.15]			.20 (1.10) [.31]	1.02	.21	1956–82
− .04 (− .14) [− 1.10]			.43 (4.31) [.20]	2.02	.49	1949–83

Table 8.7   Correlates with Broad Money Growth: Specification 3

Country	Const	C = DM Intercept Shift	RDM2 Foreign Assets	$\overset{\bullet}{\Pi}$ Import Prices	IC
			Foreign Variables		
Austria	.095	.0005	.50		− .12
	(7.72)	(.03)	(2.50)		(−1.06)
		[.009]	[.465]		[−.22]
Belgium	.04	.028	.05		− .17
	(2.40)	(1.99)	(.29)		(−2.31)
		[.42]	[.04]		[−.39]
Canada	.06	.07	.28		.04
	(3.06)	(2.68)	(.50)		(.25)
		[.53]	[.07]		[.043]
France	.09	− .01	.38		.09
	(3.44)	(−.64)	(1.42)		(.98)
		[−.14]	[.346]		[.25]
Germany	.12	− .046	.25		− .30
	(7.05)	(−2.51)	(1.42)		(−4.56)
		[−.52]	[.194]		[−.507]
Italy	.12	.07	− .08		− .10
	(6.74)	(1.60)	(−.27)		(−1.73)
		[−.80]	[−.05]		[−.343]
Japan	.19	− .005	− 1.47		− .12
	(4.19)	(−.06)	(−.96)		(−.88)
		[−.035]	[−.0338]		[−.325]
Netherlands	.14	.033	− .42		− .054
	(6.58)	(1.95)	(−1.19)		(−.66)
		[.52]	[−.225]		[−.134]
Sweden	.05	− .01	.49		− .14
	(2.79)	(−.55)	(.92)		(−1.30)
		[−.096]	[.212]		[−.301]
Switzerland	.07	− .01	.39		− .28
	(5.67)	(−.63)	(.59)		(−2.49)
		[−.093]	[1.28]		[−.42]
United Kingdom	.067	.066	.18		− .053
	(3.09)	(1.19)	(−.43)		(.31)
		[.46]	[−.08]		[.063]
United States	.05	− .021	1.63		.04
	(.670)	(−1.31)	(1.68)		(.76)
		[−.12]	[0.08]		[.05]

	Domestic Variables					
• W Nominal Wages	• WRP Real Wages	DG Actual Govt. Deficit	DDIG Adjusted Deficit	DW	R^2	Interval
	.002 (1.17) [.001]	.54 (1.12) [.268]		1.46	.25	1956–81
	.007 (3.54) [.56]	.077 (.31) [.08]		2.15	.41	1957–82
	.09 (.15) [2.94]	.32 (.55) [.124]		1.92	.31	1949–82
	.008 (1.69) [.434]	.56 (.69) [.189]		1.63	−.056	1960–82
	−.0015 (−.55) [−.167]	.37 (.70) [.138]		1.56	.61	1951–82
	.003 (1.53) [.255]	−.11 (−.29) [−.135]		1.09	.33	1956–82
	−.0006 (−.09) [−.026]	−1.30 (−.84) [−.44]		2.71	−.083	1956–79
	−.0002 (−.08) [−.02]	−1.0 (−2.99) [−.70]		1.03	.28	1961–82
	.002 (.73) [.0004]	1.14 (3.48) [1.22]		1.35	.44	1960–80
	.001 (.77) [.1104]	−.40 (−.38) [−.07]		1.38	.17	1950–82
	.0006 (−.12) [−.018]	−.40 (−.37) [−.15]		1.05	.14	1956–82
	−.12 (−.52) [−3.02]	1.74 (4.34) [0.379]		1.71	.53	1949–83

Table 8.8 Correlates with Broad Money Growth: Specification 4

Country	Const	C = DM Intercept Shift	RDM2 Foreign Assets	$\overset{\bullet}{\text{II}}$ Import Prices	IC
			Foreign Variables		
Austria	.10	.010	.54		−.19
	(10.61)	(.88)	(2.61)		(−1.74)
		[.17]	[.502]		[−.34]
Belgium	.05	.006	.05		−.18
	(4.36)	(3.87)	(.30)		(−.30)
		[.09]	[.041]		[−.41]
Canada	.089	.06	.40		−.051
	(4.41)	(2.98)	(.16)		(−.33)
		[.46]	[.102]		[−.055]
France	.09	−.005	.33		.016
	(3.60)	(−.31)	(1.19)		(.16)
		[−.071]	[.30]		[.044]
Germany	.11	−.03	.18		−.33
	(6.68)	(−1.67)	(.99)		(−5.18)
		[−.34]	[.14]		[−.56]
Italy	.12	.05	−.01		−.09
	(9.17)	(3.51)	(−.05)		(−1.90)
		[.57]	[−.006]		[−.31]
Japan	.20	−.07	−.58		−.06
	(3.45)	(−1.21)	(−1.00)		(−.49)
		[−.50]	[−.363]		[−.163]
Netherlands	.10	.014	−.005		−.014
	(0.31)	(.69)	(−1.63)		(−.14)
		[.22]	[−.295]		[−.035]
Sweden	.11	.011	−.15		−.12
	(6.31)	(.52)	(−.26)		(−.96)
		[.10]	[−.065]		[−.26]
Switzerland	.08	−.02	.43		−.28
	(5.78)	(−1.46)	(.68)		(−2.52)
		[−.18]	[1.42]		[−.42]
United Kingdom	.07	.077	−.18		.03
	(3.62)	(2.56)	(−.44)		(.20)
		[.54]	[−.015]		[.035]
United States	.075	.011	.51		−.08
	(8.53)	(.87)	(.51)		(−1.96)
		[.062]	[.025]		[−.103]

	Domestic Variables					
$\overset{\bullet}{W}$ Nominal Wages	$\overset{\bullet}{WRP}$ Real Wages	DG Actual Govt. Deficit	DDIG Adjusted Deficit	DW	R^2	Interval
	.002 (1.07) [.172]		−.66 (−.35) [−.081]	1.38	.21	1956–81
	−.18 (−2.45) [−14.45]		.043 (.84) [.147]	2.17	.43	1957–82
	−.077 (.14) [−2.52]		.19 (1.89) [.30]	2.3	.38	1949–82
	.007 (1.40) [.38]		−.69 (−.84) [.321]	1.63	−.045	1960–82
	−.0009 (−.34) [−.10]		−.26 (−1.28) [−.173]	1.74	.62	1951–82
	.002 (1.50) [.17]		.01 (.38) [.077]	1.07	.34	1956–82
	−.001 (−.18) [−.044]		.18 (.44) [.176]	2.75	−.11	1956–79
	−.005 (−1.63) [−.51]		.10 (.9) [.16]	.99	.19	1961–82
	−.002 (−.77) [−.19]		.20 (1.24) [.392]	1.54	.10	1960–80
	.0006 (.31) [.066]		1.0 (1.28) [.23]	1.31	.21	1950–82
	.0003 (.068) [.009]		.20 (1.06) [.30]	1.04	.17	1956–82
	−.26 (−.99) [−6.54]		.44 (3.48) [.21]	1.91	.46	1949–83

Notes

1   Wage-push explanations continue to dominate the political science literature. See, for example, David R. Cameron, "Social Democracy, Corporatism, Labour Quiescence and the Representation of Economic Interest in Advanced Capitalist Society," in *Order and Conflict in Contemporary Capitalism,* ed. John H. Goldthorpe (Oxford: Clarendon Press, 1984), pp. 143–78; and Colin Crouch, "Conditions for Trade Union Restraint," in *The Politics of Inflation and Economic Stagnation,* ed. Charles S. Maier and Leon Lindberg (Washington, D.C.: Brookings Institution, 1984), pp. 105–39.

2   See David R. Cameron, "The Politics and Economics of the Business Cycle," in *The Political Economy,* ed. Thomas Ferguson and Joel Rogers (New York: M. E. Sharpe, 1984), pp. 237–62; and James Buchanan and Richard Wagner, *Democracy in Deficit* (New York: Academic Press, 1977).

3   All we argue is that controllability of the money supply is technically feasible. Control theory teaches that one may use one tool, such as the money supply, to attempt to achieve some target level for *only one* ultimate variable such as inflation or unemployment. Many central banks may not meet their announced targets when they try to use monetary policy to achieve multiple goals, such as interest rates and unemployment as well as inflation. This type of behavior can lead to "stop-go" macropolicy, and is part of the time-inconsistency problem. For a useful recent analysis of this issue and references to the literature, see Kenneth Rogoff, "Reputational Constraints on Monetary Policy," *Carnegie-Rochester Conference Series on Public Policy* 26 (1987): 141–82. For an international view of experiences with monetary targeting, see Leroy O. Laney, "An International Comparison of Experiences with Monetary Targeting: A Reaction Function Approach," *Contemporary Policy Issues* 3 (Fall 1985): 99–112.

4   For recent empirical support for this statement for a number of major industrial countries, see Michael R. Darby et al., *The International Transmission of Inflation* (Chicago: University of Chicago Press for the National Bureau of Economic Research, 1983).

5   See, for example, Robert J. Gordon, "World Inflation and Monetary Accommodation in Eight Countries," *Brookings Papers on Economic Activity* 2 (1977): 409–77; Basil J. Moore, "The Endogenous Money Stock," *Journal of Post Keynesian Economics* (Fall 1979): 49–70; and Thomas D. Willett and Leroy O. Laney, "Monetarism, Budget Deficits, and Wage Push Inflation: The Cases of Italy and the U.K.," Banca Nazionale del Lavoro *Quarterly Review,* no. 127 (December 1978): 315–31.

6   See, for example, Michael Parkin, "Where Is Britain's Inflation Going?" *Lloyd's Bank Review,* July 1975, 1–13. Parkin emphasizes budget deficits, while John Hicks, "What Is Wrong with Monetarism?" *Lloyds Bank Review,* October 1975, 1–13, and Lord R. A. Kahn, "Thoughts on the Behavior of Wages and Monetarism," *Lloyd's Bank Review,* January 1976, 1–11, emphasize wage and import price-push factors. See also Basil J. Moore, "The Endogenous Money Stock," *Journal of Post Keynesian Economics,* Fall 1979, 49–70, for arguments supporting the wage-push view.

7   For critical discussion of the vicious circle debate and extensive references to the

literature, see Thomas Willett and Matthias Wolf, "The Vicious Circle Debate: Some Conceptual Distinctions," *Kyklos* 36 (1983): 231–48.

8   The global monetarist school includes economists such as Arthur Laffer, Ronald McKinnon, and Robert Mundell. For critical discussion and references, see Marina von Whitman, "Global Monetarism and the Monetary Approach to the Balance of Payments," *Brookings Papers on Economic Activity* 3 (1975), and Thomas D. Willett, *International Liquidity Issues* (Washington, D.C.: American Enterprise Institute, 1980), plus the papers and discussion in David I. Meiselman and Arthur B. Laffer, eds., *The Phenomenon of Worldwide Inflation* (Washington, D.C.: American Enterprise Institute, 1975).

9   Robert Triffin, "The International Role and Fate of the Dollar," *Foreign Affairs* (Winter 1978): 273.

10 For empirical analyses contradicting the global monetarist view that the international liquidity explosion of the early 1970s was the dominant cause of the world monetary expansion during that period, see Darby et al., *International Transmission*, p. 336; Leroy O. Laney and Thomas D. Willett, "The International Liquidity Explosion and Worldwide Inflation: The Evidence from Sterilization Coefficient Estimates," *Journal of International Money and Finance* 2 (August 1982): 141–52; and Richard Sweeney and Thomas D. Willett, "Eurodollars, Petrodollars, and World Liquidity and Inflation," in *Stabilization of the Domestic and International Economy*, supplement to the *Journal of Monetary Economics* (Amsterdam: North Holland, 1977), pp. 277–310.

11 See Moore, "Endogenous Money Stock."

12 For further discussion on this point, see Willett and Laney, "Monetarism."

13 See, for example, Parkin, "Where Is Britain's Inflation Going?"

14 This proposition that the choice of tax versus deficit financing of government expenditures makes no difference for real GNP growth is called the Ricardian equivalence theorem, named after David Ricardo, who first stated but apparently did not believe in the empirical relevance of the theorem. To hold, the theorem requires not only highly informed, forward-looking citizens but also the expectation that deficits are temporary, not permanent. For discussion of this literature and evidence that much of the U.S. budget deficit should not be considered transitory, see W. Michael Cox, "Inflation and Permanent Government Debt," Federal Reserve Bank of Dallas *Economic Review*, May 1985, 13–26; and J. Harold McClure and Thomas D. Willett, "Understanding the Supply Siders," in *Reaganomics*, ed. William Craig Stubblebine and Thomas D. Willett (San Francisco: Institute for Contemporary Studies, 1983), pp. 59–69. Of course, even if the equivalence theorem held, there could be a relationship between budget deficits and monetary expansion via the types of optimal tax considerations discussed by McClure and Willett in chapter 6 of this volume. For additional recent empirical studies of budget deficit–monetary expansion relationships see Stuart Allen and Michael Smith, "Government Borrowing and Monetary Accommodation," *Journal of Monetary Economics* 12 (November 1983): 605–16; A. J. Brown, *World Inflation since 1950: An International Comparative Study* (Cambridge: Cambridge University Press, 1985); David R. Cameron, "Does Government Cause Inflation? Taxes, Spending, and Deficit," in *The Politics of Inflation*

and Economic Stagnation, ed. Leon N. Lindberg and Charles S. Maier (Washington, D.C.: Brookings Institution, 1985), pp. 224–79; Gerald P. Dwyer, "Money, Deficits, and Inflation," in *Understanding Monetary Regimes,* ed. Karl Brunner and Allan Meltzer, *Carnegie-Rochester Conference Series on Public Policy* 22 (1985): 197–206; Kevin B. Grier and Howard E. Neiman, "Deficits, Politics, and Money Growth," *Economic Inquiry* 25 (April 1987): 201–14; Michael Hamberger and Burton Zwick, "Deficits, Money, and Inflation," *Journal of Monetary Economics* 7 (January 1981): 141–50; Dennis L. Hoffman, Stuart A. Low, and Hubert H. Reinberg, "Recent Evidence on the Relationship between Money Growth and Budget Deficits," *Journal of Macroeconomics* 5 (Spring 1983): 223–31; Douglas H. Joines, "Deficits and Money Growth in the United States: 1872–1983," *Journal of Monetary Economics* 16 (November 1985): 329–51; Robert King and Charles Plosser, "Money, Deficits, and Inflation," in *Understanding Monetary Regimes,* ed. Brunner and Meltzer, 147–96; M. Levy, "Factors Affecting Monetary Policy in an Era of Inflation," *Journal of Monetary Economics* 7 (November 1981): 351–73; W. Douglas McMillin, "Federal Deficits, Macrostabilization Goals, and Federal Reserve Behavior," *Economic Inquiry* 24 (April 1986): 257–70; William Niskanen, "Deficits, Government Spending, and Inflation," *Journal of Monetary Economics* 4 (August 1978): 591–602; Organization for Economic Cooperation and Development, *Budget Financing and Monetary Control* (Paris, 1982); and Aris A. Protopapadakis and Jeremy J. Siegel, "Government Debt, the Money Supply, and Inflation: Theory and Evidence from Seven Industrialized Economies," *Journal of International Money and Finance* 6 (April 1987): 31–48.

15 Even this is far from a perfect measure, however. For discussion of many of the conceptual and measurement issues involved, see Alan S. Blinder and Robert M. Solow, "Analytical Foundations of Fiscal Policy," in *The Economics of Public Finance* (Washington, D.C.: Brookings Institution, 1979); Frank DeLeeuw and Thomas M. Holloway, "The Measurement and Significance of the Cyclically Adjusted Federal Budget and Debt," *Journal of Money, Credit, and Banking* 17 (May 1985): 233–42; Robert W. R. Price and Patrice Muller, "Structural Budget Indicators and the Interpretation of Fiscal Policy Stance in OECD Economies," *Economic Studies,* no. 37 (Autumn 1984): 28–71; Robert Barro, *The Behavior of U.S. Deficits,* National Bureau for Economic Research, Working Paper no. 1309 (Cambridge, Mass., 1984). Some have argued that deficits should be further adjusted to remove the effect of inflation. See, for example, Gerald P. Dwyer, "Inflation and Government Deficits," *Economic Inquiry* 20 (July 1982): 315–29.

16 The basic data source was the International Monetary Fund's *International Financial Statistics.* Indices for labor earnings were taken from the OECD's *Main Economic Indicators.*

17 For discussion of differences in monetary aggregate definitions, see Ralph C. Bryant, *Money and Monetary Policy in Interdependent Nations* (Washington, D.C.: Brookings Institution, 1980), pp. 18–38. For discussion of the relative appropriateness of various definitions for a number of countries, see Gordon, "World Inflation," pp. 409–77.

18 See, for example, Thomas M. Havrilesky, Robert H. Sapp, and Robert L.

Schweitzer, "Tests of the Federal Reserve's Reaction to the State of the Economy: 1964–74," in *Current Issues in Monetary Theory and Policy,* ed. Thomas H. Havrilesky and John T. Boorman (Arlington Heights, Ill.: AHM Publishing, 1975), pp. 466–84; as well as R. Abrams, R. Froyen, and R. M. Waud, "Monetary Policy Reaction Functions, Consistent Expectations, and the Burns Era," *Journal of Money, Credit, and Banking* 12 (February 1980): 30–42; and Stanley W. Black, *Politics versus Markets: International Differences in Macroeconomic Policies* (Washington, D.C.: American Enterprise Institute, 1982).

19   For elaboration on the distinction between these different purposes, see the exchange between Ira P. Kaminow, "Politics, Economics, and Procedures of U.S. Money Growth Dynamics," in *Political Economy of International and Domestic Monetary Relations,* ed. Raymond E. Lombra and Willard E. Witte (Ames: Iowa State University Press, 1982), pp. 181–96, and Laney and Willett, "International Liquidity Explosion."

20   We did not focus on the monetary base. This decision reflects the assumption, underpinned by the empirical evidence, that the money multiplier is sufficiently stable on an annual basis to enable the authorities to achieve with reasonable accuracy a desired monetary aggregate target. See, for example, Michele Frattiani and Mustapha Nabli, "Money Stock Control in the EEC Countries," *Weltwirtschaftliches Archiv* 15 (1979): 401–24.

21   We should note, however, that the choice of operating procedures may influence the degree of monetary accommodation of various pressures. For example, the use of the federal funds rate as an intermediate target by the Federal Reserve in the 1960s may have led to a greater likelihood that upward wage or deficit pressures were accommodated. See Leroy O. Laney and Thomas D. Willett, "Presidential Politics, Budget Deficits, and the Money Supply in the United States, 1960–1976," *Public Choice* 60 (1983): 53–69.

22   Discussion on the impact of the choice of intermediate-level factor proxies on the coefficient estimates is presented by Abrams, Froyen, and Waud, "Monetary Policy Reaction Functions," pp. 30–42.

23   In earlier work on this subject our specification focused primarily on first differences in the money supply and on cyclically adjusted budget deficits. Here, the cyclical adjusted deficit, $DD1$, is the residual of the equation in which we allowed a shift in the real income slope after 1972. Specifically, $DD1$ represents the residuals of the following equation:

$$DEF = A_0 + A_1 \cdot DRY + A_2 \, DMDRY$$

DRY is the first difference in real income and $DMDRY$ is an interaction variable between the dummy DM (equal to 1 after 1972) and DRY. A summary of these initial results is presented in King Banaian, Leroy O. Laney, and Thomas D. Willett, "Central Bank Independence: An International Comparison," Federal Reserve Bank of Dallas *Economic Review,* March 1983, 1–13.

24   One disadvantage of this approach is that it deflects focus from the problems of multicollinearity among the pressure variables, which Willett and Laney found to be quite important for their earlier analysis of the comparative explanatory power of

wage-push and budget deficit pressures in Italy and the United Kingdom. See Willett and Laney, "Monetarism."

25 For further discussion of beta coefficients, again see Willett and Laney, "Monetarism."

26 While most published work to date has focused on the industrial countries, some study of these issues for the developing countries has also begun. Recent work at Claremont on Korea, Kuwait, and Nigeria has found significant effects of budget deficits on monetary expansion (although the strength and linkage appears to be a good bit less in Korea). These countries were also found to have sterilized the effects of international reserve flows on domestic monetary expansion to a substantive degree. See Mohammed Ghuloum, "A Model of the Monetary Sector of Kuwait" (Ph.D. dissertation, Claremont Graduate School, 1984); Eli Gaura, "Causes of Inflation and Monetary Expansion in Nigeria, 1960–1982: Some Empirical Evidence" (M.A. thesis, Claremont Graduate School, 1985); and Sang Man Lee, "The Controllability of the Money Supply in a Developing Country: The Case of Korea" (Ph.D. dissertation, Claremont Graduate School, 1985).

27 For further discussion on these issues, see Leroy O. Laney, "More Flexible Exchange Rates: Have They Insulated National Monetary Policies?" *Voice* of the Federal Reserve Bank of Dallas, February 1980, 6–18; and Leroy O. Laney, Christopher D. Radcliff, and Thomas D. Willett, "Currency Substitution: Comment," *Southern Economic Journal,* April 1984, 1196–1200.

28 See Gordon, "World Inflation."

29 See Nathaniel Beck, "Domestic Politics and Monetary Policy: A Comparative Perspective" (Paper presented at the meeting of the American Political Science Association, Chicago, September 1983); and Edmund J. Sheehey and Mordechai E. Kreinin, "Inflation Dispersion and Central Bank Accommodation of Supply Shocks," *Weltwirtschaftliches Archiv* 121 (1985): 448–59.

30 See Stanley W. Black, "The Use of Monetary Policy for Internal and External Balance for Ten Industrial Countries," in *Exchange Rates and International Macroeconomics,* Jacob A. Frenkel, ed. (Chicago: National Bureau of Economic Research, University of Chicago Press, 1983): 189–225.

31 See Darby et al., *International Transmission.*

32 See Gordon, "World Inflation"; and Sheehey and Kreinin, "Inflation Dispersion."

33 Given these strong negative findings, we do not need to explore the tricky issues of causation which would be raised by positive findings. On this issue, see Willett and Wolf, "Vicious Circle."

34 See Sheehey and Kreinin, "Inflation Dispersion."

35 See Black, *Politics versus Markets;* and idem, "Monetary Policy." See also Gordon, "World Inflation."

36 Subsequent research by Merzkani does find stronger evidence for real wage accommodation in France, Japan, and the United States. See Mohand Merzkani, "Budget Deficits, International Pressures, and Monetary Accommodation: A Theoretical and Empirical Study for Six Countries (France, Germany, Italy, Japan, United Kingdom, and United States): 1960–1985" (Ph.D. dissertation, Claremont Graduate School, 1987).

37 See Michael Parkin, "Oil Push Inflation," Banca Nazionale Del Lavoro *Quarterly Review,* no. 137 (1980): 163–85; and Abdelhak Lamiri, "Policy Accommodation Responses of Major OECD Countries to External Price Shocks" (Ph.D. dissertation, Claremont Graduate School, 1988).

38 See Willett and Laney, "Monetarism."

39 Our results support Beck's finding in "Domestic Politics" of concordance between fiscal and monetary policy for the United States, but not his result of nonconcordance for Germany. On the latter, our findings are more in line with the arguments of Bruno S. Frey and Friedrich Schneider, "Central Bank Behavior: A Positive Empirical Analysis," *Journal of Monetary Economics* 7 (May 1981): 291–315, that fiscal policy will tend to dominate monetary policy in Germany.

40 As an example of such an extreme cost-push view, see Peter Wiles, "Cost Inflation and the State of Economic Theory," *Economic Journal* 83 (June 1983): 377–98. For estimates of wage equations and findings of autonomous elements in European wage increases in the late 1960s, see George L. Perry, "Determinants of Wage Inflation around the World," *Brookings Papers on Economic Activity* 2 (1975): 403–35; and Gordon, "World Inflation."

41 This particular statement is by Richard Cooper in a comment on Thomas Willett's paper in "Commentaries," in *Eurocurrencies and the International Monetary System,* ed. Carl H. Stem, John H. Makin, and Dennis E. Logue (Washington, D.C.: American Enterprise Institute, 1976), p. 252, but is typical of many statements on the subject. See also Hicks, "What is Wrong with Monetarism?"

42 For the use of causality testing in our context, see Gordon, "World Inflation"; and for general methodological discussion see Rodney L. Jacobs, Edward E. Leamer, and Michael P. Ward, "Difficulties with Testing for Causation," *Economic Inquiry,* July 1979, 401–13; Arnold Zellner, "Causality and Econometrics," *Carnegie-Rochester Conference Series on Public Policy* 10 (1979): 9–54; Daniel L. Thornton, "The Government Budget Constraint with Endogenous Money," *Journal of Macroeconomics* (Winter 1984): 57–67; and Charles E. Wainhouse, "Empirical Evidence for Hayek's Theory of Economic Fluctuations," in *Money in Crisis: The Federal Reserve, the Economy, and Monetary Reform,* ed. Barry N. Siegel (San Francisco: Pacific Institute, 1984), chap. 2, pp. 37–71.

43 For the United States, see also Phillip Cagan, "Imported Inflation, 1973–74, and the Accommodation Issues," *Journal of Money, Credit, and Banking* 2 (February 1980): 1–16.

44 See, for example, Ann F. Friedlander, "Macro Policy Goals in the Postwar Period: A Study in Revealed Preference," *Quarterly Journal of Economics* 87 (February 1973): 25–43; and John H. Makin, "Constraints on Formulation of Models for Measuring Revealed Preferences of Policy Makers," *Kyklos* 29 (1976): 709–32.

45 On the theory of encompassing groups see Lars Chalmfors, "The Roles of Stabilization Policy and Wage Setting for Macroeconomic Stability—The Experience of Economies with Centralized Bargaining," *Kyklos* 39 (1985): 329–47; Mancur Olson, *The Rise and Fall of Nations* (New Haven: Yale University Press, 1982); idem, "Beyond Keynesianism and Monetarism," *Economic Inquiry* (July 1984): 297–323; and for corporatist analysis see Suzanne Berger, *Organizing Interests in Western Europe:*

Pluralism, Corporations, and the Transformation of Politics (Cambridge: Cambridge University Press, 1981); Crouch, "Conditions for Trade Union Restraint"; John H. Goldthorpe, ed., *Order and Conflict in Contemporary Capitalism* (Oxford: Clarendon Press, 1984); Peter Gourvitch, Andrew Martin, George Ross, Christopher Allen, Stephen Bornstein, and Andrei Markovits, *Unions and Economic Crisis: Britain, West Germany, and Sweden* (London: Allen and Unwin, 1984); Walter Korpi, *The Democratic Class Struggle* (New York: Methuen Inc., 1983); Leon N. Lindberg and Charles S. Maier, *The Politics of Inflation and Economic Stagnation* (Washington, D.C.: Brookings Institution, 1985); Kerry Schott, *Policy, Power, and Order: The Persistence of Economic Problems in Capitalist States* (New Haven: Yale University Press, 1984); and Philippe C. Schmitter and Gerhard Lehmbruch, *Trend Toward Corporatist Intermediation* (London: Sage Publications, 1980). For recent empirical evidence on short-run inflation-unemployment trade-offs, see, for example, Marian E. Bond, "Exchange Rates, Inflation, and Vicious Circles," International Monetary Fund *Staff Papers* 27 (December 1980): 679–711; Jeffrey D. Sachs, "Wages, Profits, and Macroeconomic Adjustment: A Comparative Study," *Brookings Papers on Economic Activity* 2 (1979): 269–319; Charles L. Schultze, "Real Wage Rigidity in Europe: Reality or Illusion," in *Other Times, Other Places* (Washington, D.C.: Brookings Institution, 1986), pp. 27–56; and David Grubb, "Topics in the OECD Phillips Curve," *Economic Journal* 96 (March 1986): 55–79.

Part Two

The Political Business Cycle

9 Politico-Economic Models of Macroeconomic Policy: A Review of the Empirical Evidence

Friedrich Schneider and Bruno S. Frey

Introduction

For over a decade there has been considerable interest in the topic of political business cycles. While there is a wealth of empirical research to support the view that macroeconomic conditions have important influences on voter attitudes and on election outcomes,[1] the numerous empirical studies which tested for systematic business fluctuations coinciding with election periods in the major industrial countries have found mixed results at best.[2] While the latter controversy has involved a great deal of technical debate about the role of rational expectations and appropriate statistical techniques (see chapter 10 of this volume as well as Kirchgässner 1984a, 1984b), we believe that a major reason that the patterns of economic activity predicted by the initial political business cycle models have not been so clearly visible is that these initial models were based on too simple views of the objectives of governments. Contending with political business cycle views of political influences on macroeconomic policies is the conception of some writers that political parties have important ideological or support group–based policies—for example, that conservative parties are more concerned about inflation than unemployment while liberal parties have the opposite priorities.

We believe that both perspectives are important and can be combined within the framework of broader politico-economic models. One set of these models would predict that political business cycle behavior will tend to dominate in elections which the government fears may be close, while "ideological" objectives will dominate when elections are expected to be safe. On this view, governments may behave in a consistent manner, but because of these multiple objectives the resulting behavior will be more complex than predicted by the simple models.

Politico-economic models of the macro economy and political process can be developed by assuming that the government maximizes its own utility subject to various constraints.[3] The government receives utility from carrying out its ideological program. A government formed by a left-wing party (or parties) may, for example, be assumed to increase the budget (in order to enlarge the domain of the state), while a right-wing government wants to decrease it (in order to keep the size of government small and to strengthen private market activities). The most important constraint the government faces is political: it may stay in power only if it is reelected. There are also important economic constraints which determine how policy instruments affect the economy, as well as the budget and balance of payment constraints (in the case of fixed exchange rates). Government is also restricted in its activity by administrative and legal constraints, for example, by the public bureaucracy which resists structural changes in expenditure programs as much as possible and has an interest in continually increasing public expenditures.

Hence, a model of a politico-economic system emphasizes the interdependence of the economy and policy by taking into account that the electorate's voting decision depends on the state of the economy (among other political issues), and that the government can influence its reelection prospects by altering the state of the economy. These relationships are sketched in figure 9.1.

Figure 9.1 shows how the state of the economy (as represented by major economic indicators such as the rate of unemployment, the rate of inflation, and the rate of growth of real income) influences the voters' evaluation of government performance: the worse (better) the economic conditions are, the less (more) satisfied the voters are with the government, assuming that the voters hold it (at least partly) responsible for the economic situation.

In the "political" sphere (polity) the institutional characteristics of the particular politico-economic system determine how much the government depends on the voters' wishes, i.e., how much a government must expect a change in its reelection prospects. Furthermore, the figure shows that the government uses its policy instruments (public expenditures and

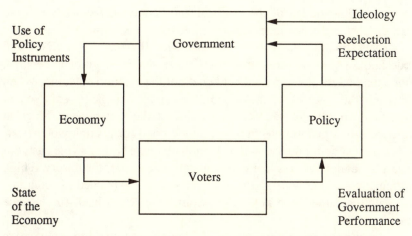

Figure 9.1   Politico-Economic System with Monopolistic Government

tax rates) considering both its reelection prospects and its ideology. The lower loop in figure 9.1, which leads from the economy to the polity to represent the voters' behavior, is termed the "evaluation function." The upper loop, which leads from the polity back to the economy to represent the government's behavior, is termed the "policy function."

The main purpose of this study is to give an overview of the current state of research on voters' behavior and on government's reactions as they relate to representative democracies. Some short remarks are added for authoritarian regimes. Furthermore, the behavior of additional actors (like the central bank and interest groups) will be analyzed in this framework. Finally, shortcomings of the current state of research are pointed out and some concluding remarks are drawn.

Voters' Behavior in Evaluating Government's Performance

Most studies in the politico-economic context—as just described—deal solely with voters' behavior concerning the evaluation of the government's (and in some also the opposition's) performance at a general election or at polls.[4] The main emphasis lies on what determines the election decisions of voters. The answer to this question is crucial for a government to know, because if the government wants to stay in office, it should have some knowledge of the political and economic factors which are used as most important determinants in a voter's decision.

The economic theory of voter behavior (Downs 1957; Riker and Ordeshook 1968) assumes that each voter makes a rational decision which maximizes the expected net benefit of the election outcome. When doing this the voter has to make two decisions: should he (or she) vote at all, and if so, should he vote for or against the government. Since to participate in a general election is a public good for a single voter (i.e., he has almost no influence on the election outcome with his vote cast, but to cast the ballot has considerable nonnegligible costs), the observed high participation rate at general elections can only be explained in economic terms with a rather high net benefit from the election itself for a single voter.[5]

Voters participating in general elections are assumed to evaluate the government in terms of its past performance over the last legislative period, or even longer. To undertake this evaluation of government's performance, the voter considers those economic and political developments for which he thinks government is (at least partly) responsible. As this information process is costly for the voter, he will use those economic and political factors which he already knows or he can obtain easily. Aggregate economic indicators which fulfill these propositions include the rate of inflation and of unemployment, the growth rate of disposable income, and the burden of taxation and of other government activities as well as government services like transfer payments. Political factors include both interior and exterior political events, such as foreign crises and domestic affairs (scandals of politicians, etc.). For the economic side it is fairly easy to investigate empirically whether these variables have an influence on voters' decisions, but for the political factors it is very difficult to find appropriate variables capturing these influences.[6]

The empirical investigation of the evaluation function started almost simultaneously at the beginning of the seventies with the econometric estimation of popularity functions (for the United States, Mueller 1970, and for Great Britain, Goodhart and Bhansali 1970) and of election functions (for the United States, Kramer 1971). These studies focused primarily on the strength of the influences of changes in the economic situation on the popularity of American presidents (and of British governing parties) or on the outcomes of congressional and presidential elections in the

United States. In these studies, the following general evaluation function was used:

$$APPR_t = F[\alpha \cdot APPR_{t-1}, (1 - \alpha) \cdot \sum_{i=1}^{n} (ec.var.)^i_{t-p},$$

$$(1 - \alpha) \cdot \sum_{j=1}^{m} (pol.var.)^j_{t-p}],$$

(1)

where APPR stands alternatively for two evaluation indicators: (1) the approval rate from popularity figures for a government, and (2) the rate of support of a government in an election; t stands for the time interval and p indicates how much time is needed before changing economic and political factors influence the two evaluation indicators; the parameter α, with $0 \leq \alpha \leq 1$, is a "discount factor" for voters' memory: if voters more or less evaluate *only* the current government performance then α approaches to 0, but if past government's performance counts a lot, α will have a value close to 1. The discount parameter can be interpreted as a measure of how myopic voters are when judging the government. With the already mentioned economic and political variables, it can be examined whether (and if so, how strongly) a change in the economic (political) situation affects the evaluation of a government.

Results of Aggregate Vote and Popularity Studies

The results of vote functions are considered first, as these look at the direct influence of economic and political influences on election outcomes. For the purposes of this study, only the economic influences are presented in table 9.1.[7] The table clearly shows that, in most cases, the rate of inflation and of unemployment and the growth rate of real income have a statistically significant impact on election outcomes—but none of these variables has a dominant influence over the others. This holds especially for the United States, where we have four studies of presidential elections for roughly the same time period: Kramer (1971) concludes that inflation and growth of real income have a significant impact. On the other hand, Fair (1978) finds only a significant influence of the real per capita income or of the rate of unemployment (if only one is included in the estimation equation). Niskanen (1979) shows a significant impact of

Table 9.1   The Influence of the Economic Situation on Election Outcomes in Representative Democracies

Dependent variable (Period)	Author	Lagged dependent variable Kind of estimation	Rate of inflation Specification and time lag
United States			
Vote share of Republican party (1896–1964)	Kramer (1971)	— ML	−0.41* Actual rate in the election year
Vote share of presidential candidate of Democratic party (1916–1972)	Fair (1978)	0.19** GLS	—
Log [vote share of presidential candidate in power] (1896–1972)	Niskanen (1979)	— OLS	—
Vote share of presidential candidate in power (1896–1976)	Kirchgässner (1981)	0.49** GLS	−0.12** Squared value in the election year
Denmark			
Vote share of bigger party in power—developed from long-term average (1920–1973)	Madsen (1980)	— GLS	−0.43* Actual value in the election year
Norway			
Vote share of governing party (1920–73)	Madsen (1980)	— GLS	−0.36* Actual rate in the election year
Sweden			
Vote share of governing party—developed from long-term average (1920–73)	Madsen (1980)	— GLS	−0.22 Actual rate in the election year
France			
Vote share of left *opposition* parties (1920–73)	Rosa (1980)	— OLS	0.20* Three years averaged values

Notes: In this table only the results of the economic factors are reported. R̄² corrected coefficient of determination; *df* = degrees of freedom. *ML* = maximum likelihood estimation; *GSL* =

Rate of unemployment Specification and time lag	Rate of income or GNP Specification and time lag	Rate of per capita federal taxes Specification and time lag	$\bar{R}^2$ df
		—	
−0.001 Change of first differences in the election year	0.27* Real, per capita value in election year		0.78 [27]
—	1.16** Real, per capita value in election year	— 	— [11]
—		−0.31* Log [real value]	0.73 [14]
—	1.51* Log [real, per capita value, average over legislative period]	—	—
−0.19 Change of first differences in the election year	—	—	0.28 [13]
−0.10 Actual rate in the election year	—	—	0.09 [13]
−2.40* Change of first differences in the election year	0.73** Actual rate in the election year	—	0.47 [13]
0.02** Three years averaged values	−0.08** Three years averaged values	—	0.80 [16]

general least squares estimation; and *OLS* = ordinary least squares estimation.* $p < .05$, two-tailed.   ** $p < .01$, two-tailed.

per capita income and of the rate of federal per capita tax. Finally, Kirch-gässner (1981) explains the vote share of American presidents by the squared rate of inflation only, and no other economic variable is significant. One reason for these quite different results may be the long time period over which the empirical studies were undertaken, with the consequences that structural changes (like the world economic crisis of 1928–29) may cause the instability in the estimation results.

For Denmark and Norway, Madsen (1980) finds *only* a significant influence of the inflation rate on the vote share for the government party or parties. For Sweden, he shows a significant impact of the rate of unemployment or of real income. Only in the case of France (Rosa 1980) do all three economic variables have a significant impact on the vote share of the left opposition parties, with the strongest influence being the inflation rate.[8] On the other side *no* statistically significant influence of the economic situation on the election outcome is found by Whiteley (1980) for Great Britain and by Inoguchi (1980) for Japan.

A comparison of the results of the vote functions between the countries may not be very useful because the time period investigated, the type of specification, and the variables included in the estimation are too different in the various studies. However, the results for the majority of the countries show that the economic situation has an important influence on the election outcome, but just how strong this influence is and which economic factors are most crucial is difficult to tell.[9]

As it is very important for a government to regularly know the evaluation by the voters of its performance in terms of the current and past, government will use the instrument of polls at regular intervals; polls on government performance are undertaken in most western countries on a monthly basis. Using polls a government can see how voters' evaluations change when the effects of its policy changes are perceived by the voters. Therefore most authors concentrate their studies on the question of which political and economic factors have an influence on government's popularity and how strong and quantitatively important they are. Today, there are more than seventy studies of the economic and political impact on government's popularity (to the authors' knowledge), most of them concentrating on the United States, Great Britain, France, and Germany. As it is not possible (and may not be very useful) to survey all of them, we will focus here on what we believe are the most important results recently published.

In table 9.2 the influence of the economic situation on the popularity of presidents in France and in the United States is reported, and in table 9.3 the estimation results of popularity functions of governing parties are given. Table 9.2 clearly shows that the rates of inflation and of unemployment and the growth rate of real income have a significant impact on a president's popularity in France and in the United States. The interesting question now is which economic variable is the dominant one. For France the results of the three studies differ:[10] Whereas Lewis-Beck (1980) finds that the inflation rate has the strongest impact (in quantitative terms), Hibbs (1981) concludes that the growth of income and the rate of unemployment are the dominating economic factors. Lafay (1984a) reaches a similar result as Hibbs and additionally finds a significant impact of the exchange rate. For the United States a clear picture emerges: The rate of unemployment and/or growth rate of real income are the dominating economic factors on presidential popularity (Schneider 1978 and Hibbs 1982a). Considering only the influence of unemployment and inflation on presidential popularity, the following result shows up: from President Kennedy to President Nixon the elasticity of unemployment is greater than for inflation, whereas for the popularity of Presidents Ford and Carter the opposite holds.[11] Furthermore, the impact of the economic situation on presidential popularity has increased remarkably over time: From Kennedy to Carter the popularity elasticities for unemployment and income almost doubled (from -0.22 to -0.36 and from 0.27 to 0.45, respectively) and for inflation the elasticity rose from -0.05 to -0.53.

Considering the results of the economic situation on the popularity of the governing party (or parties) in four European and three Asian states, again a clear picture appears: The rate of inflation and of unemployment as well as the growth rate of real income (or a similar measure) have a significant impact on the popularity of the parties in government. Moreover, with the exception of Japan, in all other countries the rate of unemployment has a quantitatively larger effect on government popularity than the rate of inflation. This means that the voters blame the government more strongly for an increase in unemployment than for an increase in inflation. The growth rate of income is quantitatively of smaller importance—again, with the exception of Japan, where the estimated coefficient has almost the same size as the one on the inflation rate. When a balance of payments (or a similar) variable is included, as in the studies for Australia, Denmark, France, Great Britain, and New Zealand, it turns

Rate of unemployment	Rate of income	Tax burden (total taxes/GNP)	Change of the exchange rate or balance of payments	$\bar{R}^2$
Specification and time lag	Specification and time lag	Specification and time lag	Specification and time lag	df
−0.56* Actual rate, lagged two months	—	—	—	0.73 [217]
−0.01** Actual rate	0.017** Actual rate real, per capita, disp.	—	—	— [29]
−0.103** Actual rate, lagged one month	0.029** Actual rate, lagged one month	—	−0.0253** Amount francs per U.S.-$; one-month lag	0.77 [104]
−5.43** Actual rate, two quarters lag	—	—	—	0.85 [25]
−3.89** Actual rate, two quarters lag	—	—	—	0.90 [24]
−0.017*** log[rate(t)/ rate(t-1)] .	0.015** log[rate(t)/ rate(t-1)] real, per capita income	—	—	— [60]
−0.017	0.273			
−0.143	0.394			
−0.249	0.392			
−0.382	0.553			
−0.356	0.452			

**These elasticities are averages over the period each president was in office and should be interpreted as rough indicators of how sensitive voters react to a change in the economic situation under a certain president.

Table 9.3   The Influence of the Economic Situation on the Popularity of
Parties in Government

Dependent variable: Popularity Period	Author	Lagged dependent variable Kind of estimation	Rate of inflation Specification and time lag
Australia Governing party(ies) 1960:2–1977:2 quarterly data	Schneider Pommerehne [1980]	0.66** OLS	−0.47* Actual rate, one quarter lag
Denmark Governing party: Social Democrats 1957:2–1968:1 quarterly data	Paldam/Schneider [1980]	0.67** GLS	−0.41* Difference between t and t-4
Germany (West) Governing party: Christian Democrats 1951:1–1966:10 monthly data	Kirchgässner [1976]	0.67** TSLS	−0.20** Actual rate
Governing parties: SPD + FDP 1970:3–1976:10 monthly data	Kirchgässner [1977]	0.61** GLS	−0.09* Actual rate
Great Britain Head of the govt. (POP-GOV – POP-OPP) 1955:3–1977:4 quarterly data	Pissarides [1980]	0.52** GLS	−0.57* First difference between t and t-1
Japan Governing party(ies) 1960–1976 30 observations	Inoguchi [1980]	— OLS	−0.68** Actual rate
New Zealand Head of the govt. party (POP-GOV – POP-OPP) 1970:1–1981:IV quarterly data	Ursprung [1983]	0.28* MLS	−0.35** Actual rate of change of inflation
Sweden Social Democrats 1967:3–1976:9 monthly data	Jonung/ Wadensjoe [1979]	0.88** OLS	−0.10* Actual rate one month lag

*POP-GOV (POP-OPP) means popularity of the government (opposition) party(ies); for further notes see

Rate of unemployment Specification and time lag	Rate of income Specification and time lag	Tax burden (total taxes/GNP) Specification and time lag	Change of the exchange rate or balance of payments Specification and time lag	R^2
−1.13** Actual rate, one quarter lag	0.05* Actual rate, real, per capita one quarter lag	—	0.04* Change of 1st differences; balance of payments	0.69 [55]
−0.73** Difference between t and t-4	0.19* Rate of real wages; difference between t and t-4	0.51* Difference between t and t-4	0.10 Difference between t and t-4; real balance of payments	0.92 [35]
−0.43** Actual rate	—	—	—	0.84 [174]
−0.31** Actual rate	—	—	—	0.76 [85]
4.55** Reciprocal value, lagged two quarters	0.26** Rate of consumption expenditures	−0.45* Actual rate	0.26** 1st difference between t and t-1; balance of payments	0.66 [80]
—	0.59* Actual rate lag: t-2	—	—	0.54 [27]
−2.12** Actual rate	0.07 Rate of growth of real, per capita GDP	—	0.36** Surplus of balance as share of GNP	0.78 [37]
−0.73** Actual rate, one month lag	—	—	—	0.91 [111]

tables 9.1 and 9.2.

out that it has a significant and quantitatively important effect in Great Britain, France, and New Zealand. We can conclude that in some countries with serious balance of payments difficulties (like Denmark or Australia), it seems to be of little interest to the voter. One reason may be that voters find it difficult to understand what balance of payments problems are. Another variable, the burden of taxation, which is included in three studies (Australia, Denmark, and Great Britain), indicates that when the tax pressure reaches a critical level it becomes an important factor, too.[12]

One matter not discussed so far in tables 9.2 and 9.3 is whether voters evaluate government's performance by just looking at the recent state of the economy or by looking further back into past government economic performance. The empirical results are mixed in this respect: Hibbs (1981, 1982a) and Hibbs and Madsen (1981) conclude from their studies for France, Germany, Great Britain, Sweden, and the United States that voters evaluate economic performance by comparing a president's/government's cumulative record over the past to that of his/its predecessors. Hibbs finds that the weights attached to the current and past economic events are estimated to decline geometrically at a rate g (as the decay rate parameter), with $g \approx 0.8$ in most studies. This high value of g (close to 1) in Hibbs' studies implies that past outcomes play an important role in current political judgments of governments by the voters. Similar results are reached by Chappell (1983) and by Chappell and Keech (1984a), who conclude that voters are *even* concerned with the future consequences of current economic policy choices and are aware of the nature of constraints imposed by economic reality. On the other hand, other researchers (Kirchgässner 1984b, Pissarides 1980) conclude from their results that voters are to a certain extent myopic and have limited knowledge of the workings of the economy, so that mainly the economic events in the current year play a significant role when voters judge a president's/government's record. Hence, the question of how "rational" or "myopic" voters are remains open and needs further research.

Whether voters should *at all* consider economic conditions as a criterion for evaluating government performance has been questioned by Stigler (1973). He argues that if voters are rational, no relationship between economic conditions and election outcomes may be expected in the United States, as the parties are so broadly based that there is no difference between them with respect to the goals of full employment, price stability, and growth of income. Moreover, strong versions of the modern theory of rational expectations completely deny such a relationship. If government, according to the Lucas-Sargent policy ineffectiveness proposition, cannot influence the real economic situation[13] and if—as Stigler already proposed—the electorate has rational expectations and knows about the inability of the government, why should they hold the government responsible for cyclical fluctuations in the economy? This view is supported by some researchers (e.g., Stimson 1976; Yantek 1982; Norpoth and Yanteck 1983a, 1983b) who—using modern time series methods—do *not* find any significant relationship between economic variables and the popularity of U.S. presidents or of political parties in power in Germany.

Stigler's view, however, has in turn been questioned by others[14] and the rational expectations in this strong version was criticized, too (e.g., McCallum 1980; Sims 1982). Moreover, the latest studies done by Norpoth (1984), Whiteley (1984), and Kirchgässner (1985a, 1985b) find that unemployment and inflation *do* have a significant and quantitatively important effect on government popularity—using the same modern time series methods (like the Box-Jenkins analysis and Granger causality tests).

From the empirical results surveyed so far, we can conclude the following: Most studies find a statistically significant and persistent relationship between the economic situation in a country and the evaluation of a president/government, which results in a quantitatively important impact of economic variables on a president's/government's popularity or approval rate at elections. The better (worse) the economic situation is, especially before elections, the more the government's popularity or re-election chance increases (decreases). But the strength of this influence varies considerably between countries and over time. Besides different country-specific voter attitudes toward economic events (e.g., the great fear of Germans about inflation), one reason for this change may be different expectations voters form about economic events over time.

Results of Disaggregated Popularity Studies

Most research on the influence of economic conditions on popularity has dealt with the electorate as if it were a homogeneous group. Different groups of voters (the different income classes, for example) can be expected to be differently affected by changes in the economy. This section looks at studies which analyze whether or not different groups of voters also evaluate the president's performance differently as the economy changes, exhibiting different levels of sensitivity to changes in unemployment and inflation.

Various researchers, such as Alt (1984), Alt and Chrystal (1983), Hibbs (1982b, 1982c), and Schneider (1978), have come to the conclusion that a changing economy differentially affects voters belonging to different income classes. Members of lower income classes favor an economic situation with low unemployment even if this means a relatively high rate of inflation. In contrast, people in upper income brackets are mainly interested in the opposite situation, i.e., low inflation at the possible cost of high unemployment. The authors put forward the following arguments: High income recipients are more concerned about inflation because they are more seriously affected by it (e.g., their money holdings depreciate in value, there is increased uncertainty about property values). Unemployment is a less serious problem for upper income groups because in general they enjoy greater job security. Low income recipients are most concerned with unemployment because they are much more in danger of being dismissed and of having to incur the cost of finding a new job (search and mobility cost, costs of uncertainty). As nominal wage rates are expected to reflect inflationary movements quite closely and automatically, the lower income groups have little incentive to be concerned about price stability.

These hypotheses have been empirically tested (Schneider 1978) using monthly popularity data of the U.S. presidents Nixon and Ford for voters belonging to seven different income classes ($POPP\text{-}YC1 =$ \$0–2,999 annual income to $POPP\text{-}YC6 =$ \$20,000 and above annual income). The empirical results for the impact of the economic variables of unemployment and inflation on presidential popularity are presented in figure 9.2. These estimates clearly support the theoretical hypotheses advanced. Figure 9.2 shows that the size of the inflation coefficient continuously rises from -1.00 to -2.60 as we move from low to high income groups. The opposite movement holds for the unemployment coefficient (with an exception for the first income group, where the estimated coefficient has a value of -2.9): it continuously falls from -4.44 to a value of -1.84. These results clearly demonstrate that high income recipients react more negatively to inflation and low income recipients to unemployment, and such a differential evaluation corresponds well to their private interests.[15]

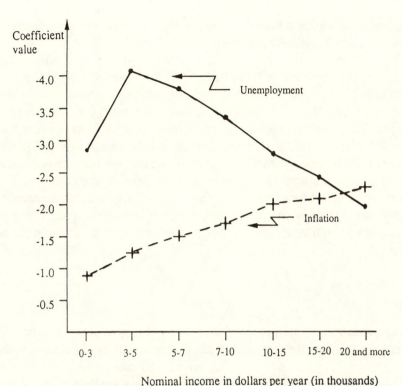

Figure 9.2 Coefficients of the Rate of Unemployment and the Rate of Inflation: U.S. Presidential Popularity for Seven Different Groups of Voters, 1969–76 (Monthly Estimates)

Government Behavior in Representative Democracies

As already mentioned, in a representative democracy with discontinuous elections every third to fifth year, the government can be considered to be in a special position of power similar to that of a monopolist. It has various advantages in comparison to the opposition, the most important of which is the opportunity to influence the course of the economy before elections. The government has considerable discretionary power which it can use to carry out its ideological programs. When political survival is seriously threatened, government is forced to undertake a vote-maximizing policy at election time. At other times, however, the government is free to pursue its ideological goals.

The behavior of a government undertaking only a vote-maximizing policy in a representative democracy has been modeled both in the context of a Phillips curve framework and of the whole economy. The best known is by Nordhaus (1975) (see also Lindbeck 1976 and MacRae 1977), who assumes that the government maximizes its vote share V at election time T. This vote share depends on the past experience of the voters with unemployment U and inflation $\dot{p}$. The voters are thus taken to make the government responsible for the course of the economy. Past economic experiences have less influence on the vote decision; the discount factor thus measures the speed with which voters forget. The government's vote share at election time accumulated over the election period $(0,T)$ is

$$V(T) = \int_0^T u[U(t), \dot{p}(t)]e^{\varrho t}dt, \tag{2}$$

where u measures the instant evaluation of the government's policy, an increase of unemployment and inflation being damaging, of course, to the government ($u_U < 0$, $u_{\dot{p}} < 0$). The government has control over the rate of unemployment, but is constrained by the (expectations) augmented unemployment-inflation trade-off.

$$\dot{p} = f(U) + \alpha\dot{p}^e; f'(U) < 0, 0 < \alpha < 1 \tag{3}$$

$$\frac{d\dot{p}^e}{dt} = \beta(\dot{p} - \dot{p}^e); \beta > 0 \tag{4}$$

Maximizing the vote share at election time (2), subject to the constraint of the economic system (3, 4), determines the government's optimal policy: the unemployment rate is increased immediately after the election in order to push down both inflation and inflation expectations, thus shifting the Phillips curve towards the origin. Before the election, unemployment is reduced, and the cost in terms of an outward shifting Phillips curve arises only after the election. The government is thus able to increase its vote share by deliberately destabilizing the economy, a phenomenon known as the "political business cycle." The fact that the government may find it advantageous to actively produce a business cycle stands in sharp contrast to the "Keynesian" notion of a benevolent government which as a matter of course has an interest in economic stabilization.

Since Nordhaus's ground-breaking study, a large theoretical and empirical literature on the political business cycle has emerged. For example, Kirchgässner (1978, 1984a, 1984b) and Minford and Peel (1982) have derived the specific features of politico-economic cycles when governments pursue ideological goals subject to an election constraint, and when voters are *not* myopic and learn to understand the creation of the cycle. The "typical" form of the political business cycle (recession after an election and upswing before the next election) is the basis of some empirically oriented papers which try to investigate whether such a cycle does systematically exist. Using quarterly data for the period 1949–74, McCallum (1977) directly examines the relationship between the patterns of unemployment and phase of the electoral cycle in the United States. He concludes that the explanatory power of an autoregressive equation for the unemployment rate for *no* administration significantly improved by the addition of a variable indicating the phase of the electoral cycle. Similar results are reached by Laechler (1978, 1982), Beck (1982b), and Thompson and Zuck (1983). Contrary to these findings, MacRae (1981) concludes that there is some empirical evidence in the U.S. postwar periods (especially during the Kennedy and Johnson administrations) for a politically motivated business cycle. In favor of a politico-economic business cycle is the study of Maloney and Smirlock (1981), too. Moreover, Paldam (1981b) has made extensive empirical tests and again found some evidence of a political business cycle in aggregate real and price variables for the OECD countries over the period 1948–75.

An interesting empirical example of a vote-maximizing policy is provided by Wright's (1974) cross-section analysis of federal government expenditures for U.S. states during the economic depression of 1933–40. The "value" of every state to the federal government depends upon the comparison of the traditional vote share (V_{io}) of the president's party (during this time the Democrats) with the vote share attainable (V_i) by generating income per capita in state i through appropriate public expenditures:

$$V_i = V_{io} + bY_i, \tag{5}$$

where b indicates the effectiveness of additional income generation Y_i upon the vote share received V_i. A state has no "value" (in this sense) if the Democrats expect to receive a majority anyway ($V_{io} > 50\%$), or if it is impossible to bring the actual vote over 50% by income generation. Based on this idea, a priority index can be constructed which takes into account the case under which any state can be won. It is hypothesized that the federal government allocates public expenditures according to this priority index, i.e., not according to "needs" of the individual states, but rather according to the partisan interest of the administration in power. Statistical estimation indeed shows a significant effect of this priority index on federal public expenditures—strongly confirming the idea that the administration in power wants to be reelected.

On the basis of a complete macroeconomic model of the United States, Fair (1975) has derived the vote-maximizing policy of a president. According to his estimates, the presidential vote share depends on the growth rate of real GNP only (a result which has not been found by other researchers). Moreover, voters only consider GNP in the election year, i.e., they completely discount the state of the economy in previous years. Under these conditions, it turns out that it is advantageous for the president to create a marked politico-economic cycle: the president maximizes votes and his reelection chance if he undertakes a strongly restrictive policy in the first part of the election period and a strongly expansionary policy in the second part. It turns out, however, that American presidents in the postwar period have not followed such a policy, i.e., the vote-maximizing use of instruments has weak explanatory power.

The studies mentioned so far mostly try to explain government behavior at election time or assume that government is maximizing votes all the time. As already argued, and if we intend to explain actual (observed) government behavior over a whole legislative period, then we have to broaden the approach and take into account that a government has considerable discretionary power which it can use to carry out its ideological programs. Hence, the basic assumption of the studies by Frey and Schneider[16] is that government maximizes its own utility in pursuing certain ideological goals.[17] However, even if we assume that it is very difficult for a government party (or parties) to be thrown out of office in the middle of a legislative period, government is still subject to various constraints in trying to achieve its ideological goals, of which the most important is the reelection constraint. Thus the government faces a dynamic maximization problem of when to undertake what kind of fiscal policy action in order to maximize its utility.

As the government is not able to resolve this problem, we assume that it will behave in a satisficing manner and that it takes the results of popularity surveys as the best current indicator of its reelection chance. If the current popularity, measured by the lead over the opposition, is high and/or there is plenty of time until the next election, government will use its various fiscal instruments to pursue its ideological goals.

Considering ideologically motivated party programs, a left-wing government will generally increase public sector activity in comparison to a right-wing government, including new and/or expanded spending programs. Socialist/labor governments in general explicitly state preferences for low unemployment and social reforms, the latter resulting in more spending on education, welfare, and health care systems.[18] Conservative (right-wing) governments state preferences for a low inflation rate and a much smaller level of growth in current and future government activities and for a strengthening of private sphere activities.

To investigate the ideological goals of U.S. presidents is a much more delicate task, because in the American political system the ideological differences of the Republican and Democratic party are quite often difficult to distinguish. Hibbs (1977) and Tufte (1978) found evidence that ceteris paribus the unemployment level is lower under Democratic administrations compared to Republican ones. Hibbs concludes that "the interadministration difference in government-induced unemployment level is about 2.4% considering the post-war administrations" (Hibbs 1977, p. 1486). Hibbs's work has been criticized by Beck (1982a) for exaggerating the differences. For example, Beck found that some Democratic administrations had higher unemployment than some Republican administrations. On the other hand, Chappell and Keech (1984b) find again that the unemployment rates differ significantly between the Democratic and Republican administrations. In general these results provide some evidence that Democratic administrations state and pursue preferences for a lower unemployment rate compared to Republican ones.

If the reelection chances are low, as indicated by a significant decline of government popularity below those of the opposition(s) and/or the next election is close, the government will concentrate on securing reelection rather than pursuing its ideological goals, which in any case it can hope to put into effect only by remaining in power. For this purpose, the government—regardless of who is in power—will undertake such a taxing and spending policy which maximizes the chance of being reelected, counting on the voters' short memory. The concrete fiscal policy undertaken will depend on voters' evaluation of government's economic preference and their preferences over the various taxing and spending items. Our main conclusion is that if a government fears to lose the next election, *any* government will switch to a common fiscal policy, i.e., one which is clearly preferred by a majority of voters. After an election, such a common (popular) fiscal policy is given up for a more ideologically oriented one.

Econometric estimates of government behavior as just described have been undertaken for Australia, Germany, Great Britain, and the United States. The main results of these studies are presented in table 9.4.[19]

From the mid-fifties up to the mid-seventies, the results shown in table 9.4 clearly indicate that the governments in all four countries studied undertake expansionary policies when they fear not being reelected in the forthcoming elections (i.e., they are in a state of popularity deficit). They tend to increase exhaustive and transfer expenditures and decrease taxes in order to stimulate the economy and hence reduce unemployment and increase personal income—a policy which showed up to be the most popular considering the results of the vote and popularity functions discussed earlier. If government can use its various fiscal instruments to pursue its ideological goals, i.e., when it feels secure about being reelected, left-wing governments (Labour in Australia and Great Britain, and Social Democrats in Germany) have a tendency to increase the size of government by raising expenditures and taxes. On the other hand, right-wing governments (Country/Liberal in Australia, Christian Democrats in Germany, Tories in Great Britain, and Republicans in the United States) tend to decrease the size of government by cutting expenditures and lowering the tax burden when their reelection is not in danger.

The results have been criticized by Alt and Wooley (1982), Chrystal and Alt (1979, 1983) and Alt and Chrystal (1983) for Great Britain and by Ahmad (1983) for the United States. Chrystal and Alt propose a permanent income hypothesis for the spending behavior of the British government. They argue that governments plan expenditures to grow in proportion to expected levels of income. These expenditures plans are not easily changed—they are too "sticky" to react to short-term fluctuations of national income in order to create an upswing and thus help the government to secure reelection. Ahmad argues that the function describing the presidential policy response has to contain both economic *and* political

Table 9.4 The Use of Fiscal Policy Instruments for Securing Reelection or Reaching Ideological Goals in Representative Democracies

Country Use of instrument Period	Author	Fiscal policy instruments		
		Expenditures for goods and services	Transfer payments to private households	Total tax revenues
Australia				
Reelection effort	Pommerehne/ Schneider (1980)	+ **	+ **	− *
Ideological goals				
Country/Liberal		− *	−	− *
Labour		+ *	+ *	+
1960:2–1977:2				
quarterly data				
Germany				
Reelection effort	Frey / Schneider (1979)	+ *	+ *	− *
Ideological goals				
Christian Democrats		− *	− *	− *
Social Democrats		+ *	+ *	+ *
1951–1976				
yearly data				
Great Britain				
Reelection effort	Frey / Schneider (1978a)	+ **	+ **	− **
Ideological goals				
Conservative		− *	−	−
Labour		+ *	+ *	+
1962:1–1974:4				
quarterly data				
United States				
Reelection effort				
Ideological goals	Frey /			− *
Repub. president	Schneider	+ **	+ **	±
Demo. president	(1978b)	− *	− *	−
1953:1–1976:4		+ *	+	
quarterly data				

Notes: + (−) means a expansive (contractive) use of fiscal policy instruments on the expenditure side—vice versa for the revenue side; ± = undecided use. All instruments are estimated by including various other constraints such as budget or cost-push factors).
*p < .05, two-tailed.   **p < .01, two-tailed.

determinants for each policy instrument. Ahmad maintains that Frey and Schneider (1978b) disregard economic influences on presidential policy. According to Ahmad, a president *always* and *immediately* reacts to changes in economic conditions irrespective of whether he feels his re-election is in danger or not.

Against Alt and Chrystal's objections, Frey and Schneider (1981a, 1982, 1983) argue that the authors give no reason why the British Government (Tory and Labour) should desire to keep expenditures a stable share of anticipated national income. "Explaining" government expenditures by national income of the same period is rather uninformative and does not allow one to make any true prediction of what government intends to do. Against Ahmad's criticism Schneider and Frey (1983) argue that Ahmad fails to convincingly argue why a president in the United States should have an incentive to react immediately whenever economic and political conditions change. Only if a president wants the "good of society" and thus acts like a "benevolent dictator" would such behavior make sense (against the evidence collected in public choice).

As it is always possible to disagree about theoretical approaches, one crucial test is how the different models work to explain reality, using the test of the true ex post forecasts which have been undertaken for the two countries.[20] Whereas the politico-economic model for the United States by Frey and Schneider yields clearly superior forecasts over the one by Ahmad, it is an open question in the case of Great Britain whether the Chrystal and Alt model or the one by Frey and Schneider leads to superior forecasts.[21] Both studies claim to demonstrate this, but as they use different data and time periods, it is difficult to come to a final conclusion.

Summarizing the results of this part, we clearly see that governments in representative democracies undertake those fiscal policies which are popular for a majority of voters when they feel that their reelection is in danger. If this is not the case then they can pursue their ideological goals, such as reducing the size of government by cutting (certain) expenditures and lowering the tax rates—a policy which President Reagan immediately undertook when he came into office in 1981.

A Politico-Economic Model of
Eastern Authoritarian Regimes

The general relationship found between economic conditions and government behavior in representative democracies also obtains for polities with an authoritarian structure: no government, not even the most dictatorial, is completely independent of the support by the population. *Every* government therefore has an interest in meeting the population's economic desires *up to a certain degree*. In every type of dictatorship, the government has greater scope to suppress the population's wishes than in a democracy, but it must nevertheless consider the fact that it may be overthrown if the population is too dissatisfied with the developing economic and political situation. In that case, it must step up repressive measures in order to keep down the likelihood of a revolt. Such a policy often requires large resources in terms of manpower (police, soldiers, informers) and finance, which cannot be used for other purposes. Even an authoritarian government is therefore forced to decide whether it is not more advantageous in terms of its own goals (utility maximization) to reduce the danger of being overthrown by improving the economic and political conditions, rather than to use additional resources to increase suppression.

A politico-economic model along these lines has been developed for the socialist countries of eastern Europe (excluding Yugoslavia and Albania, as well as the Soviet Union) for the period 1961–76 by Lafay (1981). In these countries, the government's popularity with the population cannot be measured by election outcomes because the voters effectively have no choice between competing programs and policies, nor are any public opinion surveys available. An indirect indicator of the government's popularity is the frequency with which politicians in power change. A frequent change of the members of the government is a sign of trouble and may therefore be taken to indicate that there is increased tension between the government and population. It is indeed found that a decrease in the growth rate of real wages is followed by more rapid changes among the members of government. The governments of the planned Eastern European countries tend to react to such mounting dissatisfaction in the population by easing their investment programs. The capital investment plans are revised downwards in order to make it possible to grant the population a more rapid rise in real wages. When these measures are successful the population is (relatively) more supportive of the government. Once the situation of the government is stabilized, the orthodox plans are reestablished by curtailing the growth of real incomes in order to raise the investment. The interaction between the government and the population thus leads to a politico-economic cycle which is comparable to the political business cycle found in Western industrialized democracies.

Additional Actors in Politico-Economic Models

The politico-economic models discussed so far consider only two actors, the voters and the government, and hence leave out important other decision makers, such as the central bank, and interest groups (including the public bureaucracy). To overcome this shortcoming, some research in this direction has been undertaken:

1. Frey and Schneider (1981b) have demonstrated that the model used for the government (utility maximization subject to constraints) is also suitable for explaining central bank behavior and therewith monetary policy, with the decisive constraint on the central bank being the possibility of conflict with the government. The authors hypothesize that in the case of conflict, the government is for various reasons in a more powerful position, and the central bank has to yield to its politically motivated demands in order not to lose its independence. The following hypotheses have been tested in this respect for Germany, with good results: In the case of conflict over the direction (expansionary or contractionary) of economic policy with the government, the central bank follows government policy with a certain time lag—specifically, it employs an expansionary monetary policy in accordance with the government's expansionary fiscal policy in the case of a reelection effort. In the case of no conflict with the government, the central bank pursues its own utility by employing a restrictive policy, i.e., increasing interest rates and decreasing credit in order to combat inflation.[22]

2. In most representative democracies the existing institutional conditions give great power to organized interests. There are politico-economic models stressing the activity of organized interests (van Winden 1981, Borooah and van den Ploeg 1983), and there are at least several areas relevant to macroeconomic policy in which the influence of pressure groups on the government has been specifically studied by politicometric research:

a. Schneider and Naumann (1982) and Schneider (1985) have shown that the positions which interest groups take on specific economic policy issues have a significant effect on referenda outcomes in Switzerland, ceteris paribus. Not surprisingly, those interest groups with large numbers of members (trade union confederations, farmers' unions) have more impact at *this* level of the polity than those with only few members (business and banking associations), which find it more advantageous to exert pressure at other levels of the political process, mainly through the public bureaucracy.

b. Trade union behavior is not independent of purely political factors as has been demonstrated by Gärtner (1977, 1978, 1981a, 1981b) for the case of the Federal Republic of Germany and the period 1960–76. The rate of increase of wage rates moves cyclically with elections: The trade unions ceteris paribus ask for smaller wage increases if the party in power (Social Democrats) is ideologically close to them. This behavior can be explained by an effort to contribute to keeping a government in power which is basically favorable to the trade union interest. On the other hand, if the government is politically right-wing, the trade unions see no reason to restrict their wage demands; they may even be particularly aggressive in order to reduce the government's reelection chance.

c. An area in which organized interest groups are particularly active and successful is tariffs. Within the framework of a newly developing international political economy based on public choice,[23] tariff setting has been analyzed as the result of a "game" between protectionist and free-trade interests (Findlay and Wellisz 1982, 1983). Politometric research has been able to show that the activity of interest groups strongly contributes to explaining the temporal development as well as the structure between industries of existing tariffs, particularly for the United States.[24]

In general, this discussion demonstrates that there are fruitful efforts to incorporate additional actors in politico-economic models. This line of research may also widen the aspect under which government and voters act, so that their role may be modified, when *additional decision makers are fully integrated* in politico-economic models.

Concluding Remarks and Shortcomings
of the Current Research

The current stage of research of politico-economic relations between voters and government in representative democracies allows us to draw the three following conclusions:

1. In representative democracies the economic situation has important influences on voters' evaluation of a president/government, which shows up in a statistically significant and quantitatively important influence of macroeconomic variables (such as unemployment, inflation, and disposable income) on a president's/government's popularity. The better (or worse) the economic situation in voters' eyes, the more a president's/government's popularity increases (decreases).

2. Government behavior depends on economics and politics. The basic proposition of the politico-economic model, that governments are interested in putting their selfish goals into practice in the political contest, i.e., to be reelected and to reach ideological goals, fares well compared to the competing proposition that governments are directly interested in the state of the economy as such (presumably to further the welfare of the population). However, government behavior is not solely determined by the need to survive but also by ideological considerations. The differentiation between the state of a popularity deficit before an election, in which the government is forced to undertake a popularity-increasing policy in order to be reelected, and the state of a popularity surplus, in which the government can allow itself to pursue ideologically motivated objectives, seems preferable to the (crude but still popular) assumption that the government constantly undertakes a vote-maximizing policy.

Thus even though the incentives to engage in political business cycles may be quite substantial, we would not expect governments to attempt to pursue such a pattern systematically at each election, as assumed in the initial simple political business cycle models and in much of the testing of these models. Thus we are not surprised that many studies (e.g., Mosley 1978; Golden and Poterba 1980; Beck 1982b) do not find to a great extent statistically significant patterns of a simple political business cycle. A broader view, such as is emphasized in the second generation of politico-economic models, is clearly needed. Moreover, the macroeconomic consequences and constitutional implications need to be examined, as done in the studies by Wagner (1977) and Frey (1979, 1983).

3. Governments are part of politico-economic interaction, in which a multitude of actors are participating. In the policy functions of the politico-economic models estimated, the influence of public bureaucracy and other interest groups on government can be identified to lie in the incapacity of governments to change their policy instruments quickly to the value desired if faced with stiff resistance from interest groups (e.g., the public administration has an interest in a conservative policy which enhances their position).

The current stage of politico-economic relations so far developed faces various shortcomings which can be overcome by further research:

1. In most studies, government activity is reflected only through the budget. There are, however, a great many other policy areas open to the government which it can use substitutively. If the substitution possibilities are heavily employed, the policy function as sketched above may be misspecified.

2. Informational aspects should receive more attention both with respect to voters and political actors. If, for instance, voters become increasingly aware of the fact that governments voluntarily create business cycles in order to stay in power, they may start reacting adversely to such activity. In that case, it may no longer be worthwhile for governments to create such cycles. The close relationship to the theory of rational expectations should be obvious.

3. The politico-economic models do not allow for the influence of political relations between nations. This aspect is of obvious importance, especially in the age of movements toward economic and political integration, such as the European Community. Equally, the interaction of federal units is left out of consideration. Subfederal units not only account for a large part of total public expenditures in many countries, they also influence the central government's policy.

In most of these areas, fruitful research has already begun; it may be useful to once again consider the development of this field in public choice five or ten years from now.

Notes

This is a revised and updated version of a paper presented at the Annual Public Choice Meeting in Phoenix, Arizona, and in seminars at the University of California, Santa Barbara, and at the University of Aarhus, Denmark. For most helpful and stimulating comments on earlier drafts, the authors thank Dennis Mueller, King Banaian, Howard Rosenthal, Perry Shapiro, and Thomas Willett.

1 The pioneering work in this area has been done by Mueller (1970) and Kramer (1971) for the United States and Goodhart and Bhansali (1970) for Great Britain.

2 Due to lack of space, voters' and government's behavior in direct democracies is not analyzed here. For those studies, compare Pommerehne (1978), Pommerehne and Schneider (1978), Romer and Rosenthal (1979), Schneider, Pommerehne, and Frey (1981) and Schneider and Naumann (1982).

3 The first study analyzing government behavior in this context was done by Frey and Lau (1968). For a survey of the first studies, see Frey and Schneider (1975).

4 An extensive overview of this literature is not intended here, and only the most important results will be reported. One of the best surveys of popularity and vote functions is given by Paldam (1981a). Compare also later studies by Borooah and van den Ploeg (1983), van Winden (1981), Schneider (1985), and Kirchgässner (1986).

5 It should be noted here that the economic theory of voter behavior by itself is not able to explain satisfactorily why voters actually vote, i.e., why we observe such a high participation rate at general elections in representative democracies. But given the fact that many people do vote on other grounds (a sense of duty, etc.), it does help to explain variations in the level of voter turnout. See, for example, Tollison and Willett (1973).

6 In some studies, like Hibbs (1977, 1982a, 1982b, 1987), Kernell (1978), and Fair (1978), an attempt is made to consider political factors not only by dummy variables but also by such quantitative indices as the number of Americans killed in the Vietnam War or a newspaper index for the Watergate scandal.

7 In all of these studies, political factors are mainly used to control for noneconomic influences, and they are mostly modeled by dummy variables.

8 A quantitatively strong and highly significant influence of the economic situation on the election outcome of the vote share of parties in the four Reichstag elections of the German Weimar Republic between 1930 and 1933 is found by Frey and Weck (1983). They conclude from their estimation results that if unemployment had not risen from 14 percent of employed workers in July 1930 to 52 percent in January 1933, the Nazi party would have received 24 percent instead of 44 percent of the vote in March 1933.

9 Fair (1978) and Kirchgässner (1981) deal extensively with the problem of the specification of election functions, their stability, and their interpretation. Another test of stability, ex post forecasts of U.S. national election results using the Kramer equation, is done by Atesoglu and Congleton (1982). From the quite good predictive performance of the Kramer election equation they conclude that the general economic conditions have a systematic and predictable effect on national congressional

elections. The same conclusion is reached by Kirchgässner (1981) whose ex post predictions of the U.S. presidential election come very close to the actual outcomes.

10 A comprehensive survey of the vote and popularity studies undertaken in France is given by Lafay (1984a).

11 The elasticity between unemployment and popularity means that if unemployment varies by 1 percent in the year 1977, the popularity of President Carter drops by 0.36 percent.

12 Hibbs and Madsen (1981) include a tax pressure variable also for Sweden and find a significant and quantitatively important impact on the popularity of the governing party or parties.

13 Compare, e.g., Lucas (1976), Sargent (1976), and for a survey of the new macro-economic approach, Begg (1982).

14 See the controversy between Stigler (1973) and Okun (1973). The discussion has been continued with the studies by Arcelus and Meltzer (1975), Bloom and Price (1975), and Goodman and Kramer (1975).

15 For a further disaggregation up to the behavior of single voters, compare Kiewiet (1983) and Kiewiet and Rivers (1985) and the literature mentioned there.

16 Compare Frey and Schneider (1978a, 1978b) and Pommerehne and Schneider (1983).

17 When undertaking such a policy, government will only consider the preferences of its partisan voters, i.e., a share of the whole electorate which usually is much less than the majority.

18 Hibbs (1977) and Alt (1984) present empirical evidence that labor governments in Britain ceteris paribus achieve lower unemployment levels than conservative governments.

19 Due to lack of space the exact specification of the fiscal policy instruments (expenditures and tax side) and detailed estimation results are not reported here (see the original studies mentioned in the text and in the table). It should be noticed that in some studies the use of the fiscal instruments is simultaneously estimated for the expenditure and tax side and that in all studies other economic and political constraints are considered beside the reelection constraint (e.g., the budget constraint, the influence of the public administration).

20 For Germany a confrontation of a "pure" econometric model developed by Krelle (1974) with a full-scale model of politico-economic interaction is undertaken by Frey and Schneider (1979). In the competing model the policy variables, e.g., expenditures, are a function of lagged taxes and lagged GNP. The true ex post forecasts of the politico-economic model are clearly better than the one achieved by the pure econometric model.

21 A comparison of forecasts of different politico-economic models for Great Britain is done by Hibbs (1983), where he finds that his approach yields the best forecasts.

22 Similar studies of central bank behavior have been undertaken for France by Lafay and Aubin (1984b) and for the United States by Laney and Willett (1983). For both countries the authors reach the conclusion that the central bank supports the government's expansionary policy for getting reelected with an appropriate monetary policy.

23 For a survey, see Frey (1984) and Frey and Schneider (1984).
24 See, for example, Caves (1976), Baldwin (1976), and Magee (1982).

References

Ahmad, Kabir V., "An Empirical Study of Politico-Economic Interaction in the United States." *Review of Economics and Statistics* 65/1, 1983, 170–77.

Alt, James E., "Election and Economic Outcomes in Britain." mimeographed, St. Louis: Washington University, 1984.

Alt, James E., and Alex K. Chrystal, *Political Economics*. Los Angeles: University of California Press, 1983.

Alt, James E., and John Wooley, "Reaction Functions, Optimization and Politics: Modelling the Political Economy of Macroeconomic Policy." *American Journal of Political Science* 26/4, 1982, 709–40.

Arcelus, Frank, and Alan H. Meltzer, "The Effect of Aggregate Economic Variables on Congressional Elections." *American Political Science Review* 69/4, 1975, 1232–65.

Atesoglu, H. Sonmer, and Roger Congleton, "Economic Conditions and National Elections, Post Sample Forecasts." *American Political Science Review* 76/4, 1982, 873–75.

Baldwin, Robert E., *The Political Economy of U.S. Trade Policy*. New York: Center for the Study of Financial Institutions, Graduate School of Business Administration, New York University, Bulletin 1976-4, 1976.

Beck, Nathaniel, "Parties, Administration, and American Macroeconomic Outcomes." *American Political Science Review* 76/1, 1982a, 83–93.

———, "Does There Exist a Political Business Cycle?" *Public Choice* 38/2, 1982b, 205–12.

Begg, Daniel H. K., *The Rational Expectations Revolution in Macroeconomics*. Oxford: Phillips Allen, 1982.

Bloom, Howard S., and H. D. Price, "Voter Response to Short-Run Economic Conditions: The Asymmetric Effect of Prosperity and Recession." *American Political Science Review* 69/4, 1975, 1266–76.

Borooah, Vani K., and Frederik van den Ploeg, *Political Aspects of the Economy*. Cambridge: Cambridge University Press, 1983.

Caves, Richard E., "Economic Models of Political Choice: Canada's Tariff Structure." *Canadian Journal of Economics* 9, 1976, 278–300.

Chappell, Henry W., Jr., "Presidential Popularity and Macroeconomic Performance: Are Voters Really So Naive?" *Review of Economics and Statistics* 65/3, 1983, 385–92.

———, and William R. Keech, "A New View of Political Accountability for Economic Performance." *American Political Science Review* 78/4, 1984a, 1104–38.

———, "Party Differences in Macroeconomic Policies and Outcomes." Chapel Hill: University of North Carolina, 1984b, mimeographed.

Chrystal, Alex K., and James Alt, "Endogenous Government Behavior: Wagner's Law or Goetterdaemmerung?" In *Current Issues in Fiscal Policy*, ed. S. T. Cook and P. M. Jackson. London: M. Robertson, 1979, 224–59.

———, "Some Problems in Formulating and Testing a Politico-Economic Model of the United Kingdom." *Economic Journal* 91, 1981, 730–36.

———, "The Criteria for Choosing a Politico-Economic Model: Forecast Results for British Expenditures 1976–79." *European Journal of Political Research* 11/1, 1983, 113–24.

Downs, Anthony, *An Economic Theory of Democracy*. New York: Harper and Row, 1957.

Fair, Ray C., "On Controlling the Enemy to Win Elections." *Cowles Foundation Discussion Paper* 397, 1975.

———, "The Effect of Economic Events on Votes for President." *Review of Economics and Statistics* 60/2, 1978, 159–72.

Findlay, Ronald, and Steven Wellisz, "Endogenous Tariffs: The Political Economy of Trade Restrictions and Welfare." In *Import Competition and Response*, ed. Jagdish N. Bhagwati. Chicago: University of Chicago Press, 1982, 223–43.

———, "Some Aspects of the Political Economy of Trade Restrictions." *Kyklos*, 1983, 231–49.

Frey, Bruno S., "Economic Policy by Constitutional Contract." *Kyklos* 32/2, 1979, 307–19.

———, *Democratic Economy Policy*. Oxford: Basil Blackwell, 1983.

———, *International Political Economics*. Oxford: Basil Blackwell, 1984.

Frey, Bruno S., and Larry J. Lau, "Towards a Mathematical Model of Government Behavior." *Zeitschrift für Nationaloekonomie* 28/2, 1968, 355–80.

Frey, Bruno S., and Friedrich Schneider, "On the Modelling of Politico-Economic Interdependence." *European Journal of Political Research* 3/4, 1975, 339–60.

———, "A Politico-Economic Model of the United Kingdom." *Economic Journal* 88, 1978a, 243–53.

———, "An Empirical Study of Politico-Economic Interaction in the U.S." *Review of Economics and Statistics* 60/2, 1978b, 174–83.

———, "An Econometric Model with an Endogenous Government Sector." *Public Choice* 34/1, 1979, 29–43.

———, "A Politico-Economic Model of the U.K.: New Estimates and Predictions." *Economic Journal* 91, 1981a, 737–40.

———, "Central Bank Behavior: A Positive Empirical Analysis." *Journal of Monetary Economics* 7, 1981b, 291–315.

———, "Politico-Economic Models in Competition with Alternative Models: Which Predicts Better?" *European Journal of Political Research* 10, 1982, 241–54.

———, "Do Governments Respond to Political Incentives?" *European Journal of Political Research* 11/1, 1983, 125–26.

———, "International Political Economy: A Rising Field." *Economia Internazionale* 37/3–4, 1984, 3–42.

Frey, Bruno S., and Hannelore Weck, "A Statistical Study of the Effect of the Great Depression on Elections: The Weimar Republic, 1930–1933." *Political Behavior* 5/4, 1983, 403–420.

Gärtner, Manfred, "Die Phillipskurve und staatliches Beschaeftigungsziel im Zeitalter der Globalsteuerung." *Jahrbuecher für Nationaloekonomie und Statistik* 192/3, 1978, 481–503.

———, "Eine oekonomische Analyse ideologischer und politisch-institutioneller Bestimmungsfaktoren gewerkschaftlicher Lohnpolitik." In *Staat und Wirtschaft*, ed. C. C. Von Weizsaecker. Berlin: Duncker and Humblot, 1977, 69–90.

———, "Politik und Arbeitsmarkt. Eine Uebersicht ueber ausgewaehlte Makrotheorien." *Zeitschrift für die gesamte Staatswissenschaft* 137, 1981a, 252–83.

———, "A Politicoeconomic Model of Wage Inflation." *The Economist* 129, 1981b, 183–205.

Golden, David, and John Poterba, "The Price of Popularity: The Political Business Cycle Reexamined." *American Journal of Political Science* 24/4, 1980, 696–714.

Goodhart, Charles A. E., and R. J. Bhansali, "Political Economy." *Political Studies* 18/1, 1970, 43–106.

Goodman, Samuel, and Gerald H. Kramer, "Comment on Arcelus and Meltzer." *American Political Science Review* 69/4, 1975, 1277–85.

Hibbs, Douglas A., Jr., "Political Parties and Macroeconomic Policy." *American Political Science Review* 71/4, 1977, 1467–87.

———, "Economics and Politics in France: Economic Performance and Mass Political Support for Presidents Pompidou and Giscard D'Estaing." *European Journal of Political Research* 9/2, 1981, 133–45.

———, "On the Demand for Economic Outcomes: Mass Political Support in the United States, Great Britain and Germany." *Journal of Politics* 44/4, 1982a, 426–62.

———, "The Dynamics of Political Support for American Presidents Among Occupational and Partisan Groups." *American Journal of Political Science* 26/2, 1982c, 312–32.

———, "Economic Outcomes and Political Support for British Governments Among Occupational Classes: A Dynamic Analysis." *American Political Science Review* 76/2, 1982c, 259–79.

———, "An Evaluation of Competing Time-Series Models of Voting Intentions via Ex-Post Forecasting Experiments: The Case of Great Britain." Cambridge: Harvard University, 1983, mimeographed.

———, *The Political Economy of Industrial Democracies*. Cambridge: Harvard University Press, 1987.

———, and Henrick Madsen, "The Impact of Economic Performance on Electoral Support in Sweden, 1967–1978." *Scandinavian Political Studies* 4/1, 1981, 33–50.

Inoguchi, Tanaka, "Economic Conditions and Mass Support in Japan." In *Models of Political Economy*, ed. Paul Whiteley. London: Sage Publications, 1980, 121–54.

Jonung, Lars, and Eskil Wadensjoe, "The Effect of Unemployment, Inflation and Real Income Growth on Government Popularity in Sweden." *Scandinavian Journal of Economics* 81/2, 1979, 343–53.

Kernell, Sam, "Explaining Presidential Popularity." *American Political Science Review* 72/2, 1978, 506–22.

Kiewiet, D. Roderick, *Macroeconomics & Micropolitics*. Chicago: University of Chicago Press, 1983.

———, and Douglas Rivers, "A Retrospective on Retrospective Voting." In *Economic Conditions and Electoral Outcomes*, ed. Heinz Eulan and Michael S. Lewis-Beck. New York: Agathon Press, 1985, 207–31.

Kirchgässner, Gebhard, "Rationales Waehlerverhalten und optimales Regierungsverhalten." Konstanz, Germany, Ph.D. dissertation, University of Konstanz, 1976.

———, "Wirtschaftslage und Waehlerverhalten." *Politische Vierteljahresschriften* 18/2–3, 1977, 510–36.

———, "Zur Struktur politisch-oekonomischer Konjunkturzyklen." *Staat und Wirtschaft*, Schriften des Vereins für Socialpolitik, N.F., vol. 102, ed. Carl Christian von Weizsaecker. Berlin: Duncker und Humblot, 1978, 427–50.

———, "The Effect of Economic Events on Votes for President—Some Alternative Estimates." Zurich: Swiss Federal Institute of Technology, 1981, mimeographed.

———, *Optimale Wirtschaftspolitik und die Erzeugung politisch-ökonomischer Konjunkturzyklen*. Meisenheim: Hain, 1984a.

———, "On the Theory of Optimal Government Behavior." *Journal of Economic Dynamics and Control* 8, 1984b, 167–95.

———, "Rationality, Causality, and the Relation Between Economic Conditions and the Popularity of Parties, An Empirical Investigation for the Federal Republic of Germany, 1971–1982." *European Economic Review* 28, 1985a, 243–68.

———, "Causality Testing of the Popularity Function: An Empirical Investigation for the Federal Republic of Germany, 1981–1982." *Public Choice* 45/2, 1985b, 155–73.

———, "Economic Conditions and the Popularity of West German Parties." *European Journal of Political Research* 14/4, 1986, 421–39.

Kramer, Gerald, "Short-term Fluctuations in U.S. Voting Behavior, 1956–1964." *American Political Science Review* 65/1, 1971, 131–43.

Krelle, Wilhelm, *Erfahrungen mit einem oekonometrischen Prognosemodell fuer die BRD*. Meisenheim am Glahn: Hain-Verlag, 1974.

Laechler, Ulrich, "The Political Business Cycle: A Complementary Study." *Review of Economic Studies* 45, 1978, 131–43.

———, "On Political Business Cycles with Endogenous Election Dates." *Journal of Public Economics* 17, 1982, 111–17.

Lafay, Jean-Dominique, "Empirical Analysis of Politico-economic Interaction in the East European Countries." *Soviet Studies* 23/3, 1981, 386–400.

———, "Important Political Change and the Stability of the Popularity Function: Before and After the French General Election of 1981." University of Poitiers, Poitiers, 1984a, mimeographed.

———, and Chaubert Aubin, "The Positive Approach to Monetary Policy: An Empirical Study of the French Case." University of Poitiers, Poitiers, 1984b, mimeographed.

Laney, Leroy O., and Thomas D. Willett, "Presidential Politics, Budget Deficits, and Monetary Policy in the United States: 1960–1976." *Public Choice* 40/1, 1983, 53–69.

Lewis-Beck, Martin S., "Economic Conditions and Executive Popularity: The French Experiment." *American Journal of Political Science* 24/2, 1980, 306–23.

Lindbeck, Assar, "Stabilization Policy in Open Economics with Endogenous Politicians." *American Economic Review, Papers and Proceedings* 66, 1976, 1–19.

Lucas, R. E., "Econometric Policy Evaluation: A Critique." In *The Phillips Curve and Labor Markets*, ed. Karl Brunner and Alan H. Meltzer. Amsterdam: North-Holland, 1976, 19–64.

McCallum, Bennet T., "The Political Business Cycle: An Empirical Test." *Southern Economic Journal* 43/3, 1977, 504–15.

———, "Rational Expectations and Macroeconomic Stabilization Policy: An Overview." *Journal of Money, Credit, and Banking* 12/4, 1980, 714–46.

MacRae, Duncan, "A Political Model of the Business Cycle." *Journal of Political Economy* 85, 1977, 239–63.

———, "On the Political Business Cycle." In *Contemporary Political Economy*, ed. Douglas A. Hibbs, Jr., and Heino Fassbender. Amsterdam: North-Holland, 1981, 169–84.

Madsen, Henrick J., "Electoral Outcomes and Macro-Economic Policies: The Scandinavian Cases." In *Model of Political Economy*, ed. Paul Whiteley. London: Sage Publications, 1980, 15–46.

Magee, Steven P., "Protectionism in the United States." Austin: Department of Finance, University of Texas, 1982, mimeographed.

Maloney, Kevin, and Martin Smirlock, "Business Cycles and the Political Process." *Southern Economic Journal* 47/2, 1981, 377–92.

Minford, David, and Patrick Peel, "The Political Theory of the Business Cycle." *European Economic Review* 6/2, 1982, 253–70.

Mosley, Paul, "Images of the 'Floating Voter' and the Political Business Cycle Revisited." *Political Studies* 2/4, 1978, 375–94.

Mueller, John, "Presidential Popularity from Truman to Johnson." *American Political Science Review* 64/1, 1970, 18–34.

Niskanen, William A., "Economic and Fiscal Effects on the Popular Vote for the President." In *Public Policy and Public Choice*, ed. D. W. Rae and Thomas J. Eismeier. London: Sage Publications, 1979, 93–120.

Nordhaus, William A., "The Political Business Cycle." *Review of Economic Studies* 42, 1975, 169–90.

Norpoth, Helmut, "Politics, Economics, and Presidential Popularity." Stony Brook: State University of New York at Stony Brook, 1984, mimeographed.

Norpoth, Helmut, and Thom Yantek, "Macroeconomic Conditions and Fluctuations of Presidential Popularity: The Question of Lagged Effects." *American Journal of Political Science* 27/4, 1983a, 785–807.

———, "Von Adenauer bis Schmidt: Wirtschaftslage und Kanzlerpopularitaet." In *Wahlen und politisches System, Analyse aus Anlass der Bundestagswahl 1980,* ed. Max Kaase and Hans-Dieter Klingemann. Opladen: Westdeutscher, 1983b, 136–51.

Okun, Arthur M., "Comments on Stigler's Paper." *American Economic Review* 63/2, 1973, 172–80.

Paldam, Martin, "A Preliminary Survey of the Theories and Findings on Vote and Popularity Functions." *European Journal of Political Research* 9/1, 1981a, 181–99.

———, "An Essay on the Rationality of Economic Policy: The Test Case of the Election Cycle." *Public Choice* 37, 1981b, 287–98.

———, and Friedrich Schneider, "The Macro-Economic Aspects of Government and Opposition Popularity in Denmark, 1957–1978." *Nationalokonomisk Tidsskrift* 118/2, 1980, 149–70.

Pissarides, Christopher A., "British Government Popularity and Economic Performance." *Economic Journal* 90/3, 1980, 569–81.

Pommerehne, Werner W., "Institutional Approaches to Public Expenditure: Empirical Evidence from Swiss Municipalities." *Journal of Public Economics* 9, 1978, 255–80.

Pommerehne, Werner W., and Friedrich Schneider, "Fiscal Illusion, Political Institutions, and Local Public Spending." *Kyklos* 31, 1978, 381–408.

———, "Does Government in a Representative Democracy Follow a Majority of Voters' Performances?—An Empirical Examination." In *Anatomy of Government Deficiencies,* ed. Horst Hanusch. Heidelberg: Springer, 1983, 61–88.

Riker, William H., and Peter C. Ordeshook, "A Theory of the Calculus of Voting." *American Political Science Review* 62/1, 1968, 25–42.

Romer, Thomas, and Howard Rosenthal, "The Elusive Median Voter." *Journal of Public Economics* 12/1, 1979, 143–70.

Rosa, Jean J., "Economic Conditions and Elections in France." In *Models of Political Economy,* ed. Paul Whiteley. London: Sage Publications, 1980, 101–20.

Sargent, Thomas J., "A Classical Macroeconomic Model for the United States." *Journal of Political Economy* 84/2, 1976, 207–37.

Schneider, Friedrich, *Politisch-oekonomische Modelle: Theoretische und empirische Ansaetze.* Koenigstein: Athenaeum, 1978.

———, *Der Einfluss von Interessengruppen auf die Wirtschaftspolitik: Eine empirische Untersuchung für die Schweiz.* Bern: Haupt, 1985.

Schneider, Friedrich, "Public Attitudes Toward Economic Conditions and their Impact on Government Behavior." In *Economic Conditions and Electoral Outcomes,* ed. Heinz Eulau and Michael Lewis-Beck. New York: Agathon Press, 1985, 15–31.

Schneider, Friedrich, and Bruno S. Frey, "An Empirical Study of Politico-Economic Interaction in the United States: A Reply." *Review of Economics and Statistics* 65/1, 1983, 178–82.

Schneider, Friedrich, and Joerg Naumann, "Interest Group Behavior in Democracies: An Empirical Analysis for Switzerland." *Public Choice* 38/2, 1982, 291–304.

Schneider, Friedrich, and Werner W. Pommerehne, "Politico-Economic Interaction in Australia: Some Empirical Evidence." *Economic Record* 56/1, 1980, 113–31.

Schneider, Friedrich, Werner W. Pommerehne, and Bruno S. Frey, "Politico-Economic Interdependence in a Direct Democracy: The Case of Switzerland." In *Contemporary Political Economy,* ed. Douglas A. Hibbs, Jr., and Heino Fassbender. Amsterdam: North-Holland, 1981, 231–48.

Sims, Christopher A., "Policy Analysis with Econometric Models." *Brookings Papers on Economic Activity* 1, 1982, 107–64.

Stigler, George J., "General Economic Conditions and National Elections." *American Economic Review, Papers and Proceedings* 63, 1973, 155–60.

Stimson, J. A., "Public Support for American Presidents: A Cyclical Model." *Public Opinion Quarterly* 2311, 1976, 1–21.

Thompson, William, and Gary Zuck, "American Elections and International Electoral-Economic Cycle: A Test of the Tufte Hypothesis." *American Journal of Political Science* 77/2, 1983, 364–74.

Tollison, Robert, and Thomas D. Willett, "Some Simple Economics of Voting and Not Voting." *Public Choice* 28/1, 1973, 59–71.

Tufte, Edward R., *Political Control of the Economy.* Princeton: Princeton University Press, 1978.

Ursprung, Heiner W., "Macroeconomic Performance and Government Popularity in New Zealand." Wellington, N.Z.: Victoria University of Wellington, 1983, mimeographed.

Van Winden, Frans, *On the Interaction between the State and Private Sector: A Study in Political Economics.* Pasmans: s'Gravenhage, 1981.

Wagner, Richard E., "Economic Manipulation for Political Profit: Macroeconomic Consequences and Constitutional Implications." *Kyklos* 30/3, 1977, 395–420.

Whiteley, Paul (ed.), *Models of Political Economy.* London: Sage Publications, 1980, 155–60.

Whiteley, Paul, "Macroeconomic Performance and Government Popularity in Britain—The Short Run Dynamics." Bristol: University of Bristol, 1984, mimeographed.

Wright, Gavin, "The Political Economy of New-Deal Spending: An Econometric Analysis." *Review of Economics and Statistics* 56/1, 1974, 30–39.

Yantek, Thom, "Public Support for Presidential Performance: A Study of Macroeconomic Effects." *Polity* 15/2, 1982, 268–78.

10 Does the Political Business Cycle Dominate U.S. Unemployment and Inflation? Some New Evidence

Stephen E. Haynes and Joe Stone

Introduction

The received theory of the political business cycle assumes that by maximizing voter utility through appropriate macropolicy the incumbent president maximizes his (or his party's) probability of reelection. The solution to the optimizing problem is a desired time path for unemployment (and inflation) that follows a four-year cyclical pattern, with unemployment declining prior to the election and rising again early in the next term, and with inflation peaking only after the election.[1] This politically motivated manipulation of the economy is feasible because macroexpansion tends to reduce unemployment and stimulate growth relatively quickly (with a delay of about one to two quarters) but generates higher rates of inflation only with a considerable lag (after about one to two years). As a consequence, the beneficial aspects of the manipulation can occur prior to the election, while the associated inflationary costs do not become apparent until after the election.

For the electoral model to be helpful in understanding macroeconomic fluctuations, unemployment and inflation need not follow perfect four-year sine waves correctly aligned with the election quarter, i.e., with unemployment lowest before every election and inflation highest after every election. Economic outcomes are undoubtedly determined by a wide range of factors, only one of which may be political in origin. What is important in evaluating the model is whether a significant proportion of the variation in economic outcomes averaged over the past thirty years or so can be explained by the model, and if so, how important is the electoral source of variation relative to other sources.

What evidence is there for the political business cycle? How significant is it? It is useful to begin with Gordon's application of standard demand and supply nomenclature to the model of the political business cycle.[2] The demand side of economic outcomes relates voting behavior to economic outcomes; the supply side relates responses of policymakers (and hence economic outcomes) to voting behavior. Previous tests of the demand side of the model, i.e., the responses of voting behavior to economic conditions, are generally supportive.[3] In fact, the relationship between voting behavior and economic conditions is challenged only by some political scientists and by proponents of strict rational expectations. For example, the latter group argues that even if voters would prefer a political business cycle (perhaps due to differences in time preference between the median voter and the marginal investor/borrower), economic agents will anticipate the full consequences of economic policies. Under these circumstances, a politically induced business cycle is not possible—expectations of economic agents will frustrate macroeconomic policy, and governments will foresee the futility of attempts to induce a political business cycle.

On the supply side of the model, i.e., the response of policymakers and economic outcomes to voting behavior, earlier evidence is mixed.[4] However, more recent research indicates that four-year electoral variables significantly enter policy reaction functions.[5] The evidence provided by Laney and Willett, for example, suggests the electoral cycle has a significant direct influence on federal deficits. This influence is then transmitted to monetary policy by policy reactions of the Federal Reserve. Thus, although there is no direct electoral influence on monetary policy, a significant indirect link is established by monetary reactions to politically induced movements in fiscal policy. Prior to 1979 this indirect link was virtually assured, since the Federal Reserve tended to accommodate changes in federal deficits as part of its policy of targeting interest rates. It is still too early to tell if the apparent abandonment of interest rate targeting in 1979 has diminished the link found by Laney and Willett.

In spite of the accumulating evidence supporting both demand and supply effects of the electoral business cycle, formal evidence that economic *outcomes* follow a four-year electoral cycle is weak. Relatively informal evidence suggests the significance of such cycles for the United

States, yet more formal tests fail to provide support.[6] Thus Hibbs concludes that "macroeconomic policies and outcomes do not consistently exhibit easily identified short-run electoral cycles."[7]

There are two related difficulties in testing for a political business cycle in economic outcomes. The first concerns how precise the pattern of low unemployment just prior to the election and high inflation afterward must be for the model to be "correct." This difficulty is illustrated in figures 10.1 and 10.2, where unemployment and inflation for the United States from 1951 to 1980 are plotted separately. The pattern of unemployment in figure 10.1 (unemployment is measured as a four-quarter moving average of the annual percentage change in unemployment) shows that

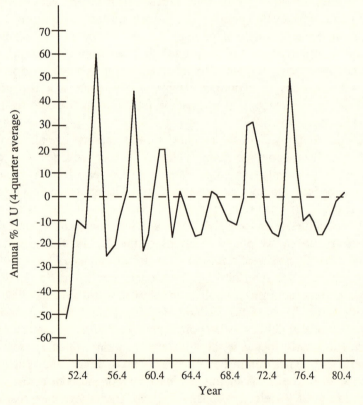

Figure 10.1   Plot of Unemployment Rate (Annual %ΔU, Averaged over Four Quarters) 1951.2–1980.1

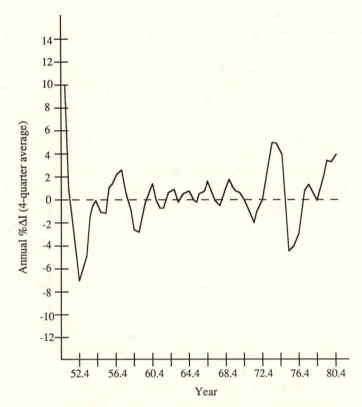

Figure 10.2   Plot of Inflation Rate (Annual %ΔI, Averaged over Four Quarters) 1951.2–1980.1

unemployment is relatively low approaching some elections, but not others. The plot of inflation in figure 10.2 (inflation is measured as a four-quarter moving average of the annual percentage change in inflation) provides evidence which is even more mixed. These figures indicate that, even if the electoral model is useful, no simply deterministic pattern should be expected in unemployment and inflation because there are many sources of variation in the two series.

The second difficulty is that the model does not merely predict low unemployment before an election and high inflation after an election. Economic outcomes are not "free" variables which can be easily manipulated by macropolicy for only two or three quarters every four years. They are sluggish variables determined by a wide range of factors and usually respond only gradually and moderately to any single force. As a consequence, the model also yields predictions in nonelection years—high unemployment and low inflation roughly two years before (and after) each election, and intermediate levels of unemployment and inflation both one and three years before (and after) each election. Thus, movements in economic outcomes over all sixteen quarters of the presidential term should be examined.

In this chapter we argue that previous tests of the electoral influence on unemployment and inflation are misspecified because they deal inadequately with these two difficulties. We present tests which (1) measure how influential electoral factors are in explaining the variation in economic outcomes relative to other determinants and (2) examine the behavior of unemployment and inflation over the entire sixteen quarters of a presidential term. The specific questions we answer based on these tests are

1. Is there a significant four-year cycle in unemployment (and in inflation)?
2. If there is a significant four-year cycle, is it aligned appropriately with the presidential election quarter, i.e., with the trough in unemployment occurring just prior to the election and the peak in inflation occurring after the election?
3. How significant is the four-year cycle in relation to other cycles that might be present?
4. Is unemployment negatively related to subsequent rates of inflation, as implied by our specification of aggregate supply (the Phillips curve)?
5. Is inflation positively related to subsequent rates of unemployment, as implied by our specification of aggregate demand?
6. Is there a significant negative covariation between unemployment and inflation at the four-year cycle?

We begin in the next section by presenting a simple model of the supply of electoral cycles. Then we conduct univariate tests of the periodic movements in unemployment and inflation and the timing (or phase alignment) of these movements in relation to the electoral cycle. In spirit, these univariate tests are similar to earlier tests of the business cycle, where economic time series are described by a set of waves or cycles with different periodicities.[8] We also compare our tests to recent studies that examine movements in unemployment and inflation for only several quarters prior to each election. Next we explore the periodic covariation between unemployment and inflation. The final section of the chapter summarizes our main conclusion—the *dominant* cyclical variation and covariation in United States unemployment and inflation between 1951 and 1980 occurs at a four-year cycle aligned appropriately with the four-year electoral cycle, i.e., the four-year trough in unemployment occurs just prior to the election quarter, but the four-year peak in inflation does not occur until several quarters after the election (consistent with the political-economic structure of the model).

Model

This section develops a simple three-equation model of the supply of electoral cycles. Our theoretical objective is to provide the economic details needed not only to demonstrate the economic predictions of the model of the political business cycle but also to guide the specification of our empirical tests in the remaining sections. The aggregate supply relationship between unemployment and inflation, i.e., the Phillips curve, is adapted from Pippenger:[9]

$$I(t) = -\frac{1}{a}U(t-1) - \frac{b}{a}\Delta I(t) + z_1(t), \tag{1}$$

where $I(t)$ is the inflation rate in period t, U is the unemployment rate, Δ is the difference operator, z_1 is an error term, and a and b are positive constants. $\Delta I(t)$ is a naive representation of inflationary expectations, demand-induced supply shifts. Exogenous supply shocks are captured by $z_1(t)$. Based on the assumption that expected and actual rates of inflation converge in the long run, the term $(b/a)\Delta I(t)$ implies that the Phillips curve becomes steeper the longer the time horizon. To see this, solve equation (1) for $I(t)$:

$$I(t) = [-\frac{1}{a}U(t-1) + z_1(t)] / [1 + \frac{b}{a}(1-L^{-1})], \tag{1'}$$

where L^{-1} is a one-period lag operator. Equation (1') implies that inflation is an exponentially declining distributed lag of unemployment, i.e., that the Phillips curve has a slope equal to zero in the short run, $(-1/a)/$

$[1 + (b/a)]$ in the intermediate run, and $-1/a$ in the long-run steady state. Thus, the Phillips curve is steeper in the long run than in the short run.

Equation $(1')$ includes standard Keynesian and monetarist models as special cases. The Keynesian special case is obtained by setting the parameter b equal to zero, which implies the intermediate- and long-run Phillips curves are identical with a slope of $-1/a$. The monetarist special case is obtained by setting parameter a equal to zero, which implies the intermediate-run Phillips curve has a slope of $-1/b$, but the long-run curve is vertical.

The aggregate demand relationship is described by

$$U(t) = C(L) I(t) + D(L) M(t) + z_2(t), \tag{2}$$

where $M(t)$ is one or more macropolicy variables, $z_2(t)$ is an error term, $C(L)$ equals $\Sigma c_{t-i} L^{-i}$ over i greater than zero, $D(L)$ equals $\Sigma d_{(t-i)} L^{-i}$ over i greater than zero, and $c_{t-i} (d_{t-1})$ are positive (negative) constants. Exogenous demand shocks are captured by $z_2(t)$. The model predicts that the unemployment response to a supply shock, $z_1(t)$, will occur substantially after the price response. Thus, unemployment in equation (2) is related only to lagged inflation. The impact of macropolicy on unemployment may begin rapidly; hence, unemployment is related to present and past values of macropolicy.

The policy reaction function is

$$M(t) = fE(t) + G(L) I(t) + z_3(t), \tag{3}$$

where $E(t)$ is the presidential electoral variable, $z_3(t)$ is an error term, $G(L)$ equals $\Sigma g_{t-i} L^{-i}$ over i greater than zero, $f(g_{t-i})$ is a positive (negative) constant. The presidential electoral variable, $E(t)$, generally increases prior to the election and decreases after the election. The precise four-year pattern of $E(t)$, however, could vary. For example, $E(t)$ could equal 1 the two years before an election and -1 thereafter, follow a sine wave with a four-year period that peaks prior to the election, or follow a more complicated pattern.[10] The inflation term, $I(t)$, is included because macropolicy may also reflect countercyclical objectives (for similar reasons, unemployment could also enter equation [3]). This effect can be distinguished from the impact of macropolicy on prices implied by equations (1) and (2)—whereas macropolicy is directly related to subsequent movements in inflation through equations (1) and (2), inflation is inversely related to subsequent movements in macropolicy in equation (3).

The three-equation model contains three endogenous variables [$U(t)$, $I(t)$, and $M(t)$] and four exogenous variables [$E(t)$ and the three error terms]. Since contemporaneous two-way causality is not present between any pair of endogenous variables, the model is recursive.[11] The effect of macropolicy, for example, is first on unemployment and then on prices. The reduced-form equations of the model imply the systematic variation in $E(t)$ causes systematic movements in macropolicy which lead to four-year cyclical movements in unemployment and inflation. Since macropolicy influences unemployment and inflation through a complicated dynamic process (eqs. [1] and [2]), macropolicy could follow a more complicated pattern than a simple four-year cycle, yet still cause simple four-year cycles in unemployment and inflation. The alignment of the four-year cycles in unemployment and inflation should be consistent with both $E(t)$ and the dynamic responses of the model. In particular, $E(t)$ induces macropolicy that reduces $U(t)$ prior to the election and increases $I(t)$ after the election.

Univariate Tests

The model in the previous section predicts that unemployment and inflation exhibit strong four-year cycles, with the timing of the cycles consistent with the political model of the business cycle. This section tests these and related predictions regarding the reduced-form correlation between unemployment and inflation using quarterly data for the United States from 1951.1 to 1980.1. The unemployment rate, $U(t)$, is the logarithm of the official U.S. unemployment rate, and the inflation rate, $I(t)$, is the logarithmic difference (annualized) of the U.S. consumer price index. The data are seasonally unadjusted.[12]

As an initial test for the existence of strong four-year cycles, the spectral density function of each series is computed. This statistic formally decomposes the variance of a series by length of cycle, hence permitting a direct comparison of the variation of each series across cycles.[13] Table 10.1 records spectral density estimates for unemployment and inflation for cycles of one year and longer. The variance in each series peaks at the four-year cycle, where it differs significantly from white noise (i.e., exceeds the 95 percent confidence interval for white noise). For each

Table 10.1 Spectral Density Estimates
(1951.1 to 1980.1)

Period in years	Unemployment	Inflation
∞	.536	.825
8.00	.996	1.127
4.00	1.487	1.138
2.67	1.093	.584
2.00	.724	.187
1.60	.308	.168
1.33	.074	.206
1.14	.028	.088
1.00	.011	.040

Note: The .95 percent interval for white noise is from 1.09 to .218.

series, comparison of this four-year estimate to the two adjacent estimates (at periods of 8 and 2.67 years), suggests the four-year variation is dominant for unemployment, but that longer cycle movements are also strong for inflation. This evidence at the four-year cycle is entirely consistent with the predictions of the electoral model of the business cycle. Reestimation by subsample and with alternative filtering procedures does not alter these findings.

As a second test for strong four-year cycles in unemployment and inflation, the autocorrelation function of each series is computed. This statistic records the correlation coefficient between a variable [e.g., $X(t)$] and its lagged value [$X(t-k)$] for various lags. If the variation in each series is dominated by a four-year cycle, the autocorrelation function should follow a damped sine wave pattern with a period of four years.[14] Table 10.2 records autocorrelation estimates for the two series for twenty lags. Consistent with theoretical predictions, as the lag length increases the autocorrelation estimate for unemployment declines from 1, turns negative, and then becomes positive, completing the damped sine wave pattern in precisely four years. The estimate for inflation is similar, but the pattern is less regular and has a period slightly longer than four years. This evidence suggests the strong four-year variation depicted in the spectral density estimate in table 10.2 is dominant for unemployment, but might be somewhat weaker relative to the 4.5-year cycle for inflation.

To relate the timing of the four-year cyclical movement in each se-

Table 10.2   Autocorrelation Estimates
(1951.1 to 1980.1)

Lag	Unemployment	Inflation
0	1.000**	1.000**
1	.829**	.518**
2	.494**	.438**
3	.130	.336**
4	−.168	.057
5	−.296**	.056
6	−.292**	−.052
7	−.254**	−.198
8	−.207	−.278**
9	−.185	−.226
10	−.211*	−.152
11	−.215*	−.073
12	−.163	−.107
13	−.051	−.069
14	.109	−.130
15	.262**	−.090
16	.345**	.048
17	.253**	.165
18	.261**	.173
19	.028	.108
20	.082	.095

*$p < .05$.   **$p < .01$.

ries to the four-year presidential election cycle, each series is regressed against a four-year sine wave sixteen times—once for every possible lagged correlation. For example, the sine wave (initially aligned to peak in the third quarter of the election year) is contemporaneous in the first regression, shifted ahead one quarter in the second regression, etc. To the extent that unemployment and inflation are periodic with a four-year cycle, the correlation coefficient across the sixteen regressions should move smoothly between a maximum and minimum, with the maximum (minimum) coefficient occurring when the dependent variable and sine wave are just in phase (out of phase). By choosing the regression that maximizes (or minimizes) the correlation coefficient and by examining the time delay between the dependent variable and the sine wave, one can date the peaks and troughs of the four-year cyclical component in each series relative to the election quarter (the fourth quarter of the fourth year of a presidential term).

For both unemployment and inflation, the correlation coefficient between the two series and the sine wave for the sixteen regressions is summarized in table 10.3. (In regression one, the sine wave peaks in the third quarter of the election year; in regression two, the sine wave is shifted ahead one quarter, i.e., peaks in the fourth quarter of the election year; etc.) The evidence is strikingly consistent with the electoral model. For both unemployment and inflation, the correlation coefficient across the regressions moves smoothly between the maximum and minimum values (each significant at the 1 percent level). In addition, the timing of the pattern is entirely consistent with the structural linkages between unemployment and inflation embodied in the electoral model. Unemployment troughs in the third quarter of the election year (the strongest *inverse*

Table 10.3 Correlation Coefficients with Four-Year Sine Wave (1951.1 to 1980.1)

Regression	Unemployment	Inflation
0	−.335**	.055
1	−.313**	.152
2	−.245*	.224*
3	−.141	.259**
4	−.000	.257**
5	.109	.217*
6	.224*	.145
7	.302**	.045
8	.335**	−.055
9	.313**	−.152
10	.245*	−.224*
11	.141	−.159**
12	.000	−.257**
13	−.109	−.217*
14	−.224*	−.145
15	−.302**	−.045

Note: In regression zero, the sine wave peaks in the third quarter of the election year; in regression one, the fourth quarter of the election year; etc.
$*p < .05.$ $**p < .01.$

correlation between unemployment and the sine wave [−.335] occurs in regression one). Inflation peaks in the second quarter subsequent to the election (the strongest *direct* correlation between inflation and the sine wave [.259] occurs in regression four). This evidence indicates that the strong four-year cycles in unemployment and inflation reported in table 10.2 are indeed the result of an electoral business cycle.

Of course, sources of variation other than four-year cycles also contribute to movements in unemployment and inflation. If one repeated the regression test reported in table 10.3 for sine waves with other cycles (e.g., cycles with periods of two, three, and five years), would the largest (in absolute value) correlation coefficients compare favorably to those for the four-year cycle (−.335 for unemployment and .259 for inflation)? Table 10.4 records the largest correlation coefficient based on these alternative sine waves. For unemployment, the only coefficient significant at the 1 percent level is the one between the series and the four-year sine wave (those at the three- and five-year cycle are significant at the 5 percent level). For inflation, the coefficients associated with both the four- and five-year sine waves are significant at the 1 percent level. Consistent with the evidence using the spectral density and autocorrelation functions, the estimates in table 10.4 indicate the four-year cyclical variation is strongly significant for both unemployment and inflation, and clearly dominant for unemployment.

The final question regarding univariate analysis is why have other recent studies (for example, Beck, and Thompson and Zuck) failed to find significant electoral cycles in economic outcomes? The reason may be that the empirical procedure used in these studies differs from our procedure. These recent studies test the significance of a dummy variable defined as one for the several quarters prior to the election and zero else-

Table 10.4 Maximum Correlation Coefficient for Sine Waves of Various Periodicities (1951.1 to 1980.1)

Period of sine waves in year	Unemployment	Inflation
2	.147	.067
3	.227*	.153
4	.335**	.259**
5	.204*	.260**

*$p < .05$. **$p < .01$.

where, and hence test for restrictions of the electoral model only for several quarters prior to an election.[15] Our spectral, autocorrelation, and sine wave tests, however, permit economic outcomes to follow four-year cycles so that information from each of the sixteen quarters in a presidential election is important. This approach is more appropriate because the electoral model yields theoretical patterns in outcome variables over the entire four-year term. A full sixteen-quarter cycle is implied by the model because economic outcomes (especially unemployment) are sluggish and nonvolatile, i.e., cannot be quickly manipulated for only two or three quarters every four years.

To test whether this specification difference explains the failure of recent studies to find electoral cycles in outcome variables, we regressed unemployment and inflation on a dummy variable of ones for the second, third, and fourth quarters of the election year, and zeros elsewhere. Although the dummy in each case has the theoretically correct sign (negative in the unemployment equation and positive in the inflation equation), each is insignificant, with a t-statistic below unity (in absolute value). Thus, we conclude that recent tests for electoral patterns in economic outcomes are misspecified because they ignore a central prediction of the electoral model—that outcome variables follow four-year *cycles,* not just episodic "blips" near elections.[16]

Reduced-Form Correlation between Unemployment and Inflation

The previous section of this chapter provides empirical evidence consistent with the political model of the business cycle: strong four-year cycles in unemployment and inflation, with peaks and troughs consistent with the four-year electoral cycle. This section explores another issue regarding the supply side of electoral cycles—the reduced-form correlation between unemployment and inflation induced by politically motivated macropolicy.

If the four-year cyclical movement in the electoral variable and the consequent movements in the policy variable are strong, then the policy variable should induce shifts in equation (2) which will trace out equation (1), the Phillips curve. These shifts will correlate unemployment inversely with *subsequent* rates of inflation, a correlation which should be strongly significant, if not dominant, at the four-year cycle.

To test the time-domain lead-lag predictions of our aggregate demand and supply equations, we estimate the cross-correlation function between unemployment and inflation, with the two series expressed in innovation form.[17] As reported in table 10.5, six of eight estimates with inflation lagging unemployment are negative, the sign and dynamics supporting the Phillips curve (eq. [1']). In addition, the cumulative sum of these lagged correlation coefficients is significantly negative at the 1 percent level for every lag.[18] The fact that the inverse correlation between unemployment and subsequent rates of inflation appears strongest at a lag of three to four quarters is entirely consistent with the four-year sine wave test, which found that unemployment reaches a minimum in the third quarter of the election year, but that inflation peaks in the second quarter of the year after the election (i.e., three quarters later). This consistency in timing between the univariate behavior of the series (based only on the four-year variation in each series) and their covariation (based on effects from all cycles) provides additional evidence that economic outcomes are strongly influenced, if not dominated, by electoral influences.

For the other side of the cross-correlation function, i.e., with unemployment lagging inflation, four of eight estimates are positive and two are significant (at lags six and seven). These positive correlations with

Table 10.5 Cross-Correlation between Unemployment and Inflation (1951.1 to 1980.1)

Lag in quarters	Inflation lagging		Unemployment lagging	
	Correlation estimate	Cumulative estimate	Correlation estimate	Cumulative estimate
0	−.032		−.032	
1	−.372**	−.372**	−.025	−.025
2	−.118	−.490**	−.022	−.027
3	−.124	−.614**	.078	.051
4	−.198*	−.812**	−.005	.046
5	.006	−.806**	.074	.120
6	−.007	−.813**	.189*	.309*
7	.098	−.715**	.325**	.634**
8	−.122	−.837**	−.073	.561*

Note: Data for each series have been formally prewhitened.
*$p < .05$.   **$p < .01$.

unemployment lagging inflation suggest that aggregate demand (eq. [2]) is identified—movements in z_1 induce shifts in equation ($1'$), which trade out equation (2). Estimates by subsample for both demand and supply are similar, even for the 1970s.

To determine the cycle(s) at which this Phillips curve relation is most significant, we compute the coherence square between the two series. This statistic formally decomposes the coefficient of determination (R^2) between two series by length of cycle.[19] Estimates of the coherence square for cycles of one year and longer are presented in table 10.6. The coherence square is significant at the 1 percent level for cycles of 2.67, 4.00, and 8.00 years, with the dominant estimate at four years. Consistent with the findings in the previous section, this evidence further suggests the short-run Phillips curve trade-off between unemployment and inflation (and the associated cyclical variations) observed in the U.S. results largely from shifts in aggregate demand, induced by politically motivated macropolicy, tracing out aggregate supply. In addition, the insignificant coherence square at the long-run, infinite cycle is consistent only with the monetary natural rate hypothesis predicting no permanent trade-off.[20]

Conclusion

Research into the model of the political business cycle can be grouped into two categories: (1) studies of the demand for electoral cycles and (2)

Table 10.6 Coherence Square between Unemployment and Inflation (1951.1 to 1980.1)

Period in quarters	Coherence square
∞	.301
8.00	.636**
4.00	.815**
2.67	.491**
2.00	.061
1.60	.056
1.33	.144
1.00	.307

Note: Data for each series are formally prewhitened.
**$p < .01$.

studies of the supply of electoral cycles. Empirical demand research generally shows consistent evidence that voting behavior responds systematically to macroeconomic conditions. Although early studies of supply have been mixed, recent research indicates that policymakers' reaction functions do in part depend on electoral cycle variables. This study explores the next obvious question regarding the model of electoral cycles: Are these demand and supply responses important enough to induce strong if not dominant electoral cycles in the variation and covariation of United States unemployment and inflation?

To answer this question we empirically investigate two sets of implications of the supply side of the electoral model of business cycles using quarterly U.S. data from 1951 to 1980. First, we explore the univariate behavior of unemployment and inflation. Spectral density and autocorrelation estimates indicate the dominant cyclical variation in these series occurs generally at the four-year cycle. Furthermore, regression tests indicate the series are aligned with the electoral cycle—unemployment troughs in the third quarter of the election year and inflation peaks in the second quarter of the year after election. These and dummy variable tests indicate that recent studies into economic outcomes, which claim that electoral influences are insignificant, are misspecified by ignoring the electoral model predicts four-year *cycles* in economic outcomes.

Second, the chapter explores the policy-induced covariation between unemployment and inflation. Cross-correlation estimates support a standard short-run Phillips curve, with unemployment inversely correlated with subsequent rates of inflation (consistent with the univariate timing test), and cross-spectral estimates indicate this correlation is strongest at the four-year cycle.

In summary, we conclude that the dominant cyclical variation and covariation in unemployment and inflation for the U.S. from 1951 to 1980 stems from politically induced macropolicy. Two important issues remain: (1) whether electoral cycle macropolicy has been the result of deliberate incumbent manipulation of the inflation-unemployment trade-off, or simply the result of a congressional bias toward deficits leading into elections in combination with Federal Reserve board accommodation; and (2) how these apparent electoral business cycles relate to other well-known partisan differences in monetary and fiscal policies.

Notes

1 For descriptions of the basic model, see W. D. Nordhaus, "The Political Business Cycle," *Review of Economic Studies* 42 (1975): 169–90; B. Frey and F. Schneider, "On the Modeling of Politico-Economic Interdependence," *European Journal of Political Research* 3 (1975): 339–60; K. J. Maloney and M. L. Smirlock, "Business Cycles and the Political Process," *Southern Economic Journal* 48 (1981): 377–92; and P. Minford and D. Peel, "The Political Theory of the Business Cycle," *European Economic Review* 17 (1982): 253–70.

2 R. M. Gordon, "The Demand and Supply of Inflation," *Journal of Law and Economics* 18 (1975): 807–36.

3 See, for example, G. H. Kramer, "Short-Term Fluctuations in the U.S. Voting Behavior, 1896–1964," *American Political Science Review* 65 (1971): 131–43; R. C. Fair, "The Effect of Economic Events on Votes for the President," *Review of Economics and Statistics* 60 (1978): 159–73; and studies in D. A. Hibbs and H. Fassbender, eds., *Contemporary Political Economy* (Amsterdam: North-Holland, 1981).

4 For example, see empirical studies in Hibbs and Fassbender, *Contemporary Political Economy.*

5 Maloney and Smirlock, "Business Cycles," and L. O. Laney and T. D. Willett, "Presidential Politics, Budget Deficits, and Monetary Policy in the United States: 1960–1976," *Public Choice* 40 (1983): 53–69.

6 See Nordhaus, "Political Business Cycle," for early supportive evidence. For more formal tests which are not supportive, see J. Alt and A. Chrystal, *Political Economy* (Berkeley: University of California Press, 1983); N. Beck, "Does There Exist a Political Business Cycle: A Box-Tiao Analysis," *Public Choice* 38 (1982): 205–9; O. Eckstein, *The Great Recession with a Postscript on Stagflation* (Amsterdam: North-Holland, 1978), chap. 4, pp. 39–48; D. MacRae, "A Political Model of the Business Cycle," *Journal of Political Economy* 85 (1977): 239–63; B. T. McCallum, "The Political Business Cycle: An Empirical Test," *Southern Economic Journal* (1978): 504–15; and W. R. Thompson and G. Zuk, "American Elections and the International Electoral-Economic Cycle: A Test of the Tufte Hypothesis," *American Journal of Political Science* 27 (1983): 464–84.

7 Hibbs and Fassbender, *Contemporary Political Economy,* p. 8.

8 For example, see J. Schumpeter, *Business Cycles* (New York: McGraw-Hill, 1939); and J. Akerman, "Political Economic Cycles," *Kyklos* 1 (1947): 107–17.

9 J. Pippenger, "Monetary Policy, Homeostasis, and the Transmission Mechanism," *American Economic Review* 72 (1982): 545–54.

10 Laney and Willett, "Presidential Politics," find the electoral variable that enters their policy reaction function most significantly equals 1 the two years before the election, and − 1 after the election.

11 We also assume the error terms of the model are uncorrelated.

12 The data are from Organization for Economic Cooperation and Development, *Main Economic Indicators* (Paris), various issues.

13 Any stationary time series can be decomposed into a sum of sine waves of differing periods, amplitudes, and phase shifts (see G. M. Jenkins and D. G. Watts, *Spectral*

Analysis and Its Applications [San Francisco: Holden-Day, 1968], chap. 6). To make the series stationary and reduce seasonal components, yet not alter cyclical components, the two series were seasonally differenced—for example, for inflation, $I(t) - I(t-4)$. Alternative filtering procedures (first differencing, quasi-differencing, and first differencing and seasonally quasi-differencing) and varying the number of lags does not alter our general conclusions. Estimates were computed using Bio Med computer program BMD02T.

14 A second-order autoregressive model describing each series can yield four-year cycles in the spectral density function and a damped four-year sine wave in the autocorrelation function; see the discussion of second-order AR models in George E. P. Box and G. M. Jenkins, *Time-Series Analysis: Forecasting and Control* (San Francisco: Holden-Day, 1970), pp. 58–63.

15 These studies are usually based on the "Box-Tiao" intervention model.

16 Experimentation with other simple patterns of the dummy variable also led to insignificant estimates.

17 Each series was prewhitened by regressing the series on a distributed lag of past values out eight quarters, and then obtaining the residuals or innovations. This approach is consistent with rational expectations over a two-year time horizon, and controls for omitted third variables to the extent these variables are captured by the past history of the series. For a recent theoretical attempt at reconciling the rational expectations framework and the four-year myopia required for the electoral business cycle model, see Minford and Peel, "Political Theory." For a statement of the usefulness of lead-lag information in identifying macroeconomic relationships compared to explicit inclusion of other third variables, see S. E. Haynes and J. A. Stone, "A Neglected Method of Separating Demand and Supply in Time Series Regression," *Journal of Business and Economic Statistics* 3 (1985): 238–43.

18 The cumulative sum of the lagged cross-correlation estimates is computed for a test of the sign and significance of the lag, since the standard chi-square test is silent regarding the sign.

19 More formally, the coherence square between two series measures by cycle the percentage variation of one series that can be explained by that of the other series (see Jenkins and Watts, *Spectral Analysis*, chaps. 8–9). For an explanation (based on a comparison of theoretical to empirical cross-spectral statistics, including the phase) of why this estimate reflects identification of aggregate supply and not aggregate demand, see S. E. Haynes and J. A. Stone, "The Dynamic Links between Inflation and Unemployment: Some Empirical Evidence," in *Time Series Analysis: Theory and Practice,* ed. O. D. Anderson (New York: North-Holland, 1983), pp. 125–36.

20 For a formal demonstration of this conclusion, see Haynes and Stone, "Dynamic Links."

11 Political Business Cycles and the Capital Stock: Variations on an Austrian Theme

Peter Lewin

Most economists are at least vaguely familiar with the Austrian theory of the business cycle (sometimes also referred to as the Mises-Hayek theory).[1] This theory, whose popularity has diminished over the years, relies on the distortion of interest rates by government financing activities to explain the business cycle. Interest rates that are "too low" signal an increase in the price of capital goods relative to consumer goods that cannot be maintained. The ultimate result is an abandoning of investment projects that once seemed profitable (at lower interest rates).

One of the problems with this theory is that it implicitly uses a two-commodity model—capital and consumer goods. And although this is not meant as a literal depiction of the economy, it raises the following question: If it is assumed that economic agents know the model, then how do we explain the mistakes that generate the cycle? This paper is a brief attempt to integrate the Austrian theory with aspects of public choice theory in a multisector description of how the capital structure[2] can get distorted by political decisions and thereby exaggerate, if not cause, economic cycles.

The capital structure can be understood only in terms of the individual plans from which it derives. A production plan involves the combining of individual capital goods and labor resources in order to produce particular outputs. The significance of understanding capital in terms of plans is twofold. First, the plans provide the reference points for interpreting any given capital structure. Second, when plans fail they will be revised and the capital structure will be changed.

The success or failure of an individual production plan depends crucially on the nature of other individual plans in the market. Only if all plans are consistent with one another will they all succeed. Plan inconsistency implies plan failure. Plan failure implies plan revision, which implies capital reshuffling. Plan revision is the root of changes in the capital structure.

The perfect consistency of all individual production plans is a most unlikely occurrence. In any modern economy, production plans are almost certain to be, at least in part, inconsistent. This means that producers will experience less than complete fulfillment of their expectations. (Indeed, some surprises may be pleasant ones.) In the economy as a whole many firms will be planning and replanning their production activities. Out of their interaction with the economic environment will emerge a flow of goods and services; successful plans are rewarded, unsuccessful plans are punished. Those capital combinations that prove themselves survive at the expense of those that do not. In a perfectly stable economic environment this would mean that a stable capital structure, consisting only of sustainable capital combinations, would eventually be established. All production plans would become consistent with one another. We may refer to this as a "sustainable capital structure."

In reality no capital structure is perfectly sustainable. Its existence would imply the absence of technological progress. The normal course of economic progress implies the unavoidable failure of some plans and the reallocation of resources. The market process tends toward the integration of capital into a sustainable structure, but because change is incessant, the process is never complete. The stability of a market economy rests in the final analysis on the dominance of capital integrating forces over forces of disintegration. The latter exist, but we should normally not expect them to predominate. There should, by the law of large numbers and the law of markets, be at least as many gains as losses. Successes should at least balance failures. The predominance of failures in one period, followed by the predominance of successes in another, is one way of characterizing an economic cycle. It is thus something of a mystery. Though we expect errors to occur, we should not a priori expect them to occur en masse. What then explains the "clustering of errors" characteristic of recession?

Part of an answer surely has to do with the existence of plan complementarity and capital specificity and durability. Insofar as plans depend on each other for their success, the failure of one set of plans may set in motion a series of failures. Since plans embody specific durable capital that cannot be rapidly depreciated, plan failures imply capital losses. There is thus a cumulative process of the kind that Keynes envisioned that accompanies the capital regrouping process. Cycles, in the sense of retrospectively identified coherences of selected economic aggregates, are probably an inevitable feature of market economies.

There is reason to believe, however, that economic policy exaggerates the concentration of errors in time and space. The logic of modern political processes suggests that biases exist that push the economy toward the successive adoption and abandonment of unsustainable capital structures. In a majoritarian democracy with frequent elections, the incentives facing policymakers favor the sponsorship of specific investment projects. Votes can be "bought" with promises of subsidies for the needy projects of their constituencies. The individual politician will attempt to secure for his/her constituency the largest possible subsidies consistent with the demands of other politicians and consistent with constitutional financial constraints. This involves supporting the production plans of some producers at the expense of others. It is entirely rational for producers so favored to respond by investing in capital combinations whose success depends on the promised support, as long as they believe that the support is likely to be enduring. Because of the free rider problem there is a tendency for the total demand for subsidies to exceed the revenue available from taxation and fees. The likely result is high real interest rates (to finance government debt) and inflation.

The real value of these government subsidies tends to diminish over time for a variety of reasons. First, if there is inflation there will be cost increases on subsidized projects. However, this may be general and may be anticipated. Even if anticipated, the production plan may still be implemented because of attractive short-term gains and because once the project is started increasing appropriations may be forthcoming. Second, those projects financed by subsidies tend to be losers; that's why they need the subsidies. As the real value of the subsidies decline, legislators have a tendency to increase the money value of subsequent appropriations, and subsidies grow. There comes a point when the financing spiral must be broken, however. This will take the form of a political crisis, a stock market panic, or some other event brought about by escalating debt, rising taxation, or accelerating inflation (all three are symptoms of the same problem). By encouraging the formation of a capital structure that cannot be sustained, policymakers sow the seeds of recession. The cluster of errors responsible for a recession is inherent in the cluster of government supported projects. When the statistical history of the period comes to be written a political-economic cycle is observed.

Notes

1   See, for example, F. A. Hayek, *Monetary Theory and the Trade Cycle* (reprint, New York: Augustus M. Kelly, 1966), and *Prices and Production*, 2d ed. (New York: Augustus M. Kelly, 1967).
2   Ludwig M. Lachmann, "Complimentarity and Substitution in the Theory of Capital," *Economica* 14 (May 1947): 108–19; reprinted in *Capital, Expectations, and the Market Process* (Kansas City: Sheed Andrews and McMeel, 1977) and *Capital and Its Structure* (Kansas City: Sheed Andrews and McMeel, 1978).

Part Three

The Political Economy of Monetary Policy

12 Problems Inherent in Political Money Supply Schemes: Some Historical and Theoretical Lessons

Lawrence H. White

Economists today generally recognize that stagflation and other aspects of contemporary monetary disorder are principally the results of the behavior of government monetary agencies. The behavior of government monetary agencies can only be understood as the result of the basic incentives and constraints facing their managers. Yet the problems associated with government control over the quantity of money are often discussed as though they stem merely from the personalities of those in charge, or at worst from minor organizational design flaws, remediable by implementation of a new and improved operating blueprint for government management of the money supply. In particular, economists and political analysts have typically discussed programs for "depoliticizing" supply of money without challenging government's monopoly control over the business of supplying basic money. These authors evidently believe it possible to take the "politics" out of money creation without taking money creation out of the province of government, or in other words, that a government authority for controlling the quantity of money can be run apolitically.

There is good cause for believing the opposite. However unpleasant the idea may be, the problem of political influence over money may not realistically be resolvable at a shallow level. This essay aims to elucidate the reasons why undesirable political influence may be inherent in government supply of money. The reasons are clearly suggested by branches of economic theory, specifically by theories of seigniorage, bureaucracy, and the political business cycle. The relevant theories are critically examined below. The history of government monetary authorities or central banks may suggest reasons even more clearly. If the exercise of official influence over money was the purpose for which central banks were legislated into existence, then stripping them of their power would leave them without a rationale for government support. It seems extremely unlikely that monetary machinery erected to manipulate the money supply for reasons of state could be turned into the best apparatus for serving the public's interest simply by issuing the operator a new instruction manual, or even by tightening a few loose joints. Some pieces of relevant history are considered in the next section.

The Political Origins of Central Banks

Political influence over the supply of money, with its various features generally judged to be regrettable, is not something new to the twentieth century. It has been present ever since ancient monarchs learned to raise revenue by monopolizing and then debasing the metallic coinage of their realms. In more recent times democratic bodies have passed legislation creating central banks for the purpose of exercising official influence over monetary and credit conditions. Considerations of state finance are crucial, though their influence is sometimes indirect, in explaining why governments have historically fostered the establishment of national monetary authorities and have arrogated to these monopoly agencies the production of a good—money—which the competitive market system readily supplies.

When central banks were established in the nineteenth and early twentieth centuries, it was certainly not for the purpose of manipulating macroeconomic variables according to the full-employment precepts of recent decades. The Keynesian notion of demand management did not yet exist. (Or more accurately, its nineteenth-century proponents had no influence and were dismissed as inflationist cranks.)[1] Nor were central banks invented for the purpose of generating seigniorage through simple additions to the stock of outside money. National economies were not yet on fiat monetary standards which allow the stock of outside money to be permanently expanded by means of the printing press or a central bank balance sheet entry. International gold and silver standards prevailed.

It is no accident that the emergence of central banks antedates the emergence of fiat money, for central banking is a precondition for fiat money. Fiat money cannot be established completely de novo because the acceptance of a money is a social convention that takes time to develop. The universal acceptance of gold and silver by the nineteenth century resulted from a long historical process of traders converging on them as the most marketable of all commodities.[2] Paper currencies and deposit monies made their initial appearance as claims to precious metal held by bankers.[3] The liabilities of central banks were initially of the redeemable sort too, as they would otherwise not have been accepted absent forced-tender status. Given a monopoly of the supply of bank note currency in a region, however, a central bank could terminate the region's gold standard and turn its own liabilities into the most basic money available by repudiating its obligation to redeem them for gold and silver. The Bank of England left the gold standard in 1797, returned in 1821, and abandoned it again in 1931. The Federal Reserve system was relieved of its redemption obligations toward domestic residents in 1933, and toward foreign central banks in 1971.

The Bank of England, to take the world's leading central bank during the era of the classical gold standard (up to 1914), was founded in 1694 purely as a conduit for government borrowing. King William III, his credit low, urgently needed funds to finance an ongoing war with France in defense of his throne. As a clever means of attracting funds, subscribers to a £1.2 million loan to the government were incorporated as the Governor and Company of the Bank of England. A "bank" with little but government debt as an asset, and little but equity and the government's working balances on the other side of the balance sheet, could hardly be apolitical. As Walter Bagehot wrote, it was a "Whig Finance company . . . founded by a Whig government . . . in desperate want of money."[4] Having created for itself a devoted pet bank, the English government found it easy and attractive to bestow exclusive privileges upon it. The exclusive possession of the government's balances, meager at first, later became a source of great prestige to the bank. In 1697 the bank's corporate charter was made exclusive: no other bank could be incorporated (given limited liability) while the Bank of England remained in operation. The field was left open to partnerships, but these were at a legal disadvantage. In 1708, as a quid pro quo for buying further government debt, Parliament delivered the decisive blow against the natural development of banking in England. It barred any bank of more than six partners from issuing bank notes, or any other negotiable securities dated shorter than six months, while the Bank of England existed. This was crucial in restricting competition with the bank, because public holding of bank notes was the major source of bank funding in the eighteenth and nineteenth centuries.

As a result of political interventions, then, the Bank of England enjoyed a legal monopoly of note issue in London, Britain's financial center. For a long while it was the sole deposit banking corporation in England as well. Given its unnatural advantages, the bank quite understandably acquired a special role in the monetary system, a role eventually identified by Bagehot and others as central banking. In particular the other banks in the system came to hold Bank of England notes and deposits in place of gold reserves, while the bank correspondingly became sole holder of the nation's gold reserves. Bagehot himself incisively traced this development to the bank's legal privileges:

> With so many advantages over all competitors, it is quite natural that the Bank of England should have far outstripped them all. Inevitably it became *the* bank in London; all the other bankers grouped themselves round it, and lodged their reserve with it. Thus our *one*-reserve system was not deliberately founded upon definite reasons; it was the gradual consequence of many singular events, and of an accumulation of legal privileges on a single bank which has not been altered, and which no one would now defend.[5]

It is certainly true, as Bagehot suggests, that no single mind designed in detail the institutional outcome of this process, nor could one have done so. Nonetheless the sponsors of banking legislation were neither unaware of nor indifferent toward the centralizing tendency they were promoting. Sir Robert Peel, sponsor of the well-known Bank Charter Act of 1844 that finally clinched the Bank of England's central position, was candid as to his government's aim: "We think it of great importance to increase the controlling power of a single Bank of Issue."[6] A disinterested rationale for centralization was provided by the Currency School's business cycle doctrines. On closer inspection, however, it becomes evident that the weaknesses in the monetary system that the Currency School proposed to remedy by centralizing regulation were due to the centralizing regulations already in place. Fundamentally the act was designed to cement a close fiscal relationship between bank and state that had served both well and promised to continue doing so. The act's major provisions were in fact proposed to Peel by the two chief officers of the Bank of England.[7] The bank gained extended privileges, increased security of tenure, and greater opportunities to expand. The government could presumably look forward with even greater assurance to having a ready buyer for its debt in any circumstance that might arise.

The story behind the establishment of the Federal Reserve system as the central bank of the United States is similar in important respects to the account just given of the development of central banking in England. Key roles were played by the fiscal needs of the government and by the intended consequences of interventionist measures designed to meet those needs. Unlike England, the United States had no continuously operating government-sponsored bank that was given a central banking role as the banking industry developed. The Federal Reserve was established quite late in the game as an institution for supplementing an already developed banking system. Nonetheless, the Federal Reserve Act of 1913 and the Banking Act of 1935 bear important parallels to Peel's act of 1844. All were deliberate attempts to remedy by centralization the shortcomings of a banking industry whose dysfunctions arose from banking regulations designed to promote the sale of government debt.

Restrictions on entry into banking were imposed by state governments in America from the earliest days. The legislatures of several states extracted some of the monopoly rents thus created by requiring the purchase of state debt as a condition of obtaining a bank charter. The so-called free banking laws of the antebellum period regularized this system by granting the right to issue bank notes to all applicants who purchased approved bonds as collateral and met other enumerated requirements.[8] The federal government appropriated the bond collateral scheme in the National Bank Act of 1863, seeing it as a handy way to force-feed its Civil War debt to the banking system. In conjunction with a crushing tax on state bank notes, the act forced issuing banks to purchase federal government bonds to be held as collateral. The bond collateral provision had an unintended consequence that eventually provided the prime motivation for the Federal Reserve Act fifty years later: it made the supply of circulating currency notoriously "inelastic." The proportion of the money stock taking the form of bank notes was not free to vary in response to public demand because the quantity of notes banks could circulate was governed instead by the inflexible stock of federal debt. Bank customers could not convert demand deposits into bank notes during those periods when many wanted currency rather than deposits. This may seem like a minor inconvenience, but it had a major ramification. Denied bank note currency, depositors instead withdrew the outside currency serving as bank reserves, which in turn reduced by a multiple the volume of deposits banks could maintain. Hence a simple demand that could have been met, absent the bond collateral requirement, by an inconsequential change in the mix of bank liabilities gave rise instead to financial stringency and sometimes "panic" as the reserve drain pressured banks to contract their liabilities and assets.[9]

Some reformers, most notably the sponsors of the American Banking Association's "Baltimore Plan" of 1894, recognized the principal root of the banking system's problems and called for an end to the bond collateral restriction. A more influential group, however, proposed somewhat superficially to treat only the most visible symptom, namely, the occurrence of systemwide reserve drains, by establishing an official institution for making additional reserves available to the banks in periods of heavy currency demand.[10] Rather than peel away restrictions, Congress chose to add the Federal Reserve system as an agency for "rational" management of banking crises under the aegis of the federal government. Initially the Fed's legislative mandate was merely to supplement the gold standard occasionally, and not to supersede it permanently, as a source of the nation's reserve money. Its capacity as a sponge for federal debt was rather limited. But with Franklin Roosevelt's executive order abrogating the domestic gold standard in 1933, and with the Banking Act of 1935 explicitly authorizing open market operations and centralized control over the system, the Fed gained a mandate to accommodate the Treasury's borrowing needs and a virtually unconstrained capacity to do so.[11] The vestigial remains of gold convertibility were finally eliminated in 1971.

The Political Incentives of Central Banks

The timing and institutional details of our arrival at the current monetary regime in America—a system of fiat money produced wholly at the discretion of an unconstrained government central bank—were in many respects the accidental outcome of a sequence of unique historical events. Yet it is not accidental that an ever-expanding federal government with ever-expanding revenue needs and macroeconomic designs has taken ever-increasing control over the creation of basic money. Today there is absolutely no tangible constraint on the Fed's capacity to expand the nominal stock of outside money (a.k.a. the monetary base or high-powered money, consisting of fiat currency plus commercial bank deposits at the Fed). The federal government can, through the Fed's open market operations, create any nominal quantity of new outside money at will. (It can also destroy outside money, but the historical record shows a decided bias toward expansion.) This power can be used in pursuit of at least three different governmental objectives: (1) When the Fed purchases federal debt and rebates the Treasury's interest payments back to the Treasury ("monetizes" the debt), the federal government can expand its command over the economy's goods and services without increasing its effective debt obligations or explicit taxation. The greater the rate of creation of fiat money, up to a certain revenue-maximizing rate, the greater the transfer of wealth from the private sector to the government. Assuming the marginal resource cost of nominal base money creation to be essentially zero, the government gains $1 in profit, called "seigniorage," for each $1 of debt monetized during a given period.[12] The by now traditional theory of seigniorage elucidates the economic limits to government's profit from exploitation of this power.[13] (2) The Federal Reserve can expand its own command over goods and services, rather than the Treasury's wealth, by spending its interest earnings rather than rebating them. Economists have only recently begun to explore the implications and evidence for this bureaucratic discretionary profit–maximizing model of money creation. (3) The Federal Reserve can attempt to manipulate the money supply so as to influence macroeconomic conditions in timely and favorable fashion for the purpose of enhancing the political prospects of the Congress, the president, and itself. For the benefit of the Congress and the president this means stimulating the economy just prior to an election, creating a political business cycle. On its own account this means maintaining a credible public "posture" of "fighting" recession, inflation, high interest rates, appreciation (or depreciation) of the dollar, or whatever else a consensus of opinion ranks as the top policy priority.[14]

Seigniorage

The theory of seigniorage alerts us to expect systematic inflation under a regime of political money supply.[15] It has been plausibly argued that the United States government, unlike some other national governments, has not been pursuing a policy aimed single-mindedly at maximizing its sei-gniorage revenue from new money creation over the past three decades.[16] Perhaps we should not expect to find seigniorage being maximized, if taxes in general are being levied at less than revenue-maximizing rates. Even if correct, however, this finding would by no means make the broader theory of seigniorage irrelevant to an understanding of the Fed-eral Reserve's behavior. It would be difficult to explain, without acknowl-edging the government's revenue from issuing additional base money, why the stock of base money and the price level have consistently risen quarter after quarter.[17] Political business cycle theory in its most general form does not indicate any such upward bias.[18]

The government's incentives in raising revenue by means of sei-gniorage may also give us some insight into why monetary expansion has been so irregular. The rate of base money growth has varied substantially from quarter to quarter and even from year to year. For example, during the first six months of 1983 the adjusted monetary base grew at 12.0 percent per annum; during the next six months at a 6.3 percent rate; dur-ing the first six months of 1984 at 11.0 percent; during the next six months at 3.8 percent; during the first six months of 1985 at 10.0 per-cent.[19] On a simple one-parameter theory of money demand this vacilla-tion could reflect seigniorage maximization only if the Fed believed that the inflation sensitivity (or nominal interest rate elasticity) of base money demand were varying.[20] There is no obvious reason why it should have believed this. A more satisfactory explanation introduces the idea that money demand is positively related to the variability of inflation.[21] The government then raises the real demand for its base money, and hence its real seigniorage, for any given average inflation rate by gyrating the ac-tual inflation rate above and below that average. It can cause these gyra-tions by varying the growth rate of the monetary base just as it did from 1983 through mid-1985.

It is moreover possible to supplement the traditional theory of sei-gniorage in various ways in order to explain why the government would aim at less than what is apparently the maximum available seigniorage. An obvious way is to assume that government is benevolent, so that it aims at a (model-defined) social welfare–optimizing rate of seigniorage rather than the maximum attainable rate. At least two problems under-mine this approach, however. First, even if other distorting taxes are pos-itive, the welfare-optimizing rate of seigniorage is zero in models where money is an intermediate good (a transaction cost–reducing medium of exchange). Secondly, even a benevolent monetary authority, if it has discretion to pursue inflationary finance (or to attempt temporary reductions in unemployment) through surprise inflation, may be driven to produce excessive inflation.[22]

It is alternatively possible to explain actual monetary expansion less than the apparent maximum while retaining the less question-begging assumption that government acts in its own pecuniary interest. Such an explanation continues to highlight the likelihood of systematic inflation under a discretionary fiat money regime.

In the traditional approach, as exemplified by Martin J. Bailey's classic contribution,[23] the seigniorage a government can raise depends on the scale of the real demand to hold the money it issues (this is its tax base) and on how sensitive this demand is to anticipated inflation (how quickly the tax base shrinks as the tax rate is raised). Attention is focused on steady states in which the known inflation rate is expected to persist indefinitely. We may supplement this by considering a stochastic setting. The sensitivity of real base money demand to a bout of inflation ought to be lower when periods of high inflation are considered unlucky draws, i.e., are expected to be followed by a reversion to low inflation, than when they are not. Individuals and firms will not readily invest in expensive cash-economizing devices or routines if high inflation is expected not to persist. Government's real seigniorage revenue from a period of high inflation will therefore be greater if it is expected to adhere to a more moderate base money creation policy in the long run. The short-run (and measured) elasticity of real money demand will be less than the long-run (true steady-state) elasticity. A government recognizing this, and projecting that at any future date it might place an unusually high value on real seigniorage, for example because it might be at war, has a purely selfish incentive to pursue "moderate" money creation. This means abstaining during peacetime from expanding the monetary base at a rate as high as the apparent steady-state seigniorage-maximizing rate.

The Federal Reserve as
Maximizer of Its Own Income

An alternative way to explain actual rates of monetary expansion, while retaining the assumption of rationally self-interested government, corresponds to the second possible objective for monetary expansion that we have identified: the enrichment of the Federal Reserve itself. This approach alerts us to the inflationary dangers of a politicized money supply stemming from a slightly different source than that identified by the traditional theory of seigniorage. In a model elaborated by Mark Toma, the management of the monetary authority aims to maximize its discretionary profits.[24] The Federal Reserve's profits are the difference between its "earnings" from holdings of Treasury bills (which it purchases by creating the new base money) and the minimal expenditures necessary to provide and maintain the stock of outside money.[25] Because Federal Reserve officials cannot directly pocket these earnings as dividends or profit-sharing bonuses, they can consume them only by padding authority expenditures. Unnecessary expenditures may take the form of high salaries, lavish offices and other amenities, travel budgets, vanity publications, or excessive numbers of employees.[26] The Fed would be unable to pad its budget in these ways only if congressional monitoring of its consumption were costless. In fact, in the absence of competition, there is no way of knowing the minimum cost at which a product can be produced. Hence the Congress could never have a firm benchmark for judging unnecessary Fed expenditures.

The Federal Reserve rebates its earnings over and above its expenditures back to the Treasury.[27] It is sometimes concluded that the Fed has no incentive to expand the monetary base because its retained earnings from the marginal dollar of seigniorage must be zero. But this conclusion would follow only if monitoring of marginal Fed consumption were costless. If monitoring is costly at the margin of consumption, the Fed *is* in a position to "skim" some portion of the marginal seigniorage dollar into its own budget. Toma finds econometrically that in fact the Federal Reserve's expenditures have risen with its income, even after its service output and wage costs are taken into account, suggesting that a nonnegligible amount of "skimming" is going on.[28] The Fed then does have an incentive to promote monetary expansion on its own behalf. In its implications for the observed rate of money creation this theory is equivalent to the standard theory of seigniorage maximization.

Toma extends this model in an attempt to explain why the monetary authority may not aim for the maximum seigniorage apparently attainable.[29] The reason is that the current management of the authority may be constrained by potential competition from alternative management teams.

Suppose that the next best team promises to produce base money with a total burden (welfare loss from its inflationary tax on cash balances plus its operating expenditures) just equal to the welfare burden of the seigniorage-maximizing rate of money creation. Suppose also that the current management is constrained to impose a burden on the public no heavier than the alternative team's, lest it be replaced. If it were to choose the seigniorage-maximizing rate of base money creation, the authority would then be constrained to zero expenditures, necessary or unnecessary. In order to maximize its discretionary profits (consumed through unnecessary expenditures) subject to the constraint, the authority must chose a rate of base money creation below the unconstrained revenue-maximizing rate. It can then pad its budget to an extent equal to the public's welfare gain from the reduced inflationary tax on cash balances, leaving the public no more (and no less) burdened than it would be under the alternative team.

The kernel of truth in this modification of the model is that the management of a monetary authority in a democracy may certainly be constrained in its monetary expansion and consumption by a fear of being generally perceived by the public as an engine of inflation and den of high living. This perception could indeed lead to popular demand for the termination of its tenure, provided that an alternative monetary regime were widely envisioned, as it did in Andrew Jackson's day.[30] But at present the Fed is clearly not tightly constrained by public, let alone by congressional, recognition of less burdensome alternative monetary regimes. After all, the regime of freezing the monetary base certainly exists as a viable alternative which could be operated with minimal administrative expense. If this were the benchmark the Fed had to meet, it would have to shrink the monetary base, providing the benefit of actual appreciation to base money holders.

Given that efforts at monetary self-education and the exertion of political pressure for a less inflationary monetary regime have concentrated individual costs, while the benefits are diffuse and not fully appreciated, we should expect most citizens (and congressmen) to be understandably ignorant and unconcerned with monetary reform.[31] The Fed therefore enjoys a fairly long leash. Unusually high inflation may shorten the leash by awakening individuals to the possible benefits of altering the present monetary regime, and the Fed may therefore feel occasionally compelled to restore its honor by notching back the inflation rate, but the leash is dangerously long nonetheless. The long-term trend in the inflation rate since 1960, despite recent moderation, seems definitely upward.

Political Business Cycles

Political business cycle theory alerts us to the possibility that a political money supply regime poses not only the danger of secular inflation but also the danger of destabilization of real output and employment in pursuit of reelection. Early versions of the theory developed scenarios in which a government artfully slides the economy along long-run and short-run Phillips curves in order to attain for a fleeting preelection moment the combination of unemployment and inflation rates most favored by voters.[32] These models assume that voters myopically focus on the recent macroeconomic past when choosing between incumbents and challengers, which may or may not be borne out empirically.[33] But the assumption deserving the most serious scrutiny is that the incumbent government has sufficient *control* and *knowledge* to move the economy off the long-run Phillips curve in the desired direction in a timely manner.

The ability of government in principle to control the economy so as to stimulate output and reduce unemployment every four years has been cogently challenged by proponents of "rational expectations" macroeconomics. In the expectations-augmented account of the Phillips curve, the ability of government to manufacture a boom through expansionary monetary policy depends upon its ability to create *surprisingly* high inflation. Underanticipated inflation distorts the output and hiring decisions of firms and the job acceptance decisions of workers and so initiates a reduction of unemployment below the natural rate. High inflation that is fully expected has no such effect. If the federal government were to follow a policy of methodically increasing the inflation rate every fourth year, participants in output and labor markets would have to be somewhat dull witted not to catch on to that policy and to revise their inflationary expectations accordingly. Once they caught on, no systematic inflation surprises would occur, and no systematic increase in real output or reduction in unemployment would be produced by quadrennial jumps in the rates of monetary expansion and inflation.[34]

The government's policy strategy may, however, not be so methodical and transparent that market participants can see through it well enough to completely neutralize it. The strong form of the rational expectations policy ineffectiveness proposition relies inter alia on the assumption that economic agents form their expectations using "the relevant theory." This "relevant theory" has to include knowledge of the monetary authority's decision rule and its perception of its own constraints. In the model of Robert J. Barro and David B. Gordon, for example, agents can form rational expectations of monetary expansion and inflation only because they know unambiguously the form and parameters of the misery function (defined over inflation and unemployment rates) that the monetary authority is trying to minimize, and know unambiguously the slope of the expectations-augmented Phillips trade-off that the monetary authority believes it faces.[35] To the extent that a monetary authority in the real world can successfully disguise or misrepresent its readiness to trade surprise inflation for temporarily lower unemployment, however, it can still exploit the short-run Phillips trade-off. Thus, if anyone takes its announcements seriously, the Fed has an incentive to *talk* a tougher anti-inflation line than it actually follows, to disclaim monetary aggregates when they indicate expansiveness in excess of its announced targets, and to insist that any disinflation that occurs is intentional while any acceleration of inflation is due to forces beyond its control.

It may take the members of the public time to learn what to expect from the monetary authority, particularly when there has been a change in its actual or announced[36] preferences, perceptions, or operating policies, so that an exploitable misanticipation of inflation may be created for a given preelection year. The public is unlikely to see perfectly (at the margin) through the authority's smoke, especially if the authority does not accelerate monetary growth with perfect regularity prior to every election. If some incumbents fail to arrange an election-year boom through timely monetary expansion, this irregularity allows the public to be less than convinced that its inflationary expectations should be hiked as an election approaches, and so enhances the ability of other incumbents to exploit the relatively low inflationary expectations of an unsuspecting populace.[37]

Whereas the rational expectations critique takes exploitable Phillips curve models of political business cycle theory to task for assuming the public to be implausibly dim, it is also possible to criticize those models for assuming the government to be implausibly clever and single-minded. For one thing, the requisite knowledge for a successful political business cycle includes at least a rough ability to forecast the lags with which innovations in monetary growth impinge on real output, unemployment, and inflation. It is unlikely that the accuracy of past forecasts by the United States federal government has been any better than *very* rough.[38] The argument that the monetary authority may lack the knowledge required to create a successful political business cycle is, of course, basically an extension of the familiar argument that the authority lacks the knowledge necessary to dampen business fluctuations of nonmonetary origin, i.e., to fine-tune the economy. The size and timing of monetary injections that will maximize electability is no less difficult to estimate than the size and timing that will minimize discrepancies between the stock of base money and the shifting quantity of base money demanded.

Even keen awareness of its own forecasting inaccuracy, however, cannot be relied upon to prevent an administration from *trying* to generate a favorably timed business cycle. It may intelligently perceive that the expected vote–maximizing policy lies *in the direction* of speeding up monetary growth at *some* point, say ten quarters before the election day, although it may recognize its ignorance as to precisely by how much and when.[39] If the public has come to anticipate this acceleration of the money supply, the policy becomes all the more necessary in order to avoid a negative monetary surprise. Inaccuracy of forecasts may simply help account for the failure of some recent presidents to successfully engineer their own reelection.

A significant modification of political business cycle theory, also arising from a more skeptical view of the central government's cleverness, consists in recognizing that not all cycles attributable to monetary surprises need to be the result of an intentional macroeconomic policy. A particular business cycle may instead be the *unintended* consequence of an innovation in monetary policy that happens to disturb macroeconomic equilibrium. A jump in the rate of monetary expansion may, for example, be produced by the pursuit of greater short-run seigniorage. Richard E. Wagner has suggestively written that variations in the price level may be "merely [a] by-product of political efforts designed to modify the structure of relative prices," i.e., designed to redistribute wealth and buy votes through targeted expenditure of seigniorage revenues.[40] Macroeconomic discoordination would then be synchronized with elections when attempts at redistribution were concentrated near election time. As redistributive spending intensifies, inflationary finance through monetary expansion intensifies. Newly created money, injected by government spending into specifically favored sectors, stimulates economic activity in a temporary and definitely lopsided way. The historical applicability of this model remains a topic for future research. But its immediate plausibility, owing to its consistency with the incentives and powers of those ruling a modern democratic government with a ready apparatus for money creation, makes the model a cogent addition to the reasons for believing that political money supply regimes are radically flawed.

Conclusion

This essay has tried to bring together a number of relevant points about the history and theory of central banks as government agencies. History (as exemplified by British and U.S. experience) indicates that central banks did not emerge for "natural" economic reasons, but instead for reasons of state. A monopoly historically created by political intervention, and today thoroughly harnessed to the central government, should not surprise us when it serves political ends. Economic theory suggests what those ends may be, and how a central bank can serve them. It can help finance government spending by creating new batches of money year after year, and will be all the happier to do so if it can spend some of this money on its own perquisites. It can try to help reelect incumbents by timing the creation of money in accordance with approaching elections, either to bend macroeconomic variables or to finance special-interest spending. In pursuing any of these ends the central bank is being used as a tool by those holding political power and is not serving the interests of the citizens compelled to use government-issued money.

Notes

I am indebted to King Banaian, Gregory Christainsen, Milton Friedman, Thomas Willett, and members of the research department of the Federal Reserve Bank of St. Louis for comments and discussion. The C. V. Starr Center for Applied Economics provided clerical support.

1 These proponents in Great Britain included Thomas Attwood and Sir John Sinclair. On Attwood as a proto-Keynesian whose policy proposals were uninfluential see Frank W. Fetter, *The Development of British Monetary Orthodoxy 1797–1875* (Cambridge: Harvard University Press, 1965), pp. 74–77.

2 The classic theoretical account of this process is Carl Menger, "On the Origin of Money," *Economic Journal* 2 (June 1892): 239–55.

3   See George A. Selgin and Lawrence H. White, "The Evolution of a Free Banking System," *Economic Inquiry* 25 (July 1987): 439–57.

4   Walter Bagehot, *Lombard Street: A Description of the Money Market* (London: Henry S. King, 1873), p. 94.

5   Ibid., pp. 99–100.

6   Speech of May 6, 1844, in *Hansard's Parliamentary Debates,* 3d ser., vol. 74 (London: T. C. Hansard, 1844), col. 742.

7   John Clapham, *The Bank of England,* 2 vols. (New York: Macmillan, 1945), 2:178–79. On Currency School doctrines and the weakness in the English monetary system see Lawrence H. White, *Free Banking in Britain* (Cambridge: Cambridge University Press, 1984), pp. 38–54.

8   However, many states allowed a broad range of collateral in addition to home state bonds. See Arthur J. Rolnick and Warren E. Weber, "Inherent Instability in Banking: The Free Banking Experience," *Cato Journal* 5 (Winter 1986): 877–90.

9   See Alexander Dana Noyes, *History of the National-Bank Currency* (Washington: Government Printing Office, 1910), and Milton Friedman and Anna J. Schwartz, *A Monetary History of the United States, 1867–1960* (Princeton: Princeton University Press, 1963), pp. 168–69. Evidence that the public wanted currency in general rather than outside currency in particular may be found in the ready public acceptance of currency issued (illegally) by clearinghouse associations during the panics of 1873, 1884, 1890, 1893, and 1907. See Richard H. Timberlake, Jr., "The Central Banking Role of Clearinghouse Associations," *Journal of Money, Credit, and Banking* 16 (February 1984): 1–15.

10 Timberlake, "Central Banking," p. 14; Vera C. Smith, *The Rationale of Central Banking* (London: P. S. King, 1936), pp. 133–46.

11 On Fed accomodation of Treasury needs, see Robert J. Shapiro, "Politics and the Federal Reserve," *Public Interest* 66 (Winter 1982): 119–39.

12 Here seigniorage is defined as the *profit* to government from *additions* to the stock of base money. Contrast this to the definition used by some economists, which identifies seigniorage as an *implicit stream* of interest savings to government from the *existing* stock of its non-interest-bearing liabilities outstanding. The former definition is appropriate where the central bank issues irredeemable (fiat) money, because such issues are permanent and are not really liabilities. Under this definition no seigniorage is captured during a period in which the stock of base money remains constant.

13 Martin J. Bailey, "The Welfare Cost of Inflationary Finance," *Journal of Political Economy* (April 1956): 93–110; David Chappell, "On the Revenue Maximizing Rate of Inflation," *Journal of Money, Credit, and Banking* 13 (August 1981): 391–92. The real revenue-maximizing limit is established, as with other taxes, where the shrinkage of the tax base (here, real demand to hold fiat money) begins more than to offset the increasing tax rate (rate of monetary expansion or inflation).

14 On the "number one evil" syndrome, see William Poole, "Monetary Control and the Political Business Cycle," *Cato Journal* 5 (Winter 1986): 685–99.

15 See especially H. Geoffrey Brennan and James M. Buchanan, *Monopoly in Money and Inflation* (London: Institute of Economic Affairs, 1981).

16 See chapter six in this volume. J. Harold McClure, Jr., and Thomas D. Willett, "Inflation Uncertainty and the Optimal Inflation Tax," Claremont Center for Economic Policy Studies Working Paper (Claremont, Calif.: Claremont Graduate School, 1987), show that taking into account plausible negative effects of inflation on output, due to inflation uncertainty, dramatically lowers estimates of the revenue-maximizing rate of inflation.

17 Explanations resting on the assumption that prices are nowadays inflexible downwards entirely beg the question.

18 In fact, with a stable long-run Phillips curve, an adaptively shifting short-run Phillips curve, and an election-day voter preference map centering on zero current inflation and current unemployment below the natural rate (for models with this structure, see note 31 below), the vote-maximizing strategy over the electoral cycle entails *deflation* on average. In that way the stage is set for moving, just prior to the election, "northwest" along a short-run Phillips curve adapted to deflation, to a point combining zero inflation with unemployment as far below the natural rate as desired.

19 Courtenay C. Stone, untitled note, Federal Reserve Bank of St. Louis *U.S. Financial Data,* July 5, 1985, 1.

20 In the Bailey model the seigniorage-maximizing rate of monetary expansion does *not* vary with the *scale* of real money demand, contrary to what has been suggested by at least one author, but only with its sensitivity to the inflation rate (which varies percentage point for percentage point with the rate of monetary expansion).

21 Such a positive relationship is found empirically by Benjamin Klein, "Our New Monetary Standard: The Measurement and Effects of Price Uncertainty 1880–1973," *Economics Inquiry* 13 (December 1975): 461–84. The result can be theoretically derived if the demand for money is properly specified as a function of the expected real rate of return on money rather than the expected rate of inflation, because the expected real rate of return on money is greater for a more variable rate of inflation (holding the mean constant). For example, inflation at 25 percent every period means a real rate of return on money of 0.80, whereas inflation at 50 percent half the time and zero the other half (averaging the same 25 percent) means an average real rate of return of 0.83 (the average of 0.67 and 1.00), a payoff more than 4 percent higher. See Benjamin Eden, "On the Specification of the Demand for Money: The Real Rate of Return versus the Rate of Inflation," *Journal of Political Economy* 84 (December 1976): 1353–59.

22 The first point is made by Kent P. Kimbrough, "Inflation, Employment, and Welfare in the Presence of Transactions Costs," *Journal of Money, Credit, and Banking* 18 (May 1986): 127–40. The second is made by Robert J. Barro, "Inflationary Finance under Discretion and Rules," *Canadian Journal of Economics* 16 (February 1983): 1–16. This is an application of the general point that period-by-period decisions by a government authority may easily lead to a suboptimal equilibrium, made by Finn E. Kydland and Edward C. Prescott, "Rules Rather Than Discretion: The Inconsistency of Optimal Plans," *Journal of Political Economy* 85 (June 1977): 473–91.

23 Bailey, "Welfare Cost."

24 Mark Toma, "Inflationary Bias of the Federal Reserve System: A Bureaucratic Perspective," *Journal of Monetary Economics* 10 (September 1982): 163–90.

25 The Federal Reserve and the Internal Revenue Service are the only two profit-making agencies of the federal government. The Fed "makes money" by literally making money.

26 See William F. Shughart II and Robert D. Tollison, "Preliminary Evidence on the Use of Inputs by the Federal Reserve System," *American Economic Review* 73 (June 1983): 291–304. One Federal Reserve economist I have communicated with argues to the contrary that Fed salaries and amenities are "notoriously" below those available in the private sector.

27 Toma, "Inflationary Bias," pp. 166–67, explains the origin of this arrangement.

28 Ibid., pp. 185–88.

29 Ibid., pp. 170–71.

30 One Jacksonian theorist who called for abolition of the Bank of the United States because he saw it as a source of monetary instability and corruption, and because he had the alternative regime of free banking clearly in mind, was William Leggett. See Leggett, *Democratick Editorials: Essays in Jacksonian Political Economy*, ed. Lawrence H. White (Indianapolis: Liberty Press, 1984), pp. 63–188.

31 On the costs in inflation and the failure of economists to understand them, see Axel Leijonhufvud, *Information and Coordination* (New York: Oxford University Press, 1981), pp. 227–89. The same "free rider" problem applies to the individual congressman as to the rationally ignorant citizen because his district would capture very little of the benefit were he to incur the costs of monitoring the Fed more closely.

32 William D. Nordhaus, "The Political Business Cycle," *Review of Economic Studies* 42 (April 1975): 169–90; C. Duncan MacRae, "A Political Model of the Business Cycle," *Journal of Political Economy* 85 (April 1977): 239–63.

33 See chapter 9 of this volume.

34 Bennet T. McCallum, "The Political Business Cycle: An Empirical Test," *Southern Economic Journal* 44 (January 1978): 504–15, tests for correlation between unemployment and phase of the U.S. electoral cycle by adding variously constructed electoral proxies to regressions of unemployment on three lagged unemployment terms using quarterly data. His results are unfavorable to the Nordhaus hypothesis that an electoral unemployment cycle exists. Nordhaus has found an unemployment cycle analyzing annual U.S. data in a nonparametric way. Daniel J. Richards, "Unanticipated Money and the Political Business Cycle," *Journal of Money, Credit, and Banking* 18 (November 1986): 447–57, regresses unanticipated money (M1) growth proxies on an electoral timing dummy variable, and finds that polical business cycle–type monetary policy appears to have existed in the period 1960–74 but not in 1975–84.

35 Robert J. Barro and David B. Gordon, "A Positive Theory of Monetary Policy in a Natural Rate Model," *Journal of Political Economy* 91 (August 1983): 589–610. Where the public remains in the dark about how monetary policy is formed period by period, and the monetary authority lacks a model of how the public forms its expectations, however, there may be no rational expectations equilibrium to the game in which the monetary authority tries to outwit the public while the public tries to guess how expansive the authority will be. See Roman Frydman, Gerald P. O'Driscoll, Jr., and Andrew Schotter, "Rational Expectations of Government Policy:

An Application of Newcomb's Problem," *Southern Economic Journal* 49 (October 1982): 311–19.

36 In the Barro-Gordon model it would be irrational for people to take seriously what the monetary authority *says* about its own policies, because they already know what it is really up to. Perhaps in our world people should likewise totally discount Federal Reserve statements. Nonetheless, many people apparently do not.

37 Growth in the aggregate M1 was slightly lower in the third year than in the first year of the presidential terms of Gerald Ford and Jimmy Carter (by 0.6 and 0.8 percentage points, respectively). Both were defeated in bidding for a second term. Richard Nixon and Ronald Reagan, by contrast, enjoyed third-year M1 growth 3.1 and 4.1 points higher than first-year growth. Both were reelected. Data from Allen R. Thompson, *Economics* (Reading, Mass.: Addison-Wesley, 1985), pp. 848, 854, 864.

38 It would be surprising, after all, for the government's forecasters to be better than those in the private sector.

39 For a journalist's historical account of election-timed presidential manipulation of U.S. money growth, see Maxwell Newton, *The Fed* (New York: Times Books, 1983). Kevin B. Grier, "Presidential Elections and Federal Reserve Policy: An Empirical Test," *Southern Economic Journal* 54 (October 1987): 475–86, has adduced econometric evidence for the existence of a cyclical pattern in U.S. monetary growth consistent with political business cycle theory. The pattern shows reduction of money growth in the seven quarters after a presidential election, followed by increasing growth rates up to the next election. The pattern is not explained away by fiscal policy variables.

40 Richard E. Wagner, "Economic Manipulation for Political Profit: Macroeconomic Consequences and Constitutional Implications," *Kyklos* 30 (Fall 1977): 395–410. See also Gerald P. O'Driscoll, Jr., "Rational Expectations, Politics, and Stagflation," in *Time, Uncertainty, and Disequilibrium,* ed. Mario J. Rizzo (Lexington, Mass.: Lexington Books, 1979).

13 Two Monetary and Fiscal Policy Myths

Thomas Havrilesky

Introduction

Over the years the standard view of monetary and fiscal policy has been dominated by two myths. The first myth is that the Federal Reserve is an independent, politically neutral institution. This particular illusion repeatedly surfaces in various policy discussions. In the section which follows I shall review two new pieces of hard evidence which refute this concept. This is important because the premise of an independent, apolitical Federal Reserve obfuscates research and debate.

The second myth is that monetary and fiscal policy systematically attempt to maximize social welfare. This myth is on its last legs. It has been replaced by the more realistic premise that monetary and fiscal policy are manipulated so as to maximize the election chances of the incumbent government. It is posited that monetary policymakers manipulate their instruments so as to effect electorally favorable swings in market rates of interest, unemployment, and inflation. This political approach thus explains the ambiguity of monetary policy pronouncements and wide swings in money growth. However, most political models do not try to explain when and how pressures are brought on the monetary authority to affect unemployment or interest rates. The next section of this chapter reviews some new papers that develop the hypothesis that electorally motivated income redistribution propels financial regulatory and fiscal policy and that monetary policy is used periodically to compensate for their adverse macroeconomic effects. If this is the true mission of monetary policy, income redistribution models are a most promising way to identify monetary regimes and eliminate the naivete that permeates the literature on macroeconomic policy modeling.

Administration Influence on Monetary Policy

Costs and Benefits

The question of who has the greatest influence on the Federal Reserve is of no small interest. Later in this section I present new evidence that, despite formal control over the Federal Reserve enjoyed by Congress, the administration often obtains the monetary policy that it wants. When viewed in terms of the costs and benefits to the parties involved, this perspective also has a good deal of intuitive appeal.

The costs to administration officials of influencing the Fed officials would seem to be quite low because both groups understand the technical aspects of monetary policy and have frequent close contacts with one another. The benefits to the administration from such influences can obviously be formidable, as reflected in the theory of the political business cycle and corroborated by reaction function studies which reveal shifts in monetary policy under different administrations.

The costs to Federal Reserve leaders who would resist signals from the administration can be imposing.[1] The Federal Reserve system's autonomy, budgetary hegemony, and supervisory authority would clearly be endangered if its leaders defied the Oval Office (or Congress). Therefore, in tacit exchange for its continued existence it is entirely reasonable to propose that the Federal Reserve must provide the administration with the monetary policy it desires and must alternately serve as the administration's whipping boy for macroeconomic misfortunes. In addition, I believe that this reciprocity requires that the Fed also must serve as the administration's "sound money oracle," ceremoniously warning the White House not to succumb to pressures for lower interest rates. The latter posturing helps the Federal Reserve to solidify its nonpartisan image, gives the administration a continuing excuse to avoid pressures for easier money, and, most importantly, sets the stage for successful periodic monetary surprises, whenever they are desired by the administration.

The costs that recalcitrant Fed leaders could impose on the administration are usually minimal. Because it was formed as a quasipublic organization, it is often said that the Federal Reserve has been able to build a constituency in the financial services industry.[2] Some researchers have argued that this constituency gives the Fed latitude in policy formulation. This may be true in bank regulatory matters where electoral consequences are rather remote and where policy, as described in the next section of this chapter, has led to the technical insolvency of such a large number of depositary institutions that the Fed may enjoy considerable leeway to respond as "crisis manager." However, in monetary policy too much is immediately at stake electorally to allow the Federal Reserve to stray beyond its ceremonial oracle/whipping boy role.

In contrast to the administration's control, Congress is not nowadays generally thought to have a strong grip on the reins of monetary policy.[3] The vote-producing benefits from a congressperson's involvement in monetary policy are typically minor compared to alternative, pork-barreling, activities. The costs of effective involvement in monetary policy are high because the issues are technical and contact with Fed officials is limited to occasional hearings and infrequent bills to modify Federal Reserve responsibilities.

Signaling

In a recent paper, I developed an index of signaling from the administration to the Federal Reserve, *SAFER*.[4] The index is predicated on the fact that there are frequent direct communications between administration and Federal Reserve officials on formal and informal levels. While these communications are seldom explicitly revealed (as it would jeopardize the Fed's nonpartisan, sound-money facade), it is assumed that the financial press extracts and disseminates in an unbiased manner the monetary policy content that is of value to financial market participants.

The index derives from all *Wall Street Journal* articles for the period from September 1, 1979, to December 31, 1984, which mention the views of any administration official on monetary policy. (After 1984 there was a pronounced dearth in signaling.) Each article was retrieved and evaluated either $+1$, -1, or 0, based on whether the official wanted either ease, tightness, or no change in monetary policy. Independent checks revealed that no eligible articles were missed in the first pass and only a negligible number were improperly evaluated. The *SAFER* index is the simple weekly sum of these articles.

In ordinary least squares regressions, cumulative three-week totals of this signaling index (*SAFER*) were found to have a statistically significant impact on the first differences in the narrow money supply during the third week (ΔM_t). A similar index of signals from Congress to the Federal Reserve (*SCFER*) had a marginally significant but perversely negative effect.

$$\Delta M_t = \begin{array}{c} 0.776 \\ (3.999) \end{array} + \begin{array}{c} 0.3141\ SAFER \\ (2.974) \end{array} - \begin{array}{c} 0.299\ SCFER \\ (-1.319) \end{array} \qquad (1)$$

$$DFE = 274 \qquad DW = 2.56 \qquad \bar{R}^2 = .04$$

The results corroborate the view that the administration and not Congress systematically influences monetary policy. When the index was decomposed into signals from Treasury, Council of Economic Advisors, presidential, and unidentified sources, only signals from Treasury and unidentified sources had a statistically significant impact on the weekly change in the money supply. In an estimated reaction function, monthly values of the *SAFER* index responded, significantly, as a dependent variable, to two variables which measure the state of the economy—changes in interest rates, Δi_t, and forecasted inflation, $\hat{P}_t$—but did not respond in a statistically significant way to forecasted changes in unemployment, $\Delta \hat{U}_t$:

$$SAFER_t = \begin{array}{c} 1.246 \\ (2.266) \end{array} - \begin{array}{c} 0.584 \Delta i_t \\ (-2.463) \end{array} - \begin{array}{c} 1.738 \Delta \hat{U}_t \\ (-1.385) \end{array} - \begin{array}{c} 16.255 \hat{P}_t \\ (-2.405) \end{array} \qquad (2)$$

$$DFE = 58 \qquad DW = 1.68 \qquad \bar{R}^2 = 21$$

In other estimated reaction functions, month-ending values of the money supply, as a dependent variable, did not respond to these same state-of-the-economy measures but did respond to monthly totals of the *SAFER* index. Further tests indicated Granger causality from the index of signals to the money supply.

Federal Open Market Committee (FOMC) Dissent Voting

Further evidence of the influence of central government on the Federal Reserve may be found in the dissent voting records of FOMC members.[5] Assume that all administrations typically have the well-known easy-money, inflationary bias.[6] Assume further that appointments to the Board of Governors reflect that bias but are mitigated by the need to satisfy the representational demands of constituents. This means that the FOMC as a whole will have a lesser inflationary bias than the presidency. My conjecture is that individual FOMC members whose career backgrounds are closely associated with central government, including the Federal Reserve board, will cast votes on FOMC policy directives that are consistent with that bias. They will tend to dissent on the side of ease from the mean as reflected in the directive. Individual FOMC members whose backgrounds do not indicate strong career ties to central government will tend to dissent on the side of tightness from the mean.

Time series data on the individual voting records and backgrounds of FOMC members were used to test this hypothesis. In the period from 1960 to 1983 there were 365 FOMC policy directives; of these, unanimity was achieved 180 times and there were 185 split-decision votes. In the split-decision votes there were 168 dissents on the side of tightness and 154 on the side of ease.

There was a remarkable consistency in the dissent voting of each member. Of all the members with more than five dissents, only one, Governor Mills, dissented more than five times on the sides of both tightness and ease. The rest of the major dissenters consistently opted either for dissent on the side of tightness or dissent on the side of ease.

In order to examine influences on the voting behavior of individual FOMC members, it was conjectured that members who had been closely identified with central government during their careers would tend to dissent from the FOMC directive on the side of ease. Two career measures suggest proximity to central government and a proclivity for dissent on the side of ease. These are the number of years the member served on the Federal Reserve board (*YRSFRB*) and the number of years the member worked for the federal government (*YRSGOV*). Career measures which indicate an absence of proximity to central government and a tendency to dissent on the side of tightness include: a binary variable indicating whether the FOMC member was a Federal Reserve president or not (*PRES*), the number of years the member worked at a Federal Reserve bank (*YRSFRBK*), the number of years the member worked in academics (*YRSACA*), the number of years the individual worked at a private bank (*YRSBANK*), and the number of years the individual worked in private industry (*YRSIND*).

To test whether training in economics influenced dissent, we included the following binary variables: whether the person had a Ph.D. degree (*PHD*), whether the member attended an Ivy League school (*IVY*), whether the member had a business degree (*BDEG*), and whether the member had a law degree (*LDEG*). We also included the number of years the member worked as an economist (*YRSECO*).

Because members, like the FOMC as a whole, try to rationalize dissent by alluding to the state of the economy, we also included standard state-of-the-economy variables for the month prior to the meeting: the change in the inflation rate (*PCH*), the change in unemployment (*UCH*), the change in the T-bill rate (*ICH*).

Using probit analysis, dissents on the side of ease were measured + 1, dissents on the side of tightness as 0. The maximum likelihood estimates and their t-statistics are reported in table 13.1. (See footnote 5.)

Of the proximity-to-central-government variables, five of the eight

Table 13.1 Dependent Variable: Individual FOMC Dissent Votes

Explanatory variable	Maximum likelihood estimate	t-statistic
Intercept	2.181	4.336
PRES	−.958	−4.336
YRSIND	−.0314	−.9831
YRSLAW	−.0301	−.5151
YRSBANK	−0.282	−1.769
YRSACA	−.0575	−3.957
YRSGOV	.0051	.2373
YRSFRB	.0296	2.7103
YRSFRBK	−.0349	−2.1157
PHD	−.0206	−.0719
IVY	−.1542	−3.828
BDEG	.4401	1.367
LDEG	.0439	.1723
YRSECO	.0020	.1742
PCH	−.0367	1.278
UCH	.7901	1.167
ICH	−.0511	−.4317

Ease dissents: 168
Tightness dissents: 154
Log likelihood ratio: 175.0

were significant at the .05 level or better, and each of these had the expected sign. The more of their career time spent away from central government—in academics, at private banks, or at Federal Reserve banks—the more members dissented on the side of tightness; the greater the number of years on the Federal Reserve Board, the more members dissented on the side of ease.

Of the variables which purport to measure familiarity with economics, only one, the presence of an Ivy League degree, influenced dissent voting (on the side of tightness) in a significant manner. Of the state-of-the-economy variables, none had statistically significant estimates. Overall, the results are consistent with the notion that administrations influence monetary policy.

Having presented evidence that Federal Reserve decisions are influenced by the administration, we now ask why the administration seeks to manipulate the economy. Much of the literature explains monetary surprises on the basis of a Kydland-Prescott game between a social welfare–maximizing Federal Reserve and wage setters, possessing different employment and inflation objectives and different information regarding private shocks to the economy.[7] The incredible ease with which these models solve the analytical problem in favor of Fed precommitment to a stable money supply feedback rule suggests that they are an inadequate way of explaining today's environment of repeated observed monetary surprises. In contrast, the assumption that the Fed is electorally motivated helps to explain the ambiguity of Fed pronouncements and large swings in money supply growth.[8] However, most electoral models do not illuminate the real sources of pressure for monetary surprise.

After over three decades of continual debate a standard article of faith for many researchers is that monetary surprises represent unanticipated Federal Reserve responses to strictly exogenous shocks, unanticipated shifts in Federal Reserve preferences for unemployment, inflation, and interest rates, or unanticipated changes in Federal Reserve operating procedures. These essentially ad hoc explanations are intellectually unsatisfying. I believe that generations of Fed watchers applying their most arcane skills will make little progress toward explaining monetary surprises within monetary regimes until this article of faith is abandoned. I will argue that more realistic models should concentrate instead on the financial regulatory and fiscal sources of periodic signals for monetary surprise.

Electorally Motivated Financial
Regulatory, Fiscal, and Monetary Policy

A major unanswered question is whether the political business cycle is caused by monetary policy's direct manipulation of short-run inflation-unemployment (Phillips curve) relations in order to affect electoral outcomes or is the incidental side effect of its pursuit of other objectives (see chapters 2, 10, and 11 of this volume). In this section I present evidence which supports the latter hypothesis from three areas: modern macroeconomic theory, a redistributive theory of financial regulation, and a redistributive theory of fiscal policy.

Modern Macroeconomic Theory

Chapters 9 and 15 of this volume present mixed evidence about whether state-of-the-economy variables really affect voting, especially in congressional elections, and about whether state-of-the-economy impacts on voting outcomes really have any effect on the desires of policymakers. This is an elemental problem because, according to the rational expectations hypothesis, even if electorally motivated governments *wanted* consistently to manipulate unemployment and real interest rates, they could not do so systematically. In addition, even if governments *could* systematically manipulate these variables, it is highly unlikely that the old-fashioned textbook image of a temporally consistent, discretionary, macroeconomic stabilization–oriented fiscal policy has any validity. In contrast to this image, according to the public choice perspective discussed below, preelection promises to change the spending, transfer, and taxation programs of government reflect primarily redistributive objectives, not macroeconomic stabilization ones.[9]

Of course, the confusion between redistributive and macroeconomic stabilization objectives that afflicts the theory of fiscal policy does not apply to the theory of monetary policy. It is clear that monetary policy may periodically be used to respond to the macroeconomic effects of various shocks. One problem for researchers is that the shocks and/or their effects on the macroeconomy are seldom strictly exogenous. For example, an exogenous shock which causes high interest rates has the effect of threatening the solvency of depositary institutions. Thus the effect to which the monetary policymaker may respond is often really a product of the regulatory policy regime and, perhaps, its interaction with (earlier) monetary policy. As another example, consider a shock which has the effect of causing high unemployment or high interest rates. The shock itself may be a lagged consequence of deliberate choices regarding spending, transfers, and taxation made prior to the latest election. Thus, while the Federal Reserve appears to be concerned about rising unemployment or rising interest rates, the regulatory and fiscal policies of government are often really antecedents of the "shocks" to whose effects monetary policy *may* respond.

The emphasis on "may" is important. If monetary policy attempted to compensate for the effects of too many shocks, it would lose degrees of freedom for producing desired short-run effects on real variables without an undesired rate of inflation. Consistent with the empirical results reported in chapter 8 of this volume, modern macroeconomic theory suggests a skepticism toward scenarios which require systematic accommodation of *any* type of shock. In addition, this type of monetary policy activism would raise inflation uncertainty and increase the risk premium that is built into real interest rates. Thus, as discussed earlier, the Federal Reserve's role as a sound money oracle, backed up by reputation- and credibility-building intervals of steady money growth, sets the stage for successful monetary surprises.

By this reasoning, intermittent responses to the effects of shocks merely give the *appearance* of Federal Reserve concern with real state-of-the-economy variables. In promoting this concerned image the Fed is perfectly free to choose the variables and assign weights to them ex post. As discussed by Lombra in chapter 14 of this volume, this seat-of-the-pants policy-making with no precommitments is in the self-protective interests of Fed leaders and the administration officials who appear to direct them.

Moreover, the periodic ex post appearance of Federal Reserve concern for the state of the economy found in reaction function studies does not generally translate into consistent statistical estimates of Federal Reserve responses to real state-of-the-economy variables. Even when separate estimates are generated for different political parties and different administrations, there is typically no intertemporal consistency. This is, of course, consonant with the logic of much of the mainstream rational expectations thinking; if consistent reactions to real state variables were uncovered by market participants, the resulting policy would be ineffective. If we really want to identify the factors that motivate monetary policy we ought to examine the regulatory and fiscal antecedents of allegedly "exogenous" shocks.

A Public Choice Theory of Financial Regulatory Policy

I am puzzled why researchers have ignored for so long the need for an economic theory of financial regulatory policy and its interface with the monetary policy regime. The chronic "omitted variables" and "inconsistent estimates" problems in empirical estimation of money demand relations are habitually ascribed to "financial innovations in a changing regulatory and monetary policy environment." Instability in velocity and other behavioral macroeconomic relations and unreliability of structural models are frequently blamed on "switches in monetary policy."[10]

Financial regulatory and monetary policy changes are not a random walk. There appear to be, for example, systematic linkages between changes in monetary policy regimes and changes in regulatory policy. For example, the (commercial loan theory of banking) monetary regime that is implicit in the Federal Reserve Act of 1913 and that fueled the Great Depression influenced the regulatory remodeling reflected in the Banking Acts of 1933 and 1935. As another example, the activist monetary policy regime that was established by the Accord of 1951 ultimately led to the regulatory revisions reflected in the Depository Institutions Deregulation and Monetary Control Act of 1980.

The conventional rationale for financial regulation is the concept of financial market failure. According to the market failure theory of financial regulation, government's goal is assumed to be to reduce an externality, e.g., either the risk of an epidemiological breakdown of the nation's payments system or the costs of monitoring banks and certifying their safety. Collapse of the payments mechanism could conceivably arise from the existence of artificially low barriers to entry which creates an underconcentrated and overspecialized financial services industry and, with a sufficiently large decrease in deposits, requires the periodic exit of a large number of depositary firms. In other words, potential large-scale breaches of deposit contracts by failed firms are viewed as a threat to the nation's payments mechanism. For decades this apparent threat as well as the need for regulator assurance of bank safety has served as a de jure justification for government's lender-of-last-resort and deposit insurance guarantees. The resulting moral hazard affords banks glowing incentives for risk taking and gives rise to a web of ancillary geographic and product line regulations. Banks in turn successfully circumvent these ancillary regulations by financial innovations which alter their form, structure, and production methods. This blend of excessive risk taking and incessant competitive change in an underconcentrated and overspecialized industry has produced a large and growing number of technically insolvent depositary institutions. Bureaucratic regulators are reluctant to shut down these institutions and to present Congress and the taxpayer with the tab, which could run into hundreds of billions of dollars. Instead of protecting the system from breakdown, regulators seem more intent on protecting their own regulatory turf.

The market failure theory of financial regulation cannot explain the persistence of large subsidies to de facto insolvent institutions at the expense of taxes on solid institutions and on taxpayers together with the persistence of a large number of banks. A public choice model of banking regulation, after Stigler and Peltzman, may be able to do this.[11]

In a recent paper[12] my colleagues and I model the political incumbent as choosing the vote-maximizing level of a subsidy for troubled banks and tax divided between solid banks and taxpayers (bank customers), all of whom foresee real income losses should bank failure occur. As the model yields the vote-maximizing number of banks, it is also a model of banking entry and exit. Comparative static experiments examine the effect of changes in political support from troubled banks, solid banks, and bank customers, arising from changes in the distribution of wealth, the distribution of voting rights, and technological changes, on the level of the subsidy, the number of banks, and the division of the tax burden. Results suggest that the emerging, politically optimal, re-regulatory package will include sizable numbers of latently troubled banks, a few financial services behemoths with heavily taxed banking entities, and another turn of the screw for the U.S. taxpayer.

Redistributive regulatory policy traditionally is seen as resulting in waste and inefficiency. The more obvious manifestations of such economic waste have adverse electoral consequences, such as low or falling levels of real per capita income.[13] These problems can often be covered up with monetary surprises that are directed at lowering real interest rates or keeping them from rising. Thus, there would seem to be a link between the regulatory regime and monetary policy. My conjecture is that the greater the losses generated by financial regulatory policy, the greater the potential for attempts at monetary surprise.[14]

Attempts at monetary surprise also seem to increase whenever interest rate shocks, excessive risk taking, and financial innovation force a critical number of financial institutions onto the garbage heap of de facto insolvency. Surprises are often justified and may even show up statistically as periodic sensitivity to high unemployment and high interest rates. Nevertheless, these may not be the true causes of monetary surprise. In order to understand monetary regimes more must be learned about the linkages between financial regulatory policy and monetary surprises.

A Public Choice Theory of
Fiscal and Monetary Regimes

In the public choice literature, as discussed in chapters 2 and 11 of this volume, political parties are often seen as making redistributive promises in order to maximize future expected votes. In a recent paper[15] I envision this occurring in the following way. A promised redistribution of income from one income class to another gains expected votes as well as cash and noncash campaign contributions from the favored class but loses expected votes and campaign contributions from the class penalized by the redistribution. Thus, the redistributive promises of a political party embodied in its fiscal policy "platform" (and in its financial regulatory policy "platform," discussed earlier) depend on the voting and cash and noncash campaign contribution support or lack of support it can expect to muster from each income class over some planning horizon. Because redistributions must be financed by higher levels of taxation, they create disincentives for productive effort. If these disincentives are unanticipated when redistributive promises are made *prior* to an election, real income will fall after that election. Monetary surprises temporarily raise the level of aggregate real income. Therefore, the role played by monetary policy in such a scheme is to compensate for expected vote losses—including those arising from the current redistribution—in future elections with well-timed monetary surprises.

This view contrasts with the idea, featured in chapter 9 of this volume, that electorally oriented fiscal and monetary policy are not as purposely redistributive as they are oriented toward improving the overall macroeconomy. This approach puzzles me since preelection promises and voter expectations regarding the unemployment and inflation goals of either party are usually similar, but their redistributive programs differ immensely, at least in the United States. In contrast, preelection redistributive promises, e.g., Social Security, Medicare, agricultural subsidies, various tax preferences, etc., are the meat of practically every presidential election campaign.

Pressures for monetary surprises emerge from the salient recognition that (fiscal and financial regulatory) redistributions distort supply decisions and lead to an undesirable low level of real income, labeled the "traditional Chicago view" by Willett and Banaian in chapter 3 of this volume. As monetary surprises temporarily increase real income, they increase expected votes. Thus the first prediction of my theory is that both conservative and liberal governments will engage in monetary surprises, as a concomitant of their redistribution policies, ceteris paribus; the greater the redistribution, the greater the surprise.

The model has a second prediction. If the conservative party is ideologically constrained not to redistribute to lower-income groups, redistribution will increase when a liberal government comes to power. Thus a newly elected liberal government will always be in greater jeopardy in the forthcoming election as the terms of trade shift with the disincentive effects. Since a newly elected liberal government faces a greater risk of losing the next election than a newly elected conservative government, it has a greater incentive to engage in postelection monetary surprises. Thus, the two predictions of the model provide a nexus between fiscal redistribution, monetary surprise, and inflation and lead to a positive theory of politics and inflation sought by Mitchell in chapter 2 of this volume.

In testing the second prediction for the 1952–1984 period by ordinary least squares regression, a variable which measured changes in the presidency from conservative to liberal, CL_{t-1}, had a marginally statistically significant, positive impact on yearly money supply growth, M_t, while changes in government from liberal to conservative, CC_{t-1}, were significant and negative.

$$\dot{M}_t = 1.391 + 0.732\dot{M}_{t-1} + 1.6677CL_{t-1} - 2.0405CC_{t-1} \quad (3)$$
$$(1.902) \quad (5.4589) \quad (1.2910) \quad (-2.7324)$$

$$\bar{R}^2 = .49 \qquad DW = 1.68 \qquad DFE = 28$$

Moreover in an estimated reaction function the apparent sensitivity of monetary policy to unemployment disappears when a change-in-government variable is introduced. These results support the prediction that changes in government from conservative to liberal produce monetary ease just after the election.

The criticism could be made that the result in equation (3) really reflects greater sensitivity to unemployment by liberal governments than conservative governments since liberals are usually elected during recessions. This contention might derive from models in which the policymaker maximizes a social welfare function whose weights on unemployment and inflation change with changes in the political party of government. However, this view is controverted by the many reaction function studies which show conservative governments such as Nixon's to be more "sensitive" to unemployment than liberal governments such as Johnson's. Moreover, correlation between monetary policy and unemployment, such as those reported by Schneider and Frey in chapter 9, does not necessarily imply causality. According to my theory, governments, liberal or conservative, engage in monetary surprise when necessary to help compensate for the adverse electoral consequences of their selected fiscal (redistribution) policy (and other shocks to the economy). Higher unemployment may be one of those consequences.

Because of the preceding criticism and because the change-in-government variable had only marginally significant effects on money growth, I tried a more direct approach and tested the first prediction of the model. This involved direct measurement of government expenditures which had an obviously less skewed distribution of benefits by income group than the distribution of earned income. I summed across government outlays on income security, veterans benefits, health, and education and, because of growth in the size of government, expressed these "social expenditures" as a proportion of aggregate income, (S/Y). Because my theory of monetary policy predicts that increases in redistribution in the direction of less inequality may have a lagged adverse effect on the level of aggregate real income and hence beget a monetary surprise, first differences in this ratio were entered into a monetary policy reaction function. The result was

$$\dot{M}_t = -0.1679 + 0.6317\dot{M}_{t-1} + 0.2086\hat{U}_t + 0.0761\hat{P}_t$$

$$(-0.1364) \quad (3.7405) \quad\quad (0.7054) \quad (0.6767) \quad (4)$$

$$+ 0.0083 \, \Delta(S/Y)_t + 1.6517CL_{t-1} + 1.7768CC_{t-1}$$

$$(1.6220) \quad\quad (1.2378) \quad\quad (-1.5498)$$

$$\bar{R}^2 = .63 \quad\quad DW = 1.91 \quad\quad DFE = 25$$

where $\hat{U}_t$ is the (autoregressively) forecasted unemployment rate, $\hat{P}_t$ is the (autoregressively) forecasted inflation rate and $\Delta(S/Y)$ is defined above. Observations are for the period from 1952 to 1984. The change in the ratio of social expenditures to aggregate income had the predicted positive (marginally) significant effect on money growth. The forecasted unemployment and forecasted inflation variables did not have a statistically significant impact on money growth. Once again, this result supports the conjecture that apparent monetary policy concern for unemployment really reflects monetary surprises in the wake of sizable redistributions.[16] Finally, as in equation (3), the estimates for the change-in-government variables are marginally significant. When these variables are removed from the reaction function, the redistribution variable continues to have a positive significant effect on money growth. Overall, the statistical results provide support for the change-in-government and redistribution predictions of my theory of fiscal and monetary policy regimes.

Concluding Remarks

The great peacetime monetary explosions of this century obviously did not develop out of the desire of (independent) monetary authorities to counter recession and unemployment. Rather, I believe most were direct consequences of the redistributive agendas that put the party (or ruling coalition) of government in power. Some parties (coalitions) came to power on the basis of promises to redistribute income to (unskilled and semiskilled) labor, for example, the labor governments in central Europe after World War I. Some governments came to power on the basis of promises to aid the urban and rural poor, for example, the "reform" governments in Latin America in the last three decades. Redistribution of these orders of magnitude cannot be financed without taxing the economic base and alienating earned income recipients. Money supply explosions reflect attempts to circumvent the electoral consequences of that alienation.

This view could give birth to the new generation of PBC models anticipated by Schneider and Frey in chapter 9. For a given monetary regime, money supply growth might oscillate between several equilibria, one reaffirming a sound-money commitment and building credibility, the others reflecting monetary policy responses to the adverse lagged electoral consequences of electorally motivated, redistributive (fiscal and financial regulatory) policy.[17] This constellation of pre- and postelection monetary policy switches clearly is consistent with the type of business cycle envisioned by Lewin in chapter 11. Depending on how the adverse consequences of fiscal and regulatory policy are distributed over time, the ensuing monetary surprises could produce the PBC correlation reported by Haynes and Stone in chapter 10. The thought-provoking reforms discussed by Mayer, White, and Willett in this volume have a far better chance of reaching fruition if the political bases of monetary surprises discussed here and in the chapters by Lewin, Mitchell, and Willett and Banaian are better understood.

Notes

I should like to thank Thomas Willett and Edward Tower for their suggestions on this chapter. Responsibility for error is entirely my own.

1 Congress could also impose these costs. As explained below, it does not, because of the relatively higher costs of and lower benefits from monitoring and influencing monetary policy.

2 One way it does this is by admitting representatives of the larger banks and bank holding companies to its councils, advisory groups, and directorates, even if, to the consternation of Congress, it violates the law. Thomas Havrilesky, "The Effect of the Federal Reserve Reform Act on the Economic Affiliations of Directors of Federal Reserve Banks," *Social Science Quarterly* 67 (June 1986): 393–401.

3 See John Wooley, *Monetary Politics: The Federal Reserve and the Politics of Monetary Policy* (New York: Cambridge University Press, 1984).

4 Thomas Havrilesky, "Monetary Policy Signaling from the Administration to the Federal Reserve," *Journal of Money, Credit, and Banking* 20 (February 1988).

5 For further refinement of the preliminary results reported below, see Thomas Havrilesky and Robert Schweitzer, "A Theory of FOMC Dissent Voting with Evidence from the Time Series," in *Political Economy of American Monetary Policy,* ed. Thomas Mayer (Cambridge: Cambridge University Press, forthcoming).

6 See Robert Barro and David Gordon, "Rules, Discretion, and Reputation in a Posi-

tive Model of Monetary Policy," *Journal of Monetary Economics* 12 (July 1983): 101–21.

7   See, for example, Matthew B. Canzoneri, "Monetary Policy Games and the Basic Role of Private Information," *American Economic Review* 75 (1985): 1056–70.

8   Alex Cukierman, "Central Bank Behavior and Credibility: Some Recent Theoretical Developments," Federal Reserve Bank of St. Louis *Review* (May 1986): 5–17.

9   I am troubled by the notion that leftist governments find it consistently in their self-interest to be more sensitive to unemployment than conservative ones. The premise, as I understand it, is that upper-income groups weather recession with less relative deterioration in their wealth than lower-income groups. Despite survey evidence that lower-income individuals are more concerned about unemployment than upper-income ones, this premise seems a bit tenuous. An alternative explanation is offered later in this chapter.

10 Thomas Havrilesky, "Monetary Modeling in a World of Financial Innovation," in *The Payments Revolution: Emerging Public Policy Issues*, ed. Elinor Solomon (Dordrecht: Nijhoff-Kluwer, 1987), pp. 159–88.

11 George Stigler, "A Theory of Regulation," *Bell Journal of Economics and Management Science* 2 (1971): 3–21, and Sam Peltzman, "Toward a More General Theory of Regulation," *Journal of Law and Economics* 19 (1976): 211–40.

12 Thomas Havrilesky, "Market Failure and Public Choice Theories of Banking Regulation and Deregulation," *Research in Financial Services: Public and Private Policy* 1 (forthcoming 1988).

13 Inefficient aggregate economic outcomes depend on the condition that the size and long-run effects of redistributive policies are not fully foreseen by voters when they are proposed. This condition will hold if voters are myopic or if they incorrectly assume that only economic rents will be taxed.

14 The interface between a public choice theory of financial regulatory policy and monetary policy surprises closely resembles the connection between fiscal and monetary policy discussed below. For example, in the 1960s and 1970s electorally motivated financial regulatory policy redistributed income to home owners and the housing industry. During periodic credit crunches the vote-reducing costs of this policy required periodic attempts at monetary surprise.

15 Thomas Havrilesky, "A Partisanship Theory of Fiscal and Monetary Policy Regimes," *Journal of Money, Credit, and Banking* 19 (August 1987): 308–25.

16 This explains the persistence of the myth of low unemployment or real interest rate goals for the monetary authority, for example, in the recent overlapping generations literature which uses games between the Federal Reserve and market participants to explain monetary surprises, e.g., Canzoneri, "Monetary Policy Games." The present paper suggests that the Federal Reserve has no such goals independently of signals from the administration which seeks relief from the adverse electoral effects of its own fiscal and financial regulatory policies—relief that may be found through monetary surprises.

17 Thomas Havrilesky, "The Electoral Cycle in Fiscal and Monetary Policy," *Challenge* (May 1988).

14 Monetary Policy: The Rhetoric versus the Record

Raymond E. Lombra

For decades the makers of U.S. monetary policy have gathered every four to six weeks in Washington to make monetary policy. All the rhetoric, including periodic Federal Reserve reports to the Congress on monetary policy decisions and even minutes of the policy-making meetings, indicate a fervent, abiding desire by policymakers to make policy both less inflationary and less procyclical. With the record of the 1950s and 1960s disappointing to policymakers themselves, it is not surprising, given such desires, that by the early 1970s, the Fed (and a number of other central banks) came to believe that formulating and implementing an improved monetary policy would be facilitated by altering the basic interest rate strategy guiding policy decisions. In particular, it was argued that by shifting policy guides so as to stabilize and lower the growth of the money stock, and the various monetary aggregates more generally, a less inflationary and more stabilizing policy performance would emerge.

Good intentions aside, the 1970s were characterized by outcomes that differed considerably from announced plans and objectives and thus a remarkably low correlation between the rhetoric and the record: the trend rate of monetary growth rose, the variations around the trend remained quite procyclical, and the inflation and unemployment rates both rose, on average. Some ascribe these outcomes to "bad" policy, while others attribute them to bad luck (e.g., oil price "shocks," a "mysterious" decline in productivity growth, and the weather). Beleaguered policymakers, quite unwilling to plead guilty to malpractice, downplay their powers and responsibility by emphasizing the complexity of the economy, the apparent breakdown and unreliability of important structural relationships (e.g., the money demand function), the monetary control problems created by financial innovation, the lack of fiscal discipline, and bad luck.

That much has been written on these issues in recent years is testimony both to the importance of a professional "sorting out" and to the lack of a broad-based consensus on the causes, and hence the cures, of the economic malaise the U.S. economy has experienced periodically over the last twenty-five years. Against this background, the present chapter provides a largely diagnostic and positivistic analysis of the policy-making process (there being no shortage of normative analyses). The resulting "field guide" to policy-making should help to explain the low correlation between the rhetoric and the record and thus contribute to a narrowing of the gap between theory (political and economic) and practice. The central theme developed is that the confluence of short-run political pressures and economic considerations—such as uncertainty, the short time horizons of policymakers and their constituents, and the associated tendency to discount both forecasts and the longer-run cumulative effects of current policy actions—contributed to procyclical policies in the short run and an inflationary bias over the longer run. Such considerations suggest there are fundamental impediments to substantial, sustained progress in the design and conduct of policy, and that such barriers cannot be analyzed or handled within the realm of economics alone.

Proximate versus Ultimate Causes of Economic Developments

Since economic instability persists, it is natural to ask whether actual policy has been an aggravating or moderating factor. The answer to this question, despite thousands of computer printouts and volumes of analysis, remains elusive. Policymakers argue they "lean against the wind," while others argue they often "lean with the wind." William McChesney Martin, for example, a former Fed chairman, once reportedly likened the Fed to someone who removes the punch bowl at a party just as the fun begins. In contrast, Edward Kane argues, "The Fed has come to function like a chaperone at a fraternity party. It legitimizes the process without changing it very much."[1]

In general, alternative views of what drives policy and enhances or limits its effectiveness are rooted, at least implicitly, in various competing theories of inflation and stagflation. The alternatives may be usefully classified, for our purposes, as essentially nonmonetary or monetary. The nonmonetary theories usually emphasize one or more of the following as driving forces behind the trend (or underlying) rate of inflation and fluctuations around the trend: oil price shocks, productivity shocks, agricultural price shocks, fluctuations in money wages, fiscal policy instabilities, international linkages (openness), and rising aspirations and associated societal conflicts over the distribution of income. The common thread linking all such theories is that while monetary policy is understood to be potentially powerful and can from time to time be an independent source of alterations in aggregate demand, it is viewed as a mostly passive force, largely accommodating the financial requirements generated by the factor(s) believed to be the *ultimate* cause(s) of economic fluctuations. Imploring the Fed to "do better" is thus misplaced and ineffective; monetary policy is largely endogenous and thus only a *proximate* cause of most economic fluctuations.

As Ira Kaminow has forcefully argued, the problem with these nonmonetary theories of inflation and stagflation is that the nested hypothesis concerning the conduct of monetary policy, and thus the process linking the money stock to the "exogenous" ultimate cause(s), is usually unspecified and untested, and therefore incomplete.[2] Mindful of this missing link, statistical analysis of the relationship between nonmonetary variables and variables influenced by or controlled by monetary policymakers (e.g., monetary growth, reserve growth, and changes in short-term interest rates) has begun to appear.[3]

The other class of theories shares the common bond of monetarism. Major economic fluctuations and sustained inflation are ascribed to the Fed's unwillingness to stabilize monetary growth around a lower trend. When, in response, the Fed argues that such a policy is difficult to implement in the face of financial innovation and shifting economic and financial relationships, the debate shifts to technical matters of monetary control; how can the Fed change its regulations and its procedures to tighten its control over money and, therefore, improve its ability to deliver a more stable policy? In effect, according to monetarists, the Fed is a key proximate and ultimate cause of economic fluctuations and inflation.

I have long found the resulting literature on reserve requirements, reserve accounting, discount window policy, and nonborrowed reserves vs. monetary base vs. federal funds rate approaches to monetary control somewhat of a puzzle. It is generally agreed within this literature that these issues are important in assessing and improving the degree of short-run (week-to-week and month-to-month) monetary control. Accordingly, and without denying the usefulness of adopting various changes in Fed procedures and regulations, it is extremely doubtful that the secular rise in inflation in the 1970s and associated secular decline in monetary discipline can be attributed to technical aspects of policy-making or to defects in the "plumbing" linking Fed actions to monetary growth. Even though most would probably agree that the current set of procedures and regulations are suboptimal and inefficient, the available research clearly suggests that the Fed could still control monetary growth within a relatively narrow range over periods of six to twelve months. Perhaps monetarists, facing Fed intransigence and the truism that the long run is nothing but a series of short runs, simply want to keep the Fed's feet to the fire in an ongoing "war of attrition." Alternatively, it may be that the plumbing gets more attention than it deserves because the political-sociological factors are harder to handle, it is easier to get agreement on technical issues, and research dealing with noneconomic factors may be considered less "scientific" and hence attract less attention to an author's work. Whatever the motivation for such research, the fact that such control has not been consistently exercised and that policymakers have been reluctant to adopt reforms which could improve short-run monetary control does raise some fundamental issues.

Despite the Fed's formal adoption of monetary aggregates as intermediate targets in 1970 and rhetoric proclaiming a commitment to control monetary growth, I would argue that the record—that is, the failure to consistently exercise such control—does reveal something about the Fed's thinking (preferences?) *and* the thinking (preferences?) of their principals (the president and the Congress). Examinations of the policy process indicate that the Fed frequently vacillates on the analytical significance of the monetary aggregates. Sometimes the monetary aggregates (individually or collectively) are alleged to be important strategic variables to be controlled. At other times, the monetary aggregates are viewed as information (indicator) variables to be used along with other data in setting policy instruments.[4] Distinguishing clearly between these alternative roles for the aggregates, and the associated scope for policy-maker discretion, would seem to be crucial and logically prior to the formulation and implementation of policy. If the aggregates are to be controlled, policymakers should respond to a divergence of actual mone-tary growth from target by resetting their instruments accordingly. If, in contrast, the aggregates are information variables, then a deviation of actual monetary growth from target might be tolerated. Absent an analyt-ical consensus, the resulting ambiguity and vacillation frustrated com-munication among policymakers and their principals and contributed to inconsistencies and circularities in policy formation. The periodic wid-ening of target ranges for the monetary aggregates, proliferation of targets, shifting emphasis accorded particular aggregates, several redefi-nitions of the aggregates, and adjustments to the base periods from which target paths are computed, however technically motivated, are manifes-tations, in part, of the shifting role of monetary growth in guiding policy decisions as the U.S. economy undergoes change.

A basic theme of this chapter is that such behavior by policymakers cannot be analyzed or understood in purely economic terms. To blame only the Fed for the evolution of policy and associated economic out-comes is to accept the dubious proposition that the Fed is independent and/or omnipotent. It will be argued below that the proximate causes of monetary control problems are not independent of the constraints (actual or perceived) generated by the political and economic environment within which policymakers operate.

The Role of Economics and Political Science in Policy Analysis: Some First Principles

Since economics and political science are both social sciences broadly concerned with behavior, it is not surprising that members of both disci-plines devote considerable effort to analyzing the behavior of policymak-ers. Unfortunately, such efforts by one discipline are often viewed with considerable disdain by the other, if not ignored completely. (How many economists read the *American Political Science Review?*) Turf problems aside, it is unlikely that our understanding of the policy process is en-hanced by such professional squabbling.

At the conceptual level, Beck has suggested a starting point for understanding how economics and political science can play complementary roles in policy analysis: "The discipline of economics can deal with the question of how different economic policies lead to different economic outcomes, but it cannot explain the basis for the rankings of the various economic outcomes."[5] Simply put, policy actions would comprise the exogenous variables for economists and the endogenous variables for political scientists.

While specialization and a division of labor are usually desired developments, destined to increase efficiency and productivity (economic and intellectual), it can be argued that policy analysis needs more integration. The problem with an unduly narrow conception of policy for economics has been aptly summarized by Hirsch and Goldthorpe: "Confronted by political and social disturbances, economists . . . have slid easily and often unthinkingly into the assumption-cum-conclusion that the non-economic factors are the extraneous variables that can be expected in the end to adapt to an overriding and objective economic reality. Technical remedies are available and adequate; all that is necessary is for them to be accepted at the political and popular levels."[6] A discomforting result of such an approach, which emerges from at least one branch of economic analysis relevant to the present examination, has been identified by Maier: "Monetarism focuses on keepers of the printing press and summons them to abstinence, but rarely explains what pressures sustain or overcome their resolution."[7]

Proceeding on the premise that a more pluralistic approach to policy analysis will yield a more complete understanding of "what they do and why they do it," the following sections examine the role of and interaction among political and economic forces bearing on the monetary policy process.

Political Aspects of U.S. Monetary Policy

In the process of making policy, the Fed implicitly or explicitly selects goals and chooses a method or procedure (e.g., a monetary aggregates approach or an interest rate approach) for pursuing its goals. Then, in executing policy, the Fed's manipulation of its instruments (open market operations, reserve requirements, and the discount rate) is guided by the operative set of goals and procedures. Making such decisions independent of political considerations is difficult to imagine.[8]

On a normative level, the incongruity between apolitical policy and our democratic form of government is obvious. Ideally, one would expect elected officials to specify the goals (ends) that the Fed should pursue. The Fed might then be left considerable discretion in selecting the means to achieve such ends.[9] On a positivistic level, since the set of goals, procedures, and instrument settings comprising a given policy strategy has nonneutral effects on the body politic, it is not surprising that "enlightened" self-interest leads individuals or groups to rank policies differently. As Kane argues,

> Some opinions are better informed and less self-serving than others, but all of them are affected by the owner's perspective as an interested member of various political and economic groups. Perspectives on macroeconomic issues [including policy] differ markedly between creditors and debtors, between workers and employers, between job holders and the unemployed, between landlords and tenants, between a product's producers and its consumers, between bureaucrats and the public that pays their salaries, between Fed staff economists and their counterparts in academe, and between incumbent politicians and those seeking to unseat them.[10]

The different perspectives and the alternative policy rankings which flow from them constitute ongoing sources of pressure which policymakers seek to selectively fend off or embrace. That monetary policymakers engage in such political activity is undeniable. How it affects policy decisions per se is somewhat less obvious.

Goal Selection

The selection of economic goals and the weight each is to receive is presumably logically prior to the formulation of policy. But where do the goals and weights come from? Few would argue that the deliberately vague and often contradictory directives (suggestions?) contained in various pieces of legislation in any serious way guide or constrain policymakers. While the resulting ambiguity and lack of specificity imparts an incompleteness and thus indeterminacy to the policy process, some argue such ambiguity and incompleteness is a necessary part of, and actually facilitates, policy-making:

> We have a political process precisely because people have multiple goals that somehow must be reconciled into a single course of government action. The resultant course of action may be called a policy, but that term is misleading if it is regarded as implying one mind, one will, and one theory. Legislation requires ambiguity in the statement of goals so that coalitions can be formed in support of it, and each group can believe that the legislation serves its own special purposes.[11]

> The first rule of the successful political process is, "Don't force a specification of goals or ends." Debate over objectives should be minimized partly because ends and means are inseparable. More important, the necessary agreement on particular policies can often be secured among individuals or groups who hold quite divergent ends.[12]

Succinctly stated, the economist's ideal, scientific approach to policy-making—specify objectives, develop alternatives, assess costs and benefits of options, chose policy—is viewed as unreasonable, unnecessary, and unattainable; within the context of complex problems, all analysis will be incomplete.[13] Thus, "disjointed incrementalism"—a kind of enlightened "muddling through"—is perhaps the most that can be hoped for, and calls for complete policy processes firmly grounded in economic analysis are naive.

If "good" policy-making consists only of being able to make decisions, the virtues of ambiguity and incompleteness follow. However, if the standard against which policy decisions are to be judged is defined in terms of the economic outcomes such actions help to produce, then ambiguity, a shifting compromise among multiple goals, and the associated confusion of means and ends would seem to impede rather than facilitate the making of "good" policy.[14]

A careful reading of the *Memorandum of Discussion* from Federal Open Market Committee (FOMC) meetings—a nearly verbatim transcript available through March 1976—makes it painfully obvious that the FOMC, as a group, did not have a specific set of ultimate objectives guiding the formulation of monetary policy. Of course, everybody was for "low" inflation and "low" unemployment, and individual members no doubt had specific quantitative income, employment, and price objectives in mind as they each spoke and voted on the policy options under consideration. However, the failure to flesh out the specific objectives, weights, and trade-offs conditioning each FOMC member's policy preferences contributed to FOMC decisions where it was not clear to the policymakers themselves in which direction policy was moving or why.

The November 1970 FOMC meeting is a typical example. The committee was of two, diametrically opposed minds. Some felt monetary restraint should be exercised to slow inflation, while others favored a more stimulative policy stance that would give priority to reducing the unemployment rate. Faced with such conflict, the usual practice was to modify the wording of the directive—the set of instructions guiding open market operations, transmitted by the FOMC to the manager of the Fed's portfolio of securities—and/or adjust the various policy alternatives slightly so as to generate unanimous or near-unanimous approval. Despite a nearly even split of policy views at the November 1970 meeting, a directive was agreed to by an 11–1 vote. Unfortunately, it was not clear to the policymakers themselves whether the actions approved would, over the near term, have a greater tendency to slow inflation or to stimulate the real sector of the economy. Divided over the appropriate direction for policy, the consensus reached was an illusion and a reflection of a type of policy paralysis which frustrates the achievement of objectives and contributes to stagflation over time.

The policy process in place at the Fed, and the unspoken disagreement it facilitates, is successful in the sense that policies are adopted. However, the ad hoc approach to goal selection (and policy-making) has not consistently produced economic outcomes satisfactory to economists, large segments of the body politic, or to policymakers. To avoid misunderstanding, it is important to emphasize that eclecticism is not the issue. With a committee making decisions, eclecticism is probably inevitable. Moreover, given uncertainty and some nonzero probability that various competing theories are "true," it may well be optimal to pursue a policy that blends theories so as to minimize the maximum error. The use of more than one theory or objective to guide policy is not the central issue; eclecticism implies a fleshing out of theories and implications which did not generally occur. As Benjamin Friedman has argued, "Policymakers must first determine what they are doing and why, before they set about doing it."[15] The alternative is inherently self-defeating.

Intermediate Target Selection

As is well known, the Fed and other central banks employ an intermediate target approach to policy-making; the basic features of this approach, along with the evolution of Fed policy over the past thirty years, are depicted in the Appendix. The advisability of employing such an approach, and the case for and against certain interest rate and monetary aggregate variables typically considered as candidates for intermediate targets, has spawned a voluminous professional literature.[16] Considerably less attention has been accorded the role that political factors play in influencing such decisions.

Analytically, the failure to specify explicit quantitative goals, as outlined above, renders the selection of a "dial setting" for a particular intermediate target variable problematic. Such incompleteness or indeterminacy is deliberate. In addition to facilitating decision making internally, it helps shift the focus of policy discussions externally away from politically sensitive goals (ends) to more technically related issues regarding means. Since everyone is for "sustainable, noninflationary growth," the basic issues to be decided involve the procedures and tactics to be utilized in pursuing this ill-specified goal.

Despite numerous hearings and other exchanges on monetary policy, it is obvious that the Congress and the president have not pressed the Fed to adopt a more complete and explicit strategy. The reason, as argued persuasively by Kane, is that "overseeing a complete strategy would undercut Fed 'independence' and implicate incumbent elected officials in monetary policy before the fact";[17] "Whenever monetary policies are popular, incumbents can claim their influence was crucial in their adoption. On the other hand, when monetary policies prove unpopular, they can blame everything on a stubborn Federal Reserve and claim further that things would have been worse if *they* had not pressed Fed officials at every opportunity."[18] Given the internal and external payoffs yielded by incompleteness, its continued existence is hardly surprising.

Politically, the choice of specific intermediate target variables is not independent of the public's perception of what the Fed's proximate role is. As Kane argues, "in the popular mind and in the financial press, the Fed is a politically beleaguered institution whose chief task is to act as the arbiter of nominal interest rates."[19] This perception, along with the distributional effects of changes in interest rates, and the continuing tendency to link "high" interest rates with "tight" policy and "low" interest rates with "easy" policy, generates an understandable desire by policymakers to put some distance between their actions and fluctuations in interest rates. Such considerations have undoubtedly played an important role in central banks' adoption of various monetary aggregates as intermediate targets.[20] Frank Morris, president of the Federal Reserve Bank of Boston, confirms this conjecture: "We know that in targeting interest rates the Federal Reserve is subject to a lot more political pressure than it is in targeting a variable which is not politically sensitive, such as the money supply; . . . this is the kind of political sheltering which we should not want to give up."[21]

Policy Execution

Grandiose or not, plans, however formulated, must eventually be transmitted into actions. How much is lost in the translation has been the subject of an expanding empirical literature attempting to link movements in various variables under the Fed's control to a fairly long list of economic variables (e.g., the inflation rate, the unemployment rate, wage growth, the budget deficit, oil prices, etc.) and political variables (e.g., political party in office, proximity of an election, etc.). Recognizing the possible interdependencies among the various economic and political variables, and the possibility that policymaker responses to such variables may be somewhat idiosyncratic instead of systematic across time, application of an increasingly sophisticated arsenal of statistical techniques has become commonplace.

Taken together, the results of these statistical studies, and some thoughtful and insightful case studies, are consistent with the notion that Fed actions through the early 1980s, consciously or not, were primarily the joint product of a complicated confluence of *short-run, domestic* political and economic forces.[22] However, the sensitivity of the empirical results to the time periods, variables, and techniques employed suggests that the Fed does not follow simple rules in reacting to such forces. Rather the Fed is "flexible." Such flexibility is the political fruit borne by the incompleteness of the Fed's strategy; it serves to "stabilize" the short-run political environment while running the risk of destabilizing the economic environment over the longer run. Free to respond flexibly to various political and economic pressures in the short run, the resultant actions of policymakers have been characterized as myopic. However, if those affected by policy—the electorate and thus incumbent politicians—are themselves myopic, as the (mis)management of fiscal policy, for example, clearly suggests, long-run destabilization is not perceived as a problem. Thus, imploring the Fed to "take the long view" is politically naive. Failing to come to grips with an abiding focus on the short run, proposed changes in procedures, even if adopted, may alter the form but not the substance of policy-making.

Economic Factors Conditioning
U.S. Monetary Policy

Whether motivated by the pursuit of economic, political, or social goals, policymakers must confront certain economic realities. *First,* policy operates with a lag; actions taken today initiate a dynamic process of adjustment and reaction in the financial and real sectors of the economy. The resulting passage of time between policy actions and their several effects requires one to distinguish analytically between the short-run period of time (say a year) encompassing the enactment of policy and its initial effects, and a longer-run period characterized by the gradual emergence of the more enduring effects of policy. Such a conceptualization leads directly to the *second* point: the short-run effects of policy on the financial and real sectors of the economy can differ markedly from the longer-run effects. In the short run, for example, a stimulative policy (particularly if unanticipated) will usually lower interest rates, stimulate aggregate demand, and lower unemployment. Over the long run such a policy stance will raise the inflation rate, inflationary expectations, and all nominal magnitudes (e.g., nominal interest rates and nominal wages) and have little or no effect on real magnitudes (e.g., real output and employment). How long it takes for such "policy neutrality" to emerge is, of course, the central focus of ongoing research on how rational economic agents form their expectations and how such expectations affect behavior.

Third, uncertainty is pervasive. More specifically, policymakers' (and economists') knowledge of key structural relationships (such as the

slope and stability of the short-run Phillips curve), despite an ever growing empiricism in policy analysis, is severely limited. As recently summarized by an eminent econometrician, "the theoretical model and
empirical results under discussion do not, unfortunately, lead to any
simple resolution of the main disputed points in macroeconomics."[23] The
apparent fragility of received empirical work and associated forecasting
errors implies that the effects of policy on the economy, especially in the
short run, are somewhat unpredictable.

Fourth, the openness of an economy has a fundamental influence
on the effectiveness and proper conduct of monetary policy.[24] No open
economy is immune from foreign disturbances, many of which may be
inherently unpredictable and whose effects may be difficult to analyze.
Domestically, the effectiveness of interest rate ceilings, reserve requirements, and other policy instruments are weakened by the widening of the
opportunity set available to borrowers and lenders which accompanies
international financial integration. In addition, exchange rate fluctuations
influence the short-run effects of policy on real output and prices. More
generally, openness increases the difficulties associated with determining
the size, source, and duration of disturbances and thus tends to weaken
the ability of policymakers to measure, assess, and react to emerging
developments.

Given knowledge deficiencies, openness, and associated uncertainties concerning the lagged effects of policy on the economy, how do policymakers make policy? To begin, however uncertain policymakers are,
they must still have some basic underlying view of the determinants of
economic activity and thus of how policy (monetary and fiscal) affects the
economy. Understandably reluctant to be pinned down on their precise
views—another manifestation of the Fed's flexibility—the Fed's "model"
is not published in any official release. Rather, it must be gleaned from
various documents the staff prepares for FOMC meetings, containing analyses of past, present, and prospective economic developments, and from
policymaker discussions contained in the minutes (*Memorandum of Discussion*) of FOMC meetings.

The consensus view of the relationship between policy, inflation, and
unemployment prevailing within the Fed in the 1970s followed a mainstream, *closed-economy,* neo-Keynesian track.[25] In general, assuming the
economy was operating below its potential, it was believed that policy-
induced alterations in aggregate demand first affected inventories, pro-

duction, capacity utilization and unemployment; with a lag, these "real" effects, and associated changes in labor market conditions, affected wage demands and, therefore, unit labor costs; changes in unit labor costs, in turn, explained systematic, "underlying" variations in the inflation rate, as opposed to transitory, shock-induced variations. Changes in interest rates, operating through wealth, cost of capital, and availability channels, are the cutting edge of monetary policy within this view of the transmission mechanism. Moreover, given the long lag believed to exist between policy actions and inflation, and thus between policy and a change in inflationary expectations, short-run, policy-induced changes in nominal interest rates are equated with changes in real rates.

Given the above view of the transmission mechanism linking Fed actions with inflation, policy decisions were conditioned by the belief that current policy actions would not materially alter the near-term (four- to six-quarter) inflation outlook and that real output and employment would bear the brunt of restrictive policies in the short run. Therefore, fighting inflation was viewed as "costly" in the short run in terms of lost output and employment. An unmistakable implication has been suggested by Wallich: "Differences on the relative evils of inflation and unemployment are wide, and they tend to be associated with different evaluations of the cost of dealing with either. It would be a rare advisor [or policymaker] who believes inflation could be dealt with at moderate costs but prefers expansion, or who sees the cost as enormous but nevertheless proposes to incur them."[26]

However sensible this general neo-Keynesian view may be, an unfortunate characteristic of the specific forecasts produced by the staff was that the projection errors were large over the two- to four-quarter horizons one would normally expect to dominate policymaker deliberations. In addition, the forecasts were biased in the sense that real GNP tended to be overestimated, while inflation was underestimated. A failure to take adequate account of policy-induced changes in inflationary expectations, and an attendant failure to distinguish between changes in nominal and real interest rates in the formulation and execution of policy, is consistent with the tendency to overestimate the real effects of policy and underestimate the nominal effects.

The *size* of the errors led policymakers to discount the forecasts heavily. This imparted a short-run bias to policy discussions and a resulting focus on current rather than projected economic conditions in selecting among policy alternatives; that is, policymakers usually acted as if no lag existed between policy actions and effects. Given the actual lagged effects of policy actions, such a focus undoubtedly contributed to procyclical policies.

The *biasedness* of the forecasts, reflecting the staff's inability to pin down the slope of the short-run Phillips curve, and the short-run focus resulting from the size of the errors, contributed to an emphasis on the real output effects of various policy actions which dominate in the short run, rather than the price effects which dominate over the longer run. Such an emphasis in turn contributed to a failure to adequately assess the longer-run cumulative effects of policy actions on prices.

Taken together, the size and biasedness of the errors, and the underlying analytical framework they reflected, reinforced the tendency of policymakers to give considerable weight to short-run developments in formulating and implementing policy—a tendency already firmly rooted in the system of political arrangements within which the Fed continues to operate. That the resulting confluence of short-run political pressures and economic considerations contributed to procyclical policies in the short run and inflationary policies over the longer run is difficult to refute.

The Fed has, of course, heard much of this before. The typical response has been to point to knowledge deficiencies and limitations to what monetary policy can itself accomplish. Operationally, it is argued that such considerations point to the need for caution, illustrate the wisdom of eschewing bold, decisive action, and emphasize the benefits of being prepared to respond flexibly to emerging developments. Although superficially appealing, a critical problem with "successive approximation" or "Micawberism" is easily illustrated. Midway through a recovery, for example, we typically observe that the unemployment rate is still relatively high, the inflation rate is relatively low, the economy is expanding fairly rapidly, interest rates have fallen, and monetary growth has accelerated. Amid arguments that the economy is operating well below its potential, that the recovery is fragile, and that inflation has been dealt a decisive blow, policymakers are understandably reluctant to slow monetary growth and encourage a rise in interest rates. After all, uncertainties do exist and a prudent person, it is alleged, should at this stage of the cycle be prepared to err on the side of doing what is necessary to sustain the expansion. Yet, since policy operates with a lag, engineering a "soft landing" for the economy, characterized by sustainable, noninflationary growth, requires policymakers to "throttle back" on the degree of stimulus being provided well before available data point unambiguously toward the need for such an adjustment of policy. That this has seldom occurred needs no documentation. Moreover, it is not obvious that such deft adjustments could be consistently engineered in the short run–oriented political environment within which the Fed operates, even with very reliable forecasts.

Toward a Narrowing of the Gap between the Rhetoric and the Record: Some Cautionary Reflections

Proposals designed to improve the Fed's performance abound. One class of proposed remedies is technical in nature, involving various reforms of the Fed's procedures and regulations. Broadly speaking, such suggestions share a common flaw; they ignore or downplay the political role the Fed plays within the current set of institutional arrangements and, therefore, the political factors which influence their actions. Simply put, it is quite unlikely that technical adjustments *alone,* however well grounded in economic theory, can sever or substantially alter the relationship between the proximate and ultimate causes of economic fluctuations. Kaminow's assessment of the Fed's October 6, 1979, announcement of a change in operating procedures (see the Appendix), designed to improve monetary control, nicely summarizes the relevant issues:

> If the fundamental cause of monetary excesses has been a technical inability to control money, then a technical solution of the sort adopted on October 6th may well succeed. The old money control procedures were extremely imprecise and a shift to control through bank reserves could easily improve precision and give the Federal Reserve added ability to slow money growth and inflation in an orderly fashion.
>
> But there are those that believe that inflation impulses go deeper than Fed technique. Economic aspirations are soaring past our ability to deliver. And when the political process directly or indirectly presses the Fed to chase unobtainable goals for economic growth, the central bank responds with the printing press. Political pressures of course need not be as obvious as direct orders from the President or Congress. Fed officials are hardly immune from the more subtle influences of the political mood and climate in the country.

If excessive money growth has been a response to recurring political pressures for expansive policy, then the October 6th package did nothing to get at fundamental causes of inflation. It neither relaxed the pressures nor increased the Fed's ability to resist them. To the contrary, the package responds well to the political mood of the moment and so offers no particular hope that overexpansion is not again around the corner if the politics begin to push that way.

The Fed deserves high marks for moving toward better money control procedures on October 6th. That move has the potential for adding enormously to monetary stability. But it will do little to slow politically inspired inflation. To do that we need to more effectively insulate the money-creation process from political influence, and that's a bigger job than the Fed can be expected to do on its own.[27]

Recognizing that purely technical reforms may alter the form but not the substance of policy-making, another class of proposals focuses on the political forces and administrative arrangements governing the conduct of policy. Such proposals range from calls for increased policy coordination of monetary and fiscal policy, to proposals requiring increased disclosure, specificity, and accountability in the policy-making process, to legislative or constitutional remedies, including, for example, defrocking the Fed and making it part of the Treasury, and/or the enactment of a monetary rule.

The attractiveness of increased policy coordination is obvious. However, deeper reflection reveals some potential problems. Suppose we have two sets of policymakers (monetary and fiscal), neither has a corner on the truth, and at a moment in time each has a different concept of what is best for society, different forecasts, different theories regarding how policy affects the economy, and, therefore, different preferred policies. Hedging bets and minimizing the possibility of major policy errors might well suggest less rather than more coordination. Moreover, as Alan Blinder has pointed out in an insightful discussion of policy coordination, "Dispersion of power is one safeguard against misuse of power, in economic policy as elsewhere. We know that checks and balances can sometimes lead to stalemate or to conflicts between different branches of government, but in many cases we view this as a reasonable price to pay for protection against abuse of power."[28]

The political argument can also be extended by noting that increased coordination would come perilously close to implicating fiscal policy-makers in monetary policy before the fact. The resulting erosion of the Fed's "scapegoat" role (discussed above) represents a real impediment to proposals calling for more coordination. Similar problems also afflict proposals designed to increase the specificity characterizing the Fed's formulation and reporting of its policy plans, and its accountability to the president and the Congress regarding the execution and effectiveness of policy. The question which needs to be addressed is, To whom is the Fed now accountable and how will proposed changes alter existing relationships?[29] More fundamentally, if the problem with Fed policy is simply that it does not pursue the goals and carry out the policies desired by its principals—the Congress and the president—straightforward remedies exist to increase the Fed's incentive to do so. I take the often amateurish "oversight" of monetary policy by the Congress and its attendant failure to require more disclosure, specificity, and accountability, along with its free-wheeling violation of budgetary plans and resolutions, as telling indicators of underlying preferences and perceived constraints.

Lest one be accused of being unduly negative, a degree of pessimism in these matters does not in my judgment necessarily render research on the policy process, technical or otherwise, nugatory. First, scientific work should not be tightly constrained by what appears politically feasible today; history is replete with examples of reforms (e.g., flexible exchange rates) previously thought unacceptable. Second, as Willett and Laney have argued, positivistic analysis which indicates that political forces have shaped policy does not imply that the only way to engender a less destabilizing policy is to deal directly with underlying political and social forces. It can be argued that the boundaries (constraints) defining the possible scope of Fed actions in the short run are neither unduly narrow nor wholly exogenous. Incentive structures can be altered and marginal improvements may well be possible. Moreover, institutional arrangements are not immutable over the longer run and learning does occur.

The notion that increased specificity plus increased accountability for the Fed *and* its principals will enhance the credibility of economic policymakers and contribute to improved policy performance is quite appealing and deserves to be pursued. More specifically, since disclosure is an essential element of accountability, the policy process needs to be opened up if we are to secure constructive policy discussions and assessments. The Fed has traditionally resisted more openness on the grounds that it would mislead the public and interfere with a free-wheeling, frank exchange of views among policymakers and between policymakers and their staffs. On the former, Havrilesky is surely correct: "Guesswork and possible misinterpretation by private market decision-makers is a reflection of Federal Reserve secrecy rather than an aberrant psychological proclivity by market participants to be mislead and to overreact."[30] As for the contention that less secrecy would inhibit discussion internally, the virtual absence of such exchanges under current arrangements suggests that the previously discussed relationship between ambiguity and flexibility is a better explanation for the Fed's reluctance.

The Fed does now report to Congress the range and "central tendency" of FOMC members' expectations for GNP, inflation, and unemployment for the period twelve to eighteen months ahead. Further movement on this front would be most desirable.[31] Nonetheless, profound difficulties emanate from what might be called "time inconsistency." Simply put, there is a lack of congruence (consistency) between the relatively short time horizons of policymakers and their constituents and the longer time horizon linking policy actions and their several effects. The associated tendency to apply high discount rates to both forecasts and longer-run effects of current policy actions, coupled with a dynamic economy that is often changing in ways imperfectly understood, represent fundamental impediments to substantial progress.

Post-1979 Monetary Policy: Dramatic and Decisive Improvement or Business as Usual?

Some, including the Fed, contend that inflation has been dealt a decisive blow by post-1979 monetary policy and that sustainable, noninflationary growth is within reach *if* budget deficits can be reduced dramatically. Central to this thesis is the notion that the Fed's 1979 change in procedures (see the Appendix) and the performance of policy since then represent a watershed for U.S. monetary policy. The analysis developed above would lead one a priori to be rather skeptical of such a conclusion.

The general features of the 1979 change in procedures, like many such reforms, were conceived earlier and born in a crisis setting. The perception of political and economic observers and policymakers was that inflation, and perhaps policy, were out of control. Focusing on the near term, the Fed, for its part, believed that a substantial rise in interest rates would be needed to brake (break?) the economy, slow down monetary growth, and reduce inflationary pressures and inflationary expectations. Viewed against this background, the change in procedures was a tactic to engineer a significant reduction in monetary growth and increase in interest rates, and, at the same time, put some distance between the Fed's actions and the financial, economic, and political repercussions. Focusing on the longer term, the change can be viewed, in part, as another step toward finding "a better place to stand" so as to more effectively fend off expansionary pressures.[32]

It is interesting to note that several members of the FOMC (in private communications with the author) have indicated that the details and full ramifications of the changes in procedures (especially the role of the discount rate and changes therein) were not clear to them nor, in their judgment, to most FOMC members at the time or for months thereafter. Such contentions, along with the observable swings in policy since 1979, raise important questions about the real significance of, motivation for, and permanence of this or indeed any change in Fed procedures. As explained in the Appendix, actual (as opposed to announced) policy procedures from late 1982 on bear little resemblance to the October 1979–late 1982 experience.

Looking Ahead

We tell our students that policymakers are guided by "the" public interest. Of course, we know better; since there is no single public interest, policymakers, in effect, mediate among often competing, organized private interests. Admitting the existence (necessity?) of shifting compromises among multiple objectives, however reluctantly, greatly complicates policy analysis, whether positivistic or normative. As Woolley argues,

> The Federal Reserve's relationships with other actors are marked by a tension between its nominal political independence and the kind of tasks it is called upon to perform in the economic system. It is asked to be politically neutral while regulating an economic system that is not neutral in results. It is expected to act on the basis of reflective scientific judgment in an environment that stresses political responsiveness. It is asked to make technically correct decisions despite conditions of economic uncertainty that make it difficult to avoid

errors and despite a highly conflictual scientific debate as to what correct policy is.[33]

Various shortcomings in the economic analysis underlying policy-making—e.g., the failure to take adequate account of inflationary expectations, forecasting errors, and frequent vacillation on the causal significance of the monetary aggregates—and technical defects in regulations and monetary control procedures have undoubtedly contributed to an erratic policy record. That policymakers are forced to operate in an environment characterized by considerable uncertainty over structural relationships and the path of the economy is undeniable. However, the core issue, ignoring the political environment for the moment, is what is the "best" policy strategy to follow in the face of such uncertainty. A basic tenet of constrained optimization theory is that short-run policy reactions should become smaller and more cautious as the degree of uncertainty increases. Given uncertainty about supply and demand in both the real and financial sectors, the theory does not specify precisely what reactions should be reduced in the face of uncertainty. Nonetheless, the thrust of the theory, combined with the political pressure flowing from the perception that central banks are the arbiters of nominal interest rates, has led the Fed (and most other central banks) to optimize subject to perceived constraints imposed by the political and economic environment by stabilizing or moderating fluctuations in nominal interest rates in the short run.

That the subsequent adjustments in interest rates have often been unduly small and delayed, contributing to an aggravation of cyclical fluctuations, is well documented. Thus, despite the lip service and periodic commitment to reserve and monetary aggregate objectives, pervasive uncertainty and the confluence of political and economic forces pose a formidable barrier to far-reaching and lasting alterations in procedures and practices. Perhaps Lindbeck is correct: "The main problem is not that we are unable to understand analytically what is happening, but rather that the institutional and the discretionary policies that are necessary for macroeconomic stability seem to be politically difficult to implement."[34] Taken together, the Fed's scapegoat–lightning rod role, firmly embedded in the institutional structure governing the formulation, implementation, *and* evaluation of policy, and an abiding focus on the short run go a long way toward explaining the low correlation between the Fed's rhetoric and the record.

Looking ahead, many have argued that a closer correspondence between the rhetoric and the record would enhance the "credibility" of policymakers and, simultaneously, through the salutary effect on expectations, reduce the impediments to achieving a noninflationary growth path for the economy. Unfortunately, designing *viable* reforms to produce or induce a closer correspondence appears quite formidable. Moreover, theoretical arguments aside, "credibility" is a slippery concept: "We do not know how to measure it, certainly do not know how to produce it, and have only the foggiest notion of whether or to what degree it is absent or present."[35]

Criticisms of policy are seldom in short supply. Particularly noteworthy is the fact that widespread agreement that policy is on the wrong course is often accompanied by considerable disagreement about what policymakers are doing or should do. This has several unfortunate consequences. First, Wallich may well be right: "The credibility of monetary policy with the public is damaged by comment from the profession implying that monetary policy is a simple matter that, with a little intelligence and goodwill, could reliably produce predictable results."[36] Second, the criticisms may have the effect of canceling each other out and obscuring some broader agreement on what can and cannot be accomplished with monetary policy. Third, the ongoing debate over technical matters largely ignores the political-institutional structure and incentives which govern the environment within which policy is conducted. Deciding whether monetary policy is part of the inflation-stagnation problem and can be part of the solution depends on facing rather than finessing the factors which have contributed to the lack of correspondence between the Fed's rhetoric and its record. Continuing failure to do so will produce an intellectual (analytical) paralysis mirroring the paralysis which has often gripped the conduct of policy.

Appendix: The Evolution of Fed Policy

Since the Fed's famous Accord with the Treasury in 1951, the strategy and tactics used by the Fed in the formulation and implementation of policy have passed through at least four distinct stages.

The 1950s and 1960s

During this period, policy was framed in qualitative terms; policymakers would vote for an "easier" or "tighter" policy, decide to "lean against the wind," etc. Such intentions were translated into policy actions producing fairly modest changes in money market conditions. The broad outline of this approach to policy is depicted in figure 14.1. The solid lines and arrows indicate the predominant direction of causation once policy actions are undertaken. The dotted lines indicate the monitoring and feedback which occur as policymakers observe incoming economic data and adjust policy in light of the objectives ("full" employment, price stability, etc.) being pursued.

Critics argued that the strategy was vague and that its analytical foundations were weak. Many called for more quantification and for policymakers to give more weight to controlling the growth of the money stock in formulating and implementing policy. Policy outcomes in the last half of the sixties, ongoing research, and the ascendency of Arthur Burns to the Fed chairmanship led to the next stage.

The 1970s

Beginning in 1970, the money stock became an official "intermediate" target of, and therefore guide for, Fed policy. The term "intermediate"

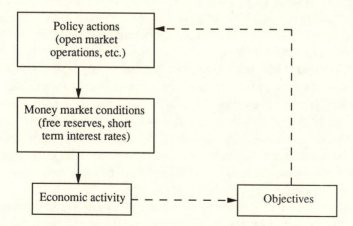

Figure 14.1   Leaning Against the Wind Strategy: 1950s and 1960s

means that the money stock lies between the Fed's instruments and the ultimate targets (or objectives) in the transmission mechanism linking policy to the economy. Control over the money stock was exerted by manipulating the federal funds rate; if money growth was deemed excessive (inadequate), the funds rate was raised (lowered).

Selecting the correct funds rate—correct in the sense of being likely on average to be consistent with the Fed's money stock targets and final objectives—proved difficult for the Fed's forecasters. More fundamentally, policymakers seemed unwilling to move the funds rate sufficiently; as the solid line running from the funds rate to the economy in figure 14.2 indicates, most policymakers believed interest rates were the cutting edge of policy (the money stock was a useful way to "index," communicate, and "discipline" policy).

The tendency to delay or moderate rate movements, whether for political or economic reasons, contributed importantly to the continuation of destabilizing policies. Many argued that the form but not the substance of policy-making had changed; policymakers were still preoccupied with money market conditions, as indexed by the funds rate.

October 1979 to Mid- or Late 1982

Designed to improve the Fed's control over monetary growth, the volume of reserves thought to be consistent with the Fed's money stock target became the proximate guide for policy actions. Instead of deliberating the "appropriate" change in the funds rate whenever the money stock deviated from its target, adhering to a given reserve path in the face of such a deviation would lead to an automatic (and often large) adjustment in the funds rate. Simply put, if money and reserve demand rose, the funds rate—the "price" of reserves—would have to rise to equilibrate supply and demand. During the seventies, in contrast, the supply of reserves was usually adjusted to moderate the effect of a shift in demand on the funds rate. The automatic adjustment accompanying the change in procedure was in turn expected to lead to a quicker return of the actual money stock to its target path (fig. 14.3).

Over the period, the variance of the money stock and interest rates increased, the economy experienced two recessions, and the inflation rate fell dramatically. As 1982 unfolded, it became clear that this mixed rec-

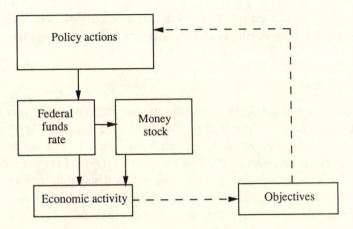

Figure 14.2   Interest Rate-Oriented Strategy: 1970s

Figure 14.3   Reserve-Oriented Strategy: October 1979 to Mid- or Late 1982

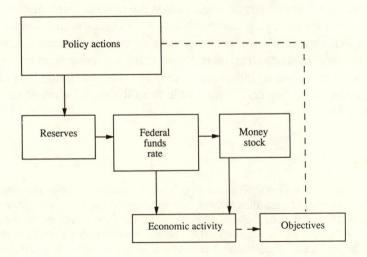

ord and the murky domestic and international outlook was leading the Fed to rethink its procedures and basic policy stance once again.

From 1982 to Date

Perceived weaknesses in the domestic and international economies led the Fed to ease policy significantly from mid-1982 through the spring of 1983. As monetary growth accelerated and interest rates declined, the U.S. economy recovered. With money stock growth (M1) exceeding its target by a wide margin, the Fed pointed to distortions introduced by ongoing innovations and deregulation, shifted target ranges, base periods, and the emphasis accorded various aggregates (M1, M2, M3), and argued for "flexibility" in responding to emerging developments in such uncertain times. That the Fed had again altered its approach to policy was clear. Given the relative stability of the Federal funds rate over most of the year, many argued the Fed had returned to the discarded strategy of the seventies. Seemingly engaged in "successive approximation," clear guideposts for the future conduct of policy—an anchor—were not yet in evidence. By 1986, the huge trade deficit and the depreciating dollar were on center stage. In 1987 the inflation rate rebounded significantly. As the new Fed chairman Alan Greenspan took office in August 1987, the Fed had abandoned its monetary targets, and policy discussions were being heavily influenced by emerging developments, both domestic and foreign. One thing was clear, however: policy actions were again directed at maintaining the level of short-term interest rates thought conducive to maintaining real growth, subduing inflationary pressures, and stabilizing the dollar. A cynic would say we had learned little from the experiences of the 1960s and 1970s.

Notes

I would like to thank Thomas Fox, Thomas Havrilesky, James Herendeen, Will Mason, Thomas Mayer, Allan Meltzer, Marvin Rozen, Frederick Struble, Michael Wasylenko, Thomas Willett, and seminar participants at Penn State and the Federal Reserve Bank of Kansas City for extremely helpful comments on an earlier draft of this chapter.

1   Edward Kane, "External Pressure and the Operations of the Fed," in *Political Economy of International and Domestic Monetary Relations,* ed. R. Lombra and W. Witte (Ames: Iowa State University Press, 1982), p. 212.

2   Ira Kaminow, "Politics, Economics, and Procedures of U.S. Money Growth Dynamics," in *Political Economy of Monetary Relations,* ed. Lombra and Witte, pp. 181–96.

3   See, for example, James Barth, Robin Sickles, and Philip Wiest, "Assessing the Impact of Varying Economic Conditions on Federal Reserve Behavior," *Journal of Macroeconomics* 4 (Winter 1982): 47–70; Nathaniel Beck, "Politics and American Monetary Policy: 1955–1982" (University of California, San Diego, April 1983, typescript); Thomas Havrilesky, "A Theory of Monetary Instability," in *The Political Economy of Policy-Making,* ed. M. Dooley, H. Kaufman, and R. Lombra (Beverly Hills: Sage Publications, 1979), pp. 59–88; Thomas Willett and Leroy Laney, "Technical versus Political Causes of Monetary Expansion," in *Political Economy of Monetary Relations,* ed. Lombra and Witte, pp. 203–7, and references cited therein.

4   See Raymond Lombra and Michael Moran, "Policy Advice and Policymaking at the Federal Reserve," *Carnegie-Rochester Conference Series on Public Policy* 13 (1980): 9–68; and Nicholas Karamouzis, "The Role of International Linkages in the Conduct of U.S. Monetary Policy: 1970–77" (Ph.D. dissertation, Pennsylvania State University, 1984).

5   Beck, "Politics and American Monetary Policy," p. 1.

6   Fred Hirsch and John Goldthorpe, eds., *The Political Economy of Inflation* (Cambridge: Harvard University Press, 1978), p. 2.

7   Charles Maier, "The Politics of Inflation in the Twentieth Century," in *Political Economy of Inflation,* ed. Hirsch and Goldthorpe, p. 39.

8   See, for example, Keith Acheson and John Chant, "Bureaucratic Theory and the Choice of Central Bank Goals," *Journal of Money, Credit, and Banking* 5 (May 1973): 637–55.

9   For an illuminating and wide-ranging discussion, see Will E. Mason, *Clarification of the Monetary Standard* (University Park: Pennsylvania State University Press, 1963).

10 Kane, "External Pressure," p. 222.

11 Martin Rein and Sheldon White, "Can Policy Research Help Policy?" *The Public Interest* 49 (Fall 1977): 123.

12 Charles Schultze, *The Politics and Economics of Public Spending* (Washington, D.C.: Brookings Institution, 1968), p. 47.

13 See Charles Lindbloom, "Still Muddling, Not Yet Through," *Public Administration Review* 39 (Nov./Dec. 1979): 517–26, and Aaron Wildavsky, *The Politics of the Budgetary Process* (Boston: Little, Brown, 1979).

14 On shifting compromises, see Jack Knott, "Uncertainty and Federal Reserve Decision Making" (Michigan State University, 1983, mimeographed).

15 Benjamin Friedman, "Empirical Issues in Monetary Policy: A Review of Monetary Aggregates and Monetary Policy," *Journal of Monetary Economics* 3 (January 1977): 100.

16 See, for example, Ralph Bryant, *Money and Monetary Policy in Interdependent Nations* (Washington, D.C.: Brookings Institution, 1980); Ralph Bryant, *Controlling Money: The Federal Reserve and Its Critics* (Washington, D.C.: Brookings Institution, 1983), and the literature cited therein.

17   Edward Kane, "Selecting Monetary Targets in a Changing Financial Environment," in *Monetary Policy Issues in the 1980s* (Kansas City: Federal Reserve Bank of Kansas City, 1982), p. 193.

18   Edward Kane, "Politics and Fed Policymaking: The More Things Change the More They Remain the Same," *Journal of Monetary Economics* 6 (1980): 206–7.

19   Kane, "Politics and Fed Policymaking," p. 200.

20   Gerald Bouey, "Monetary Policy—Finding a Place to Stand" (Per Jacobsson Lecture, Toronto, September 1982).

21   Frank Morris, "Defining the Issues," in *Interest Rate Deregulation and Monetary Control* (Proceedings of a conference sponsored by the Federal Reserve Bank of San Francisco, 1982), p. 14.

22   The statistical studies include Barth, Sickles, and Wiest, "Assessing the Impact"; Beck, "Politics and American Monetary Policy"; and Willet and Laney, "Technical versus Political Causes." The important case studies are Thomas Mayer, "A Case Study of Federal Reserve Policymaking: Regulation Q in 1966," *Journal of Monetary Economics* 10 (1982): 259–71; and Thomas Mayer, "Federal Reserve Policy in the 1973–1975 Recession: A Case Study of Fed Behavior in a Quandry," in *Crises in the Economic and Financial Structure,* ed. P. Wachtel (Lexington, Mass.: Lexington Books, 1982), pp. 41–83. For an illuminating discussion of these and related issues, see John Woolley, *Monetary Politics: The Federal Reserve and the Politics of Monetary Policy* (New York: Cambridge University Press, 1984).

23   Christopher Sims, "Policy Analysis with Econometric Models," *Brookings Papers on Economic Activity* 1 (1982): 137.

24   Jacob Frenkel and Michael Mussa, "Monetary and Fiscal Policy in an Open Economy," *American Economic Review* 71 (May 1981): 253–58.

25   See Lombra and Moran, "Policy Advice," and Karamouzis, "International Linkages." As Wallich notes, however, even here politics apparently plays a role: "Monetarism has enjoyed a considerable vogue among politicians, understandably, since it tends to absolve them from responsibility for the consequences of poor fiscal policy. In that view, most of the responsibility rests with the Federal Reserve, which therefore tends to acquire some Keynesian leanings [including an emphasis on fiscal policy] in self defense." Henry Wallich, "Policy Research, Policy Advice, and Policymaking," in *Political Economy of Monetary Relations,* ed. Lombra and Witte, p. 243.

26   Wallich, "Policy Research," p. 243.

27   Ira Kaminow, "The Fed May Not Have Shed Its Easy-Money Bias," *American Banker,* October 24, 1979, 4. Of course, the inflation rate dropped sharply following the back-to-back recessions in the early 1980s. The question is whether this reflected simply a change in Fed procedures, is support for the "great man" theory of "good" policy-making (given the ascendency of Paul Volcker to the Fed chairmanship), or is intimately connected to the changed political climate indicated by the election of Ronald Reagan.

28   Alan Blinder, "Issues in the Coordination of Monetary and Fiscal Policy," in *Monetary Policy Issues,* p. 19.

29   Knott, "Uncertainty."

30 Thomas Havrilesky, "Informationally Optimal Monetary and Fiscal Policy," *Financial Review* 17 (November 1982): 262.

31 See U.S. House of Representatives, Committee on Banking, Finance, and Urban Affairs, *Monetary Policy Report—1983*, 98th Cong. 1st sess., December 1983.

32 Bouey, "Monetary Policy."

33 Woolley, *Monetary Politics*, p. 12.

34 Assar Lindbeck, "Stabilization Policies in Open Economies with Endogenous Politicians," *American Economic Review* 66 (May 1976): 18.

35 Phillip Cagan, "Discussion," in *Monetary Policy Issues*, p. 78. For an insightful review of recent attempts to deal with the problems Cagen raises, see Alex Cukierman, "Central Bank Behavior and Credibility—Some Recent Developments," Federal Reserve Bank of St. Louis *Review*, May 1986, 5–17.

36 Wallich, "Policy Research," p. 243.

15 Politics and Monetary Policy

Nathaniel Beck

The economist Richard Cooper once remarked, "I have never been able to understand the impasse between the monetarist and the sociological explanations of inflation. I have always assumed the money supply to be sociologically determined."[1] While it is not clear how the money supply is sociologically determined, Cooper's remark becomes sensible on substituting the term "political" for "sociological." Political institutions (central banks) can determine the money supply. In spite of this, there is no agreed-on theory of the politics of monetary control. In this chapter I explore several political explanations of monetary policy. While none of those explanations will be found totally satisfactory, several together may lead to a satisfactory political account of monetary policy. Understanding the political factors that underlie monetary decisions should aid both diagnosis and cure of the ills besetting our economy.

The standard economics view of monetary policy is that it is a technical question. In the next section I attempt to show that such a view is overly narrow. Following that I consider various political accounts of monetary policy. These can focus either on the internal politics of a central bank or on the relationship of the bank to other political actors. The first treats the bank like any other bureaucracy and looks at the incentives of the bank to either curb or cure inflation; the second considers the bank to be the agent of either the executive or legislative branch and must therefore consider incentives faced by those political actors as well as the monetary authorities.

The primary incentive of all political leaders is to be elected (or reelected) and it is that incentive which this chapter treats in most depth. Particular attention will be paid to the role of the Federal Reserve in aiding presidential reelection. Do the monetary authorities help create a "political business cycle"? If not, do they try to offset such cycles? I also focus on electoral incentives in the relationship between Congress and the Fed. To what extent can monetary policy be used to aid the electoral efforts of some legislators?

The various explanations are compared in the conclusion. These explanations are then used to examine some proposed reforms of the Fed and of monetary policy-making in general.

Monetary Policy Is Not Apolitical

Central banks appear to make technical decisions about an arcane subject. Much of the debate over monetary policy is a debate about the adequacy of forecasts and models, the constancy of the velocity of money, or where errors arise in IS-LM curves. Each of these technical arguments, however, has consequences for the well-being of social groups; in making technical decisions, central banks must make trade-offs between those groups. This trade-off is not often made explicitly; it is, instead, implicit in the resolution of technical debate. It is impossible for technical understanding of the economy *alone* to determine monetary policy. The science of economics can explain the consequences of various policies; one must also be a student of politics to explain why a particular policy is chosen.

Monetary policy can be considered a problem in control theory with central bankers maximizing an objective function subject to a series of economic constraints. Economics can elucidate the nature of those constraints, but the source of the objective function must lie in the realm of politics. We think it uncontroversial that the central bank should fight inflation. But how quickly? At what cost? How serious is inflation anyway? Economists have trouble even assessing the cost of inflation.[2] But even if economists could assess the cost, given that those who gain from lower inflation are typically not those who bear the cost of fighting inflation, the question of whether the fight against inflation is worth it must be a political (distributional) question.

Why is it even controversial that the money supply is politically determined? Politics is often thought of as dealing with parties and elections. Central banks do not seem to engage in such partisan politics;

indeed, rules governing the Fed are designed to insulate it from partisan politics. But a nonpartisan Fed is not the same thing as an apolitical Fed.

The very attempt to take monetary policy out of the partisan arena is itself a political act. Central banks are insulated from partisan politics because constitution makers fear the outcomes that a partisan central bank would produce. The attempt to return to a gold standard, for example, is simply an attempt to guarantee that groups that are hurt by discretionary monetary policy (which presumably leads to higher rates of inflation) will win at the expense of groups that bear the cost of anti-inflationary policy.[3] Groups that think of monetary policy as being apolitical are less likely to turn to the political arena when they are hurt by that policy.

The idea that monetary policy is apolitical should be seen as an ideological statement, and the persistence of this view can be best explained by Gramsci's notion of ideological hegemony.[4] Hegemony "is founded on a simple premise: that modern man is not ruled by force alone, but also by ideas. . . . Those who obey, must, to some degree, share the values and standards of their 'superiors,' and consent to their own subordination."[5] From a positive perspective, apolitical monetary policy is an impossibility. The question is not whether monetary policy is political, but how politics affects policy.

In this essay I assume that central banks[6] are rational actors maximizing some utility function subject to constraints. Most economists have traditionally assumed that the maximand is social welfare, that is, central banks make monetary policy to bring about the combination of unemployment and inflation that society most prefers. We may call this the "public interest" theory of monetary policy. Modern welfare economics has shown that, in general, the concept of a social welfare function is problematic, at best; the public interest theory of monetary policy gives no account of how the central bank arrives at its particular conception of social welfare. Here we enter the realm of politics.

There are two ways of politicizing the basic model. Following Kane, more variables representing other goals of the bank could be added to the maximand.[7] A central bank might wish to maximize, for example, its budget or its political autonomy in addition to some measure of economic welfare. Central banks are, from this perspective, concerned with both social and private welfare. Alternatively, politics might affect the bank's conception of social welfare. Under left-wing regimes, for example, central banks might be concerned more with unemployment, while under right-wing regimes they might be more concerned with fighting inflation.

Adopting either of these perspectives on monetary policy makes it necessary to study the relationship of the central bank to other important political actors. The private welfare of the bank is influenced by the executive, the legislature, the private banking sector, and other interest groups. These actors will also have influence on the central bank's conception of what policies are in the public interest. In this essay the relationship between central banks and these political actors is considered. I start with the relationship between the central bank and the executive branch.

Monetary Policy and the Executive

The simplest explanation of central bank behavior is that the bank is the agent of a unitary central government dominated by the executive; understanding monetary policy is identical to understanding general economic policy. Frey and Schneider take this approach in modeling the Bundesbank; they assume the bank must defer (with some time lag) to the fiscal authorities. Sherman Maisel, former governor of the Federal Reserve, reports that the president has much influence on the Fed; Robert Weintraub, who was until his death the leading congressional staff expert on the Fed, makes a similar observation.[8]

Legislation about the Fed does not mandate deference to the president. Governors of the Fed have long (fourteen-year) terms, and regional bank presidents cannot be removed by the president. In addition, the Fed controls its own budget. Finally, the only legal obligation of the Fed is to report its activities and intentions; other than a vague charge which effectively says that the Fed must act in the public interest, it is legally free to make policy as it sees fit. In the short run neither the president nor Congress can force the Fed to do anything.

Legalities aside, the real political resource of the Fed, like that of the Supreme Court, is its legitimacy. Most political actors *that are aware of the Fed* accord it the right to make monetary policy, even when that policy is costly to some groups. On the other hand, the Fed is obscure; its legitimacy is with bankers and other financial actors, not the mass public. Unlike the Supreme Court, the Fed's legitimacy has no constitutional basis. When the Fed clashes with a president's legitimate claim to execute economic policy, the president would clearly have the advantage in terms of mass communications.

In a struggle between the Fed and the president, the Fed could mobilize certain resources, particularly in the financial community, a community which, as we have seen in the fight over withholding of taxes on interest, has substantial political resources. These resources could make the struggle costly to the president. But it seems clear that if we compare the political resources of the executive and the central bank, the executive is likely to win any fights with the central bank *when the executive desires to use its resources.*[9] Any major struggle between the Fed and the president would likely be resolved in a similar manner to the New Deal fight between Roosevelt and the Supreme Court; seeing the handwriting on the wall, the Fed would, to save its limited authority, accede to presidential demands.

The relative strengths of the president and the Fed vary with changing circumstances. If the president is perceived as being weak and incompetent, and the chairman of the Fed is perceived as competent, then the political calculus has changed. Similarly, if international economic events make defense of the dollar vital, the Federal Reserve may well have extra political advantage. The fight between the Fed and Treasury over pegging government bonds in 1951 led eventually to the Accord which represented partial triumph for the Fed over Treasury.[10] It is possible, hypothetically, that Paul Volcker could have defeated Jimmy Carter in a political struggle. No chairman could have barred Franklin Roosevelt from financing World War II via the printing press, and Chairman Martin was not able to stop Lyndon Johnson's financing of the war in Vietnam in the same manner. The Accord and hypothetical Volcker-Carter examples are the exception.

In other countries the relative powers of the central bank and the central government may vary from the U.S. pattern, but it is difficult to imagine any central government losing an important fight with its central bank. Institutional arrangements will affect the cost of that struggle and the exact nature of its outcome. The relative legal independence of the Bundesbank or the Bank of Switzerland will give those banks more of an advantage in relation to their central governments than the more dependent central banks of either the United Kingdom or France enjoy. Other factors will also affect outcomes. For example, the national consensus in both Switzerland and Germany about the horrors of inflation will give any political actors fighting inflation a tremendous advantage. But it is hard to imagine even the Bundesbank or the Bank of Switzerland triumphing on a vital issue over an elected government.

What does the central government want its central bank to do? Current theory suggests that politicians wish to be reelected. Executives desire an economic policy in support of that goal and monetary policy would be no exception. The conventional wisdom in 1983–84 was, for example, that Paul Volcker would not allow monetary policy to interfere with economic growth in late 1984. It would be surprising if, given two equally plausible policy choices, any central bank chose the policy more likely to lead to the incumbent's defeat. When in 1983 Volcker had to decide whether M1 was a reliable guide to policy, either answer was plausible. The advantage to the Fed in not tightening monetary policy based on a possibly unreliable M1, a policy that would have slowed a recovery important to Reagan's chances of reelection, seems clear-cut.

This type of electoral sensitivity is unlikely to damage the Fed. Since the Fed's action is plausible, it can be explained in the neutral, technical language of economics. The Fed's legitimacy is party based on its appearance of being nonpartisan; policy actions which can be justified on a nonpartisan basis are less likely to threaten that legitimacy.[11] Moreover, even if the incumbent loses, his successor is unlikely to punish the Fed for its electoral actions since the successor will wish the Fed to give him the same benefit of the doubt in close decisions four years hence.

Elections and Monetary Policy

What type of monetary policy will maximize a president's chance of reelection? Can the president "convince" the Fed to carry out that politically optimal policy? These two questions are logically distinct; I begin with the first.

Political scientists do not agree on a theory of elections. There are two distinct paradigms, and within each paradigm there are several distinct theories. One paradigm takes voters preferences as given, with candidates choosing electoral strategies to maximize their chance of winning, given those preferences. This is similar to the standard economics paradigm where consumers have preferences and firms make maximizing decisions constrained by those preferences. The alternative paradigm sees entrepreneurial politicians shaping electorates and elections. Voters are not lumps of clay waiting to be molded, but political leaders can determine the form and content of the debate. This perspective is similar to the view of consumers and firms held by the marketing profession.[12]

Economic policy has electoral consequences in either paradigm. The leader-driven paradigm makes no prediction about the form of a politically optimal monetary policy. A good political leader may be able to convince voters that some short-term harsh medicine is necessary for the long-term health of the economy; alternatively, a political leader may be able to fashion a campaign around the theme that the economy is doing poorly now. (The Republican campaign of 1982, stressing stay the course, is an example of the former; the Republican campaign of 1980, stressing the "misery index," is an example of the latter.) Studying the 1982 election, Jacobson concluded that "economic issues exercise no simple mechanical influence over voting decisions. How they affect voters depends in good part on how they are presented by candidates and other activists during the course of the campaign. . . . In 1982, Republicans were able to make responsibility for inflation (in districts with Democratic incumbents) and the future success or failure of Reagan's programs (in districts with Republican incumbents) the dominant economic questions."[13] Monetary policy may be an important issue in a campaign, but a good political leader could stress the long-term virtues of tight policy or the short-term benefits of easy policy. This paradigm does not, in general, predict the direction or form of monetary policy that incumbents will desire.

The voter-driven paradigm, in its most general form, also makes no specific predictions about politically optimal monetary policy. Most theories in this paradigm predict that the current state of the economy will have some effect on the election; however, perceived competence to manage the economy and expectations about future economic performance may have greater influence on the vote decision. For example, expectations about whether Reaganomics would work was a much better predictor of the vote in 1982 then were perceptions of whether the economy was performing well in 1982. We do not know whether economic problems in 1980 or perceptions that Carter would have been incompetent to solve economic problems during his second term contributed more to Carter's defeat. It is difficult to disentangle these two sources of the vote since the state of the economy is a partial guide to the economic competence of the incumbent. The state of the current economy is not, however, the only guide that voters have to the future. For example, in 1982 two-thirds of the electorate thought that Reaganomics would eventually work, while a similar percentage thought that Reaganomics had hurt the economy so far.[14] The voter-driven paradigm, like the leader-driven paradigm, is too general to predict how electorally motivated incumbents should shape monetary policy.

The Political Business Cycle

Some theorists, such as Nordhaus and Tufte, have made more specialized assumptions about the relationship of the economy and voting.[15] This specialization does allow predictions about the form of a "politically optimal" economic (and monetary) policy. Both Nordhaus and Tufte assume that voters are nearsighted (or economically naive) and have short memories. Under those assumptions, only recent economic events are strongly connected to the vote decision. While past economic events may have some effect on the vote, it is assumed that expectations about the future state of the economy have no effect. Under such assumptions it is possible for presidents to induce a "political business cycle" which reaches its peak right before the election. The inflationary consequences of such a cycle are paid after the election and hence have no effect on the current election.

The Nordhaus and Tufte theories differ on the exact shape of the political business cycle, with the Nordhaus theory being more sophisticated. Presidents will, according to Tufte, attempt to make short-term changes in economic policy right before the election to induce a short-term boom. In particular, transfer payments should increase dramatically in the third quarter of election years; monetary policy should be easier in the year before an election. Economic policy, for Tufte, is electorally motivated only right before elections.

Nordhaus, using an optimal control model of a Keynesian economy, shows how an electorally motivated incumbent should manipulate policy over his entire term to maximize his chance of reelection. Early in his term, the president can bring about a recession to drive down inflationary expectations. Late in his term he can engineer a boom; the inflationary costs of that boom will be paid after the election, thanks to the early recession.

Both the Nordhaus and Tufte theories suggest a politically optimal monetary policy. Nordhaus suggests tight money early in a term followed by easy money toward the end of that term; Tufte suggests ease toward the end of a term. While there is disagreement on the length of the lag between monetary actions and variables such as unemployment and inflation, there clearly is some such lag. Under the Tufte theory monetary policy should ease about a year before election day; under the Nordhaus theory easing should begin even earlier. The consequence of this policy is excess inflation after election day. The political business cycle theories make concrete predictions about monetary policy. Are these predictions accurate? Do they stand up to theoretical scrutiny? I start by looking at the assumptions made about voters.

The assumption of economic naivete is consistent with most studies of voting. Following Downs, most theorists have assumed that information is costly to voters and hence they will, rationally, remain relatively ignorant about economic theory and predictions based on that theory. Information about the current state of the economy is easy and cheap to obtain, so most voters would be able to take the current economy into account in deciding how to vote. The Nordhaus-Tufte view of voters is not theoretically implausible.

Moving from theory to empirical research, most time series studies relating the state of the economy to electoral outcomes have found a strong relationship. Summarizing this literature, Kiewiet concludes that "the finding of a positive relationship between economic performance and electoral outcomes is quite robust.[16] This literature tells us that in bad economic times incumbents are more likely to lose.

The survey evidence on this question presents a different picture. Jacobson and Kernell, discussing congressional elections, conclude that "the notion that the economy influences the vote through its effect on personal finances . . . receives almost no support from studies of individual voting behavior.[17] They do find some evidence in the literature of a relationship between general economic conditions and the vote, but conclude that "economic variables explain little additional variance in the vote once other variables are taken into account. Only voters' assessments of the relative economic competence of the two parties are regularly connected in an important way with the voting decision."[18]

The Jacobson and Kernell evidence is based on congressional, not presidential, elections. It is possible that the state of the economy may be a clearer issue in presidential elections, since local issues may muddy the waters in congressional elections. In British national elections, Alt found that "people saw clearly the [economic] developments that were taking place, and people expected developments in advance and thus were able to discount the worst of them."[19]

The empirical findings do not provide strong support for the Nordhaus-Tufte view of voters. The state of the economy probably does affect the incumbent's chance of reelection, but the relationship between the economy and the election is more complex than the assertion that incumbents are reelected if the economy is booming on election day. It certainly is possible that some voters may be affected by the state of the economy on election day, and that these voters may provide the margin of victory. Politicians appear to be risk averse concerning their reelection; inducing a boom on election day may turn a close defeat into a victory. Even if most voters are more sophisticated than Tufte or Nordhaus suggest, politicians still may attempt to induce a political business cycle. Do they? Do they do so using monetary policy?

The evidence for a political business cycle is not strong. Most researchers have not found a tendency for unemployment to fall before elections or inflation to rise after elections.[20] Most researchers have not found a tendency for fiscal policy or transfer payments to vary in a manner that would induce a political business cycle.[21] Alt and Chrystal sum up that "no one could read the political business cycle literature without being struck by the lack of supporting evidence."[22] Their conclusion must, however, be qualified by noting that more recent research has found evidence of politically cyclic fiscal policy.[23] In any event, there has been little research on whether monetary policy has been used to induce a political business cycle.

The first suggestions of such a cycle were for the Nixon reelection of 1972. Presumably Arthur Burns, a close political confidant of Richard Nixon, using his power as chairman, pressed the Fed to keep interest rates low to fuel the boom of 1972; the inflation of 1973–74 was partly a consequence of this policy. Others have challenged this interpretation of 1972 Fed policy, and it is difficult to assess the cause of a given single event.[24] Moving beyond the single case of 1972, would we expect the Federal Reserve to pursue policies leading to a political business cycle?

Monetary policy can be changed quickly. Unlike fiscal policy, the number of actors in the monetary policy-making process is small, so bargaining can be done quickly. Monetary theory suggests that the first consequence of monetary ease is an increase in output, with the inflationary costs of that increase being paid later. While it is debatable whether monetary policy can have a long-run effect on output, this debate is irrelevant given the short-run perspective of the political business cycle theory.

If monetary policy can be used to induce a political business cycle, it can also be used for conventional short-run stabilization purposes. Given our knowledge of elections, it may be that a stabilization policy of damping out cycles is electorally superior to a policy of inducing political business cycles. The former policy is also less risky, since it cannot be used as an issue by a challenger.

Monetary ease before an election might help an incumbent's chance of reelection. Can the president obtain such a policy? The Fed is legally independent of the president. The president cannot compel the Fed to follow a political monetary cycle. Such a cycle would, instead, have to be the outcome of a political bargain. Could the Fed be persuaded to ease monetary policy before elections?

The costs to the Fed of engaging in such manipulations might be substantial. The Federal Reserve, like the Supreme Court, has few formal powers; it does have legitimacy. This legitimacy comes both from an appearance of technical expertise and a perception that the bank does not engage in partisan politics. Loss of this legitimacy would make it difficult for the Fed to inflict pain on the economy in the name of fighting inflation. If the Fed were seen as merely another partisan actor, its legitimacy would be undermined. But that is a risk which proponents of the political business cycle theory expect the Fed to run every four years.[25]

Empirical studies also find little evidence of a Fed-caused political monetary cycle.[26] Looking at the instruments of monetary policy, I failed to find a significant impact of the 1972 election on the federal funds rate, and over a series of elections from 1964 through 1984 failed to find a significant increase in bank reserves or a decrease in interest rates before those elections. My research and that of Kevin Grier does, however, find a cycle in M1.[27] While Grier interprets this as a Fed attempt to influence elections, I find the cycle to be generated principally by fiscal policy.

In my analysis the Fed passively coordinates monetary policy with fiscal policy, regardless of whether fiscal policy is electorally motivated or not. The Fed does not actively manipulate monetary policy for electoral purposes, but it does not offset the president's manipulation of the economy. Through coordination of monetary and fiscal policy, the Fed acquiesces to electorally motivated economic policy.

This interpretation tells us much about the relative power of the president and the Fed. In my view the president is insufficiently powerful to force the Fed to work for his reelection, but the Fed is afraid to use its tools to undo nonmonetary presidential manipulation of the economy. The Fed is not completely dominated by the executive but its powers vis-à-vis that executive are limited.

Both Allen and Laney and Willett fail to find direct evidence of an electoral cycle in M1. Using different methodologies, they both find that the Fed is more likely to coordinate monetary policy with electorally motivated fiscal policy than it is with fiscal policy in general. Using a methodology similar to Allen's, my research did not find an increase in coordination between monetary and fiscal policy as election day drew near. It seems likely that the failure of the Fed to offset electoral cycles generated outside the Fed will be the most fruitful area of research on political monetary cycles.

Other central banks, such as the Bank of England and the Bank of France, are more directly under the control of the central government. They do not have to be persuaded to do anything. As agents of the central government their nonpartisan appearance is perhaps less vital to their role. However, there is no strong evidence for a political monetary cycle in either the United Kingdom or France.[28] My research, for example, failed to find a decrease in short-term interest rates before British elections. Even dependent central banks do not seem to make monetary policy to help their government's reelection campaign.

Links between Political Parties and Monetary Policy

The political business cycle theories assume that economic policy is made with an eye on the next election. Alternatively, policy may fulfill promises made in the last election. The clearest predictions in this vein are made by the party control model of Hibbs.[29] In this model parties represent stable coalitions (or classes) with each coalition having a clear preference about economic policy. After an election, the winning party makes policy in accord with its coalition's preferences.

Initially, Hibbs showed that countries dominated by left-wing parties have less unemployment and more inflation than do countries dominated by right-wing parties, and, in countries with party alternation, left-wing parties produce less unemployment than do right-wing parties. Turning to the monetary arena, this means that central banks should ease monetary policy when left-wing parties control the government.[30]

There is support for this proposition in the arena of monetary policy, although there are disagreements about the size of the effect.[31] My research shows that in the United States, adjusted reserves grow about 2 percent faster under Democrats than they do under Republican presidents; in Germany, the base grows faster under the liberal Social Democrats than it does under the more conservative Christian Democratic chancellors. Minford and Peel show for the United Kingdom that the money supply grows faster under Labour prime ministers. In addition, both the Bank of England and the American Federal Reserve have been willing to accommodate fiscal policy. Since left-wing governments usually show higher deficits, this leads to easier monetary policy under left-wing governments.

The party control model is vulnerable to two types of attacks; it assumes that executives have both too little and too much leeway. Presidents are constrained by both the international and domestic private economies; this constraint may force them into policies that do not benefit their coalition. Lindblom and most Marxist writers argue that the nature of investment in a capitalist economy requires all politicians to pursue policies favored by capitalists.[32] On a less cosmic level, international economic factors in 1982 forced the Socialist Mitterrand to pursue traditional right-wing deflationary policies. My research shows that during the economic crisis of the 1970s, left-wing governments in the United Kingdom and Germany pursued tight monetary policies. The Labour government of Callaghan turned to monetary targeting to get IMF aid for its persistent balance of payments problem. The weakness of the dollar contributed to the Fed's shift toward monetarism in 1979, notwithstanding the Democratic party's control of the White House. The president's party matters less in times of economic crisis.[33]

Alternatively, the president may, in normal times, have much more room to maneuver than the Hibbs theory suggests. A strategic politician might use this room to rebuild and strengthen his coalition for the next election. The party control model assumes that parties represent stable coalitions with stable economic preferences. Some parties in some countries may be class based; in two-party systems, neither party can afford to be dominated either by a single ideology or social class if it wishes to win elections.[34] If we think of each party as taking part in an ongoing game, it has an incentive to change its coalition to enhance its chances in future elections. To provide a satisfactory account of economic policy, we need some combination of the strategic, electorally motivated theories and the theories which assume that parties carry out their promises. Political entrepreneurship is missing from both the electoral- and party-motivated theories.

Political entrepreneurs see themselves as operating in a world of flux; this flux provides opportunities for either building or rebuilding winning coalitions. As in the political business cycle theory, entrepreneurs build their coalitions with an eye to the next election; as in the party control model, entrepreneurs who do not keep their promises find it difficult to hold their coalitions together. The world of the political entrepreneur is considerably more complicated than the world of the election or party oriented theories. A president may attempt to enlarge his coalition by making appeals to supporters of the other party (as in Jimmy Carter's move to an anti-inflationary policy in early 1980); much of the action may not be in the general election with coalitions battling for control of the nomination (as in 1980, where Carter's commitment to free trade was contested by Edward Kennedy's commitment to a policy of high employment); entrepreneurs may even attempt to redefine the economic struggle (as in Ronald Reagan making inflation, not unemployment, the primary economic evil).

This model is so rich that it no longer makes specific predictions about economic policy. We need to search for models that are more complex than those of Tufte and Hibbs but which still make falsifiable predictions. One new possibility has been suggested by the recent work of James Alt.[35] He argues that when parties come to power they carry out their economic promises if they have made any. Over time, however, constituents forget what promises were made, and the pressure of the next election may cause the incumbent leader to follow economic policies without reference to his party's position. Alt has applied this proposition to unemployment rates with success.

This model can be used to make sense of some seeming contradictions in the relationship between presidential party and monetary policy in recent times. Monetary policy in the early years of both the Carter and Reagan administrations is consistent with the party model, while policy in the latter part of their administrations is not. All of this is, however, consistent with the Alt model. Woolley also provides some more quantitative (but preliminary) evidence for the Alt hypothesis applied to U.S. monetary policy over the last quarter century.[36]

The Alt model allows presidents to have different goals and face different constraints at different points during their term. This is clearly an important step toward a more sophisticated model. Ultimately such a model will probably be electorally based, but it will also have a more sophisticated treatment of the internal politics of the central bank, and treat links between the bank and important political actors outside the executive branch. In the following sections I sketch out some of the important elements which I believe this more sophisticated model must include. I start by considering theories which stress internal political explanations.

Organizational and Bureaucratic Explanations

The executive-oriented theories treat central banks as agents of the executive; the internal politics of the bank are irrelevant in these theories. Organizational and bureaucratic theories assume that explanations of monetary policy lie in studying the incentives faced by the central bank. Bureaucratic theorists assume that central bankers maximize their own private welfare. There is no reason to assume that private and social welfare coincide. Rational central bankers, from the organization perspective, face a complex world filled with risk and uncertainty where there is little agreement on values and little time to settle those disagreements; minimizing decision costs has a strong effect on policy. Both theories attempt to provide short-run explanations of monetary policy. I begin with the organizational approaches.[37]

Organization Theory

Organization theorists stress the limited knowledge and analytic capabilities of decision makers facing a very complex world; they also stress the difficulty of settling disagreements based on differing values. Lindblom has suggested a strategy he calls "disjointed incrementalism" to deal with these problems. It has the following hallmarks:

1. Analysis is limited to a few policy alternatives which differ incrementally from the status quo
2. These policies are analyzed for only a limited number of consequences
3. There is joint analysis of both values and empirical questions
4. The strategy remedies ills rather than seeking positive goals
5. The strategy proceeds by a sequence of trials, errors, and revisions
6. Different policymakers undertake different parts of the analysis[38]

Disjointed incrementalism appears to be an excellent description of Federal Reserve policy-making. The economy is complex and there is substantial doubt about the validity of the various economic theories and models. It appears that the Fed looks at the economy, decides whether there are problems on the horizon, and if so, makes a small change in an operating instrument to head off that problem. It then sees if that change seems to have had the desired effect, and continues on its iterative sequence of trials and errors.

Disjointed incrementalism serves the needs of a central bank which has no consensus on values and no way of coming to consensus. How should the central bank value unemployment versus inflation? No other political body can instruct the Fed about appropriate trade-offs. According to Lindblom no agreement on values is necessary; it is, however, often possible to obtain agreement that some incremental policy change is desirable. The minutes of the Fed often suggest that there has been agreement on policy without any agreement about underlying values or theory; often this agreement is to do whatever was done last month.

Following incrementalist logic, the Fed is overly likely to continue to do what it did last month in the absence of any compelling reason to do otherwise. This compelling reason must be an immediate problem, not a theoretical proposition. There is a time lag before changes in monetary policy are felt in the economy. Thus a change in policy in reaction to changes in the economy may be too late. An incrementalist Fed will often continue a course for too long because it does not believe its predictions about turning points in the economy; as a consequence policy may sometimes be procyclic.

Those economists who view monetary policy-making as a problem in optimal control will always be disappointed with the Fed. For example, Benjamin Friedman writes that "an obscurantist framework designed to facilitate unspoken disagreements among the policymakers about how policy operates can only be self-defeating. Above all, the policymakers must first determine what they are doing and why, before they set about doing it."[39] The incrementalist defense of the Fed is that these demands are unrealistic; they require too much information and value consensus. The incrementalist does not defend the Fed by arguing that its policies are optimal but rather that it has arrived at a set of procedures to allow it to make policy in a complex world.[40]

Bureaucratic Theory

The bureaucratic approach to monetary policy is similar to the organizational approach in that it treats the monetary authorities as real-world policymakers. Unlike the organizational theorists, bureaucratic theorists assume that central bankers are interested in maximizing their own, not the public, welfare.[41] For example, central bankers may be interested in maximizing their discretion or their budget or their chance of a lucrative job in the private sector; none of these necessarily leads to socially optimal policy.

Milton Friedman has used bureaucratic theories to explain the failure of the Fed to follow monetarist principals. He argues that "bureaucratic inertia" explains Fed policy-making and that this inertia results from the absence of a "bottom line." The absence of a bottom line allows the Fed to pursue its own private interests.[42]

Much of this argument is based on the work of Chant and Acheson and the more recent work by Toma and by Shughart and Tollison. Following Niskanen, they postulate that the Fed's objective is to maximize its discretionary budget. Since the Fed's income is derived from interest earned on its portfolio of securities, it therefore purchases too many securities. The Fed purchases securities by creating more bank reserves; in effect it increases its income by creating more money. Hence the Fed's budget-maximizing strategy leads to more inflation.

The Fed returns about 90 percent of its earnings to the Treasury; at the margin it turns over all additional earnings. Thus it is not obvious why there should be an inflationary bias. There is evidence that the Fed spends more when its "wealth" increases, but there is no empirical evidence that it makes policy to increase its wealth. Bureaucrats clearly desire larger budgets, but the link between this goal and inflation has not been convincingly demonstrated.

Chant and Acheson argue that central banks wish to maximize their flexibility and minimize their probability of being blamed for errors. To do this, central banks choose less visible, nonquantitative instruments which allow them to deny responsibility for the consequences of their decisions. This explains, for example, the Bank of Canada's penchant for "moral suasion" rather than more visible, quantitative measures.

The Chant and Acheson argument explains the Fed's inability to agree on a single monetary indicator and the wide target range for their several monetary targets. Since 1975 the Fed has been obligated to appear before Congress to justify its policies; the use of multiple indicators and wide target ranges saves the Fed the embarrassment of having to admit that it missed its targets. According to Pierce, "the growth rate ranges for each aggregate were sufficiently wide to be virtually assured of having at least one of the five aggregates within its range 12 months ahead."[43]

Maximands other than budget size or flexibility are possible. Kane posits that the Fed wishes to maximize its influence and prestige. Until 1980 banks could leave the Federal Reserve system with a resulting loss of power and prestige to the Fed. Kane argues that discount rate policy was made to encourage banks to stay in the system; as a consequence discount rates were too low and access to the discount window too easy. In particular, seasonal borrowing privileges may have been instituted by the Fed to entice small banks to stay in the system.

The bureaucratic theory is a good antidote to the older view that monetary authorities simply maximize the public interest. A more complete theory of central banking would have monetary authorities maximizing some combination of public and private interest. In rejecting the public interest view, we should not hastily assume that central banks are only concerned with their private interest. It is important to specify carefully the nature of private interests and to show their relationship to policy. Toma and Shughart and Tollison stress narrow self-interest (personal salary, personal prestige, and personal power within the Fed); Chant and Acheson and Kane stress political self-interest. At present, the latter approach seems more fruitful for the study of monetary policy-making. To examine those political interests, we must look at the interaction of the Fed, Congress, and interest groups.

Interest Groups, Congress, and Monetary Policy

The Fed may be thought of as an agent of the president. Alternatively, it can be conceived of as an actor in a larger political universe. In this universe the Fed interacts with interest groups, such as bankers, builders, and labor. While these groups devote some effort to lobbying the Fed directly, most of their pressure comes indirectly through Congress. This is because the various lobbies command few resources needed by the Fed.[44]

However, the banking sector can have a direct effect on monetary policy, since many Fed officials have spent some time in that sector, and the Fed, both in Washington and through the regional banks, deals with banking groups on a daily basis. Thus it seems likely that some of the general assumptions of the banking sector will rub off on the Fed, and we would expect the Fed to share more attitudes with the banking sector than it does with, say, labor. In particular, we would expect the Fed to worry more about financial soundness (and inflation) relative to unemployment than does the typical member of Congress.[45]

The various interest groups concerned with monetary policy control resources desired by members of Congress. Congress, in turn, controls resources desired by the Fed. The various interest groups can put indirect pressure on the Fed through direct pressure on Congress. The Fed was created by an act of Congress; it can be changed by another such act. In particular, the independence that the Fed so prizes could be limited by Congress; for example, Congress could subject the Fed to the annual appropriations process. Thus the Fed must, in addition to trying to make good policy, worry about what Congress wants the Fed to do. The leading theory about Congress is that its members, more or less single-mindedly, want to get themselves reelected; the Fed must worry about how its actions affect those reelection chances.[46] Legislators who want to be reelected desire credit for policies that their constituents like; they gather electoral aid from interest groups by supporting the appropriate policies.

Barry Weingast has argued that the various agencies can be best viewed as agents of Congress, agents that are more or less well controlled by their principals, the Congressional committees.[47] Kevin Grier has applied this perspective to the Fed, arguing that we can best understand changes in monetary policy by looking at changes in the preferences of the Fed's principal, the Senate Banking Committee.[48] Grier's work differs with most prior research in the area, which found little if any congressional influence on monetary policy.[49]

While Grier has shown that monetary policy can be predicted by the liberalism of the Senate Banking Committee for the period 1961–80, my research finds that this conclusion does not hold up when the sample period is extended through 1984 (when conservative Republicans controlled the committee). In addition, the House Banking Committee appears to have no influence on the Fed for either sample period. This is damaging to the Weingast and Grier hypothesis since the House committee has usually taken a more active role in monetary policy than has the Senate committee. Given the weight of prior evidence and the lack of consistent findings, we should not regard the Weingast-Grier perspective as anything more than an interesting hypothesis that requires much more empirical research before being accepted.

Edward Kane views Congress and the Fed as having an implicit bargain: the Fed accepts blame for a bad economy in return for a grant of independence.[50] However, when monetary policy causes too much electoral pain to Congress, the Fed must reverse course (or risk the wrath of Congress and in particular a loss of independence). The Fed causes Congress electoral pain when interest rates rise, because groups that are hurt by such a rise (the housing and automobile sectors, among others) have important political resources. The assumption here is that the beneficiaries of anti-inflationary policy are not well organized while those who pay the costs of fighting inflation are politically well organized, and that Congress is much more sensitive to the interests of the latter.

The Kane bargain seems plausible, although at this point it is a matter of conjecture about the relative powers of the "low interest" and the "anti-inflationary" lobbies. The elderly appear to be a politically powerful group in the United States, and they would appear to favor both tight money and low rates of inflation. With new types of mortgages, savings and loans that were once part of the low interest lobby may now be shielded from many of the problems that come with increasing interest rates. Presumably, much but not all of "Wall Street" is also concerned with the long-term soundness of the American currency.

More generally, both the Kane and the Weingast-Grier arguments raise another question that is difficult to answer: Why doesn't Congress, while maintaining the distance it typically maintains from most agencies, take more control over the Fed by subjecting it to the annual appropriation process? Congress could still use the Fed as a whipping boy, while making it harder for the Fed to ignore the wishes of Congress. If Congress were to do this, its members could reap electoral rewards by interceding for constituents in nonmonetary dealings with the Fed (such as bank mergers).

Carrying this argument further, why doesn't Congress treat monetary policy like it treats fiscal policy, i.e., why doesn't Congress get into the business of credit allocation? The electoral rewards from being able to move credit toward a favored constituent ought to be as great as the electoral rewards from writing a tax loophole for that constituent. Day-to-day monetary policy could still be made by the Fed, and setting general guidelines for monetary policy is no more difficult than setting such guidelines for fiscal policy. Can anyone imagine Congress creating the Internal Revenue Service with no more guidance than to collect revenue in the public interest?

While there is no clear answer to this question, it may be fruitful to think of Congress's role in the making of monetary policy as an institutional solution to a prisoners' dilemma—individually maximizing behavior leads to an outcome where everyone is worse off than they might have been had they cooperated. A stable currency may be a collective good. Individual members could improve their electoral fortunes by having Congress become more involved in the monetary policy process. The result of such individually rational decisions might well be an unstable currency, an outcome which few legislators desire.

The problem with this type of explanation is that we need to find some incentive mechanism which leads individual members towards cooperation. It is difficult to find such mechanisms; Mayhew and Fiorina have shown us how clever Congress is at devising strategies that result in their electoral advantage. If Congress were establishing the Fed today, it probably would subject it to the annual appropriations process. But the Fed is not being newly established today. The budgetary independence of the Fed resulted from a compromise in 1913 between those who wanted a central bank controlled by private banks and those who wanted a central bank controlled by the Treasury Department. This compromise created the Fed as a quasi-private agency in control of its own budget. Open market operations have led to Fed revenues greatly exceeding outlays.[51]

Given this history, it is easier to understand why Congress has not subjected the Fed to budget control. The rules set up by Congress give the Fed political resources which it has used to fight against legislation which would limit its independence. In particular, the Fed has been able to mobilize member banks and others in what Arthur Burns has called the "Fed family" (directors of reserve banks, former Fed officials) to successfully lobby against bills which would increase congressional control over the Fed. The success of this effort may be a testament to the political prowess of the Fed as well as to the various congressional rules and norms which make it difficult for a majority to easily change the status quo.

Fiorina has argued that Congress attempts to shift responsibility from itself to the various agencies for policies that generate more political costs than benefits.[52] Monetary policy may be such a policy, since the benefits of good policy (low inflation) are diffuse while the costs of such a policy are borne by a few well-organized groups (e.g., the automobile and housing sectors). More congressional influence on monetary policy may simply be seen as generating more electoral costs than benefits to individual members of Congress.

Another possibility is that all the good which Congress can obtain from economic policy can be obtained from fiscal policy. Congress needs only one tool to give out specific goods (and prevent specific bads). Thus monetary policy can be used in a nonspecific manner, with groups that are hurt by monetary policy obtaining relief from Congress in the form of either tax relief or subsidy. In general it might be argued that a legislature needs only one form of particularistic economic policy, and in the United States it happens, for various reasons, to be fiscal policy.[53]

Finally, congressional inaction may be a consequence of the large investment in time a member must make to become knowledgeable about monetary policy. So far no congressional entrepreneur has successfully made a career out of working to increase congressional control over the Fed (although some, such as Wright Patman, have made a career out of attacking the Fed). Whether the Fed can continue to survive attacks on its fiscal independence as it becomes more politically visible remains to be seen.

Thus, while there is much merit to the Kane argument, and in particular to the part that has the Fed shrewdly aware of its political assets and liabilities, the theory is incomplete. Congress appears to treat monetary policy differently than it treats other types of economic policy; it seems almost to avoid getting involved in the making of such policy. The Kane theory, which treats the Fed like any other agency, cannot account for the special way in which monetary policy is made.

Conclusion

Any theory of monetary policy must take into account the relative powers of the central government and the central bank; even relatively independent banks like the Bundesbank or the Federal Reserve must, more or less, follow general government economic policy. For understanding long-run monetary policy, we must understand the policies of the central government. However, in the medium run, the more or less becomes important, and in the short run, monetary policy is the province of the central bank. Even in the long run, monetary policy is sufficiently different from fiscal and other types of economic policy that it must be considered separately.

For the short run, the bureaucratic and organization theories are adequate. Agencies tend to run with standard operating procedures, and those procedures can probably be best understood as responses to the complexity and uncertainty inherent in real-world policy-making. These standard operating procedures typically work to maximize bureaucratic self-interest, not the public interest. Unfortunately, understanding short-run policy-making tells us little about the politics of monetary policy; it also is of limited help in dealing with such questions as "why stagflation?" Questions such as this require looking at the longer run as well.

In the medium run the monetary authorities are heavily constrained by the central government, although there will be some room for maneuver. We would expect the central bank to both desire to fight inflation (that in some sense is its mission) and also to preserve its independence. Thus it will most desire room for maneuver when overall economic policy is expansive. Unfortunately, fighting expansive policy is likely to lead to threats on central bank independence.

The resolution of this conflict depends on the relative strengths of the bank and the government, and how many resources each side wishes to devote to that conflict. If the central bank is held in high regard and the central government is not, then the bank may win; similarly, if important political actors agree that defense of a sound currency is vital, then the bank has an advantage. These conditions enabled the Fed to pursue contractionary policies from 1979 through 1982. Conversely, in times of national emergency, such as a severe depression or war, no central bank will be able to stand in the way of government policy that is dealing with that national emergency. No central bank, for example, could fail to pursue inflationary policy in helping fight a major war; probably the Fed had little choice in using inflationary means to finance the war in Vietnam.

In the long run, monetary policy is only special in that there is nearly universal agreement on the importance of a reasonably sound currency. Thus, while most advanced industrial societies seem to have been willing to formulate fiscal policy with an eye for short-run political advantage, this does not seem to have been the case for monetary policy. There appears to be a widespread, albeit not universal, agreement that we do not wish to make monetary policy via normal political processes.

The debate on whether political authorities should directly control the money supply is ancient. The most eloquent voice calling for such control today is that of Milton Friedman, but support has come from modern political liberals such as Lester Thurow as well. Friedman argues that we already have the bad consequences of direct political control of the Fed without its benefits.[54] These bad consequences include the use of monetary policy as an electoral tool. The advantages of political control have to do with making the monetary authorities accountable to the electorate and more generally the nature of policy-making in a democracy. In Friedman's view it is better to have the Fed work at the behest of an elected official than to have it maximize its own private interest.

The arguments presented here indicate that we should be cautious in accepting this type of reform. While the Fed does not actively create monetary policy to aid presidential reelection, neither does it actively work to undo other presidential economic policies that serve electoral purposes. Similarly the Fed shows some real independence from Congress. Making the Fed an executive agency might have real consequences. These consequences will be of primary importance in the medium run, since in the long run central banks must obey the dictates of the political system. This is not to argue that such a reform is bad, but only that it has costs as well as benefits.

Notes

Professors Thomas Borcherding, Morris Fiorina, John Goodman, Gary Jacobson, Raymond Lombra, Thomas Mayer, John Mendeloff, Thomas Willett, and King Banaian provided helpful comments.

1   Cited in Fred Hirsch and John Goldthorpe, eds., *The Political Economy of Inflation* (Cambridge: Harvard University Press, 1978), p. 1.

2   Deborah Frohman, Leroy Laney, and Thomas Willett, "Uncertainty Costs of High Inflation," *Voice* of the Federal Reserve Bank of Dallas (July 1981): 1–9.

3   Throughout this essay I assume that any monetary policy helps some groups and hurts others. While economists are divided on the costs of inflation, it clearly seems to impose some deadweight costs, that is, lower rates of inflation could potentially make every group better off. In the discourse of welfare economics, a lower rate of inflation may well be a potential Pareto improvement. There is little reason to expect, given current political arrangements, that those who gain from the lower rate of inflation would transfer enough of their gains to those who pay the costs of anti-inflationary policy to make the losers better off, that is, the potential Pareto improvement may not be an actual Pareto improvement. The analysis holds if the politico-economic game makes side payments difficult and costly.

4   See, e.g., A. Gramsci, *Selections from the Prison Notebooks* (London: Lawrence and Wishart, 1971).

5   J. Famia, "Gramsci's Patrimony," *British Journal of Political Science* 13 (1983): 327–64.

6   Central banks differ. Most of this chapter treats the U.S. Federal Reserve. Where relevant, other central banks will be discussed. An adequate political theory of monetary policy ought to be able to account for policy in more than one country. For more general discussion about the differences among the major central banks, see the discussion and references in chapter 21 of this volume.

  For the purposes of this essay I treat central banks as unitary actors, ignoring political divisions within the bank. Fed decision making is dominated by its chair, so this assumption is at least plausible for the United States.

7   Edward Kane, "Selecting Monetary Targets in a Changing Financial Environment," in *Monetary Policy Issues in the 1980s* (Kansas City: Federal Reserve Bank of Kansas City, 1982).

8   Bruno Frey and Friedrich Schneider, "Central Bank Behavior: A Positive Empirical Analysis," *Journal of Monetary Economics* 7 (1981): 291–315; Sherman Maisel, *Managing the Dollar* (New York: W. W. Norton, 1973).

9   This caveat is necessary. Weak but single-minded political actors can defeat powerful actors because the weak actor can afford to devote its resources to a single struggle, whereas the strong actor must divide its attention. In addition, the strong actor may not feel that it is worthwhile to devote scarce political resources to what it sees as a minor struggle; for the weak actor, no political struggle with the strong actor is minor.

10   George Bach, *Making Monetary and Fiscal Policy* (Washington, D.C.: Brookings Institution, 1971), pp. 78–85.

11 We should be wary of extending this too far. Any decision, no matter how partisan, can probably be clothed in technical language. The more partisan decisions are clothed in technical language, the less useful that disguise. Even this minimal form of electoral sensitivity is not costless.

12 For examples of the first paradigm, see S. Popkin, J. Gorman, C. Phillips, and J. Smith, "Comment: What Have You Done for Me Lately? Toward an Investment Theory of Voting," *American Political Science Review* 70 (1976): 779–805; Morris Fiorina, *Retrospective Voting in American National Elections* (New Haven: Yale University Press, 1981); D. Roderick Kiewiet, *Macroeconomics and Micropolitics* (Chicago: University of Chicago Press, 1983); Anthony Downs, *An Economic Theory of Democracy* (New York: Harper, 1958). Works in the second paradigm include Peter Gourevitch, "International Trade, Domestic Coalitions and Liberty: Comparative Responses to the Great Depression of 1873–1896," *Journal of Interdisciplinary History* 8 (1977): 281–313; idem, "Breaking with Orthodoxy: The Politics of Economic Responses to the Depression of the 1930's," *International Organization* 38 (1984): 95–130; Thomas Ferguson, "From Normalcy to New Deal: Industrial Structure, Party Competition, and American Public Policy in the Great Depression," *International Organization* 38 (1984): 41–94; and to some extent Gary Jacobson and Samuel Kernell, *Strategy and Choice in Congressional Elections*, 2d ed. (New Haven: Yale University Press, 1983).

13 Gary Jacobson, "Reagan, Reaganomics, and Strategic Politics in 1982: A Test of Alternative Theories of Midterm Congressional Elections" (Paper presented at the annual meeting of the American Political Science Association, New York, September 1983), p. 23.

14 See Jacobson, "Reagan, Reaganomics, and Strategic Politics."

15 William Nordhaus, "The Political Business Cycle," *Review of Economic Studies* 42 (1975): 169–90; and Edward Tufte, *Political Control of the Economy* (Princeton: Princeton University Press, 1978).

16 Kiewiet, *Macroeconomics and Micropolitics*, p. 154.

17 Jacobson and Kernell, *Strategy and Choice*, p. 9.

18 Ibid.

19 James Alt, *The Politics of Economic Decline* (Cambridge: Cambridge University Press, 1979), p. 270.

20 Evidence against an unemployment cycle is in Nathaniel Beck, "Does There Exist a Political Business Cycle?" *Public Choice* 38 (1982): 205–09; Bennett MacCallum, "The Political Business Cycle: An Empirical Test," *Southern Economic Journal* 45 (1978): 504–15; Martin Paldam, "Is There an Election Cycle?: A Comparative Study of National Accounts," *Scandinavian Journal of Economics* (1979): 323–42; William Thompson and Gary Zuk, "American Elections and the International Electoral-Economic Cycle: A Test of the Tufte Hypothesis," *American Journal of Political Science* 27 (1983): 464–84. The latter two studies are comparative in nature. Haynes and Stone do find that unemployment follows a cycle with a trough in the quarter when an election takes place. See chapter 10 of this volume.

21 Golden and Poterba fail to find that either fiscal policy or transfer payments in the United States follow the pattern predicted by Tufte; Winters et al. have similar find-

ings for a wide range of transfer payments. Frey and Schneider and Maloney and Smirlock do find that fiscal policy may induce a political business cycle. All these studies are for the United States. Frey and Schneider have replicated their results for the United Kingdom and West Germany. See David Golden and James Poterba, "The Price of Popularity: The Political Business Cycle Reexamined," *American Journal of Political Science* 24 (1980): 696–714; R. Winters, C. Johnson, P. Nowosadko, and J. Rendini, "Political Behavior and American Public Policy: The Case of the Political Business Cycle," in *Handbook of Political Behavior,* ed. S. Long (New York: Plenum, 1981); Bruno Frey and Friedrich Schneider, "An Empirical Study of Politico-Economic Interactions in the United States," *Review of Economics and Statistics* 60 (1978): 174–83; and K. Maloney and M. Smirlock, "Business Cycles and the Political Process," *Southern Economic Journal* 48 (1981): 377–92.

22 James Alt and Alec Chrystal, *Political Economy* (Berkeley: University of California Press, 1983), p. 125.

23 Stephen Haynes and Joe Stone, chapter 10 of this volume; and Nathaniel Beck, "Elections and the Fed: Does There Exist a Political Monetary Cycle?" *American Journal of Political Science* 31 (1987): 194–216.

24 The allegation that Burns acted in this way was first made in print by Sanford Rose, who alleged that when the Fed refused to go along with easier policy, Burns left the room and, on returning, said that he had just spoken to the White House; at that point, the Fed caved in. See Sanford Rose, "The Agony of the Fed," *Fortune* 90 (July 1974): 180–90. Former Fed governor Sherman Maisel argues that the White House put pressure on the Fed to increase the money supply to bring about a boom. See Maisel, *Managing the Dollar,* pp. 267–68. The Rose story has been denied by several governors, such as James Robertson, who were not Burns's allies. See James Robertson, "Letter," *Fortune* 90 (August 1974): 113. Both Woolley and I give reasons to distrust the Rose allegation, although Newton supports it. Newton's sole new evidence is an interview with Sanford Rose, the originator of the allegation. See John Woolley, *Monetary Politics: The Federal Reserve and the Politics of Monetary Policy* (New York: Cambridge University Press, 1984); Nathaniel Beck, "Presidential Influence on the Federal Reserve in the 1970's," *American Journal of Political Science* 26 (1982): 415–45; and Maxwell Newton, *The Fed* (New York: New York Times Books, 1983).

25 Chairman Martin felt that it was so important to avoid even the suspicion that monetary policy had partisan motivations that during his tenure the Fed attempted to avoid any change in policy before a presidential election.

26 Evidence for a monetary cycle has come from Allen, Grier, Laney and Willett, and Maloney and Smirlock. The Maloney and Smirlock study suffers from severe omitted variable bias. Evidence against a cycle may be found in my work and in Golden and Poterba and Luckett and Potts. See Stuart Allen, "The Federal Reserve and the Electoral Cycle," *Journal of Money, Credit, and Banking* 18 (1986): 62–66; Kevin Grier, "Presidential Elections and the Federal Reserve," *Southern Economic Journal* 54 (October 1987): 475–86; Leroy O. Laney and Thomas D. Willett, "Presidential Politics, Budget Deficits, and Monetary Policy in the United States: 1960–1976," *Public Choice* 40 (1983): 53–69; Maloney and Smirlock, "Business Cycles"; Beck,

"Presidential Influence" and "Elections and the Fed"; Golden and Porterba, "Price of Popularity"; and D. Luckett and G. Potts, "Monetary Policy and Partisan Politics," *Journal of Money, Credit, and Banking* 12 (1980): 540–46.

27   Grier, "Presidential Elections and the Federal Reserve"; Beck, "Elections and the Fed."

28   My evidence is in Beck, "Executive Influence on Monetary Policy: A Comparative Perspective." Woolley provides evidence for both the United Kingdom and France; see Woolley, "Political Factors in Monetary Policy." Interestingly, both Woolley and I find the strongest evidence for electoral manipulations of monetary policy in Germany, which has an independent central bank. The evidence for Germany is, however, not strong.

29   The clearest statement of the class/party/policy model is in Douglas Hibbs, "Political Parties and Macroeconomic Policy," *American Political Science Review* 71 (1977): 1467–87. See Nathaniel Beck, "Parties, Administrations, and American Macroeconomic Outcomes," *American Political Science Review* 76 (1982): 83–93, and Alt and Chrystal, *Political Economy,* for a discussion and critique of that model.

30   Hibbs does not discuss specific policy instruments. It is possible that left-wing governments could accomplish their goals through fiscal policy alone. Given the influence of the president on the Fed, and the rigidity of fiscal policy, monetary policy should be important in the party control model.

31   Evidence for the United States comes from Nathaniel Beck, "Politics and American Monetary Policy: 1955–1982," *Journal of Politics* 46 (1984): 787–815; and G. Potts and D. Luckett, "Policy Objectives of the Federal Reserve System," *Quarterly Journal of Economics* 82 (1978): 525–34. My evidence for the United Kingdom and West Germany is from Nathaniel Beck, "Executive Influence on Monetary Policy: A Comparative Perspective" (University of California, San Diego, 1983, mimeographed). Other evidence for the United Kingdom is from P. Minford and D. Peel, "The Political Theory of the Business Cycle," *European Economic Review* 17 (1982): 253–70. Evidence on five European nations is in Andrew Cowart, "The Economic Policies of European Governments, Part I: Monetary Policy," *British Journal of Political Science* 8 (1978): 285–311.

32   Charles Lindblom, *Politics and Markets* (New York: Basic Books, 1977).

33   Gourevitch argues that policy response to the Great Depression was determined more by whether a party was in power in 1929 than by the ideology of that party. Some left-wing parties favored demand stimulus policies while other socialist parties (in the United Kingdom and Germany) rejected those policies. See Gourevitch, "Breaking with Orthodoxy."

34   For example, the British Labour Party of the early 1980s is more ideological and class based than either of the two major American parties. The recent British election demonstrates some of the difficulties of ideological, class-based parties.

35   James Alt, "Political Parties, World Demand, and Unemployment: Domestic and International Sources of Economic Activity," *American Political Science Review* 79 (1985): 1016–40.

36   John Woolley, "Political Manipulation of the Economy: Another Look at Monetary Policy with Moving Regression," *Journal of Politics,* forthcoming.

37 The bibles for organizational approaches are James March and Herbert Simon, *Organizations* (New York: John Wiley and Sons, 1958), and Charles Lindblom, "The Science of Muddling Through," *Public Administration Review* 19 (1959): 79–88. See also Aaron Wildavsky, *The Politics of the Budgetary Process*, 3d ed. (Boston: Little, Brown, 1979). For an application to the Volcker Fed, see Jack Knott, "Uncertainty and Federal Reserve Decision Making" (Paper presented at the annual meeting of the American Political Science Association, New York, September 1983).

38 Charles Lindblom, "Still Muddling, Not Yet Through," *Public Administration Review* 39 (1979): 517–26.

39 Benjamin Friedman, "Empirical Issues in Monetary Policy: A Review of Monetary Aggregates and Monetary Policy," *Journal of Monetary Economics* 7 (1977): 100.

40 An economic analysis consistent with this position is that of Ralph Bryant, *Controlling Money* (Washington, D.C.: Brookings Institution, 1983). He examines several possible operating strategies for the Fed in the light of different monetary theories. He argues that a good operating strategy is one that is robust to errors about underlying theory. In particular, monetarist strategies, which do well if the underlying monetarist assumptions hold, appear to perform poorly if those assumptions are violated.

41 The leading work here is William Niskanen, *Bureaucracy and Representative Government* (Chicago: Aldine, 1971). For applications to monetary policy, see John Chant and Keith Acheson, "The Choice of Monetary Instrument and the Theory of Bureaucracy," *Public Choice* 12 (1972): 13–33; and Mark Toma, "Inflationary Bias of the Federal Reserve System," *Journal of Monetary Economics* 10 (1982): 163–90. Evidence in support of Toma is given in William Shughart and Robert Tollison, "Preliminary Evidence on the Use of Inputs by the Federal Reserve System," *American Economic Review* 73 (1983): 90–93, 180–90.

42 Milton Friedman, "Monetary Policy: Theory and Practice," *Journal of Money, Credit, and Banking* 14 (1982): 98–118.

43 James Pierce, "The Myth of Congressional Supervision of Monetary Policy," *Journal of Monetary Economics* 4 (1978): 364.

44 Interest groups' major resources are votes, campaign finances, and information; only the last is relevant to a central bank, and presumably lack of information is not its problem. Sometimes interest groups provide jobs for helpful officials, but few high Fed officials leave for jobs in the private sector. Moreover, the most common route to a position on the board of governors is now graduate work in economics, followed by a Fed staff position (or another public position). As of this writing, only one of the seven governors is closely associated with the private banking sector.

45 This is one of Lindblom's arguments for the privileged position of business. See Lindblom, *Politics and Markets*.

46 The leading work on an electorally motivated Congress is David Mayhew, *Congress: The Electoral Connection* (New Haven: Yale University Press, 1974). Applications of this perspective to the Congress-agency relationship are in Morris Fiorina, *Congress: Keystone of the Washington Establishment* (New Haven: Yale University

Press, 1977). John Woolley, *Monetary Politics,* chap. 9, discusses the Fed's successful efforts to limit congressional initiatives on monetary policy in the 1970s.

47 Barry Weingast, "The Congressional-Bureaucratic System: A Principal-Agent Perspective (With Applications to the SEC)," *Public Choice* 44 (1984): 147–92.

48 Kevin Grier, "Congressional Preference and Federal Reserve Policy" (Center for the Study of American Business, Washington University, 1985, mimeographed).

49 See, for example, Pierce,"Myth of Congressional Supervision," or Robert Weintraub, "Congressional Supervision of Monetary Policy," *Journal of Monetary Economics* 4 (1978): 314–62. Other sources are cited in Woolley, *Monetary Politics.*

50 Edward Kane, "Politics and Fed Policy-making: The More Things Change, the More They Remain the Same," *Journal of Monetary Economics* 6 (1980): 199–212; and Kane, "Selecting Monetary Targets."

51 A good discussion of the early debates over Fed independence is A. Jerome Clifford, *The Independence of the Federal Reserve System* (Philadelphia: University of Pennsylvania Press, 1965). Lester Chandler, *Benjamin Strong, Central Banker* (Washington, D.C.: Brookings Institution, 1958), discusses the Fed's revenue problems and their solution during its formative years. For a brief review of Fed history, see Woolley, *Monetary Politics,* chap. 2.

52 Morris Fiorina, "Legislative Choice of Regulatory Process: Legal Process or Administrative Process," *Public Choice* 39 (1982): 33–66.

53 I am indebted to Morris Fiorina for this argument.

54 Milton Friedman, "Monetary Policy."

Part Four

Proposals for Reform

16 Evaluating Proposals for Fundamental Monetary Reform

Thomas Mayer and Thomas D. Willett

Introduction: The Need for Fundamental Monetary Reform

Our monetary institutions have clearly not worked well over the past several decades. Of course a nontrivial portion of the poor macroeconomic performance during this time was due to a combination of adverse shocks and mistaken policy responses. There is good reason to hope that the next several decades will not produce as many shocks and that macroeconomic policy officials have learned a good bit from past mistakes. Still, we do not share the confidence of Franco Modigliani that to achieve price stability for the future all that we need to do is "pick a world in which a tenfold rise in oil prices is out of bounds and then put stabilization policies in the hands of competent and dedicated Keynesians to whom the president listens."[1]

In our judgment the short time horizon fostered by the political environment of policy-making makes inevitable a tendency toward inflation, which will be held in check under discretionary policy-making only for relatively brief periods of time. Recent experience in a number of countries including the United States and the United Kingdom has shown that the worst-case political scenarios which predicted ever-escalating inflation under democratic institutions were too pessimistic. The democratic process is capable of putting a limit on the magnitude of inflationary excesses. However, the costs imposed before this check became effective have been enormous, as have those of restoring a much lower rate of inflation. For the types of informational reasons discussed earlier in this volume, this democratic check is likely to work only with a considerable lag; and with the spotlight removed from inflation, the condition conducive to its reemergence reappears. Again, we might expect that with continued abuse, the lags in effective anti-inflationary responses would tend to shorten; but even if this does occur, the transitional instability costs will be high. Thus we believe that there is a strong case for seriously considering reforms in our institutions for monetary policy-making designed to reduce the likelihood of the continuation of this unstable process.

Such a reform has to address the issue of how much flexibility and discretion the Fed should have. Should it be constrained from doing what it thinks is best? This question is addressed in the following section and answered in the affirmative. We go on to the major types of proposals which have been proposed to substantially reform our process of monetary policy-making.

One type of proposal which has attracted a good deal of recent attention is to eliminate the Fed's autonomy by bringing it formally under the president's control. Another is to impose a monetary growth-rate rule or a price stability rule on the Fed. There has also been increased interest in returning to traditional ways of trimming a central bank's autonomy, the gold standard or another commodity standard, as well as proposals for new types of commodity standards. There have also been much more radical proposals to eliminate the Fed's control over the money supply entirely by privatizing the creation of money. After discussing these we turn finally to the types of reform proposals which have drawn the strongest support from economists in recent years, money growth rate and price stability rules. We also discuss several modified versions of such rules. We conclude with a discussion of whether monetary reform proposals should be set by congressional legislation or written into the Constitution.

The Costs of Flexibility

Keynesians typically advocate giving the Fed great flexibility. As Stephen Goldfeld has put it, "simple semantics suggests that a more flexible rule is to be preferred to a fixed rule. By extension, discretion which in some sense offers the most flexibility should be better still."[2] The case for flexibility seems obvious. Flexibility lets you do either what an inflexible rule would require, or something else, if that is better. Hence the results of a flexible policy must be at least as good, and will often be better, than the results of a policy that is constrained by a rule. Flexibility allows policymakers to take account of new information that was simply not available at the time when a rule was set.

This argument is clear and simple—and wrong. It both assumes too much and proves too much. It proves too much because if it were correct few, if any, commitments would be made; marriages would not exist, nor would longer-term business contracts. Judges could modify laws to fit particular cases and could impose any sentence they considered appropriate.

It also assumes too much for two reasons. First, it assumes behavior that is time-consistent and ignores the possibility that decision makers may give in to short-term pressures or inducements and, hence, act in ways which are not consistent with longer-run interests.[3] Such an overemphasis on the short run should not be dismissed as irrational and hence unlikely. Relinquishing a short-run benefit is painful, and a rational person will, at least to some extent, avoid this pain even at the cost of relinquishing part of a long-run objective. Moreover, if irrational time preference exists, then an inflexible rule has a decided advantage. For example, persons on a diet frequently adopt regimes that limit their short-run flexibility. Someone who decides to have dessert only at dinner and not at lunch is not necessarily less rational than someone who adopts the flexible system of ordering dessert whenever the marginal utility of dessert seems above average to him, and refusing it when its marginal utility seems below average. Human behavior is subject to many pressures, and a reasonably rational person is not some superman who always overcomes these pressures completely, but a person who takes his or her own weaknesses into account.

Not only are policymakers, like the rest of us, sometimes shortsighted, but they also, like other people, tend to overemphasize the importance of what they do and to adopt policies that optimize their particular task but cause damage to the larger interest. In the early 1950s the Treasury Department opposed a needed change in monetary policy out of narrow concern about the federal debt. In the 1960s and 1970s the Fed slowed down needed changes in interest rates out of a concern about upsetting financial markets.

Policymakers are also likely to be too optimistic and overemphasize their capabilities. The way we select our policymakers does not favor shrinking violets. Usually it takes not only ability but also luck to become a policymaker, and those who have been lucky in the past are likely to overestimate their ability to overcome any obstacles to their policies.

For such reasons there is a serious principal-agent problem at work. Monetary policy is an area in which it is particularly difficult for the general public (the principals) to monitor effectively the actions of their agents (the monetary authorities), and there are many reasons to believe that political pressures will motivate monetary authorities to weight short-term considerations too heavily, resulting in contributions to longer-term instability. Such concerns gave rise to our current structure of independence of the Federal Reserve. Although the Federal Reserve Act was a carefully drafted compromise that tried to insulate the Fed from too much political pressure, it has not been successful. As other papers in this volume have shown, it has not sufficiently insulated the Federal Reserve from political pressures, while at the same time it leaves the public without any direct avenue to check the Fed's inflationary propensities. Thus there is a case for considering rules to help control performance. Such rules may be needed even if the policymakers are honest and public-spirited as we believe Federal Reserve officials have been. A thoroughly decent policymaker faced with excess aggregate demand is surely tempted to postpone the painful decision to become more restrictive and throw many thousands out of work.

Beyond this, flexibility creates uncertainty. One person's flexibility may be another person's uncertainty. Replacing our present laws with a simple law saying "all bad people should be jailed for as long as a judge thinks appropriate" would certainly provide courts with sufficient flexibility. But it would create great uncertainty for others.

In addition, there is an indirect benefit to abandoning flexibility. Paradoxical as it may seem, by restricting its own freedom of action the government gains some control over others'. The government wants the private sector to do certain things which the private sector is willing to do only if it can be certain that inflation will be curbed. Some examples of this are investors buying more long-term bonds, thus fostering long-term investment, or wage earners being willing to settle for smaller wage increases because they are less afraid of inflation eroding their wages. The government can generate such longer-term commitments only by convincing the public that inflation will actually be curbed. But since words are cheap, the public faces a danger; once people have made their commitments on the assumption that inflation will stop, the government may want to follow more inflationary policies again. The only way out is for the government to commit itself by tying its own hands.

Hence we believe that the pendulum has swung too far in the direction of flexibility. It is not surprising that during the Great Depression, when the gold standard enforced an inflexible regime of deflation on many countries, flexibility seemed like a panacea. But the Great Inflation has taught us that flexibility has its costs. One is that the Fed becomes subject to political pressures.

If the Fed has not behaved in a satisfactory way, perhaps its independence should be reduced or eliminated. Both supply-siders and liberal Democrats have advocated this because they think that the Fed is generally too restrictive. And Milton Friedman, though he does not believe that the Fed has been too restrictive, does agree that the Fed is too independent:

> My examination of that experience impresses me with the unbelievable strength of bureaucratic inertia in preventing the system from learning from experience. . . . The problem is somehow rooted in the institutional structure of the Federal Reserve System. . . . The only two alternatives to a continuation of the Fed's present policies that do seem to me feasible over the longer run are either to make the Federal Reserve a bureau of the Treasury . . . or to put the Federal Reserve under direct Congressional control.[4]

All in all, there are four major arguments for depriving the Fed of its independence. One is philosophical: monetary policy, like other major policies, should be under the control of democratically elected officials. A second argument is that the president is held responsible for economic conditions—he should therefore be given control over the main tool of economic policy. Third, if monetary and fiscal policies are made by different parts of the government they will be uncoordinated. Fourth, if the Fed is not responsible to elected officials it lacks a much needed "bottom line" and is therefore subject to the various bureaucratic dysfunctions which were discussed in the previous chapter.

How valid are these arguments? The philosophical one is not convincing. The public should have a right to delegate certain decisions to officials appointed by its elected representatives. The argument that the president has responsibility for economic conditions ignores the fact that even with our "independent" Federal Reserve system he already has control over the main thrust of monetary policy.[5] The argument about coordinating monetary and fiscal policy is also weak. When there is great uncertainty and chance for error, then there is something to be said for uncoordinated policies. It is sometimes better to try to run off in two directions at once than to rush off full steam in the wrong direction.[6] Besides, how can monetary policy be lodged in the same part of government as fiscal policy, when fiscal policy is itself split between Congress and the administration? But the argument that under the current arrangement the Fed lacks a needed "bottom line" is both valid and important.

Yet giving the administration or Congress direct control over the Fed has its dangers too. The beneficial effects of a restrictive policy come with a lag, but the painful effects come sooner. This is a dangerous combination if the public is myopic. Moreover, it seems "obvious" that an expansionary monetary policy can lower interest rates in the short run, and that a lower interest rate is a "good thing." Hence the present arrangement under which those who face elections every few years can claim that they lack control over the Fed has something to be said for it.

Friedman's view that eventually the public would learn about monetary policy (and therefore be immune to demagogic appeals on this issue) is plausible. But "eventually" can be a long time. As is often the case, Friedman's policy recommendation may be sound for the long run, but painful in the short run. And given a reasonable discount rate, the short-run pain could well outweigh the long-run benefits. Clearly even if, at present, there is no political business cycle, putting monetary policy under the direct control of Congress or the administration could generate one. Furthermore, as is discussed in chapter 21 of this volume, those industrial countries whose central bank is directly responsible to the government have tended to have worse, not better, records of inflation.

One possible compromise would be to grant the president the explicit authority to publicly give the Fed its marching orders on two occasions during each term, once right after the inauguration and once right after the midterm election. Since the unfavorable effects of wrong monetary policies are likely to show up within two years, the president would not be under any temptation to ask for a popular—but unsound—policy.[7]

Should We Return to a Gold Standard?

The type of fundamental monetary reform which appears to be receiving the greatest public attention currently involves proposals to return to some form of gold standard.[8] While the gold standard has the advantage from a conservative perspective of representing a return to a previous type of system rather than the adoption of a new one, we find little else to commend it as a first-best solution. Advocates of some form of gold standard have generally compared it with a system of discretionary management. On this basis one can argue that even when effects on unemployment as well as inflation are taken into account, the average experience of the gold standard of the late nineteenth and early twentieth centuries compares favorably with our experience of the last two decades. Published comparisons by both advocates and critics of economic performance under gold and discretionary monetary management have frequently painted quite different pictures. By varying the time periods selected, the performance criteria emphasized, and the choice for treatment of periods with limited roles for gold (such as the 1930s and the postwar Bretton Woods years) as gold or discretionary periods, vastly different impressions can be given. A balanced assessment, we believe, suggests that on average U.S. economic performance under the last episode of the full-fledged classical gold standard of the late nineteenth and early twentieth centuries was not as good as during the first two decades of the postwar period. However, it was better than the performance of the last two decades.[9] Thus favorable references to the historical experiences of the gold standard, while frequently painted in too rosy a manner, are not without some basis.

It is certainly true that we did not experience the type of sustained rapid inflation under the gold standard that we have had since the mid-1960s. But should this be attributed to the gold standard? It seems as plausible to argue that we were on the gold standard because we did not then have the political pressures for expansionary policies that we experience now. At that time, when unemployment rose sharply the government was not under as much pressure to "do something" as it is now. Furthermore, wages and prices displayed considerably greater downward flexibility in the days of the gold standard than they do now.[10] Thus, when demand fell, more of the effect was on prices and less on unemployment. Under modern conditions, the abandonment of the gold standard would be a likely response to deflationary pressures.

This is not to deny that a gold standard would provide *some* barrier to inflationary policies. It would require a government that undertakes such policies to bear the political costs of leaving the gold standard. But it is difficult to know how great these political costs would be. Such a political judgment is hard to make, particularly since it may depend upon the specific circumstances and personalities at the time. For example, a skilled demagogue might obtain political capital from leaving the gold standard by presenting it as a move to protect the country's welfare from the machinations of wicked foreigners who wish to steal the country's gold.

Moreover, when one compares the gold standard not exclusively with our current fiat money system (as has been done by most gold standard advocates) but also with the current system supplemented by a law embodying a price level (or inflation rate) rule, it seems doubtful that the gold standard would be the better barrier against inflation. Voters buy groceries, not gold or foreign exchange! A modern gold standard, that is, a gold bullion standard rather than a gold coin standard, would not impinge on people's direct experience; there might be little awareness of its existence and hence little opposition to abandoning it. A monetary growth rate law *might* therefore be as good—or better—a barrier as a gold standard, since the opposition party could represent any attempt to repeal such a law as an attempt by the government to gain additional resources at the expense of the public. Given the increased frequency with which countries have gone off, or substantially modified, their commitments to gold in the current century, it seems quite unlikely that a new commitment to gold would be more durable or believable than some type of constitutionally mandated monetary rule.

Furthermore, the case for a gold standard as a first-best system of constraint over monetary expansion in the United States is quite weak in terms of a forward-looking assessment of the economic performance it would be likely to generate. In effect, adoption of a gold standard among the major industrial countries would make the rate of monetary expansion in the United States dependent on developments in the global demand and supply for gold and in the U.S. balance of payments. The first set of conditions would determine the global monetary supply, while balance of payments developments would influence monetary conditions in the United States relative to other countries.

Neither of these conditions is likely to be a consistently good guide for monetary policy. There have been substantial shifts in underlying demand and supply in the gold market (even ignoring speculative factors),[11] and also in the factors which influence the U.S. balance of payments and equilibrium exchange rate. From the standpoint of the theory of optimum currency areas, the United States is the classic case of a country whose international sectors should be adjusted to its domestic sectors rather than vice versa, i.e., one which should adopt flexible rather than fixed exchange rates.[12] As Alexandre Lamfalussy has recently argued, there may be a good case for small open economies to focus on exchange rates rather than monetary rules as anti-inflation devices, but this case does not apply to a large economy like the United States.[13] For the United States some type of direct monetary rule or set of constraints should be far superior.

Conceptually, it might be possible for the United States to go on some form of gold standard unilaterally, with a flexible exchange rate between a gold-backed dollar and other currencies. The operational difficulties of such schemes could be considerable, however, and the price level in the United States would become much more sensitive to the official price of gold chosen and to shifts in the global demand and supply of gold, since the effects would be concentrated on the United States rather than being spread out over a number of countries.

Recently some advocates of a return to gold have begun to criticize other possible approaches to monetary restraint by attacking the idea that there are any meaningful monetary aggregates which could be controlled directly. In terms ironically reminiscent of the traditional Keynesian arguments for interest rate rather than money supply targets, this view asserts that financial innovations are so dynamic that the relationships between any of the monetary aggregate figures and economic activity are not sufficiently stable to be used as effective control mechanisms for the economy. For example, Arthur Laffer has recently argued that

> while restricting the growth of the money supply theoretically could bring inflation under control, practical application is not within reach. The structure of modern financial institutions does not lend itself to the levered control of monetary aggregates by the Fed.
> . . . In short, the structure of financial institutions worldwide renders the Fed virtually powerless to control the growth rate of the money supply. The private sector's ability to shift demand deposits

into money market funds, Eurodollar accounts or even credit cards implies that private actions can substantially, if not fully, offset the intended effects of Fed policy.[14]

Arguments that the major monetary aggregates in the United States cannot be controlled with a tolerable degree of accuracy over quarterly or annual periods do not enjoy much empirical support,[15] while the fact that fluctuations in the money multipliers keep money supply aggregates from being precisely controllable on a weekly or monthly basis carries little policy significance. However, shifts in the demand for money (velocity) due in considerable degree to innovations in financial practices and the financial instruments available do present a serious challenge to the case for simple monetary growth rules.

This problem will be discussed below. It should be noted, however, that the gold standard advocates who make such arguments appear to have overlooked that such financial innovations would cause the same kinds of problems of fluctuations in the velocity of gold-based money as with fiat money. Indeed, as Allan Meltzer has recently argued, velocity was frequently more variable under the gold standard than it has been during the recent period of discretionary money and flexible exchange rates.[16] As Henry Simons noted in his classic piece on rules versus discretion,[17] the elimination of this as a potential problem would require the outlawing or stringent regulation of financial instruments which would be close substitutes for money balances at the margin. Such regulation would surely be inconsistent with the principles of freedom and market efficiency advocated by most proponents of a return to gold.

A More General Commodity Standard

As was indicated above, a major drawback of the gold standard is that it directly stabilizes the price of only a single, quite unimportant commodity, gold. This does little good if the relative price of gold in terms of other goods and services varies substantially. And given the vagaries of gold discoveries and of the demand for gold if other nations adopt (or abandon) the gold standard, such substantial variations in the relative price of gold cannot be ruled out.

An obvious solution to this problem would seem to be to stabilize not the price of gold but the prices of a wide variety of basic raw materials. Let the government stand ready to buy, at a previously determined price, a bundle containing a fixed amount of certain commodities. As it does so, its purchases raise prices directly; and more importantly, since it buys these bundles with newly created money, the money supply increases, thus raising the price level back to its previous equilibrium. Similarly, during an inflation the government sells such bundles out of its storehouses, thus raising supply and also decreasing the quantity of money. Such a plan was advocated by Benjamin and Frank Graham.[18]

A somewhat similar scheme was advocated recently by Robert Hall.[19] However, in his system the government would not actually hold bundles of commodities. This has several major advantages. First, it avoids the cost of locking up resources in warehouses and storage dumps as well as the actual cost of taking care of the stockpiles. Second, it avoids the danger that producers of the stored commodities would pressure the government to increase purchases for the stockpile. Third, there would be no danger of running out of commodity bundles due to the government's attempt to keep their prices down. (It was just this sort of thing that forced the abandonment of the gold standard.)

The Hall proposal does not rely on the government holding commodity bundles because of Hall's important insight into how commodity standards function. A gold standard, for example, does *not* require the government to hold, and stand ready to sell, gold. It merely requires that the government define the dollar as equal to a certain amount of gold and enforce the right of creditors to be paid in either dollars or gold. Then, suppose that there is some "inflation" in the sense that the prices of goods and services rise relative to dollars, but not in terms of gold. Gold is now more valuable. Hence creditors demand to be paid in gold. As a result, the price of gold rises relative to the price of goods, that is, the prices of goods fall again in terms of gold. And with the dollar defined as a certain amount of gold, prices must fall in terms of dollars too, so that the inflation is stopped.

In Hall's scheme the government sets the price of a commodity unit consisting of fixed amounts of aluminum, ammonium nitrate, copper, and plywood. Hall chose these four commodities because in the past their prices have moved in close unison with the cost of living. Hence, stabilizing their prices would be similar to stabilizing living costs. The government is therefore, in effect, setting the dollar price of the cost of living.

Hall's system has an operating rule adapted from one proposed by

Irving Fisher in 1920. Again consider the gold standard. Suppose that the supply of gold increases enough to raise prices *in terms of gold* by, say, 10 percent. Fisher's rule would then offset this decline in the value of gold by raising the amount of gold per dollar, so that in terms of dollars the prices of goods and services would be constant. Hence Hall would institute a rule such as "every month depress the dollar price of the resource unit by one-twelfth of the amount by which the most recent CPI exceeds the target level."[20] Hall prefers an adjustment of one-twelfth to a full adjustment each month to prevent shifts that might be too disruptive.

Hall's scheme is ingenious. But would it work? Hall himself is not certain that it would work better than our current monetary system:

> Blunders are just as possible under a commodity standard. The dollar price of the resource unit is a policy instrument similar in many respects to the money stock in our current system. It would have been tempting to raise the dollar price for the same reasons and under the same circumstances as we actually raised our money stock. . . . Under proper management, a fiat money system could promise long-run price stability through exactly the same kind of adaptive policy.[21]

Whether Hall's system would provide a better barrier against unwise policies than our current system is impossible to say; we know much too little about how the political process operates.

There is, however, one critical aspect of Hall's system that one *can* say something about. This is his assumption that the price of his commodity unit would continue to track the cost of living. What Hall did was to select four commodities whose prices have done so in the past. But the past is precisely that—the past. There is no assurance that these prices will behave in this way in the future. Goodhart's Law (named after Charles Goodhart) states that any previously observed regularity breaks down as soon as it is used for policy. One reason for this is that when the policy changes, the incentives of the private sector change too, so that it now behaves differently. This is probably not relevant here. But another reason for Goodhart's Law is the following: Suppose that you observe a thousand commodity prices for fifty years. Suppose further that these commodity prices on the average behave entirely randomly with respect to the cost of living. Nevertheless, the chance is high that one of them will closely track the cost of living over these fifty years. But there is no reason to think that in the fifty-fifth year this particular price will track the cost of living any better than any other price does.

Hence, Hall has not provided any strong evidence that his system would provide reasonable price stability. But this does not mean that it should be dismissed out of hand. Given the poor way our current system functions it may not be fair to demand such proof of any rival system.

The Currency Competition Approach

A much more radical approach to depoliticizing the money supply process has been recently advocated by Friedrich Hayek and taken up by a number of economists, including Larry White.[22] In its strongest form this competitive money approach argues that there is no need for government production of money in the first place. The private sector could provide monetary assets, and competition would keep the rate of private money creation from being excessive. Most economists have argued that because of such considerations as externalities, economies of scale, and high information cost of monitoring, the competitive provision of money would exhibit serious market failures and contribute to monetary instability. Advocates of private competitive money have argued that such critiques and their related conclusion that government monopoly provision of money is required have been based on flawed analysis. Further, competitive money advocates cite historical experiences such as the episode in Scottish banking history where purely private money production was not associated with monetary instability, and have offered interesting reinterpretations of the U.S. free-banking experience which suggest that private money systems per se need not be as unstable as traditional analysis has concluded.[23]

In somewhat less radical versions this approach suggests the legalizing of private money production to compete with government production. The ability of individuals to switch easily to other forms of money is seen as offering a major restraining force on government propensities to inflate. We believe that this recent body of research and analysis has made important intellectual contributions. However, while we agree with many of the criticisms of the earlier literature made by the competitive money advocates, we do not think that these criticisms convincingly dispose of all of the concerns about market failures in this area. We share the concerns expressed by Michael Melvin in chapter 18 that informational problems would be likely to keep competition from producing stability in this type of economic activity. We should stress, however, that even if one does believe that serious market failures would result from prohibiting government provision of money, it does not follow that unconstrained monopoly money production by government is the appropriate alternative. Indeed, we believe that the need to create an improved set of institutions to control monetary policy is great. Experiments with monetary reform should not be taken lightly, however, and should be approached with a risk averse attitude. Thus, even if we believed that the odds were ten to one that a competitive money regime would not produce the type of monetary instability we observed in the United States in the second quarter of the previous century, we do not believe that these odds would be high enough to justify such an experiment given the possibility of adopting other approaches discussed below.

We are much more sympathetic to proposals to reduce the government barriers which discourage competition from the private provision of domestic monetary services and from foreign currencies. The efforts of such competition, however, seem to us unlikely to provide the equivalent of fundamental monetary reform. The effects of rapid depreciation of their currency on the foreign exchange market has in a number of instances prompted national governments to shift gears and adopt more prudent macroeconomic policies, but such discipline has been sporadic and far from sufficient to ensure the adoption of consistently stable subsequent policies.[24]

We share Melvin's view that the historical evidence on direct international currency substitution suggests that such competition is not as potent a restraining force on inflationary propensities as advocates of currency competition have suggested. By the same token, however, international currency substitution does not appear so far to have been the strong source of monetary instability that some economists have alleged or predicted.[25] Thus while it might make the operation of a simple monetary rule more difficult, we believe that there may be considerable merit to proposals aimed at removing restrictions on currency competition. We believe that the evolution of greater currency competition would be likely to be a slow process which would do relatively little to control inflationary tendencies in the near future, but removal of restrictions would likely be desirable on microeconomic efficiency grounds, and over time the experience with currency competition could provide useful information for the evaluation of the more radical proposals.

At present, however, we feel that the best candidates for fundamental monetary reform are limited to those proposals which would place some type of restraint on the scope for discretionary actions by the monetary authorities.

A Monetary Growth-Rate Rule

Among economists perhaps the most frequently discussed alternative to our current monetary policy arrangement is to eliminate the Fed's discretion by requiring it to follow the simple rule of increasing the money stock (or the monetary base) at a fixed rate, say 4 percent. Milton Friedman is the best-known proponent of such a rule, a rule which is the hallmark of hard-core monetarism.[26] Such monetarists do not argue that stable money growth would be an ideal monetary policy and that it would eliminate all economic fluctuations. They do not deny that an ideal central bank equipped with perfect knowledge would be better. But such a central bank does not exist and, hard-core monetarists argue, a central bank that tries to reduce economic fluctuations usually exacerbates them. It follows that a monetary growth-rate rule need not be carved in stone. Perhaps five hundred years from now the Fed will be able to do better.

The desirability of a stable growth-rate rule depends not only on how well the Fed manages monetary policy, but also on the (trend-adjusted) stability of velocity, since a stable monetary growth rate would translate variations of velocity into point-for-point variations in nominal GNP. Hence, the experience of the early 1980s when velocity fell (instead of rising at its previously established 3 percent trend) seems, at first glance, to sweep away the case for a monetary growth-rate rule. But only at first glance. Proponents of the monetary rule can reply that had such a rule been put into effect in, say, 1960, then this sharp break in velocity would not have occurred. A major reason for the rise in velocity in the 1970s was that inflation, by raising nominal interest rates, was raising the cost of holding money and hence raised velocity. Similarly, a major reason for the decline in velocity in the 1980s was that with the end of high inflation nominal interest rates fell. Had a monetary growth-rate rule been in effect, inflation would have been much less severe in the 1970s, and there would then have been much less disinflation in the 1980s. As a result, any break in the trend of velocity would have been much less pronounced.[27]

Although the behavior of velocity in the 1980s therefore does not invalidate the case for stable money growth, we do not recommend such a rule, because velocity has not been all that stable historically. And even small declines in the trend of velocity can cause severe recessions. Suppose, for example, that the trend of velocity falls from 2 percent to 1.5 percent. As a result, each year aggregate demand falls by 0.5 percent below the level that was anticipated when the monetary growth rate was set. Since prices are slow to adjust to changes in aggregate demand, such a continuous decline in aggregate demand would generate substantial unemployment for several years.

A variant of the traditional monetary growth-rate rule therefore looks more promising. This is to adjust the growth rate of the money supply (or of the monetary base) to take account of previously observed changes in velocity.[28] For example, if velocity fell by 2 percent in the prior period, then in the current period the money growth rate, instead of being, say, 4 percent, would be 6 percent. A change in the trend of velocity would therefore do damage for only one period. At the same time, such a rule would maintain the two major advantages of the traditional monetary growth-rate rule: the Fed would avoid making forecast errors because it would no longer use forecasts, and it would be essentially deprived of its discretion. It could not generate inflation by raising the money growth rate.[29]

Although a growth rate rule prevents the Fed from becoming an engine of inflation, many economists object to either the traditional or the velocity-adjusted version of the monetary growth-rate rule because these rules leave virtually no room for discretionary policies to meet supply shocks or liquidity crises. These objectives can be met either by adding sections of the Federal Reserve which would be given limited amounts of authority for monetary expansion for stabilization and lender-of-last-resort functions, as has been proposed by Jurg Niehans, or by providing a wider band of target outcomes within which the monetary authorities are given scope for discretion.[30]

While the technical provisions of such proposals could vary considerably, they all share the common characteristic that if successful they would increase substantially the weight given to achieving price stability in the formulation of monetary policy. Advocacy of this objective need not require a normative judgment that price stability is in some sense more desirable than the other traditional goals of monetary policy, such as full employment and even interest rate stability. The real issue is that monetary policy acts with much quicker effects on these latter variables than on prices, but that the slower effects on prices tend to be lasting while the quicker effects on interest rates and unemployment tend to be only temporary. Given the pressure toward adopting a short time horizon which seems virtually inevitable in the operation of the political process, the pressures for short-run monetary accommodation (which is excessive from a longer-run perspective) seem inescapable. This is a fundamental problem from a long-run view even if one is concerned about employment and not inflation. Thus, the essential characteristic of monetary reform efforts in our judgment should be efforts to increase the weight given to price stability in the formulation of monetary policy.

One approach which has been suggested is simply to initiate a mandate that Federal Reserve officials include in their oaths of office a promise to give primacy to promoting price stability.[31] By focusing on intent rather than outcomes one could avoid problems of needing to specify particular price indices and allowable ranges of deviations, etc. (Particular provisions to allow Congress to override this directive in emergencies might be provided, however.)

The key question would be the enforceability of this approach. Without further provisions, the ultimate enforcement mechanism would be impeachment, a blunt instrument. However, it can be argued that most officials take their formal oaths of office seriously and this would offer some self-enforcement.

If this were felt to be an insufficiently strong enforcement mechanism then one of the compromise provisions for controlling the rate of monetary expansion could be added as an enforcement mechanism. For example, if average inflation rates moved above a target range, then the rate of growth of the monetary base could be required to be strongly constrained until inflation fell back within the target range. Direct actions against monetary officials would only be initiated if they failed to follow this procedure. Desires to avoid being placed in such a straitjacket should give the monetary authorities strong incentives, however, to become progressively less accommodative as inflation rose above the middle of the target range. Thus this approach could provide a more continuous set of incentives to avoid excessive accumulative accommodation while allowing the authorities to "earn" greater scope for discretion by typically staying well within the target ranges.[32]

One might alternatively argue for an approach which just directly penalizes officials for poor macroeconomic performance. For example, Thomas Havrilesky has suggested levying a fine on the Fed commensurate to its misses of unemployment and inflation goals set for it.[33] We believe, however, that it would be difficult to design an effective method of implementing this type of approach. One problem with the proposal is that the Fed may justifiably claim that it is not to blame when supply shocks raise inflation and unemployment, and when demographic changes raise the unemployment rate. Second, since the Fed turns over most of its earnings to the Treasury, moderate fines might not bother the Fed. Third, were Congress to consider such a law, we might well wind up with the Fed becoming subject to congressional budget appropriations, which would give inflationists in Congress greater influence over the Fed.

A related suggestion is sometimes made. Why not link the pensions of the president, the Fed chairman, and congresspeople to macroeconomic performance? Unfortunately, it is hard to imagine that Congress would agree to adjust its own pensions that way, particularly as it could be argued that Congress is not responsible for increases in oil prices, etc. Moreover, given the low salary of the Fed chairman (relative to the alternative positions typically available to such people), a law of this type would restrict the supply of available candidates for the chairmanship largely to those who have considerable independent incomes or have built up sufficient pension equity elsewhere.

Securing agreement on some such type of system to induce monetary restraint will be difficult, but the costs of failing to do so could be enormous.

The Constitutional Constraints Approach

Ordinary legislation may not be a sufficient constraint on discretionary policy. What one Congress has done another Congress may undo. Hence someone undertaking investment that will be worthwhile only if prices are stable may be reluctant to invest even if Congress orders the Fed to maintain price stability or sets a stable monetary growth-rate rule.

A "constitutional provision" does not only mean provisions enshrined in a formal, written constitution. They can be rules that everyone "just knows" the government will obey. Civil liberties are more secure in Britain, which has no written constitution, than they are in Russia, where they are written into the constitution. Informal constitutional rules can be effective. But informal constitutional provisions are difficult to establish, usually being the result of slowly evolving tradition. No such tradition currently exists for macroeconomic policy. Hence, if such policy rules are to have constitutional protection they must be written into the formal Constitution. Should this be done? Although the current controversy on this issue centers on fiscal policy, we will deal here only with the monetary policies that we have already discussed.

Some economists and legal scholars have been opposed to the type of constitutional amendment that would be required.[34] Thus a leading constitutional scholar, Laurence Tribe, writes:

> First, the Constitution embodies fundamental law and should not be made the instrument of specific social and economic policies. . . . As Justice Holmes wrote . . . "a Constitution is not intended to embody a particular economic theory. . . ." Experience, no less than intuition, counsels against the incorporation of particular social or economic programs into the Constitution. . . . Slavery is the only economic arrangement our Constitution has ever specifically endorsed. . . . It has demeaned our Constitution.[35]

Similarly, Paul Samuelson states:

> A constitutional amendment cannot by its nature provide the flexibility . . . that is necessary in so imperfect a science as economics. There is much historical experience with laudable attempts to specify for all times the permitted parameters of economic policy. . . . Without exception—whether it be the case of the automatic gold standard, the many central bank gold reserve clauses . . . the pegged exchange rates . . . each such attempt at permanent finetuning has resulted in specific economic crises and inefficiencies.[36]

One could reply to the first of these objections that some economic clauses can meet the criterion of being "fundamental law" in the sense that they provide the legal protection that people need to make long-term arrangements and that a number of economic provisions and prohibitions are, in fact, contained in the Constitution.[37]

Does such a proposal meet the criticism that it would enshrine a particular economic theory, a theory about which we cannot be certain? To answer that the Constitution already contains clauses dealing with matters that cannot be established with great certitude is merely a debating point. A more serious answer must distinguish between the more general proposition that price stability is desirable and the more specific proposals to bring about price stability.[38]

Although it is certainly possible, it seems extremely unlikely that subsequent research will show price stability to be undesirable, particularly if price stability is modified to allow for some inflation in the case of supply shocks. Hence, one might well make a case for that type amendment.

But it is much harder to make a strong case for specific proposals to generate price stability, such as the adoption of a stable monetary growth-rate rule or a return to the gold standard. The uncertainty about how such systems of rules would work is just too great. Thus we welcome the latest generation of more flexible types of proposals which were discussed at the end of our preceding section on money growth and price rules.

We believe that such "compromise" proposals should be given serious consideration. While these would not score as high on the criterion of simplicity, we believe that there is considerable scope for such compromise proposals which are not exceedingly complicated and could be relatively easily understood without the need for substantial economic expertise.

It is important that the whole endeavor of analyzing possible fundamental monetary reforms be approached in such a spirit of compromise. Given the seriousness of such reforms they should enjoy widespread support. With the wide range of views of economists on macroeconomic issues, there is little hope of ever reaching broad agreement on optimal policy rules. But that need not, and in our judgment should not, be the objective of such reform. Rather we believe that it is essential that economists search for a reasonable set of constraints which would be acceptable to a broad range of experts, rather than seeking to impose their own preferred solution.

This is an important example of the dictum that the search for the best should not be allowed to become the enemy of the good. Of course there is always the danger with compromise that the worst rather than the best features of alternative opportunities would be combined. We believe that this could be avoided, however. Keynesians and monetarists, for example, should see if they could agree to accept Keynesian concerns about variability of velocity and the desirability of some accommodation of supply shocks along with monetarist concerns that restraints need to be placed on the scope for discretionary monetary policy to avoid escalating inflation. The result would be more scope for discretion and accommodation than monetarists would find ideal; but in return, the scope for discretion could be sufficiently limited so that a repeat of the escalating inflation of the 1960s and 1970s would be unlikely. That would be no small contribution from monetary reform.

Notes

1 Franco Modigliani, "Opportunities and Implications of a Return to Fixed Exchange Rates—Is Gold an Answer for International Adjustment?" in *The Future of the International Monetary System*, ed. T. Agmon, R. G. Hawkins, and R. M. Levich (Lexington, Mass.: Lexington Books, 1984), p. 46.

2 Stephen Goldfeld, "Rules, Discretion, and Reality," *American Economic Review* 72 (May 1982): 361.

3 See, for example, the emphasis on this connection in Geoffrey Brennan and James Buchanan, *The Reason of Rules: Constitutional Political Economy* (Cambridge: Cambridge University Press, 1985). For further discussion of the short time horizon typically displayed in the political process, see chapter 1 of this volume.

4 Milton Friedman, "Monetary Policy: Theory and Practice," *Journal of Money, Credit, and Banking* 14 (February 1982): 102, 103, 118.

5 See John Woolley, *Monetary Politics* (New York: Cambridge University Press, 1984); and Robert Weintraub, "Congressional Supervision of Monetary Policy," *Journal of Monetary Economics* 4 (April 1978): 341–63.

6 See Alan Blinder, "Issues in the Coordination of Monetary and Fiscal Policies," in *Monetary Policy Issues in the 1980s* (Kansas City: Federal Reserve Bank of Kansas City, 1982), pp. 3–34. See also the comments by William Poole and James Tobin in the same volume, pp. 35–46.

7 See Thomas Mayer, "The Structure and Operation of the Federal Reserve System: Some Needed Reforms," in *Compendium of Papers Prepared for the Fine Study*, vol. 2 (U.S. Congress Committee on Banking, Currency, and Housing, 94th Cong., 2d sess., 1976), pp. 669–726.

8 For discussion of the recent report of the U.S. Gold Commission established by Congress, see Anna Schwartz, "Reflections on the Gold Committee Report," *Journal of Money, Credit, and Banking* 14 (March 1982): 538–51.

9 For recent evaluations of the gold standard experience and its relation to the more recent macroeconomic record, see, for example, the numerous contributions conveniently collected in Michael Bordo and Anna Schwartz, eds., *A Retrospective on the Classical Gold Standard, 1821–1931* (Chicago: University of Chicago Press, 1984); Barry Eichengreen, ed., *The Gold Standard in Theory and History* (New York: Methuen, 1985); Barry Siegel, ed., *Money in Crisis* (Cambridge, Mass.: Ballinger, 1984); and "The Search for Stable Money," *Cato Journal* 3 (Spring 1983). See also

chapter 7 of this volume, which argues that the postwar Bretton Woods period should be considered a regime of discretion rather than gold for the United States.

10 See Phillip Cagan, "Changes in the Recession Behavior of Wholesale Prices in the 1920s and Post World War II," *Explorations in Economic Research* 2 (Winter 1975): 54–103; and Jeffrey Sachs, "The Changing Cyclical Behavior of Wages and Prices," *American Economic Review* 70 (March 1980): 78–90.

11 Likely to be particularly undesirable are the recent supply-side proposals to gear monetary policy to short-term changes in gold or other commodity prices. See, for example, Marc A. Miles, *Beyond Monetarism* (New York: Basic Books, 1984). As has long been discussed in the economic literature, such short-term price rules are likely to be dramatically unstable. For recent critical analysis see C. Alan Garner, "Commodity Prices and Monetary Policy Reform," Federal Reserve Bank of Kansas City *Economic Review* (February 1985): 7–22; R. W. Hafer, "Monetary Policy and the Price Rule: The Newest Odd Couple," Federal Reserve Bank of St. Louis *Review* (February 1983): 5–13; and Karl Brunner, "Has Monetarism Failed?" *Cato Journal* 3 (Spring 1983): 23–62.

12 On the theory of optimum currency areas, see Edward Tower and Thomas D. Willett, *The Theory of Optimum Currency Areas and Exchange Rate Flexibility,* Special Papers in International Economics, no. 11 (Princeton: Princeton University, 1976); and for a specific application to the United States, see Thomas D. Willett, "United States Economic Interests in Crawling Peg Systems," in *Exchange Rate Rules,* ed. John Williamson (London: Macmillan, 1981). It should be noted that the rational expectations revolution does not undercut the traditional criteria of optimum currency areas as has sometimes been alleged in the recent literature. See Thomas D. Willett, "Macroeconomic Policy Coordination Issues under Flexible Exchange Rates," *Ordo: Jahrbuch für die Ordnung von Wirtschaft und Gesellschaft* 35 (1982): 137–49.

Ronald McKinnon has recently argued that because of international currency substitution, a gold standard–type rule for the United States to gear monetary policy to maintain a constant exchange rate would be desirable. See, for example, Ronald McKinnon, "Currency Substitution and Instability in the World Dollar Standard," *American Economic Review* 72 (June 1982): 320–33. However, the empirical evidence strongly suggests that international currency substitution has not been as important an influence on the United States as McKinnon's original analysis suggested and that changes in equilibrium real exchange rates are much too important for the United States to make this a desirable strategy. On these issues, see the analysis in Sven Arndt, Richard J. Sweeney, and Thomas D. Willett, eds., *Exchange Rates, Trade, and the U.S. Economy* (Washington, D.C.: American Enterprise Institute, 1985); Allan H. Meltzer, "Size Persistence and Interrelation of Nominal and Real Shocks: Some Evidence from Four Countries," *Journal of Monetary Economics* 17 (January 1986): 161–94; and Thomas D. Willett, "U.S. Monetary Policy and World Liquidity," *American Economic Review* (May 1983): 43–47.

13 See Alexandre Lamfalussy, "Rules versus Discretion: An Essay on Monetary Policy in an Inflationary Environment," Bank of International Settlements *Economic Papers,* no. 3 (April 1981).

14 Arthur B. Laffer, "Both Monetary Goals Can Be Met," *Los Angeles Times*, August 25, 1981, sec. 4, p. 3.

15 See, for example, Anatol B. Balbach, "How Controllable Is Money Growth?" Federal Reserve Bank of St. Louis *Review* 63, no. 4 (April 1981): 3–12. On the influence of the Eurodollar market and international currency substitution on U.S. monetary conditions, see Marvin Goodfriend, "Eurodollars," Federal Reserve Bank of Richmond *Economic Review*, May/June 1981, 12–19; Willett, "Monetary Policy and Liquidity"; and references cited in these works.

16 See Allan H. Meltzer, "Monetary Reform in an Uncertain Environment," *Cato Journal* 3 (Spring 1983): 93–112.

17 See Henry C. Simons, *Economic Policy for a Free Society* (Chicago: University of Chicago Press, 1948).

18 For a critique of the Graham plan, see Milton Friedman, "Commodity Reserve Currency," in *Essays in Positive Economics*, ed. Milton Friedman (Chicago: University of Chicago Press, 1952), pp. 669–726.

19 Robert Hall, "Explorations in the Gold Standard and Related Policies for Stabilizing the Dollar," in *Inflation: Causes and Effects*, ed. R. Hall (Washington, D.C.: National Bureau of Economic Research, 1982), pp. 111–22.

20 Ibid., p. 119.

21 Ibid., p. 121.

22 For discussion and references to the pro–currency competition literature, see White's chapter 19 in this volume. For critical analyses, see Milton Friedman and Anna Schwartz, "Has Government Any Role in Money?" *Journal of Monetary Economics* 17 (January 1986): 37–62; and chapter 18 of this volume. For discussion of proposals for indexing and basket currencies and separation of the medium of exchange and unit of account functions of money, see Leland B. Yeager, "Stable Money and Free Market Currencies," *Cato Journal* 3 (Spring 1983): 305–26.

23 We should note that the recent reinterpretations of the U.S. free banking era, while quite interesting, do not directly address the issue of the macroeconomic effects of monetary instability over this period, thus they are not necessarily inconsistent with some of the earlier analysis of the monetary instability of this period. See, for example, Thomas D. Willett, "International Specie Flows and American Monetary Stability, 1834–1860," *Journal of Economic History*, March 1968, 28–50.

24 While we believe that such considerations suggest that floating rates may in fact provide more discipline than pegged rates with no accompanying constraints on monetary policy, this discipline is unlikely to prove sufficient. For further discussion, see Thomas D. Willett and John Mullen, "The Effects of Alternative International Monetary Systems on Macroeconomic Discipline and the Political Business Cycle," in *Political Economy of International and Domestic Monetary Relations* (Ames: Iowa State University Press, 1982), pp. 143–59; and Thomas D. Willett, "A Public Choice Analysis of Strategies for Restoring International Economic Stability" (Paper presented at the Konstanz Conference on New International Arrangements for the World Economy, Konstanz University, 1987, forthcoming in conference volume).

25 See Arndt, Sweeney, and Willett, *Exchange Rates;* and Thomas D. Willett et al.,

"Currency Substitution, U.S. Money Demand, and International Interdependence," *Contemporary Policy Issues* 5 (July 1987): 76–82.

26 For a review of the development of monetary rules, see G. Macesich, *The Politics of Monetarism* (Totowa, N.J.: Rowman and Allanheld, 1984).

27 For discussions of the behavior of velocity, see John Judd and John Scadding, "The Search for a Stable Money Demand Function: A Survey of the Post-1973 Literature," *Journal of Economic Literature*, September 1982, 993–1023; and Federal Reserve Bank of San Francisco, *The Proceedings of the Conference on Monetary Targeting and Velocity* (San Francisco, December 4–6, 1983).

28 Some proposals also adjust for changes in real income growth. For an early proposal, see Martin Brofenbrenner, "Statistical Tests of Rival Monetary Rules," *Journal of Political Economy* 69 (February 1961): 1–14. For more recent ones, see Bennett T. McCallum, "Monetarist Rules in the Light of Recent Experiences," *American Economic Review*, May 1984, 388–91; Allan H. Meltzer, "Overview," in *Price Stability and Public Policy* (Symposium sponsored by the Federal Reserve Bank of Kansas City, Jackson Hole, Wyo., August 2–3, 1984), pp. 209–22; and Robert E. Weintraub, "What Type of Monetary Rule?" *Cato Journal* 3 (Spring 1983): 171–84.

29 For further discussions of this growth-rate rule, see Allan Meltzer, "The Limits of Short-Term Stabilization Policy," *Economic Inquiry* 25 (January 1987): 1–14; and Thomas Mayer, "Replacing the FOMC by a PC," *Contemporary Policy Issues* 5 (April 1987): 31–43.

30 See Jurg Niehans, *The Theory of Money* (Baltimore: Johns Hopkins University Press, 1978), chap. 12; Axel Leijonhufvud, "Constitutional Constraints on the Monetary Powers of Governments," in *Constitutional Economics*, ed. R. B. McKenzie (Lexington, Mass.: Lexington Books, 1984); and Thomas D. Willett, "A New Monetary Constitution," in *The Search for Stable Money: Essays on Monetary Reform*, ed. James Dorn and Anna B. Schwartz (Chicago: University of Chicago Press, 1987), pp. 145–60. Some proposals recommend using nominal income rather than prices as a medium-term target variable. For discussion of the relative merits of these two types of target variables, see Robert Barro, "Recent Developments in the Theory of Rules versus Discretion," Conference Papers, Supplement to *Economic Journal* 96 (1986): 23–37; and Robert Hall, "Macroeconomic Policy under Structural Change," in *Industrial Change and Public Policy* (Symposium sponsored by the Federal Reserve Bank of Kansas City, Jackson Hole, Wyo., August 24–26, 1983), pp. 85–112.

31 See Thomas Mayer, "Using the Constitution to Fight Inflation," *American Banker*, November 29, 1979, 11–12.

32 See Willett, "New Monetary Constitution."

33 Thomas Havrilesky, "A New Program for More Monetary Stability," *Journal of Political Economy* 80 (January/February 1972): 171–75.

34 Liberal political scientists and sociologists often object to the establishment of any type of economic rules as displaying a preference for market over political outcomes which conflicts with their hostility to the market. Thus, for example, Brian Barry in "Political Ideas of Some Economists," in *The Politics of Inflation and Economic Stagnation*, ed. Leon N. Lindberg and Charles S. Maier (Washington, D.C.: Brook-

ings Institution, 1985), refers to economists who advocate rules as "constitution mongers" (p. 316), and states boldly that "the workings of the market are not in fact conducive to the well-being of the majority of the population" (p. 31). In the concluding paper in the same volume, Charles Maier and Leon Lindberg, "Alternatives for Future Crises," pp. 567–88, the authors argue against rules on the grounds that "efforts to depoliticize the marketplace tend to be spurious. They usually entail a one-sided buttressing of profits and managerial prerogatives" (pp. 587–88). Apart from the particular political and economic views which such statements espouse, we believe that these authors fundamentally miss the mark by casting things in all-or-none terms: the market and rules versus the political process. While we share the views of most economists that the use of a market economy brings benefits to the vast majority of individuals, few economists favor complete laissez-faire. What we discuss is the role of government in a market economy. Likewise, all rules do not work the same. In the long run, we believe that the vast majority of people, workers and managers alike, are harmed by inflation and hence that efforts to establish a framework of rules to diminish inflationary tendencies need not have highly skewed long-run distributional effects.

35 Laurence Tribe, "Issues Raised by Requesting Congress to Call a Constitutional Convention to Propose a Balanced Budget Amendment," *Pacific Law Review* 10 (1979): 628–29.

36 Paul Samuelson, "Prepared Testimony," U.S. Congress, House Committee on the Judiciary, Subcommittee on Monopoly and Commercial Law, *Hearings,* March 27–28, May 17, June 12–13, October 11, 1979, and May 1, 1980, 96th Cong., 1st and 2d sess., pp. 21–22.

37 Examples include prohibition on interstate trade barriers, export taxes, and the issue of money by the states. On the Constitution's treatment of monetary issues and the changing legal interpretation of these provisions over time, see chapter 17 of this volume.

38 For further discussion of constitutional aspects of economic issues, see the contributions and references in Richard B. McKenzie, *Constitutional Economics* (Lexington, Mass.: Lexington Books, 1984), and Brennan and Buchanan, *Reason of Rules.*

17 Fiat Money and the Constitution: A Historical Review

Gregory B. Christainsen

The trifling economy of paper, as a cheaper medium, or its convenience for transmission, weighs nothing in opposition to the advantages of the precious metals . . . it is liable to be abused, has been, is, and forever will be abused, in every country in which it is permitted. . . .—Thomas Jefferson[1]

Introduction

With the arrival of the bicentennial of the U.S. Constitution, there is renewed, intense discussion of the original intentions of the Founding Fathers.[2] There is also much discussion as to whether existing policies and institutions are consistent with those intentions, and whether those intentions should govern us today. This paper examines constitutional arrangements with respect to money in light of renewed interest in so-called free banking. It is argued that *if* one takes an original-intent view of the Constitution, a reasonable case can be made that the most important powers and activities of the Federal Reserve system are unconstitutional. Even if there seems to be little chance that the current court system would strike at the very existence of the Federal Reserve system, those who want to add *new* monetary clauses to our Constitution might do well to look at what happened to the ones we already have.

The Founding Fathers' Original Intentions

There were, of course, many expressions of ambivalence about the Constitution at the time it was being written and debated.[2] The concept of "original intent" must therefore be forever nebulous to some degree. There can be little doubt, however, that broadly speaking the Constitution was originally intended to be a document for a classically liberal government in the spirit of philosophers such as Locke and Hume, of whom people like Madison were avid followers. Aside from providing a limited number of what economists today refer to as "public goods," it was argued that government should promote the ideal of the Rule of Law, of which the Anglo-Saxon common law was regarded as the imperfect embodiment. Even in its public goods activities, government was supposed to act in ways consistent with the Rule of Law in the sense that the goods provided were supposed to be truly "public" in nature, and the means of raising revenue were supposed to be nondiscriminatory. As long as private individuals acted in accordance with the Rule of Law, they were to be free to do as they pleased, with a system of markets evolving as a result of their actions.

In the sphere of money and banking, this classical liberal conception would, in the absence of special considerations, call for a system of "free banking." Individuals would be free to define whatever monetary units they liked, and to see what prices and quantities would obtain for these units in the marketplace—subject again, of course, to the law in the form of general rules regarding property (and torts) and contracts (and fraud).

Throughout history a variety of standards of value have been proposed and tried in the monetary marketplace—shells, salt, and, more commonly, metals such as gold, silver, and copper. Systems of convertible bank notes and other financial instruments have evolved on top of these standards of value. If the monetary marketplace were to be completely free, it is arguable that government should not even grant particular standards legal tender status, and it should certainly not manipulate the rates of exchange among different monies. Under the Rule of Law government would simply have the duty to enforce the real terms of whatever lawful contracts individuals willingly negotiated.[3]

The actual words that the Constitution contains regarding money can be given several conflicting interpretations if taken out of context, however. Under a variety of interpretations, the power of an agency such as the Federal Reserve to issue an intrinsically valueless, irredeemable currency with legal tender status—"fiat money"—appears perfectly legitimate. Article I, section 8 says that the Congress has the power "to coin money, regulate the value thereof, and of foreign coin, and fix the stan-

426 | Proposals for Reform

dard of weights and measures." Article I, section 10 says, "No state shall coin money, emit bills of credit; make any thing but gold or silver coin a tender in payment of debts."

Putting these words in a modern context, one could argue that article I, section 8 simply gives Congress authority over the money supply; "to coin money" may be interpreted simply to mean "to make money," of whatever form. If that section is also taken to mean that Congress is to have the power to try to manipulate exchange rates between domestic and foreign monies, there cannot be much question of the constitutionality of the most important present-day activities of the Federal Reserve, to whom Congress has delegated its alleged monetary authority.

In the same context, article I, section 10 may be interpreted as having put restrictions only on individual states. It does not by itself appear to limit the authority of *Congress* to "coin" money, emit "bills of credit," or declare something other than gold and silver to be legal tender.

In the context in which those words were written, however, their meaning is very different from that suggested above. The Constitutional Convention was called for the express purpose of revising the Articles of Confederation. Both the Constitution and the Articles of Confederation were, in turn, written in the context of eighteenth-century Anglo-Saxon common law, of which Sir William Blackstone was widely regarded as the most authoritative expositor. In this context, the phrase "to coin" has a narrower meaning than the phrase "to make." It means: "to fashion pieces of metal into a prescribed shape, weight, and degree of fineness, and stamp them with prescribed devices, in order that they may circulate as money."[4] In other words, in granting the power "to coin" money, the Constitution simply gives Congress the authority to operate mints. Article IX of the Articles of Confederation said: "The united states in congress assembled shall have the sole and exclusive right and power of regulating the alloy and value of coin struck by their own authority, or by that of the respective states."

The very word "money" was used in a narrower sense than it is today. In the latter half of the eighteenth century, the standard definition was "[m]etal coined for the purpose of commerce."[5] The word "dollar," which is used in a few places in the Constitution, was understood to refer to the silver Spanish milled dollar. After the Constitution was ratified the value of the dollar was set at 371.25 grains of fine silver, which, in turn, was declared to be legally equivalent to 24.75 grains of fine gold.[6] It would therefore not be incorrect to say that the United States had adopted a *silver* standard (the dollar) and a *bimetallic system*, with gold and silver trading at an official exchange rate of 15 to 1 (371.25 / 24.75).

Such a monetary system was consistent with the common law as enunciated by Blackstone, which declared only gold and silver to be legal tender.[7] Blackstone spoke of a metal as "most proper for a common measure, because it can easily be reduced to the same standard in all nations."[8] "The denomination, or the value for which . . . coin is to pass current, is . . . in the breast of the king. . . . In order to fix the value, the weight and fineness of the metal are to be taken into consideration together."[9] It should be noted here that Blackstone's "fix the value" is synonymous with the phrase "regulate the value" used in article I, section 8 of the Constitution.[10]

There should therefore be little doubt—and as we shall see, Supreme Court justices for at least the first one hundred years of the Constitution's reign had little doubt—that the provisions in article I, section 8 mentioned above were intended only to provide a means for certifying the lawful conversion of bullion into coin, thereby applying to money the same control Congress was given with respect to weights and measures generally.

A proper interpretation of section 10 of article I, which denies the states certain monetary powers, hinges on still other provisions of section 8. Under the Articles of Confederation (article IX), Congress had the explicit power "to borrow money or emit bills on the credit of the united states." Article I, section 8 uses the same language except that the phrase "or emit bills" was eliminated. It should be clear from a reading of James Madison that "bills" were to be distinguished from "notes."[11] In the usage of Madison and others of the time, the latter included fixed-term, interest-bearing obligations, while the former were payable on demand and usually interest free. Congress was thus given the power to issue notes and other securities in order to obtain credit, but it was not given the power to issue paper currency.

The first draft of the Constitution gave the legislature of the United States the power to "emit bills."[12] On August 16, 1787, however, the convention moved to strike this power from the Constitution,[13] and in Madison's account, "[s]triking out the words . . . cut off the pretext for a paper currency, and particularly for making the bills a tender either for public or private debt."[14] The Founding Fathers had seen the devastating effects of the fiat monies issued during their lifetimes.

Thus, article I, section 10 simply denies the states powers that had already been denied the federal government. On August 28, 1787, twelve days after the vote to deny Congress the power to issue fiat money, Roger Sherman, who in 1752 had fought to bar paper money in Connecticut, and Oliver Ellsworth, a key player in the August 16 debate, introduced the motion that ultimately carried.[15]

The Record of Legal Interpretation

Today, however, it is the official position of the U.S. Treasury that article I, section 10 denies the states the power to issue fiat money, but that, since there is no clause in the Constitution which *explicitly* prohibits Congress from issuing it, Congress may do so![16] Note the inversion here of the Constitution's Tenth Amendment. Whereas the Tenth Amendment reserves to the states those powers not expressly granted to the federal government, the Treasury's position is that, though fiat money powers were denied to the states, the federal government has such powers.[17]

The First and Second Banks of the United States, incorporated in 1791 and 1816, respectively, issued bills of credit early in the life of the new republic. These banks were set up to help manage the finances of the federal government, which owned about one-fifth of their stock. Under a strict interpretation of the Constitution, one might argue that their actions were therefore unconstitutional, but they were in fact run along essentially commercial lines. The banks' bills and other obligations were binding and enforceable against the respective corporations, not the U.S. government, and they were not legal tender for any private debt, or for any debt of the U.S. government; creditors could not be required to accept payments in the form of notes of these banks unless they had specifically contracted to do so. Moreover, the banks' directors were personally liable for excessive corporate debts, and they had no power to purchase public debt.

The chartering of such banks by the federal government was declared constitutional by the Supreme Court in *McCulloch* v. *Maryland*, decided in 1819. The case did not, however, speak directly to the constitutionality of fiat money.

It was left to the "greenbacks" issued to help finance the Civil War, and which claimed the status of legal tender, to provoke the litigation that determined the fate of paper money. *Hepburn* v. *Griswold,* decided in February 1870, was the first Supreme Court case that focused directly on the constitutionality of the greenbacks' claim to legal tender status. In the absence of legal tender status, creditors need not accept debased bills from debtors unless they carry some discount from their face value. Once vested with legal tender status, however, creditors must accept even undiscounted bills. In *Hepburn,* the Court ruled that a debtor could not discharge an $11,250 obligation incurred before the legal tender legislation by simply paying the creditor greenbacks whose combined face value matched the nominal debt owed. The debtor was told that she would instead have to pay the greenback value of 11,250 statutorily defined *gold* dollars, the view being that one greenback dollar had less real value than one gold dollar. Chief Justice Chase, the very man who as treasury secretary had lobbied for the issuance of the greenbacks after the onset of the Civil War, declared that the legal tender clause in the greenback legislation was unconstitutional with respect to debts incurred before the legislation was enacted.

In May 1871, however, in *Knox* v. *Lee,* the Court overturned the *Hepburn* decision and ruled that the legal tender clause in the greenback legislation *was* constitutional with respect to debts incurred *either* before or after the legislation was enacted. A change in the Court's composition[18] during the intervening fifteen months resulted in a five-to-four decision. Still, the majority opinion argued that "[t]he legal tender acts do not attempt to make paper a standard of value,"[19] and Justice Bradley's concurring opinion claimed that the greenback legislation "is a pledge of the national credit. It is a promise by the government to pay dollars; it is not an attempt to make dollars. The standard of value is not changed. . . . "No one supposes that these government certificates are never to be paid."[20]

The source of the power to emit bills of credit, whether or not they constituted legal tender, was never made clear, notwithstanding claims that the bills were essential to "government self-preservation" during a time of war. As already discussed, the Founding Fathers did not intend for Congress's borrowing power to extend to bills of credit. Chief Justice Chase declared in an earlier case that "it is settled by the uniform practice of the government and by repeated decisions, that Congress may constitutionally authorize the emission of bills of credit."[21] But no decision was ever cited in support of this contention.

In 1875 Congress passed the Resumption Act, which, among other provisions, required the redemption in coin of greenbacks presented after January 1, 1879. In 1878, however, new legislation was introduced restricting the withdrawal of greenbacks from circulation! The Treasury interpreted the 1878 legislation as giving it the authority to reissue greenbacks in denominations different from those it had previously redeemed. A creditor's refusal to accept greenbacks reissued after they had been earlier redeemed in gold coin led to *Juilliard* v. *Greenman*, decided by the Supreme Court in 1884. The U.S. Treasury and lower courts cite this decision to the present day in defense of fiat money.

In *Juilliard* the Supreme Court took the position that greenbacks with legal tender status could be issued whenever Congress chose, whether wartime or peacetime. The decision relied heavily on idiosyncratic views of two of the Constitution's clauses, the clause in article I, section 8 that grants Congress borrowing power, and the so-called Necessary and Proper Clause.[22] Justice Strong in *Knox* and Justice Gray in *Juilliard* endorsed Justice Marshall's (1819) interpretation of the latter clause. According to Marshall, "let the end be legitimate, let it be within the scope of the constitution, and all means which are appropriate, which are plainly adapted to that end, which are not prohibited, but consist with the letter and spirit of the constitution, are constitutional."[23] In his dissent in *Knox,* Justice Field noted that the clause "only states in terms what Congress would equally have had the right to do without its insertion in the Constitution."[24]

In a general sense, the scope of the Necessary and Proper Clause was thus *not* a point of contention in either *Knox* or *Juilliard*. Instead, the Supreme Court sought to find an already-acknowledged power (Congress's alleged borrowing power being one candidate) to which the Necessary and Proper Clause could be applied as support. In neither the *Juilliard* nor the *Knox* case did the Court claim that the power in article I, section 8 to "coin" money means that Congress has the power to "make" money in any form it likes.

Salmon Chase, first as treasury secretary, and then as chief justice of the Supreme Court, was sympathetic to the greenbacks' issuance in light of the exigencies of wartime finance. He spoke of the Constitution's permitting "all legislation essential to the prosecution of war with vigor and success."[25] In the peacetime circumstances of the *Juilliard* decision, the only additional claim that could be—and was—made is that the granting of legal tender status to the greenbacks was an *inherent* power of government—"one of the powers belonging to sovereignty in other civilized nations."[26] Furthermore, the Court opined that the conditions under which the Necessary and Proper Clause could be invoked were themselves a legislative rather than a judicial matter![27] Recall again, however, the Tenth Amendment. It was the framers' intent to limit the federal government to certain clearly enumerated powers; if the Constitution is silent about a particular power, the federal government does not have it.

Even the *Juilliard* case did not quite complete the victory of fiat money. The decision said that Congress could, in peacetime as well as wartime, emit bills with legal tender status, but it still did not relieve Congress of the responsibility for maintaining the ultimate redeemability of its issues in terms of specie.

The phrase "ultimate redeemability" is admittedly vague; the date of redemption can always be postponed under a liberal interpretation of Congress's borrowing authority. It is arguable, however, that the victory of fiat money was not really complete until June 1968, because only then did Congress declare that silver certificates, though legal tender, would no longer be redeemed by the federal government in silver, which was the Founding Fathers' original standard of value. As for gold, it was, of course, largely outlawed from private possession from 1934 to 1974.

In recent years no case challenging the monetary powers of the U.S. government has reached the Supreme Court, though there have been several challenges in lower courts.[28] In the 1980s, the state legislatures of Alabama and Washington have passed resolutions challenging the constitutionality of the Federal Reserve Act and the Federal Reserve's power to create money, respectively.[29]

Concluding Remarks

Perhaps the most important point to make in the context of modern-day concerns about political business cycles is that, in the long run, no constitution can be effective in promoting its authors' intentions in the absence of a consensus ideology that focuses the pressure of public opinion on those contemplating constitutional breaches. The usefulness of such an ideology is most obvious in cases such as that of article I of the U.S.

Constitution, the monetary clauses of which almost invite misinterpretation. Even in cases where constitutional rules seem clear-cut, a supporting ideology is essential in order to prevent misinterpretations by future generations, who may use words in a different way than we do. So while modern-day monetary reformers are to be applauded for their attempts to devise new constitutional rules conducive to a free and prosperous economy, we must realize that their efforts are necessary, but not sufficient.

Notes

1 *The Writings of Thomas Jefferson,* ed. Paul L. Ford (New York: G. P. Putnam's, 1898), 9:416.

2 For a more detailed discussion of this topic, and for additional leads to the relevant primary source material, see George Bancroft, *A Plea for the Constitution of the United States* (Sewanee, Tenn.: Spencer Judd, 1982); Kenneth W. Dam, "The Legal Tender Cases," *Supreme Court Review,* 1981, 367–412; Gerald T. Dunne, *Monetary Decisions of the Supreme Court* (New Brunswick, N.J.: Rutgers University Press, 1960); James Willard Hurst, *A Legal History of Money in the United States, 1774–1970* (Lincoln: University of Nebraska Press, 1973); Henry Mark Holzer, *Government's Money Monopoly* (New York: Books in Focus, 1981); F. A. Mann, *The Legal Aspect of Money,* 4th ed. (Oxford: Clarendon Press, 1982); Henry G. Manne and Roger L. Miller, *Gold, Money, and the Law* (Chicago: Aldine, 1975); Arthur Nussbaum, *Money in the Law* (Chicago: Foundation Press, 1939); and Edwin Vieira, *Pieces of Eight: The Monetary Powers and Disabilities of the United States Constitution* (Atlanta: Darby, 1983). See also Bernard H. Siegan, *The Supreme Court's Constitution* (New Brunswick, N.J.: Transaction Books, 1987), chap. 2.

3 Assuming the existence of taxes, government would also have to decide what media would suffice as payment of those exactions.

4 See *Black's Law Dictionary* (St. Paul: West Publishing, 1979), p. 236.

5 See, for example, Samuel Johnson, *A Dictionary of the English Language* (London: W. Strahan for J. and P. Knapton, 1755), and subsequent editions.

6 Vieira, *Pieces of Eight,* p. 98.

7 In a strict sense then, the monetary system established by the Founding Fathers was not one of "laissez-faire," insofar as it gave gold and silver a privileged status, and insofar as it set an official rate of exchange between them. One might argue, on the other hand, that the acceptance of gold and silver was so widespread that the codification into law of their acceptability in payment of debts—legal tender status—was justifiable. The establishment of an official exchange rate for gold and silver (15 to 1, in 1792) was less consistent with classical liberal principles.

8 William Blackstone, *Commentaries on the Laws of England* (New York: William E. Dean, 1838), 1:206.

9 Ibid., p. 208.

10 See the definition of "regulate" in *Black's Law Dictionary,* p. 1156.

11 See Max Farrand, ed., *Records of the Federal Convention* (New Haven: Yale University Press, 1937), 2:310. See also p. 309, where Gouverneur Morris makes the same distinction.

12 See Jonathan Elliot, *The Debates in the Several State Conventions, on the Adoption of the Federal Constitution, as Recommended by the General Convention at Philadelphia, in 1787* (Philadelphia: J. P. Lippincott, 1937), 1:226.

13 Ibid., p. 245.

14 Farrand, *Records of the Federal Convention*, p. 310. The vote was nine to two. Of the eleven delegates whose remarks Madison reported, ten clearly put forth the view (irrespective of how they voted on the motion) that striking the phrase in question would deny Congress any power, under any circumstances, to create paper money. The eleventh delegate, Nathaniel Gorham, did not make himself clear; he did, however, vote to strike the phrase in question. See Vieira, *Pieces of Eight*, pp. 72–75.

    Hurst observes that Charles Pinckney, a "framer" of the Constitution but not one of the voters on the above motion, said later that "if paper should become necessary, the general government still possess the power of emitting it," but it is worth noting that Pinckney was the one who submitted the draft of the Constitution from which the phrase in question was struck. See Hurst, *Legal History*, p. 15, and Elliot, *Debates*, p. 145.

15 "In short, although it may have been inconvenient to the proponents and constitutional defenders of legal tender paper money, it is difficult to escape the conclusion that the Framers intended to prohibit its use." Dam, "Legal Tender Cases," p. 389. Dam was formerly Harold J. and Marion F. Green Professor in International Legal Studies and Provost, University of Chicago.

16 Readers wanting a copy of a letter from an assistant treasury secretary to a U.S. senator on this matter should get in touch with the author.

17 According to Madison in *Federalist* 45, the powers of the federal government were to be "few and defined . . . exercised principally on external objects, as war, peace, negotiation and foreign commerce. . . ." As for the federal government's duty to "provide for the general welfare," fiat money was obviously not what the Founding Fathers had in mind. In fact, the clause got into the Constitution by accident because, in Madison's words, of "inattention to the phraseology occasioned doubtless by its identity with the harmless character attached to it." See Farrand, *Records of the Federal Convention*, vol. 3, p. 486.

18 President Grant's role here was very controversial. See Charles Fairman, *Reconstruction and Reunion* (New York: Macmillan, 1971), pp. 713–63.

19 *Knox* v. *Lee*, 79 U.S. 533.

20 Ibid., pp. 560–62.

21 *Veazie Bank* v. *Fenno*, 75 U.S. 548.

22 "The Congress shall have Power . . .[t]o make all Laws which shall be necessary and proper for carrying into Execution . . .[its enumerated] Powers."

23 *McCulloch* v. *Maryland*, 17 U.S. 316, 421. Quoted in 79 U.S. 539 and 110 U.S. 441.

24 *Knox* v. *Lee*, 79 U.S. 640.

25 *Ex parte Milligan*, 71 U.S. 139.

26   *Juilliard* v. *Greenman,* 110 U.S. 450.
27   Ibid.
28   Vieira, *Pieces of Eight,* pp. 295ff.
29   Ibid., p. 385.

18   Monetary Confidence, Privately
Produced Monies, and Domestic and
International Monetary Reform

Michael Melvin

I have now no doubt whatever that private enterprise, if it had not been
prevented by the government, could and would long ago have provided the public with a
choice of currencies, and those that prevailed in the competition would have prevented
both excessive stimulation of investment and the consequent periods of contraction.[1]

1. Introduction

Economic history indicates that monies have long been provided by governments. Recently, several monetary reform proposals have called into
question the desirability of this long-standing fact of economic life. The
introductory quote by Hayek is an excerpt from his widely discussed *Denationalization of Money* monograph. Following Hayek, several others
have contemplated similar issues and concluded that there are real gains
to be realized by the private production of money, particularly with regard
to the incentives that lead a money issuer to cause inflation. It will be
argued that the analysis of this issue may be faulty in several respects. It
is important to reconsider the determinants of confidence in money that
breed a tremendous inertia in monetary institutions that is not easily overcome in the short run. It is also important to realize the political realities
along with the economic realities. I believe that many writers have offered
utopian recommendations regarding the appropriate national and international monetary system.

Beyond the discussion of government monopoly versus privately
produced money, there are additional, closely related topics regarding in-

ternational monetary reform and the nature of competition between monies which will be addressed. It is my belief that the nature of competition between monies has been oversimplified or incorrectly analyzed by many researchers.

While Hayek has received much deserved attention, he was not the first nor the only writer in the late 1970s to consider the issue of competitive monies and the role of government. The question was first considered by Klein, and then later by Girton and Roper and by Vaubel.[2] These papers analyzed the historical acquiescence of the general public to governmental monopolies in money in the context of an analysis of current policy decisions. In a review of this literature, Edwards states that one must ask "why government monopoly of money issuance is necessary in the first place and why so few good answers are forthcoming."[3] Edwards suggests that Milton Friedman has argued that the government monopoly is necessary because competing money producers would have the incentive to issue money to the point where it becomes useless because "each firm maximizes its profits by increasing output to the point that the cost of producing the next unit threatens to exceed its market value. Since the cost of printing money is virtually zero, he argues that competitive supply would force the value of money to zero, at which point money is useless."[4] However, this argument by Friedman is really not applicable to the current debate regarding competing monies, as Friedman was explaining why competition in *homogeneous* monies is unworkable, and as Edwards himself is careful to point out, competing currencies must be distinguishable. The appropriate question concerns the reasons for government monopoly money given the possibility of competition among unique currencies. This is addressed in section 4 below.

The reform proposals of the 1970s and 1980s have often followed in the private money tradition of Hayek, elaborating and offering recommendations for a specific form of competitive money in a "free banking" system, some elements of which will be considered in section 4.[5] Yeager has suggested a variant of Hayek's system where private monies are convertible into gold not at fixed gold currency exchange rates, but by "whatever quantity [of gold] had a fixed purchasing power over the goods and services composing a specified bundle."[6] Related studies by Black, Fama, Greenfield and Yeager, and Hall have offered creative views of alternative competitive monetary systems.[7] Our goal is to analyze the applicability of this family of proposals and consider the real world implications for domestic and international monetary reform.

Let me be clear from the start that I don't object to removing impediments to private money, I just doubt that such schemes would succeed in achieving the benefits claimed by their proponents. Specifically, I argue that it is unlikely that privately produced money would displace government money. In this regard I am not alone. While my analysis is founded on the economic behavior of private market participants, Mundell considers the political realities and arrives at a similar conclusion. He argues, "Whatever the merits of a free enterprise competitive money are . . . , I do not see any political path through the transition to its enactment, and I must, therefore, discard the idea as a distraction more suitable for gardens of Utopia than for a world of *real politique,* where the proposal is not worth a 'Hayek.'"[8]

The analysis will be developed in the following manner: section 2 considers the nature of competition between monies including international currency substitution. In section 3 I analyze the determinants of confidence in money and show how institutional rigidity in money use is to be expected. Section 4 considers the implications of the foregoing analysis for privately produced monies. In section 5 I discuss alternative international monetary arrangements and the benefits from a dollar-based system. Finally, section 6 offers a summary along with my conclusions.

2. The Nature of Competition between Monies

In the policy discussions below, there is a presumption that demanders face choices between alternative monies. This section deals with the determinants of money demand in the competitive framework. Only after these determinants are understood can the policy problems be carefully addressed. It is often argued that switching between various currencies results primarily from inflation differentials, as money demanders substitute away from a high-inflation currency to a low-inflation currency. It is likely, however, that competition between alternative monies depends much less upon average inflation rates and more on the unpredictability of these rates. The average inflation rate is unlikely to be an important competitive force influencing the currencies of the major industrial countries because much of the money stock, broadly defined, yields a competitive rate of interest. Thus only non-interest-bearing, high-powered money should be expected to be demand sensitive to varying inflation rates. Since actual currency is such a small part of the domestic money supply and, in the international context, foreign holdings of a nation's high-powered money are usually trivial, both domestic and international currency substitution should be relatively unaffected by average inflation rates. This point has often been overlooked in political economy discussions of the seigniorage generated for the United States by the international roles of the dollar. Section 5 will explicitly consider this issue.

We refer to the relationship between inflation predictability and money demand as the "inflation uncertainty competitive effect." Earlier theoretical work on the effect of price predictability in a competing monies framework has indicated that increased price uncertainty has theoretically ambiguous effects on the demand for money.[9] The empirical work done in this area indicates that the effect of inflation variability on money demand depends upon whether we analyze moderate or high inflation cases. Klein finds a positive effect for the U.S. over the last century, Frenkel estimates a zero effect of uncertainty for the German hyperinflation, and Blejer finds a negative effect for the rapid inflation samples of postwar Argentina, Brazil, and Chile.[10] Cassese provides an interesting synthesis. He finds evidence (albeit weak) of a negative effect for three high-inflation countries—Argentina, Brazil, and Chile—along with evidence of a positive effect for three moderate-inflation countries that maintained exchange rates pegged to the U.S. dollar—El Salvador, Guatemala, and Honduras. These seemingly contradictory findings are consistent with the competing money framework developed by Klein, in that the relationship between money demand and price uncertainty should move from positive to zero to negative as the interest elasticity of money demand increases.[11] With a linear money demand curve, we would expect to be in a more elastic region during hyperinflation.

Since money demand studies have focused on domestic demand functions, it is not surprising to find little evidence regarding the competitive (negative) effect of inflation uncertainty on money demand outside of hyperinflations. However, the international demand for money services, in a context of competing international monies, is likely to be much more interest elastic than the domestic demand, so we would expect to find the competitive effect. Melvin finds evidence of international currency substitution on the basis of this inflation uncertainty competitive effect for the Western European nations.[12] The basic approach of such empirical tests is to modify the standard domestic money demand function to include proxies for inflation uncertainty. For example, in a recent study of Latin American switching between domestic currency and U.S. dollars, Melvin has estimated several money demand functions to test for the significance of changes in domestic inflation uncertainty relative to dollar inflation uncertainty.[13] Since the derivation of the money demand function is fully discussed by Melvin, we simply present a representative estimated function here. A quarterly money demand function for Bolivia over the 1973.1–1982.3 period, during which dollar deposits were allowed in Bolivian banks, is as follows (t = statistics in parentheses):

$$\log M^d = \underset{(4.47)}{3.60} + \underset{(2.09)}{.184 \log y} + \underset{(12.31)}{.941 \log P} - \tag{1}$$

$$\underset{(-1.91)}{.138 \log r} - \underset{(-4.69)}{.148 \ Q/Q_d}$$

$$\bar{R}^2 = .972 \quad SE = .081 \quad D.W. = 1.87 \quad \rho = \underset{(1.51)}{.27}$$

where M^d = real money demand, y = real income, P = price level, r = Bolivian interest rate; and Q/Q_d is the "quality" of peso balances relative to dollars as measured by the inflation uncertainty associated with each currency. The Q variables are created as the standard errors of moving first order autoregressive equations of the inflation rate. That is, the uncertainty at any period t is proxied by the standard error of the residuals of the AR process estimated over the previous 12 quarters. The coefficient of $-.148$ suggests that for every 1 percent increase in peso inflation uncertainty relative to dollar inflation uncertainty, the demand for pesos falls by approximately .15 percent—a value statistically significant from zero. As was mentioned above, domestic demand studies found little evidence regarding the competitive (negative) effect of inflation uncertainty on money demand outside of hyperinflations, but in a framework allowing for international substitutability between monies, there is significant evidence of the inflation uncertainty competitive effect for both Latin America and Western Europe.

Thus, there is some evidence for currencies competing on the basis of inflation stability in the portfolios of money demanders. Yet, as we will discuss below, such switching may occur largely with respect to the function of money as a store of value rather than as a medium of exchange.

Furthermore, it is unlikely that we should expect to observe significant currency substitutability outside of a regional framework like that provided in Western Europe or the United States and Latin America. So the evidence presented in support of the inflation uncertainty competitive effect should not be interpreted as suggestive of a high degree of competition between currencies in general. While it would be instructive to estimate equation (1) for a large set of countries in both a regional and interregional framework, such work is beyond the scope of this paper and is left for future researchers. I simply wish to offer empirical support for my claim at the beginning of this section that currencies will compete on the basis of the variability of inflation.

3. Monetary Confidence and Institutional Inertia

Proponents of international currency reforms often seem to assume a degree of competition between international monies that simply does not exist in the real world. While there is some evidence of substitutability between currencies within a region, the existence of competitive switching between dominant monies in general has not been empirically verified. One reason for rigidity in accepting new monies is the importance of consumer confidence in a money, i.e., the credibility of the money issuer in fulfilling explicit or implicit promises regarding supply. Monetary confidence cannot be created overnight merely by an announcement of a promise regarding future behavior. It must be built up gradually with successful performance over time. Economists have too frequently believed that money merely is whatever "society" (operationally defined as the relevant policymaker) wishes it to be. However, market participants require more than official assurances at a particular moment, as anyone who remembers the period preceding exchange rate adjustments during the fixed rate period knows. Demand depends upon the existence of consumer confidence in the money, and confidence creation is not a free good.

Building confidence in any particular "brand name money" may be considered as an investment in "brand name capital." This may be done by "guaranteeing" convertibility of money into commodities or high confidence monies so that the stocks of such commodities or monies held as reserves represents the confidence-creating investment. Thus, commodity money produces consumer confidence by placing a physical constraint on money production and hence on the possible unanticipated depreciation. But of course, convertibility guarantees are not the only way to produce confidence. We observe the major vehicle currencies in the world today as having "earned" that role by successful past performance. It is the importance of this past monetary behavior that implies the very gradual evolution of a currency to "high confidence" status. Thus, the introduction of a new brand name to the market, be it Europa, SDR, or whatever, involves selling costs analogous to those borne by a producer of consumer goods introducing a new product. Just as a purchaser of new automobile tires requires quality assurance in the form of a warranty or contractual obligation on the seller, the money demander seeks quality assurance from the new money supplier. Tires with a long reputation for sound performance will not find consumers as interested in legal quality guarantees, and so it is with monies. The fact that nominal fiduciary monies may be costlessly produced on the margin implies nothing about the marginal cost of creating real cash balances. The latter, of course, refers to the confidence-creating or selling costs needed to build real balances.

Historical evidence suggests that monetary confidence and new dominant monies evolve very slowly in the marketplace and are not easily substitutable once established. In other words, the historical evidence suggests that the switching of the public to a new medium of exchange appears to be highly inelastic with respect to the currency's inflation rate. Even in the extreme cases of the post-World War I hyperinflations, individuals did not switch heavily to competing currencies.[14] Although individuals often reduced their real holdings of the inflating currency, competing currencies were not widely held as alternative media of exchange.

It is important here to make the distinction between the use of money as a store of value and the use of money as a medium of exchange. It is clear that during hyperinflations large quantities of foreign currencies (e.g., dollars and pounds) were illegally held as stores of value.[15] It is likely that such large amounts of foreign exchange were held not only because they were a hedge against inflation (any unregulated interest-bearing foreign or domestic asset could have served this function better) but also because the hyperinflating countries happened to be politically unstable. In this sort of climate, it is understandable that individuals would wish to be uncharacteristically liquid in a stable country's currency. In any event, foreign monies were not held in these cases to satisfy a medium-of-exchange demand for money.

4. Natural Monopoly Implications for Privately Produced Monies

Many arguments have appeared to support the case for government monopoly in money production. Gurley and Shaw and Patinkin have argued that competitive private production would yield an indeterminant price level.[16] Friedman, Pesek and Saving, and Johnson have argued that competitive private production of nondistinguishable money is inflationary and could lead to an infinite price level.[17] In addition, there are arguments reviewed by Vaubel related to money issuance as an efficient source of government revenue, economies of scale in money production or use, and externalities related to the public good aspects of money as a unit of account and medium of exchange.[18]

As emphasized in Klein and Melvin, it is important to consider the costs involved in money issuance to best understand the natural monopoly aspects of money production.[19] The confidence-creating selling costs associated with creating real balances are generally fixed costs such as holding stocks of precious metals or high confidence currencies, maintaining an army, purchasing an impressive marble building, or spending resources in any fashion that allows the creation of the equilibrium level of confidence. The marginal production costs of increasing real balances are negligible. Thus, we have a familiar economic problem in that setting price equal to marginal cost gives us a price less than average cost so that there is a short-run profit incentive to overissue. The large fixed cost and small or zero marginal cost of creating money suggests that the money industry is essentially a natural monopoly or that it is economically efficient for there to be a single money within a trade area.

Vaubel points out that even if the money industry is a natural monopoly, there is no justification for restrictions on entry, and certainly no reason why government, in particular, should be granted the monopoly.[20] If a competitive situation were allowed, we would observe the market determination of the optimal money—"Only if a governmental producer of money can prevail in conditions of free entry and without discriminatory subsidies is he an efficient natural monopolist."[21] The point I wish to argue is that we should expect the government to prevail in the competition. We observe government-produced money, not just because of barriers to entry, but also because government-produced money can have attributes which contribute to social efficiency in the sense of reducing the social cost of producing real money balances. The world has long been characterized by dominant monies produced by governments. Hayek (and others) wonders "why people should have put up for so long with governments exercising a power over 2,000 years that was regularly used to exploit and defraud them."[22]

The key to the puzzle is gained by first realizing the natural monopoly aspects of money production given by the high fixed costs and small marginal costs associated with producing real money balances. The creation of positive real balances is made possible by consumer confidence in money. The creation of such confidence generally involves fixed costs to the money producer such as holding stocks of precious metals or employing responsible people. The importance of these fixed costs can be illustrated by the following analysis. If P_N represents the price of a unit of nonpecuniary money services (N) and P is the price of goods in terms of the money (M) in question, then the real rental price of a unit of money services produced by M is

$$P_N/P = (i - r_M)/[(dN/dM)P], \tag{2}$$

where dN/dM is the marginal product of M in producing money services, and $(i - r_M)$ represents the difference between the return on a bond yielding nonpecuniary money services (i) and the return on money (r_M). The term $(i - r_M)$ represents the opportunity cost of holding a unit of money, and in equilibrium, will equal the value of nonpecuniary services provided by a marginal unit of M.

If monetary confidence is costless to produce, then competition between the private money producers should result in

$$(i - r_M) = dC/d(M/P),$$

where the right-hand term is the marginal cost of producing real balances. However, if confidence creation involves fixed costs incurred by the firm, then

$$(i - r_M) > dC/d(M/P)$$

will result in the firm earning a normal return on its confidence-yielding investments. In the competitive money industry, firms should face a perfectly elastic demand schedule with respect to the real rental price of money services, as defined in equation (2). This indicates that if the firm follows a policy resulting in the erosion of consumer confidence, so that the productivity of this money is reduced (or dN/dM falls), $(i - r_M)$ will also fall to maintain the constant real rental price of money services.

But $(i - r_M)$ is an important element in the determination of the seigniorage earned by the competitive firm. In any period, if the marginal cost of producing real balances equals zero, then $(i - r_M)(M/P)$, represents the real seigniorage to the money producer from the existing stock of real balances. But of course this is not the only way in which seigniorage can be generated. By increasing money growth faster than anticipated, a current transfer of resources to the money producer is realized. If $\dot{M}$ represents the actual growth of the money stock (in percentage per annum), and $\dot{P}^*$ the expected inflation rate, then the real revenue from current money creation is equal to

$$[\dot{M} - \dot{P}^*](M/P)_0,$$

where $(M/P)_0$ represents beginning of period balances.[23]

With costly information, so that there exist lags in adjusting expectations to current money growth,

$$d\dot{P}^*/d\dot{M} < 1, \tag{3}$$

and the lower the adjustment of expectations, the greater the potential gain to the producer from unexpectedly increasing $\dot{M}$. As the potential gain from such a policy of deception increases, we should expect the market to respond as consumers will demand greater quality assurance. The competitive money producer will invest in the confidence backing his brand name up to the point where the marginal cost equals the increase in the present value of the seigniorage resulting from the money issued. Therefore, if the producer return from unexpectedly large money surprises is great, then the return to producing high-quality money must be commensurately high to allow sufficient seigniorage on existing balances to forestall any such surprises.

Specifically, if the money producer promises to increase the money stock at an annual rate of g percent, consistent with a stable rate of inflation $\dot{P}^*$, then the present value of the future stream of seigniorage (discounted at rate i) is represented by

$$V = (M/P)_0 \int_0^t e^{(i-r_M)t}\, e^{-i_t}\, e^{g_t} dt = (M/P)_0 \int_0^t e^{(g-r_M)t}\, dt, \qquad (4)$$

where $(M/P)_0$ is beginning period real balances. Equation (4) suggests that $(g - r_M) > 0$ will be required to insure producer performance, especially when we consider that the alternative for the producer is to follow a deceptive policy where $\dot{M} > g$.

Private money producers will produce the kind of stable-valued, high-confidence money desired by Hayek and others if

$$(M/P)_0 \int_0^t e^{(g-r_M)t} dt > \alpha[\dot{M} - \dot{P}^*](M/P)_0. \qquad (5)$$

So if the present value of the future stream of seigniorage resulting from issuing money at the promised rate g exceeds the returns from a one-time deception in the current period, we would expect to see privately produced high-confidence monies. We haven't observed such monies in the past due to the costs of detecting current cheating, as $(d\dot{P}^*/d\dot{M}) < 1$ as in (3). These costs suggest that the potential short-run gain from a one-shot overissue will be quite high, so that the right-hand side of (5) will be large. But if the right-hand side is large, it follows that the left-hand side must be larger still. Thus it appears that the private unregulated contractual solution would imply a very high "premium" or seigniorage to assure producer performance.

Klein and Leffler analyzed the role of market forces in assuring contractual performance and state that the quality-assuring price "can be thought of as 'protection money' paid by consumers to induce contract performance."[24] The fact that the private contractual solution yields an extremely high equilibrium return for the producer implies that the government production of money may be more efficient. Klein and Leffler argue that "when explicit contract costs are high and the extent of short run profit from deceptively low quality supply and hence the quality assuring price premium is also high, vertical integration may be the cheapest arrangement."[25] For the money industry, vertical integration in the sense of government-supplied money is the standard solution. In this industry the costs of individually contracting for privately produced high-quality money are prohibitive. The essentially zero marginal cost of money production, along with the high cost of the prepurchase determination of quality for a particular money (it would be difficult for the individual demander to determine a money producer's deception), implies a large potential for cheating and thus a large quality-assuring price premium. It is this large premium required by private producers of a quality money that suggests that quality is realized more cheaply through government production.

Monetary reform advocates who believe that the public would quickly embrace a private money alternative to government-produced money are ignoring the realities of the market. Any money will have its ultimate usefulness dependent on public confidence in the monetary unit. The fact that private money issuers promise to maintain convertibility of their money into specie does not invalidate our analysis. These money issuers will pay to maintain large stocks of gold in order to build confidence in their money. In his free banking proposal White recognizes the importance of credibility of the issuing bank when he says, "It is one thing to print up notes and to *initiate* their circulation; it quite another to *maintain* their circulation in a competitive environment."[26] White considers three areas of importance in maintaining the circulation of a firm's notes: (1) Firms will compete in terms of ease of note redemption by offering longer hours, more branches, and the like. (2) Firms may offer interest-bearing notes to encourage their use. (3) Firms must convince the public of their reliability. This third area is the one we emphasize as leading to the greater efficiency of government-issued money. According to White,

> under a system of private bank notes convertible at par into specie, the primary aspect of reliability is the assurance that convertibility will not be delayed or denied on account of the bankruptcy, illiquidity, or fraud of the issuing bank. Confidence-bolstering expenditures would include construction and maintenance of an impressive bank edifice, publicity of the bank's sound financial health, "image" advertising and whatever else might reassure note-holders that theirs are not the notes of a fly-by-night outfit.[27]

It is the presence of such costs—largely fixed costs—which lead to the large quality-assuring premium required by private issuers. Do reformers believe that such costly "confidence-bolstering expenditures" can be provided without a commensurate payment to the private money issuer?

In chapter 19 of this volume White argues that no natural monopoly arises from the money producer incurring large fixed, relative to marginal, costs. His reasoning is that the money issuer's confidence capital "would seem to be proportional to the real money balances he has in circulation, because his potential gain from cheating is proportional to his existing circulation."[28] White suggests that the gold stock backing the money must rise in proportion to the money in circulation, so marginal costs are high. However, this seems untrue. All the money issuer must do is create confidence initially and sustain this confidence. Such confidence creation would seem to be produced by an initial large investment by the money issuer followed by prudent behavior. Ironically, White supports this argument when he later states "note holders have no need to observe the size of the gold reserve so long as they feel assured of continued redeemability."[29]

Regarding the historical evidence, private money supporters often refer to the free banking episodes in the United States and Scotland as supportive examples. As a most eloquent spokesman, White has used the Scottish experience to take issue with my assertion that the costs of individually contracting for privately produced high-quality money are prohibitive. He states, "Redemption contracts, as carried on the faces of private bank notes during historical episodes for free banking . . . are cheap to write and enforce. A note holder denied redemption can simply be granted a lien against the issuing bank."[30] This is a very naive argument in support of contracting for high-quality money. How does the promise to redeem a private bank note differ from a promise to redeem a corporate bond or honor any other private contractual agreement? Bonds sell at a discount that, in part, reflects a default risk premium. Does the promise to redeem a bond guarantee a high quality bond? If I join a health spa, does the spa's contractual promise to provide services for a future period guarantee the provision of these services? Of course not. Health spas have often closed and defaulted on their contracts, even while selling new memberships up to the time of closure. Bonds have become worthless, even though the bond certificate still promises redemption. If White and others wish to argue that private money contracts differ in some relevant way from other private contractual arrangements, they have yet to establish the argument. The simple promise of redemption does not guarantee high-quality money. Furthermore, the fact that such promises were honored in eighteenth-century Scotland may not be relevant for twentieth-century financial markets. Enforceability is not the issue. The bankruptcy courts handle a large volume of private, enforceable contracts daily. Unless the private money issuer receives a sufficient premium to exceed the gain from a deceptive overissue, we should expect contract defaults. Since this premium is likely to be high, we will observe government-issued money emerging as a more efficient solution.

The long history of governmental monopoly in money production is not the result of societal ignorance. The "need" for this monopoly power is not a "myth," as Hayek suggests, that has become "so firmly established that it did not occur even to the professional students of these matters ever to question it."[31] A private solution to the production of money could, no doubt, be established. Such a solution could also yield the high-confidence, stable-valued money desired by Hayek and others, but only at a very high cost. Thus in my judgment, the history of money production observed over the past two thousand years is likely due more to economic efficiency than to two thousand years of ignorance or coercion.[32]

5. International Monetary Arrangements

In previous sections the argument is developed as to why we would expect government money to potentially be more efficient than privately produced money. The analysis of section 4 was largely couched in terms of the domestic economy, but the foregoing analysis offers insights into international monetary reform as well. In this section we will explicitly consider the implications of our analysis for multicountry monetary arrangements.

First, we consider the implications for currency unions, the best example being the European Monetary System, or EMS. The natural monopoly aspects of money production suggest that it is economically efficient for there to be a single money within a trade area. Vaubel recognizes this when he says, "Since it is, finally, undisputed that lines of production that are subject to permanently declining cost must at some stage be nationalized (or in the international context, be unified), the fact that currency competition will lead to currency union must be regarded as desirable."[33]

The large economic gains from a common money indicate the potential benefits offered by European monetary union. But if effective European monetary coordination is to exist, a dominant money is necessary. If this money is not to be the mark, the obvious alternative is the dollar. The essential economic benefit of a monetary union could readily be obtained by fixing convertibility of each of the European national currencies at a given exchange rate into a dominant U.S. dollar and permitting denominations of European bank deposits in dollars. Had the United States not produced unexpected increases in the dollar money supply in the late 1960s and 1970s, the postwar trend toward such an international dollar standard would perhaps have continued.

Mundell points out that the political push for a substitute European monetary unit has proceeded very unevenly. Periods characterized by unstable U.S. policy rekindle interest in a Europa currency, but "European monetary integration seems to unravel whenever the Federal Reserve moves to or stumbles onto adept monetary policy. As long as the dollar provides a satisfactory international medium and the Federal Reserve good monetary leadership, taking into account external consequences of its action on the exchange rates and the price of gold, the other powers seem content to accept U.S. monetary leadership."[34] It is easy to understand why the European authorities' interest in developing a Europa currency falls with an increasingly stable dollar. A dollar standard, in a sense, gives the Europeans the best of both worlds. They have some of the major benefits of a unified currency area without having to give up the seigniorage on the domestic currency stock which a parallel European currency may largely require. A Europa currency would likely create a seigniorage flow that would be used to finance the European Community's expenses rather than accrue for the discretionary use of individual nations. Even if seigniorage should not be viewed as part of a theoretically optimal tax policy, real-world events suggest that many governments view seigniorage as a useful source of short-run revenue.[35] Therefore, during periods of dollar stability, the EMS seems to work quite well in the eyes of most European officials—as long as the dollar provides a stable anchor for their currencies, why incur the costs of moving to a parallel European currency? It is no accident that from May 1983 to July 1985 the EMS set a record for exchange rate stability. The prevailing strength of the dollar and the concurrent attractiveness of the United States as a haven for short-term, speculative capital flows relative to West Germany allowed the EMS to experience a record number of days without a currency realignment.

However, what if U.S. monetary policy became unstable again? What would then happen to the dollar in terms of its role in world finance? First we should acknowledge that the dollar gained its dominant international position, as sterling before it, not by legalistic coercion, but voluntarily in the marketplace. The combination of past and prospective performance induced the world to demand dollars as an international money. It is this same past and prospective performance criteria that can cost the dollar, as it did sterling, its dominant position.

Since past performance largely determines confidence in monies, it is not surprising that the poor performance of the dollar in recent decades has not eroded the dollar's dominant position.[36] In terms of the analysis of this article, the dollar has not seriously depreciated its "brand name capital" yet, but the fortunes of the pound remind us that this position is hardly a perpetual right.

An important question is, Which currency would substitute if we wanted to reduce the dollar's role? Heller and Knight's data indicate that the mark has risen in terms of official reserve portfolio share. We know that the Swiss franc has been a popular currency due to its stability, but can we expect either of these currencies to assume the role of dominant money?

The fact that the Germans, Japanese, and Swiss have resisted this movement is evidence of perhaps two phenomena. First, the dominant money producer with a large domestic relative to foreign sector finds that international shifts in demand for its money will have small repercussions on domestic operations relative to the effects a more open economy would face. Second, the seigniorage return to being the dominant international money must be small, at least relative to the costs imposed on the country.

Regarding the seigniorage issue, the fact that we have not observed countries competing for the role of dominant money seems to provide evidence that the seigniorage return is low. Fischer's estimates of seigniorage as a fraction of total government revenue (including seigniorage) average approximately 6 percent for the industrial countries over the 1960–78 period. However, since this is an unweighted average, it is a misleading indicator of the seigniorage accruing to the reserve currency countries. For the industrial countries, seigniorage as a fraction of total government revenue ranged from approximately 10 percent for Italy to 1.9 percent for the United Kingdom and 2.1 percent for the United States. If one looks outside the industrial countries, the figure ranges as high as 46 percent for Argentina. So while seigniorage has been a very important source of government revenue in some countries, this does not appear to be true for the dominant currencies.

Of course, what is relevant for being an international money producer is not the seigniorage earned from domestic money holdings but rather the seigniorage resulting from foreign holdings of the money. Since foreign holdings of a dominant money would likely include a large stock of interest-bearing deposits relative to actual currency, it is rather difficult to estimate seigniorage from any past international holdings of a dominant money like the U.S. dollar. The problem is compounded further by the existence of the Eurodollar market. Such offshore market balances have no reserve requirement and so have almost trivial backing in terms of U.S. high-powered money. The result is a very large stock of U.S. dollar denominated deposits which yield no seigniorage return to the United States.

Equation (4) stated the expression for the present value of the real future stream of seigniorage. The present value of the nominal seigniorage accruing to the money producer in any particular year may be expressed as

$$ S = M_0 \int_0^t e^{(i - r_M - c)}_t \, e^{-i}_t \, dt, \tag{6} $$

where c is the cost of producing money (assumed equal to zero in [4]). If we focus on the most likely international money producer, the United States, most of the international holdings of dollar denominated money balances are in the form of interest-bearing deposits as mentioned above. If these deposits are yielding a competitive rate of interest so that $r_M + c = i$, then the flow seigniorage from such holdings equals zero. It would seem likely that the only way a significant seigniorage return could be earned from producing an international money is if countries chose to follow a process of dollarization as discussed by Fischer. We would only expect a country to adopt a foreign money as a last resort in a situation where the domestic authority has lost all hope of effectively controlling the domestic money stock. In such an extreme case, what could the United States expect to earn from such foreign holdings of dollars?

Assuming that $r_M = c = 0$ for currency, equation (6) is modified to

$$S = C \int_0^t e^{it} e^{-it} \, dt = C, \tag{7}$$

where C represents issued currency holdings. So equation (7) reduces to $S = C$, or the nominal value of seigniorage is equal to the outstanding stock of currency held abroad. We may estimate the potential flow rate of seigniorage as

$$\dot{C} = \varepsilon_y \dot{y} + \varepsilon_p \dot{P}, \tag{8}$$

where $\dot{C}$, $\dot{y}$, and $\dot{P}$ represent percentage changes in currency holdings, real income, and the price level, respectively; ε_y is the income elasticity of currency demand; and ε_p the price elasticity. Theory as well as past empirical evidence suggests that $\varepsilon_p = 1$, $\varepsilon_y = \frac{1}{2}$ are reasonable values.

Suppose Mexico adopted the U.S. dollar for domestic use.[37] If $\dot{P}$ equals the average Mexican inflation rate over the 1976–81 period of 22 percent and similarly $\dot{y}$ is the average growth of real GDP of 6 percent, then using these values along with the elasticities discussed from (8) we find the average change in currency balances to be 25 percent (the actual change in peso currency balances over the 1977–81 period equals 29 percent). Applying this growth rate to the dollar equivalent of peso currency balances outstanding in 1981 implies a flow seigniorage return to the United States of approximately $2.9 billion, which is less than .5 percent of total U.S. government revenue for this period. It must be realized that such an estimate represents a maximum seigniorage return and almost certainly overstates any realistic outcome.[38]

We have not observed any complete dollarization, and it seems unlikely that a country with an established national currency would allow its currency to be completely replaced by the dollar. Thus for any single country, one would adjust downward the seigniorage return given by equation (8) according to the fraction of total currency use the dominant international money would likely take. We would also not expect $\dot{P}$ to be as high as the Mexican experience. If there were complete dollarization, then the U.S. inflation rate would be the relevant $\dot{P}$. Furthermore, the key variable for the international money producer contemplating alternative policies is the *expected* seigniorage return from maintaining a given level of quality associated with the dominant money. Therefore, equation (8) should properly be considered in a probabilistic setting, so that we discount the outcome of (8) to arrive at the expected value. Considering the very low prior probabilities most would attach to the prospects of a dominant money gaining a significant share of any nation's currency balances, it seems obvious that the expected seigniorage return to maintaining a high-confidence international money is quite low. In this case, recent action by the United States (and the United Kingdom before it) of disinvesting or consuming part of its monetary confidence capital may be a wealth-maximizing policy.

Since there is plausible evidence that countries have not been competing for reserve currency status, it is understandable that the European nations have considered the formation of an alternative system. Had the United States maintained the monetary confidence it had invested in the dollar, there would have been little incentive to ever discuss the creation of a European currency. Suppose the members of the EMS adopt a parallel currency called the Europa. What are the prospects for such a currency? Some advocates of the Europa believe that since the currency is to be price indexed and hence inflation-proof, it will quickly drive the European national currencies out of circulation. Historical evidence suggests this will not be the case because monetary confidence and new dominant monies evolve very slowly in the marketplace and are not easily substitutable once established. The analysis presented in this paper suggests that proponents of international currency reforms often seem to assume a degree of competition between international monies that simply does not exist in the real world.

If we assume that alternative monies (including a newcomer like the Europa) are perfect substitutes, then the pronouncements of the Europa's supporters would of course come true. While the degree of substitution between currencies is an empirical question, the nonpecuniary factors determining the choice of currency used are likely to be nontrivial across countries. The analysis of the potential attractiveness of a European parallel currency which largely considers differential yields on alternative monies to reach a conclusion of rapid and wide acceptance completely ignores the overwhelming empirical evidence on the degree of inertia that historically is present in these matters, as discussed in section 3.

One can see similarities between arguments supporting the creation of a European currency and the arguments that led to the creation of SDRs. Beside making the assumption that "money is merely what society wants it to be," the proponents of SDRs were also implicitly assuming that the IMF had unlimited brand name or monetary confidence capital. The key theoretical point is that real SDRs, like the real value of any new European parallel currency, cannot be merely "created outright," i.e., net wealth cannot be created out of nothing. Thus, we should not make the utopian assumption that institutional and informational constraints can be altered costlessly or that a money, especially a newly proposed money, possesses unlimited monetary confidence and that its demand and market share will therefore depend solely on its current price or the inflation rate in terms of the money.

6. Summary and Conclusions

Monetary reform involves political as well as economic concerns. Practical reform proposals must consider the political implications of economic actions and consequences. In this chapter the nature of competition between monies has been analyzed with a goal of understanding why government-produced money is likely to dominate privately issued money. This competitive focus also is relevant for analyzing existing and potential international monetary relationships. Competition between alternative international monies does not occur primarily on the basis of average inflation rates but rather on the basis of the predictability of these rates. While empirical evidence of this inflation uncertainty competitive effect exists in a regional framework, it does not follow that what is used as the medium of exchange in a country is quite sensitive to inflation uncertainty. Most likely, any competitive switching among monies will be in terms of the function of money as a store of value. Historical evidence suggests that what is used as the medium of exchange is invariant over a wide variety of inflationary experiences.

A major reason for the slow acceptance of new monies is the importance of consumer confidence in a money or, specifically, confidence in the credibility of the money producer regarding future supply. Since the confidence-creating selling costs associated with creating real balances are generally fixed costs, the money industry is essentially a natural monopoly. Given the declining-cost nature of money production, competitive money producers would have an incentive to overissue money unless they earned sufficient seigniorage to insure a policy of providing a stable-valued money. Since the private unregulated supply of money would require an extremely high seigniorage, the government production of money may be more efficient. This is not an argument against allowing privately produced money. If government-issued money could not survive in competition, then it should not survive. I have no problems allowing private money, but I believe government money would emerge as the more socially efficient. This does not imply that the current arrangement of discretionary monetary policy is necessarily the optimum. The current monetary framework could be dominated by alternative government schemes such as a monetary rule.

The last section considers various international monetary arrangements. While the dollar is clearly the world's major currency, it is recognized that the dollar gained its dominant international position voluntarily in the marketplace, and this same market can take away the dominance (as it did with sterling). If the dollar did seriously lose favor, it is not at all clear what would replace it, as we have not seen countries competing for the dominant currency position. Two distinct reasons are offered why other countries have resisted the assumption of a larger reserve currency role. First, the dominant money producer with a fairly open economy will find that international shifts in the demand for its money will have large repercussions on domestic operations. Second, the seigniorage return for being the dominant international money must be small, at least relative to the costs imposed on the country. This suggests that the German, Japanese, and Swiss policies of discouraging the international use of their currencies should be expected to continue. The large size and relatively closed nature of the vast U.S. domestic markets compared to any other nation make the United States the natural dominant money producer. It is safe to say that the major reserve currency status of the dollar was conferred by the market and not mandated by government decree. The decline of sterling and rise of the dollar was a market response to the performance of the two currencies and the changing relative position of

9   The two effects of an increase in price uncertainty (which lowers the "quality" or monetary service stream from money) are (1) an increase in the demand for money necessary to produce any given monetary service flow (the substitution in production effect) and (2) a decrease in the demand for money due to an increase in the implicit price of monetary services (the competitive complementarity in consumption effect). For the seminal work in this area, see Benjamin Klein, "The Competitive Supply of Money," *Journal of Money, Credit, and Banking* 6 (1974): 243–58; and idem, "The Demand for Quality-Adjusted Cash Balances: Price Uncertainty in the U.S. Demand for Money Function," *Journal of Political Economy* 85 (1977): 691–716.

10 Klein, "Quality-Adjusted Cash Balances"; Jacob A. Frenkel, "The Forward Exchange Rate, Expectations, and the Demand for Money: The German Hyperinflation," *American Economic Review* 67 (1977): 653–70; and Mario I. Blejer, "The Demand for Money and the Variability of the Rate of Inflation: Some Empirical Results," *International Economic Review* 20 (1979): 545–49.

11 Anthony Cassese, "The Variability of Inflation and the Demand for Money under Different Monetary Regimes" (Paper presented at the meeting of the Western Economic Association, San Diego, June 1980).

12 Michael Melvin, "Currency Substitution and Western European Monetary Unification," *Economica* 52 (1985): 79–91.

13 Michael Melvin, "The Dollarization of Latin America: A Market Enforced Monetary Reform," *Economic Development and Cultural Change*, forthcoming, 1988.

14 Of the seven hyperinflations studied by Cagan, only for 1923 Germany did substantial amounts of unauthorized currencies issued by local governments and private organizations circulate. But, surprisingly, these illegal substitute currencies were dominated in the hyperinflating unit. See Phillip Cagan, "The Monetary Dynamics of Hyperinflation," in *Studies in the Quantity Theory of Money*, ed. Milton Friedman (Chicago: University of Chicago Press, 1950). Also, Barro's estimates of the fraction of transactions conducted without domestic money during hyperinflation, that is, conducted with a substitute money or barter, are quite low. For example, at an inflation rate of 10 percent per month this fraction was only 0.05. See Robert Barro, "Inflationary Finance and the Welfare Cost of Inflation," *Journal of Political Economy* 80 (1972): 978–1001.

15 In Frank K. Graham, *Exchange, Prices, and Production in Hyperinflation: Germany, 1920–1923* (Princeton: Princeton University Press, 1930), and Constantine Bresciani-Turroni, *The Economics of Inflation* (New York: Kelley, 1968), the ratio of foreign to domestic real money holdings in Germany in October 1923 is estimated to be between five and thirteen to one. Although reported estimates vary a great deal from month to month and are rather unreliable, these figures should give us some general idea of the large magnitude of foreign currencies held.

16 John G. Gurley and Edward S. Shaw, *Money in a Theory of Finance* (Washington, D.C.: Brookings Institution, 1960); and Don Patinkin, "Financial Intermediaries and the Logical Structure of Monetary Theory," *American Economic Review* 51 (1961): 95–116.

17 Friedman, *Monetary Stability;* Boris P. Pesek and Thomas R. Saving, *Money,*

Wealth, and Economic Theory (New York: Macmillan, 1967); and Harry G. Johnson, "Problems of Efficiency in Monetary Management," *Journal of Political Economy* 76 (1968): 971–90.

18 Roland Vaubel, "The Government's Money Monopoly: Externalities or Natural Monopoly," *Kyklos* 37 (1984): 27–58.

19 Benjamin Klein and Michael Melvin, "Competing International Monies and International Monetary Arrangements," in *The International Monetary System,* ed. Michael Connolly (New York: Praeger, 1982).

20 Vaubel, "Money Monopoly."

21 Ibid., p. 47.

22 Hayek, *Denationalization of Money,* p. 29.

23 The seigniorage from current money creation may be viewed as $[d(M/P) / (M/P)_0]$ $(M/P)_0 = [\dot{M} - \dot{P}](M/P)_0$. If money demand is a function of anticipated inflation $(\dot{P}^*)$ rather than actual $\dot{P}$ (certainly the nominal interest rate i incorporates $\dot{P}^*$ rather than $\dot{P}$), then the seigniorage earned will depend upon $\dot{P}^*$. For a given $\dot{P}^*$, there is a particular quantity of money demanded. If expectations adjust quickly so that a higher $\dot{M}$ is quickly reflected in higher $\dot{P}^*$, money demand falls, P increases and the seigniorage gained is smaller.

24 Benjamin Klein and Keith B. Leffler, "The Role of Market Forces in Assuring Contractual Performance," *Journal of Political Economy* 89 (1981): 640.

25 Ibid., p. 635.

26 White, "Free Banking," p. 282.

27 Ibid.

28 White, chap. 19 of this volume, p. 472.

29 Ibid., p. 473.

30 Ibid.

31 Hayek, *Denationalization of Money,* p. 29.

32 Beyond my analysis, Allan H. Meltzer, "Monetary Reform in an Uncertain Environment," *Cato Journal* 3 (1983): 93–112, has argued that a monopoly central bank may be more efficient than a free banking system by lowering the levels of risk and uncertainty that society bears. The absence of a Federal Reserve–style lender of last resort to free banks is the major risk factor. Meltzer argues: "The absence of a lender of last resort increases the cost of maintaining 'free', competitive banking. A competitive producer of money bears an avoidable risk. To survive, the producer must receive compensation. Interest rates are raised by the risk premium, so the capital stock is smaller and income is lower under competitive banking" (p. 110).

33 Roland Vaubel, "Free Currency Competition," *Weltwirtschaftliches Archiv* 113 (1977): 433–61.

34 Mundell, "International Monetary Options," p. 191.

35 In discussing the benefits and costs of switching from a domestic to a foreign money (referred to as "dollarization"), Fischer concludes that the seigniorage costs involved would be so substantial that "dollarization is, therefore, not a development to be welcomed from the viewpoint of a single nation's interests." See Stanley Fischer, "Seigniorage and the Case for a National Money," *Journal of Political Economy* 90 (1982): 191.

36 H. Robert Heller and Malcolm Knight, *Reserve Currency Preferences of Central Banks,* Princeton Essays in International Finance, no. 131 (Princeton University, International Finance Section, Department of Economics, 1978); and Deborah L. Allen and Leroy D. Laney, "The Global Dollar: Trends and Issues in Official and Private International Finance," *Annals of the American Academy* 460 (1982): 29–37.

37 Melvin, "Dollarization," describes the partial dollarization of Mexico.

38 The analysis ignores any stock seigniorage gains resulting from a one-time shift into dollars. But since any "dollarization" is likely to occur gradually, and it is extremely unlikely that any nation would ever completely stop producing money and allow dollars exclusively, the stock gains are unlikely to change the basic conclusions below.

19 Depoliticizing the Supply of Money

Lawrence H. White

Recognition of the dangers posed by the political incentives of government monetary authorities, dangers examined in earlier chapters of this volume, has prompted a wide array of proposals for partial or full depoliticization of the money supply process. This chapter evaluates these proposals. The next two sections examine the question, raised by programs for partial depoliticization through central bank independence or legislated monetary rules, of whether any government money-creating agency can really be sealed off from internal and external political agendas. If not—if an apolitical government monetary authority is chimerical—then a nongovernmental monetary system clearly demands consideration. Accordingly, the succeeding section inquires into the feasibility of free market monetary arrangements, finding that public-goods and natural-monopoly arguments made against competitive private provision of money are not compelling. A final section concludes by suggesting that if the choice between governmental and market monetary institutions turns on the question of which sort of institution can more credibly be bound by contract to perform as desired, then market institutions have the advantage.

An "Independent" Central Bank

Perhaps the mildest of proposals for monetary regime change is the suggestion that the central bank should enjoy greater "independence" from the direct control of elected officials. Independence is supposed to enable the central bank to resist the partisan demands of the legislative and executive branches of government for inflationary finance and for election-year monetary stimulus. If this were true, however, it would also mean that the management of an independent monetary authority is able to resist all other demands, e.g., those of the public (to whatever limited extent it could discover and obey them). Being directly answerable to no one is certainly a comfortable situation. For this reason the officials of any central bank are themselves likely to be found in the forefront of those advocating independence for the agency. As Edward R. Tufte has commented, "The rhetoric of depoliticization [in the sense of independence] is itself a political weapon, inspired by agencies seeking to prevent external political control and to permit them quietly to serve the interests of their own constituencies."[1] An independent central bank's private constituency—presumably the large commercial banks—will generally have a private agenda which is not identical with the preferences of the common holders of money. The supposed influence of commercial banks over the Federal Reserve system, through their nominal ownership of the regional reserve banks, has been offered as an explanation of the Fed's continual emphasis on current credit market conditions (e.g., the use of interest-rate targets) in the making of short-term policy decisions.[2] It is difficult to separate commercial bank influence from Treasury influence here, however, given that the Treasury is continually concerned with marketing interest-bearing debt. In any event, the prospect of a central bank beholden to the commercial banks is not much cheerier than that of a central bank beholden to Congress.

The degree to which a government-sponsored central bank in a democracy can ever be independent from the control of the legislative and executive branches of government is, of course, severely limited. Congress created the Federal Reserve system, and can rewrite its mandate at any time as it has in the past. Knowing this, the Federal Reserve's management cannot afford to be unresponsive to congressional pressures. The same is undoubtedly true of any other legislatively created central bank. The managers of a government monetary agency, particularly when they are political appointees like the governors of the Federal Reserve, may well lack even the conception that their own objectives might properly differ from the legislature's or the administration's objectives. Much less have they any strong incentive to resist political pressures (which may simply appear to be helpful suggestions) from these sources.

Constraining the Central Bank by a Monetary Rule

Numerous reform proposals more far-reaching than "independence" for the central bank, and more likely to make a perceptible difference, have been made under the rubric of monetary "rules" or a "monetary constitution." These proposals would not eliminate a government monetary role, but would limit the monetary authority to the robotlike administration of a fully specified set of instructions for base money creation. The best-known plan of this sort at present is undoubtedly still Milton Friedman's 1959 program for adhering permanently to a prespecified steady and low growth path in the M1 or M2 measure of the stock of money.[3] Other writers have recommended more complex plans whereby the authority would adjust the target path in response to realized shifts in the growth rate of real national income or velocity, so that demand-induced deviations in the purchasing power of money would be counteracted. Still others have variously suggested that some index of purchasing power should be the explicit target on which the authority's sights are trained, with a feedback rule governing weekly base money creation.[4]

It would be impossible in the space available here to consider critically the technical aspects of each of these plans in any adequate detail. Instead a generic feature of these plans may be singled out: all of them suppose that the mind of man can design a government bureau which, once off the drawing board and staffed with real self-interested residents of the nation's capital, will function more or less as planned and will generate sufficient political support for its own perpetuation. Each designer must tacitly assume, in other words, that his plan represents a roughly stable political-economic equilibrium in the face of internal and external pressures for piecemeal modifications. The attempt to design a pressure-proof agency confronts at least three difficulties. It must be possible to specify the bureau's routine tightly enough for its mandate to require little interpretation, since extensive interpretation could serve as a means of subverting the rule in the interests of the staff itself, the legislature, the executive branch, or a private constituency. The operation of the rule must leave no interest group wanting and able to revise it through a plausible appeal to a later session of the legislature. And it must be possible to establish a disciplinary mechanism which will effectively prevent departures from the legislated instructions, whether intentional or due merely to innocent error.

The hypothesis that all these conditions can indeed be satisfied by the legislated version of a given rule cannot be empirically falsified, of course, without trying the experiment. (It cannot be decisively falsified even then. It could always be argued that the rule failed only because the effort to implement it wasn't sincere enough.) Perhaps with enough academic input the legislative or constitutional amendment process really can give birth to a single-mindedly apolitical government agency for controlling something as consequential as the money supply. But the logic of bureaucracy does not offer much encouragement. Nor does history offer a single apparent precedent.[5]

The power of money creation is so extremely tempting for government to exploit that continual public vigilance (incurring of monitoring and enforcement costs, in other words) would be necessary to hold a government agency possessing that power to a prescribed routine. There is a free rider problem here, which is more pronounced the more costly the rule is to monitor, in that most members of the public will rationally choose to let others bear the burden of keeping well informed about the conduct of the monetary agency. Keeping well informed would be all the more difficult because a monetary agency that naturally wanted to escape tight constraints on its behavior in order to pursue its own agenda would have an incentive to pollute the available information on its conduct, making public accounting more difficult. So long as an agency existed to expertly administer the monetary rule, the public would have to be well informed enough to see through all of the superficially plausible rationalizations the agency might offer for deviations from the monetary rule, such as, the deviation is really just a measurement error, or due to a distortion in the aggregate being measured, or is really not a deviation from the *spirit* of the rule, or is justified by events unforeseen by the framers of the rule. To arrive at an informed opinion on each separate case is implausibly costly for many members of the public to undertake.

To be economically monitored and enforced, and hence workable, a monetary rule must be so plain and straightforward that violations are transparent. Once in operation, the simpler the rule, the less the public needs to know to detect violations. A solid public consensus must hold "dogmatically" that the rule is never to be violated as a matter of principle. Such a consensus would not be easy to form in any case, but it would be less difficult to form the simpler and more clear-cut the rule. For these reasons a no-feedback rule stands a better chance for effectiveness than a price level feedback rule or a velocity shift–adjusted money growth rule. A zero money growth rule stands a better chance than a fixed positive growth rule, and a rule of freezing the monetary base stands a better chance than one of freezing a wider monetary aggregate.[6]

Freezing the monetary base would be uniquely easy to enforce because it is the only "monetary rule" which, like the First Amendment to the U.S. Constitution, does not direct government to perform any positive task. It merely proscribes what the federal government shall *not* do: it shall not expand the stock of monetary instruments issued by itself. Because there is no positive money creation power assigned, no money-creating agency whatsoever would be needed. The Federal Reserve system could readily be eliminated as a branch of government once its open market desk was closed down and its rediscount window shuttered.[7] The Fed's bank regulatory activities could either be terminated or transferred to another federal agency. Its check-clearing and wire-transfer facilities could be privatized quite practicably. Check-clearing operations were entirely private before the advent of the Fed, are in large part privately run in the United States today, and are entirely private in Canada and other nations. Privatization would require only that the stock of member banks in the twelve district reserve banks be treated as genuine ownership shares. The Bureau of Engraving and Printing might be allowed the job of replacing worn currency, or a plan might be devised to allow currency issued by private banks to displace government currency, so that the stock of high-powered money would come to be held exclusively as bank reserves.[8]

Any monetary rule less strict than freezing the monetary base quite obviously allows open market operations to continue being conducted, and therefore allows some government monetary agency to exist which has the function of altering the stock of base money. Under any growth rule for a wider monetary aggregate the agency is charged with offsetting changes in the relevant money multiplier; under any positive money growth rule it is charged with adding regularly to the stock of base money. The dynamics of government growth give good reason to fear that the very existence of a government money creation agency, no matter how circumscribed its initial activities, represents the thin edge of a very powerfully propelled wedge. The agency's officials can lend the weight of their expert opinion to the case for giving them greater powers to perform functions which only they, purportedly, truly understand.[9] The modification of an existing agency's operating routine is certainly less likely to encounter pitched public resistance than the creation of an entirely new agency.

This "thin edge" problem—the worrisome potential for degeneration of any legislated barriers against discretionary behavior by an existing monetary authority—cannot be dismissed by saying that we need not worry about attempts to erode the barriers until they occur. One fundamental benefit promised by a monetary rule is the assured environment it would provide, by *precommitting* the monetary authority to a predictable path of behavior, for private planning based on firmly held inflation-rate expectations.[10] The transitional drawbacks of disinflation, for example, are generally understood by economists to be less severe the more credible is the monetary authority's commitment to a disinflationary path, because greater credibility allows prudent agents more promptly to moderate the nominal prices and wages they demand in long-term contracts. If the public widely considers a particular legislatable monetary rule to be fragile and unreliable because they perceive that it may not survive political and bureaucratic pressures, then the adoption of the rule will not provide the benefit of a credible precommitment. It may even be worse than no rule. The pursuit of a low inflation policy rule in a setting where the public cynically expects high inflation is a recipe for unnaturally high unemployment and depressed real output.

There is a second respect in which a legislated monetary rule will fail to provide its advertised benefits if its long-term political survival is not sufficiently credible. A common argument for adopting a fiat money regime governed by some designed rule constraining growth in the stock of fiat money, rather than adopting a commodity-based regime (e.g., a gold coin standard) governed by demand and supply conditions in the market for the money commodity, is that rule-constrained fiat money can provide an equivalent nominal anchor at a lower resource cost.[11] Fiat money provides a social windfall, so the argument goes, by freeing the existing stock of monetary gold to be used for industrial and consumptive purposes and by releasing resources devoted to augmenting the stock of monetary gold through mining and prospecting to be used in other industries. These events require, however, that the relative price of gold be lower under the fiat money regime than under the gold coin standard. During our current experiment with fiat money this has not happened. The relative price of gold is higher, apparently due to the demand to hold gold coins and bullion as a hedge against fiat money inflation, implying that industrial and consumptive uses are more restricted and that mining and prospecting activities are greater.[12] Whether the relative price of gold would be lower under a *rule-constrained* fiat money regime depends on whether the political survival of the rule is credible enough to discourage substantial speculative holdings of gold. In view of the "thin edge" problem, it may unfortunately be the case that no rule whose administration requires the existence of a government monetary agency can achieve the requisite survival credibility.

Taking the logic of the "thin edge" problem a bit further, it is possible to doubt that even freezing the monetary base removes the power of money creation far enough from the hands of government to constitute a politically stable arrangement. Freezing the base establishes an "authorized issue" for the central government. At a later date it might plausibly be argued that since the level is arbitrary, there is no reason for not raising it to meet some pressing government expense. As a historical illustration, the second batch of fiat greenbacks issued to finance the U.S. Civil War met with less opposition than the first (which Congress had promised would be the only batch). The first batch was itself justified by reference to the precedent of the moneylike Treasury notes issued in the previous decades.[13]

A slightly outlandish analogy may make the point even more clearly.[14] The approach to monetary reform that consists of giving a discretionary monetary authority unsolicited advice for better policy is like the approach of a team of Wild West railroad detectives who, confronting a gun-toting gang in the midst of robbing a train, attempt to persuade the gang through reason that they really should be using their guns in a less threatening manner. Success is unlikely given the other side's incentives.[15] Advocacy of a legislated rule for monetary growth is like demanding that the gang holster its guns and promise to leave them holstered. This arrangement is a bit better, but still not nearly so reassuring to the train passengers as the natural solution, familiar from old Western films, of demanding that the gang drop its guns. Leaving the loaded guns within easy reach makes it all too easy for the antagonists to seize an opportunity to break their promise, so that extremely vigilant attention to their behavior remains necessary. The strongest form of a monetary rule, freezing the monetary base, might be likened (at the expense of stretching the analogy even further) to a policy of allowing the outlaws to keep their guns provided that they throw down their bullets. The stability of that arrangement is certainly greater than the stability of a weaker gun-holstering rule, but arguably it may not go quite far enough toward removing the ultimate threat and reassuring the passengers.

A Free Market Monetary System

The analogue of the drop-your-guns approach in monetary reform is the proposal that government be completely removed from the money supply business. In its place a free market monetary system would prevail, shaped and disciplined not by a legislated blueprint but by rivalrous competition among money producers for consumer patronage. Historical precedent and monetary theory together suggest that the common money emerging from such a competition would be currency and checking accounts issued by commercial banks or banklike financial firms. The money's spendability and purchasing power would be secured by contractually guaranteed redeemability into a standard basic asset, either a commodity money or an equivalently acceptable privately produced asset held by all banks and used as a clearing medium among them.[16] Because it represents depoliticization of the money supply in the most thorough conceivable form, this system merits consideration by anyone who recognizes the drawbacks of a political monetary regime. Unless a free market monetary system somehow inherently fails to provide money with generally desired features that a legislatively designed system clearly would provide, competition among private suppliers provides the best means of meeting the preferences of money users. In fact, this conclusion should be unsurprising, given that the virtues of competitive markets are widely recognized when the supply of other private goods and services is at issue.

It has been argued in several ways that a free market monetary system may inherently fail to perform in a desirable fashion. These arguments have often been made on a purely theoretical level, with their proponents neglecting to examine the historical evidence on market freedom in monetary institutions in order to see whether the projected ill effects really did occur. The available evidence that is most relevant comes from the clearest episode of monetary freedom on record, namely, Scotland's twelve-plus decades of experience with free banking prior to 1844 (at which date the Parliament in London moved to assimilate Scottish banking to the English central banking system by barring the entry of new currency-issuing banks). This evidence in fact shows a rather dramatically successful system flourishing in the absence of significant government intervention.[17] The so-called free banking era in the United States appears, in the light of recent work in economic history, to have been an era of decentralized but by no means unregulated currency supply. While it was not so chaotic as previously believed, the era's undeniable shortcomings can be attributed to its characteristic state-imposed regulations, particularly bond collateral restrictions on bank note issues and barriers to branch banking.[18]

Theoretical cases for "market failure" in the provision of money generally fall into one of two categories: (1) arguments claiming that money, or some aspect of money, is a public good or a source of nonappropriable external effects; or (2) arguments proposing that the supplying of money is a natural monopoly due to economies of scale in production. (Some authors have pointed to "social economies of scale" in the *use* of money, but these economies are more appropriately considered to fall into the category of external effects.) Both sets of arguments have been examined by Roland Vaubel, who concludes that neither of them makes a valid case for exclusive government provision of money. In Vaubel's words, "externality theory fails to provide a convincing justification for the government's monopoly in the production of (base) money," and "since, finally, we cannot even be sure that money or the currency unit is a natural monopoly, the case against restrictions of entry is overwhelming."[19] The even stronger conclusion is warranted, however, that no convincing case for the necessity or social desirability of *any* government involvement has been made.

The public-good or externality argument is rather obviously not applicable to money as a medium of exchange, since the liquidity or ready spendability services of money accrue exclusively to its owner and not to others. It might be nonetheless argued that an individual's use of a *common* medium of exchange confers nonappropriable external benefits to others who can now trade with him more cheaply, and that therefore a free market monetary system will underproduce the quality characteristic of commonness or general acceptability in exchange media. This argument runs up against the historical fact that the market did *not* fail to produce commonly accepted media of exchange prior to government involvement in money. Gold and silver emerged spontaneously as nearly universal monies because of strong *private* incentives for individuals to use as exchange media the commodities that other traders most readily accept.[20] If we assume that some fraction of the transactions cost savings accomplished through use of a common money are enjoyed by the marginal user, the remainder being enjoyed by those with whom he transacts, then there is no divergence between what is privately optimal and what is "socially optimal" in the static choice among exchange media.[21]

The most that could be argued on grounds of transaction cost externality is that market convergence on a common money may occur too slowly because of limited information about the exchange media accepted by one's potential trading partners.[22] If this argument went through, it might be used to make a utilitarian case for collective subsidy of convergence-speeding information additional to the information that would be privately produced. It could not be used to justify government imposition of a monetary standard by edict, however, because an unbiased market process is necessary in order to discover what type of money traders will find most suitable. In order to enhance "social utility," of course, government would have to know (how would it?) what information was in fact socially valued more than its cost of production even in the absence of any revealed willingness to pay for it, and would have to spend less (what would limit it?) on its production than the information was worth. But even if that were possible, government's limited publicity role would disappear entirely once the economy had fully converged on a common money. Private provision of money suffers no informational externality problems once a monetary standard has emerged.[23]

It might be argued, however, that the informational problems of convergence to a monetary standard do not lie entirely in the past. There are two cases to consider. The first case is one of transition away from the current government fiat monetary system, which was of course arrived at through political intervention rather than market evolution. If that system is to be phased out deliberately in favor of a system allowing private competition in the supply of outside money, then the question of establishing a new monetary standard arises. There is a strong utilitarian case to be made for minimizing calculational and transactional confusion in the transition by having the government, as it disengages from production of fiat dollars, take minimally interventionist steps to favor a particular new standard upon which the market economy could then rapidly converge. Obvious steps include announcing its intention to use a particular new unit for its own accounting and transactions.[24] If a precious metallic standard is to be favored, fiat dollars can also be made redeemable for the metal, so that an initial stock of the new outside money is made immediately available. This transitional step, by absorbing and retiring fiat dollars, solves the problem of a collapsing demand for Federal Reserve notes that might otherwise impose considerable losses on their holders.[25]

The second case involves an economy already on a monetary standard allowing private production of outside money. The question of establishing a new standard may arise if the purchasing power of the existing monetary unit begins to fluctuate considerably or deteriorate rapidly. (Presumably this would be an unanticipated development, because instability would militate against a standard's adoption in the first place.) The market's tendency to stick with an existing standard, each individual waiting for others to go first in getting a new system off the ground, may prevent the expeditious emergence of a new money.[26] For plausible private monetary standards, however, the hypothesized problem may well never arise. For an indexed or commodity basket standard, purchasing power instability is virtually ruled out by definition. For a more pedestrian gold or other single-commodity standard, there are both theoretical and historical reasons for having confidence in the stability of the monetary unit. The theory of commodity money demonstrates that potential changes in the purchasing power of the monetary unit are dampened by the price elasticity of supply and nonmonetary demand for the money commodity. A fall in the purchasing power (relative price) of gold, for instance, whether due to a fortuitous gold discovery or a fall in the demand for outside money, is impeded by the reduced quantity of gold that will be mined and the increased quantity that will be demanded for nonmonetary purposes at any lower price. An ongoing fall in the value of gold due to continually greater cost reductions in gold mining than in other industries is fairly implausible, and so is a nonrecurring but sharp fall in the modern world where there is little prospect of a purely fortuitous major gold discovery. For a nonrenewable resource whose reserves are known, economic theory suggests that under competitive conditions the relative price of the resource will rise over time at a rate somewhat less than the real rate of interest (the difference depends on the marginal cost of extraction). The gold standard automatically generates an approximation to the "optimum quantity of money," as holders of gold-denominated money may thereby enjoy a mild ongoing appreciation in the value of their cash balances. The

history of the classical gold standard may contain some noteworthy episodes of variation in the purchasing power of the monetary unit, but the
overall picture from 1821 to 1914 is indeed one of mild secular appreciation in the value of money, with deviations from trend strikingly smaller
than under subsequent monetary systems.[27]

The argument that money production is a natural monopoly is sometimes based on a confusion between the market tendency to converge on
a single monetary *standard* and the prevalence under natural monopoly of
a single *producer*. In a setting of competition among *noncommodity* monies, if each producer's brand of money were to constitute its own standard, the tendency to converge on a single standard might well favor the
survival of a single producer of outside money for reasons quite distinct
from natural monopoly in the usual sense of unlimited economies of
scale. This result does not occur, however, where market forces lead producers to denominate their monies according to the same standard, as
should be expected even in the case of irredeemable monies.[28] Where a
commodity money unit constitutes the monetary standard, it is clearly
feasible to have multiple producers of money unless there are genuine
natural monopoly characteristics present. Many competing mines can
produce the same precious metal, many competing mints can produce
standardized coins from that metal, and many competing banks can offer
bank notes and checkable deposits redeemable for those coins. It would
seem to be a historical question whether unlimited economies of scale
operate at any of these levels of money production, and the historical
evidence indicates that they do not.[29]

It has been argued on various theoretical grounds, however, that natural monopoly must be present in money production. For one, stochastic
economies of scale have been identified in banking (declining inside
money "production" costs).[30] These economies undoubtedly do exist, but
beyond some point they are evidently swamped by diseconomies of coordinating a large banking firm or of "selling" inside money balances.
More provocatively, Michael Melvin, drawing on the work of Benjamin
Klein, has deduced natural monopoly in money from the belief that the
costs of creating consumer confidence in the trustworthiness of the issuer,
necessary in order to "sell" real money balances, are largely fixed costs.[31]
In Melvin's own framework, however, it is natural to believe that these
costs are *not* fixed, but rise with the quantity of real balances to be sold.
The "confidence capital" an issuer must acquire, in order to convince the

public that he will not find it profitable to cheat them through overexpansion, would seem to be proportional to the real money balances he has in circulation, because his potential gain from cheating is proportional to his existing circulation. If so, then confidence-bolstering expenditures are not a fixed cost, no natural monopoly exists on this account, and no case has been made for government over private provision.[32]

Melvin makes a related argument for government provision that also deserves to be considered here. He argues that "the costs of individually contracting for privately produced high-quality money are prohibitive," i.e., performance contracts between issuer and money holder cannot be cheaply written and enforced. To achieve a stable private money, therefore, a large premium (in the form of zero interest on cash balances and steady erosion of purchasing power through inflation) would have to be continually paid to a private money issuer, a sort of "protection money" fee, to make it relatively unprofitable for the issuer to take the one-shot gain available from a surprising flood of money production. This large premium then "suggests that quality is realized more cheaply through government production."[33] Even granted the initial premises, however, the comparative cheapness of government production does not follow unless it can be shown that an equally large protection premium does not have to be paid to a government producer to assure quality. If the government has an uncertain tenure and therefore a shorter time horizon or higher discount rate than a private firm, as Klein has noted to be the case,[34] then the quality-assuring premium necessary for stability with government money production would be even higher than the premium necessary with private production, assuming effective performance contracts to be prohibitively expensive in both cases. Melvin seems to believe that the money-holding public as a body can relatively cheaply contract or "vertically integrate" with government for good performance so that a high premium can be avoided. But on this belief it would appear quite puzzling that in fact no constitutional "contract" currently limits the U.S. government's monetary behavior, which in recent years has been far from good. The discussion above concerning the difficulties inherent in monitoring, enforcing, and preserving an explicit rule binding a government monetary agency suggests that explicit performance contracting costs with government may indeed be prohibitive.

Fortunately the initial premise that Melvin adopts, that "the costs of individually contracting for privately produced high-quality money are prohibitive," is empirically false. Redemption contracts, as carried on the faces of private bank notes during historical episodes of free banking in such words as "the ABC Bank will pay to the bearer on demand one pound sterling," are cheap to write and enforce. A note holder denied redemption can simply be granted a lien against the issuing bank.[35] Swift and certain enforcement of redemption ensures that bank notes are a high-quality money, their purchasing power equal to that of the specie or other assets to which they are claims. Accordingly, de facto redeemability of private money makes Melvin's analysis irrelevant. Bank note issuers on a gold standard do not, contrary to what he asserts, have to "maintain large stocks of gold in order to build confidence in their money" directly; note holders have no need to observe the size of the gold reserve so long as they feel assured of continued redeemability.[36] The reserve is instead held to meet stochastic redemption outflows as they occur, and thereby indirectly (through a good track record) to help provide quality assurance. Though some expenditures are necessary to convince the public that a bank is not a fly-by-night affair, convertibility eliminates the need for confidence capital of the Klein-Melvin sort. Convertible private money therefore does not require that money holders bear a high cost in the form of a protection premium paid to money issuers. In fact the opportunity cost of holding currency was definitely lower under historical gold-standard free banking regimes than it is today, because lower inflation made for lower nominal interest rates on alternative assets.[37]

Conclusion

In chapter 12 of this volume we explored the incentives of a political money issuer unbound by an enforceable performance rule. The first half of the present chapter examined the question of whether any durable and credible rule could be fastened onto a political money supplier. Finally, in considering the feasibility of private money production, we have been led to ask a similar question about private issuers: Can they be effectively contractually bound to good performance? Our conclusion turns out to be one of skepticism toward the potential for enforcing any explicit rule (other than freezing the money base) for properly "depoliticized" monetary behavior by the central government. There is, after all, little or no precedent for such a thing, at least under fiat money regimes. (It remains to be understood why some central banks are less mischievous than others today.) On the other hand, we find that there exists at least one effectively enforceable contractual arrangement—convertibility—which makes desirable monetary behavior quite credible for competitive private issuers of money. The road away from political business cycles and the political economy of stagflation, toward a depoliticized and responsible set of money institutions, would therefore seem to point rather clearly in the direction of private contractual arrangements for the supply of money. It is simply too difficult to believe that a government can be more easily held to its promises than a private firm in a competitive environment.

Notes

I am indebted to King Banaian, Gregory Christainsen, Roger Garrison, John R. Lott, Jr., Milton Friedman, Anna J. Schwartz, Thomas Willett, and members of the Austrian Colloquium at New York University for comments and discussion, and to the C. V. Starr Center for Applied Economics for clerical support.

1   Edward R. Tufte, *Political Control of the Economy* (Princeton: Princeton University Press, 1978), p. 139.
2   See Milton Friedman, "Should There Be an Independent Monetary Authority?" in *In Search of a Monetary Constitution,* ed. Leland B. Yeager (Cambridge: Harvard University Press, 1963), p. 238.
3   Milton Friedman, *A Program for Monetary Stability* (New York: Fordham University Press, 1960), esp. chap. 4. Recently, Friedman has progressed to the advocacy of zero growth in the stock of base money, abolition of the Fed, and thorough deregulation of banking, as "the best real cure" for the instability of the current monetary regime. See idem, "Monetary Policy for the 1980's," in *To Promote Prosperity*, ed. John H. Moore (Stanford: Hoover Institution Press, 1984), pp. 40–54.
4   See the discussion of such proposals in Pamela Brown, "Constitution or Competition: Alternative Approaches to Monetary Reform," *Literature of Liberty* 5 (Autumn 1982): 17–18. The set of rules focusing on purchasing-power index targets includes recent "supply-side" proposals for linking open market operations to the price of gold.
5   The principal "rule of the game" under the international gold standard, i.e., convertibility at a fixed parity, was not the creature of legislative design. Central banks empowered to deviate from that rule were not free from political influence. Conversely, the durability and credibility of the classical gold standard was enhanced, I would hypothesize, by the fact that the Bank of England was privately owned.
6   See Friedman, "Monetary Policy," pp. 48–50, for a base freeze proposal and the argument that "zero growth has a special appeal on political grounds that is not shared by any other number."
7   The desk closing would require an end to the pointless (after a base freeze) activity

of rolling over Treasury securities in the Fed's portfolio as they mature. This could be accomplished by a simple bookkeeping change involving the Treasury.

8   For such a plan, see G. A. Selgin, *The Case for Free Banking: Then and Now,* Cato Institute Policy Analysis series, no. 60 (October 21, 1985). Privatization of the district Federal Reserve banks has long been advocated by Richard H. Timberlake.

9   Richard H. Timberlake, "Legislative Construction of the Monetary Control Act of 1980," *American Economic Review* 75 (May 1985): 101–2, provides a case study of this process in action: "Fed officials in their testimony to congressional committees persistently and doggedly advanced one major theme: the Fed had to have more power. . . . By misdirection and subterfuge, the Fed inveigled an unwary Congress into doing its bidding."

10   On monetary rules as precommitments, see Robert J. Barro and David B. Gordon, "A Positive Theory of Monetary Policy in a Natural Rate Model," *Journal of Political Economy* 91 (August 1983): 589–610.

11   The best-known estimate of the resource costs of a commodity standard is probably Milton Friedman's figure of 2.5 percent of annual net national product (*Program for Monetary Stability,* p. 5). That estimate assumes mandatory 100 percent reserves against all of M2, however. With historically reasonable fractional reserve ratios the figure falls to about one one-hundredth of Friedman's, namely, 0.014 to 0.028 percent (depending on assumptions about the secular trend in velocity). See Lawrence H. White, *Free Banking in Britain* (Cambridge: Cambridge University Press, 1984), p. 148.

12   This point is made by Roger W. Garrison, "The 'Costs' of a Gold Standard," in *The Gold Standard: An Austrian Perspective,* ed. Llewellyn H. Rockwell, Jr. (Lexington, Mass.: D. C. Heath, 1985). As this is being written the dollar price of gold is above $470 per troy ounce. Deflating by the GNP deflator, this is equivalent to more than $142 per ounce at 1967 prices, at which time the official price of gold was $35 per ounce, and more than $58 per ounce in 1929 terms, at which time gold was $20.67 per ounce.

13   For excerpts from the congressional debate over the initial issue of greenbacks, see Herman E. Krooss, ed., *Documentary History of Banking and Currency in the United States,* 4 vols. (New York: Chelsea House/McGraw-Hill, 1977), 2:1267–1321. On Treasury notes as a precedent for greenbacks, see Richard H. Timberlake, *The Origins of Central Banking in the United States* (Cambridge: Harvard University Press, 1978), pp. 85–86.

14   The analogy is due to Roger W. Garrison, "Gold: A Standard and an Institution," *Cato Journal* 3 (Spring 1983): 236, though he may wish to disclaim the extensions made here.

15   Robert J. Barro, "United States Inflation and the Choice of Monetary Standard," in *Inflation: Causes and Effects,* ed. Robert E. Hall (Chicago: University of Chicago Press for the National Bureau of Economic Research, 1982), p. 109, aptly comments: "Telling the Federal Reserve to select substantially different values—usually lower values—for monetary growth seems similar to urging firms and households to choose different numbers for prices, employment, production, and so on. As in the

private sector, it is reasonable to view the Fed's monetary decisions as emerging from a given structure of constraints and rewards." This is the point of the analogy. It is *not* intended to suggest that Federal Reserve officials are personally malicious characters.

16 For some of the present author's previous writings on this topic, see Lawrence H. White, "Competitive Money, Inside and Out," in *The Search for Stable Money*, ed. James A. Dorn and Anna J. Schwartz (Chicago: University of Chicago Press, 1987); and idem, "Free Banking as an Alternative Monetary System," in *Money in Crisis*, ed. Barry N. Siegel (San Francisco: Pacific Institute for Public Policy Research, 1984). See also George A. Selgin, *The Theory of Free Banking* (Totowa, N.J.: Rowman and Littlefield, 1987). For a somewhat different perspective that nonetheless may fit within the institutional pattern predicted here, see Robert L. Greenfield and Leland B. Yeager, "A Laissez-Faire Approach to Monetary Stability," *Journal of Money, Credit, and Banking* 15 (August 1983): 302–15.

17 See White, *Free Banking in Britain*, chaps. 2, 5. For earlier accounts see Rondo Cameron, *Banking in the Early Stages of Industrialization* (New York: Oxford University Press, 1967), chap. 3; and Vera C. Smith, *The Rationale of Central Banking* (London: P. S. King, 1936), chap. 2.

18 The chief contributions to this new scholarship are Hugh Rockoff, "The Free Banking Era: A Reexamination," *Journal of Money, Credit, and Banking* 6 (May 1974): 141–67; Arthur J. Rolnick and Warren E. Weber, "Free Banking, Wildcat Banking, and Shinplasters," Federal Reserve Bank of Minneapolis *Quarterly Review* 6 (Fall 1982): 10–19; idem, "New Evidence on the Free Banking Era," *American Economic Review* 73 (December 1983): 1080–91; idem, "The Causes of Free Bank Failures: A Detailed Examination," *Journal of Monetary Economics* 14 (November 1984): 267–91; idem, "Instability in Banking: Lessons from the Free Banking Era," *Cato Journal* 6 (Winter 1986): 877–90; and Robert G. King, "On the Economics of Private Money," *Journal of Monetary Economics* 12 (July 1983): 127–58.

19 Roland Vaubel, "The Government's Money Monopoly: Externalities or Natural Monopoly?" *Kyklos* 37 (1984): 45, 47. Vaubel does, however, leave open the possibilities that peripheral forms of government intervention (deposit insurance, lender of last resort, subsidization of marginal bank accounts in undermonetized economies) might be justifiable, and that government ought to be allowed to compete as a money supplier. The case for a completely free market monetary system would need to rebut these arguments as well.

20 The classic account of the convergence process set in motion by the discovery of these incentives is Carl Menger, "On the Origin of Money," *Economic Journal* 2 (June 1892): 234–55.

21 Vaubel's argument to this effect regarding choice among established monies ("Government's Money Monopoly," pp. 41–44) applies equally to choice among premonetary media of exchange, at least to the extent that we can view these choices statically.

22 This argument has, indeed, been made by Stephen O. Morell, "Exchange, Money, and the State: An Essay on the Limits of Government Involvement in Monetary Affairs" (Auburn University, 1983, typescript).

23 Vaubel, "Government's Money Monopoly," p. 41, draws a similar conclusion: "However, where, like in the industrial countries, all economic agents do use money, transaction cost externalities of using money cannot be Pareto-relevant."

24 Leland B. Yeager has argued for these steps in "Stable Money and Free-Market Currencies," *Cato Journal* 3 (Spring 1983): 319, 324. Yeager calls them a "non-coercive nudge," but it is doubtful that a measure which would presumably require payment of taxes in a particular form should be called "non-coercive."

25 Leland Yeager, "Deregulation and Monetary Reform," *American Economic Review* 75 (May 1985): 105, sees "no satisfactory answer" to the collapsing dollar problem in a transition to the non-commodity-money competitive payments system he favors.

26 I am indebted to Gregory Christainsen for bringing this problem to my attention.

27 For graphical evidence on the historical behavior of the purchasing power of gold see Michael David Bordo, "The Gold Standard: Myths and Realities," in *Money in Crisis,* ed. Siegel, pp. 212, 213, 215. For elaboration of the depletable resource theory of a gold standard, see Michael David Bordo and Richard Wayne Ellson, "A Model of the Classical Gold Standard with Depletion," *Journal of Monetary Economics* 16 (July 1985): 109–20. On both the theory and the history, see Hugh Rockoff, "Some Evidence on the Real Price of Gold, Its Costs of Production, and Commodity Prices," in *A Retrospective on the Classical Gold Standard, 1821–1931,* ed. Michael D. Bordo and Anna J. Schwartz (Chicago: University of Chicago Press for the National Bureau of Economic Research, 1984), pp. 613–49, esp. pp. 619–20.

28 F. A. Hayek, *Denationalisation of Money,* 2d ed. (London: Institute of Economic Affairs, 1978), pp. 123–24, imagines that the typical private producer of irredeemable money will promise to stabilize its purchasing power in terms of a particular index, so that other producers could easily adopt the same "standard" by targeting the same index. In the Greenfield-Yeager system the unit of account (or payment "standard") is divorced from the media of exchange, so that a single standard is clearly compatible with a plurality of issuers.

29 Vaubel, "Government's Money Monopoly," p. 47 n. 37, cites several relevant studies and concludes: "Historically, competition has not tended to destroy itself in the money-producing industry." For evidence on competitive private mints, see Donald H. Kagin, *Private Gold Coins and Patterns of the United States* (New York: Arco, 1981); for evidence on competitive bank note issuers, see White, *Free Banking in Britain,* pp. 23–49, 146.

30 See Ernst Baltensperger, "Economies of Scale, Firm Size, and Concentration in Banking," *Journal of Money, Credit, and Banking* 4 (August 1972): 467–88.

31 Benjamin Klein, "The Competitive Supply of Money," *Journal of Money, Credit, and Banking* 6 (November 1974): 447–49; Michael Melvin, chapter 18 of this volume.

32 I am indebted to John R. Lott, Jr., for discussion on this point. The tenability of Klein's confidence-capital equilibrium has been cast into sharp doubt by Bart Taub, "Private Fiat Money with Many Suppliers," *Journal of Monetary Economics* 16 (September 1985): 195–208.

33 Melvin, chap. 18, p. 446.

34 Klein, "Competitive Supply of Money," pp. 449–50.

35 In the Scottish system this was known as the note holder's right of "summary dili-
gence." See S. C. Checkland, *Scottish Banking: A History, 1695–1973* (Glasgow:
Collins, 1975), p. 121. During the United States' so-called free banking era, state
legislatures sometimes legalized suspensions of gold redemption, but that is quite
different from inherently costly enforcement.

36 The competing Scottish banks did not find it necessary to advertise the size of their
gold reserves. Having unlimited shareholder liability for their debts, which was both
enforceable and enforced, however, new banks did advertise the names of their
wealthy shareholders.

37 Even in American "free banking," in which redemption was not so easily enforced
in practice, the average note holder loss from bank suspensions and failures
amounted to less than the loss from a 2 percent inflation rate (Rockoff, "Free Banking Era," p. 151).

20 Fedbashing and the Role of Monetary Arrangements in Managing Political Stress

Edward J. Kane

In politically or economically difficult times, incumbent U.S. politicians engage in a bipartisan practice that has come to be called Fedbashing. They pointedly blame the economic ills of the country on the "misguided" monetary policies of an "independent" Federal Reserve system. Far from acknowledging a prior role in encouraging Fed officials to select the very policies they currently wish to disavow, Fedbashers seek to distance themselves from policies that are currently unpopular with potential swing voters. Other things equal, the more dissatisfied polls show swing voters to be with any aspect of the national economy, the closer the date of the next election, and the tighter a Fedbasher's election campaign, the more abuse he tends to heap upon the Fed.

What makes the game work is that Fed officials take their bashings manfully. Typically, their only defense is to point out that fiscal policy and such unforecastable events as financial innovations or oil shocks cause monetary policymakers insuperable difficulties. This gracious acceptance of blame supports the perception that monetary policy is a delicate (even arcane) art and increases the credibility of Fedbashers' collective efforts to heap political guilt for questionable policies onto the Fed.

In turn, Fed officials profess an unswerving resistance to political influence and accept the role of scapegoat for two reasons: because the structure of decision making at their agency depersonalizes blame and because serving as scapegoats lets them preserve a series of valuable bureaucratic privileges that make scapegoating credible in the first place. These privileges include budgetary autonomy for the agency, potentially long terms of office for agency leaders, an extraordinary degree of public recognition, and a broader turf and policy keyboard than competitive financial regulators enjoy at the Office of the Comptroller of the Currency, the Federal Deposit Insurance Corporation, and the Securities and Exchange Commission.

Because U.S. political parties lack discipline and different parties may control the presidency and one or both houses of Congress, the resulting incentive system is designed to favor not one *party* over the other, but incumbent politicians over their challengers. In a system in which a well-disciplined party with a parliamentary majority rules all phases of a country's national government, incumbents in the "out" party have little reason to scapegoat officials of the central bank. Instead, they have a clear interest in pinning the blame for unpopular policies squarely on the opposing party.

Fedbashing and Fed Policy Choices

Fedbashing is a three-handed game staged for an audience of potential voters at critical points in unfolding business and electoral cycles. Players represent Congress, the executive branch, and the Fed, whose participation reflects their shared responsibility for macroeconomic and financial events. On the Fed side, players seek both to fulfill an ongoing and multidimensional stabilization mission whose pursuit has politically significant redistributive effects and to extend (or at least to preserve) an inherited set of special bureaucratic privileges. Congressional and administration players seek to coax the Fed into adopting current settings for monetary policy targets (especially interest rates) that their side deems to be politically optimal, while blaming the Fed for any and all unpopular economic developments that the electorate may currently associate with *past* monetary policies.

Congressional and administration players initiate all plays. Their object is twofold: to exculpate themselves from unpopular policies after the fact and to influence the Fed's current choice of policies without surrendering the option to deny responsibility for these policies at a future date. Because the Fed's special bureaucratic status is not rooted in the Constitution, it may be changed by a simple act of Congress. In effect, Fedbashing is played under rules (the Federal Reserve Act and the Employment

Act) that Congress owns and may redesign at any time. Fed and administration players must adapt their play to the continuing possibility of
congressionally instigated changes in the rules of the game.

If a majority of both houses of Congress were to regard their institutional self-interest as better served by an alternative structure for monetary policy-making, they would be free (subject to the complication of
having to override a presidential veto) to enact this new structure. In
particular, they could at any time choose either to supervise monetary
policy much more closely or to surrender authority over monetary policy
entirely to the executive branch. In repeatedly refusing to institute a
clearly accountable structure (or unambiguous mandate) for monetary
policy decision making, Congress reveals its continuing preference for
the Fedbashing process.[1] Although at various times different presidents
might prefer different arrangements, except in the 1930s and prior to the
Treasury–Federal Reserve Accord of 1951, reforming the Fed has not
occupied an important place on any president's agenda.

Exposed as they are to the discipline of Fedbashing, Fed officials
face goals and restraints that are both political and economic in origin.
Significant monetary policy decisions temporarily redistribute income,
creating winners and losers among the electorate. It is precisely the tem-
porariness of these effects that makes the option of ex post deniability so
valuable to incumbent politicians. Fed policymakers cannot escape making trade-offs between the short-run and long-run performance of the national economy and between alternative patterns of costs and benefits for
various special interests. This leads them not only to explore the political,
bureaucratic, and economic consequences of alternative policies but also
to work hard at selling the policies they adopt to society at large. At the
time that they are made, monetary policy decisions must make political
as well as economic sense.

Concluding that monetary policymakers respond to political as well
as economic pressures is not the same thing as attributing ignoble motives
to decision makers at the Fed. In a democratic society, where else can a
policymaker look for the public good to be defined except in the expression of political forces? Fed officials are no less dedicated and well inten-
tioned a set of public servants than one finds anywhere else in federal
government. Moreover, one need not assume that, in responding to political forces, Fed officials engage in acts of conscious and explicit political

calculation. An animal trainer can control beasts that are not even capable of rational calculations by manipulating a system of straightforward rewards and punishments. Similarly, incumbent federal politicians can control Fed behavior by maintaining a political environment of carrots and sticks that are arranged and rearranged to see to it that the best that Fed officials can do for their institution is to make more or less the very choices that politicians wish them to make.[2] (Ironically, on important issues governors and Federal Reserve bank presidents appear to be similarly animal-trained by whips and favors administered by the chairman of the Federal Reserve Board.)

Political rewards and punishments range from private and public expressions of approval or disapproval to supporting or opposing legislative changes that Fed officials do or do not want enacted. Legislative rewards focus on expanding the Fed's policy turf and instrumental keyboard, as exemplified by the 1980 extension of Fed reserve requirement authority to nonbank deposit institutions and the Fed's perennial request for the right to pay interest on reserve balances. Legislative punishments consist of withholding keenly desired rewards and imposing various restrictions on the Fed's inherited span of control or on its budgetary and policy autonomy.

The Role of Committee Hearings

An essential place in the Fedbashing process is held by congressional hearings convened sporadically to consider mechanical rules for dictating policy decisions to Fed officials and structural reforms that would reduce the Fed's special bureaucratic privileges. By reminding Fed officials of the vulnerability of their agency's special privileges to an organized congressional attack and of the value of being able to repulse such an attack with a presidential veto, these hearings fan Fed interest in maintaining good relations with congressional leaders on both sides of the aisle and, especially, in staying on the good side of the president and his staff. They also permit the Fed to flex its own muscles, by letting the chairman scare off support for measures he strongly opposes by publicly branding them as serious threats to the macroeconomic or financial stability of the nation. In charting a policy course whose perceived effects on interest rates alternately promote and harm the interests of some politically powerful economic sectors, Fed officials need to be able to control to some extent the ways in which they are attacked by important players.

Past cycles of committee hearings confirm the value of the game to bashers and bashed alike. In recent years, although Congress has repeatedly threatened to impose systematic oversight procedures, it has enacted a series of minor adjustments in Fed powers and responsibilities. In the words of Lombra, these marginal changes in the structure of the Fed's responsibilities to Congress "alter the appearance but not the reality of [monetary] policy making."[3] Adjustments in requirements for reporting Federal Open Market Committee policy decisions to Congress and in the reach of Fed reserve requirements have been token changes, just large enough to keep activist congressional reformers such as congressmen Jack Kemp and Wright Patman working at the game. If a similarly marginal adjustment is made this year, it is likely to focus on the secrecy of FOMC decision making, legislating an improvement in the timing and content of reports on policy decisions taken by the FOMC. Such a change, though potentially helpful in lessening uncertainty in financial markets, stands a long way from giving the Fed a clear and realistic policy mandate and making the Fed explicitly accountable either to Congress or to the president for achieving it. If we assume that structural adjustments in the Fed's powers are perceived as politically optimal by those empowered to make them, Congress and the president have repeatedly reaffirmed the political value of the Fed's lack of accountability to them.

It is no accident that, through the Fed's seventy years of existence, Congress and the president have remained content *not* to force the Fed to submit openly to their wills. By leaving the Fed's high command a substantial amount of ex ante discretion, elected politicians leave themselves room to blame the Fed ex post for whatever aspects of its policies happen to go wrong. This conception supports a "scapegoat" theory of the bureaucratic structure of the Fed.[4]

In offering ritualistic defenses against congressional and executive branch criticisms, Fed leaders cannot fail to appreciate that political benefits accrue to them from allowing incumbents to use their institution as a scapegoat. Their patient acceptance of such criticism contributes to the stereotype of Fed decisions as a continuing series of policy errors. Although Fed officials would rather not be seen as a collection of inveterate bumblers, the valuable bureaucratic privileges that politicians grant them for bearing this opprobrium make the game worthwhile.

Political Aspects of the Problem
of Federal Reserve Reform

Deflections from the target growth rates for monetary aggregates that the Fed has published since 1975 show that the central bank's relative concern for fighting inflation and fighting unemployment tends to vary over the business cycle. So do popular rankings of these same goals.[5] The issue is whether shifts in the Fed's relative priority between these goals take place in response to shifting political constituencies shaped by changes in public opinion. In episodes where they relax a long-standing emphasis on fighting inflation, Fed officials are generally influenced by a developing conflict between their duty to resist inflation and their duty to maintain confidence in the liquidity and integrity of financial institutions. Because the current system of federal deposit insurance effectively subsidizes the taking of exotic forms of financial risk, a sustained period of high interest rates tends to undermine the solvency of important nonfinancial borrowers and of bank and thrift institution lenders. Increases in interest rates tend to reduce the market value of deposit institution assets more quickly and more extensively than they affect the value of their liabilities. On other occasions, presidential suggestion appears to play an important role. Although many authors have addressed the question of how to account for changes in Fed policy priorities, definitive empirical tests are impossible.[6] Keeping the details of board and FOMC policy debates secret prevents outsiders from testing theories of Fed policy choices against data on the Fed's policy process.

By making it harder for market participants to ascertain what the Fed is trying to do, such secrecy probably proves economically counterproductive. This suggests that the principal benefits of secrecy to the Fed are political.

What puzzles me about those who labor hardest at restructuring the Federal Reserve is their presumption that the issue of central banking reform is predominantly an economic one. Reformers typically attempt only to show that a particular change in the performance criteria or structure of Federal Reserve decision making would lead to better macroeconomic policy performance. The catch is that, evaluated over a full business cycle, a great *many* different structural reforms can be shown to lead to better policy. The deeper question is why politicians didn't adopt one of these fundamentally better arrangements years ago. The answer is twofold. First, important segments of the electorate perceive themselves as having a distributional interest in preserving the status quo. Second, supporters of different reforms let efforts to promote their particular idea of the "best" become the enemy of the good. By not addressing the effects of political incentives, advocates of monetary or credit growth rules, of strict price level or national income targeting, or of returning to the gold standard permit their various schemes to cancel each other out. Efforts to erect competitive reform frameworks generate a lobbying turbulence that makes it hard for any single reform scheme to make more than token headway.

If proposals for asserting congressional authority over monetary policy are to have a substantial chance for success, their sponsors must find a way to undo the political and bureaucratic incentives that make current arrangements so cozy both for incumbent politicians and for the Fed. The Fed's acceptance of contradictory goals and its discretionary use of a self-selected bevy of intermediate policy targets let it reverse its economic priorities suddenly in response to the ebb and flow of political pressure with minimal embarrassment. FOMC secrecy and the Fed's structural ambiguity permit Fed officials to fuzz over the important political compromises they effect between goals desired by different sectors and let these compromises be made with minimal short-term political stress for elected politicians. Moreover, the large staff of professional economists whose research on policy issues is directed by the Fed helps the institution's leadership even to shape the agenda of contemporary research on monetary policy. Unless they are willing to risk career penalties, these staff members focus their research on what Lombra calls issues of policy "plumbing" (such as the effects of using different arrays of intermediate targets or of moving from contemporary to lagged accounting for reserves and back again) rather than on the broader issues comprised in the politics of Fed policy-making.[7]

Fed leaders make uncomfortable compromises between their need to respond to immediate political pressure and their desire to improve the long-run performance of the national economy. Political goals and constraints complicate the dilemmas inherent in the Fed's economic policy mission. Over short accounting periods, macroeconomic goals such as high employment and low inflation require contradictory actions. Nondiscretionary policy rules (such as gold standard or monetary growth rules) are naive, brute-force ways of reducing the myopic bias that day-to-day political pressure and macroeconomic lags tend to impart to monetary policy.

By focusing on narrow indices of policy performance, a policy rule would serve as a mechanism for ensuring consistent decisions across business and electoral cycles. At the same time, a rule would require Congress to commit itself both to review on a continuing basis the appropriateness of the rule adopted and of the levels at which associated policy triggers are formally set and to monitor systematically Fed compliance with the rule. These oversight responsibilities would implicate congressional authorities in monetary policy selection, greatly reducing their ability to duck the blame for unpopular policies after the fact.

To accept a policy rule, Congress would have to surrender two options whose vote-gaining power it has valued in the past: (1) the option of scapegoating Fed officials for problems of macroeconomic performance and (2) the option of responding quickly at various stages of the business cycle to changes in the electorate's consensus view of what monetary policies are appropriate. Advocates of rules need to recognize that continual divergences between the current thrust of monetary policy and consensus views of the economy's short-run need for monetary stimulus or restraint would generate an uncomfortable degree of political heat. A policy rule would be hard to sustain because political frustration would accumulate against it. Over a typical business cycle, it would engender political costs that professional politicians cannot be expected to wish away.

A policy rule establishes consistency in policy priorities over time both by forestalling myopic policies for redistributing income to curry votes and by undermining inherited procedures for responding to distributional grievances. Rules retard reversals of policies that sectoral interests suffering foreseeable and especially unforeseeable policy burdens possess the political clout to win. Procedures which threaten to leave aggrieved parties feeling powerless are politically dangerous. Congress is unlikely to want to deprive losers of the power to use the political system to protect themselves against anticipated and unanticipated losses occasioned by monetary policy. Any rule that Congress could bring itself to adopt is likely to be full of loopholes to forestall the buildup of political pressure not only against the rule, but especially against the larger political system of which it is a part.

Prospects for Monetary Reform

A central bank is inescapably a political institution. Its macroeconomic mission has important distributional overtones. With the major exceptions of West Germany and Switzerland (countries whose postwar constituencies against inflation have proved unusually strong), politicians in advanced countries have chosen to bind their central banks into the formal political process far more tightly than U.S. politicians have secured the Fed.

Although limited autonomy was given to the Fed ostensibly as a way to assure less inflationary monetary policies, the fragility of the Fed's special bureaucratic privileges has turned its quasi-independent status into a political leash. If U.S. politicians' only goal was to give our country better macroeconomic performance over the representative business cycle, they would long ago have made themselves and Federal Reserve officials more directly accountable for short-run central bank behavior. Among the simpler ways to accomplish this would be to give the Fed chairman cabinet status or to make the secretary of the Treasury and the chairman of the Council of Economic Advisers full-fledged members of the FOMC. Putting the Fed under more *explicit* short-run political pressure would greatly lessen politicians' ability to disclaim responsibility for past policy decisions. For political parties and would-be career politicians, enhanced responsibility for the consequences of monetary policy would establish incentives to look past the boundaries of the current swing in the business cycle.

Most incumbent politicians revel in the political benefits of Fedbashing. Presidents and congressional leaders will keep the game running as long as the political benefits of Fedbashing exceed its political costs. The balance of benefits and costs improves slightly whenever voters place the same party in control of the presidency and both houses of Congress. However, even at these times presidential politics and the lack of discipline in the congressional wing of U.S. parties make scapegoating attractive to incumbents in the majority party. To achieve substantial and permanent progress, voters must develop and communicate sufficient concern about economic performance to overcome the symbiotic relation that now exists between elected politicians and the Fed. For this to occur, either the public must learn to see through biennial and quadriennial efforts to scapegoat the Fed or critics of the Fed must agree on a unified plan for making the Fed clearly accountable to politicians so that in turn politicians become accountable for Fed behavior. As it is now, macro-economists squander too much of their energies trying to show that the performance criteria and reporting requirements that they would impose on the Fed are better than those proposed by competitive reformers. Inter-necine squabbling among sponsors of sensible alternative central banking arrangements serves to shorten the political leash under which the Fed operates and, by keeping the public in a state of confusion about how monetary policy works, to strengthen the Fed's institutional capacity both to act eclectically and to serve as an after-the-fact scapegoat for unpopular macroeconomic events. As long as would-be monetary reformers pas-sionately shout down one another's ideas, their efforts serve to mystify the task of monetary policy-making and to keep Fed officials battling politically to preserve their special bureaucratic status. Sadly, the level of the noise they make about alternative targeting schemes and performance criteria tends to drown out these critics' far more telling concerns about the absence of a clear line of political accountability for Fed actions.

Notes

The author wishes to thank Richard C. Aspinwall, Benson Hart, and Raymond Lombra for a long series of instructive conversations on these issues. Valuable comments were also received from Robert L. Hetzel, Thomas Willett, and John T. Woolley. The views expressed in this paper are the author's and should not be construed as representing those of the National Bureau of Economic Research.

1 Edward J. Kane, "New Congressional Restraints and Federal Reserve Indepen-dence," *Challenge,* November/December 1975, 37–44; Robert Hetzel, "The For-mulation of Monetary Policy" (Federal Reserve Bank of Richmond, May 1984); John Woolley, *Monetary Politics: The Federal Reserve and the Politics of Monetary Policy* (New York: Cambridge University Press, 1984).

2 Edward J. Kane, "External Pressure and the Operations of the Fed," in *Political Economy of International and Domestic Monetary Relations,* ed. R. Lombra and W. Witte (Ames: Iowa State University Press, 1982), pp. 211–32.

3 Raymond Lombra and Michael Moran, "Policy Advice and Policymaking at the Federal Reserve," in *Monetary Institutions and the Policy Process,* ed. Karl Brunner and Allan Meltzer, Carnegie-Rochester Conference Series on Public Policy, vol. 13 (1980), pp. 9–68.

4 Edward J. Kane, "Politics and Fed Policymaking: The More Things Change the More They Remain the Same," *Journal of Monetary Economics* 6 (April 1980): 199–211.

5   Stanley Fischer and John Huizenga, "Inflation, Unemployment, and Public Opinion Polls," *Journal of Money, Credit, and Banking* 14 (February 1982): 1–19.

6   Hetzel, "Formulation of Monetary Policy"; Ira Kaminow, "Politics, Economics, and Procedures of U.S. Money Growth Dynamics," in *Political Economy of Monetary Relations,* ed. Lombra and Witte, pp. 181–196; Edward J. Kane, "Selecting Monetary Targets in a Changing Financial Environment," in *Monetary Policy Issues in the 1980s* (Symposium sponsored by the Federal Reserve Bank of Kansas City, Jackson Hole, Wyo., August 9–10, 1982), pp. 181–206; George G. Kaufman, "Monetarism at the Fed," *Journal of Contemporary Studies* 12 (Winter 1983): 27–36; Lombra and Moran, "Policy Advice"; Lombra, chapter 14 of this volume; Thomas Mayer, "Federal Reserve Policy in the 1973–1975 Recession: A Case Study of Fed Behavior in a Quandary," *Crisis in the Economic and Financial Structure,* ed. Paul Wachtel (Lexington, Mass.: Lexington Books, 1982), pp. 41–83; James Pierce, "The Political Economy of Arthur Burns," *Journal of Finance* 34 (June 1979): 485–96; Woolley, *Monetary Politics.*

7   Raymond Lombra, "Discussion," in *Monetary Policy Issues,* pp. 215–22.

21 Subordinating the Fed to Political Authorities Will Not Control Inflationary Tendencies

King Banaian, Leroy O. Laney,
John McArthur, and Thomas D. Willett

1. Introduction

The idea that the political process is likely to operate with an inflationary bias is not new. Concerns that government might put pressure on the agency responsible for printing money to pay government bills underlay the creation of the Federal Reserve system as an agency independent of the executive branch in the United States.[1] The emergence of the prolonged inflation of the last several decades suggests that the institutional implementation of these concerns may have been deficient, and has thereby generated considerable interest in recent years in possible reforms of the Fed.

The independence of the Federal Reserve was created only by congressional legislation, not constitutional guarantee. As is discussed in chapters 14, 15, and 20 of this volume, there is strong evidence that the Fed has been influenced by political pressures.[2] Members of the Fed's congressional oversight committee have frequently emphasized that the Fed should be independent of the executive branch but not of the views of Congress,[3] while many observers have argued that in practice the influence of the executive branch has been even greater than that of Congress (see chapter 13 of this volume).

Proposals for reforming the Fed have been motivated both by concerns that it has not been independent enough and has accommodated too much inflation, and by concerns from other quarters that the Fed has not been politically responsive enough and has failed to be sufficiently accommodative to hold down unemployment. While concerns about the inflationary bias of the Fed may have been reduced somewhat by the success of the Volcker Fed in dramatically reducing the rate of inflation in the 1980s, the appointment to the Federal Reserve Board of several supply-siders with an expansionist bias has raised questions about the durability of our current low rate of inflation, even under a conservative Republican administration; and a number of newspaper articles have raised the question of whether Volcker's replacement Alan Greenspan would be likely to follow expansionary policies in 1988 in order to help Republican election chances.

Apart from how Federal Reserve officials respond to various types of political pressures and their own views of how the economy operates, some critics have focused on direct bureaucratic incentives for these officials to follow inflationary policies in order to increase the Fed's budget. These critics depict the Fed as an active promoter of, rather than a more passive respondent to, inflationary pressures.[4] As we discuss in section 2, we do not believe that these bureaucratic explanations of the Federal Reserve as a major initiator of inflation carry much explanatory power. Thus, we conclude that marginal reforms bringing the Federal Reserve budget under direct political control are unlikely to provide a significant check on inflationary pressures, and could indeed increase them by making the Federal Reserve even more susceptible to political pressures. We also briefly consider the effects of proposals to limit budget deficits and conclude that while such measures should help reduce inflationary pressures, they would not be sufficient to eliminate them. Thus such measures should be considered as possible complements to, but not substitutes for, monetary reform.

In section 3 we briefly discuss the two most fundamental types of reforms meant to reduce the discretionary power of the Federal Reserve currently being discussed. One type seeks to reduce discretion by making monetary policy directly responsible to the political process, while the second seeks to remove the formulation of monetary policy entirely from the political process through the adoption of monetary rules or a return to some form of gold standard, or even to surrender monetary creation to the private banking sector. The various major candidates for this second type of reform are evaluated in other chapters in this part of the volume. In section 4 of this chapter, we argue that an evaluation of the experiences of the other major industrial countries should make us wary of the argument that making the Federal Reserve more directly responsible to the political process would be likely to improve macroeconomic policy-making and reduce inflationary tendencies. To raise this cautionary note one need only compare the high average inflation rates of countries like England, France, and Italy, where the central bank is directly responsible to the government, with the lower rates of Germany and Switzerland, where greater independence is found (see table 21.1). The Appendix presents a more detailed statistical analysis which finds central bank independence to be strongly associated with lower average rates of inflation.

Our major point in this analysis is not to defend the current institutional structure of monetary policy-making in the United States but rather to argue that marginal institutional reforms are unlikely to be very effective. Moreover, we contend that proposed reforms that would make monetary policy directly responsive to the political process are not only unlikely to be effective in restraining inflation but are, if anything, more likely to increase inflationary pressures.

2. Bureaucratic Budget
Maximization and Seigniorage

There has been a resurgence of interest in the last few years in bureaucratic analysis of central bank behavior.[5] Two recent articles (by Mark Toma and by William Shugart and Robert Tollison) have argued that bureaucratic desires to increase the size of their empires have induced the leaders of the Federal Reserve to engage in more rapid monetary expansion in order to increase the revenue available for expenditures on Fed activities.[6] Concerns on this score would suggest the simple institutional change of making the Fed's budget subject to the normal appropriation and review processes. The danger in such an approach of course is that it would increase the scope for direct political leverage over the Fed.

We agree with the monitoring costs view that suggests a possible scope for "excessive" Federal Reserve expenditures, but we do not believe that the current institutional arrangements generate substantial incentives for the Federal Reserve to engage in more rapid monetary expansion to finance such expenditures. In the typical bureaucratic environment—where expenditures are budget- or revenue-constrained—we would expect attempts at such behavior. But the normal operations of the Federal Reserve generate so much revenue that only a small fraction of it is spent by the Fed, the remainder being turned over directly to the Treasury. Furthermore, there has been no particular constancy to the ratio of revenues returned. Thus as a first approximation under current circumstances, the bureaucratic expenditure benefits for the Fed generated by revenue creation would seem to be primarily inframarginal, and thus should not provide any substantial incentives for marginal increases in the rate of monetary expansion in order to facilitate greater Fed expenditures. Toma, and also Shugart and Tollison, have presented time series analyses that are consistent with their bureaucratic expenditure hypothesis; but other recent empirical work by Boyd, Strong, and Watson suggests that these results were likely due to spurious correlations generated by omitted variables.[7]

As further suggestive evidence against the empirical importance of the bureaucratic expenditures hypothesis, we note the following. Over 90 percent of the employment in the Federal Reserve system is with the regional banks. The staff of the Federal Reserve Board itself is quite small by comparison. Thus to the extent that bureau employment was a significant consideration in monetary policy-making, this might be expected to be a more important consideration for the regional bank presidents on the Federal Open Market Committee (FOMC) than for the members of the board of governors. This in turn would suggest that on average the bank presidents should favor higher rates of monetary expansion than the other FOMC members. However, analysis of the dissents from FOMC directives made by the bank presidents indicates that the vast majority of the time they have called for tighter rather than easier monetary policy.[8]

Of greater empirical importance we believe is the more traditional literature on the inflation tax, which emphasizes the government's incentives to raise revenue from seigniorage.[9] Government debasement of the currency is not a recent development and has been elevated by some writers to the status of an inevitable historical law of government behavior. An important point which such literature typically does not address, however, is why the evolution of democracy over time has not given rise to an effective check on such antisocial tendencies on the part of governments. The basis for an answer to this question lies in the public choice analysis of the limits of informed voter monitoring and control over such government actions.[10]

We are inclined to believe that such seigniorage concerns have been an important cause of inflationary policies in many historical episodes and in many other countries today (especially in the developing world), but that this has not typically been a major motivation for U.S. policy. One could argue that the financing of the Vietnam War buildup may be an example, although the major motivation here would seem to be indirect. It is commonly argued that over and above general political reluctance to increase taxes, President Johnson did not wish to call for a tax increase to finance the increased expenditures because he feared this would generate a major political debate over policy toward the war. This led to bond financing of the increased expenditures which—via the Federal Reserve concerns about interest rates—resulted in substantial monetary accommodation.

Although there has been considerable empirical controversy about the extent to which budget deficits have stimulated monetary expansion in the United States over the postwar period, our reading of the evidence to date indicates that the relationships have been highly variable but far from trivial on balance. This suggests to us that, even with the new Federal Reserve tolerance for a greater range of interest rate fluctuations, institutional reforms to limit budget deficits would probably contribute to some reduction in average rates of monetary expansion over time.[11] Again, however, such a reform would be unlikely to fully eliminate the incentives for inflationary biases. It would require either the development of a sufficiently informed and active electorate to systematically force out of office government officials who presided over highly inflationary government finance, or institutional reforms to remove or constrain discretionary powers of money creation.

3. Rules versus Democracy in Monetary Policy-making

Arguments for replacing Federal Reserve discretion by monetary rules (a return to a gold standard would be one type) are usually based either on arguments that Federal Reserve independence has not been sufficient to offset inflationary biases, or on a basic preference for rules over discretion as the basis for a free society. Most of the discussions by economists about monetary rules are concerned exclusively with whether they are likely to generate better economic outcomes than discretionary macroeconomic policies. Embracing Henry Simons's view, however, would imply a basic preference for rules as long as their outcomes were not "too much" worse than discretion, with, of course, the delineation of "too much" depending on the strength of the value judgment in favor of rules.[12]

One can also argue, as have both some monetarists (like Milton Friedman and Harry Johnson) and Keynesians (like Lester Thurow), that an independent Fed is inconsistent with democracy.[13] For example, compare the following by Thurow and by Friedman:

> Whatever its historical merit, the time has come to end the independence of the Fed. If the President is competent enough to have his finger on the nuclear button, he is competent enough to control the money supply. Presidents are elected and defeated on their economic performance. They deserve both the controls and the responsibilities that this implies. No President should be able to hide his failures behind an "erratic" money supply beyond his control. And if the charge is true, no President should have to put up with an incompetent Fed.[14]

> Is it really tolerable in a democracy to have so much power concentrated in a body free from any kind of direct, effective political control?[15]

Friedman bolsters his own negative answer to this question by arguing that the operation of an independent central bank will suffer from a dispersal of responsibility, from undue importance given to the particular personalities appointed, and from undue weight given to the views of bankers.

While these are certainly important considerations, it must be recognized that neither the United States nor any other major country has ever purported to be a pure democracy. We are a constitutional democracy, with a number of important limitations placed on the domain and outcomes of the democratic process. Limitations on democratic outcomes have been motivated by concerns about the preservation of individual freedoms (e.g., the Bill of Rights), and because in particular areas it has been judged that the special expertise needed—combined with popular political pressures to follow policies contrary to the longer-run general interest—made it desirable to insulate decision making from the direct political process. We have a long tradition of independent regulatory agencies which cover a wide range of activities.

Thus, in our judgment, the primary issue is not the legitimacy of an independent Federal Reserve as a reasonable form of government structure, but rather whether this form has proven effective in the monetary area. In general, enthusiasm for independent regulatory agencies has waned in recent years as study after study has found them to be less insulated from special interest pressures than had been hoped.[16] While the current institutional structure of the Federal Reserve is not without defenders,[17] we find good reason for concern in the analysis of the critiques.

Recent arguments have held that not only has the Federal Reserve not been very effective in restraining inflationary biases, but because of the diffusion of responsibility in the present institutional structure, prevailing bureaucratic interests have actually generated effects opposite from those intended by the designers of an independent central bank. In this view the independence of the Fed has made a net positive contribution to the validation of inflationary pressures. This has led Milton Friedman to conclude the following in the absence of adoption of a monetary rule:

> The only two alternatives that do seem to be feasible over the longer run are either to make the Federal Reserve a bureau in the Treasury under the Secretary of the Treasury, or to put the Federal Reserve under direct congressional control. Either involves terminating the so-called independence of the system. But either would establish a strong incentive for the Fed to produce a stabler monetary environment than we have had.[18]

This seems a plausible argument which deserves to be taken seriously. It may be undercut, however, by the failure of the electoral check to work efficiently. As has been discussed in a number of the preceding chapters in this volume, there are strong reasons to believe that because of voter myopia and other biases present in our collective decision-making process, democratic electoral politics do not present a fully effective check upon the propensities of government to pursue more inflationary policies than would be deemed desirable by the fully informed median voter. Indeed, as emphasized in the literature on the political business cycle, differences between short-term and longer-run inflation-unemployment trade-offs can provide electoral incentives for governments to pursue overly expansionary policies before elections. Thus, even if making monetary policy the responsibility of the executive would be an improvement over the current institutional arrangements, substantial inflationary biases would likely remain. In fact, it seems quite possible that the net effect of making the Federal Reserve more directly politically responsible would be to increase the inflationary bias.

4. Comparing the Inflationary Performance of Countries with "Independent" and Dependent Central Banks

This is an empirical question, and we do not have comparative historical experience with relevant different institutional arrangements in the United States on which to base an informed empirical judgment. We can, however, look at comparative postwar experiences of the major industrial countries to gain some empirical clues. In particular, the degree of formal institutional independence of the Federal Reserve is fairly rare among the industrial democracies. It has been matched or exceeded only in Germany and Switzerland (and possibly in Canada up to 1967). In most countries central banks are directly responsible to their governments in monetary policy formulation (although they, of course, retain various degrees of bureaucratic influence).[19] Thus we can compare the inflationary experiences of the dependent versus the independent central banks.

The first study to make such a comparison (by Michael Parkin and Robin Bade)[20] concluded that the inflationary performance of the Federal Reserve fits better with the higher inflation tendencies of the dependent central banks than with the lower inflation tendencies of the German and Swiss central banks. This conclusion is not inconsistent with Friedman's argument in one sense. Making the Federal Reserve more directly responsible politically would at least not necessarily contribute to increased inflationary tendencies, even if the Parkin-Bade study did not suggest that such an institutional reform would substantially reduce them.

In a recent paper, however, we found that the Parkin-Bade findings are not robust.[21] They depend crucially on the choice of exchange rates as their indicator of inflationary tendencies and on the time period when their study ended. Both extending the time period to later data now available, and using alternative inflation indicators, suggest that the inflationary performance of the Federal Reserve comes much closer to those of the German and Swiss central banks than to those of the dependent central banks. (See table 21.1 for comparative inflation rates, money supply, and

Table 21.1   Price Level, Money Supply, and Nominal GNP Growth in
Eight Major Countries: Average Annual Rates of Change, 1960–84

Country	Implicit deflator inflation	Narrow money supply growth	Nominal GNP growth
Germany	4.3	8.0	7.6
Switzerland	4.8	6.5	7.6
United States	5.3	5.9	8.8
Canada	6.2	9.9	10.6
Japan	5.4	13.8	13.2
France	7.5	10.6	11.8
United Kingdom	8.8	9.2	11.2
Italy	10.7	16.4	14.7

nominal GNP growth.) This suggests that, while the independence of the
Federal Reserve has not been an ideal check against inflationary tendencies, reforms are not sufficient to substantially reduce these tendencies.
Moreover, making the Fed more directly politically responsible could be
a move in the wrong direction. Based on simple comparative historical
experience, the inflationary pressures of election politics would seem to
be even greater than those of the current bureaucratic politics.

We must, of course, be quite tentative in concluding that the current
independence of the Fed has made a modest net contribution toward reducing inflation. While the comparisons just considered are certainly consistent with the view that central bank independence has had a restraining
influence on inflationary tendencies, it is possible that there may, in fact,
be other factors in these countries which account for lower rates of inflation. Empirical evidence can never prove that a hypothesis is correct. It
can only fail to disprove it. Thus, no empirical study can definitively
prove that central bank independence does have a restraining influence.
We can add to our subjective evidence that central bank independence is
a major restraining influence, however, if we take a number of other factors into account and still find that central bank independence has an
important statistical explanatory power.

Statistical work presented in the Appendix finds significant large
negative effects for central bank independence even after the effects of a
number of other variables (such as degree of unionization, growth of government spending, income distribution, and openness of the economy)

are taken into account. These preliminary results suggest that while some of the lower inflation rates in the countries with independent central banks may be due to other factors (for example, Germany, Switzerland, and the United States all have levels of unionization well below the industrial country average), central banking arrangements do have an influence on comparative rates of inflation.

We find no support for the view that making the Federal Reserve more directly responsible to the political process would reduce long-run inflationary tendencies. We must consider more basic reforms such as those analyzed in the preceding chapters.

Appendix:
The Relation of Central Bank Independence and Other Variables to Average Rates of Inflation

In this Appendix we extend the simple comparison of average inflation rates presented in the text to consider the effects of central bank independence in relation to a number of other factors which it has been suggested may be important influences on differences in inflation rates across countries. In this study we include variables for budget deficits, degree of openness, unionization, and income distribution and aspiration gaps which play an important role in many sociological analyses of inflation.[22]

To take these factors into account, a cross-sectional study of seventeen industrial countries was undertaken.[23] To avoid having too few observations to construct useful tests, the following research design was used. For each country, arithmetic means were taken of annual observations for the periods 1960–67, 1967–73, and 1973–80. Then all observations were pooled, yielding fifty-one observations. Where Gini coefficients (which measure the degree of income inequality) and the share of the labor force unionized are included as explanatory variables, the same number was used in each of three subsamples because of limitations in data availability.[24]

The regressions are reported in table 21.2; the dependent variable used is the percent change in the gross domestic product deflator (GDPD).[25] As a measure of the "aspiration gap," we considered the common hypothesis that higher rates of growth of per capita real gross domestic product (PCRGDP) lead to lower rates of inflation. Another source of this type of pressure can be found in the Gini coefficient. If foreign

Table 21.2 Central Bank Independence and Other Factors Hypothesized to Influence Differences in Inflation Rates

Independent variable	Dependent Variable: Inflation (*GDPD*)	
	Equation (1)	Equation (2)
Growth (*PCRGDP*)	−.88008	−.85595
	(3.30)**	(3.06)**
Budget deficit	5.9647	8.4795
(*DF/S*)	(1.51)	(1.79)*
Openness (*IM/GDP*)	−.03052	−.05416
	(0.79)	(1.21)
Unionization (*UNION*)	−.01701	−.00381
	(0.66)	(0.13)
Inequality (*GINI*)	9.4035	11.903
	(0.81)	(0.98)
Central bank independence		
INDDUM	−4.0126	
	(3.32)**	
USDUM		−5.0462
		(2.39)**
GERDUM		−3.2635
		(1.74)*
SWIDUM		−2.0237
		(0.82)
CONSTANT	8.4063	7.0363
	(1.80)*	(1.38)
SEE	2.89	3.04
$\bar{R}^2$	.31	.24

Notes: SEE represents the standard error of the estimate. All other abbreviations are explained in the text. All regressions are performed by use of ordinary least squares.
*$p < .10$.   **$p < .05$.

inflationary pressures do have an impact on domestic inflation, one would expect a positive sign on the coefficient for the import share of GDP (IM/GDP). Another frequent explanation for inflation is budget deficits. The greater is an economy's savings, the less difficult it is to finance the deficit through private means and the less should be the pressure to monetize the deficit. Therefore, we used deficits as a share of savings (DF/S) as our deficit variable.[26]

Another explanation, forwarded by many cost-push theorists, is that unions originate pressures in the economy to attain large wage increases.[27] To capture this effect, union membership as a share of the labor force (UNION) is included, with a positive sign hypothesized. An alternative hypothesis has also been put forward that more corporatist states, which typically have higher levels of unionization and highly centralized collective bargaining, typically will have less inflationary problems. This would imply a negative sign on the union variable.

To study the effects of central bank independence, we add to this regression a dummy variable equal to one for the more independent central bank countries (Germany, Switzerland, and the United States, as well as for Canada for the first subperiod).

Equation (1) in table 21.2 replicates the results of our earlier study. As noted there, the growth rate of per capita real GDP has the expected correct sign and is highly significant, suggesting that larger real growth in an economy is associated with lower inflation.[28] This is consistent with the aspirations gap hypothesis. The measure of deficit pressure, DF/S, is also of the expected sign but does not quite attain statistical significance. The independence dummy, however, shows that, ceteris paribus, the three countries with independent central banks (and pre-1967 Canada) tended to have rates of inflation about 4 percent lower than the other countries in the sample. The figure is highly significant. All other variables fail to attain significant levels. The UNION variable has a negative sign suggesting that corporatism considerations may be of greater importance than union wage pressures on average, although at present such a conclusion would still have to be considered speculative.

By use of the country-specific dummies, we can investigate the decrease in inflation that might be ascribed to each independent central bank. This is presented in equation (2). All three individual country dummies have the correct sign, although in this more demanding test Switzerland's estimated reduction in inflation is not significant and that of Germany is only marginally so. Thus on this particular test, the Federal Reserve comes through as being associated with the strongest anti-inflationary effort.

We would not claim that these empirical results are sufficiently discriminating to put considerable weight on this particular result on the relative effects of the three more independent central banks. A wider range of influences should be taken into account in future studies, and problems of covariation among the independent variables can also make ascribing relative influence difficult.[29] We do believe, however, that the general pattern of substantial negative coefficients on the independent central bank variables is of some importance.[30]

Notes

This chapter draws in places on King Banaian et al., "Central Bank Independence: An International Comparison," Federal Reserve Bank of Dallas *Economic Review*, March 1983, 1–13.

1 On the origins and structure of the Federal Reserve system, see George Bach, *Making Monetary and Fiscal Policy* (Washington, D.C.: Brookings Institution, 1971); A. Jerome Clifford, *The Independence of the Federal Reserve System* (Philadelphia: University of Pennsylvania Press, 1965); Milton Friedman and Anna J. Schwartz, *A Monetary History of the United States: 1867–1960* (Princeton: Princeton University Press, 1963); John T. Woolley, *Monetary Politics: The Federal Reserve and the Politics of Monetary Policy* (Cambridge: Cambridge University Press, 1984); and the references cited in these works. There was considerable concern expressed that the Federal Reserve be independent of the private banking community as well as the government. The degree of effective independence from both of these was much less in the original operation of the system than it became with the strengthening of the Federal Reserve Board, which was established in the 1930s.

2 Those chapters contain numerous references to the literature on this subject.

3 See, for example, Henry S. Reuss, "The Once and Future Fed," *Challenge*, March–April 1983, 26–32.

4 See Mark Toma, "Inflationary Bias of the Federal Reserve System: A Bureaucratic Perspective," *Journal of Monetary Economics* 10 (September 1982): 163–90; and William F. Shughart and Robert D. Tollison, "Preliminary Evidence on the Use of Inputs by the Federal Reserve System," *American Economic Review* 73 (June 1983): 291–304.

5 For the initial postwar investigations in this area, see John F. Chant and Keith Acheson, "The Choice of Monetary Instruments and the Theory of the Bureaucracy," *Public Choice* 27 (Spring 1972): 13–33; Keith Acheson and John F. Chant, "Bureaucratic Theory and the Choice of Central Bank Goals," *Journal of Money, Credit, and Banking* 5 (May 1973): 637–55; and John F. Chant and Keith Acheson, "Mythology and Central Banking," *Kyklos* 26 (1973): 362–79. For a recent treatment in terms of the principal-agent problem, see Donald J. Mullineaux, "Monetary Rules and Contracts: Why Theory Loses to Practice," Federal Reserve Bank of Philadelphia *Business Review* (March–April 1985): 13–19.

6 See Toma, "Inflationary Bias," and Shughart and Tollison, "Preliminary Evidence."

7 John H. Boyd, "The Use of Inputs by the Federal Reserve System: Comment,"

American Economic Review 74 (December 1984): 1114–17; John S. Strong, "The Use of Inputs by the Federal Reserve System: Comment," *American Economic Review* 74 (December 1984): 1118–20; and J. W. Henry Watson, "Income Satiation at the Fed: Good for Monetary Policy, Bad for the Payments System" (University of Chicago, October 1984, working paper).

8 See Richard H. Puckett, "Federal Open Market Committee Structure and Decisions," *Journal of Monetary Economics* 12 (July 1984): 97–104. It might be argued that some pressure on Reserve bank presidents would be alleviated because, as required by the Monetary Control Act of 1980, Reserve banks now price their services to commercial banks. This source of revenue is quite small relative to total revenue of the Federal Reserve system. (In 1985, Reserve banks more than recovered costs of providing these services, but this revenue amounted to only $733 million as compared to total system income of over $18 billion. Of the latter amount, over 98 percent was returned to the Treasury.)

9 For discussion and references to this literature, see chapter 6 of this volume.

10 See, for example, James M. Buchanan and Richard E. Wagner, *Democracy in Deficit* (New York: Academic Press, 1977); and Goeffrey Brennan and James M. Buchanan, *The Power to Tax: Analytical Foundations of a Fiscal Constitution* (Cambridge: Cambridge University Press, 1980).

11 For recent evidence and references to the literature on this subject, see chapter 8 of this volume.

12 See Henry C. Simons, "Rules versus Authorities in Monetary Policy," in *Economic Policy for a Free Society* (Chicago: University of Chicago Press, 1948).

13 See, for example, Milton Friedman, *A Program for Monetary Stability* (New York: Fordham University Press, 1959); idem, "Should There Be an Independent Monetary Authority?" in *In Search of a Monetary Constitution*, ed. Leland B. Yeager (Cambridge: Harvard University Press, 1962), pp. 219–43; Harry G. Johnson, "Major Issues in Monetary and Fiscal Policies," *Federal Reserve Bulletin* 50 (November 1964), 1400–13; Edward J. Kane, chapter 20 of this volume; Robert D. Auerbach, "Politics and the Federal Reserve," *Contemporary Policy Issues* 3 (Fall 1985): 43–58; and Lester C. Thurow, "Give Reagan the Fed," *Newsweek*, March 1, 1982, 29. For a critical analysis of the relation between monetary rules and freedom, see Jacob Viner, "The Necessary and the Desirable Range of Discretion to be Allowed to a Monetary Authority," in *In Search of a Monetary Constitution*, ed. Yeager.

14 Thurow, "Give Reagan the Fed."

15 Friedman, "Independent Monetary Authority," 227.

16 See Barry M. Mitnick, *The Political Economy of Regulation* (New York: Columbia University Press, 1980).

17 See, for example, Bach, *Monetary and Fiscal Policy,* and Arthur Burns, "The Independence of the Federal Reserve System," *Challenge*, July–August 1976, 21–24.

18 Milton Friedman, "Monetary Policy: Theory and Practice," *Journal of Money, Credit, and Banking* 14 (February 1982): 118.

19 See King Banaian et al., "Central Bank Independence: An International Comparison," Federal Reserve Bank of Dallas *Economic Review* (March 1983): 1–13; Donald R. Hodgman, *National Monetary Policies and International Monetary Cooperation*

(Boston: Little, Brown, 1974); Michael Parkin and Robin Bade, "Central Bank Laws and Monetary Policies: A Preliminary Investigation," University of Western Ontario, Department of Economics, Research Paper no. 7804 (London, Ontario, 1978); Michael Parkin, "In Search of a Monetary Constitution for the European Communities," in *One Money for Europe,* ed. Michele Fratianni and Theodore Peeters (New York: Praeger, 1978); Don Fair, "The Independence of Central Banks," *The Banker,* October 1979, 31–41; and John T. Woolley, "Central Banks and Inflation," in *The Politics of Inflation and Economic Stagnation,* ed. Leon N. Lindberg and Charles S. Maier (Washington, D.C.: Brookings Institution, 1985): 318–48.

20 See Parkin and Bade, "Central Bank Laws," and Parkin, "Monetary Constitution."

21 See Banaian et al., "Central Bank Independence."

22 Earlier studies relating cross-national differences in inflation rates to such variables include Milivoje Panic, "The Origin of Increasing Inflationary Tendencies in Contemporary Society," in *The Political Economy of Inflation,* ed. Fred Hirsch and John H. Goldthorpe (Cambridge: Harvard University Press, 1978), pp. 137–60; John T. Addison and John Burton, "The Sociopolitical Analysis of Global Inflation: A Theoretical and Empirical Examination of an Influential Basic Explanation," *American Journal of Economics and Sociology* 42 (January 1983): 13–28 (which presents a very useful critique of Panic's analysis); Douglas A. Hibbs, Jr., "Inflation, Political Support, and Macroeconomic Policy," in *The Politics of Inflation and Economic Stagnation,* ed. Leon Lindberg and Charles Maier (Washington, D.C.: Brookings Institution, 1985), pp. 175–95; Rudolf Klein, "Public Expenditure in an Inflationary World," ibid., pp. 196–223; and David R. Cameron, "Does Government Cause Inflation? Taxes, Spending, and Deficits," ibid., pp. 224–79.

23 These countries were Australia, Austria, Belgium, Canada, Denmark, Finland, France, Germany, Italy, Japan, the Netherlands, Norway, Spain, Sweden, Switzerland, the United Kingdom, and the United States.

24 Observations for the Gini coefficient were formed using 1970 data, while the unionization data were taken from a 1977 survey (see George Kurian, *Book of World Rankings* [New York: Facts on File, 1977]). It seems unlikely that these measures would vary greatly over the time period under study.

25 In an earlier study (Banaian et al., "Central Bank Independence"), regression results were also reported for which consumer price inflation and the rate of growth of nominal gross national product were used as performance measures rather than GDPD. As we noted there, the results were not qualitatively affected by the change of dependent variables.

26 As is discussed in chapter 8 of this volume, actual budget deficits are not a good measure of the generation of inflationary pressures. In that chapter another budget measure, the full employment (or cyclically adjusted) deficit, is used. While there is no one clearly best adjusted measure of deficit pressures we believe that the cyclically adjusted deficit is the best measure for quarterly and annual data, while the deficit-to-savings ratio is more appropriate for data averaged over a longer time period such as is used here.

27 See, for example, the discussion and references in Cameron, "Does Government Cause Inflation?"; Colin Crouch, "Conditions for Trade Union Restraint," in *The*

Politics of Inflation, pp. 105–39; and Kerry Schott, *Policy Power and Order: the Persistence of Economic Problems in Capitalist States* (New Haven: Yale University Press, 1984).

28 Banaian et al., "Central Bank Independence."

29 For example, the countries with independent central banks also tend to have well below average levels of unionization and wage indexation. See Stanley Black, *Politics versus Markets: International Differences in Macroeconomic Policies* (Washington, D.C.: American Enterprise Institute, 1982), and "The Use of Monetary Policy for Internal and External Balance," in *Exchange Rates and International Macroeconomics,* ed. Jacob A. Frenkel (Chicago: University of Chicago Press, for the National Bureau of Economic Research, 1983), pp. 189–225. This may not make a major difference, however, as the effects of levels of unionization are ambiguous and had a negative sign in our equations, and levels of indication are probably as much or more a result of inflation as they are a contributor. The conservative versus liberal orientation of governments may also be significant; see, for example, Hibbs, "Inflation, Political Support, and Macroeconomics." For a contrasting finding that conservative governments are associated with higher rates of inflation, see Cameron, "Does Government Cause Inflation?" It is also interesting to note that the more dependent central banks have tended to make much greater use of direct credit allocations as an instrument of monetary control as opposed to the open market operations favored by the central banks in Germany and the United States. For discussions of such cross-national differences in strategies for monetary policy implementation, see Black, *Politics versus Markets,* and "Use of Monetary Policy."

30 This belief has been enhanced by the results of running several additional variations of these equations which showed a quite robust pattern of the coefficients. Variations included dropping the insignificant independent variables from the equation and the introduction of interaction terms between the independence dummies and the other independent variables. The main change in the results when the interaction terms are added is that the deficit variable becomes significant at the 5 percent level. The coefficients on the combined independence dummy varied between -3.0 and -4.4, while the coefficients for the United States separately varied between -3.6 and -5.0, and those for Germany and Switzerland varied between -2.0 and -3.3.

About the Authors

King Banaian is assistant professor of economics, St. Cloud State University, and research associate, Claremont Center for Economic Policy Studies.

Nathaniel Beck is associate professor of political science, University of California at San Diego.

John Briggs is research associate, Claremont Center for Economic Policy Studies.

Gregory B. Christainsen is associate professor of economics, California State University of Hayward.

D. B. Christenson is instructor of economics, Claremont McKenna College, and a Ph.D. candidate, Claremont Graduate School.

Patricia Dillon is assistant professor of economics, Scripps College and Claremont Graduate School.

Bruno S. Frey is professor of economics, University of Zurich.

Gottfried Haberler is a resident scholar at the American Enterprise Institute and Galen Stone professor emeritus, Harvard University.

Thomas Havrilesky is professor of economics, Duke University.

Stephen E. Haynes is associate professor of economics, University of Oregon.

Edward J. Kane is Everett D. Reese professor of money and banking, Ohio State University.

Leroy O. Laney is assistant vice president and senior economist, Federal Reserve Bank of Dallas.

Axel Leijonhufvud is professor of economics, University of California at Los Angeles.

Peter Lewin is senior vice president, Soft Warehouse Inc. of Dallas.

Raymond Lombra is professor of economics, Pennsylvania State University.

John McArthur is a Ph.D. candidate, Claremont Graduate School, and research associate of the Lowe Institute for Political Economy at Claremont McKenna College.

J. Harold McClure, Jr., is assistant professor of economics, Fordham University, and research associate, Claremont Center for Economic Policy Studies.

Pamela K. Martin is a Ph.D. candidate, Claremont Graduate School.

Thomas Mayer is professor of economics, University of California at Davis.

Michael Melvin is associate professor of economics, Arizona State University.

Mohand Merzkani is research associate, Claremont Center for Economic Policy Studies.

William Mitchell is professor of political science, University of Oregon.

Friedrich Schneider is professor of economics, University of Linz, Austria.

Joe Stone is W. E. Miner professor of economics, University of Oregon.

Arthur Warga is assistant professor of finance, Columbia University, and research associate, Claremont Center for Economic Policy Studies.

Lawrence H. White is assistant professor of economics, New York University.

Thomas D. Willett is Horton professor of economics, Claremont McKenna College and Claremont Graduate School, and director, Claremont Center for Economic Policy Studies.

Index

Library of Congress Cataloging-in-Publication Data
Political Business cycles.

Bibliography: p.
Includes index.
1. Business cycles—Political aspects—United
States. 2. Unemployment—United States—Effect of
inflation on. 3. Monetary policy—United States.
I. Willett, Thomas D.
HB3743.P67   1988   338.5'42'0973   88-7148
ISBN 0-8223-0824-X
ISBN 0-8223-0842-8 (pbk.)